Also by **Ashgate**:

MARGARET GIBSON AND JANET L. NELSON (Eds.)
Charles the Bald: Court and Kingdom

Also in the Variorum Collected Studies Series:

MARGARET GIBSON
'Artes' and Bible in the Medieval West

ROSAMOND MCKITTERICK
Frankish Kings and Culture in the Early Middle Ages

JANE MARTINDALE
Status, Authority and Regional Power: Aquitaine and France,
9th to 12th Centuries

ELIZABETH A.R. BROWN
The Monarchy of Capetian France and Royal Ceremonial

BÉATRICE LEROY
Le royaume de Navarre à la fin du Moyen Age: Gouvernement et société

ROGER E. REYNOLDS
Clerics in the Early Middle Ages: Hierarchy and Image

ROGER E. REYNOLDS
Clerical Orders in the Early Middle Ages: Duties and Ordination

G.A. LOUD
Conquerors and Churchmen in Norman Italy

E.M.C. VAN HOUTS
History and Family Traditions in England and the Continent, 1000–1200

JOSEPH F. O'CALLAGHAN
Alfonso X, the Cortes and Government in Medieval Spain

MARJORIE REEVES
The Prophetic Sense of History in Medieval and Renaissance Europe

PATRIZIA LENDINARA
Anglo-Saxon Glosses and Glossaries

VARIORUM COLLECTED STUDIES SERIES

Rulers and Ruling Families in Early Medieval Europe

To the Earlier Medieval Seminar,
the Institute of Historical Research,
in the University of London

Janet L. Nelson

Rulers and Ruling Families
in Early Medieval Europe

Alfred, Charles the Bald, and Others

VARIORUM

Aldershot · Brookfield USA · Singapore · Sydney

Published in the Variorum Collected Studies Series by

Ashgate Publishing Limited
Gower House, Croft Road,
Aldershot, Hampshire GU11 3HR
Great Britain

Ashgate Publishing Company
Old Post Road,
Brookfield, Vermont 05036–9704
USA

ISBN 0–86078–802–4

British Library Cataloguing-in-Publication Data
Nelson, Janet L. (Janet Laughland), 1942–
    Rulers and Ruling Families in Early Medieval Europe: Alfred, Charles the Bald
    and Others.
    (Variorum Collected Studies Series: CS657).
    1. Europe–Kings and rulers–Social life and customs. 2. Europe–Kings and
    rulers–Biography. 3. Europe–History, 476–1492
    I. Title.
    940. 1' 0922

US Library of Congress Cataloging-in-Publication Data
Nelson, Janet L.
    Rulers and Ruling Families in Early Medieval Europe: Alfred, Charles the Bald
    and Others/Janet L. Nelson.
    p. cm. – (Variorum Collected Studies Series: CS657).
    Includes bibliographical references (p.).
    1. Civilization, Medieval. 2. Kings and rulers, Medieval. 3. France–History–
    To 987. 4. Charles II, King of France, 823–877. 5. Charlemagne, Emperor,
    742–814. 6. Great Britain–History–Alfred, 871–899. 7. Wessex (England)–
    History. 8. Alfred, King of England, 849–899. 9. Monarchy–Europe.
    DC36. 6. N45   1999   99–29851
    940. 1–dc21   CIP

The paper used in this publication meets the minimum requirements of the
    American National Standard for Information Sciences – Permanence of
    Paper for Printed Library Materials, ANSI Z39.48–1984. ∞ TM

Printed by Galliard (Printers) Ltd, Great Yarmouth, Norfolk, Great Britain

VARIORUM COLLECTED STUDIES SERIES CS657

CONTENTS

This volume contains xii + 332 pages

PUBLISHER'S NOTE

The articles in this volume, as in all others in the Variorum Collected Studies Series, have not been given a new, continuous pagination. In order to avoid confusion, and to facilitate their use where these same studies have been referred to elsewhere, the original pagination has been maintained wherever possible.

Each article has been given a Roman number in order of appearance, as listed in the Contents. This number is repeated on each page and is quoted in the index entries.

PREFACE

The seventeen papers reprinted in this book reflect my continuing interest in rulers and royal-family politics in the early medieval West. The first six papers focus on Alfred of Wessex (reigned 871–899). Three of these were originally read at conferences (II, read in 1982; IV, in 1992, and VI, in 1991) and a fourth (I, in 1985) to the Royal Historical Society. In publishing them, I have retained as much as possible of the oral-presentational style. It will be clear that my views on Alfred have evolved and changed over the years, and for that I think no apology need be offered. The evidence is in many ways exiguous and problematic. For me, Alfred is sufficiently well-documented to make him a subject of ongoing obsessive interest – and the fact that he himself was a writer as well as a ruler adds a dimension unique for the earlier Middle Ages – yet insufficiently well-documented to make him other than baffling.[1] Most people would agree that his reign was an exceptionally important one. His dealings with Scandinavian contemporaries, and his personal concern with the written word, are aspects that have been brilliantly illuminated by Peter Sawyer and Janet Bately respectively: they are the recipients of *Festschrift* pieces reprinted here (III and V) and I will not miss the chance to reaffirm my gratitude to both. Since I wrote the papers in the present volume, two scholarly biographies, by Alfred P. Smyth[2] and Richard Abels,[3] and two substantial collections of essays on Alfred and related subjects,[4] have appeared. All these, in different ways, have deepened and altered our appreciation of the man and his reign. Further gains in understanding can be guaranteed in 1999 when the 1100th anniversary of Alfred's death is commemorated.[5] The timing of the present volume is not fortuitous.

Just as several of my papers on Alfred are more or less explicitly concerned with comparing Wessex and the Continent, so the first of the papers on Charles the Bald reprinted here (VII) launches the same comparison from the Frankish side. Other papers examine the religious and cultural concerns of Charles, his court, and his learned contemporaries (VIII, IX, X), thus doing more justice to these aspects of a remarkable reign than was possible in my brief biography of Charles.[6] The broader context of earlier medieval royal-family politics is a topic I discussed elsewhere not long ago, and it has since been brilliantly illuminated by Brigitte Kasten's recent book on Frankish sub-kingdoms.[7]

In the third group of papers, one (XI) reflects the continuation of my long-standing interest in Frankish royal women in the Merovingian period, while others (XII, XIII) extend this into a field I have been working on more recently, the reign of Charlemagne.[8] A further paper (XIV) examines the political agenda and activities of Charlemagne's court during the Aachen years. My earlier work on consecration-rites for earlier medieval kings is belatedly complemented by a short study on queenly consecrations (XV). Two final papers offer re-readings of the main ninth-century West Frankish annalistic source, the *Annals of St. Bertin* (XVI, XVII). These annals contain rich information on political ideology and practice that has yet to be fully explored and exploited.[9]

I owe thanks, first, to John Smedley, for being willing to publish this collection. Our earlier collaboration when Margaret Gibson and I co-edited our revised version of *Charles the Bald: Court and Kingdom*, (Aldershot 1990) is something I recall with pleasure. Thanks go as well to my husband Howard (alias Georges), source of both moral support and improvements to my French. *Sine quibus non* . . . This is the time and the place to record a special debt of gratitude to Bridget Taylor for all she has contributed to the smooth running of seminars at the Institute of Historical Research in the University of London. I am grateful, too, to the librarians and other staff at the IHR who together create such a congenial environment for researchers. The papers in this book all reflect, as ever, the advice, criticism and encouragement of a number of good friends. Of those based outside London, I thank especially Stuart Airlie, David Bates, Mayke de Jong, Simon Keynes, Régine Le Jan, Jane Martindale, Rosamond McKitterick, Tim Reuter, Julia Smith, Pauline Stafford, Chris Wickham, and Ian Wood. The dedication of this book indicates some of my greatest intellectual debts in the university where I've been lucky enough to spend nearly thirty years of my working life. I am particularly grateful, for all sorts of help, and for making the IHR such a fine place to think and talk history, to Susan Reynolds, to my recent research students Sarah Hamilton, Paul Kershaw, Simon MacLean (who also deserves special thanks for preparing the Index to this book), and Geoff West, to my King's colleagues David Carpenter and David Ganz, to my co-convenors Brenda Bolton, Michael Clanchy, Wendy Davies, Paul Fouracre, John Gillingham, and Alan Thacker, and to all of those, and all the others, whose participation has ensured over the years that the Wednesday seminar, and earlier medieval history, continue to flourish at the IHR, in the University of London, and far beyond it.

King's College London   JANET L. NELSON
January 1999

---

[1] See, most recently, my attempt to contextualise Alfred's spirituality, 'Monks, secular men, and masculinity, *c*. 900' in D. Hadley ed., *Masculinity in Medieval Europe* (London, 1998), pp. 121–42.

[2] *King Alfred the Great* (Oxford, 1995). See the review-articles by S. Keynes, 'On the authenticity of Asser's *Life of King Alfred*', *Journal of Ecclesiastical History* 47 (1996), pp. 529–51, and myself, 'Waiting for Alfred', *Early Medieval Europe* (1998), pp. 115–24. Cf. the reviews by M. Lapidge, *Times Higher Educational Supplement* 8 March 1996, p. 20; D. Howlett, *English Historical Review* 112 (1997), p. 942; J. Campbell, *Times Literary Supplement* 26 July 1996, p. 30.

[3] *Alfred the Great* (London, 1998). My review is forthcoming in the *Times Literary Supplement*.

[4] J. Roberts and J.L. Nelson edd., *Alfred the Wise: Studies in Honour of Janet Bately* (Woodbridge, 1997); M. Blackburn and D.N. Dumville ed., *Kings, Currency and Alliances: The History and Coinage of Southern England* (Woodbridge, 1998). In both these volumes, the contributions of Simon Keynes are outstanding. See also the valuable article of A. Scharer, 'The writing of history at King Alfred's court', *Early Medieval Europe* 5 (1996), pp. 177–206. Further important work is imminently expected on the culture of Alfred's court, on Alfred's legislation, and on his political ideas, from Anton Scharer (Vienna), Patrick Wormald (Oxford), and David Pratt (Cambridge).

[5] Scheduled events include an exhibition and major conference (8–12 September) organised at by the Wessex Medieval Centre, University of Southampton; events and an exhibition at Winchester; an exhibition at the Museum of London in September and October; and a day-conference at the Institute of Historical Research, University of London, on 26 October.

[6] *Charles the Bald* (London, 1992). Cf. also my earlier collections of papers, *Politics and Ritual in Early Medieval Europe* (London, 1986) and *The Frankish World, 750–900* (London, 1996).

[7] See my chapter, 'Kingship and royal government', in R. McKitterick ed., *The New Cambridge Medieval History*, vol. II (Cambridge, 1995), pp. 383–430; and now B. Kasten, *Königssöhne und Königsherrschaft: Untersuchungen zur Teilhabe am Reich in der Merowinger- und Karolingerzeit* (Hannover, 1997).

[8] See also my contribution, 'Making a difference in eighth-century politics: the daughters of Desiderius', in A. C. Murray ed., *After Rome's Fall: Narrators and Sources of Early Medieval History. Essays presented to Walter Goffart* (Toronto, 1998), pp. 171–90.

[9] Cf. the introduction to my translation, *The Annals of St. Bertin* (Manchester, 1991).

ACKNOWLEDGEMENTS

Grateful acknowledgement is made to the following persons, journals, institutions and publishers for their permission to reproduce the papers included in this volume: the Royal Historical Society (for chapter I); the editors and the State University of New York at Stony Brook, NY (II); the editors, Richard Barber, and Boydell and Brewer Ltd. (III, V, and XV), the editor, and the executive editor of King's College London Medieval Studies (IV), the editors, the International Society of Anglo-Saxonists, and the Board of the Medieval Institute, Western Michigan University, Kalamazoo, MI (VI); the editors and Beauchesne, Paris (VII), the editors of *Studies in Church History* and the Ecclesiastical History Society (VIII); the editors and Oldenbourg Verlag, Vienna and Munich (IX); the editors of *Médiévales*, and Presses Universitaires de Vincennes-Paris VIII (X); His Eminence the Cardinal Archbishop of Toledo (XI); the editors of *Byzantion* and la Fondation Byzantine, Brussels (XII); the editor and the Gesellschaft für mittelrheinische Kirchengeschichte, Trier (XIII); the editor and the Centre d'Histoire de l'Europe du Nord-Ouest, Université de Lille III (XIV); the editors and the Committee for Medieval Studies, the University of British Columbia (XVI); and the editor and the University of California Press (XVII).

I

'A KING ACROSS THE SEA': ALFRED IN CONTINENTAL PERSPECTIVE

I BEGIN with the quotation in my title: 'Alfred, a king across the sea'. It is actually a tenth-century label rather than a strictly contemporary one: it was used by Flodoard of Rheims in *c.* 960 when he summarized a letter sent to Alfred by Archbishop Fulk of Rheims in *c.* 890. How Fulk himself had addressed Alfred we don't know. But, according to Flodoard, what he said was 'amicable': he expressed satisfaction on hearing of the appointment of a good man, Plegmund, to the see of Canterbury, because he had heard that 'a most perverse sect' had spread among the English and Plegmund was the man to cut it down. This sect held that bishops and priests could have women secretly living with them and that anyone who wished could mate with kinswomen of his own family and have incestuous relations with women consecrated to God and have a wife and a concubine at the same time. Fulk ended by demonstrating to Alfred the error of such views.[1]

Amicable this letter certainly was by comparison with some others dispatched by Fulk to various contemporary potentates. The very next letter in Flodoard's dossier is a diatribe to the dowager Empress Richildis alleging that the 'feuds, fights, burnings, murders, and acts of lust' going on around her were diabolically inspired.[2] Fulk's tone of mingled complaint and advice resounded in a letter to Archbishop Plegmund himself where, referring to his letter to King Alfred, he thanked Plegmund for 'working, as he had heard, to cut off the incestuous heats of lasciviousness ... among that people'.[3]

The subject of Fulk's concern recurs in a letter of Pope John VIII written a few years earlier to Plegmund's predecessor Archbishop

---

[1] Flodoard, *Historia Remensis Ecclesiae*, ed. I. Heller and G. Waitz, Monumenta Germaniae Historica (hereafter MGH), *Scriptores*, xiii (Hannover, 1881), 566; trans. in *English Historical Documents*, i, *c. 500–1042*, ed. D. Whitelock (2nd edn., 1979) (hereafter *EHD*), no. 224. I should like to thank John Gillingham, Nicholas Hooper and Simon Keynes for many helpful suggestions, and Mark Blackburn and Michael Metcalf for advice on numismatics.

[2] Flodoard, 566. Compare Fulk's letter to Charles the Simple, *Patrologia Latina*, ed. J.-P. Migne, (hereafter *PL*) cxxxi, cols. 13–14.

[3] Flodoard, 568.

46

Æthelred, affirming the Church's rules on monogamy. Æthelred, it seems, had reported his worries about those who were leaving their wives and committing incest. He had also complained about the king—Alfred— who had been 'wronging the house of the Lord' and ignoring Canterbury's privileges (the date is 877/8, a difficult time for Alfred, as we shall see presently). Unfortunately there is no trace of the companion-letter of admonition which Pope John says he has sent Alfred, reminding him of his predecessors 'the most godly kings of the English' and threatening divine sanction in this world and the next if Alfred strays from their example.[4]

From John VIII too this kind of letter is not surprising.[5] What perhaps *is* surprising is that these letters constitute almost the sum total of our evidence for contemporary Continental views of Alfred. We have all been brought up to believe that Alfred was one of the great figures of the ninth century. How could Continentals have failed to notice? The question is more justified than a crudely chauvinistic 'fog in Channel—Continent cut off'. After all, several quite substantial Frankish chronicles were written during the last thirty years of the ninth century and all gave a lot of attention to the very Vikings who so preoccupied Alfred. Those responsible for the *Anglo-Saxon Chronicle* in this period show a remarkable awareness not only of Viking activity on the Continent but of the connexion between Viking fortunes on that side of the Channel and their assaults on England. For instance, the *Chronicle* for 891 records the defeat of the Danes by King Arnulf of the East Franks and in 892 reports: 'the great army which we mentioned above returned from the eastern kingdom westward to Boulogne and thence crossed over [to Kent] horses and all.'[6] Contemporary Frankish writers present a striking contrast: for them, the Vikings seem of interest only when they're on the spot. Any rationale offered for Viking appearances or departures is in terms of events in Francia. For instance, the Vikings' coming in 879 from 'over the sea' is attributed by the annalist of Saint-Vaast to their 'hearing of discord among the Franks', while their sailing away in 892 was the result of a famine in Francia: 'seeing the whole realm worn down by hunger they left Francia in the autumn and crossed the sea'—and the annalist clearly does not care where they went.[7] Hincmar of Rheims and Regino of Prüm show a similar concern with Vikings on the Continent only: the Bretons'

---

[4] Ed. E. Caspar, MGH *Epistolae Karolini Aevi*, v, 71–2; trans. *EHD*, no. 222.

[5] W. Ullmann, *The Growth of Papal Government in the Middle Ages*, (2nd edn., 1962), 219–25.

[6] *Anglo-Saxon Chronicle* (hereafter *ASC*), *s.a.* 891, 893 (*recte* 892), *Two of the Saxon Chronicles Parallel*, ed. C. Plummer (2 vols., Oxford, 1892–9), i. 82, 84.

[7] *Annales Vedastini*, *s.a.* 879, 892, ed. B. von Simson, MGH *Scriptores rerum Germanicarum in usum scholarum* (hereafter *SRG*) (Hannover, 1909), 44, 72.

resistance may be recorded approvingly, but once the Vikings decided to seek *transmarinae regiones* they vanished, it seems, from Frankish consciousness.[8] It had not always been so. In the 840s and 850s Viking attacks on England and Ireland, and victories won against them, were mentioned several times by writers in Francia.[9] Such evidence for cross-Channel contacts in the mid-ninth century seems to fit with the plans for combined operations against the Vikings that may have underlain the marriage-alliance between Alfred's father Æthelwulf of Wessex and the Carolingian princess Judith.[10] But from the 870s onwards, interest in such contacts becomes one-sided. Englishmen still traversed the Carolingian Empire *en route* for Rome.[11] English churchmen sought moral support from popes and from the archbishop of Rheims: the letters they got were responses to their own. It was the Franks whose horizons narrowed first: their chroniclers' silence on Alfred is symptomatic of that narrowing. And none of them ever thought of bringing Alfred into a Continental perspective.

In the nineteenth century, English historians were eager to compare Alfred with his Continental contemporaries, for Alfred always seemed to emerge triumphant. If no joint action between Franks and English ever was taken, that was because, according to Charles Plummer, 'Charles the Bald, a typical Frenchman in many respects, intellectually clever but caring only for the outward pomp and circumstance of empire without the strength of character to grasp and hold the reality of power, was hardly the man to carry out a consistent policy.'[12] Plummer thought Alfred could be compared with Charlemagne, but whereas 'every succeeding century has given the lie to Charles's system of a united France and Germany', 'every succeeding century has but verified more and more Alfred's vision of a united England.' Furthermore, Charlemagne's 'lax morality' and 'occasional outbursts of cruelty ... have no counterpart in our English hero-king'.[13] Only a few years after Plummer wrote, a sober comparison not of men but of institutions was published by the youthful Helen Maud Cam.[14] She followed the great nineteenth-

[8] Hincmar, *Annales Bertiniani*, *s.a.* 882, ed. F. Grat, J. Vielliard and S. Clémencet (Paris, 1964), 247; Regino, *Chronicon*, *s.a.* 892, ed. F. Kurze, MGH, *SRG* (Hannover, 1890), 138.

[9] *Annales Bertiniani*, *s.a.* 844, 850, 860; Lupus of Ferrières, *Correspondance*, ed. L. Levillain (2 vols., Paris, 1927-35), ii. 70.

[10] P. Stafford, 'Charles the Bald, Judith and England', in *Charles the Bald: Court and Kingdom*, ed. M. Gibson and J. L. Nelson (British Archaeological Reports, International ser., ci, 1981), 137-51.

[11] Flodoard, 556.

[12] C. Plummer, *The Life and Times of Alfred the Great* (Oxford, 1902), 78.

[13] Plummer, *Alfred*, 201.

[14] H. M. Cam, *Local Government in Francia and England* (1912), i, 6-17. This is an appropriate place to salute a fine, and unjustly neglected, pioneering work.

48

century historians in seeking the origins of national traits. She was struck by the resemblances between Frankish and Anglo-Saxon institutions: 'Has one country borrowed from another, or are the features they have in common part of their inheritance from a distant past, or again are the resemblances merely coincidences?' Cam looked to capitularies and laws to answer these questions, eschewing what she seems to have thought scarcely relevant — 'literary-ecclesiastical' evidence. She had little to say about the Church on either side of the Channel: hence, while her conclusion was against direct influences and towards common origins, those origins were, in her view, Germanic: only Carolingian institutions carried a 'Roman tinge'.[15]

More recently, historians have been interested in the whole range of contacts, and especially ecclesiastical, cultural and ideological contacts, between England and the Continent in the ninth century. Alfred's reign has been the focus of such work. This is the place to bring in one further (and by far the best-known) indication of ninth-century Continental reaction to Alfred, namely the single extant complete letter that purports to have been sent him from Archbishop Fulk, recommending the latter's protégé the monk Grimbald of Saint-Bertin.[16] More than forty years ago, Professor Grierson argued for the authenticity of this letter. He believed the manuscript evidence was of tenth-century date and came from somewhere in the West Country.[17] But the letter is now known to have been written out at Winchester in a mid-eleventh-century hand.[18] The *cui bono* question is therefore worth posing. Grimbald was Winchester's man and the letter does much to enhance Grimbald's reputation: it strongly suggests that Grimbald was destined for episcopal office (*pace* Drs Keynes and Lapidge, this seems to me what is meant by: 'You [Alfred] ask for Grimbald ... who is to be advanced to the care of pastoral rule') and hints at jealous ill-wishers who opposed the plan. If Grierson is right in dating Grimbald's arrival to 886 or early 887, the see in question can hardly have been Winchester, where Denewulf's episcopal dates are 879-908. It may have been Canterbury, but since Æthelred remained in office there until his death in June 888, Grimbald would then have been sent with only a promise of promotion whenever the see became vacant. Such an

---

[15] Cam, 154-6.

[16] *Councils and Synods with other Documents relating to the English Church*, I, ed. D. Whitelock, M. Brett and C. N. L. Brooke (2 pts., Oxford, 1981), i. 6-12; trans. S. Keynes and M. Lapidge, *Alfred the Great* (Harmondsworth, 1983), 182-6, with notes at 331-3.

[17] P. Grierson, 'Grimbald of St. Bertin's', *English Historical Review* (hereafter *EHR*), lv (1940), 529-61.

[18] Keynes and Lapidge, 331.

arrangement was certainly hypothesized at Winchester a century later, by which date Grimbald was the object of a local cult. Despite Grierson's assurance that 'there is nothing against [the letter] on internal grounds', the heavy emphasis on Grimbald's qualification for pastoral, that is episcopal, office suggests the possibility that the letter was forged at Winchester, perhaps during the reign of Edward the Confessor. Its criticisms of English clerical morals are echoed in the *Vita Ædwardi*, while its most striking trait, the presentation of St Remigius as the apostle of the Franks, could be the result of renewed contacts in the 1040s between Wessex and the see of Rheims.[19] At the very least, the letter has been 'improved': Fulk is hardly likely to have greeted Alfred as 'the most glorious and the most Christian king'. The bulky correspondence of Fulk's predecessor Hincmar shows Carolingians being addressed invariably in far more moderate terms.[20] If the earlier part of the letter is genuine, what Professor Whitelock called its 'arrogant and patronising tone' may be just what we could expect of a budding prince-bishop whose temporal ambitions led to his assassination in 900.[21]

But should Fulk's perspective in this letter (genuine or otherwise) also be ours? The image of Alfred as a 'suppliant' (Professor Wallace-Hadrill's word) picking up the crumbs of the Carolingian Renaissance has become firm in recent historiography.[22] Even Professor Bately, never one to underestimate Alfred, suggests a dependence of his educational 'plan' on Charlemagne's 'programme'.[23] Professor Parkes sees the *Anglo-Saxon Chronicle* as modelled on Frankish dynastic or national history-writing.[24] Some years ago, I argued that the idea of royal anointing, which I then wrongly thought unpractised in ninth-century England, came to Alfred from the Carolingians.[25] Professor Wallace-Hadrill depicted Alfred as an imitator in his legislation ('he knew that the Carolingians had found a use for

[19] *Vita Ædwardi Regis*, ed. F. Barlow (Nelson's Medieval Texts, 1962), 75-9; F. Barlow, *The English Church 1000-1066: A Constitutional History* (1963), 117, 122, 302.

[20] E.g. MGH, *Epistolae*, viii, pt. 1, ed. E. Perels (Munich, 1975), nos. 108, 131, 134, 179, pp. 52, 70, 76, 168. Compare Lupus, *Correspondance*, ii. 70.

[21] *EHD*, no. 223, p. 883.

[22] J. M. Wallace-Hadrill, *Early Germanic Kingship in England and on the Continent* (Oxford, 1971), 150, though cf. the remarks at 142.

[23] J. M. Bately, *The Literary Prose of King Alfred's Reign: Translation or Transformation?* (1980), 10-12.

[24] M. B. Parkes, 'The palaeography of the Parker Manuscript of the *Chronicle*', *Anglo-Saxon England* (hereafter *ASE*), v (1976), 149-71, at 163-6.

[25] J. L. Nelson, 'The problem of King Alfred's royal anointing', *Journal of Ecclesiastical History*, xviii (1967), 145-63; but see now Nelson, 'The earliest royal *Ordo*: some historical and liturgical aspects', in *Authority and Power: Studies on Medieval Law and Government presented to Walter Ullmann*, ed. B. Tierney and P. Linehan (Cambridge, 1980), 29-48.

it') and Mr Wormald has singled out his treason-law as notably Carolingian-inspired.[26] In the catalogue to the recent splendid Anglo-Saxon exhibition at the British Museum, Dr Webster seems to present the art and artefacts of Alfred's reign as sub-Carolingian products: while a Winchester wall-painting fragment and a reliquary get credit for 'Carolingian inspiration', the manuscript that contains the old English version of the *Pastoral Care* is rapped on the knuckles for 'rather old-fashioned provinciality'.[27] Drs Hassall and Hill surmised Frankish inspiration behind Alfred's building of double bridgeheads to block rivers against Viking access.[28] Now I have no desire to denigrate the Carolingians' achievements. But we must get them into proportion. All the Alfredian phenomena I've just listed can be explained quite well wholly or largely in terms of indigenous ideas or traditions (themselves the beneficiaries, of course, of earlier generations' contacts with Continental Europe and the Mediterranean world) without multiplying Carolingian influences beyond necessity or overloading Grimbald's baggage. Historical writing, for instance, had antecedents in England long before the 890s to inspire West Saxon annalists, while royal consecration-rites seem to have had independent histories in England and Francia predating Alfred's reign.

The Carolingian chancery is often taken as a kind of standard against which the Anglo-Saxons are measured and found wanting. Yet Charles the Bald's chancery, which produced more charters per reign-year than that of any other Carolingian, actually consisted of no more than a couple of notaries and a supervisor at any one time. Some at least of those notaries may well have been temporary staff: monks who in effect commuted between their monastery and the itinerant court, drafting charters from time to time.[29] Beneficiary diplomatic or true chancery? Modern labels create an issue where none existed. Professor Whitelock in one of her last papers, gave some of Alfred's charters the attention they deserve.[30] One notary, perhaps a Mercian, may have been responsible for three of them, each for a different beneficiary: twenty-five per cent of the total—

[26] Wallace-Hadrill, 148; P. Wormald in *The Anglo-Saxons*, ed. J. Campbell (Oxford, 1982), 155.

[27] L. Webster, in *The Golden Age of Anglo-Saxon Art, 966–1066*, ed. J. Backhouse, D. H. Turner and L. Webster (1984), 18–19.

[28] J. M. Hassall and D. Hill, 'Pont de l'Arche: Frankish influence on the West Saxon *burh?*', *Archaeological Journal*, cxxvii (1970), 180–95.

[29] My inferences from *Receuil des Actes de Charles II le Chauve*, ed. G. Tessier (3 vols., Paris, 1943–55), esp. iii. 38–93.

[30] D. Whitelock, 'Some charters in the name of King Alfred', in *Saints, Scholars and Heroes*, ed. M. H. King and W. M. Stevens (2 vols., Collegeville, Minnesota, 1979), i. 77–98, See also S. Keynes, *The Diplomas of King Æthelred 'the Unready' 978–1016* (Cambridge, 1980), 14–83.

though I admit the sample is small! We thus have the possibility that Alfred's charter-production was similar to the Carolingians'. There is less of it, but the system (if that is the word) needs no apology.

Royal resource-management is also worth a comparative glance. It is easy to smile when we find Alfred, after arranging various monetary bequests in his will, adding: 'I do not know whether there is so much money ... but I suspect so'.[31] Yet the scale of Alfred's bequests is impressive: some £2,000 or 486,000 pennies.[32] The will also lists over sixty estates among Alfred's disposable property. Asser in his *Life of Alfred* mentions the king's firm handling of his estate-managers or reeves.[33] Admittedly, there is no sign of any Alfredian estate-survey. Yet, as Mr Campbell has observed, 'quite elaborate administration is possible without written records; as indeed it was in some African states as Europeans found them.'[34] And, it could be added, as so much Carolingian government was in practice. Carolingian estate-management has seemed to some scholars impressively well-run. It depends, of course, on what impresses. Gibbon jeered at a king who troubled himself over 'the care of his poultry and even the sale of his eggs'! In any event, the concerns expressed by Charlemagne in the Capitulary *De Villis* must all too often have been stymied by the virtually insuperable problem of supervising the managers of far-flung estates rarely, if ever, visited by the king.[35] If only because Wessex was relatively compact, it seems certain that Alfred saw and knew more of his estates than the Carolingians did of theirs, and may thus have supervised his reeves more effectively than the Carolingians did their *iudices*. As for the organization of the palace and of the military household, Alfred, or at any rate the scholars about him, probably drew more inspiration from the division of episcopal revenues prescribed by Pope Gelasius I, and from the Biblical example of Solomon, than from Hincmar of Rheims' *De Ordine Palatii*.[36]

Comparing Alfred with the Carolingians, then, is no simple mat-

[31] Keynes and Lapidge, 177.

[32] As calculated by Keynes and Lapidge, 324 n. 97.

[33] *Asser's Life of King Alfred*, ed. W. H. Stevenson (Oxford, 1904), c. 91, p. 78, and c. 106, pp. 92-4; trans. Keynes and Lapidge, 102, 109-10.

[34] J. Campbell, 'The significance of the Anglo-Norman state in the administrative history of western Europe', in *Histoire Comparée de l'Administration (IVe-XVIII siècles)*, ed. W. Paravicini and K. F. Werner, Beiheft der *Francia*, ix (Munich, 1980), 117-34, at 121.

[35] Cam, 120-7; J. Martindale, 'The kingdom of Aquitaine and the "dissolution of the Carolingian fisc"', *Francia*, xi (1984), 131-91.

[36] *Decretum Gelasii*, referred to in Bede, *Historia Ecclesiastica*, I, 27 (ed. C. Plummer (Oxford, 1896) i. 48); Vulgate, III Reg., iv-v. I am grateful to Professor R. Markus and Dr D. Howlett for their suggestions here.

ter. It is difficult to determine the base-line. Helen Cam thought we might risk underestimating English local government because of the 'semblance of unity', the 'spurious efficiency' lent to the Carolingians by their more obviously Roman heritage.[37] But there may equally be a risk of overestimating Alfred's government because we lack so much of the sort of evidence that, in the Carolingians' case, shows us how wide was the gap between ideal or aspiration, and reality. We know, for instance, that Frankish counts were appointed by kings and we know what was officially expected of them; but we also know of countships that were hereditary already in the eighth century, and of counts who ignored royal injunctions. It is not a court chronicler but a rather disgruntled provincial one who tells the story of a magnate buying his way to a countship despite the existence of a sitting tenant, and having installed himself in a fortified residence, being attacked and slain by his ousted rival, who proceeded to terrorize the neighbourhood.[38]

It is this kind of evidence, culled from local charters and local, or 'unofficial' chroniclers, that provides a Continental perspective on Alfred: a perspective different from that offered by so much of the extant West Saxon evidence, and notably by the *Chronicle*, the Laws of Alfred, and the 'Alfredian' translations. This is the Continental perspective meant in the title of this paper: a vantage-point from which to re-examine sources that represent, so to speak, the Alfredian interest. It was, frankly, one of Alfred's greatest achievements to programme the responses of so many succeeding generations so effectively. He is, still, Alfred the Great! But it is the historian's job to reach behind the image: to probe the gap between ideal and reality. In Alfred's case, the Continental perspective highlights that gap, and throws unfamiliar features into high relief. Knowing what size of gap to envisage, prepared for a more complex and in some ways starker landscape, we can return to the West Saxon sources.

The ealdormen of the *Anglo-Saxon Chronicle* and the translations sound as if they always behave themselves. West Saxon kings did not have to spend time at a Carolingian court or listen to a Frankish adviser to grasp that this was good behaviour to inculcate. Thus, in the *Chronicle*, it is true, ealdormen 'appear constantly with the men of the shire'.[39] It is not the *Chronicle* but Asser who tells us of the plot of an ealdorman of Somerset against his king (no mention here

---

[37] Cam, 1. For recent surveys, see K. F. Werner, '*Missus-marchio-comes*', in *Histoire Comparée de l'Administration*, 190–239; R. McKitterick, *The Frankish Kingdoms under the Carolingians* (1983), 77–105.

[38] *Annales Bertiniani, s.a.* 867, 868, pp. 140–1. See further Nelson, 'Dispute settlement in Carolingian West Francia', in *Dispute Settlement in Early Medieval Europe*, ed. W. Davies and P. Fouracre (Cambridge, 1986).

[39] Cam, 143.

of the men of the shire).[40] Nor is it the *Chronicle* but a chance reference in a charter of Alfred's son and successor which reveals that an ealdorman, Wulfhere, lost his office and had his inheritance confiscated because 'he deserted without permission both his lord King Alfred and his country in spite of the oath which he had sworn to the king and all his leading men'.[41] The Wulfhere story is significant but it is not quite unique. Asser (and his indiscretions are so often a godsend) twice mentions defectors, in c. 53 Christians who had 'bowed themselves to the lordship of the pagans', and in c. 83 (here my translation differs from that of Keynes and Lapidge) Angles and Saxons who had been 'with the pagans but not as captives', in other words, voluntarily.[42]

Wulfhere's case can usefully be viewed in a Continental perspective; for the presence of a powerful rival lordship in the vicinity was a temptation to noble, and filial, faithlessness in the Carolingians' realms no less than in Alfred's, and far more often documented. At least for laymen, a prospective ally's paganism seems to have been no deterrent. Magnates from whom royal favour had been withdrawn, or disgruntled king's sons, sought such outside help: in the West Frankish realm from Vikings or Spanish Moors, in the East Frankish realm from Slavs, in the Italian realm, from Saracens. The outcome was often the restoration of the dis-favoured, or their kin, to the king's good grace. In other words, alliance with external enemies could be a very effective lever in rebel hands. Carolingian kings had to face frequent and serious opposition from enemies within—that is to say, from each other and from the kinsmen, often nephews, whom they tried to exclude from kingship. Rival Carolingians found noble supporters: the indeterminate succession system thus offered outlets for, and so in a sense contained, even institutionalized, aristocratic ambition. Einhard felt it necessary to stress how very few of those who rebelled Charlemagne had killed: exile was the usual penalty.[43] It was extremely difficult even for Charlemagne to deprive a faithless magnate of his patrimony. He did so

[40] Asser, c. 12, pp. 9–10; trans. Keynes and Lapidge, 70.

[41] P. H. Sawyer, *Anglo-Saxon Charters: an Annotated List and Bibliography* (Royal Historical Society, Guides and Handbooks, viii, 1968), no. 362; trans. *EHD*, no. 100. Wulfhere was ealdorman of Wiltshire, target of the Danish attack on Wessex in 877/8. His successor was in office by 887 and died in 897. 877/8 therefore seems the likeliest date for Wulfhere's defection.

[42] Asser, c. 53, p. 41; c. 83, p. 69 as amended by Stevenson, but see Keynes and Lapidge, 266. Asser apparently misunderstood the phrase in *ASC*, s.a. 886 (ed. Plummer, i. 80); but his own interpretation presumably could make sense to him and his contemporaries.

[43] Einhard, *Vita Karoli*, ed. G. Waitz, MGH, *SRG* (Hannover, 1911), c. 20, pp. 25–6.

54

deprive some unnamed nobles, 'by the judgement of the Franks' for having supported his rebellious son Pippin the Hunchback in 792. But in 797 at Aachen, Count Theodold cleared himself of treason by the very unusual expedient of the ordeal, and legally recovered his lands (I suspect he had never actually lost control of them).[44] Five years after the Hunchback's rebellion had been crushed, Charlemagne could only find peace through compromise. Louis the Pious, whose clemency was a byword, deprived rebels of their offices and in some cases their benefices, but left them their patrimonies.[45] Charles the Bald allowed penitent former rebels to recover both their patrimonies and their acquisitions (*alodes de hereditate et de conquisitu*) and any grants his father had made them. But he reserved judgement on his own grants and also on offices: on these, he said, 'I shall act as I will'.[46] The assertion was hawkish. Subsequent royal action was conciliatory, for most if not all the penitents seem eventually to have gained total restitution, or adequate compensation. But Charles' distinction of principle is revealing: in practice inherited lands and acquisitions were virtually outwith royal control. Countships and a king's own largesse were another matter.

Compare the case of Wulfhere. Alfred asserted not only the right to deprive an ealdorman of office but to confiscate his inheritance. No wonder that he took care, like Charlemagne, to have the matter decided in an assembly 'by the judgement of councillors'. The nature of our information—a subsequent grant by Alfred's son of lands that had once been Wulhere's—shows that the confiscation at least of one large estate had been carried out. Alfred's treason law, like Charlemagne's prescriptions for oaths of fidelity, was a response to the ever-present threat of faithlessness on the part of those whom the king relied on most. It came naturally to rulers on both sides of the Channel to invoke lordship as an analogy for kingship: one kind of obligation parallelled and supported the other. But Alfred's royal *familiaritas*, like that of the Carolingians, was two-faced: it smiled but it could also threaten. Referring to the time immediately after he became king, Alfred tells how he brought a dispute with his nephews (backed perhaps by their mother's kin) over some family property before the councillors of the West Saxons: 'I urged them all for love of me that none would hesitate to expound what was lawful. And I gave them my pledge that I would never bear a grudge against any one of them for declaring what was lawful.' The

---

[44] *Receuil des Historiens des Gaules et de la France*, ed. M. Bouquet *et al.* 24 vols. (Paris, 1738-1904), v. 758.

[45] *Annales Bertiniani*, s.a. 834, p. 15.

[46] MGH, *Capitularia Regum Francorum*, ed. A. Boretius and V. Krause (2 vols., Berlin, 1883-97), ii, no. 242, p. 158.

councillors were wise men: they unanimously declared Alfred's claim lawful against the claim of his nephews.[47] Was Wulfhere, the defector of (probably) 877/8 the uncle of those nephews, that is, the brother-in-law of Alfred's elder brother?[48]

The circumstances of Alfred's becoming king deserve a closer look. And here a Continental perspective has already proved helpful to Dr Stafford. It was a West Frankish chronicler's surprise at the low status of the king's wife in Wessex, plus another of Asser's indiscretions, which provoked an examination of the West Saxons' apparent preference in the ninth century for fraternal rather than filial royal succession. The downgrading of the king's wife could be identified as a strategy for inhibiting conflict between king's sons and thus making it easier for brother to succeed brother horizontally, so to speak, at the expense of vertical claimants, that is, sons of the preceding king. Such a custom, once established, might reduce tension between uncles and nephews, and could bring the realm the benefit of an adult heir rather than a child.[49]

But it does not look as if the custom was very long established in ninth-century Wessex: Alfred himself dated its origin only two generations before his own.[50] Alfred's father Æthelwulf had had five sons. The oldest, who had been sub-king of the recently acquired kingdom of Kent, predeceased him.[51] That left Kent available for re-allocation. The second and third sons were a good deal older than the two youngest. Æthelwulf reasonably left Wessex to one, Kent to the other adult son.[52] But in 860 when the older of these two died, it was not luck but good management that made the other king of both Wessex and Kent. Asser hints that Kent could have received another separate ruler at this time—presumably the next brother Æthelred. (Alfred, the youngest, was only eleven years old.) But Æthelred's hopes were thwarted when his older brother 'joined Kent to his dominion [of Wessex]—as was right'.[53] The comment is Asser's: Æthelred's view may have differed. But his luck was in when that older brother died and he was able to succeed in his turn to Kent as well as Wessex; for there was now a precedent—860— for holding onto both. Alfred was now seventeen. Did he protest? Did

[47] Keynes and Lapidge, 175.

[48] This guess assumes we can accept a genuine base to Sawyer, nos. 336 and 341, and the witness-list to Sawyer, no. 340, subscribed by 'Wulfthryth regina' immediately followed by 'Wulfhere dux'.

[49] P. Stafford, 'The King's wife in Wessex 800–1066', *Past & Present*, xc (1981), 3–27.

[50] Asser, cc. 13–15, pp. 11–14.

[51] Keynes and Lapidge, 231–2.

[52] Asser, c. 16, p. 14; *ASC*, *s.a.* 855, ed. Plummer, i. 66.

[53] Asser, c. 18, p. 17.

Æthelred, though he had young sons of his own, agree that Alfred should be his successor, clearly the implication of the title, *secundarius*, that Asser gives Alfred at this point?[54] That may only be a later inference (or gloss) on Asser's part. Perhaps Æthelred wished to avoid a family conflict; feared for the future of Wessex under a child-king, especially now with Vikings attacking? Perhaps. Or Æthelred may have been planning the succession of his own son Æthelwold, with the support of the boy's uncle, *Wulfhere princeps*. He may have calculated that given another ten years, Æthelwold would be able to secure his own succession. But Æthelred did not live another ten years. When he died in 871, it was extremely lucky for Alfred that he too could join Kent to his West Saxon dominion—'as was right'?

If horizontal, fraternal, succession had made Alfred king, he apparently did not follow the 'rule' consistently himself. It is true that his own wife kept, by Continental standards, a low profile.[55] But his plans for the next generation seem to have been of the more usual lineally-dynastic kind. He of course had no surviving brother, but he evidently lined up, probably late in his reign, the sole succession of his elder son Edward, who attests a charter as *rex* in 898.[56] Alfred seems to have been responsible not only for spreading the story of his own royal anointing as a four-year-old child by the pope in Rome, but for replicating that mythical rite in his investiture of Edward's four-year-old son, Alfred's grandson Athelstan, in 898.[57] It was probably while Alfred was still alive that a new Anglo-Saxon royal consecration *ordo* was prepared in which some stress was laid on a united realm.[58] But it may be misleading to present the 898 succession plan as Alfred's: like Charlemagne's division-project of 806, which really did break with tradition, the plan may reveal more of the ambitions of an eldest son and his aristocratic backers at a particular historic moment than of any paternal preference.[59] By 900, when he was consecrated king, Edward had probably repudiated Athelstan's mother and married Ælfflaed. It may well have been Ælfflaed for whom the Second *Ordo*'s rite for a queen's conse-

[54] D. Dumville, 'The Aetheling: a study in Anglo-Saxon constitutional history', *ASE*, viii (1979), 1–33, at 1–2, 24; Keynes and Lapidge 240, n. 56.

[55] Asser, c. 29, p. 24, names the parents of Alfred's wife, but not the wife herself. Her place in Alfred's will was relatively insignificant: Keynes and Lapidge, 177.

[56] Sawyer, no. 350.

[57] Nelson, 'The problem of Alfred's anointing'; M. Lapidge, 'Some Latin poems as evidence for the reign of Athelstan', *ASE*, ix (1981), 61–98, at 79–81.

[58] Nelson, 'The Second English *Ordo*', in *Politics and Ritual in the Early Middle Ages* (1986), 361–74.

[59] For Charlemagne's project, see P. Classen, 'Karl der Grosse und der Thronfolge im Frankenreich', in *Festschrift für H. Heimpel* (3 vols., Göttingen, 1972), iii. 109–34.

cration was first used.[60] And it was Ælfflaed's son Ælfweard whom Edward later envisaged would succeed him in Wessex.

Alfred's younger son Æthelweard, was educated in Latin.[61] He may have been destined for the Church, and the provision for him in his father's will hardly seems very generous.[62] Not for him a recreated sub-kingdom of Kent. Nor perhaps could he have been assigned the Mercian kingdom that his father acquired in the 880s.[63] For Alfred may not have had that option, any more than his near-contemporary Henry the Fowler, founder of the Saxon *Reich*, could have assigned one of his acquired *regna* to his younger son: the aristocracy there would not have stood for it.[64] Alfred's best alternative was to underwrite the régime of the Mercian Æthelred, his son-in-law. So it is hard to be sure if Alfred had, as Plummer believed, a vision of English unity, even of West Saxon/Mercian unity, or if he was just prudently adapting to circumstances. In the longer run, the interests of the dynasty might produce a re-division. Alfred might not have been disappointed could he have known of his son Edward's eventual plan to leave Mercia to one, Wessex to the other, of his own two elder sons.[65] Twenty years or so after Alfred's death, Edward hoped to cajole, or coerce, Mercian acceptance of this arrangement. As for Edward's·own brother, Æthelweard, he seems not, in the end, to have been consigned to the Church. But if he protested at his exclusion from the royal succession, the sources are silent.

In Continental perspective, such a silence looks suspicious. We know that one of Alfred's nephews, Æthelwold, like several Carolingian nephews in similar circumstances, protested at his exclusion: no sooner was Alfred dead than Æthelwold tried to gain support in Wessex. He began by seizing the *tun* where his own father was buried. Then he found help from the Northumbrian Danes. As significant are the *Anglo-Saxon Chronicle*'s hints of Kentish and Mercian complicity. But his cousin Edward slew him in battle.[66] It is presumably a tribute to Alfred's charisma that his nephew rebelled only

---

[60] Nelson, 'Second English *Ordo*', 367.

[61] Asser, c. 75, p. 58.

[62] Keynes and Lapidge, 175 (*pace* their comment at 256).

[63] See below, 60–1.

[64] J. B. Gillingham, *The Kingdom of Germany in the High Middle Ages* (1971), 9–10.

[65] *ASC* 'D', *s.a.* 924, ed. Plummer, i. 105. Compare A. Williams, 'Some notes and considerations on problems connected with English royal succession, 860–1066', *Proc. of the Battle Conference on Anglo-Norman Studies*, i (1978), 144–67, at 149–52; also S. Keynes, 'King Athelstan's books', in *Learning and Literature in Anglo-Saxon England*, ed. M. Lapidge and H. Gneuss (Cambridge, 1985), 143–201, at 187.

[66] *ASC*, *s.a.* 900 (*recte* 899), 904 (*recte* 901), 905 (*recte* 902), ed. Plummer, i. 92–4; Keynes and Lapidge, 292.

after his death. But if such conflict could be inhibited or postponed, it could not be eliminated for the Cerdicings, any more than for the Carolingians. Alfred, like Charlemagne, was a wicked uncle who pushed nephews' claims aside; but he can be claimed a successful father, at least in the sense that his sons are not known to have rebelled against him. Charlemagne too, despite the Hunchback's revolt, for the most part kept his sons' fidelity. Other Carolingians, like other Cerdicings and their descendants, did not even do as well as that.

Alfred's achievement as a father was the result of good management, as well as luck: management, that is, of his elder son whose patience he encouraged by great expectations, and of his younger whose resignation he encouraged by education from an early age for an alternative destiny; and management, also, of magnates who might goad, or seduce, princes into rebellion. Alfred's adroit use of his educational programme to promote aristocratic loyalty was pointed out some years ago by Professor Loyn, and more recently, by Professor Davis.[67] But there was more to it than 'propaganda'. The exemplary fate of Wulfhere may have acted as a deterrent to potential defectors. But Alfred's political success lay, more positively, in his capacity to hold out the prospect of rewards. It is the nature of these rewards that now requires closer definition; and a Continental perspective will allow a clearer appreciation of their significance.

The Vikings are often seen as Alfred's most formidable enemy, threatening Wessex with destruction and Alfred himself with a grisly death.[68] His achievement is usually portrayed as having been won in the teeth of Viking opposition. But the Vikings' relationship to Alfred's success may be more ambiguous, if no less crucial. Though the *Anglo-Saxon Chronicle* under-records it, the Viking onslaught on Kent immediately before, and during the early years of, Alfred's reign had important consequences for the distribution of power in southern England. Coastal attacks eliminated the Kentish ministers which Alfred's father and grandfather had sworn to protect. The communities presumably fled to the protection of their Kentish aristocratic kin. Some of their estates, however, when next recorded are held by West Saxon kings. Professor Brooks is surely right in concluding that what had taken place was 'a massive transfer of wealth from ecclesiastical to lay hands'.[69] Clearly the 'lay hands'

[67] H. R. Loyn, 'The term *ealdorman* in the translations prepared at the time of King Alfred', *EHR*, lxviii (1953), 513–25; R. H. C. Davis, 'Alfred the Great: propaganda and truth', *History*, lvi (1971), 169–82.

[68] A. P. Smyth, *Scandinavian Kings in the British Isles 850–880* (Oxford, 1977), 246–8.

[69] N. Brooks, *The Early History of the Church of Canterbury* (Leicester, 1984), 201–6. See also R. Fleming, 'Monastic lands and England's defence in the Viking age', *EHR*, c (1985), 247–65.

were not only 'royal hands'. K. F. Werner has written of 'a monarchy through whose hands wealth and power only passed and an aristocracy in whose hands they stayed'.[70] Werner of course had the Carolingians in mind. But Alfred could hardly evade similar pressures. The minister lands were, on Brooks's showing, a windfall for Alfred—which means, incidentally, that Alfred was being slightly disingenuous when he referred nostalgically to the times 'before everything was ransacked and burned'.[71] The usefulness of such windfalls for medieval (and later) kings usually lay in their availability for redistribution. Alfred may have been in a strong enough position to hold on to a substantial share of these acquisitions for himself and his son and heir: in his will Alfred left Edward 'all my booklands in Kent'.[72] The union of Kent to West Saxon dominion was there to stay. And if more of Alfred's charters had survived, it might have been possible to demonstrate what can only be guessed: that some of the Kentish windfalls had been given to powerful West Saxon supporters of Edward's sole succession. Some estates may have been leased and later resumed by the royal overlord, in a process often termed 'feudal' when it occurs on the Continent.

Alfred's acquisition of Mercia involved similar luck and good management. But at the outset of his reign, his prospects must have appeared distinctly less promising in Mercia than in Kent. In 871, Mercia was still a powerful kingdom. Even after heavy Viking incursions culminated in King Burgred's flight in 874 and the agreement of his successor Ceolwulf to pay tribute to the Vikings, this last Mercian king was far more than the mere Danish puppet-ruler implied by the *Anglo-Saxon Chronicle* in an annal clearly written up after Ceolwulf's disappearance from the scene.[73] In 877, the reduction of Ceolwulf's kingdom to the regions south and west of Watling Street may have resulted in part from Alfred's deflection of a Viking army from Wessex. The *Chronicle* tells us no more of Ceolwulf. But the last stage of his career can perhaps be reconstructed from other sources. The charter referred to above, in which Ealdorman Wulfhere's fate is recorded, states that his condemnation was pronounced by the councillors of, not just the West Saxons, but also the Mercians.[74]

---

[70] Werner, 'Bedeutende Adelsfamilien im Reich Karls des Grossen', in *Karl der Grosse. Lebenswerk und Nachleben*, ed. W. Braunfels and H. Beumann (4 vols., Düsseldorf, 1965), i. 83–142, at 122 (trans. T. Reuter in *The Medieval Nobility*, ed. Reuter (Amsterdam–London, 1978), 137–202).

[71] Prose preface to Old English version of Gregory's *Pastoral Care*, Keynes and Lapidge, 125.

[72] Keynes and Lapidge, 175.

[73] *ASC*, s.a. 874, ed. Plummer, i. 72. See P. Stafford, *The East Midlands in the Early Middle Ages* (Leicester, 1985), 109–11.

[74] Sawyer, no. 362; *EHD*, no. 100, p. 542.

The obvious explanation is that a West Saxon/Mercian alliance held good at the time: that is, surely, in 878.

There is of course no documentary evidence for this. But I think there may be some numismatic evidence. Alfred, after the large heavily debased issues of lunette-type pennies in the early years of his reign, suddenly began to mint good silver coins. And he issued them jointly with the Mercian king—the last Mercian king—Ceolwulf. Especially noteworthy among these joint-issues is the two-emperors coin (modelled on a fourth-century Roman type), whose obverse entitles Alfred 'REX ANGLO', and whose reverse design, being 'surely too complicated for wholesale production of dies', in Mr Stewart Lyon's view, shows that this 'must have been a special issue'.[75] If the special issue was for a special occasion, was that occasion a joint victory: Edington, and are the coins themselves the sole surviving evidence for the Mercians' part in that victory? Only after Edington was the flow of plunder and tribute from Wessex and Mercia to the Danes reversed, supplying the silver for Alfred and Ceolwulf to mint good pennies for the first time in their reigns. These pennies are our last record of Ceolwulf: Mercian history is a blank between 878 and 883 when we find 'Æthelred the ealdorman, enriched with part of the Mercian realm' granting lands 'with the leave of Alfred the king'.[76] According to Asser, Alfred the truth-teller had an explanation for why the West Saxons no longer had queens. But the truth-teller's *Chronicle* preferred silence when it came to explaining why the Mercians no longer had kings.

The details of Alfred's political settlement in Mercia are obscure: we do not even know when he arranged the marriage between his daughter Æthelflaed and Ealdorman Æthelred.[77] There is one possible case of a West Saxon magnate being endowed by Alfred with lands in newly acquired Mercia.[78] But in Continental perspective, another strategy seems likely too. Charlemagne annexed Bavaria by convincing enough Bavarian nobles that it was time to abandon their duke, Tassilo, and become instead the faithful men of Charles

[75] C. S. S. Lyon, 'Historical problems of Anglo-Saxon coinage (2)', *British Numismatic Journal*, xxxvii (1968), 216-38, at 236. See also R. H. M. Dolley and C. M. Blunt, 'The chronology of the coins of Ælfred the Great 871-99', in *Anglo-Saxon Coins: Studies presented to F. M. Stenton*, ed. R. H. M. Dolley (1961), 77-95, at 78-82; and M. Dolley, 'Alfred the Great's abandonment of the concept of periodic recoinage', in *Studies in Numismatic Method presented to Philip Grierson*, ed. C. N. L. Brooke *et al.* (Cambridge, 1983), 153-60. On the significance of the 'REX ANGLO' inscription, see W. Stevenson, in his edition of Asser, 151-2.

[76] Sawyer, no. 218.

[77] Stevenson, in Asser, 300.

[78] Sawyer, no. 219: see C. Hart, 'Athelstan "half king" and his family', *ASE*, ii (1973), 115-44, at 116-8.

and the Franks; and Charles the Bald acquired part of his deceased nephew's kingdom by winning over the magnates of that region.[79] Thus, presumably, Alfred won over Ealdorman Æthelred whose acceptance of his overlordship 'must have been', to quote Professor Whitelock, 'one of the greatest moments of satisfaction in Alfred's life'.[80] Alfred also attracted the loyalty of Waerferth, bishop of Worcester, who became in the 880s one of his closest allies, and the Mercian scholars Plegmund, future archbishop of Canterbury, Athelstan and Werwulf. This, at any rate, is what Asser implies when he describes how Alfred 'summoned them to him from Mercia, and exalted them with many honours and lands in the realm of the West Saxons, not counting those that Waerferth and Plegmund already had in Mercia'.[81]

There is one further hint of Alfred's way with Mercia: namely, his treatment of the minster of Abingdon in Berkshire. Two twelfth-century sources, resisting the tide of opinion favourable to Alfred, record his 'robbery by violence' of Abingdon's lands and his 'reduction' of them, 'on the advice of evil men', to 'the uses of himself and his men'.[82] Plummer was frankly incredulous: 'It is hard to believe that Alfred can have been guilty of deliberate wrong'.[83] But the Kentish minsters had succumbed to such 'uses'. Even West Saxon churches may have suffered from what, we recall, Archbishop Æthelred denounced as Alfred's 'wronging the house of the Lord': a possibly authentic charter refers to a scarcely veiled appropriation of land belonging to the bishop and community of Winchester.[84] Indeed the sheer absence of Alfredian charters endowing Winchester, or any other church, may not be accidental.

At this point, I want to return to the Continental perspective I began with: the complaints of Archbishop Fulk and Pope John about the licentiousness of English bishops, priests and laymen. How seriously should we take these complaints? Fulk's *perversissima secta* and *feminae subintroductae* (both vanish in Professor Whitelock's bland translation) sound like reminiscences of councils of the Early Church. Certainly Fulk does not link the problem of English vice with any contemporary circumstances, such as the Viking impact:

[79] *Annales Regni Francorum*, *s.a.* 787, ed. F. Kurze, MGH, *SRG* (Hannover, 1895), 78; *Annales Bertiniani*, *s.a.* 869, p. 157.

[80] D. Whitelock, 'The importance of the battle of Edington', reprinted in *From Bede to Alfred* (1980), XIII, 6-15, at 8.

[81] Asser, c. 77, p. 62.

[82] *Chronicon Monasterii de Abingdon*, ed. J. Stevenson (2 vols., Rolls ser., ii, 1858), i, 50; William of Malmesbury, *Gesta Pontificum*, ed. N. E. S. A. Hamilton (Rolls ser., lii, 1870), 191.

[83] Plummer, in his edn. of *ASC*, ii. 113.

[84] Sawyer, no. 354.

rather, for him, the problem is as old as it is English. As far as allegations of lay immorality are concerned, this is a case of the pot calling the kettle black. Fulk's own predecessor Hincmar of Rheims had written a treatise against Franks who abducted widows and nuns. In *c.* 906, Regino of Prüm devoted nearly thirty chapters of his penitential handbook to varieties of incest. In 909, the council of Trosly near Soissons denounced, lengthily, a whole gamut of sexual offences.[85] English vice was evidently Frankish as well. But perhaps Fulk, and Pope John VIII who voiced similar complaints only about the English, knew a letter of the Englishman St Boniface who on his Continental travels in the eighth century had professed embarrassment at finding the English reproached 'by both Christians and pagans for their refusal to have lawful wives'.[86] Fulk and the pope may well have preferred this authority to contemporary rapportage. There is another papal letter, however, which does seem to suggest that by contemporary Continental standards not English laymen but English clergy, bishops as well as priests, were extraordinarily laid back. John VIII urged the clergy in England to follow the example of their confrères in Rome whom he had persuaded 'voluntarily to give up the lay style of dress, voluminous—but also short'.[87] In the 870s, then, the English clergy as a body were notorious not only for having women but for dressing like laymen. I have not found that complaint about the Frankish clergy *en masse*. Nor is it easy to find cases of Carolingian bishops or monks (priests I admit are another matter) being accused of the same sexual offences as laymen. This difference in standards is I think symptomatic of a more general one: that is, the much smaller degree to which the church in England as compared with the Carolingian Empire was institutionally separate from the laity.

This contrast suggests a further dimension to the Continental perspective on Alfred: we can focus on divergent ecclesiastical responses to Viking attack. It is certainly not a question of contrasting English success with Carolingian failure. Many in England offered little or no resistance, or chose positively to collaborate: among these were monks and bishops. A minster community despoiled by Northumbrian kings had little reason to oppose their supplanters. Within a few years of the Danes' conquest of the Northumbrian kingdom, the

---

[85] Hincmar, *De Coercendo Raptu*, in *PL*, cxxv, cols. 1017-32; Regino, *De Ecclesiasticis Disciplinis Libri Duo*, II, clxxxiv-vi, cxcix, cciv-ccxx, ccxxii, ccxxiv-ccxxix, in *PL*, cxxxii, cols. 319-22, 325-30; Council of Trosly, *Acta*, ed. J. D. Mansi, *Sacrorum conciliorum nova et amplissima collectio* (31 vols., Venice, 1757-98), xviii, cols. 286-94.

[86] Boniface, *Epistolae* no. 74, ed. M. Tangl, MGH, *Epp. Selectae*, i (Berlin, 1916), 156 (trans. *EHD*, no. 178).

[87] '... sinuosum set et curtum': MGH, *Epp. Karolini Aevi*, v, 293-4 (trans. *EHD*, no. 221).

communities of St Cuthbert, and St Peter's York were actively supporting Danish overlords who for their part willingly accepted Christianity and the patronage of SS Cuthbert and Peter.[88] The evident
speed of the Danish settlement in much of England must have profited from such Anglo-Saxon attitudes. Perhaps the inmates of the
Kentish minsters fled too soon.

On the Continent, the Church in the mid-ninth century responded differently. Viking attacks on Francia were concentrated,
as it happened, on areas where the domanial régime with its increasing impositions on peasants had been becoming increasingly firmly
entrenched under Carolingian authority. And among those landlords who had done best out of the Carolingians were churches: the
great Benedictine monasteries and the bishoprics alike. Their vast
landholdings, scattered throughout the Carolingian kingdoms, replicated and sustained those of the kings who protected and sometimes endowed them.[89] In the West Frankish realm especially, the
demands for rent of monasteries with far-flung estates—the *domaines
excentriques*—promoted a circulation of coin within and between regions that helped the king to operate a realm-wide taxation system.
Churchmen, with their well-developed notion of the public good,
may have felt able to justify such royal exactions. But Danegeld hit
churches particularly hard. Therefore churchmen generally opposed
royal deals with Vikings. Individual churches were sometimes driven
to make deals of their own. But the Frankish Church as a whole—
and there is sound justification, as Dr McKitterick has shown, for
treating it as a whole—was a church militant, long schooled to the
obligation of military service. to the Carolingian state.[90] Duty and
corporate interest alike dictated firm resistance to intruders who
often scorned the saints and who, perhaps as seriously, provoked
peasant resistance that could easily become socially subversive.[91]
The case of the monks of Saint-Philibert who permanently left their

[88] *Historia de Sancto Cuthberto*, in *Symeonis Monachi Opera*, ed. T. Arnold (2 vols., Rolls
ser., lxxv, 1882–5), i. 203, 209 (trans. *EHD*, no. 6); P. Sawyer, *Kings and Vikings*
(1982), 137–8.

[89] A. Verhulst, 'La genèse du régime domanial classique en France', in *Agricoltura e
mondo rurale in Occidente, Settimane di Studio del Centro Italiano di Studi sull' alto Medioevo*,
xiii (Spoleto, 1966), 135–60; L. Musset, 'Signification et destinée des domaines excentriques pour les abbayes ... de la Gaule', in *Sous la Règle de Saint Benoit. Structures
monastiques et sociétés en France du Moyen Age a l'époque moderne*, Hautes études médiévales et
modernes, xlvii (Geneva–Paris, 1982), 167–84; J.-P. Devroey, 'Un monastère dans
l'économie d'échanges', *Annales. Économies, Sociétés, Civilisations*, xxxix (1984), 570–89.

[90] R. McKitterick, *The Frankish Church and the Carolingian Reforms* (1977). See also F.
Prinz, *Klerus und Krieg im früheren Mittelalter* (Stuttgart, 1971).

[91] *Annales Bertiniani, s.a.* 859, p. 80. See S. Epperlein, *Herrschaft und Volk im karolingischen Imperium* (Berlin, 1969), 49–50.

island monastery is almost the exception that proves the rule. Other communities fled to return and fight another day.[92]

At Corbie the young abbot had a way of 'pitching [himself] unarmed right into the midst of battle, [his] youthful energy drawn in by greed for winning'.[93] The flourishing genre of Carolingian miracle stories, often associated with temporary removals of saints' bones to save them from Viking attacks, strongly affirmed the permanence of monastic communities. Their message was one of confidence and victory. Recording a Viking raid in 860, the author of the *Miracles of St Bertin* described how the Viking chiefs themselves piled their loot for safe-keeping on St Bertin's altar (though the saint's bones had been taken away by the fleeing monks) and entrusted it to a monk who had chosen not to flee. When some of the Viking rank-and-file tried to steal the loot, they were condemned by their own chiefs for sacrilege—and hanged by the monastery gate: 'a divine manifestation, even through the judgement of infidels'.[94] The Vikings are accommodated in this writer's optimistic world-view. From the 880s when Viking armies raided northern Francia almost at will, there is plenty of evidence for the churches' will to resist and their continuing identification with kings who resisted.[95]

The problem was not lack of will on the part of clerics or laymen, but lack of co-ordination and long-term planning. And here the local horizons of the chroniclers are revealing. They thought no longer (or only nostalgically) in terms of the Frankish people, still less of the Frankish realm, partitioned as Hincmar put it into 'little bits'.[96] They thought now in terms of localities, epitomized in the strongholds of the saints. This was not the result of the imposition of local lay control on the churches. Rather the fragmentation of concerns came first, and it was the consequence of the kind of sudden collapse of royal authority to which medieval régimes were liable when a run of weak or very young kings, or short reigns, followed strong ones. After the mid-870s the Carolingians were extraordinarily unlucky in the fates of their kings: two in East, two in West Francia, all of them vigorous and able, died between 880 and 884.[97]

---

[92] P. Riché, 'Conséquences des invasions normandes sur la culture monastique dans l'Occident franc', in *I Normanni, Settimane di Studio*, xvi (Spoleto, 1968), 705-21 (reprinted in Riché, *Instruction et vie religieuse dans le Haut Moyen Age* (1981), no. 20).

[93] Lupus, *Correspondance*, ii. 138.

[94] *Miracula Sancti Bertini*, c. 2, ed. O. Holder-Egger, MGH, *Scriptores*, xv (Hannover, 1887-8), 510 (written in the 890s).

[95] P. Fouracre, 'The context of the OHG Ludwigslied', *Medium Aevum*, liv (1985), 87-103.

[96] Hincmar, *Acta* of Synod of St. Macra de Fismes, c. 8, in *PL*, cxxv, col. 1085.

[97] In West Francia, Louis III (882) and Carloman (884); in East Francia, Carloman (880) and Louis (882).

For royal authority in the Frankish heartland between the rivers Seine and Rhine, the prime object of Viking attacks, the reign of Charles the Fat (882–7) was disastrous. He lacked a personal base anywhere but Alamannia: it was no coincidence that he was fêted at Saint-Gall, where, in the 88os, Notker the Stammerer told funny stories about indigent Vikings.[98]

Monks in Francia might not have seen the joke. The reaction of churchmen there in the 88os was of critical importance: it is not just the sources' ecclesiastical slant that makes bishops and abbots appear key political actors in Francia. Great landlords and great warlords because their institutionalized place in the Carolingian régime had made them so, these men were faced with new roles: no longer as the backers, or the makers, of kings, but as territorial princes. Thus Archbishop Fulk of Rheims fortified various estate-centres belonging to his church, sought new strongholds, and came into conflict with Count Baldwin of Flanders, who instigated Fulk's murder.[99] Such rivalry itself was not new; but its significance was altered when the king was no longer in a position to hold the ring. Local priorities filled the scene. Churches lost control of their excentric domains, the kings of their fisc-lands in the provinces. The Frankish Church which for a century and a half sustained and was sustained by the kings of the Franks dissolved into many churches that had to fend for themselves as best they could, often becoming the proprietary churches of local noble families. The later Carolingians, shorn of their ancestors' carefully nurtured ecclesiastical support as thoroughly as ever the last Merovingian was shorn of his locks, were reduced to territorial princes themselves.

In the perspective of these Continental developments let us look again at Alfred—a king who, as Professor Wallace-Hadrill once observed, 'was short of bishops'; and as Asser reveals was even shorter of Benedictine monks.[100] Perhaps such shortages were a blessing in disguise. The West Saxon kingdom (and for that matter the kingdoms of Northumbria and Mercia) never had incorporated the church as had, for centuries since, the kingdom of the Franks. No Anglo-Saxon king ever made 10,000 solidi a year (or sterling equivalent) out of selling bishoprics. No Anglo-Saxon king could conceive a realm-wide *Klosterpolitik*.[101] Such Frankish power-circuits had

[98] Notker, *Gesta Karoli*, ii, cc. 18, 19, ed. H. F. Haefele, MGH, *SRG* (Berlin, 1959), 88–90.

[99] G. Schneider, *Erzbischof Fulco von Reims (883–900) und das Frankenreich* (Munich, 1975), 172–82.

[100] Wallace-Hadrill, 149; Asser, cc. 92, 93, pp. 79–81.

[101] Nelson, 'Queens as Jezebels: the careers of Brunhild and Balthild', in *Medieval Women*, ed. D. Baker (Studies in Church History, Subsidia, i, 1978), 31–77, at 52–73.

their contacts in old Roman *civitates* where saints were before the Franks ever came. *Entente* between church and Frankish kings had been fostered from the first by city-based bishops, later by suburban monks. Bede wished it so in England too. But there the truth of the matter was that gentile patriotism—the twin ideas of the *gens Anglorum* and the *ecclesia Anglorum*—did not match realities.[102] Because of the discontinuity between Roman and post-Roman régimes, because of the relatively late development of powerful kingdoms, the churches of Angles and Saxons grew up in the interstices of local aristocratic lordship. That was why ecclesiastical property was so vulnerable, why kings treated it no differently from other powerful laymen, and why the charter, the land-book, intended by churchmen to protect church property, could become in England, in the hands of the lay aristocracy, an instrument to guarantee the rights of the noble kindred.[103] The landholding of English churches corresponded to their origins in being regionalised within the old seventh-century kingdoms. There were few excentric domains. Thus the destruction of ecclesiastical landlordship in Northumbria had few repercussions elsewhere in England. As for the king of Wessex, since a realm-wide royally sustained church even within that small kingdom had never existed, its absence could not be missed. Whatever the Vikings did to churches in England, they damaged local interests, lay and ecclesiastical, rather than royal ones.

The single largest ecclesiastical lordship in England was surely that of the church of Canterbury. Its resources, like those of the Kentish minsters, had never been at the disposal of those Mercian or West Saxon kings before Alfred who had tried to dominate the south-east. Rather, the church in Kent provided a focus of resistance to successive would-be overlords.[104] Hence Viking damage here gave Alfred his opportunity: the installation of the outsider, Plegmund, signalled a new and lasting relationship between Canterbury and the West Saxon monarchy. Within Wessex itself, the church of Winchester, impoverished by the Vikings, was forced into closer dependence on the king. But neither Winchester nor Sherborne is known to have functioned as a major support for Alfred. Only in Mercia can we discern in Alfred's dealings with the see of Worcester the beginnings of an English imperial church on Carolingian lines.[105]

---

[102] See P. Wormald, 'Bede, the *Bretwaldas* and the origins of the *gens Anglorum*', in *Ideal and Reality in Frankish and Anglo-Saxon Society*, ed. Wormald (Oxford, 1983), 99–129.

[103] Alfred's Laws, c. 41, Keynes and Lapidge, 168 with 309 n. 24.

[104] Brooks, *Church of Canterbury*, pt 3.

[105] Sawyer, no. 223 (trans. *EHD*, no. 99). Eahlstan and Heahmund of Sherborne are the only English bishops known to have played a military role in the 9th century: *ASC*, *s.a.* 823 (recte 825), ed. Plummer, i. 60, 845 (recte 848), p. 64, and 871, p. 72.

The fundamental contrast between Alfred's realm and a Carolingian one is neatly epitomized in a comparison of two crises. In 858 when his West Frankish realm was invaded by a rival Carolingian, Charles the Bald's survival was due in large measure to ecclesiastical support—negatively in terms of bishops' refusal to help the invader, positively in terms of the military service provided by episcopal and monastic contingents.[106] In 878 Alfred's West Saxon realm was invaded by the Viking chief Guthrum: Alfred's survival was due to the support of the men Asser called his 'noble followers and vassals' or, in the words of a tenth-century chronicler, 'the men who used the royal feed'—Alfred's military household, his hearth-companions.[107] At this early stage in his reign, they consisted of Somerset men: Somerset had perhaps been Alfred's apanage before 871.[108] Later Assar says they came to include 'many Franks, Frisians, Gauls, pagans, Welsh, Irish and Bretons'.[109] The pagans there are significant. For they remind us that the personal loyalties of the war-band were more important at this aristocratic social level than local, or even religious, still less ethnic, communities. Alfred recruited Vikings—just as Guthrum, it seems, recruited Ealdorman Wulfhere.

A Continental perspective can help to bring Alfred's reign into sharper focus. The many ways in which the political conditions of ninth-century Wessex resembled those on the other side of the Channel are clear. But the relative underdevelopment of church—state relations in the English kingdoms as compared with the Continent emerges as a major difference. It allowed Alfred room for manoeuvre in coping with political problems which the Vikings accentuated but did not create. Where the ninth-century Carolingians sought territorial expansion by appropriating each others' kingdoms, Alfred could exploit the geography of the Viking attacks on England not only to weaken Kentish and Mercian resistance to West Saxon pressure, but to appropriate exposed church lands and use them to create a new political solidarity in his composite realm.

Comparison with Continental rulers supplies realistic criteria on which to judge Alfred's success. The effect is to magnify rather than

---

I took a rather different view of this evidence in 'The Church's military service in the ninth century', *Studies in Church History*, xx (1983), 15–30, at 18–19. Further reflection has convinced me that Hincmar's contrast between Frankish and English arrangements was more firmly grounded in contemporary realities than I allowed in 1983.

[106] Nelson, 'Charles the Bald and the Church in town and countryside', *Studies in Church History*, xvi (1979), 103–18.

[107] Asser, cc. 53, 55, pp. 41, 44; *The Chronicle of Æthelweard*, ed. A. Campbell (Nelson's Medieval Texts, 1962), 42.

[108] Perhaps implied by Asser, c. 55, as John Gillingham kindly points out.

[109] Asser, c. 76, p. 60.

reduce. 'The king across the sea', as much as any Carolingian, ful-filled contemporaries' expectations of him as lord and ring-giver. He held loyalties, noble and familial. He knew how to project himself as a ruler, in the words of the Second English *Ordo* 'stablishing his realm unitedly'. Above all, he seized his opportunities, turning others' difficulties to his own advantage. In the nature of early medieval source-material, any judgement on Alfred's moral charac-ter is risky: the 'man urgent ... in his search after the eternal verities' can't at this distance be distinguished from the hoped-for patron of his scholar-clerks or their remodelling of the philosopher-ruler (cour-tesy of Boethius) in the image of the pious king.[110] In Alfred's private history, ideal has submerged reality. But something can be recovered of his public history. Amid changing times, he could adapt policy to fortune; he was, in Machiavelli's sense, a virtuous prince.

[110] Whitelock, 'Importance of Edington', 9.

II

WEALTH AND WISDOM
THE POLITICS OF ALFRED THE GREAT*

It is a truism that every age tends to recreate the past in its own image, as myth. Since professional historians are not immune to this process, anachronism is, as Lucien Febvre said, their cardinal sin.[1] In the nineteenth century, the image of King Alfred of Wessex, round whom a thick accretion of moralising and chauvinist myth had gathered since the eleventh century, acquire a new clarity and consistency: as nation-builder and paragon of virtue, Alfred became firmly fixed in popular mythology and scholarly historiography alike.[2] A series of thousand-year anniversaries of Alfred's life coincided both with the heyday of nationalist and imperialist sentiment in Victorian England, and with the rise of History as an academic discipline.[3] In 1849, the millenium of Alfred's birth at Wantage in Berkshire was celebrated with a feast of distinguished persons in that town, and plans for a new edition of Alfred's works.[4] In 871, the millenium of his accession to the kingdom of Wessex, saw the publication of Thomas Hughes' *Life of Alfred*.[5] A prominent Christian socialist, Hughes wrote as "an Englishmen for Englishmen," offering to the co-operative movement a model of hard work, good sense, personal responsibility and patriotism. The millenium of Alfred's death was marked by popular celebrations in Winchester, where he was buried, and, soon after, by Charles Plummer's delivery at Oxford of the Ford Lectures for 1901 on "The Life and Times of Alfred the Great," published the following year by the Oxford University Press.[6]

In what remains the best and fullest study of Alfred, Plummer compared his hero to the great rulers of Europe's past, uniformly to their detriment. Marcus Aurelius had been "guilty of sad self-suppression." Charlemagne of "lax morality." There had been "something almost tradesmanlike" about Edward I, while St. Louis' very saintliness had "shed a consecration on an evil despotism, which finally exploded in one of the most hideous convulsions in history. . . . the French Revolution." Unlike all these, Alfred was "an unmixed blessing" to his people, and to posterity.[7]

Plummer's picture of Alfred was of course supported by the medieval sources. Only two pieces of evidence seemed not quite to fit. One I shall come to in a moment. The other was the twelfth-century Abingdon Chronicler's denunciation of Alfred as "a Judas piling evil on evils," who had taken lands from the monastery of Abingdon and not returned to God an adequate compensation: *imparem reddens talionem*. Plummer concluded that there must have been some mistake here: "It is hard to believe that Alfred can have been guilty of deliberate wrong."[8]

In the recent B.B.C. television series, "In Search of the Dark Ages," Michael Wood set his Alfred episode in the wartime headquarters of Winston Churchill, evoking memories of national solidarity and resistance to foreign foes: ". . . we shall fight them on the beaches. We shall never surrender." Recently, again, the Royal Historical Society in London heard a similar story from Nicholas Brooks: Alfred, he told us, forged a nation in the crucible of defeat.[9]

There have been, it is true, a few iconoclasts who have sought to dent Alfred's idealised image in recent years. Michael Wallace-Hadrill pointed out that virtually all we know of Alfred's reign, notably the *Anglo-Saxon Chronicle*'s contemporary account, emanates from the king himself or from his court circle. "We hold that Alfred was a great and glorious king in part because he tells us he was."[10] R.H.C. Davis, pursuing the implications of this remark, suggested that Alfred himself directed the production of the *Anglo-Saxon Chronicle* as propaganda, twisting the truth a little, as Winston Churchill also did sometimes, to spur on his people to an unprecedented war-effort.[11] Davis's views have aroused strong ripostes from some English scholars, notably the late Dorothy Whitelock: "Is it really possible," she asked, "that a man as urgent as Alfred in his search after the eternal verities would sink to the deliberate circulation of falsehood?"[12]

Whitelock laid some stress on the fact that Asser, Alfred's contemporary and biographer, called the king *veredicus* — a teller of the truth.[13] But the context of Asser's label is worth noting: it is a story told by Alfred, a somewhat unsavoury story, of a wicked queen, Eadburh, who had accidentally poisoned her husband King Beorhtric of Wessex (her intended victim had been a rival, "a young man very dear to the king") in 802. The purpose of this story as related by Alfred was to account for the strangely low status of the king's wife in ninth-century Wessex: "as a result of [Eadburh's] very great wickedness, all the inhabitants of the land swore that they would never permit any king to reign over them who during his lifetime invited the queen to sit beside him on the royal throne."[14] Pauline Stafford has suggested that the story justified a strategy of fraternal succession used by the mid-ninth century West Saxon kings to ensure a line of adult heirs to the throne.[15] It was a myth. Whitelock, in any event, omitted from her partial translation of Asser's *Life* the whole passage about the truth-teller's tale.

Another of her omissions was that of Asser's chapter 74, dismissed by Whitelock as "a confused account of Alfred's illnesses."[16] Certainly the organization of chapter 74 is complex; but it is not confused.[17] As a youth, says Asser, Alfred asked God to afflict him with an illness that would inhibit sexual activity: God responded with "an agonizing infirmity," piles — ideal for Alfred's purpose. Then, as he reached manhood and contemplated marriage, Alfred, logically enough, asked God to substitute a different illness, one that would be less agonizing than piles and would not render him, sexually or militarily, "useless and contemptible." This time, God sent an illness that Alfred's contemporaries could not identify. Asser describes its first attack:

> When he had duly celebrated [his] wedding which took place ceremonially in Mercia in the presence of countless persons of both sexes, and after the feasting which lasted day and night, [Alfred] was struck without warning in the presence of the entire gathering by a sudden severe illness quite unknown to all physicians. Certainly it was not known to any of those who were present on that occasion. . . . Many, to be sure, alleged that it had happened through the spells and witchcraft of the people around him; others through the ill-will of the devil . . .; others through some unfamiliar kind of fever; and yet others thought it was piles because Alfred had suffered from that since his youth.[18]

From the nineteenth century onwards, scholars have found chapter 74 hard to swallow. To some, it seemed to point clearly towards the conclusion that Asser's *Life* was a later forgery.[29] Yet Whitelock, in her otherwise very effective defense of "the genuine Asser," sought no ammunition in chapter 74. Plummer rejected it as an interpolation: "We may be glad, I think, to free the historical Alfred from the atmosphere of morbid religiosity which taints this whole passage."[20] Asser's editor, W. Stevenson, shared Plummer's feeling of revulsion, but contrived to shift the charge of "morbid religiosity" from Alfred to Asser and (since Asser was a Welshman) Celtic piety in general.[21] We begin to suspect why Whitelock decided not to include chapter 74 in the extracts from Asser in *English Historical Documents*. Even the *Life*'s most recent translators, Simon Keynes and Michael Lapidge, seem to have found chapter 74 awkward. They suspect that Alfred's illness "was in part psychological."[22]

Why have Asser's modern readers found difficulty with chapter 74? The answer lies in a perception of something incongruous here: something that has seemed to conflict with the rest of what we know about Alfred. Nineteenth- and twentieth-century people do not expect a great statesman, a great war-leader, to be so odd: to show not merely the crankiness that made Alfred rise secretly before dawn to visit sanctuaries, but the mental instability that caused him to succumb to psychosomatic illness in public.

But for Asser and his contemporaries, Alfred's illnesses were not real but heaven-sent. Far from being cause for embarrassment, to be hushed up, the terrible affliction that befell Alfred at his wedding was something to be highlighted in a work written for Alfred and, presumably, his entourage. Asser knew that the episode would make sense to an audience ready to see suffering, and its remission, as divine visitations. Alfred's public pain, like his private devotions, signalled a special closeness to God. Thus the lesson of chapter 74 for modern readers is that we must be prepared to accommodate Alfred's illnesses, and the religiosity that made sense of them, in our image of the king. We must acknowledge that our preconceptions may be anachronistic. Further, when we meet what look like contradictions, rather than shoving them under the carpet we need to inspect them particularly closely, for it is precisely here that we may find clues to the less obvious and perhaps less immediately congenial aspects and motivations of our historical subjects.

Something of a contradiction, or to us, at least, a paradox, lies at the heart of Alfred's career. He pursued, explicitly and with equal urgency, both wealth and wisdom. *Weal ond wisdom*: the pairing sounds as if it could be one of those proverbial alliterative pairings so beloved of the Anglo-Saxons. But in fact it is not a poetic cliché. It comes, of course, from Alfred's preface to the Old English version of Gregory the Great's *Pastoral Care*.[23] Alfred imagines men of the generation preceding his own, "before everything was ravaged and burnt", surveying the wealth of their churches, their treasures and books, bequeathed them by their forefathers who loved wisdom:

> It is as if they had said: "Our ancestors . . . loved wisdom and through it they obtained wealth, and left it to us. Their track can still be seen but we cannot follow it up."

And Alfred comments:

> We [meaning his own generation] have now lost both the wealth and the wisdom.[24]

Alfred declares his intention to reverse this historical process: he will make it possible for wisdom to be recovered, by promoting vernacular as well as Latin learning; and through wisdom, wealth too will be recovered.

Now while it is perfectly clear from the context — Alfred is, after all, addressing his bishops — that wisdom here has religious connotations, that the books are holy books, it is equally clear that religion, for Alfred, had material effects. There is no getting away from the concrete meaning of Old English *weal*. Etymologically, its primary reference is to moveable wealth. It was used synonymously with *hord* (hoard) and *feoh* (cattle, moveables, money). It was a glossarist's rendering of *gazofilacium* (treasury).[25] And it was the primary meaning wealth that gave rise to the secondary, extended sense of well-being, hence early modern English 'weal'. When he spoke of *weal*, Alfred meant money.

Why should Alfred's linking of money with wisdom seem odd? There is after all plenty of warrant in christian tradition for making piety a condition of, indeed a means to, material benefits. In the more optimistic passages of Scripture, the just man's rewards are vividly depicted in this world as well as the next. Solomon, a model for early medieval kings including Alfred, likened wisdom to "a treasure-store for men" ("those who use it become sharers of God's friendship"), and made Wisdom personified declare: "I shall enrich those who love me and fill up their treasure-stores."[26] Carolingian writers, much influenced by these Wisdom Books of the Old Testament, regarded wisdom as a prime royal virtue and source of benefits for kings. Through wisdom came justice, and peace.[27] But the explicit linkage of wisdom and wealth was not a Carolingian commonplace. If Alfred borrowed it from Solomon, he did so directly and not through a Continental intermediary. It was not that Carolingian kings cared less than Alfred did about material resources. But the scholars they patronized never admitted, as Alfred did, a particular concern with money. Greater Carolingian coyness or conventionality hardly account for this difference.

Nor is this the only difference between Carolingian and Alfredian concerns. There are well-known parallels between the "educational programs" of Charlemagne and Alfred.[28] But there are also contrasts. Charlemagne's overriding objective was the education of the clergy in Latin.[29] The cultural context of his efforts was a new definition of the distinctness of Latin from the evolving Romance vernaculars. With this went a new emphasis on Latin's uniqueness as a liturgical language and on its primacy as a literary and legal language too. In a Frankish Empire comprising German- and Romance-speaking populations, Latin alone could provide a *lingua franca*. But administrative considerations were not what Charlemagne put forward in his circular "about the cultivation of learning," rather, he expressed his anxiety that prayers incorrectly written and hence incorrectly said might be inoperative. The Church's indispensable function was to pray for Frankish victories, but the message could only be effective, magically, if the medium were correct Latin. While highborn lay people, including Charlemagne himself, might learn to read, they could rely on churchmen "to penetrate the mysteries of holy Writ" and to pray for them. Lay literacy was thus a spin-off rather than a central aim of Charlemagne's program.

For Alfred, by contrast, lay as well as clerical or monastic literacy was of prime importance. The learning he cultivated was expressed in the vernacular as well as in Latin, in a cultural context where the vernacular already had status as a literary and legal written language.[30] Alfred's motive, like Charlemagne's, was essentially religious: literacy was the route to wisdom. But Alfred, unlike Charlemagne, from the outset sought the active participation of laymen: "Think," he reminded his bishops, "what temporal punishments came upon us when we neither loved wisdom ourselves nor allowed it to other people." The intended beneficiaries of Alfred's programme were "all the free-born young men . . . who have the means to apply themselves [to learning]:" in other words, young aristocrats. They were to constitute the readership for the Old English versions of the books deemed by Alfred and his court scholars "the most necessary for all men to know." Asser adds the information that "nearly all" the adult aristocrats, "illiterate from childhood," also under pressure from Alfred "applied themselves in an amazing way to learning how to read". With such an audience in mind, Alfred could hardly fail to perceive the political implications of the pursuit of wisdom. He no doubt shared Charlemagne's confidence in the magical efficacy of prayer: when he recalled the times of former kings "who succeeded both in warfare and in wisdom," Alfred may have understood victory as the outcome of correct ritual performance on the part of "the religious order" as well as of piety on the part of kings themselves. But even in sketching an idealized past, Alfred envisages "men of learning" including men of "the secular order." When he comes to his own times, lay participation appears as his central concern. This characteristic of Alfred's programme, which distinguishes it so clearly from its Carolingian analogue, may provide the link between the king's preoccupation with money and his promotion of learning. Both *weal* and wisdom are worth exploring further.

Asser in his *Life of Alfred* went into some detail on Alfred's annual cash expenditure. That half of his annual income which he assigned to secular affairs was, according to Asser, divided into three, between three groups of royal *ministri*, "men who served": first the warrior retinue, second the men engaged on the king's works, making buildings or moveable items, third the visitors or guests who came to Alfred's court from far and near, "some demanding money, some not."[32] Elsewhere Asser suggests the role of money as well as of other rewards, in attracting followers to the king's military household and keeping it running well:

> Many Franks, Frisians, Gauls, pagans, Welsh, Irish and
> Bretons voluntarily gave themselves into his lordship and
> he endowed them with money and estates.[33]

Some of the Welsh princes too successfully sought Alfred's friendship:

> Those who desired to increase their worldly means got
> what they wanted; those who wanted money got money;
> those who wanted the king's *familiaritas* got that.[34]

Alfred's largesse was indeed wonderful, and Asser finds it perfectly appropriate to inform his readers (including Alfred) of his own share in it:
two Somerset monasteries (and Asser is especially interested in the
moveable wealth that went with them), "an extremely valuable silk cloak,
a quantity of incense weighing as much as a stout man," and "countless
daily gifts of wordly riches of every sort."[35]

The *Anglo-Saxon Chronicle* for Alfred's reign tells mainly of Viking
movements and the responses of the various English kingdoms under
attack. It is, of course, a West Saxon product. Successive annalists seem
to suppress West Saxon payments to buy off Viking armies: this is
something Kentishmen do.[36] But personal gift-giving by Alfred to individual Viking leaders is loudly proclaimed. Such generosity was a weapon
in the struggle, but it is portrayed as a symbol of superiority. Alfred
lavished "precious objects" on the newly-converted Viking leader
Guthrum after the battle of Edington in 878, and gave "a good deal of
money" in 893 to Hastein when his sons were baptised, and again when
they were released with their mother after capture.[37] Such gestures
established Alfred as, in the poetic eulogy of one of his bishops, "the
greatest treasure-giver of all the kings he has ever heard tell of, in recent times or long ago, or of any earthly king he had previously learned
of."[38]

We can gain a more exact impression of the scale of Alfred's giving
from the figures in his will, drawn up fairly late in the reign: a total
of nearly 500,000 silver pennies, or about Æ2,000.[39] About two-thirds
of it was bequeathed to Alfred's close kin, the rest was distributed among
magnates and the king's military retinue. Alfred's comment at the end
of the list of beneficiaries is more suggestive of the giver than the hoarder:
"I do not know for certain if there is so much — but I think so."

How had Alfred come by his 500,000 pennies? This was surely,
by early medieval standards, a remarkable quantity, amassed, moreover,
under difficult circumstances.[40] For it looks as if in the years immediately
preceding his accession in 871, and in the early years of his reign, the

"normal" resources of an early medieval king — plunder, tribute, in-coming gifts — were in quite abnormally short supply in the kingdom of Wessex, as in neighboring Mercia too. This impression arises from two kinds of evidence. First, the charters of the 860s and 870s show a striking increase in the number of references to money or treasure: so much so that instead of being rare, as in the eighth century, or quite common, as in the first half of the ninth, such references become usual in charters recording grants in these decades.[41] In other words, ostensible grants are in fact sales. This could of course just reflect changed notarial practice.[42] But the fact that mentions of money in surviving originals, after becoming so frequent in the second half of the ninth century, dwindle again in the tenth, is hardly a coincidence.[43] A correlation of land-sale with the need to meet Viking demands for money is explicit in a Mercian charter of 872. The bishop of Worcester "grants" land in Warwickshire to a king's thegn

> for his friendship, and for his pleasing money, and for
> his gift of 20 mancuses of purest gold,

and goes on to state that he does this

> on account of the immense tribute of the barbarians that
> same year when the pagans had made a base at
> London.[44]

Another charter tells a similar story, when the bishop of Winchester, unable to raise what he owed of "the tribute which our whole people was accustomed to pay the pagans," was driven to sell land to Alfred of Wessex who would then shoulder the burden.[45] Money paid to Vikings either settled elsewhere in England or departing to the Continent was money lost to Wessex.

That loss of bullion was indeed becoming a severe problem for the West Saxon kings by the 860s is confirmed by a second kind of evidence: that of coins. Alfred's elder brother and predecessor as king, Ethelred (866-71), issued large numbers of pennies of "Lunette" type, as did the Mercian king Burgred (852-74), evidently in conjunction with him.[46] The pennies of these issues, which began almost pure silver, became progressively debased, eventually being only 50%-30% fine. The early, still large, issues of Alfred were of the same type but show still further debasement, some pennies reaching a nadir of only 5-6% fine. The likeliest explanation is surely that the buying of "peace" from the Vikings had brought a fiscal crisis. This deepened during the first three years of Alfred's reign: the issues produced by Burgred in conjunction with Alfred became more and more debased until the former's abdication in 874.

But then came what D.M. Metcalf has called "an astonishing monetary comeback" represented by the coins of "Cross-and-Lozenge" type.[47] The issues were smaller, though still on quite a considerable scale.[48] But the coins were again of fine silver — a standard maintained in all Alfred's subsequent issues. The hoard-evidence suggests that, at the same time, the debased issues were demonetised: in other words, were no longer acceptable as currency. Can we date this recoinage precisely? It was organized, as in the 860s and early 870s, by the West Saxon and Mercian kings jointly, and the only firm dating derives from the reign-years of the Mercian king Ceolwulf, Burgred's successor. Unfortunately we do not know when he died: perhaps in 879, but possibly as late as 883.[49] In the joint issues of Alfred and Ceolwulf, the West Saxon output seems to have been much larger than the Mercian; nor is this surprising, given that Ceolwulf's kingdom was much smaller than Burgred's had been, covering only the southwestern part of Mercia. But Ceolwulf's contribution to the coinage is enough to belie the Anglo-Saxon Chronicle's dismissal of him as "a silly king's thegn."[50]

Why was this recoinage undertaken? It might be suggested that Alfred wished to stimulate "international" trade, that is, trade with the Vikings now settling in much of midland, eastern and northern England.[51] But this explanation may exaggerate the significance of such trade at this period, as well as attributing to Alfred priorities that are, frankly, anachronistic. "Traffic in livestock and goods" there no doubt was between Englishmen and Danes, though it could have been carried on by barter.[52] But the balance of trade could hardly have been foreseen with accuracy: a net outflow of money from Alfred's kingdom was perhaps a likelier outcome of trade across this frontier than the reverse.

It may be worth looking, instead, at the currency situation that Alfred, and Ceolwulf too, found within their own realms in the early 870s. The hoard-evidence shows that the debased coins circulated, thus were accepted, in the short run. It is indeed a remarkable fact that West

Saxon and Mercian kings could gain acceptance at all, even in the short run, for what was in effect a token coinage. But the fact of the recoinage suggests that, as so often happened in later centuries, the policy had run into difficulties; that confidence in the coinage had become shaky. This could well have meant that the use of money was declining: it seems no coincidence that we have so much more hoard evidence for the debased than for the revalued coinage. Such a decline would have worrying implications for kings used to collecting renders in cash.

But for the fullest explanation of the recoinage and the most convincing dating, we should look to politics as well as to economics. Alfred's position in 877, and Ceolwulf's too, was unenviable. It was not just that successive payments to the Vikings had beggared royal treasuries; but now the political consequences of such penury were beginning to show up. The aristocracy, like the Lord, loved a cheerful giver.[53] Alfred could not afford to be one. It seems likely that it was in the winter of 877-8, with a Viking band esconced within Wessex at Chippenhan in Wiltshire, that at least one magnate, the Ealdorman of Wiltshire had "deserted his lord King Alfred and his fatherland" to ally with the Vikings. Like the young Northumbrian nobles in the eighth century whose departure from their fatherland Bede lamented, like some ninth-century nobles in the Carolingian kingdoms, Alfred's great men must have been tempted to turn from an indigent king to a more generous ring-giver.[54] To keep their loyalty, and to reward those who stood by him (Alfred could not have foreseen, after all, that Edington in the early summer of 878 would be his last big battle), Alfred would have found it prudent to dig deeper than ever in his pockets. Ceolwulf of Mercia was in a similar position, dependent not only on Viking sufferance but on noble supporters to keep even the southern part of Mercia under his authority. How could a major recoinage fit into such circumstances?

A Continental comparison may be instructive. In 793 or 794, Charlemagne undertook a reform of the coinage, a revaluation small enough by comparison with Alfred's (only about a 30% increase in the silver content of his coins) yet expensive enough on an empire-wide scale. Why did Charlemagne do this? A number of economic historians and numismatists have alleged that the Carolingian economy was closely geared to that of the Muslim world; hence that Charlemagne's aim was to peg his pennies to Arab dinars, in order to stimulate international trade. This exercise in standing Pirenne on his head was sabotaged, with

II

characteristic coolness, by Philip Grierson, who offered a beautifully simple alternative explanation: Charlemagne decided that the weight of his coins would henceforth be based, no longer on a wheat-grain standard, but on a barley-grain one. Grierson hypothesised no deep symbolic significance in this decision, (no superseding of *Romanentum* by *Germanentum*!) but put it down to Charlemagne's passion for standardization, and the choice of penny-weight to personal preference.[55]

Grierson's picture of Charlemagne the standardizer is certainly more plausible than Charlemagne the expert in international economics. But while Grierson offers a reason for the level of the revaluation, he does not account for its timing. It is the date of the reform which points so strongly away from external factors, from Near Eastern exchange rates or inflows of bullion, and towards internal factors, to political relations within the Frankish realm. In 792, Charlemagne had faced the most serious rebellion, and perhaps the worst crisis, of his whole reign: the revolt of his own son Pippin the Hunchback, supported by a powerful faction of Frankish nobles. Charlemagne managed to crush this revolt. But a measure of his relief in so doing is the lavish scale of his treasure-giving in 793 to those nobles who had resisted the rebels' call.[56] The high cost of such gratitude implies a close-run thing.

The cost was met, I suggest, by a recoinage that was in fact, like other medieval *renovationes monetae*, a form of taxation.[57] It worked like this: you brought your 100 old pennies, each weighing, say, 1.3 grams of silver, to the mint, and you received back pennies of 1.7 grams each: not 70 new pennies, which would have left the government little better off, but perhaps 60, or even 50 pennies, which would guarantee the government (via the counts who ran the mints) a handsome profit. Evasion was precluded by the simple fact that old pennies were no longer acceptable as currency: if your money was to be worth anything, you had to pay Charlemagne's price. Resistance was precluded by the sheer new-found strength of Charlemagne's position: now if ever, with rebellion crushed, the king could recoup some of his outlay on rewarding support. Bestowal of wealth on the deserving was offset by a generalized tax on the whole realm. The coinage reform was a dramatic, and symbolic, demonstration of Charlemagne's reaffirmed power. Having distributed quantities of treasure, he proved himself in a position to acquire, hence to redistribute, still more. The political conditions which at once impelled and permitted Charlemagne to effect his reform were clearly operative in the early 790s, even before the acquisition of the fabulous Avar hoard in 796.[58]

Alfred's recoinage can now be reconsidered in the light of Charlemagne's. Its timing should, I suggest, be associated with a recent, decisive improvement in Alfred's political position. The obvious context therefore is the aftermath of the battle of Edington in 878. Though Alfred, as we saw, disbursed lavish gifts to his defeated foe, now at last there was the prospect that the outflow of plunder and tribute from Wessex had been staunched and that gifts might begin to flow back in to Alfred from new clients, Vikings and others. As important, victory had put Alfred in a position to punish a disloyal magnate, not just by deposing him from high office but by confiscation of his family lands. Politically, then, Alfred was now, for the first time in his reign, strong enough to effect a massive revaluation that must have imposed a heavy fiscal burden on his own people, and notably on those with substantial cash resources: namely, the aristocracy. The hoard evidence shows that the recoinage was effective.[59] In other words, the costs were met. Ceolwulf's joint-issues must have been the outcome of similar conditions in English Mercia: not only do they show the scope of Ceolwulf's authority, explicable, surely, only in terms of his participation in Alfred's victory at Edington, but they make it likely that Ceolwulf's life, and the West Saxon-Mercia alliance, extended beyond 879, perhaps into the early 880s. The size of the "Cross-and Lozenge" issues suggests that both Alfred and Ceolwulf were indeed able to spread the benefits of Edington over several years: not only could they withhold further payments for peace because the Vikings were now seeking loot (and land) elsewhere, but, more positively, these kings could continue to impose their new demands for wealth on their own aristocracies.

This situation was far from stable: Ceolwulf had disappeared from the scene by 883, and it is hard to escape the conclusion that Alfred, as a prime beneficiary, had something to do with this. Ceolwulf's successor Aethelred ruled as a mere ealdorman "with King Alfred's leave."[60] It may now have been possible for Alfred to reward some of his West Saxon nobles with grants of land in south-west Mercia.[61] But with Danish kings esconced and needing noble warriors just a day or two's ride away from Wessex, Alfred could not afford to neglect the cultivation of aristocratic loyalty, even after Edington. For though he had won a battle, he cannot yet have been at all sure of winning the war. His priority was still, as Asser put it, "with care and the utmost skill to exploit and hold fast to his will his ealdormen and nobles and dearest thegns."[62] To achieve this, he needed more than just material resources.

At this point, we can return to Alfred's pursuit of wealth through wisdom. Michael Wallace-Hadrill has pointed out that "the most necessary books" to render into Old English were chosen because they supplied "general instruction in the social role of christianity."[63] They were not, in any narrow sense, propaganda; but they inculcated some general principles, especially that of obedience to divinely-established authority. In this respect the translations paralleled another element in Alfred's programme, one whose purpose and success are less controversial but which has been, curiously, relatively neglected by modern historians. Asser is again our key witness. He tells us that what Alfred memorized as a child were "Saxon songs;" that what he prescribed especially for his elder children's education were "Saxon songs;" and "Saxon songs" were what he encouraged his retinue to recite and learn by heart.[64] It is no coincidence that this last reference comes in the context of Alfred's careful organization of his royal household and its upkeep: essential bases, as Asser saw, of the government of the realm.

What these Saxon songs conveyed, and hence, presumably, what Alfred wished to stress, was a distinctive Saxon, vernacular and aristocratic cultural inheritance: one that reinforced precisely those attitudes and values which suited Alfred's book. It is tempting to identify the kind of songs that Alfred had in mind with some of those still extant in the very small number of manuscripts of Old English poetry that have come down to us. This particular genre has recently been labelled "poems of wisdom."[65] In this context, Thomas Shippey uses "wisdom" to mean "an outlook on life; an understanding born of experience − a firmly-held cultural ethic." The tone of these poems is "definitive, even quasi-legal;" their "central tenets," that "misfortune is inevitable, but that men find ways of guarding against it, mitigating it, in the last resort accepting it. In this prudential process, social controls are given high importance." Thus the poems in commenting on experience also reinforce a social order in which kingship is central and obedience brings its reward. Here is a typical passage:

A king is keen for power.
Hateful to him the man who demands land,

Dear the one who offers him more!
Majesty must go with pride, the daring with the brave:
Both must wage war with alacrity. . . .
The head must influence the hand.
Treasure must wait in its hoards
And the gift-throne stand prepared
For when men may share it out.
Eager for it is he who receives the gold,
He on the high throne has plenty of it.[66]

Wisdom as a means of understanding, and so functioning well in, God's order for the world was what Alfred sought to promote. It was a social as well as a moral virtue. The message was an old one, already embedded in the mentality of his audience. The aristocracy already shared a tradition. Alfred wanted to make them more conscious and active participants in it. Wisdom would bring wealth: for the dutiful individual, due reward from the royal treasure-giver, for the wise who took counsel together, prosperity through success in war. The king's role as war-leader and dispenser of gifts was as central in these Saxon songs as in Alfred's own evocation of "happy times" when "kings both maintained peace, morality and authority at home, and also extended their territory outside."[67]

Alfred, being himself immersed in that "cultural ethic" his nobles shared, presented himself to them in terms that their "wisdom" made accessible, and validated. The myth of his royal anointing as a child at the hands of the pope contained the truth of his legitimacy as one divinely-appointed and foretold to rulership.[68] The public attacks of his mysterious illness called for, not apology, but celebration. Caesar too had suffered such attacks, according to Suetonius, while engaged in public business (and Asser may have known that).[69] But it was a similar capacity to sense the immanence of divine power, a similar wisdom, that could allow the Saxons, like the Romans, to perceive leaders, and those leaders to perceive themselves, as divinely-possessed. Finally, the wisdom to which Alfred appealed, and which he sought to foster, was not that of West Saxons alone but of Kentishmen and Mercians too. The first visitation of his illness had taken place in Mercia before Mercians we well as West Saxons, and the audience for whom Asser evoked this memorable event included Mercians also. The "happy times" Alfred aimed to restore had prevailed "throughout England," and he projected an authority over all "Englishkind." Shared culture could become part of the ideology of an English realm.[70]

Alfred presented a combination of talents and interests that his contemporaries appreciated in, even expected of, kings. We shall never understand him if we postulate mutually-exclusive or alternative images: shrewd fiscal manager or monk manqué. The ultimate anachronism would be to divorce what that skilled practitioner of early medieval politics so firmly linked together: wealth and wisdom, wisdom and wealth.

NOTES

*   This paper is substantially as read at the SUNY Colloquium on Medieval Kingship in march 1984. I should like to thank my hosts at Stony Brook for their invitation, and especially Professor Joel Rosenthal for his help and editorial patience and the Rosenthal family for their warm hospitality.

1.   L. Febvre, *Le Problème de l'incroyance au XVIe siècle; la religion de Rabelais* (Paris, 1942), (English translation B. Gottlieb, *The Problem of Unbelief,* Cambridge, Mass., 1982), cited by B. Gottlieb, "The Problem of Feminism in the Fifteenth Century," in J. Kirshner and S. Wemple (eds.), *Women of the Medieval World* (London, 1985), 336-64, at 339-40.

2.   See S. Keynes and M. Lapidge, *Alfred the Great. Asser's 'Life of King Alfred' and other contemporary sources* (Harmondsworth, 1983), 44-8.

3.   See J. L. Nelson, "Myths of the Dark Ages," in L.M. Smith (ed.), *The Making of Britain. The Dark Ages* (London, 1984), 145-58, at 147-50.

4.   It eventually appeared as the Jubilee Edition of *The Whole Works of King Alfred the Great,* ed. J.A. Giles (London, 1858).

5.   T. Hughes, *Alfred the Great* (London, 1871).

6.   *The King Alfred Millenary. A Record of the Proceedings of the National Commemoration,* ed. A. Bowker (London, 1902); C. Plummer, *The Life and Times of Alfred the Great,* (Oxford, 1902). See also W.J. Sedgefield, *King Alfred's Version of the Consolations of Boethius, Done into Modern English* (Oxford, 1900).

7.   Plummer, 200-03.

8.   Plummer (ed.), *Two of the Saxon Chronicles Parallel* (2 vols., Oxford, 1892-99), II, 113.

9.   M. Wood, *The Dark Ages* (London, 1982); N. Brooks, "England in the Ninth Cen-

tury: The Crucible of Defeat", *Transactions of the Royal Historical Society*, 5th. ser. 29 (1979), 1-20.

10. J. M. Wallace-Hadrill, "The Franks and the English in the Ninth Century: Some Common Historical Interests," *History* 35 (1950), 202-18, at 216-17 (reprinted in Wallace-Hadrill, *Early Medieval History* (Oxford, 1975), 201-16.

11. Davis, "Alfred the Great: Propaganda and Truth," *History* 56 (1971), 169-82.

12. Whitelock, "The Importance of the Battle of Edington, A.D. 878", *From Bede to Alfred. Studies in Early Anglo-Saxon Literature and History* (London, 1980), no. 13, p. 4. See also J. Bately, "The Compilation of the *Anglo-Saxon Chronicle*, 60 B.C. to A.D. 890: Vocabulary as Evidence," *Proceedings of the British Academy*, 64 (1980 for 1978), 93-129.

13. Whitelock, "Edington" 1, 6. See also J.L. Nelson, "The Problem of King Alfred's Royal Anointing," *Journal of Ecclesiastical History* 18 (1967), 33-51 at 45-7.

14. Asser, *De Rebus Gestis Aelfredi*, c. 13, ed. W. Stevenson (Oxford, 1904), 11-12; English translation, Keynes and Lapidge, *Alfred the Great*, 71. (For all quotations from Asser below, I have used the translation of Keynes and Lapidge unless otherwise stated.)

15. Stafford, "The King's Wife in Wessex, 800-1066," *Past and Present* 91 (1981), 3-27.

16. *English Historical Documents*, c. 500-1000, vol. 1 (2nd revised ed., London, 1978), 292, n. 5.

17. See M. Schütt, "The Literary Form of Asser's Vita Alfredi" *English Historical Review* 62 (1957), 209-20, at 214-15; and the far-reaching observations of D. Howlett in chapter 6 of his forthcoming study of Biblical style in Anglo-Latin texts.

18. Asser, *De Rebus Gestis AElfredi*, c. 74, ed. cit. 54-5, translation 88-9.

19. See T. Wright, "Some historical doubts relating to the biographer Asser," *Archaeologia* 29 (1841), 192-201, at 195-6; V.H. Galbraith, "Who wrote Asser's Life of Alfred?" *An Introduction to the Study of History* (London, 1964), 88-128, at 113-6.

20. Plummer, *Life and Times of Alfred*, 28.

21. Stevenson, *ed. cit.*, 294.

22. Keynes and Lapidge, *Alfred the Great*, 256.

23. Ed. H. Sweet, *King Alfred's West-Saxon Version of Gregory's Pastoral Care*, 2 vols., Early English Text Society, Original Series 45 and 50 (London, 1871-2), I, 5; English translation, Keynes and Lapidge, *Alfred the Great*, 125.

24. *Ibid.* The correct punctuation of this passage was suggested by T.A. Shippey, "Wealth and Wisdom in King Alfred's *Preface* to the Old English *Pastoral Care*," *English Historical Review* 94 (1979), 346-55, at 347-9.

25. See J. Bosworth and T. N. Toller, *An Anglo-Saxon Dictionary* (Oxford, 1882), s.v.

26. *Sap.* vii, 14; *Prov.* viii, 21.

27. H. H. Anton, *Fürstenspiegel und Herrscherethos in der Karolingerzeit* (Bonn, 1968), 97-8, 255-60, 430-31; O. Eberhardt, *Via Regia. Studien zur Smaragdus von St. Mihiel* (Münster, 1977).

28. P. Wormald, "The Uses of Literacy in Anglo-Saxon England," *Transactions of the Royal Historical Society*, 5th ser. 27 (1977), 95-114, at 106-08; J. Bately, *The Literary Prose of King Alfred's reign: Translation or Transformation?* (London, 1980), 10.

29. *De Litteris Colendis*, *Monumenta Germaniae Historica*, *Leges* Sectio 2, *Capitularia*, ed. A. Boretius, vol. 1, no. 29, p. 79 (English translation by H. Loyn and J. Percival, *The Reign of Charlemagne* (London, 1975), 63-4, curiously rendering *litterae* as "literature"!) For what follows, see further M. Richter, "Die Sprachenpolitik Karls des Grossen", *Sprachwissenschaft* 7 (1982), 412-37, and R. Wright, *Late Latin and Early Romance in Spain and Carolingian France* (Liverpool, 1982).

30. Wormald, "The Uses of Literacy".

31. *Alfred's Version of Gregory's Pastoral Care*, preface, 6, translation 126; Asser, *De Rebus Gestis AElfredi*, c. 106, 94, translation 110.

32. Asser, *De Rebus Gestis AElfredi*, cc. 100-101, 86-7 (my translation).

33. *Ibid.*, c. 76, p. 60 (my translation). I comment on the presence of *pagani*, i.e. Vikings, in Alfred's household in "A king across the sea: Alfred in Continental perspective", *Transactions of the Royal Historical Society* 36 (1986) (forthcoming).

34. Asser, *De Rebus Gestis AElfredi*, c. 81, p. 67 (my translation). *Familiaritas* certainly implies "more intimate terms" (Keynes and Lapidge, *Alfred the Great*, 96), but may refer specifically to relations within the royal household.

35. Asser, *De Rebus Gestis AElfredi*, c. 101, p. 88 (*mirabilis dispensatio*); c. 81, p. 68, translation 97.

36. *Anglo-Saxon Chronicle*, s.a. 865, ed. Plummer, *Two of the Saxon Chronicles Parallel*, I, 68 (English translation by D. Whitelock, *English Historical Documents*, 191). But for evidence that "making peace with the host" involved payments on the part of Mercians (868, 872, 873) and West Saxons (871, 876), see Keynes and Lapidge, *Alfred the Great*, 244, nn. 79, 80; 245, n. 88.

37. *Anglo-Saxon Chronicle*, s.a. 878, p. 76; 893, p. 86 (*English Historical Documents*, 196, 203.)

38. Wulfsige of Sherborne, verse-preface to the translation of Gregory's *Dialogues*, Keynes and Lapidge, *Alfred the Great*, 187-8.

39. Keynes and Lapidge, *Alfred the Great*, 177.

40. For comparable tenth-century figures, see Keynes and Lapidge, *op. cit.*, 324, n. 97. Compare also the payment by Charles the Bald to the Vikings at Paris of 7000 lb. of silver in 845: see P. Grierson, "The *Gratia Dei Rex* coinage of Charles the Bald," in M. Gibson and J. Nelson (eds.), *Charles the Bald: Court and Kingdom*, British Archaeological Reports, International Series 101 (Oxford, 1981), 39-51, at 45-8.

41. Few charters survive from the ninth century, and not all are grants. The following figures give an impression of the increased frequency of mentions of money or treasure (references are by number in P. Sawyer, *Anglo-Saxon Charters. An Annotated List* (London, 1968): of some twenty charters of Aethelwulf of Wessex (839-858), only two, S. 296, 297; of seven of Aethelberht (860-5), three, S. 327, 330, 332; of twelve of Alfred (871-99), four, S. 344, 345, 350, 355. (The last three of these show such mentions after 880 too.) For the Mercian king Burgred (852-74) and his queen, the comparable figures are seven out of ten: S. 206, 207, 208, 210, 212, 214, 1201; for his successor Ceolwulf, one out of two: S. 215.

42. Or perhaps the borrowing of a Canterbury convention: a number of Kentish charters mention payments in money or treasure: S. 332, 344, 1195, 1196, 1199, 1200, 1203, 1204, 344, 1276.

43. I owe this observation to James Campbell who presented the evidence of original charters and contemporary copies of authentic charters to a colloquium at the University of Leeds in 1979.

44. S. 1278 (English translation in *English Historical Documents*, 532.) The mancus was a unit of account, worth 30 silver pence.

45. S. 354. Whitelock, "Some Charters in the Name of King Alfred", in M.H. King and W.M. Stevens (eds.), *Saints, Scholars and Heroes. Studies in Medieval Culture in*

Honor of Charles W. Jones (Collegeville, Minnesota, 1979), 77-98, suggests that this charter "needs further attention".

46. R.H.M. Dolley and C.E. Blunt, "The chronology of the coins of Aelfred the Great, 871-99," in Dolley (ed.), *Anglo-Saxon Coins. Studies presented to F.M. Stenton on the occasion of his 80th birthday* (London, 1961), 77-95; M. Dolley, "Aelfred the Great's abandonment of the concept of periodic recoinage," in C.N.L. Brooke, I. Stewart, J.G. Pollard and T.R. Volk (eds.), *Studies in Numismatic Method presented to Philip Grierson* (Cambridge, 1983), 153-60. This and the following paragraph owe much to information generously supplied by numismatist colleagues. I am very grateful to Michael Metcalf for sharing his expert knowledge, and also to Mark Blackburn for further help.

47. Personal communication.

48. Mark Blackburn kindly informs me that no fewer than 18 different moneyers can be identified in the 25 or so "Cross-and-Lozenge" coins of Alfred, and 5 moneyers in the 8 coins of Ceolwulf II. In addition, two coins of Archbishop Aethelred of Canterbury of this type had two different moneyers.

49. The only evidence for his death comes from a post-Conquest regnal list: F.M. Stenton, *Anglo-Saxon England* (3rd. edn. Oxford, 1971), 259, n. 1. The first appearance of his successor dates from 883: S. 218.

50. *Anglo-Saxon Chronicle*, s.a. 874, p. 72, (*English Historical Documents*, 194).

51. Cf. Dolley, "Aelfred's abandonment of periodic recoinage," p. 156.

52. Treaty between Alfred and Guthrum, cc. 4 and 5, Keynes and Lapidge, *Alfred the Great*, 171-2.

53. Asser, *De Rebus Gestis Aelfredi*, c. 101, p. 88 (translation p. 106), with quotation of II Corinthians, ix, 7.

54. The evidence of the ealdorman's defection survives in a charter of 901 (S. 362) (translation in *English Historical Documents*, 541-2). For further comment on this and other comparable cases, see Nelson, "A king across the sea" (forthcoming).

55. P. Grierson, "Money and coinage under Charlemagne," in W. Braunfels and H. Beumann (eds.), *Karl der Grosse. Lebenswerk und Nachleben* (4 vols., Düsseldorf, 1965), I, 501-36, at 528-30 (reprinted in Grierson, *Dark Age Numismatics* (London, 1979), no. XVIII.

56. *Annales Laureshamenses*, s.a. 793, ed. W. Pertz, *Monumenta Germaniae Historica, Scriptores* I, 35.

57. T.N. Bisson, *Conservation of Coinage: monetary exploitation and its restraint in France, Catalonia and Aragon (c. 1000-c. 1125)* (Oxford, 1979), chapter 1.

58. The vast riches of the Avar treasure are stressed by Einhard, *Vita Karoli Magni* c. 13, ed. O. Holder-Egger, *Monumenta Germaniae Historica, Scriptores Rerum Germanicarum in usum scholarum* (Hanover, 1911), 16. See also *Annales Regni Francorum*, s.a. 796, ed. F. Kurze, *Monumenta Germaniae Historica, Scriptores Rerum Germanicarum in usum scholarum* Hannover, 1895), 98. For the date of Charlemagne's coinage reform, see Grierson, "Money and coinage," 507, 511.

59. Dolley, "Aelfred's abandonment of periodic recoinage", 153-4.

60. S. 218.

61. There is no evidence before 903, however: for the significance of S. 367, see C. Hart, "Athelstan Half-King and his family," *Anglo-Saxon England* 2 (1973), 115-44, at 116, n. 3, 118.

62. Asser, *De Rebus Gestis Aelfredi*, c. 91, p. 78 (my translation).

63. Wallace-Hadrill, *Early Germanic Kingship in England and on the Continent* (Oxford, 1971), 142.

64. Asser, *De Rebus Gestis Aelfredi*, cc. 23, 75, 76, pp. 20, 59. (I translate the passage in c. 76 rather differently from Keynes and Lapidge, *Alfred the Great*, 91.)

65. T.A. Shippey, *Poems of Wisdom and Learning in Old English* (Cambridge, 1976), esp. 18-9.

66. Quoted from the translation of *Maxims I* in S.A.J. Bradley, *Anglo-Saxon Poetry* (London, 1982), 347-8; compare Shippey, *Poems of Wisdom*, 67. See further B.C. Raw, *The Art and Background of Old English Poetry* (London, 1978).

67. Preface to Alfred's version of Gregory's *Pastoral Care*, p. 2 (translation p. 124).

68. See Nelson, "The Problem of King Alfred's Royal Anointing," *Journal of Ecclesiastical History* 18 (1967), 47-50. I believe this interpretation stands, even though I have since revised my views on the early history of royal anointing-rites in Wessex: Nelson, "The earliest surviving royal *Ordo*: some liturgical and historical aspects," in B. Tierney and P. Linehan (eds.), *Authority and Power: Studies on Medieval Law and Government presented to Walter Ullmann* (Cambridge, 1980), 29-48.

69. Suetonius, *De Vita Caesarum, Vita Julii*, c. 45, ed. M. Ihm (Leipzig, 1908), 23. Asser knew Einhard, whose *Vita Karoli* was based on Suetonius. But did Asser at least know of Suetonius himself?

II

70. Cf. P. Wormald, "Bede, the Bretwaldas and the Origins of the *gens Anglorum*," in Wormald (ed.), *Ideal and Reality. Studies in Anglo-Saxon and Frankish History presented to J.M. Wallace-Hadrill* (Oxford, 1983), 99-129.

III

RECONSTRUCTING A ROYAL FAMILY: REFLECTIONS ON ALFRED,
From Asser, chapter 2

Peter Sawyer has inclined many minds to many interesting tracks. On two where his guidance has been especially valuable, this paper attempts some further exploration: Anglo-Scandinavian interaction in the Viking Age, and early medieval kingship.[1] On both, the reign of Alfred occupies a critical point. Yet Alfred himself remains a curiously enigmatic figure. Asser's *Life*, with its account of Alfred's secret piety, and unidentified chronic illness, in some ways deepens the mystery.[2] In describing Alfred's youthful prayers for heaven-sent affliction to help him curb the lusts of the flesh, and then recording the onslaught of a second illness during Alfred's wedding feast, Asser hints at Alfred's anxieties about his own sexuality. A charter of the king's successor, Edward, reveals that Alfred had deprived a thegn of the benefice he held of the bishop of Winchester on grounds of the thegn's sexual misconduct (*stuprum*); but it goes on to say that Alfred thereafter returned the land to the bishop on receipt of a large payment.[3] Can

---

[1]   The scale of Peter Sawyer's achievement is reflected throughout the present volume. Repeated references to 'S.' numbers in the notes below indicate my debt to *Anglo-Saxon Charters, An Annotated List and Bibliography* (London, 1968). Special acknowledgement is due here for *The Age of the Vikings* 2nd edn. (London, 1971), *Kings and Vikings* (London, 1982), and 'The royal *tun* in pre-Conquest England', in P. Wormald ed., *Ideal and Reality. Studies in Frankish and Anglo-Saxon Society presented to J. M. Wallace-Hadrill* (Oxford, 1983), pp. 273–99. But Peter has always trailed inspiration *et verbo et scripto*, and this is the place to thank him for many years' worth of both. For their help and criticism on the present paper, I am very grateful to Matthew Blows, Iain Fenn, Simon Keynes, Pauline Stafford, and Patrick Wormald, and also to John Gillingham and Ian Wood. Any remaining errors are of course mine.

[2]   Asser, *De Rebus Gestis Ælfredi*, ed. W. H. Stevenson (Oxford, 1904), reprinted with a note by D. Whitelock on recent work (Oxford, 1959), translated S. Keynes and M. Lapidge, *Alfred the Great* (Harmondsworth, 1983). All page-references below are to Stevenson's edition and the translation of Keynes and Lapidge. Since 1983 the one important study on Asser has been J. Campbell's in C. J. Holdsworth and T. Wiseman, eds, *The Inheritance of Historiography* (Exeter, 1986), pp. 115–35. Despite Asser, and his exegetes, it remains true that, as W. J. Sedgefield wrote in his introduction to *King Alfred's Version of the Consolations of Boethius* (Oxford, 1900), p. vii, 'to very many intelligent people [Alfred is] a distinctly nebulous character'.

[3]   S.374. Loss of lands was the penalty for adultery in a clause tacked on to the Alfred-Ine Code in the now-burnt Cotton MS Otho B XI: see D. Whitelock's note to F. M. Stenton,

these be termed the acts of a puritan, or a cynic? We need to shun such anachronistic labels if we want to reconstruct Alfred's motives, and the politics of ninth-century Wessex. Some of the complexities and contradictions in the heart of the West Saxon royal family, and within Alfred's own family-life, have left traces in Asser, still to be seen and chased up.

Asser himself says that he wrote up the *Life* in 893, which means that the last years of Alfred's reign, so poorly-documented in other sources too, are thus not directly covered.[4] But there are obvious advantages for us in being able to pin down Asser's information to a particular point in an ongoing political story which, through internal as well as external pressures, was subject to frequent change. Further, Asser wrote within the royal *familia* (household), close to the king and his kin. From there, and from then, Asser gives a view of a recent past through which Alfred's own changing priorities can be glimpsed. For it was Alfred himself who provided Asser with 'the truth' about the history of the West Saxon royal family in the period before 866 when Asser arrived in Wessex; and it was to Alfred that Asser dedicated his work.[5] We shall not get much closer to Alfred than this.

Thanks to recent scholarship, we now know quite a lot about Alfred and his brothers, his father, and paternal grandfather.[6] We know a lot less, however, about the rest of Alfred's kin: his antecedents and coevals on his mother's side, and also his children's generation. Asser tells something; but he certainly does not tell all – which is to say that his patron and source may have been economical with the truth. If so, conflicts in the heart of the royal family – that acid test of early medieval kingship – may help explain why.

Though Asser's first chapter, on the paternal ancestry of Alfred, has often been commented on, chapter two, on Alfred's mother and maternal ancestry, has been relatively neglected. Like much of what Asser purveys, it is found nowhere else; it is hard to check, and hard to interpret.

> His mother was named Osburh, an extremely pious woman, noble in character and noble by birth: she was the daughter of Oslac, King Æthelwulf's famous butler. Oslac was a Goth by nation, for he was sprung from Goths and Jutes, namely from the seed of Stuf and Wihtgar, two brothers

---

Anglo-Saxon England, 3rd revised edn. (Oxford, 1971), pp. 309–10, n. 5. The date of the addition *could* be early in the tenth century. My thanks are due to Patrick Wormald for clarification on this text.

[4] The hole in the evidence for Alfred's last years has not attracted enough attention; but its size can be gauged by a glance at Keynes and Lapidge, *Alfred*, pp. 120, 191.

[5] Asser, pref., c.13, pp. 1, 12 (Keynes and Lapidge, *Alfred*, pp. 67, 71).

[6] See, notably, D. Dumville, 'The Ætheling', ASE 8 (1979), pp. 1–33; P. Stafford, 'The king's wife in Wessex', *Past and Present* 91 (1981), pp. 3–27; P. Wormald, in J. Campbell ed., *The Anglo-Saxons* (London, 1982), pp. 132–59; N. Brooks, *The Early History of the Church of Canterbury* (Leicester, 1985), pp. 145–7, 197–200; and references in Keynes and Lapidge, *Alfred*, p. 314, n. 3. See also J. L. Nelson, ' "A king across the sea": Alfred in Continental perspective', *TRHS* 5th series 36 (1986), pp. 45–68; and 'Wealth and wisdom: the politics of Alfred', in J. Rosenthal ed., *Kings and Kingship*, Center for Medieval and Early Studies, State University of New York, *Acta* 11 (1986), pp. 31–52.

and also companions in arms, who received control over the Isle of White from their uncle King Cerdic and Cynric his son, their cousin, and slew the few Britons who inhabited that island, those they could find there, at the place which is called Guuitgaraburhg.[7]

Stuf and Wihtgar, whose names Asser gives in their OE forms, are persons familiar to any reader of the *Anglo-Saxon Chronicle*, which records, under the year 514, their arrival and victory over the Britons, and under the year 534, that they were younger kinsman of Cerdic and given the Isle of Wight (*Wiehte ealond*).[8] The name Stuf is not attested elsewhere. The OE word closest to it is *stofn*: stem, or progeny. Wihtgar means spear-man.[9] The pair look like mythical founding fathers. Asser's editor thought that Asser got these names from the ASC; and it used commonly to be assumed that the ASC here, as elsewhere in the earliest annals dealing with the settlement of Wessex, preserved the memory of genuine historical persons and events.[10] Asser's account of the activities of Stuf and Wihtgar on the Isle of Wight does indeed show strong affinities with the information given in the ASC under the years 530 and 534. But this need not mean that Asser took his material from the ASC: both could have drawn on a common source, which need not have been very old when Asser used it.[11]

The story of Stuf and Wihtgar rooted Alfred's mother's ancestors firmly in the Isle of Wight. It may not be coincidence that Alfred's daughter, and younger son, were bequeathed lands on the Isle of Wight in Alfred's Will, perhaps lands that had come to his from his mother.[12] Asser's Guuihtgaraburhg, which the ASC calls Wihtgara byrg: 'the burh of the dwellers of Wight', may not, after all, be Carisbrooke; but the place was apparently on Wight and familiar to a ninth-

---

[7]   Asser, c. 2, p. 4. There is a striking similarity here with the *Life* of Louis the Pious by Thegan, ed. G. H. Pertz, MGH SS 2 (Hannover, 1829) pp. 585–604, where too the first and second chapters deal with the subject's paternal, then maternal, ancestry, and Louis' mother is praised in c. 2 as *nobilissimi generis* and *beatissima*.

[8]   *Anglo-Saxon Chronicle*, s.a. 514, 534, ed. C. Plummer, *Two of the Saxon Chronicles Parallel*, 2 vols (Oxford, 1892, 1899), vol.1, pp. 14, 16; *The Anglo-Saxon Chronicle: a collaborative edition*, vol. 3, MS A, ed. J. Bately (Cambridge, 1986), p. 21. References hereafter are to ASC, and, unless otherwise specified, to Plummer's edition.

[9]   Stevenson, *Asser*, p. 173 and n.1.

[10]   Ibid., pp. 170–1; Stenton, *Anglo-Saxon England*, pp. 23–4. Cf. J. N. L. Myers, *The English Settlements* (Oxford, 1986), p. 146.

[11]   Asser in c. 1 draws on a genealogy of Alfred's paternal line which circulated independently of the ASC. His version contains a significant variant which distinguishes it from that in ASC MS A: see below, p. 63, and n. 87. Asser's explanation in c. 2 of the relationship between Cerdic and Cynric, and Stuf and Wihtgar, is incompatible with the grandfather-grandson relationship between the first two men asserted in c. 1. In ASC, MS A, s.a. 534, Stuf and Wihtgar are termed *nefan* ('grandson' or 'nephew') of Cerdic and Cynric, which squares with the father-son relationship of the latter two in A's genealogy.

[12]   Alfred's Will, trans. Keynes and Lapidge, *Alfred*, pp. 175, 177, and 321. Wellow, Isle of Wight, is identified here as the bequest to Alfred's youngest daughter Aelfthryth (rather than the Wellow in Hampshire left to his eldest daughter Æthelflaed), and the first estate left to Æthelweard, Alfred's younger son, is identified ibid. p. 319, as Arreton, Isle of Wight.

century audience.[13] This, said Plummer, 'shows that Wihtgar is a mere abstraction to account for the place-name . . . [which] throws some light on the historical value of these traditions'.[14] Quite.

But suppose we assess 'historical value' in another way? Suppose we abandon the attempt to sift this material for nuggets of sixth-century fact, and instead, treat it as evidence for ninth-century fiction? David Dumville has demonstrated that reconstruction of the Cerdicing genealogy, and of the early history of Wessex, was under way in the ninth century.[15] Stoutly resisting the temptation to speculate on the reasons for such revisionism, Dumville hints that the chronologists were not immune to contemporary political pressures.[16] Some temptations are worth yielding to; and Dumville's hints are worth pursuing through Asser's chapter 2. Even historians sceptical about the factual reliability of the early annals of the ASC seem to have believed that the descent of Alfred's mother from 'the seed of Stuf and Wihtgar' was an oral tradition in her family well-established by the ninth century. This inference has been that repeated mentions of Stuf and Wihtgar were inserted into the ASC (and adapted thence by Asser) to draw flattering attention to Alfred's maternal kin.[17] But how traditional was this 'tradition'? Asser shows (and he had Alfred's word for it) that another ninth-century 'custom', namely the denial of queenly status to the West Saxon king's wife, had been formed in the course of just two generations – *moderno tempore*.[18] In Alfred's maternal *genealogia* might be seen another recent invention of tradition, its purpose to establish a distant collateral link between the house of Cerdic and Alfred's mother's family: Stuf and Wihtgar might, for instance, have been understood to be Cerdic's sister's sons.[19] Women believed (or alleged) to be distant kin were perhaps preferred royal spouses, rather than simply hard to avoid.[20] The main beneficiaries of such beliefs were one branch of the Cerdicings, who needed every bit of ancestral charisma they could lay claim to, not least to distinguish them from other branches of that sprawling line. In other words, the story of Stuf and Wihtgar and of Osburh's descent from their seed, may tell us more about the concerns of Osburh's son (and perhaps of her husband too) than about those of her own natal family.

But the oddest thing about Asser's depiction of Stuf and Wihtgar is the one I

13 Plummer, *Saxon Chronicles*, vol. 2, p. 14, accepted the identification with Carisbrooke. So too does Myers, *Settlements*, pp. 145–6. But Stevenson, *Asser*, p. 174, showed that this cannot be right. See also P. Sims-Williams, 'The settlement of England in Bede and the Chronicle', *ASE* 12 (1983), pp. 1–41, at p. 30, n. 130.
14 Plummer, *Saxon Chronicles*, vol. 2, p. 14. Cf. Sims-Williams, 'The settlement of England', pp. 25, 30.
15 D. Dumville, 'The West Saxon genealogical regnal list and the chronology of early Wessex', *Peritia* 4 (1985), pp. 21–66.
16 Dumville, 'The West Saxon genealogical regnal list', pp. 42, n. 55; 52, n. 83, 56–8; 59, n. 114; 60–1; 64–5.
17 Sims-Williams, 'The settlement of England', pp. 30, 37. Cf. K. Sisam, 'Anglo-Saxon royal genealogies', *Proceedings of the British Academy* 39 (1953), pp. 287–348, at 337.
18 Asser, cc. 13, 14, pp. 11–2. See Stafford, 'The king's wife', pp. 3–4, 7 and *passim*.
19 Stevenson, *Asser*, p. 171; Stenton, *Anglo-Saxon England*, p. 24.
20 Cf. Stafford, 'The king's wife', pp. 14–6.

have so far left unmentioned: they are Goths. The first difficulty is that this seems to contradict the ASC, whose annal for 514 is sometimes translated:

In this year, the West Saxons Stuf and Wihtgar, came to Britain.[21]

This is not actually what any manuscript says: rather, a distinction is made between the first statement, that West Saxons came to Britain and landed at Cerdicesora, and the second statement, that Stuf and Wihtgar fought with the Britons and put them to flight. The gentile origin of Stuf and Wihtgar is thus not specified here. But why does Asser identify them as Goths? And why his apparent identification of Goths with Jutes? Is Asser trying to accommodate Bede with an oral tradition (as Dumville suggests in other contexts the West Saxon genealogists may have been)?[22] Or is Asser merely muddled? While Stenton thought '[Asser's] statement . . . good evidence that Stuf and Wihtgar were Jutes', Stevenson took a different view: Asser was the victim of his 'foreign origin' and proneness to be 'led by learned associations'(!). 'Such a confusion could scarcely be made by an Englishman in the time of King Alfred', according to Stevenson, for Alfred was clear on the distinction between Gotan, 'without the erroneous *th* of the classical forms', and Jutes.[23] But though the OE Bede translated the former Gotan, the latter Geatan, Stevenson had to admit that Jutland nevertheless appears in the OE Orosius as Gotland, and ninth-century OE pronunciation could have aided a confusion.[24] Ninth-century 'Englishmen' may not have thought of Orosius' or Boethius' Goths as so remote from themselves in time or space.

In their note on Asser's statement that Alfred's maternal grandfather was a 'Goth', Keynes and Lapidge crisply observe: 'Asser is probably trying to convey the information that Oslac was of ultimately Danish extraction'.[25] Their point is well made – and more important than their lack of further comment implies. A. C. Murray has recently, and persuasively, argued that the addition of Scyld and Scef to the West Saxon royal genealogy in the late ninth century amounts to an 'attribution of "Danish" ancestors to the West Saxon kings', and that 'the Danish

---

[21] ASC, s.a. 514, p. 14; cf. also Bately, ed. cit., p. 20 and notes. The translation quoted is Stenton's, *Anglo-Saxon England*, pp. 20–1, and also that of G. N. Garmonsway, *Anglo-Saxon Chronicle* (London, 1953), p. 14. For a correct translation, see D. Whitelock *et al*, *The Anglo-Saxon Chronicle*. A revised translation (London 1961), p. 11. Dumville, 'The West Saxon genealogical regnal list', p. 44, n. 63, points out that 'there is no necessary association (such as is generally assumed) between this arrival [of the West Saxons] and the following notice of the activities of Stuf and Wihtgar.

[22] Dumville, 'The West Saxon genealogical regnal list', pp. 28 and n. 15, 41–2 and n. 55; 53–4 and n. 85, 66.

[23] Stenton, *Anglo-Saxon England*, pp. 23–4. Stevenson, *Asser*, p. 167. Cp. ibid. p. 170, for 'a great Scandinavian scholar' who seems to have been more 'confused' then Asser!

[24] Stevenson, *Asser*, p. 169. For early medieval views on the Goths and their origins, see J. M. Alonso-Nunez, 'Jordanes and Procopius on Northern Europe', *Nottingham Medieval Studies* 37 (1987), pp. 1–16, esp. p. 8 and references in n. 11, for confusion of *Getae* with *Gothi*.

[25] Keynes and Lapidge, *Alfred*, p. 230, n. 8.

presence in England was in some way a stimulus' to this genealogical creation.[26] Murray goes on: 'A Danish background was intended to give them prestige and leverage among the petty and disunited Scandinavian kings and earls of northern England and to support the claim of West Saxon suzerainty [sic] over the north . . . The Danish invasions and settlements did not lead Englishmen to disassociate themselves from the Scandinavian heroic age. On the contrary, the heroic North attracted them'.[27] This is rather less persuasive, for it smacks a little of anachronism. Not the least of Asser's advantages is his firm location at Alfred's court in the early 890s. From there, from then, did the Danes look any more 'petty', 'disunited', or indeed 'heroic', than the political scene that confronted Alfred at home?

That home scene had three important features. First, it included Scandinavians. Asser tells of *pagani* – meaning Scandinavians – enrolled at his monastic foundation at Athelney.[28] For Asser, then, the very term *pagani* was on the way to losing its religious connotation: alongside 'many Franks, Frisians, Gauls, Welshmen, Irishmen and Bretons', are the *pagani* in Alfred's household.[29] There is no evidence that conversion to Christianity as entry requirement posed any problem for Scandinavian warlords and their men.[30] Like contemporary Carolingians, Alfred needed to attract and hold a multigentile, polyglot following which then exerted a pull of its own. Hence, if Asser tells his readers that Alfred's maternal grandfather Oslac was of Scandinavian origin, he is presumably making Oslac's grandson more acceptable to local and contemporary Scandinavians, actual or potential recruits to Alfred's *familia*. Os- was of course a perfectable acceptable leading-name among contemporary Scandinavians: the ASC mentions a Danish earl Osbearn in 871, and a Scandinavian king Oscytel in 875.[31]

The second feature of the period around 893 is Alfred's new concern with areas beyond his 'English' kingdom: with Wales, with East Anglia and with the North. It is not the ASC but Asser (supported by the late tenth-century Æthelweard) who reveals this reorientation.[32] If one person of 'foreign origin' helps us here, so does another: the Continental Saxon Hrotsvitha. She believed that Alfred's granddaughter Edith was descended from the seventh-century Northumbrian king Oswald, and in celebrating Edith's marriage to Otto, son of the East Frankish king Henry I, in 929/30, Hrotsvitha claimed that Oswald's was a *stirps beata* ('blessed lineage') and that 'the whole world sang his praise'. Plummer

---

[26] 'Beowulf, the Danish invasions, and royal genealogy', in C. Chase ed., *The Dating of Beowulf* (Toronto, 1981), pp. 101–111, at 105.

[27] Ibid.

[28] Asser, c. 94, p. 81: 'paganicae gentis'. Keynes and Lapidge, *Alfred*, p. 103, translate: 'of Viking parentage'.

[29] Asser, c. 76, p. 60: 'pagani'. Keynes and Lapidge, *Alfred*, p. 91, translate: 'Vikings'.

[30] This point is made by P. Sawyer, *Kings and Vikings*, pp. 137–8. See also S. Coupland and J. L. Nelson, 'The Vikings on the Continent', *History Today* 38 (December, 1988) pp. 12–19, at 15.

[31] ASC, s.a. 871, 875, pp. 70, 74.

[32] Asser, cc. 80, 81, pp. 66–8; Æthelweard, *Chronicle*, s.a. 893, 894, 895, 899, translated Keynes and Lapidge, *Alfred*, pp. 190–1.

remarked: 'That [Edith's descent] is not genealogically correct only makes the testimony the more striking'. Plummer suggested no explanation for the 'error'.[33] But a tenth-century Continental Saxon might well have derived it as an inference from the reappearance of the saint-king's leading name among Edith's close kin. With Alfred recruiting Old Saxons and East Franks into his *familia*, and Oswald's cult already known on the Continent, it could well be that a claim like Hrotsvitha's was already being made and exploited by Alfred's entourage. In Northumbria too, which had once been Oswald's kingdom, and where the ealdorman of Somerset was sent to intervene at York in 894, Alfred might have acquired lustre from his maternal grandfather's name, Oslac – the same name as may have been borne by Oswald's own brother.[34] Os- had continued to be one of the commonest leading-names in the Northumbrian royal dynasty until its extinction in 867: the very hallmark of a *gecyndne cyning*, that is, one of the royal line.[35] It was to be Alfred's daughter Æthelflaed, lady of the Mercians, who translated Oswald's relics from Bardney to Gloucester.[36] The suggestion has been made that Alfred named his eldest daughter after Æthelflaed, daughter of the Northumbrian king Oswy and niece of Oswald.[37] Had Alfred hoped to dedicate his daughter to God as a thank-offering for victory over pagans just as Oswy did? In any event, the reappearance of an old Northumbrian royal name, and name-element, in Alfred's family might have been expected to appeal to late ninth-century Northumbrians in search of a latter-day *bretwalda*.

Heightened tensions within the royal family constitute, I think, a third feature of Wessex in the early 890s. Such tensions, ever-present, tended to surface when a king lived long enough for the next generation to challenge his position:

---

[33] Hrotsvitha, *Gesta Ottonis*, ll. 94–7, ed. P. Winterfeld, *Hrotsvithae Opera*, MGH SRG in usum scholarum, 2nd edn. (Berlin, Zurich, 1965), p. 207; Plummer, ed., *Baedae Opera Historica* (Oxford, 1896), vol. 2, p. 160, under the heading 'Miscellaneous' evidence for the cult of Oswald on the Continent. Oswald married the daughter of the West Saxon king Cynegils, Bede, *HE* III 7, but Bede gives no indication that this direct line continued beyond his son Oidilwald, *HE* III 24. K. Leyser, 'Die Ottonen und Wessex', *Frühmittelalterliche Studien* 17 (1983), pp. 73–97, at 78, has important observations on Hrotsvitha's assertion, but does not say it is an error. Perhaps Oswald *did* have descendants, who fled to their mother's kin in Wessex: note the appearance of a West Saxon *aetheling* called Oswald, ASC, s.a. 728, p. 42.

[34] Plummer, ed., *Baedae Opera Historica*, vol. 2, p. 99. It is possible, however, that the relatively late source, MS 'E' of the ASC, has been influenced by post-seventh-century appearances of the name Oslac (?including Asser, chapter 2).

[35] ASC 867, p. 68: the Northumbrians rejected King Osbryht and accepted Ælla, an *ungecyndne* king. The Os- leading name also appears in the Mercian royal line: ASC, s.a. 755, p. 50. See Sims-Williams, 'The settlement of England', pp. 22–3. For OE leading-names ('protothemes') in general, see C. Clark, 'English personal names ca. 650–1300', *Medieval Prosopography* 8 (1987), pp. 31–60, at 33–4.

[36] ASC 'C' (the Mercian Register), ed. Plummer, p. 94.

[37] The suggestion was C. S. Taylor's: see Plummer, *Saxon Chronicles*, II, p. 118, though, as Patrick Wormald reminds me, Oswy's daughter was called Ælfflaed, according to Bede. The name Eadweard given by Alfred to his son could have recalled a leading-name (Ead-) of the Northumbrian royal dynasty; but (Ead-) is also a common Kentish royal name-element. The name's appearance in the Cerdicing line anyway needs an explanation.

54

his *familia* would be exposed to the rival attractions of younger men's lordship, and his kingdom threatened by outside interventions concerted with insiders' pressures for a reallocation of power. In Alfred's case, we should be alerted to such possibilities, rather than deterred from investigating them, by the very fact that the evidence for the last years of his reign is unusually scarce. But before focussing on the 890s, we need to establish the broader context of family politics in the period.

Asser offers a rare opportunity to glimpse the role of maternal kin, and also the limits of that role, in Alfred's world. For it is thanks to Asser's chapter 2 that we know the names not only of Alfred's maternal grandfather Oslac but of his mother herself. Osburh's function in Asser's narrative is already established in her first appearance: her noble lineage accentuates and confirms her son's already illustrious birth, giving him a double link with Cerdic. Asser says that she, like her husband, favoured Alfred above their other sons: the book-memorising competition she sets them serves to highlight Alfred who, though the youngest, is the winner.[38] Osburh has no further part in Alfred's story, as Asser presents it. But the location of the book-competition in the narrative, after the account of Alfred's father's second marriage to the Carolingian princess Judith, has been thought by some commentators to make it possible that Osburh was still alive after that event, and perhaps outlived her husband: in other words, that King Æthelwulf in 856 was not a widower but a bigamist. Asser's ordering of events is not always chronological, but, despite Stevenson's hot denials, the possibility remains open that Æthelwulf repudiated, or relegated, Osburh in order to make his Carolingian alliance.[39] If Asser does not quite leave Alfred's childhood in the obscurity with which Einhard shrouded Charlemagne's, he leaves enough unclear to suggest that Osburh's story was in process of reconstruction at the time he was writing, in the late ninth century.

By specifically mentioning that Æthelwulf, 'contrary to custom', sat his Carolingian wife Judith on a throne alongside him, Asser suggests that Osburh had had no such status. Asser does not call Judith 'queen', but implies that that title was associated with enthronement.[40] The ASC explicitly says that Judith

---

[38] Asser, c. 23, p. 20 (Keynes and Lapidge, *Alfred*, p. 75).
[39] This was suggested already by J. M. Lappenberg, *Geschichte von England*, (Hamburg, 1834), vol. 1, p. 294; and rebutted by R. Pauli, *The Life of Alfred the Great*, trans. B. Thorpe (London, 1853), pp. 52–3 ('in all probability, Osburgha died before her husband set out for Rome. Her death was quiet, as her whole life had been: she had lived as the mother of her children, and not as a queen'), and by Stevenson, *Asser*, pp. 222–3 ('there is not the slightest evidence that Æthelwulf treated her in this brutal way, and his well known religious character renders the supposition that he did so a very unlikely one'). The treatment of Osburh by nineteenth-century scholars, and their difficulties in crediting Judith ('that light Frankish princess', Stevenson p. 223) with interest in her stepsons' education, reveal more about Victorian values than Anglo-Saxon attitudes. But for an exception, see the Bishop of Bristol (G. F. Browne), 'Alfred as a religious man and educationalist', in A. Bowker, ed., *Alfred the Great* (London, 1899), pp. 71–99, at 77–8, noting Judith's background at the cultivated court of Charles the Bald.
[40] Asser, c. 13, p. 11.

was given Æthelwulf *to cuene*- 'as queen'. [41] Osburh's lack of queenly status is
even more broadly hinted at in the West Frankish *Annals of Saint Bertin*: 'Æthelwulf . . . conferred on Judith the title of queen, something which had been until
then unfamiliar to him and to his people'.[42] The author of these *Annals* is
evidently retailing information given to the Franks by Æthelwulf and his entourage in 856: the West Saxons were anxious to stress the special mark of honour
accorded to their new royal bride. Pauline Stafford has argued for an otherwise
consistent demotion of the status of the king's wife in ninth-century Wessex, and
offered a plausible explanation in terms of a preference for fraternal, 'horizontal',
succession over the 'vertical' succession of sons or nephews.[43] But changing
circumstances ensured that the preference was neither consistent nor unanimous. Memories of earlier queens were not lost: even the 'highly unusual event'
of Seaxburh's one-year reign (672) was not deleted from the ASC or from the
West Saxon regnal list, perhaps because it was 'well known in West Saxon oral
tradition'.[44] According to both Asser and the ASC, Eadburh, wife of King Beorhtric of Wessex (786‑802), had been a queen.[45] Of Egbert's consort(s) nothing is
known. In Alfred's own generation, one brother, Æthelbald, married his step-
mother, Queen Judith, after his father's death, while another brother, Æthelred,
had a wife called Wulfthryth who is accorded the title *regina* in a charter of 868
(the year of Alfred's own marriage).[46] Thus, in the period before Alfred's own
reign, Osburh is the only West Saxon king's wife whose lack of a queenly title is
clear. If Æthelwulf did plan to repudiate and replace her in 855/6, it could have
suited him very well to emphasise to the Franks her lowliness and their glory
through the honourable status reserved, by contrast, for the Carolingian king's
daughter. By the late 880s, Osburh's sole surviving son may well have felt the
whole episode in need of explaining – or explaining away: hence 'the truthteller'
himself 'often' told Asser the story of the wicked Eadburh and the West Saxons'
ensuing 'perverse custom' of denying the title of queen to the king's wife.[47] At

[41] ASC, s.a. 855, p. 66.
[42] *Annales de Saint-Bertin*, ed. F. Grat, J. Vielliard and S. Clemencet (Paris, 1964), s.a.
856, p. 73. In my forthcoming translation of this work, I discuss the possibility that this
passage was interpolated into the 856 annal of Hincmar. See meanwhile Nelson, 'The
Annals of St Bertin', in M. Gibson and J. L. Nelson eds., *Charles the Bald: Court and
Kingdom*, revised edn. (London, 1990), pp. 23–40. The political context, and consequences, of Æthelwulf's Frankish marriage have been illuminated by Stafford, 'Charles the
Bald, Judith and England', ibid., pp. 139–53.
[43] Stafford, 'The king's wife', pp. 7–12, 15. Though she recognises (p. 12) that 'succession
practices change with circumstances', Stafford sees continuity 'during the ninth century',
with Judith the exception that proves the rule.
[44] Dumville, 'The West Saxon genealogical regnal list', p. 53 and n. 85.
[45] ASC, s.a. 836, p. 62; Asser, c. 13, p. 11: Eadburh was a '*pertinax et malevola regina*'.
[46] S.340. Stevenson, *Asser*, p. 201, n. 4, says this charter's source, the Winchester Cartu-
lary, is 'highly suspicious'. But the witness-list seems usable. Immediately after
Wulfthryth's attestation comes that of Wulfhere *princeps*: see below n. 58. If genuine,
Wulfthryth's title seems designed to open up the possibility of vertical succession, that is,
to assert the claims of her sons. Cf. Nelson, ' "A king across the sea" ', pp. 55–7.
[47] Asser, c. 13, p. 12. Asser adds that Alfred told him that *his* informants in turn were

the same time, Alfred may have wanted to suggest that his mother's lack of queenly status was more than compensated for by exceptional piety, ancient lineage, and a Cerdicing connexion. Hence the construction of Osburh's illustrious *genealogia* could have postdated not only her union with Æthelwulf, but her youngest son's succession: could have been, in other words, the marriage's effect, rather than its cause.

Nevertheless, it is likely, given the high value placed on maternal kin in this society, that Æthelwulf chose a wife of noble rank with politically useful connexions. If Osburh's son Æthelbald was old enough to fight alongside his father in 851, and her daughter to marry in 853, this could imply a date for the parents' union before 839, that is, when Æthelwulf was still only sub-king of Kent.[48] Osburh's father Oslac may have been related to an important Kentish noble family in which the Os- leading-name appears in the late eighth and early ninth centuries.[49] If so, this could well have recommended him further to Æthelwulf in the mid-830s. As for the linkage of Oslac's ancestors with the Isle of Wight, this could only have been encouraged by Bede's specific statement that *Cantuarii* and *Victuarii*, that is, Kentishmen and men of Wight, were alike 'of Jutish origin'.[50]

Oslac may have died soon after his daughter's marriage, since there is no record of his attesting any of Æthelwulf's charters.[51] Oslac's post of royal butler (*pincerna*) seemed problematic to Stevenson: he thought there was virtually no 'English' evidence for holders of this office during or before the ninth century, and hence no warrant for regarding it *per se* as a mark of 'loftiest birth', while 'the *pincerna* was an officer of somewhat subordinate importance in the [ninth-century] Frankish court', and hence if Oslac really was a 'great noble', his alleged job seemed an anachronism.[52] But the early evidence for 'English' butlers is better than Stevenson realised, while on the other side of the Channel, the *de Ordine Palatii* places the butler fourth, after the chamberlain, the count of the palace and the seneschal, among the officers of the Carolingian royal household,

---

veredici, that there were many of them, and that some of them were able to recall the event itself.
[48] ASC, s.a. 851, 853, pp. 64, 66. Pauli, *Alfred*, p. 42, suggests that the mother of Æthelstan, Æthelwulf's eldest son, may have been a woman other than Osburh.
[49] The death of an Ealdorman Osmod is mentioned in ASC, s.a. 836, p. 62. If he is the Osmod attesting in S.270, 271, he probably belonged to the Kentish family documented in S.1188, 1439.
[50] HE I 15. Note also the appearance of Oslac *dux* of the South Saxons granting land in Sussex in S.1184 (dated 780). Cf. S.44, 48, 49, for Osmund *rex* of the South Saxons a generation before. For Alfred's bequests in Sussex, see below, pp. 59–60.
[51] *Pace* Keynes and Lapidge, p. 229, n. 7, the Oslac who attests S.328 seems too low (ninth) on the list of lay attesters, and the date, 858, too late, for identification as the then king's maternal grandfather to seem likely. But, as Simon Keynes kindly points out to me, this is a Kentish charter.
[52] Stevenson, *Asser*, p. 164, with references to earlier literature (though slightly misrepresenting H. Brunner, *Deutsche Rechtgeschichte*, 2 vols, 2nd edn. (Munich and Leipzig, 1906, 1928), vol. 2, p. 140). An exceptional attestation of an 'English' butler in the eighth century occurs in S.57 (which, *pace* Sawyer's comment here, is not listed as 'spurious' by Stevenson at the place cited).

and all these posts were certainly held in the ninth century by men of high birth, often at an early stage in their careers.[53] The best parallel for Oslac is Odo, butler to Louis the Pious in 826, and kinsman of Count Bernard of Septimania. Odo was in an ideal position to benefit from the realignment of court factions that resulted in Bernard's appointment as chamberlain in 828: Odo himself became count of Orleans and married into the family of the counts of Paris. His daughter in turn married Louis the Pious' son Charles the Bald. (Hence the Frankish princess Judith was Odo's granddaughter.)[54] It is a coincidence that both Charles the Bald and Æthelwulf married butlers' daughters? Was Odo's example known of, or even followed, on the other side of the Channel?[55] Like Odo, Oslac attained a *Königsnähe* ('closeness to the king'), which noble birth on its own could not assure: in both cases, what the butler saw was a privileged access-route to the centre of political power. Like Odo, Oslac may have died too young to enjoy this access for long.[56]

Whatever happened to Osburh's father, evidence may exist to show another of her kinsmen as a beneficiary of her royal marriage. In 847, Osric *princeps* subscribed a West Saxon charter after King Æthelwulf and the *ætheling* Æthelbald. The unusual title, and Osric's exceptionally high placing, suggest the possi-

---

53 'English' butlers appear in S.348 (and see now Keynes and Lapidge, *Alfred*, p. 181, with comments at pp. 326–7 and 330, n. 15), where Sigewulf *pincerna* may be the same man as the Sigulf *dux* who attests S.350 (dated 898), and S.1515, the Will of King Eadred (946–56) where the listing of *discthegn, hraelthegn* and *biriele* echoes that of the *de Ordine Palatii*, c. 23, ed. T. Gross and R. Schieffer, *Fontes Iuris Germanici Antiqui* (Munich, 1980), pp. 74–6. On the problem of *de Ordine*'s authorship and date (c.820 x c.880), see Nelson, 'Legislation and consensus in the reign of Charles the Bald', in Wormald ed., *Ideal and Reality*, pp. 91–116, at 105–6. Useful general comments on Carolingian household-officers in the ninth century can be found in K. F. Werner, '*Missus-marchio-comes*', in W. Paravicini and K. F. Werner eds., *Histoire comparée de l'administration (IVe–XVIIIe Siècles)*, *Beihefte der Francia* 9 (Munich, 1980), pp. 191–239, at pp. 209 and n. 73, 236–7 and nn. 166–168; cf. Nelson, 'Public Histories and private history in the work of Nithard', *Speculum* 60 (1985), pp. 251–93, at pp. 257, n. 22 (Adalard), and 281, n. 126 (Vivian); and below, n. 55. A thorough prosopographical study has never been undertaken.
54 For Odo's career, see L. Levillian, 'Les Nibelungen historiques, II', *Annales du Midi* 50 (1938), pp. 5–66, at 31–46; Werner, 'Untersuchungen zur Frühzeit des französischen Fürstentums (9.–10. Jht.)', *Die Welt als Geschichte* 50 (1959), pp. 146–93, at 163, n. 72. Whether or not Odo was already a count in 821, he was referred to as *puer* in 826: Ermold, *Poème sur Louis le Pieux*, ed. E. Faral (Paris, 1932), 1.2346, p. 178. His daughter Ermentrude married Charles the Bald in 842: Nithard, *Histoire des fils de Louis le Pieux*, ed. P. Lauer (Paris, 1926), IV, 6, p. 142.
55 Odo's countship, and his kinship with Bernard, but not his office of butler, are mentioned by the Astronomer, *Vita Hludowici*, ed. G. Pertz, MGH SS 2, cc. 44, 45, p. 633, an author whom Asser may have known: see references in Keynes and Lapidge, *Alfred*, p. 222, n. 115. That Odo was known by his office-title may be suggested by an instruction given by Emperor Louis to *missi* in 826, *Capitularia Regum Francorum* 1 ed. A. Boretius, MGH LL 2 (Hannover, 1883) no. 155, p. 314, c. 6: 'Odo buticularius de foreste sua interrogandus est'. (Was forest-management part of the butler's official duties?)
56 Odo was killed in 834: Nithard, *Hist.* I, 5, p. 20, fighting for the Emperor, and to recover his countship.

58

bility that this man was Osburh's brother.[57] The title was also used in the late 860s by Wulfhere, who was perhaps the brother-in-law of the then king, Æthelred.[58] Osric might be further identified with the ealdorman of Dorset mentioned in the ASC for 845, and/or with the ealdorman of Hampshire mentioned in the same source, under the year 860.[59] Did he hold two ealdormanries at the same time? If so, this would begin to look like a budding territorial principality in the hands of a man who knew how to exploit his special *Königsnähe*.[60] But the asset had a time-limit: there is no record of Osric attesting as *princeps* after the 840s. In 856, he is third down the list of ealdormen, and it is tempting to link his 'demotion' with Osburh's.[61] Only in 860, in his last charter-appearance, does Osric attest second in the list of ealdormen: this is the first extant charter of Æthelberht's reign and it may be that Judith's departure allowed her predecessor's brother a brief and partial recovery of his former influence.[62] By 868, whatever position he had held at Æthelwulf's court was occupied by Wulfhere at Æthelred's.

But we can perhaps pick up one more echo of Osric, and of the characteristic leading-name of Alfred's maternal kin. The ASC, in a unique and striking narrative inserted into the 757 annal, reports the death in 786 of King Cynewulf of Wessex at the hands of his kinsman Cyneheard. The story's climax is the refusal of the king's thegns to accept any terms offered by Cyneheard, despite the fact that some of their kinsmen were with him: 'They replied that no kinsman was dearer to them than their lord, and that they would never follow his slayer'.[63] The chief of these loyal thegns is named as 'Ealdorman Osric'; and a second

---

[57] S.298. Unfortunately, all the other charters bearing Osric's attestation are of doubtful authenticity, yet even in these, his very high place on lists of attesters may be significant: S.305, 313, 1274. It should be noted that Osric's title of *princeps* is not unique in S.298's list: the title is also given to Ceorl, presumably the ealdorman of Devon mentioned in ASC, s.a. 851. p. 64. But I take the arrangement of the names in the MS, BL Cotton Charter viii, 36, to indicate that Osric is higher-placed than Ceorl. It is even possible that Ceorl's name, and title, were added later, Osric may make another appearance as *princeps* in S.319 (dated 874 but possibly altered from the original's 844), but the witness-list here is jumbled, the abbreviations used for titles are not consistent, and though other priests attest here as *prsb* or *p*, it is unclear whether *prs* too means *presbyter*.

[58] S.340, 341, and cf. 336. I raised this possibility in ' "A king across the sea" ', p. 55. It is tempting to wonder if 'Oswulf princeps' of S.39, 1439, was the brother-in-law of King Cuthred of Kent. Other men with the title 'princeps' appear in spurious charters: S.290, 292, 299, and 300. But if S.301 is reliable, 'Tuddan princeps' would repay further investigation.

[59] ASC, s.a. 845, 860, pp. 64, 68.

[60] The parallel that comes to mind to here is Charles the Bald's brother-in-law Boso: for his and other cases, see K. Schmid, 'Über die Struktur des Adels im frühen Mittelalter', *Jahrbuch für fränkische Landesforschung* 19 (1959), pp. 1–23, translated T. Reuter, *The Medieval Nobility* (Amsterdam, 1979), pp. 37–59. The prospects of such territorial formations on the Continent in this period are coolly assessed by J. Dunbabin, *France in the Making, 843–1180* (Oxford, 1985), chapter 4.

[61] S.317. Cf. also the spurious S.308, and 307.

[62] S.327, dateble to 860. My suggestion depends on the rejection of S.326, 1274 as untrustworthy.

[63] ASC, s.a. 757, on events in 786.

instance of his exemplary conduct is given a few lines further on, when Cyneheard and all his men 'were slain, all except one who was the ealdorman's
godson, and he spared his life'. The highlighting of Osric's role is no more
coincidental than the emphasis on the loyalty expected of king's thegns and the
obligations of spiritual kinship. These themes surely reflect Alfred's priorities in
the early 890s when the ASC was being put together: a point to which I return
presently.

Another probable kinsman of Alfred's on whom the characteristic Os- leading
name of his mother's *genealogia* was bestowed, is the Osweald *filius regis* who
attests a charter of 875 in third place after Alfred and the archbishop of Canterbury. Stevenson identified him as 'the son of one of Alfred's brothers'.[64] Keynes
and Lapidge suggest that he was a son of Æthelred, but it is noteworthy that the
account in Alfred's Will of the inheritance-dispute at the time of Alfred's own
succession shows only two sons of Æthelred ('the older and the younger'),
presumably the Æthelhelm and Æthelwold mentioned later in the Will, which
would mean that Osweald was not a contender along with them in 871.[65] We
have no information about other legitimate sons of any of Alfred's three elder
brothers. Osweald *filius regis* also attests two charters of 868.[66] Could he have
been an illegitimate son (or perhaps, more accurately, a son born to a woman of
low, even unfree, status), of either Æthelbald or Æthelberht? If so, he could have
been a young adult by 868; and in any case, tenth-century charters show West
Saxon aethelings attesting when still very young.[67] But if Osweald was well-
placed at Alfred's court in the early years of the reign, he was out of the running
(dead, or exiled?) by the time that Alfred made his Will, for he is not mentioned
among Alfred's beneficiaries. In any event, Osweald is a significant figure: here is
a king's son of whose existence we should have had no inkling but for the
fortuitous survival of three charters, and who, despite his possible illegitimacy,
was given the 'official' title used by such other, legitimate, kings' sons as his own
uncle and cousins. How many *æthelings* have sunk without trace?

One more kinsman of Alfred's appears prominent later in the reign: Osferth.
He is mentioned, notably, in Alfred's Will, which in its present form seems to
date from the late 890s.[68] Osferth is left eight estates, all in Sussex: considerably

---

[64] *Asser*, p. 299, n. 4 *a propos* S.1203.
[65] Keynes and Lapidge, *Alfred*, p. 322, n. 79. Cf. Alfred's Will, ibid., pp. 175, 177. See also
Dumville, 'The Ætheling', p. 11.
[66] S.340, S.1201. The 'Osweald *miles*' who attests S.348 (dating to 892) seems too low on
the list, and the charter too late, for emendation to, and identification with, Osweald to be
feasible.
[67] E.g. in S.569, 570, 745, 893. See also Dumville, 'The Ætheling', p. 14. For the
suggestion of an age-gap between Æthelbald and Æthelberht on the one hand, and
Æthelred and Alfred on the other, see Nelson, ' "A king across the sea" ', p. 55. For a
Carolingian example of youthful paternity, cf. Louis the Pious, who fathered a son and a
daughter in his early teens, before his marriage: see Werner, 'Die Nachkommen Karls des
Grossen', in W. Braunfels and H. Beumann eds., *Karl der Grosse, Lebenswerk und Nachleben*, 5 vols. (Dusseldorf, 1965–8), vol. 4, pp. 403–79, at 445–6.
[68] As implied by Keynes and Lapidge, *Alfred*, p. 174, rightly pointing out, p. 173, that the
reference to Archbishop Æthelred (died 888) provides a *terminus ante quem* only for the

more than Alfred's brother's son Æthelwold, and a much more compact bloc than the other nephew Æthelhelm. Was the bequest to Osferth in fact the core of a South Saxon subkingdom? Clearly Osferth was not, like Æthelwold and Æthelhelm, a brother's son: he, unlike them, is identified by the term *maegd* (kinsman).[69] He appears again in another document whose date, 898, may be close to that of the Will: this is the Kentish charter is which Edward attests as king.[70] Here, Osferth is second on the list of *ministri*, following Beorhtsige who is probably identifiable with Brihtsige, the son of a Mercian *ætheling*.[71] In 901, Osferth, without any title, attests next after King Edward, and in 903, again without title, immediately after Edward's younger brother Æthelweard.[72] In a doubtful charter of 909, Osferth attests next after Edward's son (and before all the ealdormen) with the title *propinquus regis*.[73] After the gap in the charter series later in Edward's reign, Osferth reappears in Athelstan's early years (thus during the period when the dynasty's descent from the saint-king Oswald was being touted) as an ealdorman at, or very near, the top of the list of lay attesters, from 926 until 934.[74] Clearly Osferth held an exceptionally prominent position at the courts of three successive kings. It is a sobering thought that none of the narrative sources mentions him at all.

What was Osferth's kin-relationship to Alfred? The one charter-attestation to specify his place in the family calls him *frater regis* in relation to Edward the Elder – 'mistakenly', comment Keynes and Lapidge, with a briskness worthy of the late Dorothy Whitelock herself.[75] But is it really out of the question that Osferth was Edward's half-brother, and thus Alfred's illegitimate son? In view of Osferth's

first three paragraphs of the Will. Two additional reasons for dating the Will to the very last years of Alfred's reign are: (i) his title in paragraph 4, 'king of the West Saxons', may be compared with that in S.350 (dated 898), on which see below, p. 64, n. 90; (ii) the Ecgwulf mentioned in the Will in terms which imply he is no longer living (Keynes and Lapidge, p. 175: '. . . property which I entrusted to Ecgwulf . . .) may be the horse-thegn whose death is mentioned in ASC, s.a. 896, p. 90 (as noted by Keynes and Lapidge, p. 289, though without the possible implications for dating the Will). If so, the bequest of this property to Winchester may have been for the good of Ecgwulf's soul. For a Carolingian parallel, see the grant of Charles the Bald to St Lucien, Beauvais, in return for prayers for the soul of Wido 'fidelis ac carissimi nobis vassalli': G. Tessier ed., *Receuil des Actes de Charles II le Chauve*, 3 vols. (Paris, 1944–55), vol. 2, no. 325, p. 217.
[69] Keynes and Lapidge, *Alfred*, p. 177.
[70] S.350.
[71] Dumville, 'The Ætheling', p. 4.
[72] S.364, 367.
[73] S.378. C. Hart, *The Early Charters of Northern England and the North Midlands* (Leicester, 1975), p. 355, notes the parallel with a phrase used in reference to Athelstan Half-King. The other charters cited by Hart as attested by Osferth (S.376, 378, 381, 382, 383) are at best dubious.
[74] In S.396 (dated 926), Osferth attests third of the *duces*; in S.400, 401, 402, 403, 412, 413, 418, 422, 393, Osferth tops the list of lay attesters; in S.407, 416, 417, 425, he attests second. Was Osward, King Edgar's *propinquus* in S.803, a descendant (?son) of Osferth?
[75] Keynes and Lapidge, *Alfred*, p. 322, *a propos* S.1286, where both Æthelweard 'filius regis' and Osferth 'frater regis' are listed above the archbishop! Cf. Hart, *Early Charters*, p. 355: the identification of Osferth here is 'certainly a mistake'.

place in Alfred's Will, and his sustained high position in the witness lists of Edward's reign and Athelstan's early years, that possibility is surely worth considering. More work needs doing on Anglo-Saxon royal naming habits. Contemporary Continental evidence shows that some names denoted greater throne-worthiness than others. Perhaps, once the criterion of legitimacy had increasingly been adopted and the circle of eligibles thus more closely drawn, to call a son by a leading-name from the father's *maternal* line was an indication of diminished suitability on grounds of illegitimate birth.[76]

It is true that Asser makes no mention of Osferth, any more than he mentions Alfred's nephews. What he offers, instead, is a picture of Alfred as the happy father of a tidy nuclear family, with just one bed-fellow – his wife – and two sons only, both legitimate, one the 'obedient' Edward, the other apparently destined for the Church. Why should Asser tell the whole story? If Osferth was a bastard son of Alfred, his existence belied the image of the chaste king portrayed in Asser's chapter 74. And yet, at the same time, it would explain the earnestness with which Alfred prayed for an illness that would inhibit sexual activity.

In the twelfth century, when lawyers were making the distinction between legitimate and illegitimate offspring more clear-cut than ever, when realms and lordships were solidifying, and when the exclusion of illegitimate sons from inheritances was becoming accepted custom, the philandering of a Henry I need produce no brood of claimants to shares in a divided realm. In the seventh and eighth centuries, kings were prolific and half-brothers fought fiercely, while the pleas of a few moralists had little effect. But the ninth century saw new tensions, new contradictions: between the persisting ways of the past, and more sustained and generalised attempts on the part of kings and noblemen as well as moralists to differentiate between legitimate and illegitimate sons and to impose stricter controls on sexual behaviour. Demographic shifts – a higher birth rate, and/or an improved survival rate for infants – and economic pressures resulting from reduced opportunities to extract plunder and tribute, are hypotheses that explain the phenomena as well as any.[77] In the Carolingian world, the claims of bastards recurrently tore apart patrimonies, kingdoms and the Frankish realm itself. Ninth-century observers did not ignore the risks of overly-narrowed descent lines, but saw too the danger of proliferating sons. There could be too much

---

[76] A possible Carolingian example of the use of a name from the father's maternal line for an illegitimate son, is Hugh son of Lothar II: Lothar's maternal grandfather was called Hugh. Thankmar, son of the East Frankish king Henry I, is another possible example. What is certain is that such names as Bernard and Hugh were used for Carolingians' illegitimate sons. For examples, see Werner, 'Die Nachkommen'. On the naming of daughters, see C. Bouchard, 'Patterns of women's names in royal lineages, ninth-eleventh centuries', *Medieval Prosopography* 9 (1988), pp. 1–32.

[77] Compare the explanations invoked by J. Wollasch, 'Parenté noble et monachisme reformateut', *Revue Historique* 264 (1980), pp. 3–24, and D. Herlihy, *Medieval Households* (Harvard, 1985), pp. 83–7, in reference to the eleventh and twelfth centuries. I hope to discuss this problem more fully in a forthcoming paper on Gerald of Aurillac.

nobilitas, too many noble youths with claims to 'equality of birth, rank and power'.[78] Among the landed elite, chastity began to be preached with a new vigour, and not only by churchmen: the noble lady Dhuoda exhorted her son 'to do service in the marriage bed', or to opt for virginity, but at all costs to avoid 'inlicita stupra'.[79] No doubt many Franks failed to live up to such prescriptions, just as many English did. But the interesting thing is that the ideal was insistently proposed, and that some laymen, at least, tried to practise it.[80] According to Asser, chapter 74, the young Alfred prayed earnestly for an illness that would keep him from lust, and, once married, was a model of fidelity. Even if Alfred was unable to avoid an occasional lapse, he aspired to chastity.

Alfred's aspiration, discussed by previous historians in terms of his individual psychology, could also be understood as a reponse to contemporary social and political pressures. Reading between the lines of the ASC, and making the most of Asser, we can glimpse those pressures in the recurrent succession-crises of ninth-century Wessex. The generation before Alfred's had seen a series of responses to the problems of acute fraternal rivalry and filial unrest: the creation of a subkingdom, rebellion, a division of the realm, stepmother-marriage. Alfred's succession to an undivided realm was not just a matter of luck. Both the ASC and, especially, Asser present Alfred in the late 860s as successor-in-waiting, and his brother's designated heir. Both the ASC and Asser neglect to mention Alfred's nephews whose claims to succeed their father Alfred set aside in 871. Both the ASC and Asser also leave out Osferth. Nor does the ASC as written up in 892 say anything about Alfred's son Edward, though by then he was probably aged over twenty. What this means is that the view from 892/3 of a narrowed-down succession line, and a future which Alfred could control, was also an aspiration rather than a reality.

Alfred's Will is explicit about its own reference to a particular point in time: there have been other wills, it says, which are now declared superseded. Implicitly Alfred acknowledges that *this* Will may also be ephemeral. Asser too reveals a moment in time: he presents Alfred, in 893, aligning Edward for the succession, but the depiction of Edward as 'obedient' reminds us of Asser's own earlier depiction of an *ætheling* who was not obedient: the 'wicked and grasping' Æthelbald who rebelled against his ageing father.[81] In other words, where Asser reveals conflict within the royal family in the previous generation, he suppresses it in

---

[78] Regino of Prüm, *Chronicon*, ed. F. Kurze, MGH SRG in usum scholarum (Hannover, 1890), s.a. 888, p. 129; but cf. the anxieties expressed by Regino s.a. 880, p. 116–7.
[79] Dhuoda, *Manuel pour mon fils*, ed. P. Riché (Paris, 1975), IV, 6, p. 228.
[80] See Wormald, 'Æthelwold and his Continental counterparts: contact, comparison, contrast', in B. Yorke ed., *Æthelwold* (Woodbridge, 1988), pp. 13–42, at 20, 35–7; and Nelson, 'A tale of two princes', *Studies in Medieval and Renaissance History* 11 (1988), pp. 105–40.
[81] Asser, c. 12, pp. 9–10: 'quaedam infamia' (Keynes and Lapidge, *Alfred*, p. 70: 'a disgraceful episode'). I follow Keynes and Lapidge in translating *pertinax* as 'grasping'.

Alfred's. Alfred is different: papally-anointed; parentally-preferred; the nobility's choice even before his brother's death.[82]

But Asser's is not the only story, even in 893. Against the ASC's silence is Æthelweard's account of the battle of Farnham in that year, in which Edward's military prowess, and popularity with a following of young warriors, are highlighted.[83] Plans for the succession must surely have been revised more than once in the course of Alfred's reign. Alfred's Will throws light on the scene in the late 890s: here Edward is lined up to inherit most of Alfred's personal property in Somerset, as well as some estates in Wiltshire and Hampshire, but no fewer than four other kinsmen of Edward's generation (his brother Æthelweard, his two cousins Æthelwold and Æthelhelm, and Osferth) are assigned parts of Alfred's personal inheritance, both in Old Wessex, where Æthelweard, not Edward, inherits estates in Dorset and the Isle of Wight, and in the acquired regions to the east, Surrey and Sussex, where again Edward received almost nothing. Edward, on the other hand, is to receive 'all my booklands in Kent'.[84] This distribution suggests that a subsequent re-partition of the expanded realm remained on the cards. The Will records a dispute between Alfred and his nephews over a particular piece of shared inherited property, probably in 871, and hints, further, at Alfred's disputed succession to the realm itself. A charter whose witness-list could suggest a date not many years after 871 actually has Alfred's nephew the *ætheling* Æthelwold attesting above his son Edward.[85]

In 897 or 898, Alfred 'invested' his little grandson Athelstan in what has been understood as a ritual of designation to succeed eventually to Alfred's expanded, composite kingdom. This may have signalled a far-sighted plan for the transmission of an undivided realm through the succeeding two generations. It may have been designed with Edward's connivance, indeed, at his insistence, for it certainly implied a narrowed descent-line excluding Edward's own brother.[86] But there is an alternative explanation: the designation of a grandson may have been Alfred's own project, its purpose to bypass Edward at least as far as the succession to Wessex itself was concerned. Dumville has observed that there are alternative versions of Alfred's genealogy at the critical point of Cerdic's successor: some include Cerdic's son Creoda, while others delete him, jumping straight from Cerdic to Cynric. Dumville comments: 'It is perhaps just conceivable that in Alfred's or Edward's reign the legitimate succession of a grandson might be thought to create an unfortunate model for Æthelwulf's other grandsons to follow'.[87] Dumville was evidently thinking of the conflicting claims of Edward

[82] Asser, cc. 8, 22, 42, pp. 7, 19, 32.
[83] Æthelweard, *Chronicon*, ed. A. Campbell (London, 1962), p. 49 (Keynes and Lapidge, *Alfred*, p. 189.
[84] See Keynes and Lapidge, *Alfred*, pp. 175–7, and map, p. 176.
[85] S.356.
[86] As I implied in ' "A king across the sea" ', p. 56, following a suggestion of Lapidge, 'Some Latin poems as evidence for the reign of Athelstan', ASE 9 (1981), pp. 61–98, at 79–81
[87] Dumville, 'The West Saxon genealogical regnal list', p. 59, n. 114.

and his cousin Æthelwold, who was, of course, also a grandson of Æthelwulf. But it is possible that the genealogists' discrepancy hints, instead, at conflict between Edward's expectations, and his own father's plans involving his grandson.[88] Alfred himself may have chosen, and perhaps dowered, Edward's first spouse, Ecgwyna (Athelstan's mother), for him, and sought thus to control her offspring. Edward seems to have married another woman, Ælfflaed, very soon after his father's death.[89] The divergent forms of the Cerdicing pedigree could reflect the views of rival camps in the mid-890s: one favouring Edward's sole succession, the other his partial exclusion in favour of his own son – that is, a redivision of the realm such as Edward himself was to try to engineer for the next generation.[90]. We know that Athelstan was brought up in Mercia by his aunt Æthelflaed: but whose idea was that – his father's, or his grandfather's? In the 890s there were several possible ways of reslicing the cake. One that had been tried before (and would perhaps be tried again by Edward for one of his own sons) was to recreate a kingdom in Kent.[91] A Kentish charter of 898 is attested by Edward as 'rex', while Alfred's title here, *rex saxonum*, seems to imply a more limited authority than the 'Anglo-Saxon' kingship asserted during the previous decade and more.[92] In this same charter, Osferth attested for the first time: he was probably behind Edward in a political as well as a diplomatic sense. Hungry *æthelings* were indeed beginning to prowl.[93] And when *æthelings* prowled, a king needed, above all, to keep the loyalty of his own thegns. Here, in the last years of Alfred's reign, was his Achilles heel: for, as the ASC poignantly records, the worst problem he confronted in 896 was the loss of 'many of the best king's thegns that were in the land'.[94] Even the bonds of spiritual kinship, pointedly mentioned in the 893 annal, as in the Osric episode recounted under 757, could not be counted on to hold.[95]

[88] For paternal intervention in an adult son's affairs to influence the royal succession in the second generation, compare Charles the Bald's attempt to disinherit his own grandsons by making Louis the Stammerer repudiate his wife and marry another woman: Regino of Prüm, *Chronicon*, s.a. 878, 879, p. 114, and Werner, 'Nachkommen', pp. 437–8. Charles at this point was hoping to beget a new son of his own, and also conferring *Königsnähe* on the kin of Louis's new wife.

[89] On Edward's marriages, see Stafford, 'King's wife', p. 13, and my comments in 'The Second English Ordo', in J. L. Nelson, *Politics and Ritual in Early Medieval Europe* (London, 1986), p. 367. Pauline Stafford kindly points out to me that Alfred might have sought to secure Ecgwyna's status, had he wanted to promote her son, and that Carolingian evidence shows kings choosing their sons' brides and providing the morning-gifts.

[90] See Nelson, ' "A king across the sea" ', p. 57.

[91] Kent had been ruled as a sub-kingdom by Æthelwulf during Egbert's lifetime, then by Athelstan during Æthelwulf's: Keynes and Lapidge, *Alfred*, pp. 15, 231–2. Edward the Elder may have planned for his third son, Edwin, to rule Kent: Plummer, *Saxon Chronicles*, 2, pp. 137–8.

[92] S.350. I am grateful to Iain Fenn for this point.

[93] I borrow (not for the first time!) the inimitable phrase of K. Harrison, *The Framework of Anglo-Saxon History* (Cambridge, 1976), p. 92.

[94] ASC, s.a. 896, p. 90: 'during those these years' – i.e. 893–6.

[95] ASC, s.a. 893, p. 86, in the context of the sons of Haesten. For earlier examples, see ASC, s.a. 878 (Guthrum-Athelstan), and Asser, c. 80, p. 67 (Anarawd ap Rhodri).

I have left to the last another problematic king's wife. Though Alfred was anxious to assert his own mother's rank (if not her queenly status), he was apparently indifferent to that of his own consort. The ASC does not mention his marriage; Asser does, but omits the name of the bride, though he says she was descended through her mother from the Mercian royal line.[96] Neither source tells us anything of Alfred's wife's activity during her husband's reign. Nor does she attest any charter of Alfred's. His Will seems to be the only document produced during his lifetime to give her name – Eahlswith; but she is not identified here even as wife, let alone queen, and in the list of kin who are Alfred's beneficiaries, she comes last of all, behind Osferth. Of the three estates bequeathed to her, two may have been already 'earmarked for the support of royal women'.[97] Thus, at the time the Will was drawn up, Ealhswith's stock with her husband seems not to have been particularly high. In 892/3, the silence of the ASC and Asser tells a similar tale.

Conversely, the ASC indicates Ealhswith's emergence from obscurity after 899, when Alfred died: her brother's death is recorded under the year 902 (recte 901), and her own death under 904 (recte 902).[98] Though only one possibly genuine charter of Edward's carries her attestation, as 'king's mother', a record of her endowment of the Nunnaminster at Winchester also survives.[99] She seems to have left her landed property to her son Edward.[100] It is tempting to suggest that Ealhswith was a consistent supporter of Edward, and to account thus for her absence in the early 890s from an historical record that was tilted against her son. When Asser says that the onset of Alfred's second, unidentifiable, illness at his wedding-feast was attributed by some contemporary observers to witchcraft, he may have been projecting back, significantly to that occasion, the atmosphere of 893.[101]

Hence perhaps the dilemma facing Alfred, and Asser, over the status of the king's wife in ninth-century Wessex. Much as Alfred wanted to cast a retrospective aura around his mother's name, in the early 890s strictly contemporary circumstances required that his own wife be kept in the background. Had Alfred at that time wished to secure the 'vertical' sole succession of his own elder son, there would have been every reason to affirm Ealhswith's status. Instead, what

---

96 Asser, c. 29, p. 24.
97 Keynes and Lapidge, *Alfred*, p. 323; cf. Stafford, 'The king's wife', p. 22.
98 ASC, s.a. 902, 904, pp. 92, 94.
99 S.363, 1560. On the record of bounds of land at Winchester, see M. Parkes, 'a fragment of an early tenth-century Anglo-Saxon manscript and its significance', *ASE* 12 (1983), pp. 129–40, at 131–2.
100 Keynes and Lapidge, *Alfred*, p. 325.
101 Asser, c. 74, p. 55: 'multi ... favore et fascinatione circumstantis populi hoc factum esse autumabant' (Keynes and Lapidge, *Alfred*, p. 89: '. . . spells and witchcraft of the people around him'). For a comparative view of witchcraft accusations in 'the intimate, ambiguous hot-house atmosphere of the court', see E. Peters, *The Magician, the Witch and the Law* (Philadelphia, 1978), pp. 9–10, 16, 112–25, esp. p. 116, noting the effect of the arrival of a new queen into a court. Paul Kershaw and Neville Wylie kindly drew my attention to the possible significance of Asser's words.

66

the evidence points to is a growing tension between Alfred and Edward, and (whether as cause or effect) attempts on Alfred's part to keep open his options on the succession. In that context, hungry *æthelings* had their advantages. Not before 898, it seems, was Edward able to secure the Kentish kingdom. In his father's Will, Edward received Alfred's booklands in Kent, and a landed base in Old Wessex too. Other *æthelings* bided their time. By 898, Asser had stopped work, and the ASC for the moment was hardly being kept up. While Edward lived on to gain immortality through a new generation of annalists after 900, prime victims in the 890s of his ambition, and of the historians' silence, were the king's wives of the preceding century.

IV

THE POLITICAL IDEAS OF ALFRED OF WESSEX

Ever since Plato recommended rulers who were philosophers, many self-proclaimed philosophers (Cicero, for instance, or Rousseau) have wished they were rulers; but not many rulers have shown much inclination for philosophy or indeed for theory of any sort. Those rulers who have tried their hands at it (James I; Mussolini) have been treated in rather patronizing terms by professional theorists in their own time and after. Usually, rulers have been happy to leave political theory to scholars—and confined their own interests to political practice. The ninth century, therefore, attracts attention as a rather extraordinary period: then, there actually were kings who were said to be lovers of wisdom, self-consciously following what they knew Plato had preached;[1] then, according to J. M. Wallace-Hadrill, 'learned kings, or at least kings who were patrons of learning, [were] the rule rather than the exception'.[2] The 'at least', however, represents quite a large concession: for patronage, and practice itself, are two different things.

---

[1] See H. H. Anton, *Fürstenspeigel und Herrscherethos in der Karolingerzeit* (Bonn, 1968), pp. 98 (noting that Alcuin quoted 'the Platonic saying' to Charlemagne by way of Prudentius and Boethius), and 247, 255–7 (for similar echoes in works addressed to Louis the German and Charles the Bald). See further P. Godman, *Poets and Emperors* (Oxford, 1987), p. 136. I should like to thank my colleagues Janet Bately and Anne Duggan for moral support and editorial patience.

[2] *Early Germanic Kingship in England and on the Continent* (Oxford, 1971), p. 129.

126

Charlemagne and several of his ninth-century successors patronized a renaissance of sorts, and their learned protégés copied out
classical works, but also wrote new ones, in a range of genres, for an
audience that included laity as well as ecclesiastics. This renaissance,
if much narrower, in content and social range, than the later medieval
one, not only hoarded but sowed.[3] Yet scarcely a single work—
scarcely more than a couple of letters, perhaps[4]—can be credited to
the authorship of a single Carolingian. We need to move far on in the
Middle Ages to find occasional instances of Continental kings who
can plausibly be credited with any literary output, let alone the literary expression of political ideas of their own.[5] This last point may
strike some readers as redundant: for modern commentators have
failed to find much in the way of political ideas in the earlier Middle
Ages at all. Systematic treatises on political themes are almost non-
existent. What there are, in the ninth-century Carolingian world, are
mirrors of princes, works of moral guidance for individual rulers; and
liturgical texts, notably king-making rites, all of them written by
clergy who naturally emphasize religious duties and ecclesiastical authority.[6] Before the twelfth-century rediscovery of Roman Law, so

---

[3] *Pace* Jacques Le Goff, *Les intellectuels au moyen âge* (Paris, 1969), p. 14: a
stimulating but overly harsh judgment from the perspective of the central
Middle Ages. The scope of the Carolingian Renaissance's achievement can
be gauged in three recent books: R. McKitterick, *The Carolingians and the
Written Word* (Cambridge, 1989); L. Nees, *A Tainted Mantle. Hercules and
the Classical Tradition at the Carolingian Court* (Philadelphia, 1991); and D.
Bullough, *Carolingian Renewal. Sources and Heritage* (Manchester, 1991).

[4] If Charles the Bald himself, rather than Hincmar of Reims, can be credited
with the authorship of two royal letters to Pope Hadrian II: see below, n. 49.

[5] For Louis IX of France, whose ideas have to be reconstructed from anecdotal
and other indirect evidence, see the papers of J. Le Goff and M. Kauffmann
in the present volume. Interestingly, Queen Elizabeth I (like Alfred) found inspiration in Boethius' *Consolation of Philosophy* and translated it into English; but much of the evidence for her political thought is second-hand.

[6] The best study in English remains J. M. Wallace-Hadrill, 'The *via regia* of
the Carolingian Age', in *Trends in Medieval Political Though*, edited by B.
Smalley, (Oxford, 1965), pp. 22–41. See further Anton, *Fürstenspiegel*; and
J. L. Nelson, 'Kingship and Empire', in *The Cambridge History of Medieval
Political Thought*, edited by J. H. Burns (Cambridge, 1988), pp. 211–51, at

runs a textbook argument , would-be theorists lacked the vocabulary and the concepts of properly political discourse. Hence, allegedly, ninth-century texts contain no concept of the state as an apparatus of institutions and public resources persisting through time, no notion of legislative sovereignty, or indeed of legislation. Instead, it's argued, there is the idea of an association of men bonded together by personal obligations to a common lord—a *Herrschaftsverband*.[7] It's been inferred, further, that such thinking about power in entirely personal terms both resulted from and strengthened the dominance of the Church over the ideology and the actual workings of early medieval kingdoms: Walter Ullmann wrote of the 'stunted sovereignty' of ninth-century Carolingians.[8] Finally, the personalizing of the political has often been linked with the privatization of power, notably in the treatment of the kingdom as a family possession to be divided between heirs.[9] (The consequences of ninth-century Carolingian divisions persisted: western Europe has repeatedly split along fault-lines created arbitrarily by a fraternal share-out in 843.) Hence royal lordship, caught between church and dynasty, was not—could not be—conceptualized in properly political terms. These arguments are persuasive: there is no disputing the centrality of personal bonds to early medieval political thinking. What can be disputed, however, is the claim that the idea of public authority, of the state, was unknown, indeed unthinkable, in the ninth century. Alongside, uncomfortably jostling, private and personal ties and obligations were public demands and duties, self-consciously affirmed by rulers who cast themselves as heirs to Constantine and Theodosius. The Carolingians and

---

218–21.

7   So, J. Fried, 'Der karolingische Herrschaftsverband im 9. Jhdt.', *Historische Zeitschrift*, CCXXXV (1982), 1–43; cf. now the comments of G. Althoff, *Verwandte, Freunde und Getreue. Zum politischen Stellenwert der Gruppenbindungen im fruuheren Mittelalter* (Darmstadt, 1990), pp. 5–9.

8   *The Carolingian Renaissance and the Idea of Kingship. The Birkbeck Lectures 1968–9* (London, 1969), Lecture V.

9   F. L. Ganshof, *The Carolingians and the Frankish Monarchy* (London, 1971), p. 247. For a different view, see Nelson, 'Kingship and Empire', p. 224.

their advisers were under the spell of Christian Antiquity.[10]

Was Alfred immune? His Laws were a gathering-together, and a writing-down, of 'the ones that our forefathers observed.... For I did not presume to set down in writing at all many of my own...'[11] This king seems the very epitome of Fritz Kern's guardian of the Good Old Law, barely claiming the power to legislate.[12] Yet, in the very same passage, there breathes a more assertive royalty: Alfred has selected from custom 'what pleased me, and rejected the others'. Further, in the Laws that follow, Alfred uses such expressions as 'we establish', 'we command', 'we declare'.[13] In other words, he makes new law even as he inscribes parts of the old. And among the new is a law of treason: for plotting against the king's life, a man is to be henceforth 'liable for his life and all that he possesses'.[14] This, Alfred may have borrowed from the Carolingians.[15] But behind both him and them were late Roman models.[16]

And behind Alfred, mediating those models, enabling him to situate himself in an insular legislative tradition, was earlier Anglo-Saxon practice. Military obligations (to serve in the army of defence, to contribute to guarding frontiers, and to bridge-building) required by eighth-century kings in Mercia and Kent, and rather belatedly by

---

10 Nelson, 'Translating images of authority: the Christian Roman emperors in the Carolingian world', in *Images of Authority. Papers presented to Joyce Reynolds on the occasion of her 70th birthday,* edited by M. M. Mackenzie and C. Roueché (Cambridge, 1989), pp. 194–205.

11 Quoted from the translation of the preface by S. Keynes and M. Lapidge, *Alfred the Great. Asser's* Life of King Alfred *and Other Contemporary Sources* (Harmondsworth, 1983), p. 164.

12 F. Kern, *Kingship and Law*, English translation by S. B. Chrimes (Oxford, 1939), pp. 70–3.

13 Cc. 34, 36, 41, 42.

14 Laws, c. [4] 5, Keynes and Lapidge, *Alfred*, p. 165.

15 The argument will be forcefully put by Patrick Wormald in his forthcoming book on Anglo-Saxon lawmaking. I am very grateful to him for discussions on this subject, and for kindly allowing me to see parts of his book in advance of publication.

16 Wormald, '*Lex scripta* and *verbum regis*: legislation and Germanic kingship from Euric to Cnut', in *Early Medieval Kingship*, edited by P. Sawyer and I. Wood (Leeds, 1977), pp. 105–38.

West Saxon kings from the 850s on, were directly modelled, as Nicholas Brooks pointed out over twenty years ago, on the public services, the *munera sordida,* of the Theodosian Code.[17] (What was 'rediscovered' in the twelfth century, incidentally, was Justinian's Code, whose fifth-century predecessor, though only patchily and selectively applied, was never lost in the earlier Middle Ages.)[18] But to the duties specified in Roman models, Anglo-Saxon kings added the obligation to perform *burh*-work, that is, to contribute to fortifying, and garrisoning, centres of settlement and/or refuge. When the Carolingian Charles the Bald (re)imposed services for the *patria* in 864, he acknowledged the inspiration not only of antiquity but also, and specifically in the context of *civitas*-fortification, of 'other peoples' (*aliae gentes*)—a clear reference to those across the Channel.[19] Undeniably here is the concept of public services for the state: Anglo-Saxon kings, in requiring these, acted as imitators of Roman Christian Emperors, but, in the form of *burh*-work, added something new.

As a child, Alfred had been taken to Rome; seen the newly built walls around St. Peter's. He had visited the court of Charles the Bald; seen his Carolingian stepmother crowned queen of the West Saxons by the archbishop of Reims. To ideas gleaned from youthful experience, he applied the hard-won knowledge of the mature student and the autodidact. The boy who learned Saxon songs by heart grew up to become aware of the limitations of memory, to become convinced of the value, and cultural prestige, of having things in writing.[20] Reared

---

17 Brooks, 'The Development of Military Obligations in Eighth- and Ninth-Century England', in *England before the Conquest. Studies in Primary Sources presented to Dorothy Whitelock,* edited by P. Clemoes and K. Hughes (Cambridge, 1971), pp. 69–84. See also E. John, *Land Tenure in Early England* (Leicester, 1964).

18 See *The Theodosian Code,* edited by I. Wood and J. Harries (forthcoming 1993).

19 *MGH Capitularia,* II, no. 273, c. 27, pp. 321–2. Cf. Nelson, 'Translating images of authority', p. 197; and eadem, 'The Franks and the English in the ninth century revisited', in *The Preservation and Transmission of Anglo-Saxon Culture,* edited by J. Rosenthal and P. Szarmach (Binghampton, N.Y., 1993), forthcoming.

20 Alfred's version of Augustine's *Soliloquies,* translated by Keynes and Lapidge, *Alfred,* p. 139.

in the values of a warrior elite, Alfred had also read vernacular books
of private prayer, had internalized Christian teachings on sexual guilt
and self-censorship. Struck down by agonizing pain, in public, at his
own wedding-feast,[21] Alfred came to interpret suffering as a heaven-
sent discipline. Like his Continental contemporaries the Emperor
Charles the Fat and Count Gerald of Aurillac,[22] Alfred found it hard
to reconcile the demands of high status in the secular world with the
otherworldly criteria offered by spiritual guides who had so often
worked in a monastic milieu. Alfred learned eventually to effect a
reconciliation of his own, despite the problems he evidently confronted in his own sexuality, and despite a military record which
could suggest a reluctance to get personally involved in the violence
of hand-to-hand fighting. In the *Gesta Karoli* written *c.* 885, Notker
reminded Charles the Fat that the *res publica terrena* 'cannot continue without marriage and the use of weapons'.[23] Alfred understood
this—perhaps warned by the fate of Charles the Fat which the *Anglo-
Saxon Chronicle*, exceptionally well-informed ('he was deprived of
the realm [*rice*] six weeks before his death [in January 888]'), implicitly attributes to his failure to prevent the Danes from 'moving
about that realm at will'. The consequence was 'the dividing of that
realm into five'—and of the four who divided Gaul and Italy 'not one
of them was born to the realm on his father's side'.[24] In 888, these

---

21 Asser, *Life of Alfred*, c. 74, edited by W. H. Stevenson (Oxford, 1904), pp.
54–5, trans. Keynes and Lapidge, *Alfred*, pp. 88–9.

22 See Nelson, 'A Tale of Two Princes: politics, text and ideology in a Carolingian annal', *Studies in Medieval and Renaissance History,* X (1988), 105–41,
at p. 132.

23 Notker, *Gesta Karoli*, ii. 10, edited by Hans F. Haefele, *MGH SRG, NS, XII*
(Berlin, 1959), 66.

24 *Anglo-Saxon Chronicle* [hereafter *ASC*] 887, translated by G. N. Garmonsway (London, 1953), p. 80. Compare the treatment of these events in the
Annals of Fulda, translated by T. Reuter (Manchester, 1992), p. 103 (MS 2
continuation), 114 (Bavarian continuation); Regino of Prüm, *Chronicon*,
edited by F. Kurze, *MGH SRG,* L (Hanover, 1890), 129–30; *Annales
Vedastini*, edited by B. von Simson, *MGH SRG,* XII (Hanover, 1909), 64–5.
The emphasis on patrilineal descent is the *ASC*'s own. Cf. a similar emphasis
in King Alfred's Will, stating a preference that his personal lands 'should
pass to the child in the male [rather than female] line': Keynes and Lapidge,

events posed questions for the Franks: who should rule? how indispensable was royal blood? what was rulership for? what were the sanctions against misrule? The *ASC*'s coverage suggests that such questions were asked insistently in England too: plentiful supplies of information were passing across the Channel at precisely this time (and the same Danish ship-warriors were active on both sides of the Channel). In 886, Alfred asked the archbishop of Reims to send him the scholar Grimbald of St-Bertin 'to superintend the administration of pastoral care': Alfred, significantly, already knew all about Grimbald and his specific talents—which of course suggests a whole prehistory of contacts.[25] Envoys from Alfred's kingdom passed through Francia, and could hardly have avoided going near if not via both St-Bertin and Reims, en route to Rome, in 883 or 884, and every year from 887 to 890.[26] There were ample opportunities here for the transmission back to Alfred's court of news, views, and food for thought.[27]

Alfred's thoughts were not simply taken over, ready-made, from the Franks, however. Dynasticism—the sense that royal power should be transmitted in a royal line—was something Alfred and the Carolingians shared: hence a common interest in genealogies;[28] hence the *ASC*'s comment on Charles the Fat cited above, and hence its pointed reference under 867 to an *ungecyndne cyning*—a king

---

Alfred, p. 178.

[25] The contents of Alfred's letter are rehearsed in the archbishop's reply: Keynes and Lapidge, *Alfred*, p. 185.

[26] *ASC* 885 (referring to an earlier embassy), 887, 888, 889, 890, pp. 80–1.

[27] For information on Scandinavian movements on the Continent in *ASC* 880–7 and 890–2 as an indication of high-level military intelligence, see R. H. C. Davis, 'Alfred the Great: propaganda and truth', *History,* LVI (1971), 169–82, at p. 174.

[28] Two full West Saxon royal genealogies are incorporated in the *ASC*, preface, and 855, pp. 2, 66; and Asser, c. 1, pp. 2–4 gives another version: see D. Dumville, 'The West Saxon genealogical regnal list and the chronology of early Wessex', *Peritia*, IV (1985), 21–66, and more generally Dumville, 'Kingship, Genealogies and Regnal Lists', in Sawyer and Wood, *Early Medieval Kingship*, pp. 72–104. For Carolingian genealogies, see K.-U. Jäschke, 'Die karolingergenealogien aus Metz', *Rheinische Vierteljahrsblätter* XXX-IV (1970), 190–218.

132

who was 'not kinned' to his predecessors.[29] But dynasticism had autochthonous roots in Anglo-Saxon kingdoms: Alfred did not have to borrow it from the Carolingians. Further, the idea of the kingdom as territory also flourished independently in England and on the Continent. It is equally clear in the detailed boundaries of the Treaty of Meersen between Charles the Bald and Louis the German in 870,[30] and in 886/7, in the no less explicitly defined boundary delineated in Alfred's Treaty with the Danish king Guthrum.[31] The notion of the realm as a territory appears in the *ASC* for 878, when the Danes promised 'to leave Alfred's realm [*rice*] without delay'.[32]

But other features differentiate Alfred's kingship from that of Continental contemporaries. The original empire of Charlemagne had been very much a Frankish affair: Frankish aggression created it, Frankish dominance maintained it. Charlemagne titled himself *rex Francorum, Gallias, Germaniam, Italiamque sive harum finitimas provintias ... regens.*[33] To the hitherto pagan conquered Saxons, Christianity, for all its potential to transcend gentile difference, was at first the *ritus dominorum.*[34] It was not Frankish, however, but Latin which Charlemagne promoted as the empire's common language; and the 'barbarous and most ancient songs in which used to be sung the deeds and wars of the kings of old', and which Charlemagne caused to be written down and preserved, were probably in Latin.[35]

---

29 Ed. Bately, p. 47, trans. Garmonsway, p. 68.
30 *Annals of St-Bertin*, translated by J. L. Nelson (Manchester, 1991), pp. 168–9.
31 Keynes and Lapidge, *Alfred*, pp. 171–2, whose dating I still prefer to that suggested by D. Dumville, 'The Treaty of Alfred and Guthrum', in his *Wessex and England from Alfred to Edgar: Six Essays on Political, Cultural, and Ecclesiastical Revival* (Woodbridge, 1992), pp. 1–27.
32 *ASC*, p. 76.
33 In the preface to the *Libri Carolini*, edited by F. Bastgen, *MGH Concilia,* II, Supplement (Hanover, 1924), 1: 'Charles king of the Franks, ruling the Gauls, Germany and Italy and also the provinces that border them'.
34 Hrabanus Maurus, *Liber de Oblatione Puerorum*, in *PL*, CVII, col. 432. Hrabanus continues: 'or rather, [the Franks] by fatherly love converted [the Saxons] to the Christian faith'.
35 Einhard, *Vita Karoli Magni,* c. 29, edited by O. Holder-Egger, *MGH SRG,* XXV (Hanover, 1911), 33: *barbara et antiquissima carmina*, translated by L. Thorpe, *Two Lives of Charlemagne* (Harmondsworth, 1969), p. 82. For a convincing rebuttal of the notion that the *carmina* were in the Germanic

Louis the Pious was committed to an ideal of rulership over 'the Christian people', and, while spurning the ancient songs, spoke Latin as if it had been his native tongue.[36] Superimposed cultural unity was never intended to forestall political dis-unity. Louis's successors, the Carolingians who were Alfred's contemporaries, were heirs to a divided *regnum*.[37] None could claim 'kingship of the Franks', for each ruled over only some of the Franks. At the same time, each ruled a population of more than one people [*gens, gentes*], hence each new realm was a multi-gentile entity. From 840 onwards, each Carolingian king called himself simply *rex*.[38] In 887, Arnulf, the illegitimate nephew of Charles the Fat, seized the kingship of the East Franks. What modern historians recognise as a key event in the formation of Germany was seen in Alfred's entourage as reviving and perpetuating a kind of imperial unity: according to Asser, notwithstanding the multiple consecrations of 888, '*imperium* remained in Arnulf's hands',[39] and the *ASC*, unlike any Continental annalist,

---

vernacular, see D. Geuenich, 'Die volkssprachige Überlieferung der Karolingerzeit aus der Sicht des Historikers', *Deutsches Archiv*, XXXIX (1983), 104–31, at pp. 113–5. For Latin in the Carolingian Empire, see J. L. Nelson, 'Literacy in Carolingian Government', in *The Uses of Literacy in Early Medieval Europe*, edited by Rosmund McKitterick (Cambridge, 1990), pp. 264–72.

36 Thegan, *Vita Hludowici imperatoris*, c. 19, edited by G. Pertz, *MGH SS*, II (Berlin, 1829), 594.

37 W. Schlesinger, 'Die Auflösung des Karlsreiches', in *Karl der Grosse. Lebenswerk und Nachleben*, edited by W. Braunfels, 5 vols (Düsseldorf, 1965–8), I, 792–857; E. Ewig, 'Überlegungen zu den Merowingischen und Karolingischen Teilungen', *Settimane di Studio del Centro Italiano di Studi sull'Alto Medioevo*, XXVII (1981), I, 225–53.

38 P. E. Schramm, *Kaiser, Könige und Päpste*, 4 vols (Stuttgart, 1968), II, 82–7 (also noting the rare exceptions). As emperors, Charles the Bald and Charles the Fat used seals with inscriptions referring to the restoration of an *imperium Francorum*: *ibid.*, pp. 84, 294.

39 Asser, *Life*, c. 85, p. 72: *imperium penes Earnulf remansit*, trans. Keynes and Lapidge, *Alfred*, p. 98 (translating *imperium* 'overall authority'), with comments at 267, rightly noting that Asser's remarks are 'derived, but also developed, from *ASC*'. Cf. *ASC* 'A' 887, edited by J. M. Bately, *The Anglo-Saxon Chronicle. A Collaborative Edition. 3: MS A* (Cambridge, 1986), p. 53: 'hi [i.e. the other four kings] cuedon thaet hie thaet [i.e. each kingdom] to his honda healdan sceoldon', literally, 'they declared that they should hold it at his hands'; cf. trans. Garmonsway, p. 80.

underlines the multi-gentile character of the force that Arnulf led to victory over the Danes in 891: 'with the East Franks and the Saxons and the Bavarians ... [he] put them to flight'.[40] For Alfred, Arnulf's East Frankish kingdom must have held particular interest because here, alone among the Carolingian successor-kingdoms, a written tradition in the Germanic vernacular had been created, and flourished, since the reign of Louis the German (840-876).[41]

Alfred's royal title always has a gentile identification—in earlier charters *rex Saxonum*, later *rex Anglo-Saxonum*.[42] Rooted in a realm of the West Saxons which, by the ninth century anyway, was not divisible, Alfred's kingship had acquired by the mid-880s a wider dimension, had become 'imperial', through the acquisition of the realm of the Angles (Mercians) alongside that of the Saxons.[43] References to 'all Englishkind' (*Angelcyn*) in the *ASC* for 886, in the introductory section to his Laws, and in the preface to the Old English *Pastoral Care*, suggest that Alfred's aim was to reinforce West

---

40 *ASC* 891, trans. Garmonsway, p. 82. Cf. *Annales Vedastini*, 891, p. 70; Regino, *Chronicon*, p. 137; and *Annals of Fulda*, trans. Reuter, p. 121, which insists that only Franks were involved in the victory.

41 Wallace-Hadrill, *The Frankish Church* (Oxford, 1983), pp. 377–89; Geuenich, 'Die volkssprachige Überlieferung'. And see below, p. 135.

42 *Rex Saxonum*, the usual title of eighth-century West Saxon kings, A. Scharer, 'Die *Intitulationes* der angelsächsichen Könige im 7. und 8. Jahrhundert', in *Intitulatio*, edited by H. Wolfram and A. Scharer, III (Vienna/Cologne/Graz, 1988), 9–74, at pp. 72–3, is the title used by Alfred in the following charters, cited from P. Sawyer, *Anglo-Saxon Charters. An Annotated List and Bibliography* (London, 1968) [hereafter Sawyer]: Sawyer, nos 321 (dated 880), 345 (882), and 350 (898), the last case perhaps explicable in terms of some loss of control during Alfred's very last years (see below, n. 45). Alfred has the title *rex Anglorum et Saxonum* (or the like) in Sawyer, nos 346 (889), 347 (891), 348 (892) and three undated charters (Sawyer, nos 354, 355, 356) very probably of the period *c.* 886–*c.* 896.

43 Cf. the comment in the *Annals of Fulda*, 869, p. 61 (and n. 11), on Charles the Bald's acquisition of (part of) Lothar II's kingdom: '[he] ordered that he should be called emperor and *augustus* as one who was to possess two kingdoms'.

Saxon-Mercian unity;[44] and that policy can perhaps be read, too, in the insertion in a royal consecration-prayer, imported from Francia arguably in the 890s, of references to 'the realm of the Angles and Saxons' and to 'establishing *unitedly* the apex of paternal glory'.[45] In fostering a united kingdom, Alfred could draw on a learned, written, tradition. Pope Gregory the Great in the 590s had mistakenly assumed that the oneness of *Britannia* persisted, under the management of *Angli*, to whose king he directed his Roman missionaries. (Gregory was known to Alfred's contemporaries as the apostle of the English). Bede used Gregory's letters to construct the idea of a single English people, with a Church to match.[46] From Bede's further notion of rulers wielding extensive *imperium* within the area that had once been *Britannia*, the learned men of Alfred's generation constructed a fully-fledged English (Anglo-Saxon) kingship borne in the ninth century by Alfred's dynasty.[47] There was also cultural substance, in another, oral and poetic, tradition, to the invented English community. Saxon songs could be understood by the Saxons' neighbours: Alfred, brought up to memorize Saxon songs, was keen to teach them to the Angles (and others) assembled at his court. Saxon songs in the genres of epic or proverbs purveyed the socially-

---

[44] *ASC* 886, p. 80; Keynes and Lapidge, *Alfred*, pp. 163–4 (Laws), and 124–5 (*Pastoral Care*).

[45] Nelson, 'The Second English *Ordo*', in *Politics and Ritual* (London, 1986), p. 365. If political pressures in the late 890s forced Alfred not only to set up a separate sub-kingdom of Kent for his eldest son but to relinquish some control of Mercian lands (see Nelson, 'Reconstructing a royal family', pp. 63–4), this would reflect later circumstances, perhaps unforeseen, certainly unwished, by Alfred *c.* 890.

[46] P. Wormald, 'Bede, the *Bretwaldas* and the origins of the *gens Anglorum*', in *Ideal and Reality in Frankish and Anglo-Saxon Society*, edited by P. Wormald (Oxford, 1983), pp. 99–129: a fundamental study. The same year saw the publication of the thought-provoking book of Benedict Anderson, *Imagined Communities: Reflections on the Origin and Spread of Nationalism* (London, 1983), who unfortunately ignores medieval antecedents.

[47] Wormald, 'Bede, the *Bretwaldas* and the origins', pp. 103–7, 120–1. In understanding the *ASC* thus, I have profited from conversations with David Howlett.

136

conservative virtues of lordship and order, loyalty and fortitude.[48] New songs could be composed in that vein and invested with wider 'English' appeal. *Beowulf* is conceivably a case in point, with its appreciation of Angles and of Scandinavians too.[49] So, certainly, are the so-called *Lays of Boethius*: Alfred's verse-rendering of the verse-sections of Boethius' *Consolation of Philosophy*.[50] The *Lays* open with an introductory section which is apparently Alfred's own composition:

In those days a leader	in Rome was living
A high-born chieftain	cherishing his lord...
A man most righteous	He was 'mid the Romans
A giver of treasure	glorious ever
wise toward this world	wishful of honour
learned in booklore:	Boethius the name was
That this hero had	that so highly was famed...[51]

This Boethius would be at home in Beowulf's world. The audience whom Alfred aimed to reach was one of Old English speakers,

---

48 T. Shippey, *Poems of Wisdom and Learning in Old English* (Cambridge, 1976), esp. pp. 18–9; Nelson, 'Wealth and Wisdom. The Politics of Alfred the Great', in *Kings and Kingship*, edited by J. Rosenthal, State University of New York Acta, 11 (New York, 1986 [for 1984]), pp. 31–52, at 44–5. See further, D. Bullough, 'The educational tradition in England from Alfred to Ælfric: teaching *utriusque linguae*', *Settimane di Studio del Centro Italiano di Studi sull'Alto Medioevo*, XIX (1972), 453–94, now reprinted in his collected essays, *Carolingian Renewal*, pp. 297–334; and P. Wormald, 'The uses of literacy in Anglo-Saxon England', *Transactions of the Royal Historical Society*, XXVII (1977), 95–114.

49 Cf. Nelson, 'Reconstructing a royal family', pp. 51–2.

50 For the alternating verse- and prose-sections, see Godman, *Poets and Emperors*, pp. 160–1. For the authenticity of Alfred's verse-version of Boethius's Metres, see K. Sisam, *Studies in the History of Old English Literature* (Oxford, 1953), pp. 293–7.

51 Translated by W. J. Sedgefield, *King Alfred's Version of the Consolations of Boethius. Done into Modern English, with an Introduction* (Oxford, 1900), p. 179, from *King Alfred's Old English Version of Boethius de Consolatione Philosophiae*, edited by Sedgefield (Oxford, 1899), p. 153.

already well-attuned to the metre and the message of Saxon songs. In transposing Boethius into a vernacular key, Alfred had already effected a transformation of function as well as form.

It is in such vernacular literature, and in Alfredian contributions to it, that I propose to look for Alfred's political ideas. Which extant texts can be called *Alfredian*? That term has been used in two senses: broadly, to cover works associated with royal patronage emanating from the king's entourage, hence including the first and second blocks of the *Anglo-Saxon Chronicle* and the Old English version of Orosius's *Histories*, and even Asser's *Life* of Alfred; narrowly, to denote works attributable to Alfred's own authorship. There are problems of definition here. We know, for instance, that Alcuin contributed substantially to the writing of 'Charlemagne's *Admonitio generalis*'.[52] Early medieval kings, like modern leaders, had their speech-writers and their ghost-writers. Hincmar wrote letters for Charles the Bald. Nevertheless Charles at least occasionally was responsible for his own correspondence.[53] And there are several reasons for believing that in Alfred's case—exceptionally—the king was indeed involved in the production of some substantial texts, the so-called Alfredian translations, made with the help of a scholarly team, but with a personal, authorial, input of the king's own.[54] In identifying 'Alfred's work', we need to be clear that translation entailed substantial interpolation: that is, the addition of sometimes lengthy passages amplifying or explicating the original, as Alfred put it, 'sense for sense'.[55] Four 'translations' produced during Alfred's

---

52 The extent of Alcuin's contribution is debated; but that it was considerable is convincingly argued by F. C. Scheibe, 'Alcuin und die *Admonitio generalis*', *Deutsches Archiv,* XIV (1958), pp. 221–9, reinforced by Bullough, *Carolingian Renewal*, p. 218, n. 46.

53 Nelson, '"Not bishops' bailiffs but lords of the earth": Charles the Bald and the problem of sovereignty', in *The Church and Sovereignty. Essays in Honour of Michael Wilks*, edited by D. Wood (Oxford, 1991), pp. 23–34.

54 For this, and for what follows, see J. M. Bately, *The Literary Prose of King Alfred's Reign: Translation or Transformation?*, Inaugural Lecture, King's College, London, 1980.

55 D. Whitelock, 'The Prose of Alfred's Reign', in *Continuations and Beginnings. Studies in Old English Literature,* edited by E. G. Stanley (London,

reign show traits of style and vocabulary which suggest, so experts tell us, a single, distinctive, authorial voice: the *Pastoral Care* of Gregory, the *Soliloquies* of Augustine, the *Consolation of Philosophy* of Boethius in both prose and verse versions, the first Fifty Psalms.[56] Three of the chosen items reflect specifically royal interests: Gregory could be seen as having written for *rectores* secular as well as spiritual;[57] the *Boethius* underlines the risks and responsibilities of high office;[58] and the Psalmist, David, was a frequently-chosen royal role-model for early medieval kings, not least Alfred's own contemporary Charles the Bald (both, like David, were youngest sons, and both, like David, had a long haul en route to power).[59] Further, of those translations, three themselves declare Alfred's input. In the preface to the *Pastoral Care*, Alfred says: 'I translated it ... as I learnt it from Plegmund, Asser, Grimbald and John'—referring to his four scholar-assistants.[60] The last sentence of the Augustine reads: 'Here end the sayings which King Alfred himself selected'.[61] The Boethius preface

---

1966), pp. 67–103, at pp. 79–80; and Bately, *Literary Prose*, esp. pp. 12–15.

[56] Whitelock, 'The Prose of Alfred's Reign', esp. pp. 71, 79, 83, 94. Keynes and Lapidge, *Alfred*, pp. 28–32, offer a succinct survey. For the Old English version of the Psalms, see P. O'Neill, 'Old English Introductions to the Prose Psalms of the Paris Psalter: sources, structure and composition', in *Eight Anglo-Saxon Studies*, edited by J. S. Wittig (Chapel Hill, N.C., 1981), pp. 20–38; and J. M. Bately, 'Lexical evidence for the authorship of the Prose Psalms in the Paris Psalter', *Anglo-Saxon England,* X (1982), 69–95. For the cultural context, see J. M. Bately, '"Those books that are most necessary for all men to know": the Classics and late ninth-century England, a reappraisal', in *The Classics in the Middle Ages*, edited by A. S. Bernardo and S. Levin (Binghampton, N.Y., 1990), pp. 45–78; and cf. Bullough, *Carolingian Renewal*, pp. 299–300.

[57] Wallace-Hadrill, *Early Germanic Kingship*, pp. 143–5; R. Markus, 'Gregory the Great's rector and his genesis', in *Grégoire le Grand, Colloques internationaux du CNRS* (Paris, 1986), pp. 137–46.

[58] See below, p. 141.

[59] See Nelson, *Charles the Bald* (London, 1992), pp. 15, 85.

[60] Keynes and Lapidge, *Alfred*, p. 126.

[61] *Ibid.*, p. 152. Though this translation survives in a single mid-twelfth-century MS in which the beginning of the preface is lost, Whitelock, 'The Prose of Alfred's Reign', p. 71, takes the last sentence as showing that 'this work is certainly Alfred's', and supports this with 'internal evidence of style'. See

states: 'King Alfred was the translator of this book'.[62] Manuscripts of two of the four take us back to, or very nearly to, Alfred's own time.[63] A century after Alfred's death, Ælfric, homilist and translator of Scripture and saints' lives into the vernacular for lay aristocrats as well as ecclesiastics, saw himself as carrying on a project Alfred had begun:

> that [unlearned men] did not know or possess the evangelical teaching among their books ... except from the books which King Alfred wisely translated from Latin into English, which are still obtainable.[64]

The survival of the Old English *Pastoral Care* in six manuscripts[65] suggests the multiplication and distribution of copies explicitly called for in the verse preface ('King Alfred commanded his scribes to produce more copies from the exemplar so that he could send them to his bishops'[66]), while the prose preface says that this, the *Pastoral Care*, is one of 'certain books which are the most necessary for all men to know'.[67] The preface to the Boethius translation foresees a similar diffusion ('He [King Alfred] beseeches ... each of those whom it pleases to read this book, to pray for him'[68]). And Alfred's biographer Asser seems to hint at this when in *c.* 106 he

---

now E. G. Stanley, 'King Alfred's Prefaces', *Review of English Studies,* XXXIX (1988), pp. 349–64.

[62] Keynes and Lapidge, *Alfred,* p. 131. See further M. Godden, 'King Alfred's Boethius', in *Boethius: his Life, Thought and Influence,* edited by M. Gibson(Oxford, 1981), pp. 419–24.

[63] London, British Library, Cotton Tiberius B.xi (see Keynes and Lapidge, *Alfred,* p. 293) and Oxford, Bodleian, Hatton 20, are MSS of the *Pastoral Care* probably written in Alfred's lifetime; London, British Library, Cotton Otho A.vi, is a tenth-century MS of the Boethius.

[64] D. Whitelock, *English Historical Documents,* vol. I, 2nd edn (London, 1979), p. 239.

[65] In addition to the two just mentioned, there are London, BL, Otho B.ii; Cambridge, University Library, Ii.2.4; Cambridge, Corpus Christi College MS 12; and Cambridge, Trinity College, R.5.22.

[66] Keynes and Lapidge, *Alfred,* p. 127.

[67] *Ibid,* p. 126.

[68] *Ibid,* pp. 131–2.

refers to the *libri Saxonici* (distinct from the orally-transmitted and memorized *carmina Saxonica* also referred to in other chapters)[69] which Alfred prescribed for ealdormen, reeves and thegns to read. Lastly there are two other works, both very closely associated with Alfred, for which the manuscript tradition is similarly widely diffused: namely, the *ASC* and Alfred's Laws. It seems impossible to deny Alfred's personal role in getting these vernacular works copied and distributed—and perhaps a little perverse to question Alfred's stimulus to their production too.[70] If Alfred did not write the Old English translations of the *Pastoral Care*, the Boethius, the Augustine and the Psalms (as well as patronizing other works including the *ASC*), then we should have to invent an author (and patron) just like Alfred.

Now, for an early medieval ruler, activity as an author is an astonishing fact, almost unprecedented—and unparalleled for centuries to come. Yet in our resolutely historical quest (shutting our ears to Derrida-esque claims of authorial demise) for Alfred as author, as well as publicizer, of political ideas, we must beware of anachronism. What is fundamental may not be most distinctive, let alone self-consciously

---

69 Asser, *Life*, c. 106, p. 94, trans. Keynes and Lapidge, *Alfred*, p. 110: 'books in English'; for *carmina*, cc. 23, 75. 76, pp. 20, 59, trans. Keynes and Lapidge, pp. 75, 91.

70 Whitelock, 'The Prose of Alfred's Reign', pp. 95–7, acknowledges Alfred's authorship of the Laws, yet is reluctant to accept his responsibility for the *ASC*'s compilation, chiefly on the grounds that the 853 annal includes 'the strange belief' that Alfred's consular investment by Pope Leo IV was a royal consecration. See also Whitelock, *English Historical Documents*, I, 123–4. On this point, Whitelock follows F. M. Stenton, *Anglo-Saxon England*, 2nd edn (Oxford, 1947), pp. 269, n. 2, and 683; and is in turn followed by Bately, 'The compilation of the Anglo-Saxon Chronicle 60 B.C. to A.D. 890: Vocabulary as evidence', *Proceedings of the British Academy*, LXIV (1980 for 1978), 93–129, at p. 128. Keynes and Lapidge, *Alfred*, pp. 40, 217–8, 278–9, incline to a similar view, but rightly distinguish between compilation and diffusion, though without explicitly stating that Alfred 'published' the *ASC*. For a different interpretation of the 853 annal, see Nelson, 'The Franks and the English in the ninth century revisited', in *The Preservation and Transmission of Anglo-Saxon Culture*, edited by J. Rosenthal and P. Szarmach, forthcoming. I hope to return shortly to the question of the *ASC*'s origins.

new. Indeed the choice of medium—translations and interpolations—
keeps us firmly within a matrix of authoritative texts. Take the single
best-known political idea with which Alfred has been credited: that
of the three orders, which appears in Alfred's version of Boethius'
Consolation of Philosophy. Here is a passage translated from
Boethius's Latin:

> Then I [Boethius] said that she [Philosophy] was well aware of how little
> I had been governed by worldly ambition. I had sought the means of
> engaging in politics so that virtue should not grow old unpraised ....
> Philosophy replied: The desire for glory, the thought of fame, is the one
> thing that could entice minds ... not yet perfected with the finishing
> touch of complete virtue ... But how unimportant such fame is.[71]

In his version of this passage, Alfred interpolates between the initial statement and the reply the following gloss on 'means of engag-
ing in politics':

> In the case of the king, the resources and tools with which to rule are that
> he have his land fully manned: he must have praying men, fighting men
> and working men... [and] he must have the means of support for his
> tools, the three classes of men: gifts, weapons, food, ale, clothing and
> whatever else is necessary for each of the three classes of men.[72]

This, it has been alleged, is the first appearance of the three orders
in the medieval Christian West. Irish influence (that explanatory *deus
ex machina*) has even been surmized.[73] But Dominique Iogna-Prat

---

71 Boethius, *The Consolation of Philosophy*, II, vii, translated by V. E. Watts
(Harmondsworth, 1969), p. 72. For Boethius' work in its context, see H.
Chadwick, *Boethius: the Consolations of Music, Logic, Theology, and Philo-
sophy* (Oxford, 1981).

72 Trans. Sedgefield, p. 41 (the passage is referred to in Sedgefield's Index, p.
247, at 'Alfred, his theory of government'); and also Keynes and Lapidge,
Alfred, p. 132.

73 G. Duby, *The Three Orders. Feudal Society Imagined*, English trans.
(London, 1980; French original Paris, 1978), pp. 99–109, taking up the argument of D. Dubuisson, 'L'Irlande et la théorie médiévale des "trois or-

and Edmond Ortigues[74] have now shown that the three orders of ancient Rome—senators, soldiers and farmers, familiar to medieval writers via Isidore—were 'baptized' by Frankish scholars in the middle decades of the ninth century. At the school of Auxerre, Haimo elaborated in his Commentary on the Book of Revelation a notion of three functional groups, substituting the priesthood for the senators. It has been suggested often enough that Continental commentaries on the *Consolation of Philosophy*, in particular that of another Auxerre scholar, Remigius, lie behind Alfred's comments on Boethius. Sceptics, notably Joseph Wittig, who elegantly demonstrated the non-dependence of Alfred's treatment of the Orpheus story,[75] have perhaps thrown out the baby with the bath water. Lateral thinking shifts the focus from Commentaries on the *Consolation of Philosophy* to the Auxerre scholars' broader agenda.[76] One such scholar, and one such work in particular, suggest the first link in the chain from Auxerre to the court of Alfred. The *Miracles of St Germain*, by Heiric, also a student of Haimo and like him author of a Commentary on Revelations, include a particularly clear exposition of the three orders theme.[77] The work was intended for the eyes of Charles the Bald and Heiric was a familiar of Charles's court in the

---

dres'", *Revue de l'Histoire des Religions*, CLXXXVIII (1975), 35–63. See also Keynes and Lapidge, *Alfred*, p. 298; and M. Godden, 'Money, power and morality in late Anglo-Saxon England', *Anglo-Saxon England,* XIX (1990), 41–66, at p. 55.

[74] D. Iogna-Prat, 'Le "baptême" du schéma des trois ordres fonctionnels', *Annales. Économies. Sociétés. Civilisations*, Janvier-Février 1986, pp. 101–26; E. Ortigues, 'L'elaboration de la Théorie des Trois Ordres chez Haymon d'Auxerre', *Francia*, XIV (1988), 27–43.

[75] Wittig, 'King Alfred's Boethius and its Latin sources: a reconsideration', *Anglo-Saxon England,* XI (1983), 157–98. But see W. F. Bolton, 'How Boethian is Alfred's Boethius?', in *Studies in Earlier Old English Prose*, edited by P. Szarmach (Binghampton, N.Y., 1986), pp. 153–68, still arguing for a Continental source.

[76] See the contributions to *L'école carolingienne d'Auxerre*, edited by D. Iogna-Prat, C. Jeudy, and G. Lobrichon (Paris, 1991).

[77] *Miracula Sancti Germani,* ii. 18, *PL* 124, col. 1254: 'some who fight, some who till the soil, and a third *ordo* whom God has chosen for his special service'.

870s.[78] Around then too, another young cleric began to make his mark in that same milieu: Fulk, favoured man among the *palatini*, to whom Charles had given, by July 877, the abbacy of St-Bertin.[79] It was from St-Bertin, via Reims, where Fulk became archbishop in 883, that Grimbald, Fulk's protégé, was called by Alfred in 886. One further bit of evidence reinforces the hypothesis that the three orders came from Auxerre to Wessex via St-Bertin: late in the 890s, a member of the St-Bertin community wrote up that saint's miracles, including an account of a victory won against the Northmen in 891:

> the Christians divided their booty into three parts: the first went to the saint's sanctuaries; the second to those who pray [*oratores*] and the poor; the third to the fighting men [*bellatores*], 'more noble' and 'humbler' alike.[80]

The author adds that the *oratores* including those unfit for fighting (*imbelles*) did more than the *bellatores* to bring about victory.

These are not Alfred's three orders; nor do they coincide with the three groups, *bellatores*, *operatores* and *advenae*, among whom (according to Asser) was divided that half of Alfred's revenues which he devoted to earthly affairs.[81] But these are variations on a theme of trifunctionality. (Even the practical means of support, the allegedly most 'Alfredian' details, food and beer, do in fact come from Continental Commentaries on the *Consolation of Philosophy*.[82]) And the

---

[78] Nelson, *Charles the Bald*, p. 234.

[79] *Ibid.*, p. 250.

[80] *Miracula Sancti Bertini*, c. 7, edited by O. Holder-Egger, *MGH SS,* XV, part 1, pp. 512–3.

[81] Asser, *Life*, cc. 100, 101, pp. 86–7, trans. Keynes and Lapidge, *Alfred*, pp. 106–7.

[82] J. C. Frakes, *The Fate of Fortune in the Early Middle Ages. The Boethian Tradition* (Leiden, 1988), p. 112. Cf. a similar interpolation about 'meat, drink and clothes', trans. Sedgefield, p. 29. For guidance to Alfred's Boethius, Frakes's fine book should now be consulted along with K. Otten, *König Alfreds Boethius* (Tübingen, 1964), F. A. Payne, *King Alfred and Boethius: an Analysis of the OE Version of the 'Consolation of Philosophy'* (Madison, 1968), and A. J. Frantzen, *King Alfred* (Boston, 1986), pp. 43–66.

144

likeliest medium for the theme's transmission to Alfred's England is Grimbald of St-Bertin. Where does that leave Alfred's 'original idea'? The question is misconceived: early medieval writers characteristically drew on authorities and made their own contributions in the ways they rearranged or marginally adapted their materials. Alfred did just that. Precisely because he was a king, and not a monk or a priest, Alfred viewed the three orders from the king's perspective, situated them in reference to royal needs. So the interpolated passage replaces ecclesiology by political thought. Alfred asked, not: how is the church composed? but: how can a king's power be exercised?[83] Because he read as a king, Alfred fundamentally reinterpreted Boethius's work, by applying an Augustinian (and ultimately Stoic) criterion: where Boethius had rejected wordly goods, including political power, Alfred, like Augustine, accepted them—on condition that (*buton*—only if—only so long as—is a characteristic and crucial Alfredian construction) they were rightly used.[84] In order to effect this reinterpretation, Alfred radically altered the figure of Fortune who occupied a central place in Boethius's original work. The concept of *wyrd* (Fate) was depersonalized, eviscerated, devalued, denied autonomy: it became simply what happens in the world—and was seen as wholly under the controlling power of God.[85] On the other hand, *woruldsaelda* (worldly goods) were *re*valued: in an interpolated passage, following his translation of *Consolation of Philosophy* II, ii, Alfred gave a little speech to personified

---

[83] Nelson, 'Kingship and Empire', pp. 239–40. Since I gave the present paper last April, Wendy Davies has very kindly allowed me to read an unpublished paper of her own on insular treatments of the three orders theme. We seem to have arrived independently (and, for me, reassuringly!) at similar conclusions as to the sources of Alfred's thought.

[84] See R.A. Markus, *Saeculum: History and Society in the Theology of St Augustine*, 2nd edn. (Cambridge, 1988), pp. 67–8, citing Augustinian works (*Responses to Diverse Questions*; *The City of God*) that may not have been known to Alfred. But the notion of right use also appears in *Soliloquies* I, iii, 7, edited and translated by G. Watson (Warminster, 1990), p. 22: '... cum illum iure oderim qui male utitur eo quod amo'. For Alfred's characteristic 'only if', see Whitelock, 'The Prose of Alfred's Reign', pp. 94–5.

[85] Frakes, *Fate of Fortune*, p. 91.

woruldsaelda:[86]

> Why do you reproach us? [they ask the Prisoner]. It was you who first
> desired us, not we you. You set us on the Creator's throne when you
> looked to us for the good you should seek from Him.... You are more
> guilty than we are ... because owing to you we are unable to do the will
> of our Maker. He lent us to you to enjoy in accordance with his
> commands.

This passage follows a crucial modification in the Boethian original: Alfred omitted personified Fortune, and substituted *Wisdom*, that
is, an aspect of God. It seems to me significant that Fortune—
unstable, capricious—was always conceived, by Classical authors,
and by their medieval and Renaissance heirs, as female,[87] while *Wisdom* in Alfred's Old English—reasonable, consistent, knowledge-
able—is male: a model of good lordship, a giver and lender of goods.
Accordingly *Wisdom*'s control over men begins when they attain
maturity—*to monnum become*[88]—and so become capable of right-
thinking, of wise use of the good they are 'lent'. The revaluing of
worldly goods thus goes hand in hand with a revaluing of earthly life,
and of the possibilities for useful activity in a patriarchal social
world.

Appropriately, the concept Alfred introduces here is that of the
tool or instrument, of men as the king's tools, and of material resources and human skills as their tools. To develop skill, Wisdom is
required: but if it is thus applied, and skills used to wise ends, then
worldly goods are to be welcomed, not rejected. What Alfred has

---

86 Trans. Sedgefield, pp. 16–7.
87 Cf. Machiavelli's well-known treatment of *Fortuna* in *The Prince*, c. xxv,
    edited by Q. Skinner, translated by R. Price (Cambridge, 1988), p. 87: 'I
    certainly think it is better to be impetuous than cautious, because fortune is a
    woman, and if you want to control her, it is necessary to treat her roughly.
    And it is clear that she is more inclined to yield to men who are impetuous
    than to those who are calculating'. See further Price's notes on *fortuna*, *ibid.*,
    pp. 104–6.
88 Frakes, *Fate of Fortune*, pp. 103–4 makes the point about maturity, without
    noting the gender component in the key terms.

done is to convert the world-rejecting message of Boethius into one of clear, if conditional, acceptance. Boethius's consolation, entirely congenial as it stood to a monastic world-view, has necessarily been adapted to a secular but still emphatically Christian one, and hence become useful in a new sense. Auxerre baptized: Alfred politicized.

In another piece of Alfredian adaptation, that politicization is given a further dimension. Boethius had indulged in a little flight of fancy:

> You'd laugh if you saw a community of mice and one mouse arrogating to himself power and jurisdiction over the others! ... Don't you stop to consider, you earthly creatures, the people over whom you think you exercise authority?[89]

Boethius's point is that humankind —all of them—are as feeble as mice and that political pretensions would therefore be as ludicrous in the one case as in the other. Here's what Alfred makes of the passage:

> Suppose you saw a mouse that was a lord over other mice, and laid down laws for them, and made them pay taxes: wouldn't you be amazed, wouldn't you shake with laughter! Yet a man's body compared with his mind is like a mouse's body compared to a man's. A man's body is frail ... but a mind with discernment cannot be harmed.[90]

Alfred draws a quite different conclusion from Boethius's, almost the opposite in fact. Where Boethius was bitterly ironic, Alfred invites to cheerful laughter and where Boethius was gloomily egalitarian, Alfred is optimistic about the capacities of men (if not those of mice). Lawgiving and tax-taking are not ludicrous in human communities precisely because a man with a discerning mind can exer-

---

[89] Trans. p. 70.
[90] Ed. Sedgefield, pp. 35–6. Cf. trans. Sedgefield, p. 36 (I have ventured my own translation above). For the term *gafol*, tax, see J. Bosworth and T. N. Toller, *An Anglo-Saxon Dictionary* (Oxford, 1898), *s.v.*

cize authority successfully.[91]

Alfred's thought can be compared, further, to Augustine's, and a rather similar contrast observed. Where in Augustine's *saeculum*, there is only peace of a kind, and the human judge's condition of ignorance is a miserable one,[92] Alfred sees power committed to him by God to be rightfully administered, and those who serve the king also have their crafts to develop and apply. Where Augustine's citizens of the heavenly city remained *peregrini*, resident aliens, in earthly cities, Alfred's three orders are fully at home in manning the king's land and, in a more personal sense, on the *laen* (leased lands) the king may give them.[93]

Alfred's ideas present another, equally striking, contrast with those who wrote mirrors of princes for the Carolingians—the exponents of *l'Augustinisme politique*. Jonas, Sedulius, Hincmar all stressed the authoritative role of bishops in directing royal power—in fact, situated that power (in Ambrosian mode) firmly within the Church. If they rehabilitated earthly kingdoms, the Carolingian writers did so on ecclesiastical terms. For them there could be no positive idea of secular power in its own right.[94] Alfred is a notable contrast. He has nothing to say in any of his Boethian interpolations about the institutional church. Bishops, priests, are unmentioned. This is true too of his other writings. And even in the *Pastoral Care* there is a tendency to shift Gregory's original sense of *rector*—bishop—to those in secular authority: kings in particular. In the Augustine translation, Alfred inserts two famous analogies. First, you can recognize God's will for you as clearly as you can recognize your lord's will in his letter and seal (*ðines hlafordes ærendgewrit and hys insegel*)—

---

91 In an interesting interpolation in his version of the *Pastoral Care*, cited by Whitelock, 'The Prose of Alfred's Reign', p. 64, Alfred makes it clear that while authority (*ealdordom*) can be seen as service (*ðenenga*), it should have nothing to do with companionship (*geferrædenne*) or equality (*efnlicnesse*) when the ruled are evil.

92 *City of God*, XIX, 6, 13.

93 Preface to *Soliloquies*, edited by T. Carnicelli (Cambridge, Mass., 1969), p. 48, trans. Keynes and Lapidge, *Alfred*, p. 139.

94 Wallace-Hadrill, 'The *via regia* of the Carolingian age'; Nelson, *Politics and Ritual in Early Medieval Europe* (London, 1986), pp. 133–71.

and once you've recognized it, you follow it, whatever the immediate sacrifice, preferring temporary loss of wealth (*welan*) to losing your lord's friendship. Second, wisdom is like the king's court: all are drawn to it, though some have a harder time getting there than others, and once there, not all get equally close to the king.[95] Here Alfred assumes readers already familiar with the king's power and with his demands—which is why he can use those to illustrate God's. Michael Wallace-Hadrill memorably remarked that Alfred was short of bishops.[96] That shortage was in fact the necessary condition for Alfred's pursuit of his own thoroughly secular but thoroughly Christian approach to politics. With more, and more authoritative, bishops at his side, breathing down his neck, Alfred could never have framed his distinctive idea of the realm as a territory within which the king wielded unique authority over resources and over men—lawgiving and tribute-taking.

As in Francia, and as in Mercia, too,[97] so in Wessex Alfred had to raise tribute to pay off Scandinavian warbands. This pressing need engendered public activity of the most concrete kind, and ideas of state power to match. Such ideas—that the state had the right and responsibility to tax in order to defend its territory, and that even churches might be required to contribute (being *quantum ad saecularia* within the remit of secular authority)—are implicit in Alfred's reform of the coinage early on in his reign, c. 875, and in his unabashed statement in a charter for Winchester that the bishop and *familia*, after receiving an estate as a bequest from King Æthelwulf but being unable to pay off their contribution to the tribute which the whole *gens* was accustomed to pay to the *pagani*, 'begged me [Alfred] to pay off the tribute and to have the land—which I did'.[98] The problem was to maintain the resources of the kingdom over time. Alfred was all too familiar with the risk of conflict within the royal

---

[95] Trans. Keynes and Lapidge, *Alfred*, pp. 141, 143–4.

[96] *Early Germanic Kingship*, p. 149.

[97] Francia: *Annals of St-Bertin*, trans. Nelson, pp. 130, 200; Mercia: Sawyer, no. 1278. For effects on the coinage, see D. Metcalf and J. Northover, 'Coinage alloys from the time of Offa to Charlemagne', *Numismatic Chronicle,* CLIX (1989), 101–20.

[98] Sawyer, no. 354.

family—hence of the risk of splitting the royal resources. Compared to the Carolingians the West Saxon royal dynasty did well in inhibiting fraternal conflict—Alfred seems anxious, anyway, to give this impression in his Will, where he recalls how he and his brother provided for each other's children in a series of agreements.[99] The *ASC* records the peaceful transmission of the kingship from one brother to the next and Asser underlines this point. Intergenerational conflict, especially between father and son, was a more serious problem. Asser reports the rebellion of Alfred's eldest brother against his father King Æthelwulf—*quaedam infamia contra morem omnium Christianorum.*[100] And in praising Alfred's upbringing of his children, Asser carefully specifies their *magna patris subjectio*—the reference seems to be to Edward in particular.[101]

Alfred himself in the Boethius translation waxes especially indignant on the subject of rebellion within the family: 'we have learned that long ago there happened a most unwonted and unnatural evil, that sons conspired together and plotted against their father'.[102] Again, this time *à propos* the Classical myth of the Giants rebelling against Jove, Alfred comments: 'Giants, sons of the earth who ruled over the earth and were, so to speak, Jove's sisters' children, were angry that he had sway over them, and sought to burst the heavens beneath him—but he sent thunders and lightnings and scattered therewith all their handiwork and themselves he slew'.[103]

Alfred firmly denied the claims of his nephews to shares in the kingdom; he tried to deny no less firmly the claims of his son to a share in the kingdom during his, Alfred's, own lifetime; and he tried to obliterate the existence of Mercia as a separate kingdom, insisting its ruler (his own son-in-law) be termed not king but ealdorman. Fi-

---

99 Trans. Keynes and Lapidge, *Alfred*, p. 174. For other aspects of conflict-control, see P. Stafford, 'The king's wife in Wessex', *Past and Present,* XCI (1981), 3–27; Nelson, '"A king across the sea": Alfred in Continental perspective', *Transactions of the Royal Historical Society,* XXXVI (1986), 45–68.

100 *Life*, c. 12, p. 9, trans. Keynes and Lapidge, *Alfred*, p. 70.

101 *Life*, c. 75, p. 58, trans. Keynes and Lapidge, *Alfred*, p. 90.

102 Trans., p. 76.

103 Trans., p. 112.

nally Alfred arranged for the single succession of one son, Edward, to his whole composite realm, and, thinking ahead to the next generation, ritually invested Edward's eldest son Athelstan, then aged four, in what looks like a replica of Alfred's investiture at the age of four, in 853.[104]

If Alfred had a clear conception of his realm as an impartible territory, he also conceived his *anweald* in terms of power over men. In his Laws, he draws a sharp distinction between free and slave; in his Boethius translation 'a mighty [*rice*] king', he says, 'should only be served by free men'.[105] Those free men involved in a special relationship of service to the ruler occupied a special position. The king offered them friendship,[106] signifying a relationship of unequals which perhaps nevertheless carried a reminder that men are by nature equal—an idea which Alfred could have read in Gregory.[107] The relationship was a personal one, each friend being the man of his lord. But it was not only personal. Alfred termed the three orders *geferscipas*—groups of *gefere*—companions.[108] The king's thegns them-

---

[104] See further, Nelson, 'Reconstructing a royal family', 63.

[105] Laws [43] 39, trans. Keynes and Lapidge, *Alfred*, p. 170, with n. 31, p. 310; Boethius, trans. Sedgefield, p. 142. See Godden, 'Money, power and morality', p. 46, arguing that Alfred consistently distinguishes between 'wealthy' (*welig*) and 'having authority' (*rice*), yet acknowledging a difficulty for his argument in one passage of the Boethius, trans. Sedgefield, p. 69, where Alfred, describing treasurers (*mathmhirdas*) as *rice*, seems to see power and wealth as going together. (Note that *rice* is both an adjective and a noun ['kingdom', 'realm'].) With the statement (p. 67): 'authority and riches [*rice*] cannot make their possessor more worthy but rather make him the less worthy, *unless* he were already good', Alfred (with a characteristic *buton*— enabling him to have his cake and eat it) paves the way for an extension of the sense of *rice* to include powerful *and wealthy* in the case of good office-holders. Godden's general argument for a semantic shift in the tenth century is persuasive, nonetheless.

[106] *Soliloquies*, trans. Keynes and Lapidge, *Alfred*, p. 142.

[107] *Pastoral Care*, II, 6, *PL*, LXXVII, col. 34, OE Version edited by H. Sweet, *King Alfred's West Saxon Version of Gregory's Pastoral Care*, 2 vols, Early English Text Society, Original Series, 45, 50 (London, 1871–2), c. 17, pp. 106–7. For friends as kinsmen, see Boethius version, trans. Keynes and Lapidge, *Alfred*, p. 133.

[108] *Alfred's Old English Boethius*, ed. Sedgefield, p. 40.

selves formed a group and the *ASC* underlined their collective importance as guardians of *burhs* and more generally as royal agents 'in the
land' (896). To the author of the 896 annal Alfred had suffered less in
the 890s from Scandinavian attacks than from the deaths of 'the best
king's thegns'.[109] But on one group of his thegns the king relied especially: his *fasselli summertunenses*—his closest retainers recruited
from Somerset (had his apanage in the 860s lain in that shire?)—who
in 878 shared his tribulations and his triumph.[110] Asser elsewhere
writes of Alfred's *dilectissimi ministri*, or his *satellites*.[111] Though
only a dozen charters of Alfred's survive, they preserve some 70 attestations of king's thegns, that is, the names of some fifty individuals.[112] These were the tools of which Alfred especially relied: all-
purpose agents of his will, bearers of his intentions, those to whom he
recited Saxon books 'and especially taught Saxon songs by heart'.
These men were bound to him by *familiaris dilectio*[113] and Alfred
shared with them his longing for wisdom. Asser hit the nail on the
head in calling these men vassals, for they are the exact counterparts
of the men on whom ninth-century Carolingians relied to run their
realms and who, precisely in the 860s and 870s and in the West
Frankish kingdom, were acquiring clear definition as individuals and

---

109 *ASC* 893, 896, pp. 87, 90.
110 Asser, *Life*, c. 55, p. 44. (Keynes and Lapidge, *Alfred*, p. 84, translate
'thegns', which obscures the particularity of Asser's term here.) Cf. also c.
53, p. 41 (*faselli*). On the term *fas(s)elus as* 'a proof of Frankish influence',
see Stevenson's note, *Life*, pp. 254–5. See also Nelson, '"A king across the
sea"', p. 67.
111 *Life*, cc. 91, 100, pp. 78, 87, trans. Keynes and Lapidge, *Alfred*, pp. 101–2,
106.
112 I consulted the witness-lists of the following charters in W. de G. Birch,
Cartularium Saxonicum, 3 vols (London, 1885–99), II, nos. 548 (Sawyer,
321), 549 (Sawyer, 352), 550 (Sawyer, 345), 565 (Sawyer, 354), 567
(Sawyer, 348), 568 (Sawyer, 356), 576 (Sawyer, 350), 581 (Sawyer, 355). In
a few cases it is unclear whether the attester is a thegn or not: hence an
approximate total. The relatively small number of repeated attestations could
suggest a high turn-over. *ASC* 893, p. 87, says that 'many king's thegns'
were killed at Buttington, for instance.
113 Asser, *Life*, c. 76, p. 60, trans. Keynes and Lapidge, *Alfred*, p. 91.

as a group.[114] Did Grimbald tell Asser, and Alfred, about *vassalli*? But would not Alfred, in any case, in his desire to exalt royal authority and hence to generalize the ideal of *service* to that authority, have recast his companions (*gesiths*) and reeves, and even his ealdormen and bishops, as thegns?[115]

That Alfred should emphasize order and authority (and not only royal authority) is hardly surprising. It is not surprising, either, that he should impose the death-penalty for one who plots against the king's life and for one who plots against his lord's life.[116] Lordship at every level was linked in a hierarchy, divinely ordained by the Lord of Lords. But what is more surprising, and equally revealing of Alfred's political ideas, is the notion that it may sometimes be justified to *resist* your lord. One very remarkable difference between Boethius's prisoner and Alfred's (whom he calls *Mod*—Mind) is that whereas Boethius asserts his innocence of the charge of conspiracy, Alfred's prisoner has indeed plotted against his lord. Here's how Alfred describes it:

> To the Romans [Theodoric] promised his friendship and that they should keep their old rights; but he kept that promise very basely ... Boethius, a man of book-learning and most truly wise in worldly wisdom, perceiving the manifold wrongs wrought by Theodoric upon ... the chief men of the Romans, began to recall ... the rights they had once enjoyed under the Caesars, their ancient lords. And so ... he began to muse and to cast about within himself how he might wrest the sovereignty from the unrighteous king and give it to them of righteous life.[117]

'Unrighteous rulers' are clearly identified: they not only 'commit

---

114 W. Kienast, edited by P. Herde, *Die Fränkische Vasallität: von den Hausmeiern bis zu Ludwig dem Kind und Karl dem Einfältigen* (Frankfurt, 1990), esp. pp. 380–4, 389–93.

115 See H. R. Loyn, 'The term *ealdorman* in the translations prepared at the time of King Alfred', *EHR,* LXVIII (1953), 513–25, and idem, 'Gesiths and thegns in England from the seventh to the tenth century', *EHR,* LXX (1955), 529–49: two important (and oddly neglected) articles.

116 Laws, cc. [4] 5, [4,2], trans. Keynes and Lapidge, *Alfred*, p. 165.

117 Trans. Sedgefield, pp. 1–2.

private deeds of savage cruelty', but 'destroy and ravage the lands subject to them'.[118] The right of resistance to such kings is consistently maintained by Alfred: it is a duty, even if it brings suffering. Indeed Alfred sees Boethius as victim not only of attachment to false goods but of his own virtue in resisting the unrighteous king:

> Theodoric would not have been displeased with thee if like his foolish favourites thou hadst shown liking of this unrighteousness.[119]

Wisdom can promise Theodoric's downfall—and so, can offer Boethius hope of restoration. But a clear distinction is suggested between justified and unjustified resistance:

> Hear now a lay of unrighteous kings. We see them seated on high seats … girt about with a great company of their thegns who are decked with belts and golden-hilted swords and wargear of many kinds…. But if thou … take away from him his company of thegns and his power, then you can see that he is just like one of the thegns who serve him, and indeed baser.[120]

If thegns depend on the king for their honour and reward, the power of the king depends on his thegns. On the other hand, resistance, withdrawal of obedience, may be unjustified—and in that case the thegns suffer, not the king. Thus when Ulysses was seduced by Circe and 'tarried with her so long that his thegns could no longer stay with him, yearning for home and being minded to punish him, they resolved to abandon him'. The result was their horrible punishment of having their bodies changed into those of wild beasts— though their minds remained those of men.[121] Alfred apparently regards withdrawal of obedience as justified only for unrighteous acts that damage the realm. A distinction between public and private actions is implicit here. Tyrannical conduct, in the style of Theodoric,

---

[118] *Ibid.*, pp. 40, 34.
[119] *Ibid.*, p. 66.
[120] *Ibid.*, p. 128.
[121] *Ibid.*, pp. 133–4.

meant flouting the old rights enjoyed by the 'chief men' of the people. But if Alfred was interested in not only chief men but all the free, he knew that chief men could very often be greedy for power, perverters of justice, neglecters of wisdom. Alfred castigates such men in his Boethius, just as Asser describes him doing in real life.[122] Alfred was prepared to remove one of them from office and confiscate his lands—the Ealdorman Wulfhere who broke his oath both to Alfred and his *patria*.[123]

With the notion of the *patria*, we come, finally, close to home—and to London. Asser says that Alfred 'restored the city of London splendidly'.[124] The evidence of coin-issues shows—or rather numismatists have recently been able to demonstrate from that evidence—that London was in Alfred's hands in the early 880s: this is what several manuscripts of the *ASC* in fact suggest, in mentioning a siege of London by Alfred in 883 during which he fulfilled a promise to send alms to Rome 'and their prayers were well fulfilled after that promise'.[125] Hence what happened in 886 was a *re*-taking, or a special celebration, or both. The *ASC* shows that the 'setting' of London was thought important at Alfred's court *c.* 891. But whatever occurred was assigned real importance *at the time* as well. In all datable

---

122 Asser, *Life*, cc. 91, 106, pp. 78, 93–4, trans. Keynes and Lapidge, *Alfred*, pp. 101, 110.

123 Nelson, '"A king across the sea"', pp. 53–4.

124 *Life*, c. 83, p. 69, trans. Keynes and Lapidge, *Alfred*, p. 97. Cf. *ASC* 886, ed. Bately, p. 53: '… gesette Elfred cyning Lundenburg'; trans. Garmonsway, p. 80.

125 *ASC* MSS B, C, D, and E. Stenton, *Anglo-Saxon England*, p. 258, n. 3, followed by Whitelock, *English Historical Documents*, I, 181, and Keynes and Lapidge, *Alfred*, p. 266, refers this 'misplaced' addition to 886. But see now Keynes, 'King Alfred and the Mercians', and M. Blackburn, 'The London mint in the reign of Alfred', both in *Kings, Currency, and Alliances: the History and Coinage of Southern England, A.D. 840–900,* edited by Blackburn and D. Dumville (Woodbridge, 1993), forthcoming. I am very grateful to Simon Keynes and Mark Blackburn for keeping me abreast of their work in advance of publication. See meanwhile Blackburn, 'The Ashdon Hoard', *The British Numismatic Journal*, LIX (1989), 13–38, at p. 16. I am also grateful to Marion Archibald of the British Museum for helpful discussion.

charters issued after 886, Alfred has the title that reflects rule over the Angles as well as the Saxons, or—to use the *ASC*'s terminology—'all Englishkind'.[126] While it's true that Asser styles Alfred *rex Angul-Saxonum* earlier in the *Life*,[127] the first chapter in which the title seems to have a strictly contemporary (as distinct from a retrospective) reference relates to 882.[128] Thereafter it appears five more times (885-7) with precise and specific chronological reference.[129] It is tempting to link the title with a 'taking of London' in or around 883. By *c.* 891, however, the 'restoration' of 886, through its association with Mercian submission signalled in the Mercian leader Æthelred's acceptance of an ealdordom (and possibly at the same time marriage to Alfred's daughter[130]) was apparently regarded at Alfred's court as the critical moment in the *re*-construction of the realm of the English, and perhaps in the hoped-for establishment of that realm's *sedes* at London.[131] And whence the revival of that notion? Via Bede, no doubt; and influenced by the fact that Alfred's grandfather Egbert had (briefly) held London in 829, and issued a commemorative coin

---

126 See above, n. 42. At this time too, Archbishop Fulk of Reims addressed Alfred as 'king of the English', but Continental usage, as in the *Annals of St-Bertin*, trans. Nelson, pp. 69, 95, 97, may well have been influenced by Gregory and Bede (there were copies of both Gregory's letters and Bede's *Ecclesiastical History* in the library of Fulk's predecessor at Reims: J. Devisse, *Hincmar archevêque de Reims*, 3 vols (Geneva, 1975–6), III, 1487, 1495).

127 Keynes and Lapidge, *Alfred*, p. 227, state that Asser uses this title 'throughout the Life'; but the references in cc. 1, 13 and 21 all relate to the time of Asser's writing, i.e. 893.

128 C. 64, p. 49, trans. Keynes and Lapidge, *Alfred*, p. 86.

129 Cc. 67, 71, 73, 83 (the reference to the 'restoration of London), 87, pp. 50, 53, 54, 69, 73.

130 The marriage-date is not known for certain, but 886 is plausible: Alfred married Ealhswith in 868, so their eldest child could have been 16 or so.

131 Only in the latter years of Alfred's reign are there hints of Winchester's (instead?) becoming something like the *sedes regni* that Aachen was for the Carolingians: B. A. E. Yorke, 'The foundation of the Old Minster and the status of Winchester in the seventh and eighth centuries', *Proceedings of the Hampshire Field Club and Archaeological Society*, XXXVIII (1982), 75–83.

to mark the occasion;[132] but also directly from papal Rome, where Alfred himself back in the 850s had surely stayed at the *Angelcynnes scole*, the *schola Anglorum*,[133] and whence Pope Gregory the Apostle of the English had dispatched his plan for the organization of the English Church. A further link thus seems to me likely between Alfred's gaining control of London and his sending of an embassy to Rome, to Pope Marinus (882-4) whose rather undistinguished pontificate went down in the *ASC* as that of 'the good pope'.[134] What had prompted Alfred to send envoys of *freondscip*? It seems possible that Alfred had revived the idea proposed by Coenwulf of Mercia some eighty years before—an idea which itself had constituted a revival of Gregory's original 595 plan—of shifting the metropolitan see to London.[135] This could help explain the flurry of diplomatic contacts with the papacy in 883/4, followed by the regular despatch of alms to Rome later in the 880s,[136] and also the sending, as well as the timing, of Alfred's request to Archbishop Fulk of Reims to send a man suitable to superintend the administration of pastoral care:[137] the synchronism—in 886—of the 'restoration' of London and the request for Grimbald as future metropolitan was no coincidence. Yet, the best-laid schemes of mice and men gang aft agley—and Alfred's plan of 886 was a case in point. By 890 he had come up with another,

---

[132] A. Vince, *Saxon London. An Archaeological Investigation* (London, 1990), p. 113, with fig. 57.

[133] A hostel, not a school: see Stevenson's comments in his edition of Asser, *Life*, pp. 243–7; Nelson, 'The Franks and the English revisited'. References to this establishment account for three (816, 874, 885) of the four other times that the term *Angelcyn* occurs in *ASC*, before 886. (The fourth, 597, clearly reflects the *ASC*'s overall theme in the context of *c.* 891, see above, n. 70, as do the references to *Angelcynnes lond* at 787, 836, 866).

[134] *ASC* 885, trans. Garmonsway, p. 80.

[135] For Coenwulf's plan, see N. Brooks, *The Early History of the Church of Canterbury* (Leicester, 1984), pp. 123–5. This possibility was explored in the University of London B.A. Special Subject Dissertation (1992) of Frances Bradshaw, whose work I gratefully acknowledge.

[136] *ASC* 884, p. 80 cf. Asser, *Life*, c. 71, p. 53, trans. Keynes and Lapidge, *Alfred*, p. 88; for the alms, see n. 26 above.

[137] This sounds as if Alfred had episcopal office (at least) in mind: Nelson, '"A king across the sea"', p. 48.

equally adroit, idea: of fusing Mercian/West Saxon unity by appointing the Mercian Plegmund to Canterbury.[138] Perhaps, though, the idea of restoring London as his metropolis had been his preferred choice: a political as well as a religious centre, a border place between Mercia and Wessex, a site with echoes of imperial Rome as well as prospects for future commercial growth.[139]

For Alfred rejected the notion that wisdom in the world and book-learning are quite separate spheres, or exclusive categories. In Alfred's book, they were compatible, and could overlap, just as worldly goods and heavenly rewards could go together. Wisdom linked them. And Alfred, like Boethius, was worldly-wise. That was why his model was Solomon: *pius, opinatissimus atque opulentissimus.*[140] *Pius*: devout, but also righteous in the sense of fulfilling worldly expectations too, hence fair-minded, generous;[141] *opinatissimus*: most worthy of renown in the sense defined by Alfred in his Boethius, *god hlisa*, worthwhile fame, distinguished from mere glory (which was by definition worthless) as being fame acquired *wearðfullice*— worthily;[142] *opulentissimus* most rich and powerful—like the good man 'given worldly goods that he might reward the good for their goodness as well as the wicked for their wickedness'.[143] Solomon, says Asser, first despised 'all renown and wealth of this world [*praesens gloria et divitiae*], and sought wisdom from God, and

---

138 Brooks, *Early History*, pp. 152–3, not, however, drawing attention to Asser's statement, *Life*, c. 77, p. 62, that Plegmund already had *honores* and *potestates* in Mercia.

139 For Alfred's interest in London, see T. Dyson, 'Two Saxon Land Grants for Queenhithe', *Collectanea Londiniensia: Studies presented to R. Merrifield*, edited by J. Bird, H. Chapman, and J. Clark (London, 1978), pp. 200–15; T. Tatton-Brown, 'The Topography of Anglo-Saxon London', *Antiquity,* LX (1986), 21–8; and the careful discussion of Vince, *Saxon London*, pp. 105–6, 124–7.

140 Asser, *Life*, c. 76, pp. 60–1, trans. Keynes and Lapidge, *Alfred*, p. 92.

141 R. Schieffer, 'Ludwig "der Fromme". Zur Entstehung eines karolingischen Herrscherbeinamens', *Frühmittelalterliche Studien,* XVI (1982), 58–75; Nelson, 'Kingship and Empire', p. 222.

142 See Frakes, *Fate of Fortune*, pp. 115–6.

143 Trans. Sedgefield, p. 157.

thereby achieved both: wisdom and renown in this world'.[144] Asser had been reading the Old Testament Book of Proverbs, especially 8:14-15: *per me reges regnant et legum conditores justa decernunt... Mecum sunt divitiae et gloria, opes superbae et justitia.*[145] Asser could also have been reading Alfred's Boethius. For the compatibility of *wisdom 7 weal*, wisdom and worldly well-being (including wealth and success in war)[146] is at the heart of Alfred's political ideas. It is a secular ethic—but entirely Christian. It is active, not passive: 'we know that no-one can accomplish anything good unless God work with him—and yet no-one should remain so idle as not to undertake something with the abilities (*cræftas*) that God gives him'.[147] Alfred wants office-holders who are (like Boethius) book-learned, and so will have learned to apply themselves (like Alfred) to the *utilitas* of the common people and not just their own.[148] But he will not deny them wealth as well.

Alfred's quest for *weal and wisdom* led him, in the 880s, to London—and I will end this paper in London, if not quite at King's College then very near it, where, a little over a century ago, the Courts of Justice were built at the point where Fleet Street becomes the Strand. Look high above the entrance to the law courts and you will see three statues: on the topmost pinnacle is Christ, source of all justice; on a lesser pinnacle, to Christ's right, is Solomon, the type of royal wisdom; on Christ's other hand, and level with Solomon, is Alfred. Today, motivated by something other than the Victorians' chauvinism, and not necessarily sharing their muscular Christianity, we can still find in Alfred's political ideas a practical wisdom worth emulating.

---

144 *Life*, c. 76, p. 61, trans. Keynes and Lapidge, *Alfred*, p. 92.

145 See Otten, *König Alfreds Boethius*, p. 31.

146 T. A. Shippey, 'Wealth and Wisdom in King Alfred's Preface to the Old English Pastoral Care', *EHR,* XCIV (1979), 346–55; Nelson, 'Wealth and wisdom', pp. 35–6.

147 *Soliloquies*, trans. Keynes and Lapidge, *Alfred*, p. 143. Whitelock, 'Prose of Alfred's Reign', p. 85, n. 1, points out that *craft* means both 'trade, art' and 'talent, ability'.

148 Asser, *Life*, c. 106, p. 92, trans. Keynes and Lapidge, *Alfred*, p. 109 (translating 'benefit').

V

'. . . *sicut olim gens Francorum . . . nunc gens Anglorum*': Fulk's Letter to Alfred Revisited

For many historians of Anglo-Saxon England, the letter of Archbishop Fulk of Rheims to Alfred has seemed a significant piece of evidence for the king's contacts and aspirations.[1] From time to time, however, the letter's authenticity has been impugned; and even those who do not doubt the letter's genuineness have found something faintly offensive in its 'arrogant and patronising tone'.[2] While the letter's 'tone' may help explain its relative neglect by English historians, its most suspicious feature also explains its near-total neglect by Continental scholars: rather than having been transmitted, like nearly all the rest of Archbishop Fulk's extant correspondence, uniquely in the form of excerpts and 'analyses' in Flodoard's *Historia Remensis Ecclesiae*,[3] this letter survives as a whole, in English manuscripts and *only* in those: an addition copied into an eleventh-century Winchester gospel-book, and, copied from that, in the probably fifteenth-century *Liber Monasterii de Hyda*.[4] The letter purports to have accompanied the Frankish

---

1 To take but two examples: D. Whitelock, *English Historical Documents*, vol. I, 2nd edn (London, 1979), no. 223, pp. 883–5; S. Keynes and M. Lapidge, *Alfred the Great: Asser's Life of King Alfred and Other Contemporary Sources* (Harmondsworth, 1983), pp. 182–6, 331–3 (notes). I am very grateful to Simon Keynes for his comments on a draft of the present paper, and for directing me to his splendid just-published edition of *The Liber Vitae of New Minster and Hyde Abbey Winchester* (Copenhagen, 1996).

2 Whitelock, *English Historical Documents*, vol. I, p. 883.

3 Flodoard, *Historia Remensis Ecclesiae*, ed. I. Heller and G. Waitz, MGH SS XIII, pp. 405–599. For the single case of additional transmission outside Flodoard's work, see below, n. 24. For Fulk's correspondence, and his career at Rheims, see now the fine study of M. Sot, *Un historien et son Eglise: Flodoard de Reims* (Paris, 1993); and for the broader genre, *idem, Gesta episcoporum. Gesta abbatum*, Typologie des sources du moyen âge occidental 37 (Turnhout, 1981), and also R. Kaiser, 'Die *Gesta episcoporum* als Genus der Geschichtsschreibung', in G. Scheibelreiter and A. Scharer (eds), *Historiographie im frühen Mittelalter* (Vienna, 1994), pp. 459–80. For Fulk's career, see also G. Schneider, *Erzbischof Fulco von Reims (883–900) und das Frankenreich* (Munich, 1975). For Fulk's work methods, see further H. Zimmermann, 'Zu Flodoards Historiographie und Regestentechnik', in K.-U. Jäschke and R. Wenskus (eds), *Festschrift für H. Beumann zum 65. Geburtstag* (Sigmaringen, 1977), pp. 200–14.

4 See the edition by D. Whitelock, M. Brett and C. N. L. Brooke, *Councils and Synods with other Documents relating to the English Church, I. AD 871–1204*, part 1: 871–1066 (Oxford, 1981), pp. 8–11, at p. 8, n. 1, and the comments of Keynes and Lapidge, *Alfred*, p. 331. See

V

scholar Grimbald to Wessex, and its main purpose was to commend Grimbald to Alfred's patronage: hence, given Grimbald's well-known connexions with Winchester, the provenance of the letter's manuscript credentials has been thought to raise the possibility of Winchester fabrication.[5] A brief review of the question may be timely: especially so in a *Festschrift* for Janet Bately, who devoted one of her earliest publications to Grimbald.[6]

The problem has been mainly approached from the Anglo-Saxon side. In a study that remains fundamental, Philip Grierson argued that 'there could have been no conceivable motive for forging [the letter], since Fulk played no part in the tradition of Grimbald's life that was current at New Minster [Winchester]'.[7] This seems the strongest argument against suggestions of Winchester forgery. It is an argument not addressed by A. P. Smyth in his recent reiteration of the case against the letter. In so far as that case involves points made by me, this may be the place to state clearly that I now think that 'the possibility' (no more) of forgery, which

also below, n. 7. For the likely date of the New Minster *Liber Vitae*, see now Keynes, *The Liber Vitae*, pp. 44–5.

5   As suggested, tentatively, by me in ' "A king across the sea": Alfred in Continental perspective', *Transactions of the Royal Historical Society* 36 (1986), 45–68, at 48–9; and now, forthrightly, by A. P. Smyth, *King Alfred the Great* (Oxford, 1995), pp. 257–9.

6   'Grimbald of St Bertin's', *Medium Aevum* 35 (1966), 1–10.

7   P. Grierson, 'Grimbald of St Bertin's', *English Historical Review* 55 (1940), 529–61. This study totally supersedes the brief remarks of C. Plummer, *The Life and Times of Alfred the Great* (Oxford, 1902), pp. 138–9, and W. Stevenson, *Asser's Life of King Alfred* (Oxford, 1904), pp. 308–9. Grierson showed that New Minster tradition on the one hand linked Grimbald directly with St-Bertin, and on the other made nothing of the Rheims connexion. Fulk's letter, on the contrary, does not mention St-Bertin and is emphatically concerned with Rheims. For the Rheims-St-Bertin connexion, see below, p. 138. But Grierson's suggestion, 'Grimbald', pp. 547–8, that the gospel-book, MS BL Addit. 34890, was of tenth-century date, and that Fulk's letter 'or at least the tenth-century copy of it' had been preserved, not at Winchester but 'at some abbey in the west of England and only became known at Winchester during the twelfth century' must now be abandoned. The scribe who wrote the gospel-book was Eadui Basan, who worked at Christ Church, Canterbury, from c. 1015 to the 1030s. For other manuscripts written by him, see M. Brown, *Anglo-Saxon Manuscripts* (London, 1991), pp. 26–7. Since he sometimes worked to commission, MS Addit. 34890 may have got to Winchester quickly; or it may have got there after the Conquest. Fulk's letter, at ff. 158–160v, was copied into the manuscript late in the eleventh century, perhaps even as late as c. 1100: the hand may not be identical with, but is similar to, the hand(s) that made additions in the late eleventh century to the *Liber Vitae* of New Minster, Winchester (Stowe 944), and to the Arundel Psalter (BL MS Arundel 60), both securely provenanced to New Minster Winchester. That Addit. 34890 was at Winchester when Fulk's letter was copied into it is further suggested by the fact that Grimbald's name at f. 159v (like Alfred's at f. 158r) is written in capitals. A little error in E. Temple, *Anglo-Saxon Manuscripts* (London 1976), no. 68, has given rise to the notion that the hand that wrote out Fulk's letter is a pre-Conquest one. This is certainly wrong. See now Keynes, *The Liber Vitae*, pp. 101–2. I am very grateful to Michelle Brown for looking at these manuscripts with me and clarifying the problems of date and provenance.

I seriously considered a decade ago, ought to be rejected.[8] My change of mind is the result of more careful thinking about the Frankish side of the matter.

That Flodoard's Register of Fulk's correspondence preserves no trace of this particular letter should not necessarily arouse suspicion of forgery. Evidence for only nine letters from Fulk to secular rulers survives, compared with thirty-six to popes: the suspicion that *should* come to mind is that Flodoard has been selective, and/or that what survived in the Rheims archive in the mid-tenth century was only part of the original archiepiscopal output. This can be checked in the case of Fulk's predecessor Hincmar: of 572 letters sent, Flodoard preserves evidence of only some 450. Amongst items preserved outside Flodoard's Register are letters of Hincmar to several Frankish kings. In Fulk's case, Flodoard preserved longer 'analyses'[9] of many fewer letters: perhaps he made a more restricted selection, or perhaps the archive was less complete anyway.[10]

Fulk's correspondence as preserved by Flodoard does, however, include the résumé of one letter to Alfred. The identifying of Alfred as *rex transmarinus* here was surely not the address-form of the original but Flodoard's own label.[11] The content of this letter shows concerns that are similar in two respects to those of the letter of recommendation for Grimbald: the appointment of a worthy archbishop of Canterbury, and clerical misconduct, against which Fulk cites texts from *sancti patres*. The certainty that Fulk wrote to Alfred in c. 890, and the apparent familiarity of this letter's tone, makes earlier correspondence plausible. It is the more so, given the evidence in the Anglo-Saxon Chronicle for close acquaintance with West Frankish affairs in the later 880s. There is no doubt that Grimbald came to Alfred's kingdom sometime in those years, and that his arrival belonged in a context of cross-Channel contacts.

Grimbald's presence at the monastery of St-Bertin can be documented in charters from 867 to 885.[12] By 877, Fulk, a palace cleric of Charles the Bald,

---

8   Even the letter's initial addressing of Alfred as *gloriosissimus et christianissimus rex anglorum* which I suggested was an eleventh-century 'improvement', ' "A king across the sea" ', p. 49, could well have been in Fulk's original. It is true that Hincmar preferred less elaborate forms of address for royalty, but a more thorough trawl through ninth-century letters shows good precedents for Frankish bishops addressing rulers in just such superlatives: e.g. MGH Epp. IV, pp. 537, 539, 540, 542, etc.

9   The term is that of Sot, *Un historien*, p. 173. Some of Flodoard's résumés are very brief, others quite long. In the one case where comparison can be made (see below, n. 24), Flodoard's 'résumé' is actually longer than the original version! It remains true to the essentials of the letter, however.

10 Cf. the thoughtful remarks of M. Stratmann, *Hinkmar von Rheims als Verwalter von Bistum und Kirchenprovinz* (Sigmaringen, 1991), p. 67.

11 Plegmund is termed *archiepiscopus transmarinus* in Flodoard's résumé of a letter from Fulk to him, *Historia Remensis Ecclesiae* IV, c. 6, p. 568 (Whitelock *et al.*, *Councils*, no. 6, p. 13, and Sot, Register of Fulk no. 53, *Un historien*, p. 166).

12 Grierson, 'Grimbald', pp. 542–3, 545 (the reference of Whitelock *et al.*, p. 6, n. 2, to pp. 544–7 of Grierson's paper is not quite right). Grimbald witnessed a charter for one of St-Bertin's dependent churches as *Grimbaldus senior*: Grierson, 'Grimbald', p. 544, sug-

'educated almost from the cradle in canonical disciplines', as Fulk himself later put it,[13] had been given the abbacy of St-Bertin. This was at once a reward for loyal service, and a political responsibility: Fulk's first extant appearance in this role was as one of the leading men left behind in Francia to keep the young king Louis the Stammerer under surveillance when Charles set off for Italy in June 877.[14] Fulk's responsibilities at St-Bertin did not prevent him from keeping his position at court – a position he retained through the brief reigns of Louis the Stammerer and Carloman, before becoming archbishop of Rheims, as Fulk recalled in a letter to Pope Stephen VI (896–7).[15] The consecration took place on 7 March 883.[16] But Fulk did not cease to be abbot of St-Bertin, hence to call on the services, scholarly and otherwise, of Grimbald. There can be no doubt of Grimbald's close contacts with, and likely frequent visits to, Rheims from 883.[17] Grimbald's arrival in Wessex is not easy to date precisely, but must be somewhat before c. 890, when Alfred himself named Grimbald as one of his scholar-helpers.[18] Grimbald is a likely candidate as agent of transmission for the Anglo-Saxon Chronicle's information about Scandinavian movements in north-eastern Gaul during the 880s. Close contacts with Rheims no doubt continued after Grimbald's move to Wessex. The Chronicle's account of events in West Francia in 887–8 adopts Fulk's perspective, both in mentioning Guy as a contender for the throne in that year (Fulk was in fact Guy's main supporter during what proved a short-lived bid) and in stressing Arnulf's persisting authority over the whole empire after its division in 888 (Fulk, after abandoning Guy for Odo, stressed

gests that the epithet indicates that Grimbald was in charge of the dependent church. Alternatively, the epithet could have been used to distinguish this Grimbald from any junior homonym(s).

13 *Historia Remensis Ecclesiae* IV, 4, p. 562 (Sot, Register no. 36, *Un historien*, p. 162). This letter can be dated to 896.

14 MGH Capit. II, ed. A. Boretius (Hannover, 1897), no. 281, c. 15, p. 359. Gifts of abbacies to palatine clerics were usual in ninth-century Francia: see Nelson, *Charles the Bald* (London, 1992), p. 62, and Index s.v. 'cleric-abbots' for examples. Fulk had already accompanied Charles on an earlier visit to Rome in 875, recalled by Fulk in a letter to Pope Marinus I (882–4), *Historia Remensis Ecclesiae* IV, 1, p. 555 (Sot, Register no. 2, *Un historien*, p. 157): he had made this pope's acquaintance 'tempore Johannis papae quando cum Karolo imperatore . . . fuerat Romae'.

15 '. . . a rege Karolo . . . in palatinis ac domesticis eius . . . assumptus obsequiis, sicque in aula palatii perseverans usque ad tempora Karlomani regis . . . nepotis eiusdem Karoli, quando a sanctis provinciae Rememnsis episcopis necnon a clero et plebe huius urbis electus sit et ordinatus episcopus', *Historia Remensis Ecclesiae* IV, 4, p. 562 (Sot, Register no. 36).

16 *Historia Remensis Ecclesiae* IV, 10, p. 575.

17 There is no need, therefore, to assume a brief period of residence at Rheims between 885 and 886. Nothing in the way Fulk speaks of Grimbald's services to his church's administration need imply permanent residence at Rheims rather than St-Bertin.

18 Alfred's Preface to the OE Version of Gregory the Great's *Pastoral Care*, transl. Keynes and Lapidge, *Alfred*, p. 126. Smyth, *King Alfred*, pp. 527–602, seems disinclined to date the Alfredian translations: cf. below, n. 22.

Arnulf's approval for Odo's kingship).[19] It has even been suggested, with some plausibility, that Grimbald conveyed to Wessex the idea of writing up a dynastic and *gens*-centred chronicle.[20] Still more telling are the indications of Frankish scholarship being transmitted via Rheims to Alfred's court to find its way into his translations. In Alfred's version of Boethius's *Consolation of Philosophy*, the idea of the three orders reflects the influence of exegetes working at Auxerre in the reign of Charles the Bald.[21] Grimbald will hardly have have been the *only* West Frank to purvey these influences and this learning. But we have Alfred's own word for it that Grimbald mattered.[22] Even without the evidence of Fulk's letter of recommendation, we could guess that Grimbald mattered to Fulk as well.

Fulk's early years as archbishop saw a series of efforts to mobilise successive popes against the appropriator of a monastery belonging to Fulk's family.[23] Two other traits emerge strongly from Fulk's correspondence. The first is his assertion of Rheims' primatial claims. Writing to Pope Stephen V in 885/6, Fulk expressed his devotion to the *sedes romana*:

I and my fellow-bishops persist even unto death in our devotion to the Roman see (*in cultu romanae sedis*) . . . as befits the see of Rheims which your

---

19 *The Anglo-Saxon Chronicle: A Collaborative Edition. 3: MS A* (Cambridge, 1986), s.a. 887, p. 53: 'hi [i.e. the other four kings] cuędon þaet hie þaet [i.e. each kingdom] to his honda healdan sceoldon', literally, 'they declared that they should hold it at his hand'; cf. transl. G. Garmonsway, *The Anglo-Saxon Chronicle* (London, 1953), p. 80. See my remarks in 'The Franks and the English in the Ninth Century Reconsidered', in P. Szarmach and J. Rosenthal (eds), *The Preservation and Transmission of Anglo-Saxon Culture* (forthcoming, 1997).

20 J. M. Wallace-Hadrill, 'The Franks and the English in the ninth century: some common historical interests', *History* 35 (1950), 202–18, repr. in his collected papers, *Early Medieval History* (Oxford, 1975), pp. 201–16; M. B. Parkes, 'The palaeography of the Parker manuscript of the *Chronicle*', *Anglo-Saxon England* 5 (1976), 149–71, at 163–6.

21 Nelson, 'The Political Ideas of Alfred of Wessex', in A. Duggan (ed.), *Kings and Kingship in Medieval Europe*, King's College London Medieval Studies X (London, 1993), pp. 125–68, at 141–4; and T. E. Powell, 'The "Three Orders" of Society in Anglo-Saxon England', *Anglo-Saxon England* 23 (1994), 103–32.

22 Given the recent attack of Smyth, *King Alfred*, on Asser's *Life of Alfred* as a forgery, I have decided to rest my case on sources other than Asser. Nevertheless, since Fulk's letter to Alfred has been the victim of a stray bullet, and the whole issue of Frankish influence on Alfredian culture a more serious casualty, it is impossible wholly to bypass Smyth's work in what follows.

23 Fulk's brother Rampo in his will had requested the refoundation of the monastery at Bonneval (dép. Eure-et-Loire, prov. Sens), founded by a *miles* also named Fulk (the uncle of these brothers?), but then appropriated by Rampo; a man from the Rouennais named Ermanfrid had married Rampo's widow and seized control of the Bonneval property, and Fulk urged that papal orders be sent to the archbishops of Rouen and Sens to discipline Erminfrid and force the return of Bonneval. See Sot, *Un historien*, pp. 157–8 (Register nos. 3, 4, 6, 7 and 8), and also pp. 125, 129, 190. The story can be pieced together from *Historia Remensis Ecclesiae* IV, 1, pp. 555–6, and *Petite chronique de l'abbaye de Bonneval*, ed. R. Merlet, Mémoires de la Société Archéologique d'Eure-et-Loire 10 (1896), 14–35. Cf. R. Le Jan, *Famille et pouvoir dans le monde franc (VIIe–Xe siècle)* (Paris, 1995), pp. 236–7.

predecessors, valuing it above all those of Gaul, endowed with the primacy, as when the Blessed Peter Prince of the apostles sent Sixtus here to be bishop of this whole region, and Pope Hormisdas willed that Remigius be obeyed as his deputy throughout all the Gauls.[24]

This elevation of Remigius to apostolic rank had been going on before Fulk's time, notably under Archbishop Hincmar.[25] In 869, masterminding the consecration of Charles the Bald at Metz, Hincmar declared:

> Louis [the Pious, Charles' father] was descended from Clovis, famous king of the Franks, who was converted through the catholic preaching of St Remigius the apostle of Franks, and baptised along with 3,000 of the Franks, not counting children and women, on the vigil of holy Easter at the metropolis of Rheims, and anointed and consecrated king with chrism got from heaven, of which we still have some . . .[26]

Fulk took this ball and ran with it – so successfully that the pope joined the game. Granting Fulk's request for recognition of his see's apostolic status, Pope Formosus (891–6) recalled that 'the blessed Remigius had been established as apostle of the Franks by the authority of the Holy See of Rome and by the grace of God'. Apostolicity carried with it the requirement of preserving true doctrine: a job for which Grimbald's scholarship, whether practised at Rheims itself or at St-Bertin, would have been invaluable. It also carried a further connotation, of responsibility for converting pagans. Fulk informed the dowager empress Richildis, in a letter severely chastising her wicked way of life ('It is the Devil, not God, who is with you!'), that he had assumed the role of St Paul: 'Quamdiu apostolus sum gentium, ministerium meum honorificabo'.[27] Missionary endeavour was already a tradition at Rheims, mission to the Franks having been followed up in 820s by mission to the Danes.[28]

This leads into Fulk's second theme: concern over Scandinavian attacks. So severe had been their infestation of the realm for the past eight years, Fulk told Pope Stephen V (885–91), that 'there seems to be no free passage for anyone far

---

[24] T. Gousset (ed.), *Les actes de la province ecclésiastique de Reims*, vol. I (Rheims, 1842), p. 520. This is the only one of Fulk's letters to survive independently of Flodoard. See Sot, *Un historien*, pp. 172–3, for a comparison of the original with the *Historia Remensis Ecclesiae* version, demonstrating Flodoard's essential accuracy.

[25] P. Depreux, 'La dévotion à saint Rémi de Reims aux IXe et Xe siècles', *Cahiers de civilisation médiévale* 35 (1992), 111–29.

[26] *Annales de Saint Bertin*, ed. F. Grat, J. Vielliard and S. Clémencet (Paris, 1965), s.a. 869, pp. 162–3, transl. Nelson, *The Annals of St-Bertin* (Manchester, 1991), p. 161. Though Charles was acquiring Lotharingia, Hincmar depicted this as a *Frankish* consecration.

[27] *Historia Remensis Ecclesiae* IV, 5, p. 566, citing Rom. xi, 13.

[28] Depreux, 'La dévotion', p. 126 asks whether Fulk was not consciously evoking the tradition of Archbishop Ebbo in Louis the Pious's reign.

beyond [their] castles'.[29] The emperor Charles the Fat was reminded forcefully of his responsibility for 'the defence and protection of the *regnum Francorum*, protected, by God's help, until now, while it was ruled by your uncle and your namesake and his sons, but since the magnates committed the realm's protection to you, everything has gone from bad to worse'.[30] 885–6 saw the year-long siege of Paris by Scandinavian attackers who raided ever more persistently in the surrounding countryside. These were indeed anxious times for custodians of the *castra Dei*.

In the light of Fulk's self-representation in the correspondence of the early years of his pontificate, then, and also against this background of pagan onslaughts, his purported letter of recommendation for Grimbald can be properly assessed. A lost letter from Alfred to which it responds can be reconstructed in entirely plausible terms. Alfred had reported his effective defence of his realm against Viking attacks, and Fulk begins by warm commendation of this king who 'attend[s] to the good of the kingdom divinely entrusted to you, seeking or safeguarding peace with warlike weapons and divine support', at the same time, 'taking care to increase the dignity of the ecclesiastical order with spiritual weapons'. The reasons for the low state of 'the ecclesiastical order' had evidently been rehearsed by Alfred himself. Fulk responds, 'you say [the reasons are]: frequent irruptions and attacks of pagans,[31] the passage of time, the neglect of bishops, and the ignorance of subjects'. Alfred, it seems, determined to improve the situation, had requested 'advice and support' from Rheims. What has sounded 'patronising' in modern ears may have simply represented the rhetoric of respectable, and respectful, *patrocinium* – rhetoric that may well echo Alfred's own. Fulk was not only able but obliged to help: just as God sent Remigius to the Franks of old, so too the English were now seeking a man from Remigius' see, imbued with his teaching. Evils deep-rooted through old custom and barbaric practices must be stamped out.[32] Rheims, 'the church over all the churches of Gaul', had the right standards and the learning to accomplish the task. But Remigius was not the only role-model invoked here: Fulk also recalled Augustine of Canterbury, 'sent by *your* apostle the Blessed Gregory'. Fulk praised Gregory's missionary strategy and emphasised its success, referring specifically to the role of papal letters in the early days in confirming the Faith, and the subsequent role of councils in strengthening it. Was it through natural

---

29 '. . . ut nemini extra castella procul liber aditus potere videtur': *Historia Remensis Ecclesiae* IV, 1, p. 555 (Sot, Register no. 6, *Un historien*, pp. 157–8, dating to 885/886).

30 *Historia Remensis Ecclesiae* IV, 9, p. 563 (Sot, Register no. 37, *Un historien*, p. 162, dating to 885).

31 Keynes and Lapidge, *Alfred*, p. 182, translate 'Vikings', which half-misses the point.

32 These topoi in reference to English kingdoms also had a prehistory going back to Boniface and beyond: see Nelson, ' "A king across the sea" ', pp. 61–2. Fulk's idea of church councils as a means of securing the progress of the faithful, Keynes and Lapidge, p. 184, both looks back to Boniface, and prefigures a similar notion in the preface to Alfred's Laws, Keynes and Lapidge, p. 163.

tact that Fulk evoked the achievements of the English Church? It seems more likely that here again he was responding to points made in Alfred's letter.

No request could be made without a counter-gift, and Alfred's to Fulk was strikingly apt: aware, whether through his own experience or through reports from English travellers, of the prevalence of wolves in Francia (which Fulk naturally called *patria nostra*), the West Saxon king had sent specially bred dogs to ward off those that threatened Fulk's 'flocks'. Fulk's neat response may also have been adumbrated in Alfred's letter: in return for the corporeal dogs, spiritual dogs must be sent – 'and especially one, Grimbald, to take charge of the administration of pastoral care' (another evocation, here, of the apostle of the English). Alfred had specifically asked for Grimbald, then, because his 'true faith and holy religion',[33] and perhaps too his political assistance to the archbishop of Rheims (Fulk said he had been *consors ministerii nostri et in omni utilitate ecclesiastica fidissimus adiutor*[34]), were known in Wessex. That speaks volumes for prior cross-Channel contacts. West Frankish scholarship, and Carolingian example, had impressed a king conscious of 'an urgent necessity . . . to direct our minds to divine and spiritual law'.[35] Alfred sent a prestigeous entourage of magnates (*proceres vel optimates tam episcopi . . . quam et religiosi laici*) to fetch Grimbald back to Wessex.

'The administration of pastoral care' implies episcopal office, and that surely is what Fulk inferred was Alfred's plan for Grimbald, whom Fulk considered 'most worthy of *pontificalis honor*'. Solemn undertakings were to be given (the letter presents this in the subjunctive mood, suggesting the promises were still to be made at the time of writing) by the members of the prestigeous entourage, 'aloud to me in the presence of all my church', in order to guarantee Grimbald's security and long-term well-being in *propria sedes*.[36] But which bishopric could have been

---

33 Keynes and Lapidge, *Alfred*, p. 185. Smyth, *King Alfred*, pp. 257–8, distinguishes sharply between scholarly work and pastoral responsibilities, insisting that the letter's 'exaggerated' emphasis exclusively on the latter 'gives this spurious document away'. I think this distinction is overstated: as the examples of Plegmund and Waerferth (and for that matter Hincmar) show, the reformer-bishop and thé scholar could be one and the same man.

34 Transl. Keynes and Lapidge, *Alfred*, p. 185: 'a companion in my administration and . . . a most reliable assistant in every ecclesiastical concern'. Grierson, 'Grimbald', p. 551, assumed that this meant Grimbald had been on Fulk's staff at Rheims; Keynes and Lapidge, *Alfred*, p. 332, n. 7, suggest that Grimbald never left St-Bertin until he went to Wessex, and that Fulk was here expressing an unfulfilled hope for Grimbald's becoming a suffragan in his province. I think St-Bertin and Rheims would have operated in tandem under Fulk's regime, and that Grimbald's *ministerium* would have entailed, *inter alia*, holding St-Bertin securely against predatory local rivals. Fulk's 'distinguished career' (so, Keynes and Lapidge, *Alfred*, p. 331, n. 1) needs to be understood in the late ninth-century West Frankish context revealed so vividly in his letters.

35 Preface to Werferth's translation of Gregory the Great's *Dialogues*, Keynes and Lapidge, *Alfred*, p. 123. For Carolingian influence in Alfred's Laws, see P. Wormald, *The Making of English Law* (Oxford, forthcoming).

36 'Viva voce in praesentia totius ecclesiae nostrae', Whitelock *et al.*, *Councils*, p. 11, Keynes and Lapidge, *Alfred*, p. 185. I am unconvinced by the argument of Keynes and Lapidge, pp. 186, 332, n. 10, that *ad propriam sedem* should be translated 'to their [i.e. the envoys'] own

in Alfred's mind? Canterbury was not vacant in the relevant time-frame, that is, c.886, and neither was Winchester.[37] Could London have been in Alfred's sights? 886 was the year in which, according to the Anglo-Saxon Chronicle, 'gesette Elfred cyning Lundenburg'[38] that is, refortified the old Roman walled city. Certainly by the 890s, when the Anglo-Saxon Chronicle was compiled, 886 had come to seem, in retrospect, the key moment in the reconstruction of the realm of the English, the moment when 'all Englishkind', Mercians and West Saxons together, acknowledged his rule, though it is clear that Alfred had had control of London rather earlier. Had Alfred just received back the envoys he had sent to Pope Marinus in 884? Had he acquired papal agreement for an old project, the shifting of the metropolitan see to London?[39] Were Grimbald's *electores* the assembled leaders of the Angelcyn at Lundenburg? Speculation aside, Fulk sent Grimbald with *some* bishopric in mind. Perhaps some delay was expected until an appropriate see became available.

In its setting within Fulk's letter-collection, this particular letter does not seem to me out of place. On the contrary: the letter's substance has the hallmarks of late ninth-century Rheims origin, and should therefore be accepted as genuine. The alleged 'arrogant and patronising tone' of the letter is considerably less striking when read in full context: Fulk, proud primate though he was, saw the *Angli* in their need as deserving his church's support, not least because the *Franci* had been there before: '. . . sicut olim gens Francorum . . . nunc gens anglorum'. This was also Alfred's point. Apostolic foundations had Faith and doctrine in common, and must collaborate. Fulk was willing to make a considerable personal sacrifice to this end. This paper has approached the issue of his letter's authenticity from the Continental side, and could not have been written without the benefit of recent Continental scholarship on Fulk's career and correspondence. Yet, frustratingly, this scholarship has ignored Fulk's letter to Alfred.[40] On the other hand, it has to be said that we *transmarini* have not always made the most of what is available on the Continent. . . . *sicut gens francorum, . . . [et !] gens anglorum* . . . So, a

home'. Cf. ' "A king across the sea" ', p. 48. I agree with Grierson, 'Grimbald', p. 549, that Fulk understood that Grimbald was to receive a bishopric, but I cannot see any reason to suppose that Fulk himself was to consecrate Grimbald as bishop. Smyth, *King Alfred*, pp. 257–8, while rejecting the letter as a forgery, insists, rightly I think, that the 'future responsibilities' it indicates for Grimbald were those of a bishop, and that the 'minders' were taking him back to his see. The final section of the letter reveals Fulk's anxieties about Grimbald's safety in the face of any (unidentified) person who 'guided by some devilish impulse with jealousy of malice and ill-will, should occasion a quarrel or incite dissension', Keynes and Lapidge, *Alfred*, p. 186.

[37] As noted by Nelson, ' "A king across the sea" ', p. 48.

[38] Bately, *The Anglo-Saxon Chronicle . . . MS A*, p. 53, transl. Garmonsway, *The Anglo-Saxon Chronicle*, p. 80.

[39] I ventured these speculations in 'The Political Ideas of Alfred', pp. 155–6.

[40] It is unmentioned by Schneider, *Erzbischof Fulco*, and by Sot, *Un historien*. M. Depreux courteously acknowledges in an additional note his having been directed to it, though he had not cited it in the unpublished Mémoire de Maitrise (Paris, 1989), on which his article draws.

V

further conclusion (which will surely commend itself to the expositor of Alfred's work in the Paris Psalter[41]) must be that the sooner the old fog in the Channel is dispelled, the better for the cultural heirs of both Carolingian and Alfredian Renaissances in the here and now.

[41] Bately, 'Lexical evidence for the authorship of the Prose Psalms in the Paris Psalter', *Anglo-Saxon England* 10 (1982), 69–95; *idem*, 'Old English prose before and during the reign of Alfred', *Anglo-Saxon England* 17 (1988), 93–138, at 130–1. I take this opportunity to thank Janet for many years of colleagueship and inspiration.

VI

THE FRANKS AND THE ENGLISH IN THE NINTH CENTURY RECONSIDERED

Before the Roman came to Rye or out to Severn strode
The rolling English drunkard made the rolling English road. . . .
A merry, a mazy road, and such as we did tread
The night we went to Birmingham by way of Beachy Head.[1]

I have taken my cue from Chesterton, not because I intend to talk about Anglo-Saxon trackways, or drinking habits, but to signal this paper's point of departure: that direct routes are not always the ones people take, nor are direct links therefore the only ones upon which historians ought to focus. Time-travelers to the ninth century need a map covering more than the English Channel. For ninth-century contacts between the Franks and the English often went a long way round: not rolling drunkenly, I hasten to add, but *carefully choosing* a route via Rome. Rome's unique combination of imperial and apostolic traditions was reinforced in the ninth century by the new historical reality of a western empire and by the papacy's newly asserted claims to jurisdictional authority. Anglo-Frankish contacts were pulled into a transalpine ellipse—and they can scarcely be understood unless we too feel the pull of Rome.

Over 40 years ago Michael Wallace-Hadrill argued that it was "Danish pressure" that "drew the English and the Franks—or at any rate their rulers—closer together than they had ever been before." It was in these "years of crisis" that "the full force of Frankish example hit England"—and Wallace-Hadrill saw the evidence in the historical writing of Alfred's reign—the Anglo-Saxon Chronicle and Asser's *Life*.[2] Twenty years later, Wallace-Hadrill developed these insights in the latter part of *Early Germanic Kingship in England and on the Continent*.[3]

Ninth-century historical writing supplies evidence for political strategies in which a motive and motor, even more powerful than common concern with external defense, was competition. Wallace-Hadrill rightly diagnosed dynastic insecurity as a major problem for all ninth-century rulers; but his account of ninth-century remedies underestimated one that I see as of fundamental importance: the renewal of empire. This necessarily embroiled Franks and Anglo-Saxons in rivalry rather than in mutual support. Which brings me back to my starting point. The rulers and leaders of both Franks and English aspired—precisely because of their insecurity—to extend and defend their power by attaching it to imperial or papal authority. Ideologically speaking, and very often literally as well, all roads led to Rome. What follows is an investigation of three cases in point. They may seem only obliquely relevant to the continental reception of Anglo-Saxon culture. In fact, they should be read as evidence of the profound impact of that culture on the Franks. For it was not only Anglo-Saxon texts[4] but also Anglo-Saxon regimes that, through a variety of personal and institutional contacts, helped to re-focus the Franks' attention on Rome in the mid- and later-ninth century. Of course, that orientation was already congenial: short of legitimacy, Pippin, the first Carolingian king, had looked to papal authority, while his successors Charlemagne and Louis the Pious had drawn heavily on sanctity imported from Rome.[5] All that is well known. Later in the ninth century, however, established receptivity stimulated further kinds of reception of Roman models and Roman inspiration. Here too—and this is less well known—Anglo-Saxon culture continued to play an essential role. The very indirectness of the evidence is testimony to contacts so pervasive, influences so thoroughly absorbed, that they had become part of the air breathed in the Frankish world.

I. IMPERIAL STRATEGIES AND ROMAN LEGITIMACY:
ÆTHELWULF KING OF WESSEX AND
CHARLES THE BALD OF WEST FRANCIA

In recent years there have been two interesting accounts of the marriage of Æthelwulf with Charles the Bald's daughter Judith and its political context, both concentrating primarily on West Saxon interests.[6] If the focus is shifted to West Francia, the scene is dominated by Charles the Bald, restless, ambitious, inventive. He suffered the first major defeat of his career in August 851 at the hands of the Bretons; Charles salvaged his pride (at least) and put relations with the Breton leader Erispoë on a new footing: Erispoë "gave Charles his hands," and Charles granted him "royal vestments" but withheld a royal title. Charles himself thus implicitly assumed a superior "imperial" position.[7] In 855 he set up his second son as sub-king in Aquitaine; and in February 856 he set up his eldest son as sub-king in Neustria (the region between the Seine and the Loire), at the same time arranging the boy's betrothal to Erispoë's daughter.[8] These relationships, reinforced by public rituals, created a family of kings and princely allies, reminiscent of the Byzantine model. Charles was no emperor yet—but he had aspirations to imitate his grandfather Charlemagne.[9] The death of Charles' eldest brother, the emperor Lothar, in 855 had been followed by a parceling out of Lothar's realm among his three sons: the eldest of them ruled, as the West Frankish annalist put it, as "so-called emperor of Italy."[10] After 855, Carolingian political relationships altered fundamentally, and north of the Alps new prospects of empire-building opened up. Charles the Bald's initiatives in later 855 and early 856 must be seen in the light of a response to the new conditions. So too must the marriage of Charles' daughter to Æthelwulf: it brought the West Saxon king into Charles' "family of kings," succeeding where Charlemagne had in a sense failed with Offa. But Charlemagne was certainly his grandson's model for (at this stage) a *Romfrei* imperial ideal.[11]

In 849–50 when the Breton chief Nominoë deposed "his" five bishops, defying their Frankish metropolitan, the Archbishop of Tours,

King Charles had, it seems, sent a trusted agent, Lupus of Ferrières, to Rome to mobilize the authority of Pope Leo IV (847–55), and it was Lupus who could then draw on papal letters in composing the conciliar admonition sent to Nominoë by the assembled West Frankish bishops.[12] Æthelwulf of Wessex took a similar tack: in 853 (or end of 852?) he "sent his son Alfred to Rome. The Lord Leo was then pope in Rome, and he consecrated him king and stood sponsor to him at confirmation."[13]

Æthelwulf's decision can be seen in part as a defensive one: contacts with Charles' kingdom had been exceptionally close during the early 850's,[14] and Æthelwulf probably knew enough of Charles' imperial vision to wish to forestall any extension of it across the Channel. But Æthelwulf's frame of mind in 853 was less likely to have been defensive than quite positively assertive: in 850, at Sandwich in Kent, his son Athelstan had "slain a great army," while the following year Æthelwulf and his son Æthelbald "inflicted the greatest slaughter on a heathen army that we have ever heard tell of" at Aclea in Surrey.[15] In 853 the Anglo-Saxon Chronicle records—immediately before the sending of Alfred to Rome—a West Saxon campaign across Mercia (at the Mercians' request) against the Welsh, and the Welsh "submission";[16] and the same annal ends with the marriage on Æthelwulf's territory[17] of Æthelwulf's daughter Æthelswith to the Mercian king. She may well have been crowned queen on this same occasion, following a Mercian precedent.[18]

There were new possibilities here. Could Æthelwulf set up his own family of kings? There is no evidence that in 853 or later he had set his face against a division of his realm: Asser c. 16 shows him dividing it in 856/58.[19] Given high mortality (Æthelwulf's eldest son, Athelstan, may have died in or soon after 851[20]) and the availability of potential sub-kingdoms, even a fourth son might hope for a realm. Contemporary arrangements were much more flexible than is often realized. Carolingian rulers who were Æthelwulf's contemporaries made and unmade succession arrangements to suit their own desires, and they created *regna* that modern historians call sub-kingdoms, without, apparently, staging formal king-makings for the recipients or conferring royal titles on them. Thus Charlemagne's eldest son and namesake got a *regnum* in 790 but was crowned king by the pope only in 800, and apparently he did not have the title *rex* before that.[21] Louis the Pious' youngest son, Charles (the Bald), got a series of *regna* in the 830's and in 838 even received a crown without actually being consecrated king, or using the title *rex* before his father's death in 840.[22] It was not clear that Lothar's son Louis would rule in Italy rather than (as Lothar himself had finally succeeded in doing) in Francia. Only on his deathbed did Lothar make his final dispositions, and (evidently to some observers' surprise) carved out a *regnum* for his youngest son.[23] Æthelwulf in 853, I suggest, invoked papal authority to legitimize a similar possibility. Like Louis the Pious, like Lothar, Æthelwulf wanted his youngest son to succeed to a share in his composite realm, and in 853 he seemed in position to secure that. While Leo did not (strictly speaking) make Alfred a king, he set the seal of throne-worthiness on him: Alfred was now a prospective, a potential heir. The claim that Alfred was "consecrated king" in 853 simply drew out the implication of papally invented rituals that were probably intended anyway to be ambiguous.[24] Whoever, c. 890, entered this statement in the Anglo-Saxon Chronicle had no intention of being controversial. The question of Alfred's truthfulness or otherwise seems to me a red herring.[25]

For two things seem certain. First, in sending Alfred to Rome, Æthelwulf was imitating Carolingian examples of the designation of kings' sons as potential heirs.[26] Charlemagne in 781 had taken (rather than sent) his third and fourth sons (aged four and three) to Rome, to be confirmed and consecrated kings by the pope,[27] and in 800 he had done the same with his son Charles the Younger.[28] Lothar I in 844 had sent his eldest son (aged eighteen) to Rome, where the pope (Sergius II) "anointed him king and invested him with a swordbelt"; and in 850, Lothar sent the same son again to Rome, where Pope Leo IV consecrated him emperor.[29] Second, Alfred was being kept in the running by being marked out for secular life; this is clear from Leo IV's own account of his reception of Alfred: as well as confirming him, he conferred the title of consul and invested him with a sword and belt.[30] In sending Alfred to Rome in 853, Æthelwulf was forging his own direct link with Leo IV and also registering his own *imitatio imperii*: just as Lothar had had his son girded with a sword by the pope, so too would the king of a West Saxon kingdom recently extended to include Kent, and Devon, and Cornwall, and already with sights set northwards to Mercia and Wales.[31] There is a striking contrast, though, with what Charles the Bald did the very next year in the case of his own four-year-old son, Carloman, the third of three sons borne by Charles' wife between 846 and 849: "Charles had [Carloman] tonsured and dedicated him to the church"—that is, he meant to exclude him from the succession.[32] Charles' plans envisaged a limitation of partibility from early on—just the opposite of Æthelwulf's. As if to underline the significance of *his* strategy, Æthelwulf himself visited Rome in 855–56, bearing gifts that rivaled those of Carolingian benefactors (a golden crown weighing five pounds, golden armrings and a gold-decorated sword, two golden statues, four silver-gilt Saxon platters, and some embroidered vestments)[33] and taking Alfred with him "for a second journey on the same route, because he loved him more than his brothers."[34]

But ninth-century royal family planning was a hit-and-miss affair; and even today strange things can happen at home when rulers take trips abroad. The involvement of Æthelwulf's eldest surviving son in a major revolt during his absence meant that Æthelwulf dropped his own quasi-imperial pretensions and instead attached himself to Charles the Bald's; that was surely what it meant to become Charles' son-in-law (though the bride's consecration, and coronation, as queen may have owed something to Æthelswith's example).[35] In 856 Æthelwulf was no longer in any position to maintain Alfred's claims to a *regnum* in the face of his elder sons' hostility: by the terms of the will drawn up during the last two years of Æthelwulf's life, his youngest son had to be content with a share of his father's personal property, and some money.[36]

II. MILITARY SERVICE, FRANKISH, ANGLO-SAXON, AND ROMAN

In the Edict of Pîtres (June 864), Charles the Bald enacted that "those who cannot perform military service in the army must, according to the custom of antiquity and of other peoples (*aliae gentes*), work at building new *civitates* and bridges and ways across marshes, and perform watch-duty in the *civitas* and on the march."[37] Despite the formulation, Charles was not referring here to *a single custom* that was both antique and practiced by contemporary foreign peoples. He was making a distinction: he recognized that while Christian Roman emperors required work on the construction of "public and sacred buildings," roads and bridges, and on the repair of walls, there was in fact no Late Antique precedent for demanding work on the building of *civitates,* that is, of walls around them; nor was there a precedent in earlier Carolingian legislation.[38] Hence Charles had to appeal, uniquely in his extensive capitularies, to an alternative model, acknowledging that in this respect the West Saxons had extended the scope of the state's demands further than the Franks themselves—and further than the Christian Roman emperors who elsewhere in the Edict of Pîtres were Charles' role models.

The earliest West Saxon charter references to the reservation of the royal right to demand fortification work—*arcis* (or *arcium*) *munitio*—belong, as Nicholas Brooks pointed out, to the reign of Æthelbald. The first appearance is in a grant of 858 to Winchester.[39] That Charles knew about a recent extension of West Saxon royal claims is entirely plausible: contacts between the two kingdoms and courts had surely been closer than ever from 856 to 860, when Charles' daughter was married to Æthelwulf, then, on his death in 858, to his son Æthelbald;[40] and in 860 a group of Danes who had crossed the Channel from West Francia (where Charles was attempting to recruit them into his service) were repulsed from Winchester—an event recorded by the Annals of Saint-Bertin as well as the Anglo-Saxon Chronicle—perhaps because *munitio arcis* had successfully been required by the West Saxon king and was already paying dividends.[41] If Æthelbald and his successor had been implementing a burghal program during those years, Charles would have heard about it—and it may well have inspired his own program in 864, implemented in the later 860's.[42]

What inspired the West Saxons? Mercian and Kentish example, no doubt. But those had been available before, yet not followed. Again the route to the answer leads via Rome. When Alfred and his large entourage[43] reached Rome in 853, Pope Leo had just the year before completed the fortifications linking St. Peter's with the city of Rome itself on the other side of the Tiber. Leo's biographer says that work teams were required from all the estates and towns in the duchy of Rome. Surviving inscriptions make it clear that each team, called a *militia*, was responsible for a stretch of wall.[44] Forty feet high with 44 towers and stretching for something over two thousand meters, the new walls protected, as well as St. Peter's, the *schola Saxonum*,[45] where Alfred surely stayed during his two visits. In the OE version of Augustine's *Soliloquies*, Alfred says there is a difference between seeing a thing and being told about it: "me þincð nu þæt ic wite hwa *R*omeburh timbrode, and æac feala oðra þincga þe ær urum dagum geweordon wæs, þa ic ne mæg ælla ariman. nat ic no ði hwa (Rome)burh timbrede þe ic self hyt gesawe."[46] He is referring to the ancient city—*ær urum dagum*; but the point perhaps had extra piquancy because everyone knew that Alfred had only *just* missed seeing a modern timbering of Rome.

III. FULK OF RHEIMS, ALFRED, AND THE ROMAN MODEL OF MISSION

Archbishop Fulk of Rheims was a key participant in the last phase of Frankish contacts with the English in the ninth century. It was Fulk to whom Alfred applied for a scholar who would help restore the learning and morale of the church in his kingdom.[47] Grimbald's arrival in 886 may not have been the necessary stimulus to the Anglo-Saxon Chronicle's production, but it seems to have contributed, sufficiently, to the annals' content. On events in 885, continental information reached Wessex from East as well as West Francia: like the East Frankish Annals of Fulda, the Anglo-Saxon Chronicle called Charles the Bald's grandson "Carl" instead of "Carloman";[48] and Asser knew that Charles the Fat had been king of the Alamans (not, *pace* Whitelock, "Germans").[49] The account of events s.a. 887 has not so much a West Frankish as a Fulk-ish slant—or to be more accurate, reflects Fulk's views on Carolingian legitimacy in 888 (but not before) and Fulk's persisting interest in Guy of Spoleto. Fulk had supported Guy for the

West Frankish throne in 887, despite Guy's lack of Carolingian blood in male or female line. Only once it became clear that Guy's bid would fail did Fulk switch his support to Odo, yet he remained keen to give the impression that Odo had become king only with Arnulf's permission: the *Annals of St-Vaast* reflect this in the story about Arnulf's sending a crown with which Odo was crowned on 13 November at Rheims— presumably by Fulk—and acclaimed by *omnis populus*, those who had previously opposed Odo now being received into "fellowship" (*societas*). Fulk had in fact pushed Guy's candidature because the two men were close kinsmen,[50] but he could offer the justification that Guy had been picked by the pope as an adoptive son.[51] Like Æthelwulf, and like the emperor Lothar, Fulk was playing the card of papal authority to legitimize a succession strategy.

The same authority underpinned Fulk's dealings with the English, as is directly evidenced in his letter to Alfred. Dorothy Whitelock resented that letter's "patronizing tone."[52] But patronage—*patrocinium*—in heaven as well as on earth was exactly the name of Fulk's game. Reading the letter to Alfred in the light of the quite substantial dossier on Fulk's career and political contacts before 886, one becomes aware of the Roman dimension to Fulk's conception of his own primatial position at Rheims. Fulk himself had been to Rome[53] (he continued to hope for a return visit that never materialized); and his first act on becoming Archbishop of Rheims early in 883 was to write to Pope Marinus, whom he already knew personally. In 884 he was writing to Hadrian III, and in 886 to Stephen V.[54] His repeated invocations of papal authority, and assertions of Rheims' primatial status, were two sides of a coin. Rheims was a Petrine foundation: its first bishop had been endowed with the primacy of Gaul by Peter himself. Peter's successors had held the see of Rheims in special honor. And the purpose and substance of this claim, in Fulk's mind, was quite literally its apostolic role. *Quamdiu apostolus sum gentium, ministerium meum honorificabo*: Fulk could quote St. Paul (Romans 11:13) with a real sense of historic unity between past and present in Rheims' specific task of mission.[55] Of Fulk's ninth-century predecessors, Ebbo had evangelized the Danes in the 820's, and Hincmar had identified St. Remi as the apostle of the Franks, inventing the tradition of Remi's baptism of Clovis that was also a royal anointing, with oil sent from heaven.[56] Fulk fused these two themes—patronage and mission—in his letter to Alfred. Of course the English had already been evangelized; they already had their apostle, Gregory (in Fulk's eyes, and he had history on his side, the *apostolus Anglorum—apostolus vester*—was modeled on the *apostolus Francorum* rather than vice versa[57]): but the English, unlike the Franks, urgently needed a second dose of mission. Alfred had knocked on the right door—"quia una est catholica et apostolica ecclesia, sive Romana sive transmarina."[58] Fulk did not quite claim jurisdiction over the church of the English, though he came close in suggesting that church councils had assembled "non solum ex vicinis civitatibus vel provinciis, sed etiam ex transmarinis regionibus." (Was Fulk thinking of the Council of Frankfurt in 794?[59]) But what he did have to offer was *patrocinium*: and Grimbald too, endowed with Remi's authority, would extend his *patrocinium* over those who received him in England—descendants of the *gens rudis et barbara* to whom Gregory's decrees had been sent. Remi's successor did not have to pose as the middleman between the English and Rome: he actually functioned as such, writing to the pope after 886 *pro quorundam susceptione Anglorum.*[60] Like Charles the Bald with Æthelwulf, Fulk with Alfred exploited his strategic location on the route to Rome. At the outset of his pontificate, with *timor hostilis* real and immediate at Rheims, Fulk could understand all too well Alfred's anxieties about the irruption of pagans: Rheims' safety was credited to St. Remi's protection—but Fulk then rebuilt the city walls. His successor, Harvey, was to take the lead in converting Viking settlers in Normandy.[61] Mission and defense were necessary responses at Canterbury or Winchester as well as at Rheims. Fulk, and Alfred, had their sights set on a more distant destination even than Rome, but *patrocinium* with all it entailed of responsibility as well as power imposed a busy agenda meanwhile—one which both Fulk and Alfred (like Chesterton[62]) contemplated with zest and ultimately with optimism.

NOTES

1. "The Rolling English Road," G. K. Chesterton, *Collected Poems*, 10th ed. (London, 1943), p. 203. I should like to thank Joel Rosenthal and Paul Szarmach for scholarly inspiration over the years, and, in reference to the present paper, for their moral support and editorial patience.

2. J. M. Wallace-Hadrill, "The Franks and the English in the Ninth Century: Some Common Historical Interests," *History*, 35 (1950), 202–18, rpt. in his collected essays, *Early Medieval History* (London, 1975), pp. 201–16, at p. 209. The title of the present paper is intended to suggest a coda to Wallace-Hadrill's work.

3. J. M. Wallace-Hadrill, *Early Germanic Kingship in England and on the Continent* (Oxford, 1969), chs. 5 and 6.

4. For that type of Anglo-Saxon cultural influence see the masterly paper by George H. Brown in the present volume.

5. P. Riché, "Les Carolingiens en quête de sainteté," in *Les fonctions des saints dans le monde occidental (IIIe–XIIIe siècles)* (Rome, 1991), pp. 217–24.

6. M. J. Enright, "Charles the Bald and Æthelwulf of Wessex: The Alliance of 856 and Strategies of Royal Succession," *Journal of Medieval History*, 5 (1979), 291–302; P. Stafford, "Charles the Bald, Judith and England," in M. T. Gibson and J. L. Nelson, eds., *Charles the Bald: Court and Kingdom*, 2nd ed. (London, 1990), pp. 139–53, stresses Æthelwulf's wish to concert a common defense policy with Charles, against Enright's view of the marriage as Æthelwulf's response to the rebellion of his son. Stafford thinks the marriage provoked the son's revolt. See below, p. 144.

7. *Annales de Saint-Bertin* 851, ed. F. Grat, J. Vielliard, and S. Clémencet (Paris, 1964) (hereafter AB), pp. 63–64, tr. J. L. Nelson, *The Annals of St-Bertin* (Manchester, 1991), p. 73. For the significance of Charles' dealings with Erispoë see now J. M. H. Smith, *Province and Empire: Brittany and the Carolingians* (Cambridge, 1992), pp. 108–15.

8. AB 855, 856, pp. 70, 856, tr. Nelson, pp. 80–82; and cf. on the latter episode the supporting evidence of charters: G. Tessier, *Receuil des Chartes de Charles II le Chauve*, 3 vols. (Paris, 1943–55), vol. 1, nos. 113, 114.

152

9. See Nelson, "Translating Images of Authority: The Christian Roman Emperors in the Carolingian World," in M. M. Mackenzie and C. Roueché, eds., *Images of Authority: Essays in Honour of Joyce Reynolds* (Cambridge, 1989), pp. 196–205. For the broader context see A. Angenendt, *Kaiserherrschaft und Königstaufe* (Berlin, 1984).

10. AB 863, 864, pp. 96, 105, tr., pp. 104, 112. Cf. AB 858, 859, pp. 78, 82, tr., pp. 87, 91, where Louis is called "king."

11. "Rome-free" empire was the phrase coined by C. Erdmann, *Forschungen zur politischen Ideenwelt des Frühmittelalters* (Berlin, 1951). See further Nelson, "Kingship and Empire," in J. H. Burns, ed., *The Cambridge History of Medieval Political Thought* (Cambridge, 1988), pp. 230–34.

12. Lupus of Ferrières, *Correspondance*, ed. L. Levillain, 2 vols. (Paris, 1935), vol. 2, Epp. 75–77, 81, pp. 16–23, 56–65. See also W. Hartmann, ed., *Die Konzilien der karolingische Teilreiches 843–859* (Hanover, 1984), MGH *Concilia* 3, pp. 185–93; and Smith, pp. 154–55. Lupus' mission may well have had several other objectives: see E. Lockwood, "Lupus of Ferrières," Ph.D. thesis Univ. of London 1992, ch. 9.

13. *The Anglo-Saxon Chronicle: A Collaborative Edition*, general eds. D. Dumville and S. Keynes, vol. 3, *MS A*, ed. J. M. Bately (Woodbridge, 1986) (hereafter ASC), s.a. 853, p. 45, tr. G. N. Garmonsway (London, 1953), p. 64. Asser, *Life of King Alfred*, c. 8, ed. W. Stevenson (Oxford, 1904), p. 7, tr. S. Keynes and M. Lapidge, *Alfred the Great* (Harmondsworth, 1981), p. 69, translates this into Latin, with additions: see below, p. 143.

14. The victory at Sandwich (ASC 851, p. 44, tr., p. 64) was recorded in northern Francia within months if not weeks of the event (AB 850, pp. 59–60, tr., p. 69); and Lupus of Ferrières wrote to congratulate Æthelwulf on his victory at Aclea (*Correspondance*, vol. 2, Ep. 84, p. 70). Further, at Æthelwulf's court, acting not just as a scribe but (if we take Lupus literally) head of the royal chancery (*Correspondance*, vol. 2, Ep. 84, p. 70, "epistolarum vestrarum officio fungebatur"; cf. vol. 1, Ep. 17, p. 98, on Charles' chancellor Louis, "epistolare in palatio gerens officium"), was a Frank called Felix, an old acquaintance of Lupus and also the recipient of a letter from him (Ep. 85) in 851. Lupus had just recovered control of Ferrières' dependent church of Saint-Josse near Quentovic, hence on the obvious route for English travelers to the Continent: see Stafford, pp. 140–41; and S. Lebecq, "La Neustrie et la mer," in H. Atsma, ed., *La Neustrie*, Beihefte der *Francia*, 2 vols. (Sigmaringen, 1989), vol. 1, pp. 405–40,

esp. 427–28. West Saxons were certainly interested in Breton affairs a generation later: ASC 885, 890; and Æthelwulf had very probably learned about dealings between Franks and Bretons very soon after the event.

15. See preceding note. Note Æthelwulf's contact right at the beginning of his reign with Louis the Pious, AB 839, pp. 28–30, tr., pp. 42–43. Could this be linked with the journey of Archbishop Wigmund of York (to whom Lupus also wrote c. 851) to Rome to collect his pallium, c. 839?

16. ASC, pp. 44–45; tr. Garmonsway, pp. 64–66.

17. Asser, *Life of King Alfred*, c. 8, ed. Stevenson, p. 8, tr. Keynes and Lapidge, p. 69: "at the royal estate called Chippenham."

18. See Stafford, p. 149 and n. 65.

19. Asser, *Life of Alfred*, ed. Stevenson, pp. 14–15: "regni inter filios suos, duos scilicet seniores, . . . divisionem ordinabiliter literis mandari procuravit." Cf. tr. Keynes and Lapidge, p. 72. On Æthelwulf's intentions see D. P. Kirby, *The Earliest English Kings* (London, 1991), pp. 198–204. I read Kirby's book only after delivering this paper; though my conclusions differ somewhat from his, I have found his discussion characteristically thought-provoking.

20. Cf. Keynes and Lapidge, pp. 231–32: "[Æthelstan] is not heard of again after 851."

21. See P. Classen, "Karl der Grosse und der Thronfolge im Frankenreich," in *Festschrift für H. Heimpel*, vol. 3 (Göttingen, 1972), pp. 109–34.

22. See Janet L. Nelson, *Charles the Bald* (London, 1992), pp. 92–97.

23. AB 855, p. 71; cf. 856, p. 73, tr., pp. 81, 83.

24. Cf. AB 869, p. 155, tr., p. 156, for symbolic papal gifts to Lothar II, and their interpretation. There is of course no question of confusing distinct liturgical rites in 853: the ambiguity centers on the status of *regna* and *reges* in kingdoms that were family firms.

25. I took a rather different view in "The Problem of King Alfred's Royal Anointing," *Journal of Ecclesiastical History*, 18 (1967), 145–63, rpt. in my essays, *Politics and*

Ritual in Early Medieval Europe (London, 1986), pp. 309–27 (cited hereafter from the reprint).

26. He may also have been mindful of the Mercian precedent of Offa, whose son Ecgfrith had perhaps been consecrated by papal legates in England; see Wallace-Hadrill, *Early Germanic Kingship*, p. 114. If so, Æthelwulf meant to go one better.

27. *Annales Regni Francorum*, ed. F. Kurze, MGH *Scriptores Rerum Germanicarum in Usum Scholarum* (Hanover, 1895), pp. 56–57.

28. Unmentioned in the *Annales Regni Francorum*, but clearly stated in *Vita Leonis III*, c. 24, *Liber Pontificalis*, ed. L. Duchesne, rev. C. Vogel, 3 vols. (Paris, 1955–57), vol. 3, p. 8; tr. R. Davis, *The Lives of the Eighth-Century Popes (Liber Pontificalis)* (Liverpool, 1992), p. 191.

29. AB 844, pp. 45–46: ". . . Hlodouuicum pontifex Romanus unctione in regem consecratum cingulo decoravit," tr., p. 57 (taking *cingulum* to imply 'sword'), and AB 850, p. 59, tr., p. 69.

30. ". . . consulatus cingulo honore vestimentisque ut mos est Romanis consulibus decoravimus," ed. A. de Hirsch-Gereuth, MGH *Epistolae* 5 (Berlin, 1899), p. 602. I argued 25 years ago that the consulship and investiture with sword were anachronisms branding the letter fragment of Leo IV an 11th-century forgery. I am now fairly sure that I was wrong: the so-called *Tract on Offices*, convincingly argued by P. S. Barnwell, "*Epistula Hieronimi de Gradus Romanorum*: An English School Book," *Historical Research*, 64 (1991), 77–86, to be an Anglo-Saxon schoolbook diffused on the Continent in the 9th century, shows *consul* a familiar term for viceroy; and for instances of papal *imitatio imperii* in the Donation of Constantine (where c. 15 specificies the papal right to appoint consuls) and elsewhere, see my "Problem of King Alfred's Royal Anointing," pp. 312–13. The appointment of Alfred as consul does fit within this context.

31. The significance of Æthelwulf's reign is underlined by P. Wormald, "The Ninth Century," in J. Campbell, ed., *The Anglo-Saxons* (Oxford, 1982), pp. 140–42, and also by Kirby, p. 195.

32. AB p. 70, tr., p. 79. See Nelson, "A Tale of Two Princes: Politics, Text and Ideology in a Carolingian Annal," *Studies in Medieval and Renaissance History*, 10 (1988), 105–41, at p. 109.

33. *Vita Benedicti III, Liber Pontificalis,* vol. 2, p. 148: "gabatae saxiscae de argento exaurato IIII, saraca de olovero cum chrisoclavo I, camisa alba sigillata olosyrica cum chrisoclavo I, vela maiora de fundato II."

34. Asser, *Life of Alfred,* c. 11, ed. Stevenson, p. 9: "iterum in eandem viam secum ducens. . . ." In my 1967 article, pp. 325–26, I mistakenly rejected Asser's unequivocal statement about Alfred's second journey. For suggestive observations on important, and hitherto neglected, evidence see S. Keynes, "Anglo-Saxon Entries in the 'Liber Vitae' of Brescia," in J. Roberts and J. L. Nelson, eds., *Alfred the Wise. Studies in Honour of Janet Bately* (Woodbridge, 1997), pp. 99–119.

35. See above, p. 142; for Æthelwulf's intentions cf. Enright, "Charles the Bald and Æthelwulf of Wessex."

36. Asser, *Life of Alfred,* c. 16, ed. Stevenson, pp. 14–15, tr., p. 72.

37. MGH *Capitularia Regum Francorum,* ed. A. Boretius and V. Krause (Hanover, 1897), vol. 2, no. 273, c. 27.

38. See N. Brooks, "The Development of Military Obligations in Eighth- and Ninth-Century England," in P. Clemoes and K. Hughes, eds., *England before the Conquest: Studies Presented to Dorothy Whitelock* (Cambridge, 1971), pp. 69–84.

39. B 495/S 1274. In this and following references to Anglo-Saxon charters, B signifies the number in W. de G. Birch, *Cartularium Saxonicum,* 4 vols. (London, 1885–99), and S, the number in P. Sawyer, *Anglo-Saxon Charters: An Annotated List and Bibliography* (London, 1968). B 451/S 298 shows Æthelwulf already reserving host- and bridge-service in 847. See Brooks, p. 81, for further references to reservation of *arcis* [*arcium*] *munitio* in B 500/S 326 (860); B 504–5/S 335 (862); and B 508/S 336 (863—for 868). To these may be added B 520/S 340 (868) and B 886/S 341 (869), both with a possibly authentic base.

40. Judith's marriage to her stepson evoked "magna infamia," according to Asser, *Life of Alfred,* c. 17, ed. Stevenson, p. 16, tr. Keynes and Lapidge, p. 73, but it is recorded without comment in AB 858, p. 76, tr., p. 86.

41. AB 860, p. 83, tr., p. 92, records the Anglo-Saxons' repulse of Danes from the Somme; ASC 860, p. 46, tr., p. 68, says they had attacked Winchester, and Asser, *Life*

of Alfred, c. 18, ed. Stevenson, p. 18, tr. Keynes and Lapidge, p. 74, adds that they fled "like women." AB 861, p. 85, tr. p. 95, records the return of this group (now naming their commander as Weland) from England. Charles seems to have employed a Dane named Ansleic as cross-Channel negotiator with these Danes while they were in England: *Miracula Sancti Richarii, Acta Sanctorum Aprilis III*, p. 456. See F. Lot, "La Grande Invasion normande de 856–862," *Bibliothèque de l'École des Chartes*, 69 (1908), 5–62, rpt. in Lot, *Receuil des travaux historiques*, 3 vols. (Geneva, 1968–73), vol. 2, p. 756, n. 1.

42. At Angoulême, *Annales Engolismenses* 868, ed. O. Holder-Egger, MGH *Scriptores* 16 (Hanover, 1859), p. 486; and at Pîtres, Le Mans, and Tours, AB 868, 869, pp. 150, 166, tr., pp. 151, 163–64. For later-9th-century royal demands for "maintenance and defence" of fortifications in Wessex see the Burghal Hidage, tr. Keynes and Lapidge in *Alfred the Great*, pp. 193–94.

43. Asser, *Life of Alfred*, c. 8, ed. Stevenson, p. 7: "magno nobilium et etiam ignobilium numero constipatus."

44. On 27 August 846 the basilica of St. Peter had been sacked by Saracens and St. Peter's tomb desecrated. Though his biographer says the pope acted on Lothar's orders, Leo himself organized the building project, celebrated its successful completion, and reaped the propaganda harvest; Frankish annalists credit the work to Leo and say nothing about the emperor. For this and Leo's other projects, including frescoes and mosaics, see *Vita Leonis IV, Liber Pontificalis*, vol. 2, pp. 123–24 and nn. at pp. 137–38.

45. On this hostel for Anglo-Saxon pilgrims and visitors see P. Llewellyn, *Rome in the Dark Ages* (London, 1972), pp. 178–79, and map at pp. 16–17.

46. *King Alfred's Version of St Augustine's Soliloquies*, ed. T. Carnicelli (Cambridge, MA, 1969), p. 97. 'Now it comes into my mind that I know who built Rome, and also many other things that happened before our days, so many that I can't list them all. It's not because I saw it myself that I know who built Rome.' Cf. the text of Augustine that Alfred is following here, quoted by Carnicelli, p. 107: ". . . unde sciremus civitates ubi numquam fuimus; vel a Romulo conditam Romam. . . ?" Augustine's point was that knowledge comes from sources other than direct experience; Alfred takes this on board but adds an allusion to his own visit to Rome.

47. Alfred's request is described in Fulk's reply: D. Whitelock, M. Brett, and C. N. L. Brooke, eds., *Councils and Synods with Other Documents Relating to the English Church,*

I (Oxford, 1981), vol. 1, pp. 6–12, tr. Keynes and Lapidge, *Alfred the Great*, "Fulk's Letter to Alfred," pp. 182–86. Despite the doubts I expressed in "'A King across the Sea': Alfred in Continental Perspective," *Transactions of the Royal Historical Society*, 36 (1986), 45–68, at pp. 48–49, about the authenticity of this letter as it stands, I have been persuaded that its substance is genuine. See below and also my "'. . . *sicut olim gens Francorum . . . nunc gens Anglorum*': Fulk's letter to Alfred Revisited," in Roberts and Nelson, eds., *Alfred the Wise*, pp. 135–44.

48. ASC 885, p. 52, tr. p. 79; cf. the Mainz Continuator of the *Annales Fuldenses* 884, ed. F. Kurze, MGH *Scriptores Rerum Germanicarum in Usum Scholarum* (Hanover, 1891), p. 101 (though not the Regensburg Continuator, 885, p. 113); see now the translation by T. Reuter, *The Annals of Fulda* (Manchester, 1992), p. 96, with comment on the divergent continuations at pp. 5–9.

49. Asser, *Life of Alfred*, c. 70, ed. Stevenson, p. 52, tr. Keynes and Lapidge, p. 87; cf. D. Whitelock, ed., *English Historical Documents*, vol. 1, 2nd ed. (London, 1979), p. 198, n. 12.

50. Flodoard, *Historia Remensis Ecclesiae IV*, c. 1, pp. 555–56, says Guy was Fulk's *affinis*; at c. 3, p. 565, his *propinquus*.

51. For Guy's adoption by Pope Stephen V see G. Schneider, *Erzbischof Fulco von Reims (883–900) und das Frankenreich* (Munich, 1975), pp. 44–45. Curiously enough, Schneider has nothing to say about Alfred.

52. *English Historical Documents*, ed. Whitelock, vol. 1, p. 883.

53. Flodoard, *Historia* IV, c. 1, p. 555—with Charles the Bald in 875–76.

54. See Schneider, pp. 30–38.

55. Flodoard, *Historia* III, c. 5, p. 566 (addressing the dowager empress Richildis). P. Depreux, *Étude sur la devotion à Saint Remi de Reims*, unpub. Mémoire de Maitrise, Paris, 1989, has invaluable comments on the 9th-century association of Rheims with mission. I am very grateful to Philippe Depreux for sharing his insights with me. He does not deal with Fulk's letter to Alfred, however.

56. AB 869, pp. 162–63, tr., p. 161. The author of the AB at this point was Hincmar himself. For Hincmar's sense of Rheims' history see Wallace-Hadrill, "History in the

VI

Mind of Archbishop Hincmar," in R. H. C. Davis and J. M. Wallace-Hadrill, eds., *The Writing of History in the Middle Ages: Essays Presented to R. W. Southern* (Oxford, 1981), pp. 43–70, esp. 48, 54–55.

57. "... sicut olim gens Francorum ... nunc gens Anglorum. ...": letter to Alfred, ed. Whitelock, Brett, and Brooke, p. 7, tr. Keynes and Lapidge, p. 183.

58. Ibid., p. 11: "... for the Catholic and Apostolic Church is one, whether Roman or across the sea."

59. To this council Alcuin brought back from Britannia a formal letter to add to the synodical letters of other *gentes*: *Annales Nordhumbrani*, MGH *Scriptores* 13, ed. J. Heller and G. Waitz (Hanover, 1881), p. 155; MGH *Concilia* 2, ed. A. Werminghoff (Hanover, 1908), i, no. 19, pp. 120–21. Cf. *Libri Carolini* IV, 28, MGH *Concilia* 2, Supplement, ed. H. Bastgen (Hanover, 1924), p. 227, on the participation at councils of "praesules duarum vel trium provinciarum—et fortasse dici potest universale, quoniam, quamvis non sit ab omnibus orbis praesulibus actum, tamen ab universorum fide et traditione non discrepat."

60. Flodoard, *Historia* IV, c. 1, p. 556.

61. D. Bates, *Normandy before 1066* (London, 1982), pp. 11–12.

62. "For there is good news yet to hear and fine things to be seen / Before we go to Paradise by way of Kensal Green" (Chesterton, "The Rolling English Road").

VII

Charles le Chauve
et les utilisations du savoir

Depuis peu l'on a redécouvert bien des aspects fondamentaux de la culture carolingienne. Qui donc, il y a trente ans seulement, se rendait compte de l'importance d'une école d'Auxerre ou d'une autre à Laon [1] ? L'intention, on le sait, de la Table Ronde du roi Arthur était de donner à tous un droit égal à parler ; il en va ainsi dans ces Entretiens où nous pouvons échanger sur des questions et des hypothèses nouvelles, comme je vais faire en jetant un pont entre histoire politique et histoire culturelle. On a insisté, à juste titre, sur l'impulsion indispensable qu'a donnée le pouvoir public, voire la volonté de Charlemagne, au décollage de la renaissance carolingienne. On a soutenu également que la vraie renaissance est en pleine déroute sous Charles le Chauve ; il a fallu admettre que dans la législation par ailleurs très riche de ce roi, il n'existe guère de sources manifestant un intérêt pédagogique [2]. Il convient évidemment de distinguer entre conditions initiales et développements secondaires : une fois mise en marche, la renaissance est-elle devenue automotrice ? Disons plutôt, passant d'une métaphore machiniste à une analyse sociologique, que les intéressés ont su poursuivre leurs affaires, leurs devoirs, parce qu'ils étaient soutenus non seulement par le roi, mais aussi par une élite parsemée, installée dans quelques villes épiscopales, monastères et grandes villas. Décentralisation qui signale la réussite même de la renaissance originale.

Mais qu'est-ce que cela implique pour le régime de Charles le Chauve ? Il est difficile de bien le connaître : pas d'ouvrage de sa plume, même ses rares lettres ont été écrites par autrui, et aucun des grands épistoliers de l'époque n'a illuminé la vie de sa cour, comme Alcuin celle de Charlemagne. Pas de biographe, très peu de détails personnels. On a par des portraits l'impression d'un visage long et lourd, mais plein de vigueur, un regard direct et franc, des yeux vifs, le menton ferme, une moustache serrée mais imposante ; image séduisante, mais peut-être trompeuse, parce que représentation stéréotypée d'un souverain idéal, influencée par des traditions artistiques de Byzance et de l'Antiquité tardive [3]. Sur sa personnalité, on n'a que des allusions indirectes, des soupçons. Ratramne, en envoyant à Charles une collection de sentences, espérait que leur brièveté les empêcherait d'ennuyer un homme si occupé [4]. Loup de Ferrières se gardait de le mettre en colère, et donna le même conseil aux moines de Saint-Amand : « J'estime qu'il est dangereux... de désobéir aux ordres du roi ». Si Loup écrit à l'évêque Enée, homme de confiance à la cour, que le roi, *doctrinae studiosissimus*, « a agréé d'un visage souriant mon vœu (de reprendre l'étude des arts libéraux) », c'est parce qu'il lui faudra des demandes réitérées pour inciter Charles à exécuter sa promesse [5]. Hincmar de Reims se sentait taquiné par un patron qui accusait les évêques de vouloir « *tota die per scripturas parabolare* » [6]. Agnellus de Ravenne le décrit, avec un goût de l'humour noir, tourmentant après la bataille de Fontenoy l'archevêque Georges, partisan des vaincus, qui rampait à ses pieds : « N'as-tu pas dit hier que Charles une fois battu, tu le tonsurerais ? Voici deux fautes que tu as commises, d'abord tu as dit ce que tu ne devais pas dire, et puis tu as menti ! » [7]. Enfin, une petite histoire assez connue, mais un peu tardive (c'est Guillaume de Malmesbury qui la raconte et s'exclame : « Quoi de plus drôle ? »). Charles le Chauve et Jean Scot sont assis à table, face à face, après un très bon repas ; le roi, voyant que l'Irlandais a commis « un écart offensant pour la compagnie des Gaulois, s'en irrita courtoisement et dit : « Qu'est-ce qui sépare le sot et le scot ? » Et de convive se faisant docteur, l'autre répliqua : « Rien que la table » [8].

Voilà donc ce Charles, ironique et irascible, mais d'une piété sincère, dévoué au culte des saints et surtout à son protecteur saint Denis [9], bon seigneur aussi, qui savait non seulement punir l'infidélité mais aussi récompenser un bon serviteur, tel ce *Wido fidelis et carissimus nobis vassallus* dont la « très grande dévotion » l'a fait plus proche *(propinquior)* du roi et dont l'anniversaire serait à jamais commémoré, grâce à des dispositions royales [10].

Mais ce roi s'intéressait-il aux choses de l'esprit [11] ? S'est-il efforcé de gouverner selon les autorités écrites, voire bibliques [12] ? Était-il un vrai protecteur des savants [13] ? S'imaginait-il vraiment *rex doctus* [14] ? C'est ainsi que l'ont vu ces derniers temps des connaisseurs tels que R. Bezzola, P. Riché, le regretté M. Wallace-Hadrill, R. McKitterick, J.J. Contreni, tandis qu'auparavant, des historiens se sont exprimés plus froidement [15]. Il reste au moins un sceptique, qui mérite d'être entendu. Dans ses deux livres récents, P. Godman a mis en doute la réalité d'un *court style*, même d'une « école du Palais » de Charles le Chauve [16]. Il a jugé déplacé l'enthousiasme d'un Riché et d'une McKitterick. Selon Godman, l'excellence de Charles le Chauve n'est qu'une supposition, fondée seulement sur des raisonnements circulaires et des témoignages partiaux. Quand beaucoup d'écrivains ambitieux prétendent qu'ils répondent dans leurs ouvrages à des sollicitations du roi, ne faut-il pas déceler ici des espoirs d'auteur ? Quand Hincmar évoque le souci royal pour la « science de tout bien » [17], n'a-t-on pas affaire aux attentes d'un évêque ? Quand un poète présente Charles comme son protecteur, comme un véritable roi-philosophe, Godman soupçonne une licence poétique, en constatant que de tous les poèmes adressés à Charles, un seul a vraiment été demandé par le roi [18]. En comparaison avec les règnes précédents, le nombre de panégyristes était réduit ; et les frères aînés de Charles étaient ses égaux comme protecteurs des poètes [19]. Argument-clé de Godman, le fameux passage dans lequel Heiric fait l'éloge du roi : « ainsi parlera-t-on à bon droit d'école pour ce palais dont la fine fleur s'exerce chaque jour autant aux arts libéraux qu'à ceux de la guerre ». Selon Godman, « Heiric affirme comme rhétoricien que le palais de Charles aurait pu être appelé une école, non pas qu'il l'était en effet ». Et Heiric lui-même « n'était pas poète de la cour », mais... un homme de Saint-Germain d'Auxerre, et ainsi typique d'une culture des centres monastiques locaux. L'école du Palais de Charles le Chauve, comme le prétendu *court style* ou la *court poetry*, est « une illusion » fondée en grande partie sur une méprise « grossière » du passage cité ci-dessus [20].

Godman a bien vu la paille dans l'œil du prochain, mais n'y a-t-il pas une poussière, sinon une poutre, dans l'œil du savant d'Oxford ? C'est lui qui voit en l'empereur Lothaire un « auditeur réceptif » pour un panégyriste recommandé par son savoir, au seul témoignage de ce panégyriste lui-même [21]. C'est lui qui nous invite à croire à un Charles le Chauve « philhellène », en invoquant le témoignage des poésies hellénisantes de Jean Scot [22]. Il admet, lui, que Charles le Chauve stimulait les travaux théologiques de Jean. Bien sûr, soyons critiques ; mais ne risque-t-on pas de jeter le bébé avec l'eau du bain ? L'important, et je crois que P. Riché l'a déjà vu [23], n'est pas tellement la localisation ou même l'existence d'une école de la cour, que le rôle du roi, n'importe où, comme intéressé à la culture et au savoir, et comme leur instigateur. Godman stigmatise « une fragmentation de la vie littéraire » [24] ; je parlerais plutôt d'une multicentricité, et je ferais ressortir la quasi-ubiquité du roi [25].

Je crois qu'il reste néanmoins un problème. Le temps qu'on a mis à recevoir l'œuvre de P. E. Schramm (et comment expliquer l'absence presque complète de traductions de ses travaux sinon par des considérations non-scientifiques ?) a retardé d'autant la redécouverte de Charles : plus qu'un mécène, vraiment un idéologue de son propre chef, maître des symboles et des rituels de la royauté, fabriquant d'images politiques durables, un « prince de la Renaissance carolingienne », non seulement au sens culturel qu'entendait Wallace-Hadrill, mais avec la signification, disons machiavélique ou burckhardtienne, du créateur d'un état comme œuvre d'art, le royaume de France en l'occurrence [26]. On verra par la suite combien la thèse de Schramm est convaincante.

Mais, a demandé récemment N. Staubach dans une étude remarquable, pourquoi ce roi si intelligent, si sage, a-t-il mené une politique si désastreuse ? Comment concilier le haut niveau spirituel avec tant de faiblesses pratiques ? Staubach a décelé ici une « relation profonde » : la politique presque déraisonnable de Charles était calquée sur une image, celle de Charlemagne [27]. Charles le Chauve avait trop bien assimilé l'enseignement des panégyristes : le *novus Karolus* des poètes a ainsi intériorisé leur idéal en se façonnant un *Selbstbild* et une *Selbstbildung*, qui ensuite domineront ses actions. Idéal impossible à réaliser. Charles est alors devenu la victime de sa propre propagande. Staubach ne tente pas pour Charles une réhabilitation analogue à celle dont les historiens britanniques ont récemment gratifié Jacques VI, autrefois dénoncé comme un imbécile lettré, maintenant admiré comme un habile homme d'État, en avance même sur son époque [28]. Non. Les bonnes notes qu'a reçues Charles dès la planche à dessin ont été non seulement compensées, mais tout à fait annulées par sa performance sur piste. A quoi bon la maîtrise de l'idéologie si elle vous pousse à la folie, voire à votre perte ? Staubach affirme qu'il fait une sorte d'analyse fonctionnaliste [29] ; mais trouve-t-on une fonctionalité quelconque dans une politique qui se liquide ?

A la place d'un Charles le Chauve « hitleresque », je voudrais montrer une autre façon de résoudre la dissonance présumée entre le roi savant et le roi politique, sans pourtant la réduire à un démasquage de *Realpolitik* sous couvert de moralité [30]. En essayant de distinguer entre le véritable *rex doctus* et le faux ressemblant et factice des flagorneurs, on est tenté bien sûr par l'exemple de Charlemagne. J'y reviendrai, mais je crois que cet exemple ne convient pas tout à fait au cas de Charles le Chauve. Comme point de comparaison, je préfère un roi contemporain de Charles, qu'on dit s'être occupé beaucoup des lettres et du savoir. Je veux parler du roi Alfred. Même si, à l'instar de Godman, on reste sceptique devant un Alfred écrivain, même si les œuvres prétendûment alfrédiennes ont été plutôt écrites par des savants de son entourage, le rôle dirigeant du roi reste incontestable [31]. Son biographe Asser verse sans doute dans la flatterie et la vantardise quand il décrit ses efforts pédagogiques et la réponse d'un roi disciple tout à l'enthousiasme de lire, de traduire et d'instruire les autres [32]. Mais on voit en fin de compte les manuscrits : la traduction en vieil anglais de la *Cura Pastoralis* du pape Grégoire, la *Chronique anglo-saxonne*, les *Lois* d'Alfred ; leur quantité et leur diffusion ne s'expliquent autrement que par une forte impulsion royale, et leurs utilisations sont en harmonie parfaite avec les buts que son biographe attribue au roi et que celui-ci annonce dans la préface à la traduction de la *Cura Pastoralis* :

> Il est venu très souvent à mon esprit... que les rois du genre anglais *(Angelcynn)* ont su et maintenir la paix, la morale, l'autorité chez eux, et étendre leur territoire à l'extérieur, et qu'ils ont réussi et dans la guerre et dans la sagesse... Nos ancêtres ont aimé la sagesse, et par là ils ont obtenu les biens *(weal)* qu'ils nous ont transmis... Mais nous, nous avons perdu et les biens et la sagesse *(weal and wisdom)* [33].

Le projet royal était donc de regagner les deux, *weal and wisdom*, les biens matériels (richesse, succès dans la guerre) et la sagesse [34]. Les deux vont de pair, leur liaison est autorisée par l'Écriture Sainte [35]. Le programme alfrédien tente ainsi de réaliser l'ordonnance divine. Rien d'irréconciliable chez Alfred entre profits matériels et profits spirituels : on a là une sorte d'utilitarisme chrétien.

Utilité aussi dans un deuxième sens. En propageant le savoir parmi les grands, particulièrement la capacité de lire et écrire en langue vernaculaire, Alfred entendait, comme dit Asser, « de la manière la plus sage possible, les convertir tous à sa volonté et au bien commun du royaume entier »[36].

En termes pratiques, les hommes qui font partie de l'assemblée des grands, le *Witan*, c'est à dire les « hommes sages », doivent étudier et s'appliquer à la sagesse. Sous le latin d'Asser, on perçoit un calembour en langue vernaculaire : ceux qui jouissent de l'office et du rang des *witan* ont négligé l'étude de la *wisdom*. La solution d'Alfred est brusque :

> Ou vous perdez vos offices et vos pouvoirs, ou vous vous appliquez de toutes vos forces à la recherche de la sagesse. Et (continue Asser) tous ces hommes s'appliquaient d'une façon étonnante à apprendre à lire... et ceux qui ne faisaient pas de progrès poussaient du fond du cœur de profonds soupirs, parce que jeunes ils n'avaient pas appris à lire, et que maintenant âgés, ils ne savaient plus s'y prendre. Voilà. Cette exigence que tous, jeunes et vieux s'adonnent à la lecture, je vous l'ai montrée afin que vous puissiez mieux comprendre le roi Alfred[37]

Et ce sont les derniers mots des *Gestes du roi Alfred*.

Des recherches récentes ont démontré le succès des efforts de ce roi. Les archives anglo-saxonnes des Xe et XIe siècles révèlent une utilisation très répandue de l'écrit dans les affaires juridiques et gouvernementales[38]. Puis l'histoire politique de cette époque, la survie du royaume fédéré qu'a créé Alfred (le Wessex dont le Kent, et la Mercie), donnent les preuves d'un deuxième succès, à la fois symbolique et sociologique[39]. Alfred visait à réformer les noblesses des petits royaumes afin de construire une nouvelle aristocratie, des cadres engagés à l'égard de la monarchie, dévoués aux objectifs du roi. Dans les traductions alfrédiennes, les *gesiths*, compagnons, ont cédé la place aux *thegns*, hommes de service. Les *ealdormen* sont dépeints comme des officiers royaux aux devoirs précis, intendants plutôt que princes territoriaux[40]. Les testaments en particulier attestent l'étroitesse des relations entre la famille royale et les grands qui vantent leur intimité avec *hlaford*, *hlæfdige* et *ætheling*[41]. Il est impossible de mesurer ce que fut la contribution d'une idéologie royale et d'une formation aristocratique, telles que les prônait Alfred avec tant d'énergie, à la naissance d'un royaume uni. Mais il est également impossible de douter de son importance. Et souvenons-nous qu'autour du roi les serviteurs connus par les documents étaient peu nombreux : ils venaient tous d'au-delà du Wessex, tel Asser, voire de la Francie comme

Grimbaud [42]. C'est par eux, dit un poète contemporain, que le roi est entré dans les *rura peregrinæ sophiæ*, « les campagnes d'une sagesse venue des pays étrangers » [43]. D'Auxerre par exemple [44].

Sans aucun doute, Alfred s'inspirait en partie des modèles carolingiens. Il connaissait certainement l'œuvre de Charlemagne, probablement aussi les traductions en langue vernaculaire faites au royaume de Louis le Germanique [45]. Cependant l'influence de Charles le Chauve devait être plus proche, plus attirante même [46]. Je crois en définitive que nous avons affaire à deux réponses analogues à des problèmes comparables [47]. J'espère ainsi démontrer que Charles le Chauve, non moins qu'Alfred, a su utiliser le savoir à des fins aussi politiques qu'intellectuelles. Si on doute aujourd'hui qu'Alfred, fils d'Aethelwulf et surtout petit-fils d'Egbert a vraiment dû se faire par lui-même comme il prétendait, on a toujours su que Charles n'était pas le créateur, mais l'héritier de la grande *renovatio* inaugurée par son grand-père [48]. En matière de culture, il suffisait d'engranger la moisson que Charlemagne avait semée. Et nombreux étaient les moissonneurs.

Mais quel rapport y a-t-il avec la politique ? Je crois que nous sommes ici dans une impasse historiographique dont nous sommes responsables. Même Staubach, même E. James ou J. Martindale, sans parler de P. Riché et de K.F. Werner, ont insisté en fin de compte sur la décomposition politique qui suivit Charlemagne, et donc sur la faillite presque inévitable de Charles [49]. Mais voici qu'arrivent sur notre chantier des matériaux importants, à peine imaginables. Ici, les spécialistes des structures domaniales, J.-P. Devroey, J. Durliat, E. Magnou-Nortier, montrent un réseau économique encore bien soutenu par un appareil d'Etat pendant le règne de Charles [50]. Là, M. Metcalf, numismate expert, offre le témoignage d'une réévaluation monétaire en 864, poursuivie très efficacement dans les émissions des années suivantes [51]. Plus loin, des archéologues comme D. Hill et B. Dearden ont contribué à des mises au point sur les fortifications de Charles le Chauve [52]. Mais avant de reconstruire, comme on a fait pour Louis le Pieux [53], la figure d'un Charles le Chauve homme d'État qui a somme toute réussi, il a fallu pouvoir se l'imaginer. Aussi devait-on reconnaître les possibilités idéologiques du savoir carolingien. Les clercs du IXe siècle, pas davantage que les humanistes italiens du XIVe, ne pouvaient imposer un programme culturel nouveau sans l'aide d'un public réceptif : à propos de cette autre renaissance, Lauro Martines fait état des relations réciproques entre intellectuels et élite sociale, et d'une prise de conscience de la part de celle-ci [54].

Au début du règne de Charles, après les développements du règne précédent, il y a eu un déplacement de l'activité culturelle de la cour vers de nombreux foyers ecclésiastiques dans les provinces. En outre il existait maintenant une classe dirigeante lettrée, qui savait lire le latin, ou au moins comprendre des textes lus en latin. Cette évolution, selon nos connaissances, s'est produite dans la Francie de l'Ouest, dans le royaume de Charles le Chauve plus que dans les autres royaumes carolingiens du IXe siècle [55]. Et pourquoi ? R. McKitterick vient de suggérer que la proximité du « latin écrit » vis à vis de la « langue romane parlée » aurait facilité la compréhension du poème du *Waltharius* par des auditeurs laïcs du IXe plutôt que du Xe siècle [56]. Mais cela s'appliquerait aussi bien à l'Italie qu'au royaume de Charles. Pourtant les textes écrits ou les lecteurs laïcs paraissent assez peu nombreux dans le *regnum italicum* de Louis II, contemporain presque exactement de Charles ; mais dans l'ancien royaume lombard, on ne voit rien qui soit semblable au rôle culturel de l'aristocratie de la Gaule mérovingienne [57]. Il a donc fallu et fondement social, et structures politiques. On distinguera naturellement entre culture littéraire proprement dite et utilisation de l'écrit en matière juridique. La culture littéraire nous renvoie nécessairement au royaume de Charles, où, semble-t-il, dès le début du règne, les auteurs pouvaient compter sur un public de laïcs qui se sentaient à l'aise avec la littérature latine et des genres diversifiés. Pendant les mois troublés qui ont suivi la bataille de Fontenoy (25 juin 841), Nithard a répondu dans ses *Histoires* aux inquiétudes des vainqueurs [58], Angilbert dans ses *Versus* a tenté de soulager les vaincus [59], tandis que Dhuoda mettait la main à son *Manuel* d'instruction morale pour son fils rallié à Charles après la bataille [60]. A peu près à la même époque, semble-t-il, un grand du camp de Charles s'interroge au sujet de la fidélité, et il écrit à l'impératrice Ermengarde. Il proteste qu'il n'a jamais fomenté de dissensions : « Je ne suis pas compagnon des démons. L'homme qui cherche seulement son propre droit ne veut pas la discorde universelle ». Ce fidèle inconnu révèle les assurances d'un lettré pour qui la morale et l'utilité politique marchent de conserve : « Je vous serai d'autant plus utile et fidèle, dit-il, que je me suis avancé dans l'étude de la sagesse » [61].

Ces lecteurs, ces auditeurs et leurs sensibilités ont contribué à créer une situation nouvelle en regard du passé proche. A la cour de Charlemagne, un gouffre s'ouvrait, et j'emprunte ici les mots inimitables de Bezzola, entre une « académie cléricale » et « une noblesse inculte,

intrigante, vicieuse, sanguinaire, féroce... », et celle-ci était personni-
fiée par ce *membrosus Wibodus* dont Théodulf s'est moqué dans un
poème célèbre [62], ou par le « repulsively realistic... hairy nobleman »
que Wallace-Hadrill a vu dans le Sacramentaire de Gellone [63]. Selon
Bezzola, Charlemagne n'a pu jeter un pont entre les deux groupes ; il
s'ensuivit une dissociation complète entre les guerriers et les clercs [64].
Mais voilà que sous Charles le Chauve, on rencontre une trentaine de
grands laïcs lettrés, la plupart dans le royaume de l'ouest, destinataires
de lettres, dédicataires de livres écrits par des clients ou possédant eux-
mêmes des livres [65]. Parmi ceux-ci, le cas le plus intéressant est sans
doute celui du comte Conrad d'Argengau, qui a emprunté à Haymon
d'Auxerre un manuscrit de l'*Histoire d'Alexandre* : Conrad était ainsi,
à sa manière, un amateur de l'Antiquité classique, il possédait lui-
même le Commentaire sur l'Ecclésiastique de Hraban Maur qu'Haymon voulait lui emprunter en échange. Tout ceci montre que le comte
en bon carolingien cherchait activement la sagesse, et plus précisément, se fit collaborateur laïque de l'école d'Auxerre [66].

Ceci suscite un petit commentaire historique. D'abord, selon
Hincmar qui malgré tout laisse percevoir les prétentions intellectuelles
de Conrad, la *scientia* de celui-ci n'était que « frivole et inutile » [67]. La
note du manuscrit cité nous empêche heureusement de partager ce
jugement injuste, d'ailleurs assez coutumier chez Hincmar. Puis on
remarque dans l'Ecclésiastique, comme dans les livres sapientiaux ou
les autres livres deutérocanoniques, ce qu'on a déjà vu chez Alfred :
une explication très matérielle de la *sapientia,* bien adaptée à la vie
séculière de la noblesse. « Fuyons la tristesse ; on n'y trouve rien
d'utile » ; « au banquet... l'homme qui sait se contente d'un verre »...,
« quant à l'utilité de la connaissance..., l'homme qui connaît beaucoup
ne cesse de s'en persuader » ; « et à propos de la vraie ou de la fausse
pudeur..., la sagesse cachée, le trésor invisible, quelle utilité ont-
ils ? » [68]. Il est vrai que le commentaire de Hraban, dont le destinataire
originel était un évêque, s'attache plutôt aux significations mystiques.
Mais le sens littéral n'y est pas négligé, surtout au sujet de l'*amicitia,*
et encore moins dans le commentaire du même Hraban sur les Maccabées, dédié, lui, à Louis le Germanique [69]. Chez le roi Alfred, mais
aussi en Francie chez Nithard, chez Dhuoda, chez le fidèle anonyme
cité ci-dessus, on constate d'ailleurs une lecture personnelle, voire laï-
cisée, de l'Ecriture Sainte ainsi qu'un *studium doctrinae* attentif aux
besoins de la vie séculière. C'est précisément la lecture de ce genre de
chaîne biblique que conseillait Loup de Ferrières au jeune Charles [70].

Conrad aussi, Hincmar l'a montré, pouvait appliquer sa « science » aux affaires publiques, dans le conseil royal.

Pourquoi supposer alors chez le comte Conrad des préoccupations extraordinaires, incongrues ? Il faudrait en réalité substituer aux Wibode francs de Bezzola des dizaines, des centaines peut-être de Conrad. Ce comte et les siens — un de ses fils est devenu comte d'Auxerre, un autre est connu sous le nom de Hugues l'Abbé —, ont bien existé au milieu du IXe siècle. Collectivement ils frayaient la voie d'un roi sage. Alfred, on l'a vu, a tenté de forger un consensus idéologique par le moyen d'une propagande écrite. Mais Charles ? Etait-il plutôt une brute comme Wibode ou, malgré son sobriquet, un « hairy Frank » ? Hébergea-t-il Jean Scot pendant trente ans seulement à cause de ses blagues ou de son savoir-faire médical ? En dépit des nombreux ouvrages qu'on lui a dédiés, Charles était-il vraiment indifférent à la culture, un mécène malgré lui ? Je n'en crois rien et ne puis suivre P. Godman : quoi qu'il en soit du laconisme des sources, je suis persuadée que Charles aussi s'est intéressé au savoir et a su l'employer à des fins à la fois culturelles et politiques.

La comparaison avec Alfred souligne encore les traits spécifiques de la Francie. Pourquoi, par exemple, Charles n'a-t-il pas comme Alfred commandé des livres d'histoire contemporaine sur son règne [71] ? En 841, Charles a en fait demandé à Nithard d'en écrire un ; mais lorsque fut réalisé l'objectif politique à court terme, le roi se désintéressa d'un écrivain plus soucieux d'histoire privée que d'histoire publique [72]. Il n'y eut pas non plus d'Annales royales : le roi réservait ses chapelains à d'autres tâches. Charles n'était pas confronté comme Alfred à la conjoncture critique d'un petit royaume récent et sans histoire, d'un roi privé d'ancêtres prestigieux et d'une lignée assurée, vivant surtout sous la menace des Vikings. Charles avait une position beaucoup plus ferme : les « Histoires des Francs » avaient donné de solides fondations au royaume, le mythe dynastique était éblouissant, et le problème normand était certainement surmontable. L'absence d'une histoire officielle à la cour de Charles tenait en somme au choix du souverain.

Charles était conscient que son aristocratie, à la différence des Saxons de l'Ouest, avait déjà entrepris la lutte contre l'*imperitia* et l'*insipientia* [73], et n'éprouvait pas le besoin de renvoyer les grands à l'école. Au contraire d'Alfred, il tenait l'Église de son royaume en bon ordre et bien en main [74]. Ayant donc à sa disposition des organes et des agents, Charles était capable d'entreprendre une nouvelle politique de formation : la nouveauté touchait moins au public concerné, l'élite franque, qu'au style et au contenu envisagés. En bref, Charles entendait se présenter en *princeps orthodoxus, imperator felix,* à l'image de Théodose [75], il voulait aussi faire des grands du royaume des *iudices* et *consiliarii* dévoués à la *res publica,* au *bonum publicum.*

Hincmar nous renseigne parfaitement sur l'institution-clé au niveau du royaume, le *placitum totius regni,* assemblée des Francs, une Table Ronde en grand [76]. Il y avait en outre des assemblées au niveau du comté, où les agents royaux s'efforçaient de poursuivre et de contrôler l'exécution des décisions prises au palais [77]. C'est à travers ces assemblées et leurs aboutissements législatifs, les capitulaires, que Charles a su articuler une politique utilitaire du savoir. Il y avait bien des conciles spécialisés où les clercs traitaient les affaires doctrinales, comme la prédestination ; mais on y était bien conscient des aspects sociaux et politiques de ces questions [78]. En réalité, la plupart des assemblées s'occupaient de questions à la fois séculières et ecclésiastiques et réunissaient côte à côte clercs et laïcs nobles, souvent d'ailleurs parents par le sang.

La réponse royale aux crises des années 850 a été une averse de capitulaires. Ainsi celui de Quierzy, du 14 février 857 ; il est presque certain qu'Hincmar en était l'auteur, mais on ne se tromperait pas à y déceler des décisions et une pensée collectives [79]. Les « chapitres » sont promulgués à l'issue d'une assemblée où évêques et fidèles du roi ont traité ensemble les « affaires utiles à l'Église et nécessaires au royaume » *(negotia ecclesiasticae utilitatis ac regni necessitatis)* ; ils sont dressés en capitulaire, copiés en exemplaires multiples (il en subsiste deux, destinés à l'Orléanais et au Ternois, chacun portant les noms des *missi* responsables, évêques et grands laïcs côte à côte [80]). Les décisions sont donc portées aux « assemblées des diocèses et comtés » *(placita in parrochiis vel comitatibus),* où « tous les agents de l'État » *(omnes reipublicae ministri)* et « tout le monde sans exception de personne, sans excuse ni délai » *(omnes sine ulla personarum exceptione vel excusatione aut dilatione)* doivent se présenter [81]. Tous doivent y entendre l'évêque, dont l'admonition doit être lue *aperto sermone,* et un exemple d'admonition est adjoint au capitulaire ; le comte alors doit faire donner lecture des « jugements de la loi pour en assurer la publicité » ainsi que des « chapitres » utiles [82]. La mention ici de la *res publica* et de l'exception de personne renvoie à la notion fondamentale dans le droit romain du bien public auquel chaque individu est subordonné, y compris le *princeps* lui-même [83]. Autre exemple, l'admonition composée par Loup de Ferrières en 857 pour l'archevêque de Sens Guenilon. Beaucoup mieux que dans le sermon-modèle d'Hincmar, on entend ici la voix d'une morale séculière, jouxtant l'enseignement chrétien. Pas question de sacrifier le maintenant au futur : « Ici *(hic)* les biens temporels échoient souvent aux gens de bien, alors qu'en l'autre monde *(alibi)*, les biens éternels viennent les couronner ». Bien sûr il ne faut pas chercher seulement les richesses temporelles, « pensons parfois à obtenir les biens spirituels », et que « nos désirs restent dans certaines limites ». Mais cette moralité implique aussi des obligations envers l'État : « Cherchons encore les vertus par lesquelles ce royaume a grandi et fleuri... ; par crainte et amour de Dieu, renonçons à poursuivre notre gain personnel, ensemble et d'un seul cœur appliquons-nous au bien commun de l'État » [84]. Voilà comment les gens du Sénonais auront été rappelés à leurs devoirs publics.

Les fidèles de Charles n'auraient pu rester sourds à cet appel. Si quelques-uns d'entre eux ont répliqué par une fin de non-recevoir en 858, leurs griefs portaient non sur la faiblesse du gouvernement royal, mais sur le poids trop lourd des charges publiques [85]. Les fidèles ont entendu mainte fois par la suite le rappel de leurs devoirs, notamment à Pîtres en juin 864 : dans un capitulaire où résonnaient les échos du Code théodosien, le roi imposait à nouveau les *munera sordida* d'autrefois. Bien avant que l'annaliste de Fulda constate en 869 que Charles « est sur le point de tenir les deux royaumes », ce roi est en passe de devenir empereur, et s'imagine déjà successeur des très illustres empereurs [86]. Il va sans dire qu'une telle conception du rôle impérial ne dépendait pas d'un couronnement par le pape.

Qui donc a su partager, vraiment comprendre une idéologie pareille ? Jean de Salerne raconte en passant dans sa Vie d'Odon de Cluny, qu'un fidèle au moins du royaume de Charles, peut-être en Touraine — il s'agit d'Abbon, le père d'Odon —, connaissait « de mémoire » les Novelles de Justinien ainsi que les « histoires des anciens » [87]. Et à vrai dire, le capitulaire de Pîtres en 864 ne rime à rien ou presque si l'on n'y suppose pas une ample connaissance de la *Lex romana* chez les fidèles qui ont contribué à l'œuvre du roi législateur. Mais ce n'est pas là seulement que les Carolingiens ont pu puiser la conception du service public. L'Écriture Sainte montrait, dans les livres apocryphes d'Esther et des Maccabées, un homme se soumettant à l'« utilité commune », puis des souverains gouvernant « comme le requiert le bien public de l'État » ou « pour le bien commun » [88]. Or nous avons vu déjà la liaison faite dans la Bible entre *utilitas* et *sapientia*.

Concluons par deux images du roi en quête de la « sagesse » utile. La première vient du *Ferculum Salomonis* d'Hincmar, commandé par le roi au dire de l'auteur [89]. Faut-il n'y voir que de la flagornerie ? Je crois quant à moi qu'on peut admettre ici une sollicitation de la part du roi. Il s'agit d'un texte bizarre du Cantique des Cantiques :

> Le roi Salomon s'est fait un trône en bois du Liban ; les colonnes, il les a faites d'argent, le baldaquin d'or, le siège de pourpre... Sortez, filles de Sion, et voyez le roi Salomon en diadème. C'est sa mère qui le couronna au jour de ses épousailles, au jour de la joie en son cœur [90].

Je ne sais si l'exégèse de *Cantique* 2, 9-11 par Hincmar a plu au roi. Mais considérons la fréquence des comparaisons savantes entre Charles et Salomon, la renommée de celui-ci pour la sagesse, l'intérêt aussi de Charles aux rituels et aux symboles, la commémoration soigneuse des anniversaires de sa mère et de ses propres noces : n'est-il pas vraisemblable que ce passage aura piqué la curiosité de notre roi ?

Enfin, et grâce encore à Hincmar, voici un aperçu de Charles à sa cour, entouré de ses fidèles. Au mois de février 859, Hincmar laisse échapper son exaspération et celle des autres fidèles [91]. Les nécessités de la guerre ont fait lâcher la meute des cavaliers et même des portefaix *(cocciones)* — on se souvient des plaintes d'Alcuin à Charlemagne sur la « furie de vos serviteurs » [92] —, qui dévastent tout dans les domaines *(villae)*. Que faire ? Hincmar craint que les admonestations des prêtres des paroisses aient peu de poids, si elles ne sont pas étayées. Il envoie à Charles copie de sa lettre synodale

> afin que vous la gardiez secrète ; puis, un jour, vous convoquerez vos fidèles en leur disant que voulez leur communiquer ce qu'il vous plaît de leur dire, et avant qu'ils ressortent de votre palais pour rentrer chez eux, vous leur délivrerez ces remontrances, suivant la sagesse que Dieu vous a donnée...

On avait donc fort à faire pour transformer ces « hairy Franks » en « société courtoise » [93]. Mais je crois que pour Charles ce n'était pas la moindre utilité du savoir.

NOTES

1. Outre les participants à ces Entretiens d'Auxerre, il faut évoquer les noms des regrettés H. BARRÉ et M. CAPPUYNS. Je reconnaîtrai par la suite mes autres dettes intellectuelles. Je remercie aussi F. GROOTHUES et G. LOBRICHON qui ont bien voulu m'aider dans la préparation du texte français de mon exposé.

2. Fait admis par P. RICHÉ, *Charles le Chauve et la culture de son temps*, dans *Jean Scot Erigène et l'Histoire de la philosophie. Colloques internationaux du CNRS, n° 561*, Paris 1977, p. 37-46, notamment 38ss. Cf. J.J. CONTRENI, *Carolingian Biblical Studies* dans *Carolingian Essays*, ed. U.-R. Blumenthal, Washington, 1983, p. 71-98, 75ss.

3. J. GAEHDE, *The Pictorial Sources of the Illustrations to the Book of Kings, Proverbs, Judith and Maccabees in the Carolingian Bible of San Paolo fuori le Mura*, dans *Frühmittelalterliche Studien* 9 (1975), p. 359-389 ; R. MCKITTERICK, *Charles the Bald and the image of kingship*, dans *History Today* (June 1988), p. 29-36.

4. *MGH, Epist. Karol. Aevi, IV, Ep. Variorum*, n° 8, p. 150.

5. LOUP, *Correspondance*, I, n° 67, p. 246-9 ; II, n° 122, p. 186-7.

6. *P.L.* 126, 97. Cf. J. DEVISSE, *Hincmar, archevêque de Reims (845-882)*, 3 vol., Genève 1975-6, II, p. 727, n. 6.

7. AGNELLUS, *Liber Pontificalis Ecclesiae Ravennatis*, c. 174 : *MGH, SSRL*, p. 390.

8. Guillaume de MALMESBURY, *Gesta Pontificum*, éd. Hamilton, *Rolls Series*, London 1870, p. 392.

9. P. RICHÉ, *Charles*, p. 41-2 ; J.M. WALLACE-HADRILL, *Early Germanic Kingship*, p. 129-133 ; ID., *A Carolingian*, p. 164-6 et 176 ; ID., *The Frankish Church*, Oxford, 1983, p. 244-7.

10. *Recueil des Actes de Charles II le Chauve*, éd. G. Tessier, II, Paris, 195, n° 325, p. 217. Cf. M. ROUCHE, *Les repas de fête à l'époque carolingienne*, dans *Manger et boire au Moyen Age. Actes du Colloque de Nice (15-17 octobre 1982)*, I : *Aliments et Société*, Nice, 1984, p. 265-296.

11. R.E. BEZZOLA, *Les origines et la formation de la littérature courtoise en Occident (500-1200)*, I, Paris, 1958, p. 196. Voir aussi P. RICHÉ, *Charles* ; ID., *Les Irlandais et les princes carolingiens aux* VIIIe *et* IXe *siècles*, dans *Die Iren und Europa*, éd. H. Löwe, I, Stuttgart, 1982, p. 735-745.

12. J.M. WALLACE-HADRILL, *A Carolingian*, p. 184 ; ID., *The via regia of the Carolingian Age*, dans *Trends in Medieval Political Thought*, Oxford, 1965, p. 22-41. Voir aussi P. GODMAN, *Poets and Emperors*, Oxford, 1987, p. 174-5.

13. R. MCKITTERICK, *Charles the Bald and the Patronage* ; ID., *The Palace School* ; J.J. CONTRENI, *Inharmonious Harmony : Education in the Carolingian World*, dans *Annals of Scholarship* 1 (1980), p. 81-96.

14. P. GODMAN, *Poets*, p. 170, et index (« Learning of Rulers »).

15. Par ex., J. DUBOIS, éd., *Martyrologe d'Usuard*, Bruxelles, 1965, p. 38. Mais cf. E. LESNE, *Histoire de la Propriété ecclésiastique*, 6 vol., Lille, 1910-1943, t. 4, p. 610 et t. 5, ch. 3.

16. *Poetry, Introduction*, p. 48 ; *Poets*, ch. IV.

17. *Scientia omnis boni : MGH, Epist.* VIII, I, n° 108, p. 53.

18. *Poets*, p. 175 ; *Poetry*, p. 63.

19. *Poets*, p. 153-4 et 167-8 ; *Poetry*, p. 56.

20. *Ita ut merito vocitetur scola palatium cuius apex non minus scolaribus quam militaribus consuescit cotidie disciplinis :* P. GODMAN, *Poetry*, p. 57-8.

21. *Poets*, p. 167.

22. *Poets*, p. 170, où P. GODMAN allègue une disposition permanente de Charles le Chauve, en évoquant un témoin de 869. Voir aussi *Poetry*, p. 59. Cf. les remarques nuancées de J.M. WALLACE-HADRILL, *A Carolingian*, p. 173, et de P. RICHÉ, *Le Grec dans les centres de culture d'Occident*, dans *The Sacred Nectar*, p. 153-154.

23. P. RICHÉ, *Charles*, p. 38. En effet, P. GODMAN repète ici les mots de J.M. WALLACE-HADRILL, *A Carolingian*, p. 168-9.

24. *Poetry*, p. 58.

25. Voir J.L. NELSON, *Charles the Bald and the Church in Town and countryside*, dans *Studies in Church History* 16 (1979), p. 103-18, réimpr. dans *Politics*, ch. 4.

26. P.E. SCHRAMM, *Der König von Frankreich*, 2 vol., Darmstadt, 1939 ; ID., *Herrschaftszeichen und Staatssymbolik*, 3 vol. Stuttgart, 1954-6 ; *Kaiser, Könige und Päpste*, 4 vol., Stuttgart 1968-71. Voir l'analyse très suggestive de J.M. BAK, *Medieval symbology of the state : Percy E. Schramm's contribution ;* dans *Viator* 4 (1973), p. 33-63.

27. N. STAUBACH, *Das Herrscherbild Karls des Kahlen. Formen und Funktionen monarchischer Repräsentation im früheren Mittelalter*, Inaugural-Dissertation der Westfalischen Wilhelms-Universität zu Münster, 1982, p. 14-9.

28. M.L. SCHWARZ, *James I and the historians : towards a reconsideration* dans *Journal of British Studies* 13 (1944), p. 114-34 ; J. WORMALD, *James VI and I : Two Kings or One ?*, dans *History* 68 (1983), p. 187-209.

29. *Herrscherbild*, p. 22.

30. Cf. les remarques de Staubach, *ibid.*

31. J. BATELY, *The Literary Prose of King Alfred's Reign : Translation or Transformation ?*, London, 1980 ; ID., *Lexical evidence for the authorship of the prose psalms in the Paris Psalter*, dans *Anglo-Saxon England* 10 (1982), p. 69-95 ; P. WORMALD, dans J. Campbell, éd., *The Anglo-Saxons*, Oxford, 1982, p. 155-159. Voir aussi l'étude fondamentale sur la législation alfrédienne par P. Wormald, à paraître : je le remercie de m'en avoir permis la lecture avant parution.

32. ASSER, *De Rebus Gestis Aelfredi*, c. 88, 89, éd. W. Stevenson, Oxford, 1904, p. 74-5, traduction anglaise dans S. KEYNES et M. LAPIDGE, *Alfred the Great. Asser's Life of King Alfred and other contemporary sources*, Harmondsworth, 1983, p. 99-100.

33. S. KEYNES et M. LAPIDGE, *Alfred*, pp. 293-4 (manuscrits de la *Cura Pastoralis*), 275-9 (*Chronique*), 303-4 (*Lois*).

34. H. SWEET, éd., *King Alfred's West-Saxon Version of Gregory's Pastoral Care*, London, 1871, p. 2-3, traduction anglaise par Keynes et Lapidge, *Alfred*, p. 124-5. Cf. ASSER, c. 76, p. 60-1 (trad. angl., p. 92) : *in hoc pium et opinatissimum atque opulentissimum Salomonem Hebraeorum regem aequiparans, qui primitus, despecta omni praesenti gloria et divitiis, sapientiam a Deo deposcit, et etiam utramque invenit...*

35. *Ecclésiaste* 7,12 : *Utilior est sapientia cum divitiis, et magis prodest videntibus solem. Sicut enim protegit sapientia, sic protegit pecunia.* Voir J.L. NELSON, *Wealth and Wisdom : The Politics of Alfred*, dans *Kings and Kingship*, éd. J. Rosenthal, Center for Medieval and Early Renaissance Studies, State University of New York, Acta, 11, New York, 1986, p. 31-52 ; J. MADDICOTT, *Trade, Industry and the Wealth of Alfred*, dans *Past and Present* 123 (1989), p. 3-51.

36. *Ad suam voluntatem et ad communem totius regni utilitatem sapientissime... annectebat :* Asser, c. 91, p. 78 (trad. angl., p. 102).

37. ASSER, c. 106, pp. 93-5 (trad. ang., p. 110).

38. S. KEYNES, *The Diplomas of King AEthelred the Unready* Cambridge, 1980 ; P. WORMALD, *Charters, law and the settlement of disputes in Anglo-Saxon England*, dans W. DAVIES et P. FOURACRE éd., *The Settlement of Disputes in Early Medieval Europe*, Cambridge, 1986, p. 149-68 ; S. KELLY, *Anglo-Saxon lay society and the written word*, dans *The Uses of Literacy in Early Mediaeval Europe*, R. McKITTERICK éd., Cambridge, 1990, p. 36-62.

39. P. STAFFORD, *The tenth-century Kingdom*, dans L. SMITH, éd., *The Making of Britain*, London, 1983, p. 117-29 ; ID., *Unification and Conquest*, London, 1989 ; S. KEYNES, *A tale of two kings : Alfred the Great and Aethelred the Unready*, dans *Transactions of the Royal Historical Society* 36 (1986), p. 195-217 ; J.L. NELSON, « *A king across the sea* » : *Alfred in Continental perspective*, *ibid.*, p. 45-68 ; ID., *The Second English Ordo*, dans *Politics* 16.

40. H.R. LOYN, *The term ealdorman in the translations prepared at the time of King Alfred*, dans *English Historical Review* 68 (1953), p. 513-25 ; ID., *Gesiths and thegns in Anglo-Saxon England*, dans *English Historical Review* 70 (1955), p. 529-49.

41. D. WHITELOCK, éd., *Anglo-Saxon Wills*, Cambridge, 1930, n° VIII-XI, XIII, p. 20, 23, 26-8, 30-2.

42. S. KEYNES et M. LAPIDGE, *Alfred* (cit. n. 32), p. 26-7, 331-3.

43. M. LAPIDGE, *Some Latin poems as evidence for the reign of Athelstan*, dans *Anglo-Saxon England* 9 (1981), p. 61-98 ; S. KEYNES et M. LAPIDGE, *Alfred* (cit. n. 32), p. 192, 338.

44. L'influence directe d'un commentaire auxerrois sur la version alfredienne de la *Consolatio Philosophiae* de Boèce a été exclue par J. WITTIG, *King Alfred's Boethius and its Latin sources : a reconsideration*, dans *Anglo-Saxon England* 11 (1983), p. 157-98. Mais voir D. IOGNA-PRAT, *Le Baptême du schéma des trois ordres fonctionnels*, dans *Annales E.S.C.* 1 (1986), p. 101-126 et E. ORTIGUES, *L'Élaboration.*

45. J. BATELY, *Literary Prose* (cit n. 31) ; S. KEYNES et M. LAPIDGE, *Alfred* (cit n. 32), p. 295-6 ; J.M. WALLACE-HADRILL, *The Frankish Church*, p. 377-89.

46. Voir les relations diverses examinées par P. STAFFORD, *Charles the Bald, Judith and England*, dans *Charles the Bald*, p. 159 ; et R. HODGES, *Trade and Market Origins in the Ninth Century, ibid.*, p. 203-23 ; cf. J.M. WALLACE-HADRILL, *Early Germanic Kingship*, p. 132, 142-3, 148.

47. J.L. NELSON, *A king across the sea*, p. 49-50.

48. Préface à la version de la *Cura Pastoralis*, trad. angl., dans S. KEYNES et M. LAPIDGE, *Alfred* (cit. n. 32), p. 125.

49. J.M. WALLACE-HADRILL, *A Carolingian*, p. 156-7 ; N. STAUBACH, *Herrscherbild* (cit. n. 27), p. 55-95 ; E. JAMES, *The Origins of France*, London, 1982, p. 174-5 ; J. MARTINDALE, *The kingdom of Aquitaine and the dissolution of the Carolingian fisc*, dans *Francia* 11 (1985), p. 131-91 ; P. RICHÉ, *Les Carolingiens : une famille qui fit l'Europe*, Paris, 1983, p. 191-202 ; K.F. WERNER, *Les Origines*, t. 1 de *l'Histoire de France*, dir. J. FAVIER, Paris, 1984, p. 416, 422. Qu'on me permette de renvoyer à mon étude, *Charles the Bald : a life* (à paraître).

50. J.-P. DEVROEY, *Réflexions sur l'économie des premiers temps carolingiens*, dans *Francia* 13 (1986), p. 475-88 ; J. DURLIAT, *Le polyptyque d'Irminon et l'impôt pour l'armée*, dans *Bibliothèque de l'Ecole des Chartes* 141 (1983), p. 183-208 ; E. MAGNOU-NORTIER, *Etude sur le privilège de l'immunité*, dans *Revue Mabillon* 60 (1984), p. 465-512.

51. D.M. METCALF, *A sketch of the currency in the reign of Charles the Bald*, dans *Charles the Bald*, p. 65-97.

52. J.M. HASSALL et D.M. HILL, *Pont-de-l'Arche : Frankish influence on the West Saxon burh ?*, dans *Archaeological Journal* 127, (1970), p. 188-95. Voir aussi les trouvailles récentes signalées par B. DEARDEN, *Charles the Bald's fortified bridge at Pîtres (Seine) : recent archaeological investigations*, dans *Anglo-Norman Studies* 11 (1988), p. 107-12.

53. R. COLLINS et P. GODMAN, éd., *Charlemagne's Heir*, Oxford, 1990.

54. L. MARTINES, *Power and Imagination. City States in Renaissance Italy*, Harmondsworth, 1983, ch. XI, XII, XIII, surtout p. 282-95, 317-31, 351. MARTINES a préféré le mot *imagination*, parce que (p. XII), « my supreme concern is with relations between dominant social groups (power) and the articulated, formal, refined, or idealizing consciousness of those who speak for the powerful. In this interplay, the workings of imagination tend to be foremost ».

55. J.L. NELSON, *Public Histories and private history*, dans *Politics* ; R. MCKITTERICK, *The Carolingians*, ch. 6. Bien sûr, les laïcs lettrés ne manquaient pas dans les autres royaumes carolingiens ; et de toute façon, les intérêts de nombreux grands laïcs — tels Conrad — recouvraient plusieurs royaumes.

56. R. MCKITTERICK, *The Carolingians*, p. 228.

57. La *préhistoire* de la culture laïque dans le royaume franc est évidemment critique : voir P. RICHÉ, *Education et culture dans l'occident barbare*, Paris, 1973 ; ID., *Instruction et vie religieuse dans le Haut Moyen Age*, London, 1981, surtout ch. VI et VII ; R. MCKITTERICK, *The Carolingians*, p. 212-7.

58. J.L. NELSON, *Public Histories* (cit. n. 55) ; ID., *Ninth-century knighthood : the evidence of Nithard*, dans *Studies in Medieval History presented to R. Allen Brown*, C. HARPER-BILL, C.J. HOLDSWORTH et J.L. NELSON éd., Woodbridge, 1989, p. 255-66.

59. *MGH, PLAC*, II, p. 138. Voir P. GODMAN, *Poetry*, p. 48-50 et 262-5.

60. Ed. P. RICHÉ, Paris, 1975. Voir J.L. NELSON, *Les femmes et l'évangélisation*, dans *Revue du Nord* 68 (1986), p. 471-85.

61. *MGH, Epist. Karol. Aevi*, t. V, Epp. Variorum n° 27, p. 343-5.

62. Theodulf, *MGH, PLAC*, I, p. 489 (trad. angl., P. GODMAN, *Poetry*, p. 160-1, avec commentaire, p. 11-2) ; R.E. BEZZOLA, *Les origines* (cit. n. 11), p. 99.

63. *Frankish Church*, p. 178. J.M. Wallace-Hadrill fait allusion sans doute au fol. 9v (fig. 4) du Sacramentaire de Gellone, éd. A. DUMAS, *C.C.S.L.* 159, Turnhout, 1981.

64. R.E. BEZZOLA, *Les origines* (cit. n. 11), p. 99, 145 ; cf. p. XXI, où l'auteur décrit en se tordant les mains « l'abîme entre l'homme d'action et l'homme de pensée ». Pour une autre manière d'interpréter nos connaissances du 9e siècle, voir J.L. Nelson, *Ninth-century knighthood* (cit. n. 58).

65. J.L. NELSON, *Public Histories*, p. 256-60, avec bibliographie citée ; R. MCKITTERICK, *The Carolingians*, ch. 6.

66. Annotation dans Paris, B.N., lat. 5716, (*Historia Alexandri* de Q. Curtius Rufus) de *Haimus monachus* qui l'envoie à Conrad et requiert celui-ci de lui prêter le Commentaire sur l'Ecclésiastique de Hraban. R. QUADRI, *Aimone*, fait les identifications d'*Haimus* avec Haymon et de Conrad avec le comte Conrad, abbé laïc de St-Germain d'Auxerre (plutôt qu'avec *Conrad comte du Vermandois*, MCKITTERICK, *The Carolingians*, p. 261 et n. 169, mais sans référence à l'article de QUADRI). Même si l'écriture de l'annotation datait du Xᵉ siècle, il pourrait s'agir, selon la graphie du nom *Chuinrado*, d'une copie d'un original du IXᵉ siècle (G. LOBRICHON). Ce Conrad était l'oncle maternel de Charles le Chauve, et le mari d'Adélaïde, fille d'Hugues, comte de Tours. Les relations de Conrad avec Auxerre

lui venaient, semble-t-il, par sa femme : R. LOUIS, *De l'histoire à la légende. Girart, comte de Vienne (... 819-877) et ses fondations monastiques*, t. I, Auxerre, 1946, p. 32-8. Selon nos connaissances, ce Conrad n'a jamais été comte d'Auxerre : outre Y. SASSIER (ci-dessus), cf. J. WOLLASCH, *Das Patrimonium*, p. 209, voir aussi aux p. 193, 207-9 ; M. BORGOLTE, *Die Grafen Alemanniens im merowingischer und karolingischer Zeit*, Sigmaringen, 1986, p. 166-8 (qui note que Conrad était dédicataire d'un poème de Walafrid, mais sans référence à Haymon). Conrad et Adélaïde se sont occupés tous deux de la *translatio* de saint Germain en 841, et de la construction d'une crypte : Heiric fait l'éloge de leur *prona et incomparabilis in nos locumque nostrum... benevolentia*. (*Miracula*, II, 8-9, p. 560-1). Parmi les fils de ce couple, Hugues est devenu abbé de St-Germain (853), et Conrad (II) comte d'Auxerre (fin 858).

67. *Annales de St Bertin*, an. 865, éd. F. GRAT, J. VIELLIARD et S. CLEMENCET, Paris, 1964, p. 95. Voir NELSON, *The Annals of St Bertin*, dans *Charles the Bald*, p. 35 ss. L'animosité d'Hincmar venait peut-être aussi d'une dispute entre Conrad et les moines de l'abbaye de St-Denis autour d'une *precaria* que Charles le Chauve et l'abbé Louis, ont voulu accorder au comte : *MGH, Capit.*, II, n° 294, p. 422-3.

68. Par exemple : *Fugienda est tristitia..., non est utilitas in illa* (*Eccl.* 30,25) ; *de conviviis... quam sufficiens est homini erudito vinum exiguum* (32,22) ; *de utilitate experientiae... vir in multis expertus cogitabit multa* (34,9) ; *de vero et falso pudore..., sapientia abscondita et thesaurus invisus, quae utilitas in utrisque ?* (41,17).

69. Commentaires de Hraban sur l'Ecclésiastique et sur les Maccabées : *P.L.* 109, 763-1126 et 1125-1256.

70. LOUP, Ep. 37, *Correspondance*, I, p. 160-5, au sujet de l'apport de la *sapientia* à la *respublica : ... eadem consilia ab ipso Domino ad utiles diriguntur effectus... Sapientem hic intelligimus, quem aut experientia docuit aut lectio erudivit aut inspiratio divina caeteris praetulit.* Cf. ci-dessous n. 84, pour les lettres 31, 46 de Loup.

71. J.L. NELSON, *The Annals of St Bertin* (cit. n. 67), (*pace* J.M. WALLACE-HADRILL, *A Carolingian*, p. 159).

72. J.L. NELSON, *Public Histories.*

73. ASSER, c. 106, p. 93.

74. Je tente de faire ressortir ce contraste dans « *A king across the sea* », p. 61-7.

75. J.L. NELSON, *Translating images of authority : the Christian Roman emperors in the Carolingian world*, dans *Images of Authority. Studies presented to J.M. Reynolds*, éd. M.M. MACKENZIE, Cambridge, 1989, p. 196-205.

76. J.L. NELSON, *Legislation and consensus in the reign of Charles the Bald*, dans *Ideal and Reality. Studies in Frankish and Anglo-Saxon Society presented to J.M. Wallace-Hadrill*, éd. P. WORMALD, Oxford, 1983, p. 202-27 (repris dans J.L. NELSON, *Politics*, ch. 5).

77. J.L. NELSON, *Dispute settlement in Carolingian West Francia*, dans *The Settlement of Disputes in Early Medieval Europe*, éd. W. DAVIES et P.J. FOURACRE, Cambridge, 1986, p. 45-64.

78. P. RICHÉ, *Charles*, p. 43-4 ; J.M. WALLACE-HADRILL, *A Carolingian*, p. 160 ; et surtout D. GANZ, *The debate on Predestination*, dans *Charles the Bald*, ch. 18.

79. *MGH, Capit.*, II, n° 266, p. 285-91.

80. *Ibid.*, p. 286, note * : les manuscrits 2-4 de Boretius dérivent d'un texte conservé à Reims, le manuscrit 5 d'un texte orléanais.

81. *Ibid., c.* 2.

82. *Legales sententiae sicut eas cognitas habent..., capitula utiles : Ibid., c.* 3 et 4.

83. Cf. J.L. NELSON, *Translating images of authority* (cit. n. 75), p. 199.

84. *Bono communi et publico certatim et unanimiter consulamus :* LOUP, Ep. 94, *Correspondance*, II, p. 102-107. Cf. Ep. 31 à Charles le Chauve, *ibid.*, I, p. 144-147, surtout p. 144 : *Communem utilitatem et oportunitatem omnium carissimam vobis omnes intellegant... ; Ep. 37, I, p. 160-165 : Tales quaerite qui publicam dilectionem...*

85. *Annales Fuldenses*, éd. F. KURZE, MGH, SS in us. schol. (1891), an 858, p. 49-50.

86. *MGH Capit.*, II, n° 273, c. 34, p. 326. Cf. J.L. NELSON, *Translating images of authority* (cit. n. 75), p. 199-201.

87. *Vita S. Odonis* c. 5 : *P.L.* 133, 45-6.

88. *Communis utilitas :* 2 *Macc*, 4,5 et 9,21. Artaxerxès gouvernant *ut reipublicae poscit utilitas : Est.* 16,9.

89. *P.L.* 125, 817-34. Voir J. DEVISSE, *Hincmar*, I, p. 54-9 ; S. TAEGER, *Zum « Ferculum Salomonis » Hinkmars von Reims*, dans *Deutsches Archiv* 33 (1977), p. 153-167.

90. *CT* 3, 9-11 (en réalité Hincmar ne commente que les v. 9 et 10) : *P.L.* 125, 819-20. J. DEVISSE, *Hincmar* (cit. n. 6), I, p. 54, n. 115, semble dater l'ouvrage entre 853 et 856.

91. *MGH, Epp.* VIII, i, n° 126, p. 63.

92. *MGH Epp.* VI, p. 242.

93. J'emprunte le titre de N. ELIAS (cf. trad. ang., *The Court Society,* Oxford, 1983). Mais je crois que cet auteur néglige un peu les précurseurs médiévaux des relations sociales qu'il a si bien décrites dans l'Ancien Régime français. Le problème des *comitatus* des guerriers affranchis de toute autorité est endémique aux temps carolingiens, comme aussi plus tard : voir les plaintes nombreuses des capitulaires : par ex. *MGH, Capit.* I, n° 18, c. 6 et 7, p. 43 (Pépin, 768) ; n° 75, p. 168 (Charlemagne, 804/ 811) ; n° 150, c. 16 et 17, p. 305 (Louis le Pieux, 823/825) ; *Capit.* II, n° 270, c. 9, p. 298 (Charles le Chauve, 860) ; n° 281, c. 19, p. 360 (Charles, 877). Il me paraît significatif que ce soit seulement après la mort de Charles, en 878, qu'Hincmar dans les *Annales de Saint-Bertin* raconte de véritables *werrae* dans la Francia de l'ouest : éd. cit., p. 222. Le point de départ de toute étude sur le sujet de la *guerre privée* face au pouvoir public dans le haut moyen âge doit être désormais S. WHITE, *Feuding and peacemaking in the Touraine around the year 1100,* dans *Traditio* 42 (1986), p. 195-263.

VIII

THE FRANKS, THE MARTYROLOGY OF USUARD, AND THE MARTYRS OF CORDOBA

The bodies of holy martyrs, which the Romans buried with fire, and mutilated by the sword, and tore apart by throwing them to wild beasts: these bodies the Franks have found, and enclosed in gold and precious stones.

FOR the author of the longer prologue to *Lex Salica*, writing in 763–4, in the reign of Pippin I, the first king of the Carolingian dynasty, the Franks' devotion to the martyrs was the secret of their success. It proved the strength of their Christian faith; it was at once the manifestation and the explanation of special divine favour. *Vivit qui Francos diligit Christus.* . . .[1]

The Franks had some justification for priding themselves on their special devotion to the cults of martyrs. Gregory of Tours, whom the Franks by the Carolingian period had come to see as the narrator of their history, also wrote in praise of martyrs.[2] That early, the feats of martyr saints were marked in Gaul by readings of *passiones* recounting their sufferings and deaths. Gregory somewhat disingenuously says that this was done to encourage the devotion of rustics.[3] But bishops, including Gregory himself, were enthusiastic devotees of martyr cults, especially of martyred bishops (since *passiones* continued a thriving genre in the seventh century not least because the activities of Frankish kings and nobles ensured a supply of new episcopal victims, it was not, in fact, only the

---

[1] 'Christ lives who loves the Franks . . .', *Lex Salica, 100-Titel Text*, prologue, *MGH.LNG*, IV, 2, ed. K. A. Eckhardt (Hanover, 1969), pp. 6–8.

[2] *In gloria martyrum* [and other hagiographical works], ed. B. Krusch, *MGH.SRM*, I, ii (Hanover, 1885), Eng. tr. R. van Dam (Liverpool, 1988), with an excellent introduction, esp. pp. 11–15, on Gregory's placing of martyrdom 'in the context of the ecclesiastical community'. For Gregory and his work in general, see G. de Nie, *Views from a Many-windowed Tower* (Amsterdam, 1987), and W. Goffart, *Narrators of Barbarian History* (Princeton, 1988), ch. 3.

[3] *In gloria martyrum*, c.63, p. 81, tr. van Dam, p. 87, '. . . mos namque erat hominum rusticorum ut sanctos dei quorum agones relegunt attentius venerentur.' On ways of hearing such stories and making spiritual use of them, see P. Brown, *The Cult of the Saints* (London, 1981), pp. 79–84.

Romans who made martyrs[4]) and of martyrs whose relics were housed in episcopal churches.[5] Frankish kings and nobles, as well as bishops, 'made' martyr cults in the other sense too: their acquisitiveness for relics was one aspect of a more general acquisitiveness. In his *Histories*, Gregory records how the Merovingian King Childebert I in 542 attacked Zaragoza and brought back the robe (*stola*) of St Vincent in triumph to Francia, founded the monastery of Saint-Germain-des-Prés and endowed it with relics, including Vincent's robe.[6] Monasteries patronized by the Frankish elite thus were natural centres for the production of martyrologies: it was probably between 615 and 629, the heyday of Merovingian power, that an expanded version of the so-called *Martyrologium Hieronymianum* was produced at Luxeuil, in Burgundy.[7]

Between about 838 and 855, no fewer than four substantial martyrologies—by Florus, Hrabanus, Wandalbert, and Ado—were produced, respectively, at Lyons, Mainz, Prüm, and Lyons again.[8] Neither the timing—the reigns of Louis the Pious and Lothar I—nor the locations were coincidental; any more than the production of the two great universal histories of the later Carolingian period in the same area was coincidental.[9] In the Frankish heartlands, called after 843 the Middle Kingdom, lay the religious foundations where a sense of Frankish identity was most strongly cultivated, and with it a sense that the Frankish realm was now the cultic centre of the Christian world. Thanks to massive transfers of relics into Francia in the reigns of Charlemagne and Louis the Pious, the Franks could now see themselves as the special custodians of the martyrs—and the martyrs as the special custodians of the Franks.[10] The

---

[4] For seventh-century *passiones* and their context, see P. J. Fouracre, 'Merovingian history and Merovingian hagiography', *PaP*, 127 (1990), pp. 3–38.

[5] See P. Brown, 'Relics and social status in the age of Gregory of Tours', in his collected essays, *Society and the Holy in Late Antiquity* (London, 1982), pp. 222–50.

[6] *Libri Historiarum X*, ed. B. Krusch and W. Levison, *MGH.SRM*, 1, 2nd edn (Hanover, 1937–51), III, c.29, pp. 125–6.

[7] Ed. G. Rossi and L. Duchesne, *Acta Sanctorum Bollandiana*, Nov. 2, 1 (Paris, 1894). Against Duchesne's attribution to Auxerre and the late sixth century, see B. Krusch, 'Nochmals die Afralegende und das Martyrologium Hieronymianum', *Mittheilungen des Instituts für oester-reichische Geschichtsforschung*, 21 (1900), pp. 1–27, at pp. 9–27. J. Dubois, *Les Martyrologes du Moyen Age latin* (Turnhout, 1978), p. 33, holds to Duchesne's views, but without mentioning the arguments of Krusch.

[8] On these, see W. Wattenbach, rev. W. Levison, *Deutschlands Geschichtsquellen im Mittelalter* [hereafter Wattenbach-Levison], 1 (Weimar, 1952), pp. 60–1; Dubois, *Les Martyrologes*, pp. 37–45; J. M. McCulloh, 'Historical Martyrologies in the Benedictine Cultural Tradition', in W. Lourdaux and D. Verhelst, eds, *Benedictine Culture 750–1050* (Louvain, 1983), pp. 114–31.

[9] H. Löwe in Wattenbach-Levison, 3 (Weimar, 1957), pp. 328–9.

[10] P. J. Geary, *Furta Sacra. Thefts of Relics in the Central Middle Ages* (Princeton, 1978, rev. edn, 1990). Cf. also M. Heinzelmann, *Translationsberichte und andere Quellen des Reliquienkultes*

The Martyrology of Usuard

political dimension was implicit in the imperial relic collection presided over by Charlemagne's sister at Chelles, with its carefully itemized pieces of martyrs from Italy, from southern and western Gaul, from Bavaria, Saxony, and Northumbria.[11] Imperial control was explicit in the decree of the Council of Mainz in 813 that no relics be authenticated without the say-so of the *princeps*;[12] and the propagandistic function of relic acquisition was especially clear in the years from 824 to 830, as Louis the Pious, Lothar, and the clerics who served (and sometimes tactfully admonished) them sought to reaffirm the special bond between the Franks and Rome.[13]

Usuard, monk of Saint-Germain-des-Prés, drew on all the martyrologies I have already mentioned (and also that of Bede) to produce one of his own—which was destined to become the most widely-diffused and influential martyrology of Western Christendom for the rest of the Middle Ages and beyond. Not all who drew on it acknowledged, or perhaps knew, that they were doing so. If all the later martyrologies derived the whole or in part from Usuard's were added up, they would, according to Usuard's editor, run to 'hundreds, even thousands of manuscripts'.[14] By cutting down on the wording of previous martyrologists, Usuard saved some space, so that, while still producing a relatively compact book, he could provide martyrs for every single day of the year, and brief biographical details for many of them. His field of vision spanned the universal Church, from Asia to Ireland and Scotland: though Usuard's sources had included Patrick and Bridget, his was the first continental martyrology (thanks probably to oral information from Irish monks) to contain entries for Fintan, Ciaran, Cainnach, and—last but certainly not least—Columba.[15]

(Turnhout, 1979), pp. 31–42, 94–9; and the useful list of no fewer than 74 items assembled by H. Fros, 'Liste des translations et inventions de l'époque carolingienne', *AnBoll*, 104 (1986), pp. 427–9.

[11] See J. Laporte, 'Reliques du Haut Moyen Age à Chelles', *Revue d'art et d'histoire de la Brie et du pays de Meaux*, 37 (1986), pp. 45–58.

[12] *MGH.L*, 3, *Concilia*, II, p. 272.

[13] See J. Fried, 'Ludwig der Fromme, das Papsttum und die fränkische Kirche', in P. Godman and R. Collins, eds, *Charlemagne's Heir. New Perspectives on the Reign of Louis the Pious* (Oxford, 1990), pp. 231–73, at p. 263.

[14] J. Dubois, *Le Martyrologe d'Usuard* (Brussels, 1965), p. 14; cf. ibid., p. 5, where Dubois stresses that Usuard's work was the 'essential link in the chain of martyrologies' leading from the Early Church to modern times. The Roman Martyrology produced in 1583, declared official by the pope in 1584, and (after successive revisions) still in use, was based on Usuard's Martyrology. See also for a concise account of Usuard's work, Dubois, *Les Martyrologes*, pp. 45–56.

[15] See Dubois, *Martyrologe*, p. 101; and for Usuard as abbreviator, pp. 105–10.

Clearly no further justification is needed for talking at this conference about the Martyrology of Usuard. But what about the immediate historical context of its production? It carries a preface, addressed to Charles the Bald, *dominus regum piissimus*, and *sapientissimus rex*: 'It should be understood [says Usuard] that I undertook this work through no *jeu d'esprit*, but rather, as was right, I obeyed your commands which as ever were directed to the welfare of the Catholic faithful.'[16] The work was dedicated to the King, because he had commissioned it. Should we take that literally? No, says Dom Dubois. 'Ce que nous savons du personnage de Charles le Chauve interdit de supposer qu'ait eu le moindre compétence pour apprécier le valeur et l'intérêt des martyrologes. . . .'[17] So the dedicatory preface reveals merely a *bon courtisan* making his pitch for patronage? Nevertheless, Dubois is clear that a copy of the work was presented to Charles—and that royal approval helps explain its exceptionally wide diffusion.[18] In what follows, I want to argue that Charles did indeed solicit the Martyrology of Usuard and that the commission makes sense in terms both of the work's general context, by reference to contemporary Frankish piety and political ideas (the two were of course inseparable), and of the work's specific context, by reference to Charles's, and Usuard's, interest in Spain and in the martyrs of Cordoba.

First, then, Charles was a plausible connoisseur of martyrologies. There was nothing perfunctory about his cultivation of martyr saints. Among earlier medieval rulers, Charles was exceptional in the intensity and range of his devotion and his grasp of its political uses. He had learned some lessons at his father's court, where Einhard glossed the significance of the arrival from Rome of the bones of SS Petrus and Marcellinus, and where Hilduin, in the 830s, explained the special potency of St Denis, 'the outstanding martyr'. As king, Charles would endow the monastery of Saint-Denis on an unprecedentedly lavish scale, instituting commemorative feasts for himself and his close kin.[19] His consecration as King of the

---

[16] Dubois, *Martyrologe*, p. 144, '. . . ut sciretur non me in hoc usum levitatis conamine, sed potius vestris, ut erat dignum, paruisse imperiis catholicorum fidelium solito consultentibus utilitati.'

[17] Dubois, *Martyrologe*, p. 38. Cf. the characteristically measured response of P. Riché, *Instruction et vie religieuse dans le Haut Moyen Age* (London, 1981), ch. 12, p. 41: 'ce jugement me paraît sévère.'

[18] Dubois, *Martyrologe*, pp. 17–18.

[19] I do not share Dubois' view, *Martyrologe*, pp. 118–19, that Usuard's treatment of St Denis, namely, the provision of two distinct feasts for the bishop of Athens (3 Oct.) and the bishop of Paris (9 Oct.), thus flouting the identification between the two made by Hilduin, argues against Charles as primary sponsor of the Martyrology's production and diffusion. As Dubois acknowledges, Saint-Germian and Saint-Denis were rival establishments (hence Usuard's

The Martyrology of Usuard

Franks took place in the Church of St Stephen the Protomartyr, at Metz. Hincmar, drawing this to the King's attention, and reminding him of his father's tribulations, struck a resonant chord: for Charles's personal piety, as reflected in his private prayer-book, centred on the likening of his own 'wounds' to Christ's, and on self-identification with the suffering David whose humiliation was a necessary route to salvation.[20] Over eighty per cent (122 out of 149) of the saints whose names appear in Charles's charters, because their churches were beneficiaries of his generosity, were martyrs listed in Usuard's Martyrology.[21] As for the personal acquaintance with the tradition of Frankish devotion to the martyrs, Charles very probably knew Gregory's work and (like his father) possessed a copy of *Lex Salica* (including the longer prologue), as, certainly, did leading members of the Frankish aristocracy.[22] If Charles wanted a martyrology, that was in line with his perception of the protective power of the martyrs and of the way martyr cults consolidated the bond between the Franks and their kings. Charles's concern had a further dimension. Previous martyrologies had been produced in the Middle Kingdom of his brother Lothar, and notably at the great centre of Lyons. Lothar died in 855. In commissioning Usuard not long after that date, Charles was staking his own claim to Lothar's inheritance as patron and as imperial head of the Carolingian house.

Even before the 850s, however, Charles had taken a keen interest in the politics of the Ebro valley region. It was dominated in the ninth century by a local *muwallad* (Muslim convert) family, the Banu Kasi, over whose successive leaders the Umayyad regime in Cordoba rarely managed to assert its control. As the long reign of the amir Abd al-Rahman II (822–52) drew to a close, the Banu Kasi were more often than not in rebellion. In

---

implicit rejection of new claims for St Denis). Charles successfully sought the benefits, and the services, of both—and celebrated Denis's feast on 9 October. Dubois' research on the manuscripts of the Martyrology shows that, in addition to the copy (plus dedication) presented to Charles, Usuard's 'original', Paris, BN, MS. lat. 13745 (without dedication), was kept at Saint-Germain, where revisions were entered (probably by Usuard himself) throughout the 860s. Dubois' argument that Usuard was already interested in martyrologies (and necrologies), and had been preparing materials for years before the late 850s seems very plausible, but strengthens, in my view, rather than weakens, the case for a royal commission to complete the work.

[20] For further references on Charles's piety, see J. L. Nelson, *Charles the Bald* (London, 1992), pp. 15, 85.

[21] Dubois, *Martyrologe*, pp. 139–40.

[22] See R. McKitterick, 'Charles the Bald and his library: the patronage of learning', *EHR*, 95 (1980), pp. 28–47; *The Carolingians and the Written Word* (Cambridge, 1989), pp. 60, 239–40, 246–9. Also Riché, *Instruction*, chs 7 and 8.

the 840s, the head of the family, Musa ibn Musa, lord of Tudela, sought an alliance with Charles: that is the probable explanation of the arrival of a Cordoban embassy at Rheims in 847 'to seek a peace with Charles'.[23] The next year, there was Cordoban backing for a rebellion in the Frankish-ruled Spanish March, which resulted in the expulsion from Barcelona of the governor whom Charles had appointed there. More serious still, the rebels included the count of Gascony, and, it seems, supported Charles's nephew and rival, Pippin, who until 849 had been a serious contender for the kingdom of Aquitaine. Only in 850 did Charles's men recover control of Barcelona.[24] It was at this point that the martyr movement began in Cordoba.

This movement certainly arose, in part, from the religious concerns of a small group of Cordoban Christians, whose activities were recorded by a local priest named Eulogius.[25] The growing appeal of Arab culture to members of the Christian elite, and the growing number of converts to Islam, seemed to require a drastic, and dramatic, response. Eulogius' friends involved themselves in public debate with Muslims, denounced the Prophet, and thus sought, and achieved, martyrdom. Between 850 and 857 there were forty-four Cordoban martyrs.

It has been suggested that 'the beginnings of the movement were largely accidental',[26] and previous commentators have dwelled (some more sensitively than others) on the religious aspects of the martyr movement.[27] It is, of course, written up by Eulogius almost entirely in

---

[23] *Annales de St Bertin*, ed. F. Grat, J. Vielliard, and S. Clémencet (Paris, 1964), p. 53, tr. J. L. Nelson, *The Annals of St-Bertin* (Manchester, 1991), p. 64. For the Banu Kasi, see R. J. H. Collins, *Early Medieval Spain, Unity in Diversity* (London, 1983), pp. 190–2, 233–4. On Musa ibn Musa, the essential study is C. Sanchez Albornoz, 'El tercer rey de España', *Cuadernos de Historia de España*, 49–50 (1969), pp. 5–49.

[24] See Nelson, *Charles the Bald*, p. 161. A key source on these events is a letter written by the Cordoban priest Eulogius to the bishop of Pamplona, ed. in J. Gil, *Corpus Scriptorum Muzarabicorum* [hereafter *CSM*], 2 vols (Madrid, 1973), 2, *Ep.* iii, pp. 497–503.

[25] Eulogius, *Memoriale Sanctorum*, ed. Gil, *CSM*, 2, pp. 366–459: Book i includes theological justification (aimed probably against local sceptics) for the cult of confessors and martyrs who 'were not dragged violently to martyrdom but came of their own accord' in protest at, for instance, the harsh treatment of church property; books ii and iii consist largely of the martyr acts proper. In the *Liber apologeticus martyrum*, ed. Gil, *CSM*, 2, pp. 475–95, written near the end of his life, Eulogius returned to the problem of voluntary martyrdom. For his *Documentum Martyriale*, see below, n. 28. E. P. Colbert, *The Martyrs of Cordoba* (Washington, 1962), offers an excellent discussion of the texts. See now also the remarkable study of R. B. Wolf, *Christian Martyrs in Muslim Spain* (Cambridge, 1988).

[26] Collins, *Early Medieval Spain*, p. 213.

[27] A. Cutler, 'The ninth-century Spanish Martyrs' Movement and the origins of Western Christian missions to the Muslims', *Muslim World*, 55 (1965), pp. 321–39, interestingly brings out eschatological aspects, and draws parallels with thirteenth-century Franciscans' ideas of

The Martyrology of Usuard

religious terms, as *acta martyrum*, with the characteristic traits of the genre: plenty of direct speech, circumstantial detail, military imagery, family drama, women.[28] At the same time, Eulogius addressed himself very seriously to the theological problem of voluntary martyrdom, and conscientiously explained away the absence of miracles associated with the martyrs' deaths.[29] But there are signs that the movement had a political context, and that that context involved the Franks. In 848, as the Cordoban embassy was returning (or had just returned) from Francia, Eulogius set off from Cordoba for Francia in search of his brothers. In a long letter recording his abortive journey (he could get no further than Zaragoza), Eulogius explained that his brothers had been exiled, apparently a short while before, and had fetched up in the East Frankish kingdom of Charles's brother and at that time close ally, Louis the German.[30] Exile smells of politics. From 850 to 852 Charles was involved in further intrigues with Musa ibn Musa. The alliance seems finally to have paid off when, thanks to Musa's pressure, the count of Gascony yielded to Charles and handed over Pippin of Aquitaine into captivity in Francia.[31] The next evidence for Frankish interest in Spain comes some five years later with the sending of a pair of monks from Saint-Germain-des-Prés to seek the body of St Vincent at Valencia.[32] On the way, they

---

mission. For a survey of the historiography and reflections on the martyrs' religious motives, see Wolf, *Christian Martyrs*, chs 3 and 9.

[28] Eulogius' *Documentum Martyriale*, ed. Gil, *CSM*, 2, pp. 459–75, was a treatise of encouragement specifically written for two women who sought martyrdom. It needs further study for what it suggests of the gender dimension to martyrdom and martyrology. Wolf, *Christian Martyrs*, pp. 65–7, cites relevant material, but neglects the dimension. It is not neglected, in the case of the rich later medieval evidence, by Miri Rubin, below, pp. 153–83.

[29] In the *Vita* written by his friend Paul Alvar soon after Eulogius' own martyrdom in 859, he is called *fauctor* [*sic*] *anelantissimus martirum*, c. 13, ed. Gil, *CSM*, 1, p. 338. Wolf, *Christian Martyrs*, pp. 77–104, rightly stresses the differences between the situation of the martyrs of Cordoba and those of the Early Church, and convincingly explains these in terms of divisions within the Cordoban Christian community: there was no collective sense of persecution to generate a receptive Christian 'audience'. (Cf. below, p. 76, and n. 44.) Wolf's concluding argument (pp. 107–19) that the Cordoban martyrdoms were provoked by profound anxieties about the preservation of Christian religious identity within Muslim society, is interestingly developed but at bottom less radical than he seems to claim. Less convincing (and unnecessary to that argument) is his contention that Eulogius, and the martyrs whose literary memorial he produced, had very different concerns. The *Documentum* is relevant here: see above, n. 28.

[30] *Ep.* iii, cc. 1, 6, ed. Gil, *CSM*, 2, pp. 497, 499–500. See also Paul Alvar, *Vita Eulogii*, c. 9, ed. Gil, *CSM*, 1, p. 335.

[31] Nelson, *Charles the Bald*, p. 162.

[32] Aimoin, *Translatio SS. Georgii, Aurelii et Nathaliae*, PL 115, cols 939–60. Aimoin, a monk of Saint-Germain-des-Prés, was Usuard's former teacher; Löwe, in Wattenbach-Levison, 4 (Weimar, 1974), p. 579.

learned that the body was no longer at Valencia (it had already been forcibly removed by the bishop of Zaragoza, who was keeping Vincent under an assumed name to deter other interested parties[33]). Instead, they were told, relics of new martyrs could be obtained in Cordoba.

One of those relic-seekers from Saint-Germain was Usuard; and the story of his Cordoban journey was recorded from his own account by his fellow monk Aimoin.[34] What it clearly shows (though this emerges less clearly from the retellings of twentieth-century hagiographers[35]) is the intimate involvement in the mission, from start to finish, of Charles the Bald. His *auctoritas* sent the two monks off,[36] and it surely lay behind their first destination—going to Spain from Paris by way of Beaune, in Burgundy, would otherwise have been a bit like heading for John o'Groats by way of Beachy Head. It happened that at Argilly, near Beaune, was the residence (*villa*) of Hunfrid, recently invested by Charles with lands and office in Burgundy and on the Spanish March;[37] also that Hunfrid had already been in contact with, indeed entered into a treaty (*foedus*) with, 'Abdiluvar', the leading man in Zaragoza, and equipped Usuard with a letter of recommendation to him. When the monks reached Zaragoza (having received more help *en route* at Barcelona from the local count, an appointee of Charles), an interpreter was available to translate Hunfrid's letter, and the local ruler 'although a barbarian faithfully obeyed his ally's command' and found the monks a group of travelling companions setting out for Cordoba—where they duly arrived on 17 March 858. Thanks to the help of the local bishop, they acquired the relics of three martyrs, George, Aurelius, and Natalie,[38] then they asked the bishop to parcel the relics and close them with his own seal 'and address them to King Charles'.[39] Returning via Zaragoza, where they were given letters for Hunfrid, and a safe-conduct, they again made for Hunfrid's *villa* in Burgundy, where they were joyfully received. Thence

---

[33] According to the slightly different version of this story by the same author, Aimoin, in the *Translatio Beati Vincentii*, PL 126, cols 1014–26, an Aquitanian monk's vision ensured that Vincent's relics were identified: they ended up in Aquitaine, at Castres (dep. Tarn): see Geary, *Furta Sacra*, pp. 61–2.

[34] See above, n. 30.

[35] B. de Gaiffier, 'Les Notices hispaniques dans le Martyrologe d'Usuard', *AnBoll*, 55 (1937), pp. 268–83; Dubois, *Martyrologe*, pp. 93–6, 128–32.

[36] *Translatio*, c. 1, PL 115, col. 941, and for the rest of the journey, see cc. 2–15, cols. 941–8.

[37] On Hunfrid's career, see further below, p. 79.

[38] Eulogius, *Memoriale Sanctorum*, II, c. x, ed. Gil, *CSM*, 2, pp. 416–30, describes these martyrdoms at length (Natalie, Aurelius' stalwart wife, is here called Sabigotho).

[39] PL 115, c. 11, col. 946, '. . . sub assignatione Karoli regis'.

The Martyrology of Usuard

they made it back to Francia,[40] where in due course they were received by the King:

> It is impossible for us to express how delighted the glorious King Charles was at the martyrs' arrival, when he had read over to himself the accounts of their passions. He was happy because Gaul had proved worthy during the period of his reign to receive such flowers . . . But he did not neglect to choose Mancio to go to Cordoba and search out on the spot the truth of what had happened. When Mancio came back, the king learned what had been omitted from the martyrs' deeds before and what was worth recording by memory or in writing.[41]

Given the genre of our information, it's not surprising that the religious aspect of these transactions takes centre stage. But the name Mancio hints at another kind of significance: this man can probably be identified with the Mancio who in the 860s was at Charles's court, along with other young nobles (they included several future bishops), and from 867 to 877 served as a royal notary.[42] The use of such a man as an emissary suggests a mission of some political importance, and that had surely been true of Usuard's mission too.

What were Charles's motives? He had had little choice over involvement in and across the Pyrenees. Once Pippin of Aquitaine had found support in that region, Charles was bound to look for counter-allies there. But the policy had a history. As a boy, Charles would have learned of successful Frankish interventions in Spain in Merovingian times; and he had his head stuffed full of his grandfather's exploits—including the story of the Roncesvalles campaign. No reader of Einhard (and Charles *was* a reader of Einhard) could fail to see the benefits to the Franks of plunder and tribute. After 843 Charles had only one frontier that seemed to offer any prospects of that sort—a Pyrenean frontier. What is only intermittently recorded by contemporary writers who aren't primarily interested

---

[40] Usuard's return is noted as a final entry under 858 in the *Annales de St Bertin*, ed. Grat, p. 79, tr. Nelson, p. 89.

[41] *Miracula* (book iii of the *Translatio*), c. xxviii, *PL* 115, col. 957. Mancio witnessed two fresh martyrdoms in Cordoba.

[42] I accept the identification with the Mancio who was one of the comrades of Radbod, future bishop of Utrecht, *Vita Radbodi Traiectensis episcopi*, *MGH.SS*, XV, p. 569. Here Mancio is said to have been the future bishop of Châlons-sur-Marne (893–908): see R. McKitterick, 'The palace school of Charles the Bald', in M. T. Gibson and J. L. Nelson, eds, *Charles the Bald. Court and Kingdom*, 2nd edn rev. (London, 1990), pp. 326–39, at p. 329. For Mancio as notary, see G. Tessier, *Receuil des actes de Charles II, le Chauve*, 3 vols (Paris, 1943–55), 3, pp. 78–9.

in these areas remote from Francia, can, in fact, be traced as a thread running through Charles's reign. He knew enough about the Umayyad regime in Cordoba to exploit its weaknesses, notably its lack of control in the Ebro valley. Conversely, the amir knew enough about Charles's tactics to be anxious to forestall his interventions—hence the rich gifts sent to Charles in 863 and 865.[43]

Now I am certainly not claiming that the Cordoban martyrs were some kind of fifth column. I do think, however, that the problems of the Umayyad regime were such that at least a faction of Spanish Christians saw sense in a resistance movement, and that the timing of their action was not fortuitous. In fact, Eulogius himself at one point suggests that political circumstances were part of the picture. He writes of 'rebellion in the provinces', of hostility against the amir Mohammed (852–86) on the part of his own people, because of his 'avarice and the tributes imposed on the Christians'.[44] Clearly Mohammed's regime in its early years looked distinctly shaky.[45] In his letter to Bishop Wiliesind of Pamplona, written c. 852, Eulogius compared his own sufferings 'under the wicked empire of the Arabs' to Wiliesind's enjoyment of 'the lordship of a Christian prince'.[46] Was the implicit aspiration here more than a pious hope? Still further north, in the land of the Franks, there may have been what seemed to Eulogius quite promising possibilities. After 849 Charles the Bald had sufficient authority in Aquitaine, and on the Spanish March, and sufficiently powerful agents in those areas, to intervene repeatedly across the Pyrenees, encouraging rebellion against Cordoba. In the longer term, Charles might have hoped to extract regular gifts from Cordoba or, at least, from the lords of the Ebro valley—a kind of *paria* system *avant la lettre*. No frontier offered better prospects. If Charles had such dreams, he was in good company: his father Louis the Pious had written to the

---

[43] *Annales de St Bertin*, 863, 865, ed. Grat, pp. 102, 124, tr. Nelson, pp. 110, 129: 'camels carrying couches and canopies'.

[44] Eulogius, *Memoriale Sanctorum*, III, cc. iv, v, pp. 441–3: 'Even the amir's concubines, so they say, hate him. . . . He also cut the soldiers' pay.' Eulogius saves his fiercest denunciations, though, for the Christian tax-farmers recruited by the amir: a significant comment on the prevalence of collaborationist attitudes among the local Christian elite. For Christians in the Cordoban bureaucracy, see Wolf, *Christian Martyrs*, pp. 11–14.

[45] The instability of the Cordoban regime in the ninth century is now penetratingly discussed by Wolf, *Christian Martyrs*, pp. 15–20, and by R. Fletcher, *Moorish Spain* (London, 1992), ch. 3. Though Wolf, p. 18, discusses the implications of an alliance between Toledans (perhaps including Christians and muwallads) and the Christian king of Asturias, Ordoño I, against Cordoba in 852–4, Frankish contacts are unmentioned in this context.

[46] *Ep.* iii, c. 9, ed. Gil, *CSM*, 2, p. 501. for the kingdom of Pamplona in the ninth century, see Collins, *Early Medieval Spain*, pp. 249–51.

The Martyrology of Usuard

leading men and the people of Merida in 826 in very similar circumstances: he sympathized with their subjection to unjust taxes—and encouraged them to resist. Further, Louis had seen the possibility of co-ordinating a Meridan rebellion with his own military efforts to quell unrest in the Spanish March: 'We shall send an army next summer to our March', he told the Meridans, 'and it will wait for you to tell it the right time to move forward.'[47] Only with hindsight can we dismiss all this as a chimera.

Usuard's mission represented, at one level, Charles's political response to the martyr movement: the encouragement of dissidents, the strengthening of a chain of command between the King's Frankish power-base and Frankish magnates down in the Languedoc and the south-west—who, in turn, had their own networks of intrigue and influence straddling the Pyrenean frontier. But Charles set his sights wider still: he would take responsibility for the *utilitas catholicorum fidelium*[48]—that is, of Latin Christians at large. Such concerns had already led Charles to commission a range of expert opinions on the burning theological issue of the 840s and 850s: Predestination. Uniquely among Carolingian rulers, Charles could appreciate both the doctrinal problem and its political implications—the threat to social order, to *princeps* as well as to *episcopus*.[49] His theologians believed him capable of understanding the 'mysteries of divine wisdom' (*divinae sapientiae mysteria*).[50] They expected him to act as arbiter.

In the 840s and 850s the *utilitas catholicorum fidelium* was also under threat beyond—but tantalizingly *just* beyond—the frontiers of Charles's share of the Frankish realm, in Spain.[51] In 847, according to the *Annals of St-Bertin*, 'all the Christians in that realm', threatened by persecution, sent Charles a tearful petition requesting his protection.[52] The author of the *Annals* at this point, Prudentius, Bishop of Troyes, was himself of Spanish

---

[47] Louis' letter, curiously neglected in recent historiography, was preserved among Einhard's letters in a unique manuscript, ed. K. Hampe, *MGH.Ep*, V, i (Berlin, 1898), pp. 115–16. Though the editor dates it '830 *in?*' Colbert, *Martyrs*, p. 134, more plausibly dates it to 826, and also notes that while Hampe rightly accepted the manuscript's 'Merida', earlier editors, incredulous at the idea of Frankish intervention in south-western Spain, emended to 'Zaragoza'.

[48] See above, n. 16.

[49] Hincmar, *Third Treatise on Predestination*, PL 125, col. 386.

[50] Ratramnus, *On Predestination*, PL 121, col. 13. The key study is D. Ganz, 'The Debate on Predestination', in Gibson and Nelson, eds, *Charles the Bald*, pp. 283–302.

[51] Cf. *Annales de St Bertin*, 843, ed. Grat, p. 45, tr. Nelson, p. 56: Charles's kingdom extended 'usque ad Hispaniam'.

[52] *Annales de St Bertin*, 847, ed. Grat, p. 54, tr. Nelson, p. 64, with n. 1 (where, however, it is wrongly suggested that the Cordoban martyr movement was already under way at this date).

parentage, and well-informed on Spanish affairs. We should take this information seriously (and perhaps no less seriously Prudentius' attribution of a role in the threatened persecution to a Frankish convert to Judaism, the former palatine clerk Bodo, who in 839 had established himself in Zaragoza[53]). Whether the activities of Eulogius and his friends were quite what Charles had had in mind is another question: living martyrs have minds of their own, which makes them hard for authorities (including those on their side) to control. By the late 850s it was a matter of naming and claiming.[54] If sponsoring Usuard's expedition promised political as well as spiritual benefits for Charles, so, too, did the commissioning of Usuard's Martyrology. Dom Dubois has been able to show that Usuard wrote the core of the work not long after his return from Spain,[55] and before he received news of Eulogius's martyrdom, which happened on 11 March 859,[56] while various scrapings-out and writings-in in Usuard's manuscript show successive additions through the 860s. The Martyrology's production can be set still more firmly in its historical frame. In 858 Charles faced the stiffest tests of his reign: he was campaigning against Northmen ensconced near Paris when, at the beginning of September, his realm was invaded by his brother Louis the German. At the turn of the year Charles overcame his enemies and achieved a kind of restoration, which he himself attributed to the intercession of martyr saints. His commission to Usuard, and his reception of the work, would fit well in the winter of 858–9 and the spring of 859 respectively. From now onwards Charles began very seriously to contem-

---

[53] *Annales de St Bertin*, 839, ed. Grat, pp. 27–8, tr. Nelson, p. 42. Bodo's ability to influence Cordoba is taken seriously by H. Löwe, 'Die Apostasie des Pfalzdiakons Bodo (838) und das Judentum der Chasaren', in G. Althoff et al., eds, *Person und Gemeinschaft im Mittelalter. Karl Schmid zum fünfundsechzigsten Geburtstag* (Sigmaringen, 1988), pp. 157–69, who points, illuminatingly, to a wider universe of relations between Jews, Muslims, and Christians, spanning the Black Sea (the Jewish kingdom of the Chasars) and the Mediterranean, within which Bodo's influence at Cordoba could become credible.

[54] The process whereby martyrs are recognized and appropriated is illuminatingly discussed in the contribution of Miri Rubin to the present volume, below, pp. 153–83, while Stuart Hall, above, pp. 2–3, points out the Early Church's difficulty in controlling living martyrs (but cf. Eulogius' *Documentum*, above, n. 28—were women easier, or less easy, than men for (male) 'namers' to control?).

[55] Usuard left Cordoba on 11 May 858, and finally arrived back to Esmans (where the community of Saint-Germain was in temporary residence) on 20 October 858; Aimoin, *Translatio*, c. 11, *Miracula*, III, c. 28, PL 115, cols 947, 957. See also above, n. 40.

[56] The date is given by Paul Alvar, *Vita Eulogii*, c. 15, ed. Gil, *CSM*, I, p. 340. Oddly, Eulogius' name is entered 'sur grattage' in Usuard's manuscript at 20 September: Dubois, *Martyrologe*, p. 306. Dubois, p. 96, discusses this discrepancy without finding any explanation. Could 20 September have been the date on which Usuard received the news?

The Martyrology of Usuard

plate the revival of a Frankish Empire which incorporated, and transcended, that of Rome.[57]

Usuard's Martyrology, like its predecessors, reflected the concerns of the Church universal. The persecutions of the early Christian past had, after all, affected every province of the Roman Empire. They had taken their toll in Italy: and it looks as if Hunfrid, who had kin in north-eastern Italy, gave Usuard the names of a group of Italian martyrs from that region by way of supplement to his Martyrology.[58] But of all those provinces, there was one whose saints found in Usuard's work *une place de choix*: that was Spain.[59] Usuard added in some cases to the information in earlier martyrologies; more significant, he added thirteen new entries on Spanish saints, such as Julian of Toledo and Isidore of Seville, on whom he had probably gained information during his visit in 858. Most striking of all, and quite certainly the result of Usuard's personal mission, were the commemorations of no fewer than thirty of the martyrs of Cordoba, on whose deaths Eulogius had been Usuard's key informant, and who finally included Eulogius himself, martyred only months after Usuard's visit to Spain.[60] I will give a single example of these new Spanish martyrs—I like to think Charles the Bald took a personal interest in this one, for the martyr's heavenly birthday was the king's earthly birthday:

13 June—the priest Fandila was beheaded and achieved martyrdom at Cordoba.[61]

---

[57] On the events of 858–9, see Nelson, *Charles the Bald*, pp. 185–93; and for Charles's political ideas, see Nelson, 'Translating images of authority: the Christian Roman emperors in the Carolingian world', in M. M. Mackenzie and C. Roueché, eds, *Images of Authority. Papers presented to Joyce Reynolds on the Occasion of her 70th Birthday* (Cambridge, 1989), pp. 194–205.

[58] As suggested by Dubois, *Martyrologe*, pp. 97–8, 121; and 'Le Martyrologe d'Usuard et le manuscrit de Fécamp', *AnBoll*, 985 (1977), pp. 43–71, at pp. 48–9, 57. This suggestion is strengthened by evidence recently signalled by U. Ludwig and K. Schmid, 'Hunfrid, Witagowo und Heimo in einem neuentdeckten Eintrag des Evangeliars von Cividale', in R. Härtel, ed., *Geschichte und ihre Quellen. Festschrift für F. Hausmann* (Munich, 1987), pp. 85–92, at pp. 90–2. (I am very grateful to Stuart Airlie for this reference.) Ludwig and Schmid follow Dubois in dating Hunfrid's 'contribution' to Usuard after 864, when Hunfrid, who had joined a rebellion against Charles, was expelled from the Spanish March and went to Italy (*Annales de Saint Bertin*, 864, ed. Grat, p. 112, tr. Nelson, p. 118). It seems to me more likely that Hunfrid supplied Usuard with the list of Italian martyrs in the early 860s as a gesture of devotion to Charles, thus as an expression of political ties through liturgical ones, *before* falling from favour. Hunfrid's Italian connections clearly pre-existed 864 and explain his flight to Italy rather than (or as well as) vice versa.

[59] Dubois, *Martyrologe*, p. 93.

[60] See above, n. 56.

[61] Dubois, *Martyrologe*, p. 246. The date was 853. Cf. Eulogius, *Memoriale Sanctorum*, ed. Gil, *CSM*, 2, pp. 444–5. See Wolf, *Christian Martyrs*, pp. 30, 115.

Charles the Bald had commanded Usuard to go through existing martyrologies and collect the feasts of the saints *in quandam unitatem*. That unity, in the minds of Charles and his Frankish contemporaries, embraced the Christians of Spain. A century after Pippin's prologue to *Lex Salica*, Charles, his sights set on an imperial title, could hope to reawaken and refocus the Franks' sense of mission through their special devotion to martyred saints. The interest of a Frankish king and would-be emperor, as well as the enterprise of a Frankish monk, ensured that the Cordoban martyrs found their place in the permanent liturgical memory of Latin Christendom. Those martyrs' fates probably helped to establish prejudices of lasting significance—to foreshadow the ending of attitudes that favoured *convivencia* in Spain; and to shape the new and distinctively bloody-minded vengefulness of the Christian West thereafter. In the eleventh and twelfth centuries there would be new *gesta Dei*, through *Franci* of a new kind who nevertheless thought of themselves as the lineal descendants of the Franks of old.[62] Oral literature had preserved the memory of Charlemagne and his paladins. Roland and Oliver and Turpin, recalled from the heroic age of martyr cultivators, were themselves recast as martyrs, and in Spain.[63] If the latter-day *Franci* who named and claimed them had Zaragoza and Cordoba ringing in their heads, *those* names also echoed through another lively medium of social memory: the Martyrology of Usuard.

---

[62] For *gesta Dei per Francos*, and for Urban II at Clermont allegedly appealing to his audience to emulate Charlemagne and Louis the Pious and the Franks, see J. Riley-Smith, *The First Crusade and the Idea of Crusading* (London, 1986), p. 25.

[63] For tales of Charlemagne and his paladins in the age of the Crusades and long after, see now J. Fentress and C. Wickham, *Social Memory* (Oxford, 1992), pp. 154–62, with the thought-provoking observation (among many), at p. 160, n. 11, that Ademar of Chabannes, writing in early eleventh-century south-western France, claimed that Charlemagne 'ruled Spain as far as Cordoba, which has a Rolandian ring to it'. The origins of the ideas of Crusade and *Reconquista* remain fruitful areas of research, not least because of their continuing resonance: see C. Morris's fine paper in the present volume, below, pp. 93–104, and F. Fernández-Armesto, 'The survival of the notion of *Reconquista* in late tenth- and eleventh-century León', in T. Reuter, ed., *Warriors and Churchmen in the High Middle Ages. Essays Presented to Karl Leyser* (London, 1992), pp. 123–44.

History-writing at the courts of Louis the Pious and Charles the Bald

"The barbarous and very ancient songs in which were sung the acts and deeds of the kings of old, he wrote down and committed to memory."[1] Thus, Einhard on Charlemagne. What Einhard does not tell us (though he surely knew all about this) is that annals were being kept at Charlemagne's court from the late eighth century onwards. This signalled a change in the meaning of the remembered past. Writing, and writing annals, meant different record-keepers, and the application of different models from Antiquity. Louis the Pious's hall at Ingelheim was adorned with themes from Orosius' Histories: "the royal hall gleamed with extensive art-work" wherein Cyrus, Ninus, Phalaris, Romulus and Remus, Hannibal and Alexander were complemented by Constantine, Theodosius, Charles Martel, Pippin and Charlemagne[2]. The man who commissioned those images knew how to read them, as he did the spiritual sense *in omnibus scripturis*. "He despised the poetic songs that he had learned in his youth."[3] Learned men — and palace clerks in particular — acquired a vested interest in keeping up, and keeping, the annalistic record. "No learned man doubts", wrote Ardo Smaragdus in his Life of Benedict of Aniane, "that it is the most ancient practice, habitual for kings from then to now, to have deeds and events written down in annals for posterity to learn about."[4] At Louis the Pious's court the bard was supplanted by the historian. Stories gave way to histories.

Historical writing wasn't new among the Franks. A line of historiographic tradition links Gregory of Tours, and Fredegar, via his continuators, to Carolingian chroniclers. But the line of tradition was a very thin one. Furthermore, though it touched those at court, it was not court-centred — until the Carolin-

---

[1] Einhard, Vita Karoli Magni, c. 29 (ed. Oswald Holder-Egger, MGH Scriptores rerum Germanicarum in usum scholarum, 1911) p. 33.

[2] Ermold the Black, In Honorem Hludowici Pii (ed. Edmond Faral, Poème sur Louis le Pieux, Paris 1964), ll. 2126—2163.

[3] Thegan, Gesta Hludowici imperatoris, c. 19 (ed. Georg-Heinrich Pertz, MGH Scriptores 2, 1829) p. 594.

[4] Ardo Smaragdus, Vita Benedicti abbatis Anianensis, prologue (ed. Georg Waitz, MGH Scriptores 15/1, 1887) p. 201.

gian period. And then, only really in the reigns — and at the courts — of Louis the Pious and Charles the Bald did the thin line become a thick cultural layer. This court-centredness has four implications worth noting. First the court was the school of princes: and since History's prime function was educational, this explains the production and the editing of historical works to educate princes and young rulers — Einhard, Freculf, Ermold, the Astronomer, Lupus, Walahfrid all belong here — and the survival of strings of historical works in manuscripts very probably made for Louis the Pious and Charles the Bald. The deeds of kings and their kin were the very stuff of history. After all, what did you find in the Biblical history-books? *Multi . . . seniores et seniorum parentes . . . Lege Regnorum et invenies plenius*[5]. Dhuoda addressed her fifteen-year-old son as he joined the retinue of Charles the Bald.

The second aspect is the very large role played by clergy — *clerici palatini, capellani*. Clerical tutors, often hand-in-glove with mothers, no doubt, asserted their claims as educational directors of princes and also of young nobles at court. The role of the prince's tutor became a metaphor for wise political guidance. Theodosius picked Arsenius to tutor his son: Wala the new Arsenius "tutored" the new young Caesar Augustus Lothar; Ermold "tutored" Pippin of Aquitaine; Walahfrid really did tutor the adolescent Charles the Bald (we can imagine them reading Einhard together). The civilising process, the process of courtization (I borrow the terms from Norbert Elias[6]) was thus also a transmission, and imposition, of the cultural values of the *clerici* onto the lay nobility. Among those values was the restoration of the Theodosian age: the signifiance of antique learning was to be realised anew, hence the social power of the learned, and of their literary production. A fullblown classical revival in a wide range of genres reflects all this. By the reign of Louis the Pious, the active participation of the lay nobility as consumers of the written word had multiplied the private as well as the public uses of literary production and expression. For the court was a competitive environment and a man needed all the help he could get. "Carolingian aristocrats knew how to value learned magicians as it [sic] valued learned chroniclers, holy men, astrologers, wandering Irish . . . and any other successful means of making their way . . .'"[7]

The third characteristic aspect of the ninth-century Carolingian court is the institutionalised political role of the nobility as counsellors. "The palace of a king is called such, not because of the materials it's built of, but because of the reasonable men who dwell therein.[8]" Saint-Simon alleged that Louis XIV's Versailles "served as the tool of a politics of despotism . . . [whereby] the highest nobles were defiled and humiliated'"[9]. Aachen, Ingelheim, Compiègne

---

[5] Dhuoda, Manuel pour mon fils, III, 8 (ed. Pierre Riché, Paris 1975) p. 168.

[6] The Court Society (trans. E. Jephcott, Oxford 1983) pp. 258—270; cf. idem, The Civilising Process (trans. E. Jephcott, Oxford 1982), ch. VIII.

[7] E. Peters, The Magician, the Witch and the Law (Philadelphia 1978) p. 26.

[8] Hincmar of Rheims, Letter sent to Louis the German on behalf of the bishops of the provinces of Rheims and Rouen ("the Quierzy Letter"), c. 5 (ed. Wilfried Hartmann, MGH Concilia 3, 1984) no. 41, p. 412.

[9] Cited in Elias, The Court Society p. 197.

were no Versailles. The fifteen-year old joining the retinue of Charles the Bald in 841 was told by his mother Dhuoda that he would find "magnates and counsellors gleaming at court" (*fulgentes in aula*). These were men to be cultivated, "for in a big house like that one, many discussions are carried on"[10]. "The Government of the Palace", a work that really frames my subject, shows the court (*palatium*) also as a governmental centre where personal and public coincided in the giving of counsel[11]. The *generalitas universorum maiorum* attended assemblies

> the more influential to frame counsel, the less important to hear that counsel and sometimes to deliberate on it and to confirm it, not because they are forced to do so, but from their own understanding and freely-expressed opinion[12].

The theme recurs in the Capitulary of Quierzy (877), where Charles the Bald, on the eve of his departure to Italy, tells his *fideles*, left behind to help Charles's son in the task of governing Francia, that they are "to attend assemblies on time and . . . each is to speak out as he thinks best"[13]. Political rivalries, played out through factions at court, and through rival courts — for from Louis the Pious's reign onwards several Carolingian courts existed simultaneously — are associated with, or represented in terms of, different policies.

This is where historical writing comes in: specifically contemporary history — deeds and events recorded more or less as they unfolded. This was what court consumers wanted. This is why historical writings multiplied, and included History. History took its place in a cultural repertoire. The Old Testament was crammed with it: *lege Regnorum* . . . The genre as transmitted by antiquity was distinct from panegyric, or satire (though it could partake of both). What distinguished history's teaching function was not just its purveying of private morals and exemplary conduct, but its direct reference to politics — to public life. Historical writing was intended to contribute to those *collationes* at the court, to the framing of counsel through debate, not just as (and not directly as) an expression of consensus, or collective self-representation, but as an instrument of sectional, even individual, interests. History was produced and consumed as a means of critique and contestation. It was the discourse of constructive criticism. But it presupposed a context, a shared frame of reference, a common perception of collective interests.

---

[10] Dhuoda, Manuel, p. 170: *In domo etenim magna ut est illa, collationes conferuntur multae.*

[11] De Ordine Palatii (edd. Thomas Gross and Rudolf Schieffer, MGH Fontes Iuris Germanici Antiqui 3, 2nd ed., 1980). The work as we have it is Hincmar's, incorporating an earlier work by Adalard of Corbie.

[12] De Ordine Palatii c. 29, pp. 84—85. Conversely, Paschasius Radbertus had denounced misgovernment in terms of the abandonment of right counsels: Epitaphium Arsenii II, c. 19 (ed. Ernst Dümmler, Abhandlungen der kaiserlichen Akademie der Wissenschaften zu Berlin, phil.-hist. Klasse, 1900) p. 90.

[13] MGH Capitularia II, no. 281, c. 22, p. 360: *Nullus in consilio tardus appareat; sed unusquisque, ut sibi melius visum fuerit, loquatur, et post omnium locutiones, quod melius visum fuerit, eligant.*

In 841—842, Nithard used that concept of *res publica* as a political weapon: specifically when criticising those who abused the public interest[14]. The term occurs most insistently in Book I, when Nithard wanted to draw attention to threats to the state during the reign of Louis the Pious: threats from Bernard of Septimania, from Lothar, and from all those who put private benefit before the common good. Nithard cast himself among the *participes secretorum* of Charles[15]. These were men with a mission to save the realm. History was written, then, not for personal development in private life, but to advance a cause — and at the same time a career — in public life. History writing was the special mode in which the learned participated in counsel: it was associated with, not alternative to, speaking, and speaking out.

And the audience? — other counsellors, who were to find in Histories a practical guide to action. Such concerns are expressed in prefaces. Freculf saw his task as arousing "some people's lazy minds", opposing useless leisure by energetic practice of writing and teaching. He hoped his work would be useful, he said. He dedicated the first of its two parts to the former chancellor Helisachar, perhaps to provide him with a stronger hand at court, and the second to the Empress Judith to help with her son's upbringing[16]. "Here as in a mirror . . . you will be able to see what should be done, and what should be avoided." Walahfrid explained that Thegan was "more effusive and more impassioned in speaking about certain opinions, noble and strong-minded man that he was"[17]. Freculf's subject-matter was the uncontentiously remote past — though even there he seemed to select some topical lessons of good rulership (which entailed patronage for good scholars) and bad rulership (the consequence of bad counsels); but Thegan wrote Louis the Pious's *gesta* while Louis himself was still alive; and though his grammar might be "von altem Schrot und Korn"[18], Thegan's subject-matter was absolutely topical, and aimed at the court constituency.

History's flourishing as a genre in the ninth century to some extent responded to the centripetal pull of courts; and the multiplication of courts partly explains the increased output of historical writing. Yet most history, clearly, was not actually produced in or at the palace. The court nevertheless had a sociological, not just a spatial, meaning[19]. A *consiliarius*, a *fidelis*, even

---

[14] Yves Sassier, L'utilisation d'un concept romain aux temps carolingiens: la res publica aux IXe et Xe siècles. Médiévales 15 (1988) pp. 17—29; Philippe Depreux, Nithard et la *Res Publica*: un regard sur le règne de Louis le Pieux. Médiévales 22—23 (1992) pp. 149—161.

[15] Nithard, Historiarum Libri IV (ed. Philippe Lauer, Paris 1926) II/5, p. 52. For *res publica*, and *publica utilitas*, see I, 1, 3, 4, pp. 4, 10; III, 2, p. 84; and IV, prologue, 1, 2, 6 and 7, pp. 116, 118, 142, 144.

[16] Freculf of Lisieux, Chronicon (Migne, PL 106) cols. 917—918, 1115—1116.

[17] Walahfrid, preface to Thegan, Gesta Hludowici, MGH Scriptores 2, p. 589.

[18] Walter Berschin, Biographie und Epochenstil im lateinischen Mittelalter, III. Karolingische Biographie, 750—920 n. Chr. (Quellen und Untersuchungen zur lateinischen Philologie des Mittelalters 10, 1991) p. 226.

[19] A point made with characteristic acuteness by Stuart Airlie, Bonds of Power and Bonds of Association in the Court Circle of Louis the Pious, in: Charlemagne's Heir. New Per-

when not at the palace, could be in touch with it and thinking about it. The court was a frame of mind. At assemblies, it acquired a physical frame as well. I have argued in earlier papers that a centrifugal force pulled away from the court in Charles the Bald's reign: in particular that after 842, Nithard abandoned the court; and that after c. 840, historical writing in the form of the "Annals of St-Bertin", the continuation of the "Royal Frankish Annals", tended to become private instead of public. A key argument was that criticism directed against Charles the Bald could not have been meant for his eyes[20]. I'm no longer so sure. In my last section, I want to review, and revise, this argument — and in fact to move on from an unreal public/private opposition, to argue that History could be court-orientated without being official history. History's critical yet reasoned and serious function distinguishes it from panegyric or satire. Does that make it less of a courtier's genre? The problem can be addressed from the opposite angle: what could a historian n o t write for a court audience? What were the limits of the sayable?

Einhard in his "Life of Charlemagne" certainly warned or criticised (depending on when you date it)[21] Louis the Pious. Heinz Löwe pointed out that Einhard was hardly flattering Louis when he wrote that Charlemagne's most outstanding proof of *pietas* was having his grandson Bernard succeed his defunct father Pippin of Italy[22]. Yet Louis had a copy of Einhard's work in his court library, and Einhard by an amazing balancing act (*mira libratio* — Walahfrid's phrase) also, miraculously (*quod maioris est miraculi* — the ironic Walahfrid again), kept in Louis's reign the high position he had had under Charlemagne[23]. Thegan inveighed against some of Louis's ecclesiastical patronage, and denounced, memorably, his favouring of the lowborn Ebbo: in such counsellors Louis believed more than he should[24]. Yet Thegan wrote, surely, to be read and relished at court, and, now that the hated Ebbo had fallen, by other counsellors.

The court was no monolith — and Louis the Pious was no Louis XIV. Nor, even, was Charles the Bald. He did occasionally say: Off with his head! But that was never, so far as we know, in response to a historian's criticism[25]. In fact, criticism surfaced in various genres of writing in Charles's reign: in the distinctly tutorial tone of one or two of Lupus's letters[26]; in Paschasius's *Epita-*

---

spectives on the Reign of Louis the Pious (814—840) (edd. Peter Godman and Roger Collins, Oxford 1990) pp. 191—204, at 193—196.

[20] Janet L. N e l s o n, Politics and Ritual in Early Medieval Europe (London 1986) pp. 181—192; 225—229.

[21] See now Matthew I n n e s and Rosamond M c K i t t e r i c k, "The writing of history", in: Carolingian Culture (ed. McKitterick, Cambridge 1993) pp. 204—208.

[22] Die Entstehungszeit der *Vita Karoli* Einhards. DA 39 (1983) pp. 85—103, at p. 102, n. 67.

[23] Walahfrid, prologue to Einhard, Vita Karoli, p. XXIX.

[24] Thegan, Gesta Hludowici, c. 20, p. 595.

[25] For examples of decapitation for treason, see Janet L. N e l s o n, Charles the Bald (London 1992) pp. 171, 212.

[26] Lupus of Ferrières, Correspondance (ed. Léon Levillain, 2 vols, Paris 1927—1935) nos. 31, 37, 46, 49, pp. 140—147, 160—165, 192—197, 202—209.

phium[27]; in Audradus's "Revelations"[28]; in Bishop Hildegar's "Life of Faro"[29]. All of these may have been seen by Charles. Nithard, commissioned by Charles to write up "the deeds done in your times"[30], never produced courtier's flattery. In Book IV his criticism of Charles is oblique: Count Adalard's abuse of the *res publica* is back-dated to Louis the Pious's reign[31]. But in criticising Louis, still more in harking back to the golden days of Charlemagne, Nithard did very effectively criticise Charles's hard times. Had Nithard retired from court when he wrote Book IV? Not necessarily. Could he ever have contemplated Charles as a reader? Perhaps yes. Why criticise Adalard so specifically unless you hope to diminish his influence? And perhaps Nithard's barbs stuck and festered: Adalard did, it seems, leave Charles's court within little more than a year of Nithard's verbal onslaught[32]. The manuscript tradition of Nithard's work is not quite as slim as I once asserted: there was apparently another manuscript, apart from Paris, BN lat 9768, and Hariulf implies that he read it at Gorze[33]. It's possible that Nithard by the time he completed his work intended it for another Carolingian's eyes: changed horses in mid-stream, as it's been plausibly argued the Astronomer did[34]. But Nithard may indeed have intended Charles himself to read his "Histories": MS Paris BN lat 9768 certainly got at some time to Soissons, and perhaps was already there in the early 860s when another of those clerical tutors, Wulfad abbot of St-Medard, could have used it, as he may well have used Einhard's "Life of Charlemagne", to educate Charles the Bald's son Carloman[35].

---

[27] See David Ganz, The *Epitaphium Arsenii* and the opposition to Louis the Pious, in: Charlemagne's Heir, pp. 537—550.

[28] Liber Revelationum (ed. Ludwig Traube, O Roma nobilis. Philologische Untersuchungen aus dem Mittelalter, Abhandlungen d. philosophisch-philol. Cl. d. Bayer. Akad. d. Wiss. 19/2, 1891) pp. 88—89.

[29] Hildegar, Vita Faronis, cc. 123—126 (ed. Bruno Krusch, MGH Scriptores rer. Merov. 5, 1910) pp. 200—203. I discuss this work briefly in "The Frankish World" (forthcoming). Hincmar's highly critical Visio Bernoldi was written after Charles' death: Migne PL 125, cols. 1115—1120; see Jean Devisse, Hincmar, archevêque de Reims, 845—882, 3 vols (Geneva 1975/6) vol. 2, pp. 821—824; and, more generally, Patrick Geary, Germanic tradition and royal ideology in the ninth century: the "visio Karoli Magni". Frühmittelalterliche Studien 21 (1987) pp. 274—294.

[30] Hist. I, prologue, p. 2: *"res temporibus vestris gestae".*

[31] Hist. IV, 6, p. 142.

[32] Nelson, Charles the Bald, p. 142, though suggesting a rather different explanation.

[33] Hariulf, Chronique de l'abbaye de Saint-Riquier III, 5 (ed. Ferdinand Lot, Paris 1894) p. 101, seems to have drawn on Nithard, Hist. IV, 5, p. 138. MS Vatican reg. lat. 235 contains the same passage, and came from St-Riquier: see Lot, ed. cit., pp. XXIII—XXVII. I am very grateful to David Ganz for drawing my attention to the significance of Hariulf's evidence, and for urging consideration of the possibility that a Carolingian might have been criticised to his face.

[34] Ernst Tremp, Die Überlieferung der Vita Hludowici imperatoris des Astronomus (1991) pp. 138—148.

[35] Lauer ed. cit., p. XV. For a St-Médard MS of Einhard's *Vita Karoli* and other historical works, see John Michael Wallace-Hadrill, Early Germanic Kingship in England and on the Continent (Oxford 1971) p. 128; Rosamond McKitterick, Charles the Bald (840—877) and his library: the patronage of learning. English Historical Review 95 (1980) pp. 28—47, at 32, n. 3. For Wulfad, see John Marenbon, Wulfad, Charles the Bald and John Scottus Eriugena, in: Charles the Bald. Court and Kingdom (edd. Margaret Gibson and Janet

I come, finally, to the "Annals of St-Bertin", which I have argued became an unofficial work after 844, and strictly for private perusal by the authors, Prudentius of Troyes, then Hincmar of Rheims, and their coteries[36]. Can this be wholly right? How then to explain entries like the 851 annal, which seems carefully constructed to gloss over Charles's humiliation at the battle of Jengland (August 851)? Or 858, which avoids explicit slating of Charles's performance at Oissel[37]? On the other hand, Prudentius does criticise his king, notably in repeating allegations that Charles paid the Slavs to attack Louis the German; and in denouncing Charles's treatment of Gottschalk[38]. Clearly, in 865, a copy of Prudentius's annals was in Charles's hands, the contents read and known by *plurimi*, a number of people[39]. Had the king been reading those pre-861 annals during their author's lifetime? Either way, Charles was clearly willing to tolerate a plurality of views, and the circulation at court of outright criticism of his own policies.

Hincmar, author of the "Annals of St-Bertin" for twenty years after 861, was Charles's counsellor and so, by definition, his occasional fierce critic. Hincmar was not always listened to by a king who had a mind of his own, and the option of seeking other counsellors. Hincmar in his Annals (after 861) shows Charles following "indispensable advice" when in 862 he organised defence against Vikings, or heeding "wiser counsels" when in 869 he moved swiftly to annex Lothar II's kingdom[40]. The rhythm of criticism in the Annals follows Hincmar's personal fortunes to some extent: he is bitter about the promotions of Wulfad and Ansegis[41], and about Charles's high-handed way with church property[42]. Annals were not the only medium Hincmar used for criticism: in 868 when his annalistic tone was on the whole distinctly more favourable to his king, he directed an extremely forthright critique in the *Pro Ecclesiae Libertatum Defensione*. He stood up to Charles when the irate king shouted at a bishop in public[43]. But Hincmar's most uncompromising criticism came in the Annals themselves. He wanted to express his disapproval of two royal actions that occurred in October 869. Charles's first wife died on 6 October. Within three days he had dispatched a special envoy to bring a new partner to court. Hincmar is extremely careful over these dates[44]. There is a parallel — but only one — later in the Annals. In 876, Hincmar detailed the chronology of

---

L. Nelson, 1st ed., British Archaeological Reports, International Series 101, Oxford 1981) pp. 375—383.

[36] Cf. above, n. 20.

[37] Annales de Saint-Bertin (ed. Félix Grat, Jeanne Vielliard and Suzanne Clémencet, Paris 1964) pp. 63, 78. Cf. my translation of these Annals (Manchester 1991) pp. 73, 87—88.

[38] Ed. Grat et al., pp. 68, 70; translation, pp. 77, 80.

[39] Hincmar to Archbishop Eigil of Sens (ed. Ernst Perels, MGH Epistolae 8/1, 1939) no. 187, pp. 194—195. See my comments in the introduction to my translation of the Annals, p. 10.

[40] Ed. Grat et al., pp. 88, 157; translation, pp. 98, 157.

[41] Ed. Grat et al., pp. 132—134 (866); p. 191 (876); translation, pp. 132—134, 191—192.

[42] Ed. Grat et al., p. 136; translation, p. 136.

[43] Migne, PL 125, cols. 1035—1070; and col. 1036 for Charles's anger.

[44] Ed. Grat et al., p. 167; translation, p. 164.

Charles's disastrous attempt to "plunder" his nephew of his inheritance: again the month was October, and the climactic date was the 8th, the battle of Andernach, where, in Hincmar's Biblically-inspired phrase, "the plunderers" — Charles and his men — "were themselves plundered". On the following day, 9 October, Hincmar notes, the empress learned of her husband's defeat[45]. In 869, and again in 876, Hincmar denounced the king's conduct in terms which the king himself could hardly mistake. For the critique employed a code — a Dionysian code — to which Charles was uniquely well-attuned. St Denis was Charles's patron-saint, to whom Charles, following in his father's footsteps, displayed lifelong devotion, and on whose patronage he relied especially in his later years[46]. St Denis's day was 9 October. In highlighting the commission of wrongdoing on those dates in October, Hincmar, surely, was writing for Charles himself. Hincmar was clear on what the king's priorities ought to be; and he took his task as counsellor seriously enough to risk Charles's wrath. In 875, he was nearly as explicitly critical in his circular letter, "Keeping Faith", as he had been in his 868 treatise on church property[47]. Given that he risked the king's wrath in these other "pièces d'occasion", given the exceptional importance he attached to the specific monitory function of History, it hardly seems likely (so I now think) that Hincmar wrote the "Annals of St-Bertin" as a private work only. Hincmar and Saint-Simon (to whom Levillain compared him)[48] were worlds apart: Hincmar as a thoroughly ninth-century figure saw History as counsel — counsel which therefore had to be given publicly, and directed at court and king. And Charles for his part appreciated that advice, even if painful, was of vital importance to the running of the realm. He was no autocrat, but rather a careful man-manager who genuinely governed by the counsel of the Franks. He had been brought up to read History, to treat it as guidance. History and practical politics alike impelled him to accept criticism and use it constructively, and to learn from his mistakes. Thus taught, Charles the Bald kept his head — which helps to explain why no critic ever, in the other sense, lost his.

[45] Ed. Grat et al., pp. 208—210; translation, pp. 196—198.

[46] See G. B r o w n , Politics and patronage at the abbey of St Denis (814—898): the rise of a royal patron saint (unpublished D. Phil. thesis, Oxford 1990) esp. pp. 330—410.

[47] De fide Carolo regi servanda (Migne PL 125) cols. 961—984, especially 979—980. See Nelson, Charles the Bald, pp. 239—240.

[48] Léon L e v i l l a i n , Introduction to the edition of the Annales de Saint-Bertin by Grat et al., p. XIV. Cf. my even more misleading comparison of Hincmar the annalist with Pepys the diarist: Politics and Ritual, p. 192.

X

LA MORT DE CHARLES LE CHAUVE

Démographie et pathologie

D'après les archéologues, l'espérance de vie au Moyen Âge était très courte, se situant autour de 28 ans pour les hommes. Pour la royauté et l'aristocratie, cependant, la durée de vie semble avoir été notablement plus longue[1]. Charles le Chauve mourut à l'âge de 54 ans et les sources concernant les trois précédentes générations de Carolingiens montrent que Charles avait effectivement toutes les chances d'atteindre ce que nous appellerions l'âge mûr[2]. Pépin le Bref vécut (probablement) jusqu'à 54 ans. Charlemagne (probablement) jusqu'à 66, mais son frère Carloman jusqu'à 20 seulement.

Pour la génération suivante, les fils de Charlemagne vécurent jusqu'à 42 ans (Pépin le Bossu), 38 ans (Charles), 33 ans (Pépin d'Italie) et 62 ans (Louis) ; ceux qui avaient embrassé la vie religieuse jusqu'à 54 ans (Drogon), plus de 40 ans (Hugues et Richbod). Un seul fils de Charlemagne (Lothaire) est mort en bas âge et la date de décès d'un autre (Thierry) n'est pas connue. La moyenne est de 44 ans. De toute cette descendance mâle, seulement deux fils périrent de mort violente.

Pour la génération des petits enfants de Charlemagne, les chiffres sont de 20 ans (Bernard), 44 ans (Nithard), plus de 47 ans (Arnulf), 60 ans (Pépin), 70 ans (Louis le Germanique), 67 ans (Louis, seul religieux), 54 ans (Charles). La moyenne est de 50 ans. De cette génération aussi, deux périrent de mort violente.

Mais la descendance mâle de Charles le Chauve présente un tableau tout autre : ses fils sont morts respectivement à 33 ans (Louis), 19 ans (Charles), 27 ans (Carloman), 14 ans (Lothaire), 10 ans pour les deux jumeaux (Drogon et Pépin) et moins d'un an pour deux autres enfants. La moyenne est de 14 ans. On peut dire que deux sont morts à la suite de violences. De ses huit fils, un seul survécut à Charles. L'espérance de vie des mâles caro-

---

1. À comparer avec les chiffres de G. DUBY, *Guerriers et Paysans, VIIIᵉ-XIᵉ siècles. Premier essor de l'économie européenne*, Paris, 1973 ; K. LEYSER, *Rule and Conflict in an Early Medieval Society : Ottonian Saxony*, Londres, 1979, p. 49-62, 92-95 ; H.W. GOETZ, *Leben im Mittelalter*, Darmstadt, 1987, p. 28.
2. Pour les chiffres suivants, voir les données de K.F. WERNER, « Die Nachkommen Karls des Grossen », dans W. BRAUNFELS dir., *Karl der Grosse. Lebenswerk und Nachleben*, t. 4, Düsseldorf, 1965, p. 442 sq. avec tableau généalogique, et ID., *Structures politiques du monde franc (VIᵉ-XIIᵉ siècles)*, Londres, 1979, chap. VII.

lingiens était donc très incertaine, davantage réduite par les maladies que par les hasards militaires.

Le rythme de vie d'un roi médiéval était épuisant. En été, quand l'activité militaire était intense, il fallait beaucoup voyager, le plus souvent à cheval, entre des étapes qui étaient souvent de courte durée. Les conditions de vie étaient spartiates. Les meilleures techniques de menuiserie ne protégeaient pas contre les courants d'air[3]. Il y avait certes des médecins, mais leur savoir n'offrait que peu de remèdes efficaces contre la maladie. Pour des raisons politiques, militaires et aussi religieuses, les rois carolingiens étaient souvent obligés d'aller en Italie. Les contemporains savaient que pour les Européens du nord les séjours prolongés en Italie présentaient des risques, surtout en été. C'est sans doute en raison de telles inquiétudes que les *primores* de Pépin le Bref se montrèrent si peu disposés à l'accompagner quand il partit en Italie en 756[4]. Si Charlemagne a choisi de commencer sa campagne lombarde en hiver malgré le difficile passage des Alpes, c'est peut-être qu'il craignait de voir se prolonger le siège de Pavie et redoutait les conséquences d'un long séjour estival. En 836-837, après que Lothaire eut été contraint de quitter l'Italie par son père, une épidémie fit périr tant de nobles francs que la cour de Louis le Pieux fut plongée dans le deuil[5]. Lothaire II mourut en Italie d'une épidémie semblable avec un grand nombre de ses hommes en juillet- août 869 ; « il voyait les cadavres de ses hommes s'entasser par centaines »[6].

Charles le Chauve ne pouvait pas ignorer le danger lorsqu'il s'apprêta à son tour à partir pour l'Italie à la fin de 875, bien que ce fût l'hiver (dès le mois de mars 876 il était reparti pour la *Francia*). On sait qu'il a souffert de maladie grave à quatre reprises dans sa vie : la première en été 858, la deuxième en automne 874, et la troisième et quatrième respectivement en juillet-août et en décembre 876. Il est possible qu'il ait contracté la malaria pendant son séjour italien de 875-876 ; en revanche on ignore tout de sa maladie de 874[7]. Il avait deux médecins dans son entourage ; le premier, Jean l'Irlandais, est signalé dans les textes du début de son règne ; le second, un Juif nommé Zédéchias, n'apparaît que vers la fin[8]. Il est intéressant de noter que Charles, au début des années 850, attribuait sa guérison d'un mal de dent aigu à l'intervention divine plutôt qu'à la médecine[9].

3. Pour l'ébénisterie du IXᵉ siècle, voir M. MACCARONE *et al.* dir., « La Cattedra lignea di S. Pietro in Vaticano », Atti della Pontificia Accademia Romana di Archeologia, ser. III, Memorie X, Cité du Vatican, 1971, surtout les articles de N. GABRIELLI, F. CORONA et E. HOLSTEIN ; P. RAHTZ, *The Saxon and Medieval Palaces at Cheddar*, Oxford, 1979, (British Archaeological Reports, British Series 65), p. 99-107, 374.

4. EGINHARD, *Vita Karoli*, ch. 6, O. HOLDER-EGGER éd., *MGH SS Rer. Germ.*, Hanovre, 1911, p. 8.

5. L'ASTRONOME, *Vita Hludovici Pii*, ch. 56, G. PERTZ éd., *MGH SS II*, Berlin, 1829, p. 624.

6. *Annales Bertiniani*, F. GRAT *et al.* éd, Paris, 1965 (désormais abrégé en *AB*), p. 156.

7. HEIRIC D'AUXERRE, *De Miraculis sancti Germani Autissiodorensis libri II*, *PL* 124 ; *AB*, p. 196-197, 206, 211.

8. G. TESSIER éd., *Recueil des Actes de Charles II le Chauve*, t.1, Paris, 1944, n° 75, p. 213 (Jean) ; *AB*, p. 216 (Sedechias).

9. TESSIER, *Recueil*, t. 1, n° 182, p. 484.

Mentalités

À l'historien moderne, Charles peut donner l'image d'un politicien pragmatique, et c'était en effet un aspect de son caractère. Il vivait cependant, tout comme ses contemporains, dans une forêt de symboles. Son livre de prières contenait des textes pénitentiels destinés à sa dévotion personnelle, et sur l'un des folios lui même était représenté prosterné devant le Christ en croix. Le David des Psaumes était un modèle particulièrement approprié à un roi qui souffrit beaucoup mais qui triompha de l'adversité. Sur la couverture du Psautier de Charles l'âme de David était représentée sous l'aspect d'un petit enfant qu'un ange tient sur les genoux[10]. Charles s'intéressait aux martyrs ; il commanda un martyrologe et envoya même un émissaire à Cordoue pour s'informer des martyrs contemporains (il y eut en effet dans l'Espagne des années 850 une vague de persécutions dont la nouvelle traversa aussitôt les Pyrénées) et pour acquérir des reliques[11]. Charles n'était pas dépourvu d'une certaine curiosité intellectuelle – par exemple, il cherchait à comprendre le sens d'un passage obscur du Cantique des cantiques, et à savoir quelles liturgies étaient utilisées à Ravenne[12]. C'est qu'il s'intéressait aux pratiques rituelles : il demanda en effet à Hincmar de composer des *ordines* de consécration pour sa fille Judith en 856 quand elle devint reine des Saxons de l'Ouest, puis pour sa femme Ermentrude en 866 (reine depuis près d'un quart de siècle, elle avait récemment perdu six de ses huit fils) et pour lui-même aussi, en 869, à l'occasion de l'acquisition de la Lotharingie. Il institua de son propre chef des cérémonies liturgiques, quand il fit célébrer par des moines et par le clergé toute une série d'anniversaires royaux, ce qui était sans précédent en Occident[13]. Plus qu'aucun autre roi du Haut Moyen Âge, il sut exploiter des relations de parentés symboliques ou spirituelles, surtout le parrainage, en tant que métaphores du pouvoir[14]. Jeune roi, il savait déjà utiliser le rituel aussi bien pour accabler ses ennemis en leur montrant la croix sur laquelle « ils avaient prêté les serments qu'ils avaient ensuite rompus », que pour rallier ses propres partisans autour d'un événement cérémoniel qu'il présentait comme un miracle – l'arrivée à temps pour Pâques 841 des *regalia* d'Aquitaine. La fête de Pâques était par dessus tout un temps de consolidation des liens entre le seigneur et ses hommes, par la distribution des largesses et par la célébration

---

10. R. DESHMAN, « The exalted servant : the ruler-theology of the prayer-book of Charles the Bald », *Viator*, t. 11, 1980, p. 385-417.
11. J. L. NELSON, « The Franks, the Martyrology of Usuard and the martyrs of Cordoba », *Studies in Church History*, t. 30, 1993, p. 67-80.
12. B. TAEGER, « Zum *Ferculum Salomonis* Hincmars von Reims », *Deutsches Archiv*, t. 33, 1977, p. 153-167 ; A. JACOB, « Une lettre de Charles le Chauve au clergé de Ravenne », *Revue d'Histoire Ecclésiastique*, t. 67, 1972, p. 409-422.
13. Voir M. ROUCHE, « Les repas de fête à l'époque carolingienne », dans D. MENJOT dir., *Manger et boire au Moyen Âge*, Actes du Colloque de Nice, (15-17 octobre 1982), t.1 : *Alimentation et société*, Nice, 1984, p. 265-296 ; O.G. OEXLE, « Mahl und Spende im mittelalterliche Totenkult », *Frühmittelalterliche Studien*, t. 18, 1984, p. 401-420 ; A. STOCLET, « "Dies unctionis". A note on the anniversaries of royal inaugurations in the Carolingian period », *Frühmittelalterliche Studien*, t. 20, 1986, p. 541-548 ; et surtout N. STAUBACH, *Das Herrscherbild Karls des Kahlen*, Münster, 1982 ; ID., *Rex Christianus. Hofkultur und Herrschaftspropaganda im Reich Karls des Kahlen*, Teil II : *Die Grundlegung der « religion royale »*, Cologne, 1993.
14. A. ANGENENDT, *Kaiserherrschaft und Königstaufe. Kaiser, Könige und Päpste als geistliche Patrone*, Berlin, 1984 ; J.M. SMITH, *Province and Empire. Brittany and the Carolingians*, Cambridge, 1992, p. 118-15.

communautaire de la liturgie[15]. Soucieux de présenter une image favorable de la royauté, Charles la fit illustrer par des artistes et des savants. Car plus que d'autres souverains de son temps il aimait de telles représentations. Parmi les motifs sculptés sur les plaques d'ivoire qui décorent son trône, se trouve un portrait du roi couronné, tenant sceptre et globe, et entouré d'anges portant des couronnes[16]. Charles se présentait ainsi comme *rex christianissimus*.

Lorsqu'il devint empereur en 875, Charles affina le rituel. Il fit chanter des laudes, en son honneur et en celui de l'impératrice, par les évêques rassemblés au conseil de Ponthion en 876[17]. D'après des Annales tenues par un Franc de l'est hostile à Charles, « il adopta des vêtures nouvelles et insolites : car il allait à l'église le dimanche et les jours de fête vêtu d'une dalmatique qui lui tombait aux chevilles, portant l'épée à la ceinture, la tête enveloppée d'un voile de soie surmonté d'un diadème. Car, méprisant les coutumes des rois francs, il préférait les gloires de la Grèce »[18]. Mais Charles n'avait pas perdu la tête. Dans le même temps il créait de lui-même une autre image, celle d'un chef dialoguant avec son peuple, « devisant avec les *minores* familièrement, écoutant leur doléances »[19]. Jusqu'à la fin Charles garda la maîtrise des deux registres : autorité et consensus.

Memento mori

L'Église au IXᵉ siècle encourageait ses fidèles à ne pas oublier que la vie est fugitive et que la mort est toujours présente[20]. Il se peut que Charles ait ressassé le récit de la mort de son père relaté dans un ouvrage qui lui avait sans doute été dédié : la vie de Louis le Pieux rédigée par l'Astronome. L'empereur y est couché sur son lit de mort en proie à la terreur : « il hurlait dans sa langue maternelle, "Hutz, hutz" – comme s'il voulait chasser les mauvais esprits »[21]. Trente-quatre ans plus tard, Louis le Germanique, demi-frère de Charles, « une nuit, vit en rêve leur père l'empereur Louis qui, plongé dans la plus grande détresse, lui adressait ces paroles en latin : "Je t'implore par notre Seigneur Jésus Christ et par la Sainte Trinité de me délivrer de ces tourments dont je pâtis pour que je puisse enfin atteindre la vie éternelle" »[22]. Le secours ne pouvait venir que des prières des moines, et Louis le Germanique, « envoya [donc] des lettres à tous les monastères... leur demandant d'urgence d'intervenir par leur prières auprès du Seigneur pour libérer une

---

15. Nithard, *Histoire des fils de Louis le Pieux*, II, 6, 8, P. Lauer éd., Paris, 1926, p. 56, 60 ; voir J.L.Nelson, *The Frankish World*, Londres, 1996, p. 85-6.

16. L. Nees, « Cathedra Petri », dans M.T. Gibson et J.L. Nelson dir., *Charles the Bald. Court and Kingdom*, Aldershot, 1990, p. 340-7, à la p. 345.

17. *AB*, p. 205.

18. *Annales Fuldenses*, F. Kurze éd., *MGH SS Rer. Germ.*, Hanovre, 1891 (désormais abrégés en *AF*), p. 86.

19. *De Ordine Palatii*, c. 35. Cf. J.L. Nelson, *Charles le Chauve*, trad. française, Paris, 1994, p. 66-70, 268-71.

20. M. McLaughlin, *Consorting with Saints. Prayer for the Dead in Early Medieval France*, Ithaca N.Y., 1994.

21. L'Astronome, *Vita Hludovici, op. cit.*, p. 648.

22. *AF*, 874, p. 82.

âme tourmentée »[23]. Un des destinataires de cette lettre était le conseiller de Charles, Hincmar archevêque de Reims[24], celui-là même sans doute qui lui avait annoncé le sort douloureux de son père dans l'autre monde. Hincmar n'arrêtait pas d'avertir Charles que l'âme après la mort se trouve « nue et seule, sans femme ni enfant, sans le confort ni la chaleur des proches et des vassaux »[25]. Comme son demi-frère Louis le Germanique, Charles ne manqua pas de solliciter l'intercession monastique.

Par ailleurs Charles vouait une grande dévotion à saint Martin, le patron ancestral des Francs et aussi celui de sa mère, Judith[26]. Il révérait aussi saint Germain d'Auxerre ; ce fut vers lui que Charles se tourna pour demander son intercession quand éclata la crise de l'hiver 858-859, puisqu'il ne pouvait pas se rendre au sanctuaire de saint Denis qu'il considérait comme son patron[27] et que son père lui avait enseigné à vénérer. Charles hérita de lui les services d'Hincmar, moine de Saint-Denis, qui le poursuivit de ses conseils tout au long de sa vie. Charles manifesta en de nombreuses occasions sa dévotion pour Denis, qui était honoré comme patron du royaume des Francs et à qui Charles devait vouer un culte *ex officio*. Mais Charles éprouvait aussi sans aucun doute une dévotion toute personnelle à son égard. Depuis son jeune âge il avait fait le vœu de protéger les reliques du saint des ravages des Vikings, fût-ce au prix de sa vie[28]. Plus tard, il se rendait volontiers à la tombe du saint, surtout à Pâques quand il le pouvait. On comprend dès lors qu'il ait choisi Saint-Denis pour sa sépulture.

Car, comme un nombre croissant de ses contemporains laïcs, Charles tenait à prendre ses dispositions pour ses propres funérailles et les commémorations. Le 19 septembre 862, il fit don à Saint-Denis d'une *villa* (à Senlis près de Paris), « pour le repos des âmes de feu notre seigneur et père l'empereur Louis et de notre mère l'impératrice Judith, et de la nôtre ». Les revenus de cette propriété étaient destinés à l'éclairage de l'église, à cinq fêtes offertes à la communauté, et à l'assistance aux pauvres. Les fêtes comportaient des banquets en commémoration de l'anniversaire de Charles (13 juin) ; du jour de son sacre (6 juin) ; du jour où, en 859, il avait repris en mains le royaume (15 janvier, date à remplacer ultérieurement par celle de son enterrement) ; du jour de l'anniversaire de mariage de Charles et d'Ermentrude (13 décembre) et de l'anniversaire de naissance d'Ermentrude (27 septembre, date à remplacer le moment venu par celle de son enterrement). Les frères devaient réciter quotidiennement cinq psaumes du vivant et après la mort de Charles, devant l'autel appelé le Trésor, « où sera notre sépulture, si Dieu le veut» *(ubi sepulturam nostram, si ita Deus voluerit, disposuimus)* ; de plus un prêtre devait célébrer tous les jours la messe pour Charles,

23. *Ibid.*, voir P. E.DUTTON, *The Politics of Dreaming in the Carolingian Empire*, Nebraska, 1994, p. 219-24.
24. FLODOARD, *Historia Remensis ecclesiae* III, 20, I. HELLER et G. WAITZ éd., *MGH SS*, 13, p. 513 ; cf. *ibid.* III, 18, p. 510.
25. HINCMAR, *Épître de Quierzy*, novembre 858, W. HARTMANN éd., *MGH Conc. III*, Hanovre, 1984, n° 41, c. 4 ; cf. Hincmar à Charles le Chauve, E. PERELS éd., *MGH Ep., VIII*, Berlin, 1939, n° 126, p. 64.
26. TESSIER, *Recueil*, t. 1, n° 61-63, p. 173-184, n° 80, p. 223-226, n° 167, p. 438-442 ; t. 2, n° 239, p. 32-41, n° 240, p. 41-45, n° 307, p. 179-181.
27. TESSIER, *Recueil*, t. 1, n° 200, p. 511-512 ; HEIRIC, *Ex Miraculis S. Germani*, II, c.102, *PL* 124, col. 1255 ; G. BROWN, « Politics and patronage at the Abbey of St. Denis (814-898) : the rise of a royal patron saint », thèse dactylographiée, Oxford, 1990, p. 330-410.
28. *Translatio Sancti Germani Parisiensis, Analecta Bollandiana*, t. 2, 1883, c. 12.

et une lampe devait brûler devant l'autel, « pour que par les mérites des saints et les prières ferventes des frères, une lumière brille éternellement pour nous »[29]. L'absence de dispositions concernant les descendants de Charles, surtout le(s) héritier(s) présomptif(s), peut surprendre. Mais aux IXe et Xe siècles des dispositions comparables à celles de Charles étaient souvent « rétrospectives », c'est-à-dire qu'elles étaient destinées aux ascendants plutôt qu'aux descendants[30].

Une deuxième série de dispositions, datant du 27 mars 875, concernait en premier lieu les célébrations commémorant la mort de Charles, celle de ses enfants et d'autres personnes. Cette charte précise que sept lampes doivent brûler à perpétuité devant l'autel de la Trinité, « derrière lequel nous souhaitons être ensevelis après avoir échappé aux lois humaines » *(post quod nos humanis solutum legibus sepeliri obtamus)*. Les lampes sont destinées au père de Charles, à sa mère, à lui-même, à sa première femme Ermentrude, à sa seconde (et présente) femme Richilde, et à toute sa progéniture vivante ou décédée, à Boson et Guy ainsi qu'à « tous les autres familiers de notre maison que leur grande fidélité nous a rendus particulièrement chers » *(reliqui familiares nostri quos maxima fidelitatis devotio nobis propinquiores effecit)*. D'autres dispositions encore prévoient quinze lampes pour l'éclairage du réfectoire, un banquet mensuel pour les moines, un banquet annuel pour commémorer la mort de Charles, de Richilde et de Boson (son frère), enfin le vêtement et la nourriture pour ceux de ses *familiares* qui choisiraient de se retirer à Saint-Denis[31]. Il a peut-être donné à l'église une antique baignoire romaine en marbre rouge qui devait lui servir de sarcophage et qui servit sans doute par la suite de fonts baptismaux[32]. Peut-être même cette baignoire avait-elle déjà servi de fonts baptismaux avant son acquisition par Charles ; s'il en est ainsi, cet objet pourrait renvoyer symboliquement à l'empire et à la renaissance. Il est possible que Charles ait ramené d'Italie cet objet magnifique, qu'il plaça à Saint-Denis au retour de sa première visite à Rome pour son couronnement, en 875-876. La tombe, illuminée à perpétuité, devait attirer tous les regards. De plus sa dotation était si somptueuse que Charles pouvait être sûr d'être commémoré pendant de longs siècles, et de jouir d'une réputation enviable à Saint-Denis.

Le contexte politique de 877

Si le premier voyage de Charles en Italie en 875-876 lui valut la couronne impériale, il fut en revanche désastreux pour le royaume de Francie occidentale puisqu'il provoqua (et permit) l'incursion de son demi-frère Louis le Germanique, dont les hommes mirent à sac la province de Reims[33]. L'absence de Charles avait donné lieu aux critiques violentes, non seulement

29. TESSIER, *Recueil, op. cit.*, t. 2, n° 246, p. 53-56.
30. On se souviendra aussi que les deux fils aînés de Charles s'étaient soulevés contre leur père en 862.
31. TESSIER, *Recueil, op. cit.*, t. 2, n° 379, p. 347-350.
32. B. DE MONTESQUIOU-FÉZENSAC, « Le tombeau de Charles le Chauve à Saint-Denis », *Bulletin de la Société des Antiquaires de France*, 1963, p. 84-88 ; A. ERLANDE-BRANDENBOURG, *Le roi est mort. Étude sur les funérailles, les sépultures et les tombeaux des rois de France jusqu'à la fin du XIIIe siècle*, Paris/Genève, 1975, p. 39 avec fig. 31.
33. *AB*, p. 199.

d'Hincmar, mais aussi du peuple, selon l'archevêque[34]. « Si Dieu le ramène sain et sauf, écrit Hincmar, peut-être Charles se ravisera-t-il et reconnaîtra-t-il qu'il faut donner la priorité à son royaume. » Les critiques d'Hincmar ne furent évidemment pas du goût de Charles, qui alla peut-être jusqu'à le soupçonner de déloyauté. En 877, à la veille du départ pour son deuxième voyage en Italie, Charles choisit d'omettre le nom d'Hincmar sur la liste des hommes de confiance chargés d'aider et de conseiller son fils Louis pendant son absence. Toutefois Charles prit soin de s'assurer qu'il n'y aurait pas de répétition du désastre de 875. Au mois de juin, l'assemblée de Quierzy avait décidé de prendre les mesures défensives qui s'imposaient, et les nobles consentirent à leur application, surtout sur le front de l'est[35]. À la fin juin, « emmenant avec lui sa femme (Richilde) et une très grande quantité d'or, d'argent, de chevaux et d'autres meubles », Charles prit le chemin de l'Italie[36].

Mais Charles ne pouvait ignorer les risques qu'il prenait en quittant son royaume. Il prit soin d'assurer la situation économique de sa femme Richilde (qui n'était pas, on s'en souvient, la mère de Louis), en prenant des dispositions pour le cas où elle lui survivrait, sage précaution pour assurer l'avenir d'une veuve qui n'aurait peut-être pas de progéniture mâle[37]. Il donna aussi des instructions concernant les fidèles qui pourraient après sa mort choisir de se retirer du monde pour se consacrer à sa mémoire[38]. Il avait recommandé avec insistance à ses exécuteurs testamentaires (*eleemosynarii*, dont Hincmar) de respecter les dispositions qui avaient été prises auparavant : les livres contenus « dans [son] trésor » devaient être partagés entre Saint-Denis, le palais-église de Compiègne et son fils Louis[39]. Il montrait du mordant et une bonne dose d'ambiguïté en déclarant : « il faut décider quelle partie de l'empire reviendra à notre fils si notre mort advient ; et s'il plaisait à Dieu de nous donner un autre fils, quelle partie doit revenir à ce dernier. Et si l'un de nos neveux se montrait digne, [nous en déciderions] en fonction de ce qui nous semble bon, à nous ou à ceux qui sont partie prenante de cette décision ». Charles laissait donc Louis dans une position précaire, et d'autres documents aussi témoignent du peu d'affection qu'il portait à son unique fils survivant, de sa méfiance envers lui, et de son souci de le placer sous surveillance pendant qu'il partirait « au service de Dieu et de ses saints »[40].

D'autres passages encore du capitulaire de Quierzy montrent que Charles avait bon espoir de rentrer sain et sauf d'Italie, et qu'il pensait sans cesse à son retour. Dans le cas où des *honores* resteraient vacants avant son retour, il avait prévu des dispositions provisoires[41]. Ceux de ses fidèles qu'il avait laissés en Francie devaient garder le contact avec lui en dépêchant régulièrement des messagers « à cheval ou à pied *(cursores pedites)*, pour le tenir au courant de tous les événements qui adviendraient dans le royaume [de

34. HINCMAR, *De fide Carlo regi servanda*, PL 125, col. 979-980.
35. *Capitulaire de Quierzy*, A. BORETIUS éd., *MGH Capit.*, II, n° 281, c. 15, p. 359.
36. *AB*, p. 200.
37. *Capitulaire de Quierzy*, MGH Capit., II, n° 281, c. 5, p. 357 cf. c. 6, au sujet des filles de Charles, et surtout sa *parvula filia*, Rothild.
38. *Ibid.*, c. 10, p. 358.
39. *Ibid.*, c. 12-13, p. 358-359.
40. *Ibid.*, cc. 12-15, 21-22, 25, 32-33, p. 359-361.
41. *Ibid.*, c. 8, p. 358.

Francia] et dont il n'aurait pas eu connaissance »[42]. Surtout, sachant d'expérience que la fausse nouvelle de la mort du roi pouvait se répandre, il les mit en garde : « si par malchance la nouvelle de ma mort parvenait aux oreilles de nos *fideles*, il ne faut pas la croire [trop] facilement »[43]. Plus révélateur encore est l'ordre intimé à Louis de se tenir prêt : « quand avec l'aide de Dieu nous serons de retour, il devra être prêt à partir pour Rome et là il devra œuvrer au service de Dieu et de ses apôtres aussi longtemps qu'il sera nécessaire, et se faire couronner roi si Dieu le veut »[44]. Ainsi il est clair que Charles avait la ferme intention de régner comme empereur en Francie et d'y résider, comme l'avait fait son propre père, tandis que Louis deviendrait roi d'Italie, et y demeurerait comme l'avait fait le plus souvent Lothaire, le frère de Charles, entre 820 et 830[45]. À propos des fonctions respectives du père et du fils, Charles suggère deux rôles militaires distincts, l'un dévolu au roi « jeune » et l'autre au roi « vieux ». Sans doute Charles pensait-il à sa propre jeunesse lorsqu'il recommanda : « puisque, grâce à Dieu, notre fils est un homme jeune, il ne devrait pas imposer de trop lourds services à tous nos hommes fidèles ; il devrait au contraire, comme nous l'avons souvent fait dans le passé, choisir avec l'aide de Dieu parmi tous nos *fideles* un [petit contingent] d'hommes vigoureux pour l'accompagner et puis il devrait attaquer nos ennemis par surprise (*inimicis nostris insperate superveniat*) et les frapper de terreur par force virile »[46]. *Viriliter perterrere*, voilà la technique militaire appropriée aux jeunes. Il était sous-entendu que Charles lui-même aurait utilisé des forces plus puissantes et les tactiques plus réfléchies de l'homme mûr. Le ton ici n'est pas vraiment nostalgique mais un rien condescendant. Charles savait pertinemment que la politique italienne à laquelle il destinait Louis n'était qu'un leurre : son but en 877 n'était que de colmater quelques brèches ; il laissait les vrais problèmes à son fils.

D'après Hincmar de Reims, Charles se trompait sur la situation politique en Francie. Les renforts qu'il attendait pendant sa campagne italienne ne vinrent jamais et un groupe de ses *magnates* jusque-là les plus loyaux – dont Boson, frère de la reine Richilde – fomentèrent une conspiration contre lui[47]. Mais, pour des raisons déjà évoquées, il faut prendre le témoignage d'Hincmar avec prudence. Aucune autre source contemporaine ne mentionne un complot, et seul l'auteur des *Annales de Saint-Vaast* affirme que Charles partit en Italie « contre la volonté de ses hommes »[48]. Et même s'il y eut un complot, Hincmar de toute évidence en exagère l'importance et déplace ses motivations. Car, comme il le laisse entendre lui-même, les comploteurs s'inquiétaient en premier lieu de l'absence de Charles et souhaitaient le ramener en Francie aussi vite que possible parce qu'ils se méfiaient de Louis (qui, on se souvient, n'était pas le neveu de Boson). Sans les renforts escomptés,

---

42. *Ibid.*, c. 25, p. 360.
43. *Ibid.*, c. 11, p. 358.
44. *Ibid.*, c. 15, p. 359.
45. J. JARNUT, « Ludwig der Fromme, Lothar I, und das *Regnum Italiae* », dans P. GODMAN et R. COLLINS dir., *Charlemagne's Heir. New Perspectives on the Reign of Louis the Pious*, Oxford, 1990, p. 249-262.
46. *Capitulaire de Quierzy*, c. 16, p. 359.
47. *AB*, p. 216.
48. *Annales Vedastini*, B. VON SIMSON éd., *MGH SS Rer. Germ.*, Hanovre, 1909 (désormais abrégés en *AV*), p. 42.

la situation de Charles en Italie devenait intenable. La menace de l'avance de son neveu et rival Carloman de Bavière avait déjà contraint Charles à abandonner Pavie pour Tortone[49]. Là il prit des dispositions pour que le pape vienne sacrer impératrice Richilde – mère de la progéniture impériale à venir –, puis il l'envoya en Maurienne par le Mont-Cenis, où elle devait l'attendre « avec le trésor ». À la mi-septembre, Carloman entrait à Pavie – et, toujours d'après Hincmar, Charles apprenait en même temps qu'une conspiration se tramait contre lui. Même s'il ne faut pas prendre à la lettre le déroulement chronologique proposé par Hincmar, une chose est certaine : dès la troisième semaine de septembre, Charles dut se résigner à quitter la Lombardie. Le pape était déjà reparti en hâte pour Rome, emportant un crucifix en or massif offert par Charles à Saint-Pierre de Rome. Quant à Charles, il reprit à son tour la route du nord « sur les pas de Richilde ». Il était désormais trop tard pour qu'il fût présent à Saint-Denis le jour de la fête de son saint patron, le 9 octobre.

Les rites et les droits de la mort

Charles avait toujours souhaité être enterré à Saint-Denis *si ita Deus voluerit*. Mais Dieu ne le voulut pas. Hincmar raconte l'histoire dans les *Annales de Saint-Bertin* :

> Charles, frappé de fièvre (le 25 septembre), but une poudre que Zédéchias, son médecin juif, qu'il aimait et en qui il avait une confiance excessive, lui avait donnée pour guérir son mal. Mais il avait bu un poison contre lequel il n'y avait pas d'antidote. Transporté à dos d'homme, il traversa le col du Mont-Cenis et arriva en un lieu appelé Brios. De là il envoya chercher Richilde qui se trouvait en Maurienne, lui demandant de venir le rejoindre, ce qu'elle fit. Le 6 octobre, le onzième jour après avoir bu le poison, il rendit l'âme dans une misérable petite hutte. Ses hommes ouvrirent son corps, retirèrent les intestins, versèrent à l'intérieur le vin et les aromates dont ils disposaient, placèrent le corps sur une civière et se mirent en route pour Saint-Denis où il avait demandé à être enterré. Mais à cause de l'odeur infecte [qui se dégageait du corps], ils ne purent aller plus loin ; alors ils le placèrent dans un tonneau qu'ils avaient auparavant enduit de poix à l'intérieur et à l'extérieur et entouré de peaux, mais tout cela ne réussissait pas à atténuer l'odeur. À grand peine ils arrivèrent à Nantua, un petit monastère de la province de Lyon, et là ils ensevelirent le corps avec le tonneau.

Quelques lignes plus loin, Hincmar ajoute que Charles sur son lit de mort avait confié les *regalia* – la couronne, l'épée et le sceptre – à la reine pour qu'elle les transmette à son beau-fils, l'héritier Louis le Bègue[50]. Le texte ne tire pas la morale de l'histoire, mais il donne une explication scientifique de l'odeur fétide. Notons qu'un chroniqueur un peu plus tardif, Réginon de Prüm, qui écrivait au début du Xe siècle, reprend l'histoire *(fama)*

---

49. *AB*, p. 215.
50. *AB*, p. 216-217. Je traite de ces rituels d'une façon plus générale dans « Carolingian royal funerals », dans F. THEUWS dir., *Rituals of Power from Late Antiquity to the Early Middle Ages*, Leyde, à paraître en 1997.

du médecin juif et ajoute que c'était un imposteur et qu'il égarait les esprits par des ruses et des sortilèges[51]. Réginon paraphrasait peut-être Hincmar, en ajoutant quelques touches fantaisistes ou, plus probablement, tous les deux s'inspiraient des témoignages oraux rapportés après la mort de Charles. Quoi qu'il en soit, tous exprimaient le rationalisme carolingien[52], ici teinté d'antisémitisme. Un autre annaliste rigoureusement contemporain, l'auteur des *Annales de Fulda*, explique lui aussi la nécessité d'ensevelir à Nantua le cadavre trop vite décomposé et nauséabond :

> (Charles) attrapa la dysenterie et périt dans de grandes souffrances. Alors que ses gardes du corps voulaient porter le cadavre au sépulcre qu'il s'était fait préparer à Saint-Denis, ils furent forcés de l'ensevelir dans un monastère en Bourgogne à cause de la terrible puanteur dégagée par le cadavre putride, devenue insupportable pour l'armée[53].

Quant à l'auteur des *Annales de Saint-Vaast*, lui aussi contemporain, il mentionne le médecin juif de Charles et sa « potion » sans faire allusion au poison. Il n'offre aucune explication de l'enterrement de Charles à Nantua et confirme laconiquement que le corps de Charles fut placé dans une sépulture temporaire en attendant d'être transporté en Francie. L'annaliste ajoute tout de même que ce transfert eut lieu « plus tard »[54].

Ces quatre sources ne montrent évidemment aucun esprit critique. Néanmoins, derrière l'histoire du cadavre putréfié que rapportent trois d'entre elles, toute personne connaissant la Vulgate pouvait reconnaître le macabre récit de la mort d'Antiochos Épiphane telle qu'elle est évoquée dans le Deuxième Livre des Macchabées, IX. 8-28. Antiochos, tyran orgueilleux et persécuteur des Juifs, fut frappé de maladie subite, puis gravement blessé en tombant de son char. Il devait être porté dans une litière, et il souffrit un sort épouvantable – la putréfaction à vif : « des vers sortaient en grouillant du corps de l'homme impie, et sa chair se dissolvait dans d'atroces douleurs alors qu'il était encore en vie ; l'odeur et la pestilence en affligeaient l'armée *(odore etiam illius et foetore exercitus gravaretur)*. Celui qui, hier encore, pensait pouvoir toucher les étoiles du ciel était à présent l'homme que personne ne réussissait à porter à cause de l'intolérable puanteur » *(... eum nemo poterat, propter intolerantiam foetoris, portare)*. Deux des quatre sources qui parlent du sort du corps de Charles font écho aux paroles de la Vulgate[55]. D'abord, les *Annales de Fulda* : « *corpus...propter foetorem nimium putridi cadaveris, quo gravabatur exercitus, in Burgundia...sepelierunt...* ». Ce qui n'a rien d'étonnant, car ce texte de Francie orientale se montre fortement et systématiquement hostile à Charles tout au long de la décennie 870. Il est plus surprenant en revanche d'en trouver l'écho dans les *Annales de Saint-Bertin* d'Hincmar : *quem pro fetore non valentes portare...*, puisque Hincmar était un Franc de l'Ouest, familier et

---

51. RÉGINON, *Chronicon*, F. KURZE éd., *MGH SS Rer. Germ.*, Hanovre, 1890, p. 113.
52. Voir H. LIEBESCHUTZ, « Wesen und Grenzen des karolingischen Rationalismus », *Archiv für Kulturgeschichte*, t. 33, 1950, p. 17-14.
53. *AF*, p. 90.
54. *AV*, p. 42.
55. Peut-être aussi dans RÉGINON, *Chronicon*, p. 113 : *quia foetor intollerabilis ex putretudine cadaveris baiulantes gravabat, compulsi sunt illud terrae mandare*. Je tiens à remercier Philippe Buc pour ses remarques très suggestives au sujet du traitement de la mort dans ces textes.

ancien conseiller de Charles. De toute évidence les annalistes du IXe siècle pouvaient compter sur leurs lecteurs pour lire entre les lignes et saisir les critiques dissimulées en d'obscures références. De telles allusions avaient déjà été à l'occasion adressées autrefois à Charles lui-même par Hincmar. On en trouve deux exemples dans les *Annales de Saint-Bertin* où Hincmar profère ses critiques en utilisant ce que j'ai appelé ailleurs le « code diony-sien » : je veux dire que par des allusions à peine voilées à saint Denis, Hincmar exprime sa condamnation de la conduite royale. La clé en est le jour de la fête de saint Denis, le 9 octobre. Ainsi à l'année 869, Hincmar attire l'attention sur le fait que Charles avait envoyé chercher une nouvelle épouse trois jours à peine après la mort de sa première femme Ermentrude le 6 octobre ; et encore en 876, Hincmar détaille les moments de la défaite de Charles à Andernach le 8 octobre, et note que Richilde apprit le désastre le 9 octobre[56]. Le récit de la mort de Charles est un troisième exemple de cette critique codée. La date du 6 octobre était aussi celle de la mort d'Ermen-trude en 869. La reine qui se trouvait au chevet du mourant était celle-là même qu'il avait envoyé chercher avec une hâte inconvenante huit ans plus tôt jour pour jour. L'insinuation – et d'ailleurs Hincmar n'avait guère besoin d'être plus explicite – est la suivante : l'enterrement de Charles à Nantua, qui eut peut-être lieu le 9 octobre, insiste sur la séparation entre le roi et son saint patron. C'était Charles lui-même qui, par sa conduite, avait perdu sa chance d'être enterré à Saint-Denis comme il l'avait depuis longtemps souhaité et soigneusement préparé. Hincmar ne dit pas que Charles eut une deuxième chance. C'est Réginon qui décrit l'exhumation de ses ossements, « après quelques années », et l'ensevelissement, cette fois enfin *honorifice*, à Saint-Denis[57].

Hincmar donne d'autres informations encore sur la mort de Charles. Lui seul de tous les annalistes révèle que la reine était présente au chevet du roi mourant et que les *regalia* furent transférés d'une manière correcte. Ce qui signifie que la royauté de Charles transcendait ses faiblesses person-nelles et que la fonction survivait à l'homme. D'autres détails suivent. Les hommes de Charles (*qui cum eo erant* ; cf. Réginon : *baiulantes* ; AF : *satel-lites*) firent tout ce qu'ils pouvaient pour porter son corps à Saint-Denis ; sur ce point les récits de Réginon, des *Annales de Fulda* et d'Hincmar sont concordants. C'est un témoignage éloquent du dévouement des hommes de Charles à leur seigneur, et nous avons déjà eu l'occasion de remarquer que Charles avait l'art d'entretenir ce lien[58]. Rien ne suggère que la mort misé-rable de Charles ait nui à son prestige. À Nantua, l'éloge flatteur d'un poète orna sa tombe. Après son transfert à Saint-Denis, Charles fut enterré à l'endroit même qu'il avait choisi, entre les autels du Trésor et de la Trinité. Il reposait, comme il en avait fait le projet, dans le sarcophage de marbre rouge. On peut supposer que ses secondes funérailles furent accompagnées de cérémoniaux élaborés ; bien que l'existence de tels rites funéraires soit controversée pour les premiers Carolingiens, des indices suggèrent qu'il ont pu exister à partir du IXe siècle. Les cérémonies funéraires d'un grand site

---

56. Cf. J.L.NELSON, « History-writing at the courts of Louis the Pious and Charles the Bald », dans A. SCHARER et G. SCHEIBELREITER dir., *Historiographie im frühen Mittelalter*, Vienne, 1994, p. 435-442.

57. RÉGINON, *Chronicon*, p. 113. Cf. *AV*, p. 42.

58. J.L. NELSON, *Charles le Chauve, op. cit.*, p. 33, 241.

cultuel comme Lorsch, où Louis le Jeune fit enterrer son père Louis le Germanique en 876, ou de Saint-Ambroise de Milan, où Louis II fut enseveli en 875, se conformaient certainement à des rituels appropriés. Il est probable que Charles n'eut pas en 877 ce qu'Eginhard appelle, à propos de la mort de Charlemagne, le *mos sollemnis* : la toilette et la préparation de la dépouille mortelle. Mais l'histoire d'Hincmar suggère une certaine connaissance des techniques d'embaumement, aussi bâclées qu'elles aient pu être dans le cas de Charles. On ne sait pas qui eut l'idée de l'embaumement – les acolytes italiens, la reine, ou peut-être même le médecin juif – mais il s'ouvrait ainsi de nouvelles perspectives pour la prolongation artificielle de la « vie » politique du roi. Les premières funérailles de Charles furent sans doute expédiées en hâte. Les Nantuais gardèrent cependant la mémoire d'une cérémonie honorable. Comme nous l'avons vu, le second enterrement à Saint-Denis fut conduit selon les volontés de Charles.

La commémoration des anniversaires n'était pas la prérogative exclusive des rois ; les abbés et les évêques, ainsi que l'aristocratie laïque, étaient aussi commémorés. Mais les dispositions de Charles étaient « officielles », attestant une *imitatio imperii* qui, dans ses dernières années, était devenue pour lui une quasi-obsession. Charles avait fait de grands projets pour la création d'une nécropole dynastique en l'église de Saint-Denis. C'est là qu'avait été enterrée son épouse Ermentrude en 869. Là aussi que furent ensevelis ses deux fils, morts en bas âge au début des années 870, années qui justement furent marquées par une certaine ambiguïté des rapports entre le mausolée et le siège de l'Empire. Dès 869, Charles espérait mettre la main sur Aix-la-Chapelle ; lorsqu'il lui fallut abandonner cet espoir, en 876, il se mit à construire à Compiègne un « Aix » des Francs de l'Ouest, un « Aix » de substitution – sa Carlopolis à lui. C'est là que fut enterré son successeur Louis le Bègue en avril 879. Pourtant rien n'indique que Charles ait eu l'intention de faire de Compiègne le mausolée des Francs occidentaux. C'est au contraire à saint Denis qu'il porta une dévotion constante tout au long de sa vie et à l'heure de sa mort. Bien que, par la force des choses, d'autres lieux aient servi de sépulture royale, aux XIIᵉ et XIIIᵉ siècles Saint-Denis s'affirma de nouveau en devenant la nécropole royale de France, grâce notamment au zèle de l'abbé Suger, ravi d'avoir pour ainsi dire dans ses registres un Charles empereur ; mais aussi grâce au zèle de Charles le Chauve, récompensé enfin à longue échéance, à sa dévotion fidèle et constante, à ses dons somptueux au sanctuaire, et enfin (ce qui n'est pas négligeable) à la présence de ses ossements.

Alain Dierkens a suggéré récemment que ce qui distinguait les obsèques des souverains occidentaux de ceux des souverains de l'Est était une série de manques : à l'ouest les rites funéraires n'étaient pas sophistiqués, il n'y avait pas d'église faisant fonction de sépulture dynastique, ni de somptueux tombeaux, pas de moyens de conserver la dépouille royale ni d'utilisation des insignes royaux dans les cérémonaux funéraires[59]. Quels qu'aient été les rites funéraires des plus anciens Carolingiens, c'est à Charles le Chauve que revient le mérite d'avoir élaboré un rituel et désigné une église servant de sépulture royale ; il a probablement aussi conçu les plans de sa tombe

---

59. A. DIERKENS, « Le tombeau de Charlemagne », *Byzantion*, t. 61, 1991, p. 156-180, en particulier p. 179.

de marbre. Des efforts furent faits pour embaumer son corps. Les insignes royaux furent transmis soigneusement à son successeur. Ce dernier point a une signification particulière, qui nous amène finalement à comprendre comment la mort de Charles fut perçue par les contemporains. Il y a une différence entre la description de la mort de Charles, particulièrement dans le récit d'Hincmar, et celle de la mort du tyran biblique Antiochos dans le livre des Macchabées. La putréfaction du corps d'Antiochos précéda sa mort, tandis que celle du corps de Charles la suivit. Les deux récits portent le même message : la tyrannie est un mal. Mais Antiochos et Charles furent des tyrans très différents, dont les caractères respectifs marquent la différence entre les Séleucides de la Bible et les Carolingiens d'Hincmar. Les souverains défiés par les Macchabées étaient mauvais par définition ; ils n'avaient aucun droit à régner à Jérusalem, ils profanaient la ville sainte. Charles, au contraire, n'avait pas toujours été fautif, il avait reçu de Dieu le pouvoir royal. La passation des insignes royaux au fils de Charles authentifiait la légitimité de la succession de Louis, et en même temps soulignait la continuité transcendante de la fonction royale, distincte de son titulaire temporaire. Hincmar ne manque pas de souligner cette continuité, ni d'expliquer le sens de sa fonction, dans l'*ordo* de consécration qu'il compose pour l'intronisation royale du successeur de Charles le 8 décembre 877 ; rituel dont Hincmar raconta en détail les préliminaires dans les *Annales de Saint-Bertin*[60].

Ainsi dans le texte d'Hincmar relatant la mort de Charles, et dans le contexte plus large de son œuvre, est exposée d'une manière dramatique la dissolution du lien temporaire entre l'homme et la fonction, entre la chair et le royaume, entre les deux corps du roi (Hincmar n'utilise pas encore les mots, mais il a compris le sens). La putréfaction du corps de Charles signifie la chute du tyran, la punition lancée par Dieu sur un simple mortel frappé dans son orgueil. Mais en même temps on peut en faire une autre « lecture » – la putréfaction symbolise la séparation du corps public et du corps privé[61]. Les insignes royaux (l'épée, les robes, la couronne et le sceptre) transmis à son fils par les mains de Richilde et par ordre officiel *(preceptum)* de Charles sur son lit de mort, représentent la continuité du royaume. Le roi meurt, le royaume est immortel.

Traduit de l'anglais par
Lada Hordynsky-Caillat et Odile Redon

---

60. *AB*, p. 219-221 ; voir R. JACKSON, *Ordines Coronationis Franciae*, vol. 1, Philadelphie, 1995, p. 110-23.

61. Cf. E.H. KANTOROWICZ, *Les deux corps du roi*, (1957) trad. française, Paris, 1990 ; G. KOZIOL, *Begging Pardon and Favour. Ritual and Political Order in Early Medieval France*, Ithaca-New York, 1992.

A propos des femmes royales dans les rapports entre le monde wisigothique et le monde franc à l'époque de Reccared[1]

C'étaient les Grecs, selon Eginhard, qui au VIIIe siècle connaissaient la proverbe suivante: Si tu as un Franc comme ami, tu ne l'as pas comme voisin [2]. Au VIe siècle, des autres gens en savaient bien la vérité. Et entre eux, les Wisigoths: depuis le débâcle de Vouillé, voisins mal à l'aise des Francs. Les razzias, les emprises de butin, constituaient les relations «normales».

Mais il y avaient aussi d'autres relations —on ne peut pas dire non violentes, mais de toute façon moins violentes. De telles relations entre Francs et Wisigoths, je veux vous esquisser d'abord l'arrière-plan politique de chaqu'un des deux associés, puis trois séries d'échanges entre eux. Ces relations forment, en tout, un reseau autour de l'evènement auquel est consacré notre congrès. Elles nous aideront, peut-être, à mieux comprendre l'importance de certains aspects de la conversion de Reccared, tout en la localisant en son contexte contemporain.

Il faut souligner, au début, malgré l'existence chez les écrivains de l'antiquité et du haut moyen âge, de quelques stéréotypes ethnographiques apparamment «nationales» —Gothi, Franci— ou même des définitions de zones culturelles —Gothia face à Romania— qu'il n'existaient point à cette époque ni de nations, ni donc de relations internationales, au sens moderne [3]. La diplomatie du VIe siècle était affaire personelle des rois et des cours —non pas des états; et les royaumes ne s'accordaient point avec des territoires «nationales». C'est un monde des gentes qu'il nous faut pénétrer— monde dirigé, formé, et aussi fractionné, déformé ainsi que réformé, par des rois et bien sur par des reines [4].

I. L'ARRIERE-PLAN DES RELATIONS FRANCO-WISIGOTIQUES

D'abord, les Francs. Si Bède en effet créa pour la posterité la gens anglorum, c'est Grégoire de Tours qui en fit de même pour les Francs —mais malgré lui. Il faut nous rappeler que ce n'était pas Grégoire qui donna le titre L'Histoire des Francs à son chef-d'oeuvre. Lui, il l'intitula simplement: *Livres d'Histoire*[5]. Grégoire considéra les Francs comme une *gens* parmi d'autres. C'est néanmoins évident que les traditions orales aussi bien qu'écrites au sujet de l'ancien temps montraient à notre historien de nombreuses groupements autour des *duces* et *regales,* installés en régions diverses. Clovis avait imposé une espèce d'unité stalinesque. Après 511, pourtant, il s'agissait encore d'un partage. Donc, le règne de Clovis apparut comme une césure brève entre périodes de divisions: comme voit très clairement Grégoire lui-même quand il se rappelle de façon nostalgique la paix clovisienne. Mais quand il parle d'un *regnum,* Grégoire le fait comme qualité personelle d'un roi individu: c'est le royaume de Clovis, plus tard le royaume de Clothaire I. À l'invers des historiens de l'époque carolingien, jamais Grégoire ne parle d'un seul *regnum Francorum,* encore moins de *Francia.* Ainsi, dans sa diatribe bien-connue contre les rois ses contemporains, Grégoire ne songe pas à une monarchie, ou à une réunification des *regna*[6]. Les rois francs eux-mêmes, en traitant entre eux, avant 558, en *caritas germanitatis,* parlaient des *communes provinciae*[7]. Un peu plus tard, dans la deuxième moitié du VIe siècle, on considérait les *regna* des feu les rois fils de Clovis comme des blocs, à être repartagés ou même recoupés en portions, mais toujours à retenir en vue: ainsi, par example, parla-t-on en 587 d'une *portio* ou d'une *pars* du *regnum* d'un roi de la génération précédente, *pars regni* qu'on voulait *in integrum redhiberi* au royaume paternel[8]. Des royaumes multiples à l'intérieure de la Gaule étaient ainsi devenus des faits acquis: royaumes multiples —et en principe royaumes égaux en fonction de parties plus ou moins égales des terrains fiscaux et des trésors qu'avaient amassés Clovis. Mais c'était un équilibre à jamais mis en danger, à jamais à retablir. Ainsi les *bella civilia* que déplora Grégoire faisaient fonction positif, en soutenant cet equilibre, out plutôt le renouvelant.

Autre moyen d'atteindre un tel résultat: c'était non seulement partager, mais en effet morceler la Gaule entre royaumes afin que chaqu'un posséderait sa partie des terrains larges au sud de la Loire. Même un accoucheur aussi résolu que M. Rouche n'a pas su faire naître l'Aquitaine au VIe siècle[9]. Au lieu d'une région discrète, y avaient-ils des morcellements succesifs: le royaume dit austrasien de Sigibert a renfermé l'Auvergne; le royaume dit neustrien de Chilpéric a renfermé la plupart de l'ouest de la France moderne, y-inclus la Gascogne. Ainsi ces deux royaumes, comme aussi le royaume dit burgonde de Gontran, étaient voisins du royaume des Wisigoths. À l'intérieur des royaumes francs suivaient des morcellements et remorcellements des régions —la Touraine, par example, faisait partie successivement du royaume de Chilpéric, puis du royaume de Gontran, puis du royaume de Childebert II— morcellements aussi des *civitates*— la *civitas* de Paris, par example, était partagée entre deux royaumes dans les années 560 entre Charibert et Sigibert, et dans les années 580 entre Childebert II et Gontran[10]. C'est évident que la recherche de ressources royales s'intensifia au deuxième moitié du VIe siècle: encore des *bella civilia.*

On remarque deux autres tendances significatives. D'une part, le *Drang nach Osten* des Francs était en effet arrêté par la résistance Saxonne, tandis qu'en Italie, les Lombards étaient en train de s'y installer. Dans quelle direction donc un roi franc pourrait-il ramener ses visées sinon vers un autre royaume franc? Ou vers l'Espagne? D'autre part, la guerre de pillage, comme moyen de gagner des ressources indispensables, pouvait s'éffacer un peu par rapport au marriage dynastique— y inclus la réception du dot qu'apporterait l'épouse. *Tu felix Austrasia nube!*

Quant'aux Wisigoths, et les tendances generales chez eux à cette époque: aborder un tel sujet devant une telle assistance —c'est vraiment apporter de l'eau à la rivière! Je ne me permets donc que d'offrir quelques observations très brèves sur deux grands traits comparatifs.

Premièrement, à propos du système de succession royale, on a dit qu'après la disparution de la dynastie Balt en 531 il n'existait plus de succession dynastique chez les Wisigoths: à sa place on trouve un système de succession élective [11]. À la longue, c'est incontestable. Mais est-ce que l'on l'aurait prévu au VIe siècle? Avouons que nous ne savons pas beaucoup des rois entre 531 et 568; des liens de parenté entre eux sont au moins possibles en quelques cas. Ce que nous savons bien c'est qu'Athanagild n'avait pas de fils: fait qu'on doit mettre en relation avec la survivance politique de la mère de ses filles, Goiswinthe. Et cette survivance, on va voir, fait ressortir un pouvoir assez intéressant de la part de cette reine. Si elle aurait mis au monde un fils, il y aurait bien eu de possibilités de fondation dynastique. Avant Clovis, qui aurait prévu la dynastie mérovingien? Sans Clothilde, femme de Clovis, qu'est-ce qui en serait devenu en 511?

Ensuite, in n'y avait pas, au VIe siècle, chez les Wisigoths, un royaume uni. De même chez les Francs, comme nous avons vu. Mais à la différence de ceux-ci, les démembrements du royaume des Wisigoths, selon une opinion très généralement reçue, provenaient d'un régionalisme pré-existent et tenace. Donc les rois des Wisigoths se heurtaient contre un problème particulier, pour ainsi dire spécifiquement espagnol: problème irresoluble. Sans vouloir pour un instant nier les particularités des régions de l'Espagne, je crois qu'il faut éviter tout déterminisme géographique. L'Espagne bien sur est un pays large, et varié, coupé par des grandes fleuves et par des montagnes. Mais n'en était-il pas de même pour la France aussi? On alléguera le témoignage de Jean de Biclar. Il décrit Léovigild vainqueur des *provinciae,* qui savait assujettir les *gentes* à sa domination [12]. Mais n'est-ce pas vrai que Jean veut faire de Léovigild l'équivalent dans l'ouest des empereurs romains dans l'est? Voici un parallélisme frappant dans les premières années de sa chronique. Si Grégoire avait passé des années à Constantinople au lieu de Tours? Si Grégoire avait écrit un chronique style Empire? Entendrait-on aussi dans ses *Historiae* encore des *provinciae* soumises? Mais je m'empresse de vous assurer que je suis loin de mépriser le témoignage de Jean de Biclar: au contraire, je suis persuadée que il faut le lire avec la même attention soutenue qu'on a donné tout récemment au récit de Grégoire. Car, après être revenu de l'est, Jean était bien placé —à Barcelone, à Biclar, à Gerona— à se rendre compte de la bipolarité fondamentale du royaume des Wisigoths: il y avait *l'Hispania citerior,* y inclus la *provincia Gothorum,* et il y avait la *provincia Galliae Narbonensis* —deux provinces faisantes ègalement parties constituantes du royaume de Léovigild, puis de Reccared. C. Higounet a dit: «S'il y a eu un époque ou il n'y a surement pas eu de Pyrénées, c'est bien le Moyen Age»— et J. Fontaine a bien ajouté que cela va pour le haut moyen âge aussi [13]. Ce qui implique une fois de plus qu'il nous faut oublier pour l'instant non seulement les configurations de l'Espagne et de la France modernes, mais l'idée même de nos états nationaux. En realité c'étaient les *reges* et *regales* et les *reginae,* qui formaient, eux et elles, les unités de cette Europe première: une Europe qui renfermait, certes, des frontières internes —mais parce que ces frontières se rapportaient aux régimes personnels, aux royaumes, elles étaient pour ainsi dire provisoires— qui risquaient toujours être redressées selon les politiques royales et les accidents dynastiques.

II. LES MARIAGES DES FILLES D'ATHANAGILD

Ce qui nous affronte aux années 560-570, c'est l'inattendu d'un rapprochement entre Francs et Wisigoths. Alors - pourquoi ce rapprochement, pourquoi ces mariages presque sans précédent entre rois mérovingiens et princesses wisigothiques? On s'adresse à Grégoire de Tours. Il nous explique que le roi Sigibert en regardant ses frères qui s'unissaient avec les femmes indignes, de couche inférieure, visa, lui, à une fille d'un roi, et ainsi dépècha des courriers au roi Athanagild [14], Après cela, le frère de Sigibert, le roi Chilpéric, voulut lui aussi une princesse wisigothique. Il y avaient eu déjà des rois d'Austrasie qui cherchèrent des princesses étrangères, chez les Burgondes, chez les Lombards, même une fois chez les Wisigoths. Mais pourquoi chercher en Espagne, et à Tolède même, en 566? Grégoire met le doigt sur deux points significatifs. Il vient de nous décrire les expériences matrimoniales d'autres rois francs: il en déplore le résultat —embarras de fils— et de fils de sang inférieur. Dans le Livre IV de ses *Histoires*, Grégoire vient de s'occuper longuement du sort affreux de Chramn, fils dégénéré de Clothaire I, rebelle contre son père. Notre auteur veut nous dire, de façon tacite, qu'en choisissant une femme de race royale, et en s'attachant à elle seule, le roi Sigibert pourrait par contre s'assurer des fils meilleurs —et en quantité maniable. Quand il écrivit ces chapitres, Grégoire en savait bien l'heureux résultat: le fils unique de Brunehaut regnait sur le royaume paternel— tandis que, parmi les fils nés des reines de Gontran, femmes de naissance inférieure, pas un seul n'avait survécu. Aux yeux de Grégoire, Jugement évident de Dieu! Quand il donne à entendre qu'il reproche à l'evêque Sagittaire d'avoir dit que les fils de servantes n'étaient pas dignes de la succession royale, et quand il affirme que l'on áppellait fils de roi les fils de roi, peut-on douter que Grégoire ironise? [15]

En décrivant les mariages espagnoles des années 560, Grégoire nous signalle un changement de vitesse dans les concurrences fraternelles de ses rois. Si Chilpéric voulut une princesse d'Espagne, c'est par cela qu'il entendit acquérir, comme l'avait fait son frère, un trésor vaste en douaire. Maintes fois dans les chapitres centrales du Livre IV, Grégoire nous montre les rois à la recherche des trésors et en les dépensants pour s'attirer des adhérents. Enfin ces rois avec leurs *sedes* au nord, à Rheims, à Paris, cherchèrent-ils à s'ouvrir des chemins au sud, des fenêtres à la Méditerranée. Ce n'est pas par hazard que Sigibert une fois marié avec Brunehaut, s'efforça de mettre la main sur Arles, ville du royaume de Gontran à la frontière du *provincia Narbonensis* wisigothique [16]. Grégoire, bien sur, ne dit rien d'une telle liaison. Il donne de ces mariages une explication typiquement francocentrique.

Quittons pour l'instant Reims, Paris, et installons-nous à Tolède. Pourquoi Athanagild s'intéressa-t-il aux propositions franques? Il avait regné déjà depuis 551, et il lui manquait de fils. Pensa-t-il aux petits-fils, comme avait pensé, un demi-siècle en avant, le grand Théodoric d'Italie? Au delà de ces rois et leurs politiques matrimoniales s'étendait un monde plus vaste que Justinien vint de ressusciter [17]. Si les Pyrénées n'existaient pas, il faut avouer que vers 560 la Méditerranée était toujours —ou plutôt encore— en place. Autour des réseaux interprovinciaux filait-on à Constantinople des super-réseaux. Les cadres impériaux se serviaient de la mer. C'était parce que Justinien y avait rentré en commande que les interventions franques en Italie avaient enfin échoué, et qu'Athanagild, tout en devant son royaume au coup de main des armées impériales, devait désormais s'occuper en vains efforts à les expulser. Mais Justinien est mort en 565. À mon avis, ce n'était pas par hazard que Athanagild entra dans ses accords avec Sigibert et Chilpéric pendant les mois suivants. La politique de Théodoric était de nouveau concevable.

Considérons pour un instant ce don dotal, ou *Morgengabe,* vraiment extraordinaire, fait à l'ainée des filles d'Athanagild, Galeswinthe. Le roi Chilpéric donna ainsi à sa femme tolétaine cinq *civitates,* ça veut dire, comtés, en trois blocs au centre et au sud-ouest de la France moderne: Limoges et Cahors; puis Bordeaux; enfin Bigorre et Béarn[18]. Les historiens du droit et des femmes franques l'ont traité comme normal[19]. Mais il faut avouer que nous savons très peu de ce qui était la coutume franque en matière dotale. Cinq *civitates* me semblent, même pour une princesse, un peu excessif. Et plus tard, la succession à cette *Morgengabe* de la soeur de Galeswinthe défunte n'était pas prise pour regulière, coutumière: il fallut, par contre, la définir par décret royal et y apposer l'assentiment des Francs[20]. Pourquoi cette dotation énorme si non comme gage pour assurer l'avenir d'un fils de Galeswinthe et Chilpéric —et ainsi d'un petit-fils d'Athanagild lui-même? Et le roi wisigoth n'espérait-t-il vivre jusqu'à voir ce petit-fils héritier d'un royaume déjà transpyrénéen?

Entre les intéressés, il y avait aussi un autre personnage: je veux dire, la reine Goiswinthe. À ce moment-ci, Grégoire de Tours n'en a rien à nous dire. Il faut nous adresser à un autre témoin: Venance Fortunat. Dans son éloge à la mémoire de Galeswinthe, il évoque en détail les relations intimes entre mère et fille —en négligeant en même temps presque complètement le rôle du père. C'est Goiswinthe qui est ici dépeinte comme particulièrement impliquée dans la politique du mariage, c'est elle qui accompagne sa fille jusqu'à la frontière— elle, enfin, dont la lamentation si attendrissante éclate aux nouvelles de la mort de la jeune épouse en pays lointain[21]. Thème littéraire, sans doute. Mais on peut bien croire que pendant les années suivantes, Fortunat avait ses raisons d'évoquer le rôle d'une reine de Tolède encore influente, et que Goiswinthe avait eu ses raisons à elle en négociant ce mariage, et en pleurant, dans la suite, son échouement. Elle aussi avait besoin de s'assurer: qui était mieux placée à calculer la survie de son mari? Veuve, sans fils, elle courrait des dangers réels. Elle serait obligée de poser son espoir en ses filles en en le petit-fils à venir. Mais, grâce à Jean de Biclar, nous savons qu'elle avait aussi ses propres ressources: quand, quelques mois seulement après le départ de Galeswinthe de Tolède, Athanagild est mort, c'était la veuve Goiswinthe qui tenait les clefs de la *provincia Gothorum* et Léovigild, en se mariant avec elle en deuxièmes noces, s'assura du *regnum citerioris Hispaniae*[22]. D'ou cette influence de Goiswinthe? On a supposé une parenté puissante[23]. Et, si Jean de Biclar n'en fait pas mention ici, on peut évoquer les preuves indirectes du rôle exercé à cette époque par des reines comme guardiennes du trésor royal[24]. C'est évident aussi, dans le cas même de la fille de Goiswinthe, c'est à dire la reine Brunehaut, et dans des cas assez nombreux pendant le haut moyen âge, que le pouvoir d'un roi défunt était censé d'adhérer dans une certaine façon à sa veuve qui pouvait le transmettre ensuite à un autre époux[25]. Ici encore, on voit chez les Wisigoths du VIe siècle des pratiques semblables à celles des autres peuples à l'époque. Avec la mort d'Athanagild, les dispositions parentales par rapport à leur descendance sont selon toute apparence bouleversées. Le roi Chilpéric, qui «aima beaucoup Galeswinthe parce qu'elle avait apporté une douaire très large», la fit tuer[26]. Evidemment, il n'y avait plus de père qui aurait pu punir son beau-fils meutrier. Et pour la mère, et la soeur de Galeswinthe: quoi faire? À l'instant, Fortunat nous présente Goiswinthe en douleur: il ne lui attribue pas de menaces vindicatives. On a fait couler beaucoup d'encre au sujet de la vendetta que poursuivit, dit-t-on, Brunehaut pur se venger de la mort de sa soeur[27]. Mais de cela, il n'y a aucun soupçon dans le récit de Grégoire, qui, tandis qu'il nous raconte que Brunehaut était accablée par les nouvelles de l'assassinat de son mari, ne nous dit rien de sa réaction à la mort de sa soeur[28]. D'ailleurs, Grégoire dit formellement que c'étaient les frères (dans le pluriel) de Chilpéric qui le punirent pour sa complicité dans l'assassinat de la reine en l'expulsant de son royaume[29]. Encore un prétexte, semble-t-il, à faire ce qu'entendaient faire de toute façon les frères de Chilpéric. Néanmoins, et Goiswinthe et Brunehaut trouvèrent des moyens de se protéger. Comme nous verrons, on n'oublia pas Galeswinthe.

Avant de quitter les années 560, on doit se demander, quel rôle jouait-elle la religion dans ces relations dynastiques? Les princesses wisigothiques étaient des ariennes, les rois francs catholiques. N'est-ce pas ce même Grégoire qui veut nous faire croire que des lignes de bataille —catholiques contre ariens— étaient dressées à l'époque? Mais l'auteur n'attribue aucune motivation religieuse ni à l'un ni à l'autre des maris francs. Dans les deux cas, Grégoire nous raconte que chacune des deux princesses fut vite convertie à la foi catholique et rebaptisée avec le saint chrême (et il ajoute que le roi Sigibert lui-même a donné un coup de main aux évêques qui ont converti Brunehaut)[30]. Et c'est tout. Grégoire n'évoque pas de problème: quand le processus de conversion va dans ce sens, c'était pour lui normal, attendu, voire providentiel.

II. GOISWINTHE, INGONDE ET LA REVOLTE D'HERMENEGILD

La conversion à la foi catholique d'Hermenegild doit une bonne partie de sa renomée historique à Grégoire de Tours, qui la donne des allures dramatiques: comme prélude à la martyre, comme préfigure inachevée à la conversion de Reccared— et comme conséquence des activités feminines[31]. D'abord, Hermenegild, prince arien, se maria avec une princesse catholique, Ingonde, fille du feu roi Sigibert: «On a envoyé la jeune fille en Espagne», nous dit Grégoire, sans dire qui c'est qui l'a envoyée. Une fois arrivée, Ingonde fut asujettie aux compulsions, puis à la main armée de la reine Goiswinthe qui voulait la faire accepter la foi arienne. Goiswinthe était la belle-mère d'Ingonde. Et c'est vrai que Grégoire nous donne ici une explication: Goiswinthe, la persuasión échouante, força sa belle fille d'être rebaptisée, en déclanchant au même temps une persécution en grand contre les catholiques dans le royaume wisigothique: indication significative de son influence si non réelle, au moins plausible. Mais Ingonde, toujours catholique en secret, mit ses efforts à la conversion de son mari. Dans cette ambiance de conflit religieux, Hermenegild se décida et à devenir catholique et à se révolter contre son pére. Ainsi Grégoire nous invite à faire un lien entre les deux affaires. Récit trés circonstancié et contemporain. Mais je suis persuadée, grâce aux recherches récentes de mes collègues Roger Collins et Ian Wood, que le récit grégorien soit de fond en comble oeuvre d'artifice, calquée sur des préconceptions au sujet de l'arianisme[32]. Et calquée aussi, n'est-ce pas, sur des stéréotypes féminines? C'est parce qu'il a déjà une idée fixe de la bonne femme catholique missionnaire auprès de son mari hérétique ou païen, que Grégoire doit ainsi dépeindre l'influence d'Ingonde[33]. C'est parce que les belles-mères sont pour ainsi dire naturellement méchantes que Grégoire décrit ainsi Goiswinthe. Et enfin, c'est parce qu'il entend découvrir derrière cette persécution un esprit malin qu'il assigne ce rôle à la reine plutôt qu'à Léovigild lui-même.

Derrière cette histoire, peut-on déceler une autre? Grégoire en effet identifie Goiswinthe comme *avia* (grandmère) d'Ingonde. C'est vrai qu'il ne dit rien de Brunehaut à cette endroit. Mais qui aurait envoyé Ingonde en Espagne si non sa mère, la reine-mère d'Austrasie et en effet régente pour son fils Childebert qui, lui, n'atteigna l'âge de majorité qu'en 585? On a prétendu que les années 576-84 étaient pleines d'humiliations pour Brunehaut. Mais j'ai noté ailleurs quelques indications de son influence politique, dont une me parait particulièrement significative dans notre contexte: le fait enregistré tout à fait en passant par Grégoire qu'en 579 ou en 580, l'évêque Elafius de Châlons-sur-Marne fut *in Hispanis in legatione directus... propter causas Brunichildis reginae*[34]. Dans le mariage d'Ingonde, donc, peut-on supposer, à mon avis, l'action maternelle de Brunehaut, et l'utilisation d'une axe féminine entre Brunehaut et Goiswinthe, sa mère —femmes toutes les deux assez soucieuses de retenir dans leurs mains les clefs de pouvoir.

C'est Jean de Biclar, autre témoin contemporain, qui nous donne deux renseignements essentiels sur Goiswinthe. D'abord, au sujet de son importance politique au début du règne de Léovigild, Jean fait supposer que c'était par son mariage avec cette veuve du roi précédent que Léovigild, dont le frère Liuva (installé, lui, en *Narbonensis*) l'avait constitué roi en *Hispania,* en 569 y étendit, puis stabilisa son pouvoir[35]. Goiswinthe, reine sans fils, put donc en effet transmettre des moyens du pouvoir *(leudes, trésor)* d'un roi à un autre. Ensuite, c'est encore Jean de Biclar qui, sans mot dire du mariage d'Ingonde, nous fait partie du fait suivant: dix ans plus tard, en 579, Hermengild se révolta *factione Goswinthae reginae*[36]. À l'invers de Grégoire, et d'une façon beaucoup plus convaincante, Jean aligne Goiswinthe avec Hermenegild, donc avec sa petite-fille aussi, en révolte contre Léovigild. Quand Ingonde fit naître un fils, on l'appella Athanagild: nom du grand-père de l'enfant, bien sur —mais aussi du mari original de Goiswinthe[37]. C'était elle qui devint ainsi le point de convergence du conflit entre Léovigild et son fils, et entre ce fils et son frère. Soit-il permis de soupçonner l'influence de Goiswinthe dans le choix de nom pour son arrière-petit-fils?

Pourquoi reposer sa confiance en Jean de Biclar? Les historiens modernes ont décelé en 579 des impulsions régionalistes, des oppositions structurales des provinces contre le centre. Ils ont sans doute raison. Mais quand même, c'est des motivations et des interêts personnels qu'évoque Jean de Biclar, des conflits au sein de la famille royale, des luttes pour le pouvoir dans lesquelles les femmes pouvaient jouer un rôle critique. Et non seulement en Espagne: il vaut la peine de remarquer encore deux fois dans la chronique de Jean —chronique du reste assez brève— la même phrase dont il décrit l'action de Goiswinthe. D'abord le roi des Lombards est tué par ses hommes *factione coniugis suae*. Puis le cousin de l'empéreur Justin II est assassiné *factione imperatricis Sophiae*[38]. Rien qu'un cliché littéraire, misogyniste? Mais non — les deux cas sont bien documentés ailleurs, et en plus, ce sont des actions de reine bien vraisemblables[39]. Goiswinthe comme ces autres utilisa des moyens existants. Autrement dit: on est porté à croire le récit de Jean parce qu'il dépeint la reine wisigothique dans les mêmes couleurs que d'autres reines du VIe siècle tardif. Couleurs nouvelles? En partie, oui. Si on peut hasar-

der une conjecture: au fur et à mesure que l'économie devint de plus en plus démoné-
tisé, que les perceptions des impôts s'amoindrirent, et que les institutions d'état devin-
rent militarisées et dé-bureaucratisées, le rôle à la cour de la femme du monarque, déjà
important dans le Bas-Empire, ne put que s'aggrandir: comme guardienne du trésor,
comme trésorière, dispensatrice aux soldats, appui des ambitieux de la familie royale[40].
L'histoire des reines haut-médiévales commence au VIe siècle, chez les Wisigoths comme
chez les Francs, les Lombards, les Byzantins: ce qui implique une ressemblance entre
les Wisigoths et ces autres quant'au système politique. À la fin, comme tout le monde
le sait, ils s'intallèrent des différences entre royauté franc et royauté wisigothique: celui-
là adopta un système de succession royale dynastique et partageable, celui-ci un système
electif et unitaire - et ainsi moins favorable au pouvoir de la reine[41]. Mais au VIe siècle tardif, ces différences étaient encore à l'avenir. Les possibilités restaient ouvertes.
D'une part, des tendances dynastiques se montraient clairement chez les Wisigoths.
D'autre part, les démembrements, les rémembrements des royaumes composites, se pro-
duisirent de l'un côté des Pyrénées comme à l'autre. Peut-être s'est-on trop appuyé sur
quelques phrases de Grégoire, phrases parfois arrachées de contexte. Nous avons vu
déjà dans le cas de la succession royale mérovingienne comment était trompeux le commentaire de Grégoire: non moins le prétendu diagnostic grégorien d'une coutume détes-
table des Goths qui tuent les rois désagréables[42]. Il me parait qu'ici encore, Grégoire,
au lieu des renseignements specifiques, préfere un aparté ironisant. C'est la contrepar-
tie exacte de sa remarque à propos de Léovigild: «il a fait tuer tous ceux qui feraient
projet d'assassiner les rois ses fils[43]».

Il y a une dernière raison à croire que Goiswinthe jouait un rôle important du
côte d'Hermenegild: c'était que Léovigild a choisi d'aborder des négotiations avec Chilpéric, meutrier de Galeswinthe[44]. À travers le recit assez obscure de Grégoire peut-on
déduire que c'était Léovigild qui prit l'initiative. Seulement l'assassinat de Chilpéric
en 584 termina brusquement toute une politique de neutralisation de l'axe Hermenegild-
Goiswinthe-Brunehaut.

III. BRUNEHAUT, RECCARED, ET NARBONENSIS

Grégoire nous montre des relations complexes entre les événements qui déroulè-
rent aux deux côtés des Pyrénées aux années 580-90: tandis que Léovigild devait faire
face à la révolte d'Hermenegild, le roi Gontran avait un problème pareil avec le prétendant Gondovald. On a justement soupçonné des interventions byzantines dans les deux
cas. C'est probable que Gontran avait exploité les évènements en Espagne: Grégoire
fait mention des navires qui vogagèrent en 585 de la Gaule à la Galicie ou Léovigild
mena une campagne féroce[45]. Peut-être Gontran fit prétexte de la mort de sa nièce
Ingonde en lanceant un assaut contre les *Gothi horrendi*: Léovigild avait vainement essayé
de le détourner en fomentant des dissensions entre les rois francs. C'est à ce moment
que Grégoire met dans la bouche de Gontran les affirmations extraordinaires que la
Septimanie fit toujours partie de la Gaule et que lui, Gontran, se fut decidé à la réinté-
grer dans sa *dominatio*[46]. Étant donné les activités de sa bête-noire Gondovald dans les
régions voisines des Wisigoths, on peut bien comprendre le point de vue de Gontran.

Il y a une autre indication que la *Narbonensis* posait des problèmes pour Léovigild à cette époque. Grégoire nous raconte que l'évêque Fronimius d'Agde était associé en quelque façon avec Ingonde, et que Léovigild a du, en conséquence, l'expulser de son siège. Originaire de Bourges, Fronimius a cherché un protecteur à la cour de Childebert et Brunehaut[47]. Cette petite histoire pourrait faire penser que la révolte d'Hermenegild trouva des soutiens en *Narbonensis* aussi. Quoi-que ça soit, le jeune Reccared envoyé en *Narbonensis* pour la défendre contre les assauts des Francs de Gontran, fit ses preuves en dévastant et le Toulousain et, beaucoup plus a l'est, la région d'Arles[48].

Mais Gontran n'était plus le prédominant des rois francs. Le meurtre de Chilpéric, tout en faisant échouer la diplomatie matrimoniale de Léovigild, renforça beaucoup la position de la reine Brunehaut. De plus, la majorité de son fils Childebert II en 585 l'a mieux placée qu'avant à faire des interventions politiques. Ce n'est qu'à ce moment-ci, selon nos connaisssances, qu'elle révendiquait la *Morgengabe* de sa soeur, la malheureuse Galeswinthe: révendication qui dut l'attirer encore vers le sud, et vers l'Espagne[49]. Brunehaut même si elle ne soutint le prétendant Gondovald, sut profiter de sa ruine. Elle attira le soutien de quelques-uns de ses anciens serviteurs; des autres, révoltés de nouveau contre Brunehaut et son fils en 587, elle écrasa complètement[50].

C'est à la lumière de toutes ces évolutions que nous pouvons comprendre le récit grégorien des faits suivants: qu'après la mort de Léovigild, la première acte de Reccared c'était de faire rapprochement avec la reine Goiswinthe en la reconnaissant comme sa «mère», puis suivant le conseil de celle-ci, Reccared envoya des ambassades et à Brunehaut et à Gontran— ce qui implique, peut-être, que malgré la prise d'Hermenegild et malgré sa mise à mort, la révolte n'était pas encore, même en 586, tout à fait supprimée[51]. Reccared sut bien établir ses priorités. Gontran par cause de ses ambitions en Septimanie n'en voulait rien d'une alliance wisigothique. Alors il fallait une alliance avec Childebert et Brunehaut. Reccared proposait maintenant qu'il se mariât avec Clodosinde, la fille de Brunehaut[52].

La reine y mit son prix. Elle reclamait déjà peut-être la *Morgengabe* de sa soeur défunte. Elle voulait aussi des terres en *Narbonensis*. Nous savons par la correspondance postérieure du Comte Bulgare de Septimanie que Brunehaut reçut de Reccared deux propriétés près de la *civitas* de Béziers: Juvignac et Corneilhan[53]. Bien que nous ne savons pas la date de cette donation, elle doit se situer, je crois, vers 587. Reccared aurait essayé de s'assurer de l'alliance de Brunehaut contre les desseins de Gontran en *Narbonensis*.

Grégoire donne encore un détail: c'est que le roi Childebert— et derrière lui, on peut voir sa mère la reine Brunehaut —donna son accord au mariage de sa soeur avec Reccared parce qu'il reconnaissait que les Wisigoths étaient convertis à la foi catholique[54]. Est-ce qu'on est ainsi autorisé à croire que Brunehaut avait en effet imposé comme condition du mariage de sa fille la conversion des Wisigoths au catholicisme? Même Grégoire ne le croit pas. Sans doute Reccared avait pour sa décisión ses raisons à lui— et parmi elles, une espèce de raison d'état. Qu'il s'occupa avec la *provincia Narbonensis*, c'est certain: s'il y avait là une dimension religieuse, c'était que Reccared s'inquiéta de quelques ariens obstinés. Grégoire raconte qu'un évêque arien (de Narbonne, paraît-il) essayait vainement de susciter un mouvement de résistance contre les décisions du Concile de Tolède[55]. Encore un fois, en 589, quand Gontran fit un dernier assaut sur la *Narbonensis*, Reccared se manifesta résolu: jamais la Septimanie ne tomberait aux mains avares de Gontran. Grégoire n'indique chez l'agresseur aucune motivation religieuse. Au contraire, il est parfaitement formel que ce qui a agité Gontran c'était l'alliance politique entre Childebert —avec, croyait-il, les conseils de Brunehaut— et le roi Reccared[56]. On pourrait dire que dans ce sens au moins, le soutien de Brunehaut était de l'essentiel pour le nouveau converti. Et ça malgré l'avortement complet du projet de mariage entre Reccared et Chlodosinde. Brunehaut menait un jeu très subtil: sans rupture avec Gontran, elle donnait à Reccared le coup de main d'une neutralité diplomatique qui liu permit de garder la Septimanie pour le *regnum* wisigothique. Brunehaut, elle, espérait retrouver un as dans sa main —si on lui envoyerait de Constantinople son petit-fils Athanagild, fils d'Ingonde.

Est-ce que l'on entend en 589 un écho lointain des plaintes d'une autre reine? Si Reccared ne se maria pas avec la fille de Brunehaut, mais s'il prit une autre femme Baddo, dame wisigothique, semble-t-il,[57] qu'est ce que cela importa pour Goiswinthe? La vieille reine-mère dut voir échouer une dernière chance d'installer au palais une autre petite-fille, autre Ingonde, si vous voulez, et retenir ainsi peut-être toute sa propre autorité. Brunehaut, à son tour, aurait peur avant tout de se voir effacée, elle, par la parution d'une autre reine à la cour, et c'est pour cela qu'elle empêcha le mariage de son fils ou de son petit-fils avec une autre femme courageuse[58]. Brunehaut éviterait en tout cas le triste sort de Goiswinthe. Est-ce que cela explique sa dernière mention dans le chronique de Jean de Biclar? Elle s'était convertie à la foi catholique comme les autres, en 587— mais la suite montrerait qu'elle faisait faux semblant. Deux ans plus tard, elle s'affronta à l'avilissement. Assister à une grande cérémonie ou ferait figure une autre reine —sa supplantatrice? Et à Tolède ou elle, Goiswinthe, avait présidé auprès de toute une série des rois pendant un demi-siècle presque? Jamais! Quand dit Jean de Biclar que Goiswinthe *vitae tunc terminun dedit,* il veut dire, je crois, qu'elle préféra la mort[59]. Mort quand même honorable —ce qui explique pourquoi elle n'empêcha pas que Brunehaut tint à son alliance avec Reccared.

Avec Brunehaut, je veux terminer. Reine franque d'origine wisigothique, elle apporta un contribu non négligeable, même si indirecte, à la conversion de Reccared. Mais elle avait aussi des horizons plus larges. Dans sa correspondance avec l'impératrice de Constantinople, Brunehaut se montra *imitatrix imperii,* protectrice, comme les *basileis,* de la foi catholique[60]. Les lettres du Pape Grégoire le Grand nous font partie du rôle tout à fait indispensable de Brunehaut dans une autre conversion du VIe siècle tardif: celle des Anglo-Saxons[61]. En Angleterre, comme en Espagne, Brunehaut eut sans doute des interêts à elle; mais en même temps, et à l'échelle de la chrétienté, elle entenda remplir les devoirs d'un souverain *felix.* Si on croit apercevoir toujours de la politique, c'était la politique augustinienne.

NOTAS

[1] Je remercie vivement JOCELYN HILLGARTH et M. DÍAZ y DÍAZ de leur invitation au Congreso: RAMÓN GONZÁLVEZ, CARMEN LLORENTE et les organisateurs de leur acceuil si chaleureux; et mes collègues hispanistes ROGER COLLINS et PETER LINEHAN de leurs conseils experts. Je remercie aussi de tout coeur IAN WOOD qui m'a demontré un nouveau GRÉGOIRE de TOURS, et GEORGES NELSON qui a bien voulu corriger mes erreurs en grammaire française.

[2] VITA KAROLI MAGNI c. 16, ed. G. Waitz, *MGH Scriptores rerum Germanicarum in usum scholarum* (Hannover 1911), p. 20.

[3] S. REYNOLDS, «Medieval *Origines Gentium* and the community of the realm», *History* 68 (1983), pp. 375-90; R. COLLINS, compte rendu de S. TEILLET, *Des Goths à la Nation Gothique* (Paris 1984), dans *Nottingham Medieval Studies* 38 (1988), pp. 176-9.

[4] J. M. WALLACE-HADRILL, *The Long-Haired Kings* (Londres 1962); idem, *Early Medieval Kingbip in England and on the Continent* (Oxford 1971); H. WOLFRAM, «The shaping of the early medieval kingdom», *Viator* 1 (1970). pp. 1-20; P. STAFFORD, *Queens, Concubines and Dowagers* (Athens, Georgia 1983); IAN WOOD, *The Problem of Princes and the Royal Succession in Merovingian Francia* (à paraître).

[5] P. WORMALD, «Bede, the *Bretwaldas*, and the origins of the *gens Anglorum*», dans P. WORMALD ed., *Ideal and Reality in Frankish and Anglo-Saxon Society* (Oxford 1983), pp. 99-129; W. GOFFART, «From *Historiae* to *Historia Francorum* and back again: aspects of the textual history of GREGORY of TOURS», dans T. F. X. NOBLE et J. J. CONTRENI eds., *Religion, Culture and Society in the Early Middle Ages; Studies in Honor of R. E. SULLIVAN* (Kalamazoo, Michigan 1987), pp. 55-76 (réimp. dans GOFFART, *Rome's Fall and After* (Londres 1989), pp. 255-74.

[6] *Historiae* V, prologue, ed. B. KRUSCH et W. LEVISON, *MGH Scriptores rerum Merovingicarum* I, part 1, 2nd ed. (Berlin 1937-51), p. 193.

[7] *Pactus Childeberti I et Chlotharii I* c. 16, *MGH Capitularia regum Francorum I* (Hannover 1883), n°. 3, p. 7.

[8] *Ibid*, n.° 6, pp. 12-4 (texte pris de GRÉGOIRE, *Hist.* IX. 20).

[9] *L'Aquitaine des Wisigoths aux Arabes, 418-781 (Paris 1979).*

[10] Hist. V, 4, 13, VII, 12, VII, 24, pp. 198-9, 207, 333, 344 (Tours); VII, 6, IX, 20, pp. 328-9, 435 (Paris).

[11] R. COLLINS, *Early Medieval Spain* (Londres 1983), pp. 36-40, 113-6. Cf. J. ORLANDIS, *Historia de España. La España Visigótica* (Madrid 1977), pp. 211-2.

[12] Jean de Biclar, *Chronica*, ed. T. MOMMSEN, *MGH Auctores* XI (Berlin 1894), pp. 212-7.

[13] C. HIGOUNET, «Les relations franco-ibériques au Moyen Age», *Comité des travaux historiques et scientifiques, Bulletin Philologique et Historique pour 1969* (Paris 1972), pp. 3-16, à 3; J. FONTAINE, «Mozarabie Hispanique et Monde Carolingien: les échanges culturels entre la France et l'Espagne du VIIIe au Xe siècle», *Anuario de estudios medievales* 13 (1983), pp. 17-46.

[14] *Hist.* IV, 27, p. 160.

[15] *Ibid.*, V, 20, p. 228. VOIR IAN WOOD, «Kings, Kingdoms and Consent», dans P. SAWYER et I. N. WOOD eds., *Early Medieval Kingship* (Leeds 1977), pp. 6-29, à 14; *idem, The Problems of Princes.*

[16] *Hist.* IV, 30, pp. 162-3.

[17] R. MARKUS, «Gregory the Great's Europe» *Transactions of the Royal Historical Society* 31 (1981), pp. 21 36. Cf. J. HERRIN, *The Formation of Christendom* (Princeton 1987), pp. 119-27.

[18] GRÉGOIRE, *Hist.* IX, 20, p. 437. Voir ROUCHE, *Aquitaine,* p. 72.

[19] F. L. GANSHOF, «Le statut de la femme dans la monarchie franque», *Receuils Jean Bodin* 12 (1962), pp. 5-57, à 27, n. 65; S. F. WEMPLE, *Women in Frankish Society* (Philadelphia 1981), p. 45. Cf. WOOD, «Kings, Kingdoms», p. 27; ROUCHE, *Aquitaine,* p. 67.

[20] GRÉGOIRE, *Hist.* IX, 20, p. 435, 437: après la mort de Gontran, toutes ces *civitates* doivent revenir «in dominatione dominae Brunichilde heredumque suorum cum omni soliditate».

[21] Venance Fortunat, *Carmina* VI, n.° v: *de Gelesuintha,* ed. F. LEO, *MGH Auctores* IV. i (Hannover 1881), pp. 136-46.

[22] *Chronica*, p. 212.

[23] ORLANDIS, *Historia*, p. 94.

[24] J. L. NELSON, «Queens as Jezebels: Brunhild and Balthild in Merovingian history», dans D. BAKER ed., *Medieval Women* (Oxford 1977), pp. 36, 40, 47; STAFFORD, *Queens,* pp. 104-6.

[25] NELSON, «Queens as Jezebels». pp. 37, 40-1; STAFFORD, *Queens,* p. 49. Cf. A. CAMERON, «The Empress Sophia», *Byzantion* 45 (1975) pp. 5-21, à pp. 17-8.

[26] GRÉGOIRE, *Hist.* IV, 28, p. 160.

[27] WALLACE-HADRILL, *Long-Haired Kings,* pp. 134-5, 205; NELSON «Queens as Jezebels», p. 40; COLLINS, *Early Medieval Spain,* p. 39.

[28] *Hist.* V, 1, p. 194.

[29] *Ibid.* IV, 28, p. 161.

[30] *Ibid.* IV, 27, p. 160.

[31] *Ibid.* V, 38, VIII, 28, pp. 244-5, 390-1; Cf. VI, 43, pp. 314-5, avec quelques réservations au sujet d'un fils révolté contre son père. Sur le témoignage de Jean de Biclar, voir K. STROHEKER, «Das Spanische Westgotenreich und Byzanz», *Bonner Jahrbücher* 163 (1963), pp. 252-74 à 259-60.

[32] COLLINS, *Early Medieval Spain,* pp. 46-9; WOOD, «Gregory of Tours and Clovis», *Revue Belge de Philologie et d'Histoire* 63 (1985), pp. 249-72.

[33] S. LIFSHITZ, «Les femmes missionnaires: l'exemple de la Gaule franque», *Revue d'Histoire Ecclésiastique* 83 (1988), pp. 5-33; B. MERTA, «Helenae conparanda regina - secunda Isebel», *Mitteilungen des Instituts österreichische Geschichtsforschung* 96 (1988), pp. 1-32.

[34] *Hist.* V, 40, p. 247.

[35] *Chronica,* p. 212.

[36] *Ibid.* p. 215.

[37] *Epistolae Austrasicae,* n.os 27, 28, 43-5, ed. W. GUNDLACH, *MGH Epistolae* III (Berlin 1892), pp. 139, 140, 149, 150.

[38] *Chronica,* pp. 213, 211.

[39] GRÉGOIRE, *Hist.* IV, 41, V, 30, pp. 174, 235-6 . Voir sur la mort d'Alboin, roi des Lombards, W. GOFFART, *Narrators of Barbarian History* (Princeton 1988), pp. 391-2, n.º 197; sur la mort du cousin de Justin II, A. CAMERON, «The Empress Sophia», p. 9.

[40] STAFFORD, *Queens,* pp. 191-7. Cf. K. HOLUM, *Theodosian Empresses; Women and Imperial Dominion in Late Antiquity* ((Berkeley 1982).

[41] Voir STAFFORD, «Sons and mothers: family politics in the early Middle Ages», dans BAKER ed., *Medieval Women,* pp. 79-100; *idem,* «The king's wife in Wessex» *Past and Present* 91 (1981), pp. 3-27; WOOD, *The Problems of Princes.*

[42] *Hist.* III, 30, p. 126.

[43] *Ibid.* IV, 38, p. 170.

[44] *Ibid.* V, 43, p. 249: VI, 18, 40, 45, pp. 287-8, 310, 317.

[45] *Ibid.* VIII, 35, p. 404.

[46] *Ibid.* VIII, 28, p. 391.

[47] *Ibid.* IX, 24, pp. 443-4. Voir L. GARCÍA MORENO, *Prosopografia del reino visigodo de Toledo* (Salamanque 1974), n.º 532, pp. 190-1.

[48] GRÉGOIRE, *Hist.* VIII, 30, p. 396; cf. JEAN DE BICLAR, *Chronica,* p. 217.

[49] Voir ci-dessus p. 2, et n. 18.

[50] GRÉGOIRE, *Hist.* VII, 43, p. 364; IX, 10, 28, pp. 425, 446.

[51] *Ibid.* IX, 1, pp. 414-5.

[52] *Ibid.* IX, 16, pp. 430-1.

[53] *MGH Epistolae* III, *Epistolae Wisigothicae* n.º 13, pp. 680-1 Voir ROUCHE, *Aquitaine,* p. 240 et n. 353 (p. 593).

[54] GRÉGOIRE, *Hist.* IX, 25, p. 444.

[55] *Ibid.* IX, 15, pp. 429-30. VOIR GARCÍA MORENO, *Prosopografia,* n.º 663, pp. 223-4.

[56] *Ibid.* VIII, 28-30, pp. 390-6.

[57] ORLANDIS, *Historia,* p. 116. C'est Baddo *gloriosa regina* qui à l'instar d'une impératrice byzantine, souscrit le profession de foi au IIIe Concile de Tolède: J. VIVES ed., *Concilios Visigóticos e Hispano-Romanos* (Barcelone-Madrid 1963), p. 10.

[58] NELSON, «Queens as Jezebels», pp. 43-4, 58.

[59] *Chronica,* p. 218.

[60] *MGH Epistolae* III, *Epistolae Austrasicae* n.os 29, 44, pp. 140, 150.

[61] GRÉGOIRE le GRAND, *Epistolae* VI, 57 (voir aussi vi, 49), VIII, 4, et surtout XI, 48, ed. P. EWALD et L. M. HARTMANN, *MGH Epistolae* I, II (Berlin 1899), I, pp. 423-4, 431-2; II, p. 7, pp. 320-1.

XII

LA FAMILLE DE CHARLEMAGNE

'Toutes les familles heureuses sont heureuses de la même façon ; toutes les familles malheureuses le sont de façons différentes'. C'est Léon Tolstoï qui l'affirme — mais peut-être Anna Karénine est-elle une autorité discutable ... Dans cette communication, je voudrais présenter deux propos sur la famille de Charlemagne — d'abord que cette famille était relativement heureuse ; ensuite — et malgré Tolstoï — que son bonheur était hors du commun, et apparaissait même un peu «bizarre» dans le Haut Moyen Âge occidental.

La famille heureuse d'abord. Parce que vivre en famille, en tant que chef de famille, entouré par de proches parents comme alliés, serviteurs, ou satellites, était le sort de tous les monarques du Haut Moyen Âge et, bien sûr, des époques plus tardives. Les rois mérovingiens étaient sans doute ainsi entourés par de nombreux parents, plus ou moins proches, à la fois alliés et concurrents : nos connaissances sont rares néanmoins sur de tels personnages — ce qui n'a pas empêché les historiens modernes de faire des conjectures, sur base onomastique par exemple. Il est en effet possible que Bertrade, mère de Charlemagne, fille d'un comte Caribert (¹), descende des Mérovingiens, mais aucun auteur du huitième siècle ne s'en préoccupa. La famille étendue, la *stirps regia*, des Mérovingiens reste presque entièrement dans l'ombre.

En ce qui concerne les Carolingiens, on attendrait plus de témoignages. Pépin, roi parvenu, avait besoin de soutiens fidèles et ses parents avaient intérêt à se joindre à lui. Le sang, dit-on

(1) *Annales Bertiniani* 749, ed. G. WAITZ, *Monumenta Germaniae Historica Scriptores rerum Germanicarum in usum scholarum* (cité ci-après *MGH SRG*) (Hanover, 1883), p. 1. Je remercie de tout cœur Alain DIERKENS qui a eu la bonté de corriger mes fautes en langue française et de me donner des conseils précieux. À lui et à Jean-Marie SANSTERRE, je dois aussi des remerciements chaleureux pour l'organisation du Colloque de Bruxelles.

en anglais, est plus épais que l'eau — et, pourrait-on dire, mieux fait pour coaguler. La fortune de Pépin devait être aussi la fortune de ses *propinqui*. Il est cependant difficile de les retrouver mentionnés dans les sources narratives. Même les auteurs des *Continuationes Fredegarii* — l'oncle, puis le cousin de Pépin — manquent à l'histoire du règne de Pépin. De ceux qui faisaient partie de la famille royale seuls s'y trouvent la reine Bertrade et ses deux fils, Charles et Carloman. Les *Annales Regni Francorum* traitent surtout des frères de Pépin, Grifon et Carloman, sources de problèmes pour le nouveau roi. Après 755, ils sont morts tous les deux. Sur les autres *propinqui* ou sur les parents de Bertrade, les *Annales* ne disent rien. C'est la famille étroite, nucléaire, que nous présentent les chroniqueurs contemporains du premier roi carolingien. Pour d'autres proches parents de Pépin, il faut se référer à diverses sources, parfois un peu plus tardives. Deux demi-frères illégitimes étaient déjà voués aux carrières ecclésiastiques ; le nouveau roi s'en servit dans les premières années du règne : Jérôme accompagna le pape Etienne II en route pour Rome en 754 (²) ; Remi devint évêque de Rouen en 755 (³). Un troisième frère (ou demi-frère bâtard ?), Bernard, ne figure pas dans les sources relatives au règne de Pépin.

On remarque deux contrastes entre la famille du roi Pépin et celle de ses ancêtres, maires du palais. D'abord, ceux-ci ont partagé avec leurs proches parents (y compris les femmes) leurs biens familiaux des régions de la Meuse et du Rhin : action typique de la noblesse franque (⁴). Mais un royaume n'est pas seulement un fonds familial. Même s'il manquait d'un principe d'*Unteilbarkeit*, le fisc (c'est-à-dire la terre publique), plus ou

---

(2) *Liber Pontificalis, Vita Stephani* c. 39, ed. L. Duchesne (Rome, 1886), vol. 1, p. 451 ; *Annales Fuldenses* 754, ed. F. Kurze, *MGH SRG* (Hanover, 1891), p. 7 ; *Vita Arnulfi*, ed. Br. Krusch, *MGH Scriptores Rerum Merowingicarum* II, p. 429.

(3) *Gesta Abbatum Fontenellensium* c. 12, ed. G. H. Pertz, *MGH Scriptores* (cité ci-après *SS*) II (Hanover, 1829), p. 286 ; Adrevald, *Miracula Sancti Benedicti, Patrologia Latina* (cité ci-après *PL*) 124, col. 918.

(4) Voir E. Hlawitschka, 'Zu den Grundlagen des Aufstiegs der Karolinger. Beschäftigung mit zwei Büchern von Matthias Werner', *Rheinische Vierteljahrsblätter* 49 (1985), p. 1-61 (réimpr. dans Hlawitschka, *Stirps Regia. Forschungen zu Königtum und Führungsschichten im früheren Mittelalter* (Frankfurt-am-Main, 1988), p. 43-103, surtout 72-100).

moins stable, qui devait servir de base solide au pouvoir royal, se distinguait nettement des biens privés. Pépin s'est fait héritier du fisc mérovingien : mais il a aussi dû transformer son patrimoine en «fisc supplémentaire» pour réduire le risque d'aliénations permanentes entre *coheredes*. Le nouveau roi a peut-être utilisé des moyens traditionnels : pour bon nombre de ses proches parents, remise de mariage, vie célibataire ou carrière ecclésiastique. Puis Pépin a ajouté de nouveaux moyens : règles canoniques qui ont restreint davantage les degrés interdits du mariage et qui ont exclu les bâtards de l'héritage familial. Aucun partage du patrimoine carolingien n'a été réalisé entre le roi Pépin et ses frères ou demi-frères. Ou bien ceux-ci moururent sans descendance ; ou bien ils étaient ecclésiastiques, dotés de biens d'Église ; dans le cas de Bernard qui restait dans la vie séculière, ses terres lui venaient, semble-t-il, de ses mariages et ses fils étaient donc héritiers de leur mère, mais non de Charles Martel ([5]).

Ensuite, dans les rituels d'accession au pouvoir, Pépin a souligné soigneusement la famille nucléaire : père, mère et deux fils. On n'a pas besoin d'une *Clausula de unctione* authentique pour être sûr — grâce à une lettre pontificale — qu'en 754, la reine Bertrade et ses deux fils furent consacrés avec Pépin par le pape ([6]). On assiste là à quelque chose de neuf parce que rien n'annonce cette espèce de succession *pre mortem* ou la participation de la reine aux rituels inauguraux mérovingiens. Pépin avait une opinion stricte sur le mariage. Il n'eut aucune maîtresse. Pépin et Bertrade menèrent une vie domestique impeccable — au moins pour la forme ([7]). Ils gardèrent à la cour leurs deux fils à la

---

(5) La mère d'Adalard, fils aîné, *adhuc tiro palatii* vers 770 était franque ; la mère de Wala, fils cadet, était saxonne : L. WEINRICH, *Wala. Graf, Mönch und Rebell* (Lubeck, 1963), p. 11-12.

(6) *Codex Carolinus* 11, ed. W. GUNDLACH, *MGH Epistolae* III, p. 505. Voir A. STOCLET, 'La «clausula de unctione Pippini regis»' : mises au point et nouvelles hypothèses', *Francia* 8 (1980), p. 1-42.

(7) Mais *Codex Carolinus* 45, p. 561, donne à entendre que Pépin a tenté une fois de se débarrasser de Bertrade : voir M. ENRIGHT, *Iona, Tara, Soissons. The Origin of the Royal Anointing Ritual* (Berlin, 1985), p. 92-3. Le mariage de Pépin eut lieu en 744, la naissance de Charles en 747 : K. F. WERNER, 'La date de naissance de Charlemagne', dans *Bulletin de la Société nationale des Antiquaires de France*, année 1972, Paris 1975, p. 116-43 (réimpr. dans WERNER, *Structures politiques du monde franc* (Londres, 1979), ch. VII).

différence de Pépin lui-même, élevé à St Denis), qui restaient
donc en relations étroites avec leurs parents.

Une seule fille a survécu aux années d'enfance : Gisèle, née
en 757. Elle avait été demandée, peut-être en 767, en mariage
par l'empereur Constantin pour son fils, puis en 770 pour le fils
du roi lombard Didier. Mais Gisèle ne s'est jamais mariée. Elle
devint abbesse de Chelles (⁸). Pour ses deux fils, Pépin a trouvé
deux femmes nobles et franques, Himiltrude et Gerberge. Tandis
que le pape en 770 voulait croire que ces unions étaient de vrais
mariages, treize ans plus tard, Paul le Diacre assurait ses lecteurs
que la liaison de Charlemagne avec Himiltrude n'avait pas été
un *legale connubium* (⁹). En tout cas, on ne sait rien de la paren-
tèle de ces femmes — *in-laws* des fils de Pépin pendant la vie
de Pépin, *in-laws* de Pépin lui-même. Pourquoi ? Il est vrai qu'un
régime nouvellement établi, toujours précaire, ne pouvait se
permettre aucun gaspillage de charisme ou de ressources maté-
rielles, qu'il fallait canaliser aussi étroitement que possible. Mais
une telle prévention patrilinéaire, dynastique, était déjà tradition-
nelle dans la monarchie franque. Pépin a reconstruit une famille
royale d'après le modèle mérovingien. Famille heureuse de la
même façon. Famille royale idéale, peut-être. Avec le règne de
Charlemagne, nous appréhendons un peu mieux la réalité.

En 768, Charlemagne était co-héritier avec son frère Carloman. Tout de suite, et en partie à cause de la politique de la
reine-mère Bertrade (¹⁰), une menace parut au sein même de la

---

(8) Voir dessous, p. 207. Selon L. Levillain, 'Les comtes de Paris à
l'époque franque', *Le Moyen Âge* 12 (1941), p. 137-205 (p. 153), Pépin avait
une deuxième fille, Rotrude. Mais elle était plutôt proche parente de Charles
Martel : E. Hlawitschka, 'Die Vorfahren Karls der Grossen', dans W. Braunfels ed., *Karl der Grosse. Lebenswerk und Nachleben*, 5 vols. (Düsseldorf,
1965-7), vol. 1, p. 51-82, à la p. 82 ; Werner, 'Die Nachkommen Karls de
Grossen', dans Braunfels ed., *Karl der Grosse*, vol. IV, p. 403-79 (p. 431).
Pépin n'a donc utilisé aucune de ses filles pour établir des liens de parenté
avec la noblesse franque. Deux autres filles sont mortes dans l'enfance : Paul
le Diacre, *Gesta Episcoporum Mettensium*, ed. Pertz, *MGH SS* II, p. 265.

(9) *Gesta Episcoporum Mettensium*, p. 265.

(10) L'auteur des *Annales Regni Francorum* 770, ed. F. Kurze, *MGH SRG*
(Hanover, 1895), p. 31, la dépeint comme *mater regum* pacificatrice ; mais
c'est elle qui a promu l'alliance de Charles avec la princesse lombarde : voir

famille royale : elle ne fut évitée que grâce à la mort de Carloman en décembre 771. Charles resta seul — en poussant un grand soupir de soulagement. C'est au début même de son règne monarchique que deux proches parents apparaissent dans son entourage. Le *propinquus* Thierry (peut-être son cousin au troisième degré) apparaît pour la première fois dans un jugement de 772 comme *vassus* du roi, puis comme comte en 775. Bernard, l'oncle de Charlemagne, fait son entrée en 773 (alors qu'il devait avoir au moins trente-deux ans) ([11]). C'est Bernard qui conduisit une partie de l'armée de Charlemagne à travers le *Mons Jovis* pendant l'hiver pour faire le siège de Pavie. Pourquoi Charlemagne avait-il besoin des services de ces *propinqui* ? Parce qu'après la mort de son frère, la veuve et les fils de celui-ci s'étaient enfui vers Pavie, en cherchant la protection du roi Didier. Ainsi la seconde ligne de la *progenies* de Pépin survivait à Carloman lui-même et le risque de division existait encore au cœur de la famille carolingienne. Les rejetons de la *stirps regia* durent opter pour un camp ou l'autre : leur appui était critique. Charlemagne s'attacha ses *propinqui* — et élimina ses neveux ([12]).

Charlemagne eut une longue vie — son règne dura quarante-trois ans — par comparaison avec les dix-huit années du règne de Pépin. Puis, à la différence de son père, Charles était un *pater familias* prolifique. Non pas polygame, bien sûr, comme l'a affirmé Mlle Konecny ([13]), mais vigoureux *serial monogamist*, peut-être parfois adultère. Face aux trois enfants de Pépin (je ne compte pas ceux qui n'ont pas atteint leur troisième anniversaire), Charles en eut quinze ([14]). Ces faits biologiques exceptionnels

S. Konecny, *Die Frauen der karolingischen Königshauses* (Vienne, 1976), p. 61-2.

(11) Voir D. Bullough, '*Albuinus deliciosus Karoli regis* : Alcuin of York and the shaping of the early Carolingian court', dans L. Fenske et al. edd., *Institutionen, Kultur und Gesellschaft im Mittelalter. Festschrift für J. Fleckenstein* (Sigmaringen, 1985), p. 73-92, aux p. 87-8.

(12) Eginhard, *Vita Karoli* c. 3, ed. G. Waitz, *MGH SRG* (Hanover, 1911), p. 6 : 'defuncto Karlomanno uxor eius ... nullis existentibus causis (!), spreto mariti fratre ... sub Desiderii regis Langobardorum patrocinium se cum liberis suis contulit'.

(13) *Die Frauen*, p. 66.

(14) Voir table généalogique, en face de la p. 211. Je remercie ma collègue Susan Kruse de son expertise avec 'Macdraw'.

impliquaient pour la famille royale non seulement une augmen-
tation, mais un changement de forme. Le père doit coexister
longtemps avec des enfants adultes. Puis la famille s'étend à trois
générations. La relation *nepos-patruus*, c'est-à-dire neveu-oncle
paternel, le plus difficile des liens de parenté au sein de la famille
royale, s'est reproduite. Dans la *Divisio* de 806, Charles demanda
à ses fils : «Quant aux petits-fils, c'est-à-dire les fils de nos fils,
nous voulons que nul d'entre nos fils ne fasse accuser devant
lui aucun d'eux [c'est-à-dire de ses neveux] ni le fasse tuer, mutiler,
aveugler ou tonsurer à contrecœur» [15]. Ces mots évoquent
pourtant le destin des princes-neveux des générations suivantes
avec Louis le Pieux, ensuite avec Charles le Chauve, puis Charles
le Simple. Type de vie familiale normal à l'époque, mais il est
inhabituel que le grand-père s'en soit préoccupé.

La famille à trois générations — avec ses complications, ses
conflits possibles — apportait bien des possibilités aux proches
parents, y compris aux parents par alliance. On connaît la belle
carrière du frère de Hildegarde, Gérold, et de ses fils [16]. Mais
on remarquera que Gérold n'est *praefectus* en Bavière que quelques années après la mort de Hildegarde [17]. Selon Notker le
Bègue, Udalric, un autre frère de la reine, a vu ses terres confis-
quées par Charlemagne tout de suite après la mort de la reine.
Pourquoi croire Notker ici ? parce qu'il était compatriote
d'Udalric et parce que son histoire, qui se rapporte à cette espèce
de *veredicus* par excellence, le bouffon, se moquait du beau-frère
du roi : «Maintenant que sa sœur est morte, Udalric a perdu
ses terres et dans l'Est et dans l'Ouest». Quelle blague affreuse [18] !

(15) *MGH Capitularia* I, no. 45, c. 18, p. 129.
(16) K. SCHMID, 'The structure of the nobility in the earlier middle ages',
dans T. REUTER ed., *The Medieval Nobility* (Amsterdam, 1978), p. 37-60,
aux p. 39-40 ; K. F. WERNER, 'Bedeutende Adelsfamilien im Reich Karls des
Grossen', dans W. BRAUNFELS, ed., *Karl der Grosse*, vol. I, p. 83-142 aux
p. 111-2. À comparer D. BULLOUGH, '*Europae pater*. Charlemagne and his
achievement in the light of recent scholarship', *English Historical Review* 85
(1970), p. 59-105, aux p. 73-84.
(17) M. BORGOLTE, *Die Grafen Alemanniens im merowingischer und
karolingischer Zeit* (Sigmaringen, 1987), p. 122-6.
(18) NOTKER, *Gesta Karoli Magni* I, c. 13, ed. H. F. HAEFELE, *MGH SRG*
(Berlin, 1962), p. 17. Sur l'humour très significatif de Notker, voir D. GANZ,
'Humour as history in Notker's *Gesta Karoli Magni*', dans E. KING et al.

Charlemagne a pleuré, puis a rendu les terres à son beau-frère. La tristesse de Charles, comme celle d'Udalric, ne dura qu'un moment. Par la suite, Charles s'entendit bien avec ses *in-laws*. Mais la promotion de Gérold, au moins, avait peut-être un rapport avec la promotion de son neveu le jeune roi Pépin, roi d'Italie mais aussi roi de Bavière. Ici le lien était celui du neveu et de l'oncle maternel : lien que Marc Bloch a depuis longtemps considéré comme particulièrement chargé d'affection dans les sociétés médiévales ([19]). La fortune de Pépin était la fortune de son oncle.

Avec les fils de Charlemagne, nous nous trouvons au centre de la famille royale, et de ses problèmes. Les relations entre père et fils sont toujours difficiles, surtout après que le fils a atteint sa majorité. Le fils aîné de Charlemagne était le fils de Himiltrude. Son nom, Pépin, implique en soi que le garçon était accepté comme digne de la succession royale. Son visage était beau, selon Eginhard, qui ajoute (d'une façon tendancieuse) qu'il était bossu ([20]). Même quand, en 781, Charlemagne changea le nom de son troisième fils, en l'appelant aussi Pépin et en le faisant roi d'Italie, son fils aîné ne protesta pas. Dans la liturgie royale, son nom continua à être commémoré ; il était donc toujours reconnu «officiellement» comme co-héritier de son père ([21]). Mais en 790, Charlemagne a promu son deuxième fils, Charles le Jeune, qui règnera désormais sur la Neustrie ([22]). Quand le Bossu se révolta un an plus tard (j'y reviendrai), Charles se trouva face à la crise la plus sérieuse du règne. Il la surmonta. Il survécut. Comment ? Par sa dureté, bien sûr, envers les rebelles — qui comptaient parmi eux, je crois, le jeune cousin de Charles, Wala, jusque là nourri à la cour et maintenant renvoyé à la campagne

---

edd., *Monks, Nuns and Friars in Medieval Society* (Sewanee, Tennessee, 1989), p. 171-83.

(19) M. Bloch, *Feudal Society* (London, 1961), p. 137.

(20) Eginhard, *Vita Karoli* c. 20, p. 25.

(21) P. Classen, 'Karl der Grosse und die Thronfolge im Frankenreich', dans *Festschrift für H. Heimpel*, 3 vols. (Göttingen, 1971-2), vol. III, p. 109-34, à la p. 118. Il y avait pourtant des gens qui déjà prenaient parti pour les fils d'Hildegarde (voir n. 43 ci-dessous).

(22) *Annales Mettenses Priores* 790, ed. B. von Simson, *MGH SRG* (Hanover, 1905), p. 78.

et au travail de la charrue ([23]). On suppose que Wala était partisan du Bossu. Mais Charlemagne se servit aussi de la *magnanimitas*, du compromis. Pour le Bossu, enfermé à Prüm, le monastère était peut-être plutôt un foyer sympathique qu'une prison. L'abbé de Prüm avait été coupable d'*infidelitas* — mais en 797 il récupéra des biens confisqués, tout comme un autre infidèle de la même région, Théodold ([24]).

En plus du Bossu, Charlemagne avait trois autres fils, légitimes, nés avant 778, donc adultes pendant la première moitié du règne de leur père. Mais après 791, on n'assiste à aucune révolte filiale. Pour un roi médiéval, ce fait est tout à fait exceptionnel. Eginhard évoque, une fois de plus, la *magnanimitas* de Charlemagne, et sa *pietas* qui l'a fait pleurer à chaudes larmes à la nouvelle de la mort de deux de ses fils en 810 et 811 ([25]). Même une famille heureuse a ses peines. De plus, c'était une famille de rois : dans les années 790, Charlemagne et ses fils portaient tous le même titre, *rex*. Il fallut distinguer l'autorité du père — roi des rois — de celle des fils ; ce qui est, au moins, une des significations du couronnement impérial de Charlemagne.

En 806, Charlemagne annonça la division de son empire. Le contexte de cette *divisio* était, pour ainsi dire, une crise annoncée. Les *primores et optimates Francorum* étaient rassemblés pour discuter 'l'établissement et le maintien de la paix' ([26]). C'est à ce moment que le cousin de Charlemagne, Wala, rentra en faveur à la cour ([27]). Charlemagne a su étouffer un conflit qui menaçait — non seulement parce qu'il avait beaucoup à donner, mais aussi parce qu'il savait faire une distribution égale. Charles le Jeune, *rex Francorum*, devait hériter de toute la Francie — arrangement

(23) Paschasius, *Epitaphium Arsenii* I, c. 6, ed. E. Dümmler, *Abhandlungen der königlichen Preußischen Akademie der Wissenschaften zu Berlin*, Berlin 1900, p. 28.

(24) *MGH Diplomata regum Karolinorum* 1, ed. E. Mühlbacher, n°s 180, 181, p. 242-5.

(25) Eginhard, *Vita Karoli* c. 19, p. 24.

(26) Classen, 'Karl der Grosse und der Thronfolge', p. 121-34, surtout 129-32.

(27) Weinrich, *Wala*, p. 18-9. À comparer : K. F. Werner, '«*Hludovicus Augustus*» : Gouverner l'empire chrétien — idées et réalités', dans P. Godman et R. Collins, edd., *Charlemagne's Heir, New Perspectives on the Reign of Louis the Pious* (Oxford, 1990), p. 3-124, aux p. 28-54.

révolutionnaire dont le regretté P. Classen a indiqué l'importance — et, à l'Est, des possibilités d'élargissement aux dépens des peuples slaves. Mais Charles le Jeune restait sans descendance — peut-être était-il célibataire. Ses frères puînés avaient, donc, des espérances (son biographe le dit explicitement dans le cas de Louis, le plus jeune) ([28]). De plus, ils régnaient déjà, chacun, sur de grands royaumes qui avaient aussi des frontières toujours croissantes. Les historiens modernes disent que vers 806 l'expansion impériale des Francs était terminée — mais qui le savait en 806 ? Pépin avait de vastes frontières vers l'est, dans l'*Avaria*, où Charlemagne était en train d'intervenir (en 805, puis en 811) dans les *controversiae Hunorum et Sclavorum* ([29]). Pépin avait là des raisons justifiées d'espérer. Il en est de même de Louis le Pieux (roi d'Aquitaine depuis 781) dans la Marche d'Espagne — où les dernières grandes acquisitions du territoire datent précisément des années 806-812 ([30]). Cette situation était donc favorable à Charlemagne : pour emprunter une phrase de Nithard (lui-même petit-fils de Charlemagne) : «*il avait de quoi dédommager ses fidèles*» — y compris ses fils ([31]). En même temps, il a su éviter la dissolution et le partage du fisc en Francie, cœur de l'Empire.

Charlemagne avait également su renforcer les bonnes relations entre ses fils et, en même temps, soulager les tensions entre eux, par une série de campagnes collectives (de Louis et Pépin en Italie en 793, par exemple ([32]) ; Louis et Charles le Jeune en Saxe en 796 ([33]) ; Louis et Pépin avec leur père en Saxe en 797 ([34]) ; Louis et Charles le Jeune avec leur père en Saxe en 799) ([35]) ; et de rassemblements familiaux, notamment à Ratisbonne en

---

(28) ASTRONOME, *Vita Hludovici* c. 20, ed. PERTZ, *MGH SS* II, p. 617. Pour Charles le Jeune, voir P. CLASSEN, 'Karl der Grosse und der Thronfolge', p. 111, 132.

(29) *Annales Regni Francorum*, p. 120, 135.

(30) ASTRONOME cc. 14-18, *MGH SS* II, p. 613-6.

(31) NITHARD, *Histoire des fils de Louis le Pieux* IV, 3, ed. Ph. LAUER (Paris, 1926), p. 124-6.

(32) *Annales Laureshamenses* 793, ed. PERTZ, *MGH SS* II, p. 35 ; Astronome c. 6, *MGH SS* II, p. 610.

(33) *Ann. Laureshamenses* 796, p. 37.

(34) *Ann. Regni Francorum* 797, p. 103.

(35) *Ann. Regni Francorum* 799, p. 106.

793 ([36]) et à Rome en 800, où seul Louis était absent (mais Charlemagne avait d'abord voulu que Louis y assiste aussi) ([37]) ; puis à Aix en 806 ([38]). Selon l'Astronome, Charlemagne vers 793 tint sous sa propre main pendant près d'une année l'éducation de Louis : il fallait que sa résidence en Aquitaine n'habitue pas le jeune homme franc à des mœurs déplorables et n'implique pas un gaspillage du fisc du royaume d'Aquitaine ([39]). Ce fisc, le père le fit reconstituer. Aussi maria-t-il son fils Louis, en lui choisissant une femme ([40]). La co-résidence de Charlemagne et de son fils Charles le Jeune était plus suivie : ils étaient ensemble en 800-1 à Rome ; en 804, 805, 806, 808, 810 ([41]). Charlemagne, selon Eginhard, était un *paterfamilias* consciencieux, et s'occupait tellement de l'éducation de ses enfants que «jamais il ne prenait ses repas, jamais il ne voyageait, sans eux» ([42]).

Voilà l'image de Charlemagne que tous connaissent. On sait bien pourquoi : pour la première fois depuis l'Antiquité, nous avons des détails non seulement biographiques sur Charlemagne lui-même, mais sur sa famille : d'abord (on ne le sait pas assez) grâce à Paul Diacre, qui dépeint le groupe familial en 783-4, et nous donne les épitaphes touchantes de Hildegarde et de deux de ses filles ([43]) ; ensuite grâce à Eginhard qui nous décrit d'une façon inoubliable la vie domestique de Charlemagne ([44]). Encore c'est une *progenies* (père et descendance) : si la famille est nombreuse, c'est parce que Charlemagne a survécu à cinq épouses, et il avait aussi quelques maîtresses. Ensuite il a survécu à son

(36) *Ann. Laureshamenses* 793, p. 35 (seul Charles le Jeune peut-être n'était pas là). Voir aussi p. 206, ci-dessous.

(37) *Ann. Regni Francorum* 801, p. 114 ; Astronome c. 10, *MGH SS* II, p. 611.

(38) *Ann. Regni Francorum* 806, p. 121.

(39) ASTRONOME c. 6, p. 610.

(40) THEGAN, *Vita Hludovici imperatoris* c. 4, *MGH SS* II, p. 591. Voir KONECNY, *Die Frauen*, p. 73.

(41) *Ann. Regni Francorum*, p. 119-25 ; *Chronicon Moissiacense, MGH SS* II, p. 258.

(42) EGINHARD, *Vita Karoli* c. 19, p. 24-5.

(43) *Gesta Episc. Mettens.*, MGH SS II, p. 265-7. Voir W. GOFFART, *The Narrators of Barbarian History* (Princeton, 1988), p. 373-8, surtout à la p. 376. (Traduction anglaise par G. HALSALL à paraître).

(44) EGINHARD, *Vita Karoli* cc. 18-20, p. 21-6 ('interior atque domestica vita').

fils Pépin d'Italie dont les filles sont venues à Aix pour être élevées chez leur grand-père. On voit ici non pas une famille étendue en direction horizontale (famille qui s'étalait comme celles des *Libri Memoriales*), mais une *genealogia* verticale comme celle décrite par Dhuoda, vers 841. En commandant à son fils : *Ora pro parentibus genitoris tui*, elle voulait dire le grand-père, la grand-mère, les oncles, les tantes. Le point central était le père. Selon Dhuoda, le premier devoir des enfants était l'obéissance au père. Le professeur Riché a justement parlé d'une religion de paternité ([45]).

Eginhard nous décrit une famille de Charlemagne sans *propinqui*, une famille pour ainsi dire étroite. C'est une famille qui vit ensemble, ou au moins qui passe beaucoup de temps ensemble. Famille heureuse — plus ou moins. Mais — et ici j'aborde la deuxième partie de cette communication — c'est une famille heureuse de façon insolite. L'indice critique en est le rôle joué par les femmes : rôle prépondérant d'abord du point de vue statistique. Lisez Eginhard : à côté de la série des reines, des concubines, de la sœur aimée de Charlemagne, (et Eginhard omet la cousine de l'empereur — Gondrade, qui, selon Paschase, était *virgo familiarior regi*) ([46]), il y avait les filles : les, trois filles de Hildegarde (Rotrude, Berthe et Gisèle), les deux filles de Fastrade (Théoderade et Hiltrude), cinq filles de concubines (Rothaide, Madelgarde, Rothilde, Gersvinde, Adaltrude), puis après la mort de Pépin d'Italie (8 juillet 810), les cinq filles de celui-ci (Adelheid, Atule, Gondrade, Berthaide, Théoderade). Quinze princesses !

Voilà pour la statistique. Mais ces femmes jouaient-elles aussi un rôle politique ? Quelques mots d'abord au sujet des reines, dont le rôle important (normal d'ailleurs au Haut Moyen Âge) a été, malgré le témoignage parfaitement explicite des sources contemporaines, un peu négligé par les historiens modernes ([47]).

---

(45) Dhuoda, *Manuel pour son fils* VIII, 14 ; X, 5, ed. P. Riché (Paris, 1975), p. 318-21, 354-5, avec l'observation de Riché, p. 27.

(46) Paschasius, *Vita Adalhardi* c. 33, *PL* 120, col. 1526.

(47) Mais voir récemment l'étude exceptionnelle de P. Stafford, *Queens, Concubines and Dowagers* (Athens, Georgia, 1984) ; J. Hyam, 'Ermentrude and Richildis', dans M. T. Gibson and J. L. Nelson edd., *Charles the Bald ; Court and Kingdom*, 2ᵉ éd. (London 1990), p. 154-68, et E. Ward, 'Caesar's Wife : the career of the Empress Judith', dans Godman and Collins edd.,

L'unique femme de Pépin père de Charlemagne, nous l'avons vu, exerçait une influence déjà grande, surtout comme veuve, auprès de ses fils. Après 768, Charlemagne répudia d'abord la mère du Bossu (elle était concubine, peut-être, plutôt que reine) ; il se remaria avec une princesse lombarde, puis la répudia aussi. La série de reines a impliqué des difficultés pour les gens de la cour de Charlemagne. Vers 771, son cousin Adalard, fils de Bernard, se trouvait *tiro* au palais, quand Charlemagne répudia sa femme lombarde contre la volonté de sa mère Bertrade et se remaria avec Hildegarde. Selon son biographe, Adalard refusa tout net «de transférer son service dans l'obéissance d'une autre» ([48]). Cet aperçu sur les liens étroits entre reine et *iuvenes* concorde avec le témoignage d'Adalard lui-même dans le *De Ordine Palatii*, où la reine est responsable des dons aux *milites* du palais ([49]). On soupçonne une histoire pareille à celle du jeune Adalard chez Benoît, futur abbé d'Aniane, confié par son père à la reine Bertrade *inter scholares nutriendum* ([50]). Benoît, aussi, devait trahir Bertrade et sa protégée, la princesse lombarde. Les deux jeunes hommes, Benoît et Adalard, ont trouvé la même issue de secours : la vie monastique. Plus tard, pendant le règne de Charlemagne, ils ont tenté, tous les deux, un retour politique, mais dans l'entourage d'autres rois : Benoît chez Louis d'Aquitaine, Adalard chez le jeune Pépin d'Italie ([51]).

Nous connaissons peu de choses de l'activité politique de la reine Hildegarde, peut-être parce que la reine-mère Bertrade restait à la cour et qu'elle a même survécu à sa bru ([52]). Hildegarde avait des relations chaleureuses avec l'anglo-saxonne sainte Leoba

---

Charlemagne's Heir, p. 205-27. À noter aussi, P. CORBET, *Les saints ottoniens. Sainteté dynastique, sainteté royale et sainteté féminine autour de l'an mil* (Sigmaringen, 1986).

(48) *Vita Adalardi* c. 7, *PL* 120, col. 1511.

(49) *De Ordine Palatii*, ed. T. GROSS et R. SCHIEFFER, *MGH Fontes Iuris germanici antiquae* (Hanover, 1980), p. 72.

(50) Ardo, *Vita Benedicti abbatis Anianensis* c. 1, ed. G. WAITZ, *MGH SS* XV (i), p. 201.

(51) Voir les remarques très suggestives de WERNER, «*Hludovicus Augustus*», p. 30-2.

(52) Hildegarde est morte le 30 avril 783, Bertrade le 12 juillet de la même année.

de Tauberbischofsheim, *consanguinea* de Boniface du côté maternel, et selon son hagiographe, conseillère favorite de la reine. Le dernier voyage de Leoba se fit à la cour à la demande de Hildegarde 'à cause de leur amitié profonde' ([53]). Il est même évident que la reine soupçonnait que la sainte était mourante et qu'elle voulait la retenir à la cour jusqu'à sa mort. Pensat-elle à profiter des reliques de son amie ? Mais Hildegarde n'a guère survécu à Leoba. La reine, après avoir mis au monde quatre fils — dont des jumeaux — et cinq filles en moins de douze ans de mariage, est morte en couches avec son dernier enfant. Paul Diacre trouva les mots justes dans son épitaphe : «Hélas, O mère des rois, hélas, la gloire et la douleur» ([54]) !

C'est à la reine qui lui succéda qu'il faut prêter une influence politique vraiment considérable : selon Eginhard, la cause de la révolte du Bossu (et d'une autre révolte, en 785) «était la cruauté de la reine Fastrade» ([55]). Quelques témoignages datant des alentours de l'an 792 viennent à l'appui d'une telle interprétation. La seule lettre personnelle subsistante de Charlemagne, écrite vers septembre 791, est adressée à Fastrade. Le roi pouvait supposer qu'elle était bien renseignée sur les sujets militaires et liturgiques. Elle voulait en savoir plus sur les victoires du jeune Pépin d'Italie contre les Avares. Elle devrait organiser des jeûnes liturgiques et des litanies à la cour à Ratisbonne, où elle avait avec elle ses jeunes filles ([56]). Ensuite, à Ratisbonne, Fastrade devait surveiller le jeune Louis le Pieux pendant tout l'hiver 791-2 ([57]). Enfin, il y a dans les *Formulae imperiales* de Louis le Pieux un troisième témoignage. Venue de la Bavière pour hiverner à Francfort, Fastrade y tenait sa cour. En sa présence, un homme, Hortlaicus, est tué parce qu'auparavant il en avait tué un autre. Tous les biens de Hortlaicus sont confisqués, et ses terres doivent

---

(53) *Vita Leobae* c. 20, *MGH SS* XV (i), p. 130. Leoba est morte en 779.
(54) Paul, *Gesta Episc. Mettens.*, *MGH SS* II, p. 266, l. 40.
(55) Eginhard, *Vita Karoli* c. 20, p. 26.
(56) *MGH Epistolae* IV (ii), *Epistolae variorum Karolo regnante scriptae* no. 20, p. 528-9. Cette lettre existe uniquement dans un manuscrit (BN lat. 2777) avec d'autres matériaux qui se rapportent à l'abbaye de Saint-Denis à l'époque de l'abbé Fardulf (c. 793-806). C'était lui qui avait démasqué le complot du Bossu : voir ci-dessous, p. 208.
(57) Astronome, c. 6, p. 610.

faire partie du fisc en effet pour le reste du règne de Charlemagne ([58]). Il est évident que la reine a effectué une confiscation
non des *beneficia* ou *honores*, mais d'une *hereditas* : chose rare
et difficile. On peut dater l'action de 793, donc, à la suite de
la révolte de Pépin le Bossu. Si Eginhard manifeste quelque
sympathie pour le révolté, s'il accable Fastrade, n'est-ce pas parce
que Fastrade était contre le Bossu, avait tenté de l'exclure de
la cour et de la succession ? En tout cas, l'épisode prouve que
Eginhard n'exagère pas l'influence politique de la reine.

Fastrade est morte en 795 — en ne laissant que deux filles,
et aucun fils. Charles se remaria une nouvelle fois. De Liutgarde
on retiendra seulement que quelques lettres d'Alcuin révèlent très
bien ses fonctions comme reine, fonctions précisées dans le *De
Ordine Palatii*. Elle prit en charge la *mansio*, c'est-à-dire l'accom-
modation royale : c'est donc à elle qu'Alcuin s'adresse pour savoir
«dans quel palais Charles va passer l'hiver». Elle était responsable
du trésor : après que son mari se fut accaparé des trésors des
Avares, c'est Liutgarde qui en fit en partie la distribution. Puis
la reine procède à un itinéraire liturgique avec ses filles : en 798,
elles sont allées à Nivelles, église de sainte Gertrude, pour y passer
la fête de l'Assomption de la Vierge. Une autre sorte de réseau
féminin (*women's network*) d'ici-bas et de l'au-delà ([59]) !

Venons-en à la sœur de Charlemagne, Gisèle, abbesse de
Chelles, la sœur bien-aimée, aux termes d'Eginhard ([60]) : c'est à
elle et au monastère de Chelles que son frère confia sa collection
véritablement impériale de reliques, récemment retrouvée ([61]).
C'est à elle aussi que Charles confia sa fille Rotrude, pour laquelle
deux mariages dynastiques avaient échoué. C'est à Gisèle encore
qu'il confia la fille du duc de Bavière Tassilon qu'il venait
d'écraser. Le célèbre Psautier, aujourd'hui à Montpellier, qui vers
790 parvint de Mondsee (en Bavière) à Chelles, nous permet

<hr/>

(58) *Formulae imperiales* n° 49, ed. K. ZEUMER, *MGH Formulae*, p. 323.
(59) ALCUIN, Epp. 50, 96, 102, 190, ed. DÜMMLER, *MGH Epp*. IV, p. 93-
4, 140, 149, 317, puis (pour la visite à Nivelles) Ep. 150, p. 246.
(60) EGINHARD, *Vita Karoli* c. 18, p. 23.
(61) J.-P. LAPORTE, *Le trésor des saints de Chelles* (Chelles, 1988), p. 115-
50. Voir H. ATSMA et J. VEZIN, *Chartae Latinae Antiquiores* XIX (Zurich,
1987), no. 682 (1-95), et D. GANZ et W. GOFFART, 'Charters earlier than 800
from French Collections', *Speculum* 65 (1990), p. 906-32, aux p. 928-32.

d'imaginer Gisèle commémorant avec la jeune bavaroise les carolingiens défunts ([62]). C'est Gisèle, *femina verbipotens*, qui a peut-être façonné l'idéologie impériale qui aboutit non seulement à Rome en 800, mais aussi à Aix en 806 ([63]). Mais revenons à la cour. Quand un jeune clerc lombard voulut dévoiler le complot du Bossu contre son père, il arriva une nuit au palais pour chercher Charlemagne. Étant passé par sept portes, le clerc parvint à la chambre du roi, chambre gardée par des femmes «qui étaient toujours avec Charlemagne pour servir la reine et les filles». (Lire la suite au deuxième livre de Notker !) ([64]). Filles non mariées, selon Eginhard, parce que leur père les aimait beaucoup et les retint chez lui jusqu'à sa mort, en disant «qu'il ne pouvait pas vivre sans leur *contubernium*». Les résultats étaient mauvais, dit Eginhard (il veut dire qu'il y avait des amoureux — et des bâtards) mais Charlemagne lui-même les dissimulait, «comme si rien de honteux ne s'était passé ...» ([65]).

Il est en tout cas vrai que pas une seule des filles de Charlemagne ne s'est mariée — pas même l'aînée, pour laquelle son père avait cherché un mari byzantin. Et après la mort de la reine Liutgarde en 800, Charles ne se remaria pas. Les femmes à la cour étaient ses filles — et une série de concubines, probablement de basse extraction. Le professeur H. Fichtenau a voulu marquer la différence entre les filles et les fils de Charlemagne, en disant que les fils «étaient trop valables pour servir de jouets, ou pour être utilisés seulement comme objets de l'amour du père» ([66]). Si on considère de plus près le mot *contubernium*, inattendu ici, puisque les auteurs de l'époque carolingienne s'en servaient pour

---

(62) A. Stoclet, 'Gisèle, Kisyla, Chelles, Benediktbeuren et Kochel. Scriptoria, bibliothèques et politique à l'époque carolingienne. Une mise au point'. *Revue Bénédictine* 96 (1986), p. 250-70 ; R. McKitterick, *The Carolingians and the Written Word* (Cambridge, 1989), p. 253-5.

(63) Alcuin, Poème 12 (l. 6), ed. Dümmler, *MGH Poetae aevi karolini* I, p. 237 ; Alcuin, Ep. 216, *MGH Epp.* IV (i), p. 359-60. Voir J. Nelson, 'Perceptions du pouvoir chez les historiennes du Haut Moyen-Âge', dans M. Rouche et J. Heuclin edd., *La femme au Moyen-Âge* (Maubeuge, 1990), p. 75-85, aux p. 80-1.

(64) *Gesta Karoli* II, 12, p. 72.

(65) Eginhard, *Vita Karoli* c. 19, p. 25.

(66) H. Fichtenau, *The Carolingian Empire* (trad. anglaise, Oxford, 1968), p. 42-3.

faire mention de la compagnie des camarades mâles, souvent en contexte militaire, on peut se demander si, pour Charlemagne, le *contubernium* de ses filles était indispensable, uniquement parce qu'elles lui ont servi de jouets *in domo sua*. Que faisaient ces *columbae coronatae* qui volaient à travers les fenêtres et dans les chambres (c'est Alcuin qui en parle) ([67]) ?

Naturellement les sources «officielles» — les *Annales Regni Francorum* par exemple — n'en disent rien. Mais, grâce aux lettres alcuiniennes — dont douze sont adressées aux filles de Charlemagne et cinq encore en font mention, et même grâce aux poètes (Alcuin, mais aussi Théodulf, Angilbert et Dungal l'Écossais), nous pouvons entrevoir une vie de cour où les femmes jouaient un rôle politique presque négligé par les historiens. Dans un poème bien connu, Théodulf décrit les filles de Charlemagne à la cour : elles ont participé aux fêtes, aux banquets, à la chasse royale, tous les rituels centraux ([68]). Dans un autre poème moins connu, Théodulf dépeint le roi («David») qui reste dans sa citadelle avec quelques jeunes filles alors que la flûte des Muses souffle des chansons. Ici c'est «Delia» — c'est-à-dire une des filles, peut-être Berthe (deuxième fille de Hildegarde et l'aînée des filles qui restent dans la vie séculière) — qui «fait rougir les Muses de Flaccus». Je crois que Théodulf se moque d'Alcuin (connu sous le sobriquet de Flaccus), «le vieux avec ses garçons qui doit quitter la ville le soir, pour revenir le lendemain» — alors que les filles restaient auprès de leur père ([69]). La plaisanterie de cette petite bataille des sexes serait d'autant plus mordante si, avec John Boswell, on prêtait à Alcuin des tendances homosexuelles ([70]). Mais c'est plus qu'une plaisanterie. Avec les filles de Charlemagne, les hommes de la cour, tel Alcuin ou Angilbert,

(67) ALCUIN, *Ep.* 244, *MGH Epp.* IV (i), p. 392 (avec allusion à Isaïe, 60, 8).

(68) THÉODULF, Carmen no. 25, *MGH Poet.* I, p. 483-9 (ll. 79-108), trad. anglaise par P. GODMAN, *Poetry of the Carolingian Renaissance* (Londres, 1985), p. 150-63. À comparer : ANGILBERT, n°s 1 et 2, *MGH Poet.* I, p. 300-3 (ll. 43-53) (trad. ang. GODMAN, p. 114-7).

(69) THÉODULF, Carmen ad Corvinianum, n° 27, *MGH Poet.* I, p. 490-3 (ll. 27-44).

(70) J. BOSWELL, *Christianity, Social Tolerance, and Homosexuality* (Chicago, 1980), p. 188-91.

veulent l'*amicitia* ou la *familiaritas* — c'est-à-dire l'amitié politique. (En plus, bien sûr, Angilbert était l'amant de Berthe). La position permanente de ces femmes au palais leur donna un énorme avantage, en tant que *potentiores*, les plus proches du souverain. On peut même suggérer que, pendant les années 790, les filles ont pris parti pour l'un ou l'autre des fils de Charlemagne ([71]). À travers la langue artificielle — presque courtoise — des poètes, on perçoit le pouvoir des *puellae*. On sait, tout à fait par hasard, grâce au biographe du pape Léon III que les filles étaient avec leur père à Rome à Noël 800. Fait qui mérite de retenir l'attention ([72]).

Malheureusement, nos sources sont inégales, et les dernières années du règne sont mal connues : plus d'Alcuin, plus de poètes ! Mais n'attendrait-on pas que dans ces dernières années, alors qu'il manquait une reine, que la *turba puellarum* fonctionnait, pour ainsi dire, comme «reine collective» et que la cour se fixait presque en permanence à Aix, vrai *palatium* unique, l'influence des filles de Charlemagne soit plus grande qu'auparavant ? C'est ce que suggère l'Astronome quand il décrit le début du règne de Louis le Pieux : «les enfants de Charlemagne» au palais — l'auteur veut-il dire «les filles» ? — s'occupent de la sépulture du souverain dé-funt. Et puis Louis, qui s'installe à Aix, doit donc chasser (je cite l'Astronome) *omnis coetus — qui permaximus erat — femi-neus.* Ces femmes en effet gênaient Louis de façon sérieuse. Leur expulsion (et celle de leurs associés mâles) était la condition préa-lable à l'établissement du nouveau régime : c'est ce que montre la violence avec laquelle Louis s'est déchaîné contre les colombes d'autrefois ; témoin aussi, la violente propagande dont se sont servis les partisans de Louis. La reconstitution de la cour devint une réforme morale. Les femmes de la cour de Charlemagne sont dépeintes comme abandonnées, ou même comme des putains : une seule d'entre elles (c'était la sœur de l'abbé Adalard) avait su rester vierge *et inter venereos palatii ardores et iuvenum ve-nustates etiam inter mulcentia deliciarum et inter omnia libidinis*

---

(71) Allusions, peut-être, par exemple dans ALCUIN poème no. 14 ; ANGILBERT, poème no. 1, *MGH Poet.* I, p. 238, 360-3. Cf. CLASSEN, 'Karl der Grosse und der Thronfolge', p. 112-3, 123.

(72) *Liber Pontificalis, Vita Leonis* c. 24, p. 8.

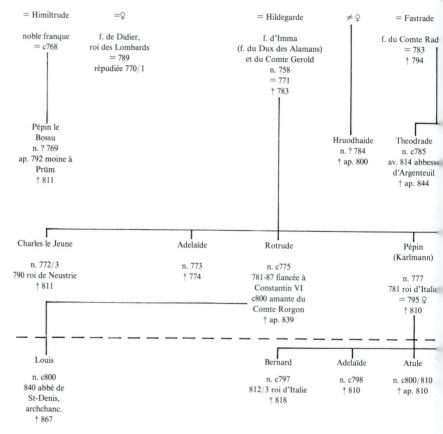

= Himiltrude

noble franque
= c768

Pépin le
Bossu
n. ? 769
ap. 792 moine à
Prüm
† 811

=♀

f. de Didier,
roi des Lombards
= 789
répudiée 770/1

= Hildegarde

f. d'Imma
(f. du Dux des Alamans)
et du Comte Gerold
n. 758
= 771
† 783

≠♀

Hruodhaide
n. ? 784
† ap. 800

= Fastrade

f. du Comte Rad
= 783
† 794

Theodrade
n. c785
av. 814 abbesse
d'Argenteuil
† ap. 844

Charles le Jeune

n. 772/3
790 roi de Neustrie
† 811

Adelaïde

n. 773
† 774

Rotrude

n. c775
781-87 fiancée à
Constantin VI
c800 amante du
Comte Rorgon
† ap. 839

Pépin
(Karlmann)

n. 777
781 roi d'Italie
= 795 ♀
† 810

Louis

n. c800
840 abbé de
St-Denis,
archchanc.
† 867

Bernard

n. c797
812/3 roi d'Italie
† 818

Adelaïde

n. c798
† 810

Atule

n. c800/810
† ap. 810

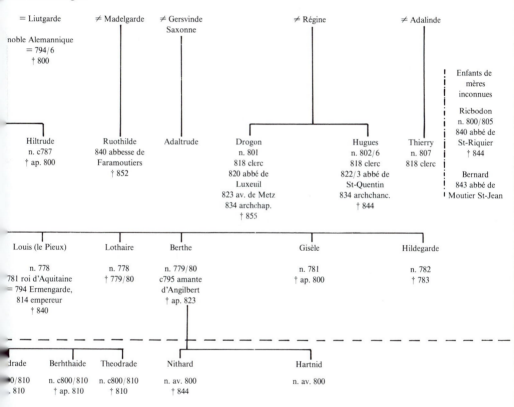

lle de Charlemagne

| = Liutgarde | ≠ Madelgarde | ≠ Gersvinde Saxonne | | ≠ Régine | | ≠ Adalinde |

noble Alemannique
= 794/6
† 800

Enfants de
mères
inconnues

Ricbodon
n. 800/805
840 abbé de
St-Riquier
† 844

Bernard
843 abbé de
Moutier St-Jean

Hiltrude	Ruothilde	Adaltrude	Drogon	Hugues	Thierry
n. c787	840 abbesse de		n. 801	n. 802/6	n. 807
† ap. 800	Faramoutiers		818 clerc	818 clerc	818 clerc
	† 852		820 abbé de	822/3 abbé de	
			Luxeuil	St-Quentin	
			823 av. de Metz	834 archchanc.	
			834 archchap.	† 844	
			† 855		

Louis (le Pieux)	Lothaire	Berthe	Gisèle	Hildegarde
n. 778	n. 778	n. 779/80	n. 781	n. 782
781 roi d'Aquitaine	† 779/80	c795 amante	† ap. 800	† 783
= 794 Ermengarde,		d'Angilbert		
814 empereur		† ap. 823		
† 840				

drade	Berhthaide	Theodrade	Nithard	Hartnid
0/810	n. c800/810	n. c800/810	n. av. 800	n. av. 800
. 810	† ap. 810	† 810	† 844	

blandimenta ... carnis spurcitias illaeso calle transire ([73]). Rappellons-nous le mot *contubernium* : mot équivoque, puisqu'en plus de son sens de 'camaraderie', il a une signification tout autre, la cohabitation sexuelle illicite. Eginhard voulait-il insinuer qu'il y avait eu des relations incestueuses entre Charlemagne et ses filles ? Il fallait, en tout cas, accabler ces femmes. Si l'*imperium femineum* de l'impératrice Irène à Byzance était monstrueux, véritablement *monstrous regiment* ([74]), le *coetus femineus* á la cour de Charlemagne n'en apparaissait pas moins monstrueux.

On sait bien que n'importe quelle cour aura ses femmes et que les femmes sont chez elles dans la *höfische Gesellschaft* ([75]). Leur rôle à la cour de Charlemagne avait cependant un caractère spécifique. Il avait permis de contenir les tensions et les concurrences — insupportables autrement — qui ont dû croître pendant un règne si long, entre père royal et fils adultes et ambitieux. Les femmes remplissaient la fonction de «canaux» de patronage et d'informations : canaux contrôlés effectivement par le souverain parce que non-formels et dépendant entièrement de sa faveur. Les femmes, et surtout les filles non mariées, étaient préparées par toute leur formation à obéir au *paterfamilias*. S'il permit des amants, tant mieux. Sinon, on gardait toujours les clés de la chambre royale, donc les clés du pouvoir. Les filles de Charlemagne constituaient un cadre fonctionnellement semblable aux eunuques de Byzance ([76]) en ce qu'elles n'offraient pas de concurrence comme héritiers du pouvoir formel, et ne produisaient pas de descendance légitime qui pourrait menacer le patrimoine. Charlemagne avait même installé des eunuques à sa cour pour garder les filles ! À la différence de ceux-là — qui étaient, selon le méchant Théodulf, *in cameris non sponte fideles* — les filles

---

(73) Voir dessus n. 46.

(74) Cf. John Knox, *The First Blast of the Trumpet against the Monstrous Regiment of Women* (Edimbourg, 1558) ; cf. *Annales Laureshamenses* 801, *MGH SS* II, p. 618, au sujet de *femineum imperium*.

(75) N. Elias, *The Court Society* (trad. anglaise, Oxford, 1983), p. 243-4.

(76) K. Hopkins, *Conquerors and Slaves* (Cambridge, 1978), p. 172-96, par exemple 196 : «The violent criticism directed against eunuchs diverted dissatisfaction which might otherwise have been aimed at the emperor ... [Eunuchs] were used as lubricants for the system».

étaient fidèles sans réserve ([77]). Charlemagne avait bien choisi. Son succès politique a beaucoup dû au *contubernium* de ses filles. L'année 814 a sonné enfin leur départ, et avec une vitesse brutale : *Felix quippe pater, flores qui germine tales egregiis mundi progenuit titulis* ([78]) ! («Père heureux qui a engendré de telles fleurs pour les titres distingués dans le monde»).

Alcuin avait raison. Mais il aurait pu ajouter : *infelices filiae*, à la mort du père.

---

(77) Théodulf, *Carmen* n° 27, *MGH Poet.* I, p. 493 (ll. 87-92).
(78) Alcuin, *poème* n° 12, *MGH Poet.* I, p. 237.

XIII

THE SITING OF THE COUNCIL AT FRANKFORT: SOME REFLECTIONS ON FAMILY AND POLITICS

Why Frankfort? The point of my question is not to ask why Frankfort is called Frankfort. Everyone knows the answer — or at least *an* answer — to that one! There is a famous story, first recorded from the telling of »credible men« in the early eleventh century, of how a deer, as if sent by God, showed the fleeing Franks an escape-route across the Main, thus enabling them to escape the pursuing Saxons via the »ford of the Franks«[1]. My question this morning is not about Frankfort's name, but rather: why was Charlemagne here, at Frankfort, in June 794? Why was it to Frankfort that he summoned what was apparently the largest assembly he had ever held, and to discuss a whole range of fundamentally important issues? Why was it here that Charlemagne chose to represent his regime to his realm, indeed to his world? Why this particular »Inszenierung«? The aim of my paper is to suggest an answer — not, I hasten to add, the only answer. No doubt there were a number of reasons for the choice of Frankfort in 794. But, since you can never have too many cooks engaged in preparing the historical broth, I shall offer this contribution to Frankfort's 1200th birthday-feast.

Nearly half a century ago François-Louis Ganshof's *Observations sur le synode de Francfort* included no observation on the siting of the council. It was, he wrote, »one of those specially important assemblies«, a sequel to that at Herstal in 779;

---

1   There is a lively painting of this episode by Leopold Bode, »Karl der Große findet die Frankenfurt«, 1888, Historisches Museum Frankfurt, reproduced in G. KAPFHAMMER, *Sagenhafte Geschichte. Das Bild Karls des Großen durch die Jahrhunderte*, Munich 1993, 52. The earliest written record of the story is THIETMAR, *Chronicon* VII 75, ed. R. HOLZMANN, MGH *SRG* N.S. IX, Berlin 1935, 490.

the meeting-place was, according to Ganshof, »la grande salle du "palais" royal«, which we should envisage on the model and scale of Ingelheim and Aachen[2]. But in 794 was there really a »grande salle du palais« at Frankfort? What w a s Frankfort in 794? Thanks to the research of Thomas Zotz and his colleagues, we know the whole history of the royal palace of Frankfort in the Middle Ages — after 794[3]. It seems to have no pre-history in terms of written evidence. Did it spring fully-equipped from Charlemagne's head?

In Charlemagne's charters, the first mention of Frankfort as a royal residence comes, punctually, in 794, on 22 February: charter 176 was issued »super fluvium Moin in loco nuncupante Franconofurd«[4]. Charter 177 is datelined 31 March and simply »in Franconofurd«. Charter 178, issued on 20 July, signals some enhancement of status: »actum in Franconofurd palatio«[5]. But you don't build a palace on the scale of Aachen or Ingelheim overnight, or even in a few months. A residence, some kind of estate-centre we must presume, had been upgraded. Frankfort had been put on the political map, where, as we all know, it would remain permanently.

This needs to be set in a context. Charlemagne's six-month stay at Frankfort was part of a shift, a *Schwerpunktverlagerung*, of the Frankish realm: the old core-area of the Merovingian *regnum* had been the Seine-Aisne-Oise region, where royal palace-residences lay thick on the ground. Charlemagne changed that — Charlemagne, note, and not his father Pippin. The shift was not therefore simply dictated by the location of the Carolingians' family-lands. Charlemagne's own residence-pattern began rather similar to his father's. It moved to centre on the Rhine-Main region, gradually at first, in the 770s, then fairly definitively, in the later 780s[6].

Why? Military reasons may seem the obvious answer. They have so often been put forward as the mainspring of Charlemagne's reign as a whole. But while they may have played a part in the eastwards shift, they can hardly be the whole story. Charlemagne had campaigned in Saxony up to 785, but from then on until

---

2 F.-L. GANSHOF, *Observations sur le synode de Francfort. Miscellanea historica in honorem A. De Meyer*, I, Louvain 1946, 306-318, at 308-309.

3 *Die deutschen Königspfalzen*, I: *Hessen*, edd. T. ZOTZ/K. HEINEMEYER/E. ORTH, Göttingen 1985, 158ff.; E. ORTH, *Frankfurt am Main im Früh- und Spätmittelalter*, in: *Frankfurt am Main. Die Geschichte der Stadt in neun Beiträgen*, hg. von der Frankfurter Historischen Kommission, Sigmaringen 1991, 9-52.

4 MGH *Dipl.* I, ed. E. MÜHLBACHER, Hannover 1906, no. 176, 238. This is an original.

5 MGH *Dipl.* I, nos. 177 and 178, 239, 240 survive only in copies of the early modern period.

6 See Table, 164-165, below. For the shift and its implications, see C.R. BRÜHL, *Fodrum, Gistum, Servitium Regis*, Cologne 1968, 20.

792, at least as depicted in the *Annales Regni Francorum*, the Saxons seemed pacified, and so too did the Bavarians after 788. In this source, for the years 789–794 there is a marked shortening of the individual annals compared with the action-packed earlier ones, and also compared with what is to come later. And for 790 and 792, there is the striking phrase: »nullum fecit iter«, »(Charlemagne) made no expedition.« The revised version of the 790 annal, written soon after Charlemagne's death, actually adds a little apology:

»Lest he should give the appearance of lassitude through inaction or time-wasting, Charlemagne travelled by boat up the Main to his palace at Salz, and then from there came back downstream on the same river to Worms again«[7].

Now that is quite a journey upstream, the best part of 200 km. on the water, and it would take quite a lot of hard work to row that far, though presumably it was not Charlemagne himself who did that hard work. Yet 789–794 was not a period for laziness, nor of quiet preparation for what was to come.

We need to appreciate the exceptionally tense and chequered character of these years, 789–794, precisely because Charlemagne's reign has so often been viewed teleologically, from Christmas Day 800, with everything beforehand leading inexorably to that extraordinary event, after which dawned a new era. Ganshof detected a more complex rhythm in the reign: there was a phase of expansion and conquest, which ended with the crisis of 778, when the newly-conquered peoples (notably the Saxons) revolted, or (in the case of Gascons, Aquitanians and Lombards) threatened revolt. This was followed by a second expansionist phase, down to 791. 791 marked the end of the »outstanding period of (the) reign, when Charlemagne widened his power, gave it a solid base, and initiated policies whose consequences were felt for centuries.« Then, problems multiplied, and Charlemagne was overwhelmed by »the second great crisis of the reign.« This is more surprising. Why should that »most decisive period in Charlemagne's ascent towards dominance over the west … and the richest in lasting results« have been followed, immediately, by crisis? Note that this second crisis is not explicable in quite the same terms as the first. True, revolt is a common feature. Otherwise, the second crisis presents something new. Ganshof listed several syptoms: in addition to trouble with the Saxons, problems in Benevento, Saracen attack in southern Gaul, there was in 792, a very serious harvest failure, which caused famine in 793. »Far more upsetting« than any of those problems, however, was a conspiracy led by »Charlemagne's favourite bastard Pippin the Hunchback«, late in 792. What were the causes? »It revealed

---

7 *Annales regni Francorum* s.a. 790, ed. F. KURZE, MGH *SRG* VI, Hannover 1895, 86-87.

in the aristocracy a feeling of discontent and opposition to royal autocracy«, and second, more speculatively, but supported by the opinion of A. Kleinclausz, »it was a sign of weariness caused by unceasing warfare«[8].

Charlemagne, Ganshof observed, in 792 was a fifty-year old: »it would seem that ... he had acquired experience and wisdom«[9]. His response was to follow better counsels, »to understand that moderation was necessary to consolidate the fruits of victory« (implying an end to forced conversions?), and to show more concern for »the interests of the Church.« The Council of Frankfort, Ganshof suggested, was symptomatic of these changed perceptions. Alcuin was the key figure; he connected the protection of the Church with the reestablishment in the West of imperial power; and so a straight line led from Frankfort to Christmas Day 800. *Quod erat demonstrandum*. More recent research seems to have shown just how prescient Ganshof was in assigning to Alcuin the role of chief ideologue in the 790s; indeed, it was a role he may have played in the 780s too[10]. Yet, curiously, Ganshof had nothing more to say about the two reasons he had identified as causes of the great crisis of 792–793. The discontented aristocracy, and their weariness of unceasing war, remained the loose ends of his argument. If these factors caused crisis in 792–793, did they diminish thereafter? Ganshof's account ignored these themes — until »the last years of Charlemagne«, when selfish nobles defied the emperor, caused »political and social defects revealing a bad government«, and altogether pushed »the Frankish state« to »the verge of decay«[11].

In the near-half century since Ganshof produced this analysis, there has been some useful tying up of ends. Karl Brunner has argued in detail for Charlemagne's success in the distribution of patronage: that is, in preventing »excessive accumulations of aristocratic power« while, at the same time, retaining the loyalty of particular noble individuals and groups[12]. As for the alleged war-weariness:

---

8   F.-L. GANSHOF, *Charlemagne*, in his collected papers, *The Carolingians and the Frankish Monarchy*, London 1970, 17-27, with reference at n. 9 to A. KLEINCLAUSZ, *Charlemagne*, Paris 1934, 203-205.

9   GANSHOF (cf. n. 8) 21. It now seems likely that Charlemagne was only 45 at this point: see K.F. WERNER, *La date de naissance de Charlemagne*, in his collected papers, *Structures politiques du monde franc*, London 1981, arguing for a birth-date of 747.

10 D. BULLOUGH, »*Aula renovata*«: *the Carolingian court before the Aachen palace*, in: *Proceedings of the British Academy* 71 (1985) 267-301, reprinted in his collected essays, *Carolingian Renewal*, Manchester 1992, 123-60; see also IDEM, »*Albuinus deliciosus regis*«: *Alcuin of York and the shaping of the early Carolingian court*, in: *Institutionen, Kultur und Gesellschaft im Mittelalter*. Festschrift für J. Fleckenstein, edd. L. FENSKE/W. RÖSENER/T. ZOTZ, Sigmaringen 1985, 73-92.

11 GANSHOF (cf. n. 8) 23-24.

12 K. BRUNNER, *Oppositionelle Gruppen im Karolingerreich*, Vienna 1979, 61. See also M. BECHER, *Eid und Herrschaft*, Sigmaringen 1993.

Timothy Reuter has stressed plunder and tribute as the incentives of Frankish aristocratic warfare and so recast the problem in terms of aristocratic recalculation of profit. He concludes that it was not until the early ninth century that the sums ceased to add up[13]. In other words, the 790s remained full of opportunities for enrichment. After all, 795 was the year when the Avar treasure came back to Francia in cartloads, making the Franks feel as if they'd been paupers before, says Einhard, so rich did they now become[14].

Further approaches suggest a periodisation of Charlemagne's reign converging on, or around, 791. Peter Godman's study of the poetry of the period shows it court-based until the early 790s, therafter dispersed to provincial locations[15]. Donald Bullough has evoked the *aula renovata*, Charlemagne's court renewed during the generation before 791, and notably in the 780s. In effect Bullough finds here, in the years leading up to 791, the developments assigned by Ganshof to the 790s: the »enhancement of *eruditio*«, the patronage of artists and scribes, the concern for reform, and, in the *Admonitio generalis* of 789, a »synthesis of ideology and administrative action … for the first time complete«[16]. That synthesis seems epitomised in the production, in 791, of the great collection of Papal-Frankish correspondence, the *Codex Carolinus*[17]; and perhaps shortly before, the writing-up of the Royal Frankish Annals and their maintenance thereafter year-by-year[18]. Yet another approach has been via numismatics: in 793 (probably) Charlemagne undertook, successfully, a coinage reform which entailed revaluing the entire currency by some 30%[19]. In the earlier Middle Ages, so far as I can see, such things were not undertaken in tranquillity: rather that a huge administrative effort was in effect a great taxation, provoked by a pressing need for money, yet at the same time an imposing demonstration of power[20]. Bearing all this in mind, I think there is still more to be said on the background to that »Schwerpunktverlagerung« with

---

13 T. Reuter, *Plunder and tribute in the Carolingian Empire*, in: *Transactions of the Royal Historical Society* 35 (1985) 75-94; idem, *The end of Carolingian military expansion*, in: *Charlemagne's Heir*, 391-405.

14 Einhard, *Vita Karoli* 13, ed. O. Holder-Egger, MGH *SRG* XXV, Hannover 1911, 16.

15 P. Godman, *Poetry of the Carolingian Renaissance*, London 1985.

16 D. Bullough, *Carolingian Renewal* (cf. n. 10) 141.

17 Ed. W. Gundlach, MGH *Epp.* III, 476, for the colophon in the unique manuscript.

18 H. Löwe, revised edn of Wattenbach/Levison II, 250-252.

19 P. Grierson, *Money and coinage under Charlemagne*, in: *Karl der Große* I, 501-536, reprinted in his collected papers, *Dark Age Numismatics*, London 1979; also P. Grierson/M. Blackburn, *Medieval European Coinage*, I, Cambridge 1986, 208-209, and P. Spufford, *Money and its Use in Medieval Europe*, Cambridge 1988, 44-73.

20 See J.L. Nelson, *Wealth and wisdom in the politics of Alfred*, in: *Kings and Kingship*, Acta XI (1986, from 1984), ed. J. Rosenthal, State University of New York, Stony Brook 1986, 31-52.

which I began. Let's take a brief look back at the first of the two serious rebellions of Charlemagne's reign. The rising of 785 was an aristocratic one, according to Einhard, »facta in Germania«[21]. That is, the rebels were located east of the Rhine. Some may have been Thuringians; but some were certainly eastern Franks. According to one version of the story, a version clearly current west of the Rhine, a key issue was the refusal of an easterner to hand over his daughter at Charlemagne's demand to the western noble to whom she was betrothed. If intermarriage could be seen (and this was how Charlemagne saw it[22]) as a way of cementing solidarity between different peoples within the enlarged realm, disputes over marriage, that is, over women, had the very opposite effect : they could tear the realm apart, as this case in 785 nearly did when the bride's father »not only swore that he'd never hand her over but also assembled nearly all the Thuringians and his own kin and they determined to defend themselves against the king of the Franks«[23]. Marriage, women and the family, then, were not things to be relegated to the sidelines of »private life«. They were the stuff of politics. I shall argue that they are a crucial part of the significance of 794. But note here too the dangers that Germania posed to Charlemagne. One of those rebellious Thuringians, haled before Charlemagne at Worms, had declared that should he and his companions be found guilty of rebellion, »then no-one will ever see you alive again on our side of the Rhine!«[24] Only Charlemagne's exceptional mildness and wisdom enabled him to swallow such insolence for the time being. Charlemagne had already anticipated the problem revealed by the revolt of 785: the tension between eastern and western Franks. In 783 Charlemagne had married an easterner, Fastrada: an alliance intended to weld the disparate parts of the Frankish *gens* together, that is, the nobility, on whom Charlemagne's power depended.

Let me first, then, underline the importance of women in royal and princely politics during the immediately preceding period. Charlemagne's mother Bertrada had been much involved in Carolingian diplomacy in 770-1: in her case, there is an interesting and fairly typical contrast between her relatively low profile in the records during her husband's lifetime, and her leap into action, and visibility, as a widow[25]. But it was not only royal widows, or queen-mothers who took such

---

21 *Vita Karoli* 20 (HOLDER-EGGER 25).

22 *Divisio regni* of 806, MGH *Cap.* I, no. 45, c. 12, 129.

23 *Annales Nazariani* s.a. 786, ed. G. PERTZ, MGH *SS* I, 41.

24 *Ibid.*, 42.

25 See J.L NELSON, *La famille de Charlemagne*, in: *Byz.* 61 (1991) 194-212. Bertrada is, however, documented, as by implication politically active, in the last year or so of her husband's life (was

very active roles. Compare the case of Tassilo of Bavaria, himself the product of one of the great scandals of the eighth century: his mother's flitting across the Rhine to marry the Bavarian duke »against her brothers' will«[26]. Tassilo's wife, Liutberg, daughter of the Lombard king Desiderius, was according to the revised version of the *Annales regni Francorum* the power behind Tassilo's throne. It was she who »constant and extreme in her hatred of the Franks since her father's exile (in 774), had incited the Huns (i.e. the Avars) to hostility against the king (Charlemagne) and to undertake a war against the Franks«[27]. Do we credit this female diplomacy? The details here seem too specific for mere misogyny. To the Frankish annalist, Luitberga was *deo odibilis* because she hated the Franks. The famous Tassilo-chalice now at Kremsmünster actually has Liutberg's name on it (along with Tassilo's), with the label *virga regalis* — *virga* not a misprint for *virgo*, but an allusion to the »rod« or family-tree of the Lombard royal line, perhaps also to Liutberg as her husband's »rod and staff«. It was she, surely, who saw to her own parents' commemoration at Salzburg[28]. Her active political role alongside her husband is evident in a Freising charter's claim that Bishop Arbeo (764–783) was punished through loss of lands after incurring »the wrath of Tassilo and Liutberg« because he was allegedly »more faithful to Charles than to them«[29]. We shouldn't be surprised, then, to find female influence at the heart of politics.

Historians, it's true, have acknowledged the importance of some features of Charlemagne's own family: the succession, and father-son relations, have been notably well-studied during the past twenty years or so by Peter Classen and Rudolf Schieffer respectively[30]. Nevertheless, the historiography of Charlemagne's reign as a whole remains dominated by two kinds of narratives: one in which warfare supplies the basic structure, just as it does in the *Annales regni*

---

his health already causing concern?): *Die Fortsetzungen der Chroniken des sogenannten Fredegar* 49-52, edd. B. KRUSCH/A. HOFMEISTER, trans. H. HAUPT, Darmstadt 1982, 318-322.

26 *Die Fortsetzungen der Chroniken des sogenannten Fredegar* 25 (KRUSCH/HOFMEISTER 294): »faciente consilio nefario noverce sue, fraudulenter … Renum transiit et ad Odilonem ducem Bagoariis pervenit (Chiltrudis) …« Hiltrude's move immediately followed her father's death (October 741). The scandal was recalled just a century later: ASTRONOMER, *Vita Hludowici* 21, ed. G. PERTZ, MGH *SS* II, 618.

27 *Annales regni Francorum*, revised, s.a. 788 (KURZE 81).

28 *Liber confraternitatum sancti Petri Salisburgensis vetustior*, ed. S. HERZBERG-FRÄNKEL, MGH *Necrologia Germaniae* I, Berlin 1888, 12, col. 29.

29 *Die Traditionen des Hochstiftes Freising*, I, ed. by T. BITTERAUF, München 1905, no. 193b, 183.

30 P. CLASSEN, *Karl der Große und der Thronfolge im Frankenreich*, III, in: *Festschrift für H. Heimpel*, hg. von Mitarbeitern des Max-Planck-Instituts für Geschichte, Göttingen 1972, 109-134; R. SCHIEFFER, *Väter und Söhne im Karolingerhause*, in: *Beiträge zur Geschichte des Regnum Francorum* (BFr. 22), Paris 1990, 149-164.

Francorum and in the first part of Einhard's *Vita Karoli*; the other in which religious reform provides the connecting thread, as we move from Herstal (779), to the *Admonitio* (789), to the Council of Frankfort and thence to the great imperial reform programmes of 802 and 813. The best modern historians manage to splice the two together, so that reform is seen (as Ganshof saw it) as a response to military problems. Fine, so far as all that goes. But to try to periodise a long reign like Charlemagne's without discussing the changing configuration of his family is like, well, *Hamlet* without the prince – but also *Lear* without the daughters, because *Lear* is a story not only of older and younger generations, but also of the eddying of power around women.

Let's come closer, at last, to Frankfort, by considering the second of the two known rebellions of Charlemagne's reign: the rebellion of the son whom Ganshof called »Charlemagne's favourite bastard«[31]. That son, Pippin, whose face was handsome though he was a hunchback, says Einhard[32], rebelled in 792. Why? Well, we can point to snippets of evidence that suggest fear and resentment of his next brother, or rather half-brother, Charles. There is a story, datable to c.790, of »serious rivalries and disputes« between Young Charles and Pippin when a quarrel arose over the order of precedence on a river-journey, perhaps associated with their father's efforts to avoid the impression of lassitude[33]! In 790 Charles had been granted a *regnum* west of the Seine, the duchy of Le Mans, the area known in the ninth century as Neustria[34]. It was a promotion of a kind: after all, Charlemagne's next two sons, Pippin of Italy and Louis of Aquitaine had been given their *regna*, and papally-consecrated to kingship over them too, as long ago as 781. Furthermore, that Pippin had originally been called Carloman and his renaming in 781 might have been thought designed on purpose to disquiet, even displace, his elder half-brother and namesake. Yet there is no evidence of incipient rebellion at that point. Pippin the Hunchback made his move in 792. There is some reason to think he won support in Bavaria[35].

---

31 GANSHOF (cf. n. 8) 21.

32 EINHARD, *Vita Karoli* 20 (HOLDER-EGGER 25): »facie quidem pulcher, sed gibbo deformis.«

33 *Miracula Sancti Goaris* 11, MGH *SS* XV, 366. See BRUNNER (cf. n. 12) 62.

34 *Annales Mettenses Priores*, ed. B. SIMSON, MGH *SRG* X, Hannover 1895, 78. See NELSON, *Gender and genre in women historians of the early Middle Ages*, in: *L'historiographie médiévale en Europe*, ed. P. GENET, Paris 1991, 149-163, at 156-160.

35 NOTKER, *Gesta Karoli* II 12, ed. H. HAEFELE, MGH *SRG*, Berlin 1962, 71-72; cf. W. BRAUNFELS, *Karl der Große*, Reinbek bei Hamburg 1972, 54. That Charlemagne had been having difficulty in establishing his power there seems indicated by his stays in Regensburg in 791-792, and by c. 3 of the Capitulary of Frankfort, ed. A. BORETIUS, MGH *Cap.* I, no. 28, 74.

Other evidence points to the Franks. The Hunchback's mother, certainly, had been a Frank[36]. The revised *Annales regni Francorum*, and Einhard, expressly mention »certain Franks«, »certain of the leading men of the Franks.« The *Annales Mosellani* interestingly specify »a very large number of the most noble Franks, younger men and older men«, as if the participation of the older group was worth noting, while that of *iuvenes* was less surprising[37]. Most interesting of all is Einhard's unequivocal and repeated statement in c. 20 of the *Vita Karoli* of the cause and origin of this revolt, as of its precursor, the revolt of 785: in both cases the cause, Einhard says, was the cruelty of Fastrada. The allegation is amplified a little in the revised *Annales regni Francorum*: the Franks who rebelled »said they could no longer bear the cruelty of Fastrada and therefore conspired to kill the king«[38].

Why disbelieve this evidence? Einhard was certainly writing long after the event. But he had joined Charlemagne's court in 794, hence, very soon after these events; and when he wrote later of 792–793 he believed, and thought that his readers would believe, that Fastrada could have determined the course of events. The same would go for the reviser of the royal Annals, whether or not that reviser was Einhard himself. There may also be some whitewashing here: exculpating Charlemagne, who was normally benign and gentle, according to Einhard, meant shifting the blame onto someone else. Fastrada, you might say, was an easy target: she left no son to defend her name (though she had two daughters, Theoderada and Hiltrude). As a woman, she was an easy butt for misogyny. But in fact there is some good contemporary evidence for Fastrada's political influence between 783, when she married Charlemagne, and 794, the date of our Council here at Frankfort.

There are several distinct types of source-material in the dossier. First, the *Annales regni Francorum*: whereas they do not record Charlemagne's previous marriage to Hildegard[39], and mention Hildegard only thrice (her accompanying Charlemagne to Italy in 774 and 780, and the record of her death in 783)[40],

---

36 Stephen III in 770 thought that Himiltrude was Charlemagne's lawful wedded wife, *Codex Carolinus* 45, ed. W. GRUNDLACH, MGH *Epp.* III, 561; only retrospectively is she labelled a concubine: PAUL THE DEACON, *Gesta Episcoporum Mettensium*, ed. G. PERTZ, MGH *SS* II, 265; *Annales Mosellani* s.a.792, ed. J.M. LAPPENBERG, MGH *SS* XVI, Hannover 1859, 497.

37 *Annales Mosellani* s.a.792 (LAPPENBERG 498): »quam plures ex nobilissimis iuvenibus seu senioribus Francorum sociati.«

38 EINHARD, *Vita Karoli* 20 (HOLDER-EGGER 26); *Annales regni Francorum* s.a. 792 (KURZE 91).

39 They also pass in silence over the king's previous marriage to the daughter of Desiderius; but cf. *Annales Mosellani* s.a. 770 (LAPPENBERG 496).

40 *Annales regni Francorum* s.a. (KURZE 40, 56-57, 64).

Fastrada rates five mentions: her marriage to Charlemagne is not only recorded, in 783, but it is located, at Worms, with the significant additional information that she had the title »queen«[41]; then in 785 we are told that Charlemagne, on return from campaigning against the Saxons, »came to Eresburg and bade his wife the lady queen Fastrada, together with his sons (probably Pippin the Hunchback, and Charles) and daughters, to join him there«[42]; under 787, the Annals, after describing Charlemagne's third journey to Rome, record: »the most gentle king joined his wife the lady queen Fastrada in the city of Worms and there they rejoiced and were happy in each other's company and together praised God's mercy. The lord Charlemagne convoked his assembly to that same city and reported to his bishops and other magnates how everything had turned out on his campaign ... and explained everything that had been done in regard to Tassilo«[43]. The revised version of this annal adds the information that Fastrada had with her already at Worms »his sons and daughters (again!) and the whole retinue whom he had left with them«[44]. In their 792 entry, the revised Annals, as we've seen, say that Fastrada's cruelty was alleged by Pippin the Hunchback and the other rebels as the cause of their revolt; and finally, both versions of the Annals record not only Fastrada's death but her burial-place[45]. This amounts, in terms of early medieval annalistic records, to a uniquely well-documented queenly career. The affective language of the 787 entry is particularly striking. So too is the link between the happy reunion at Worms of the royal couple and the location there of the ensuing assembly: »ibi ad invicem gaudentes ... ac Dei misericordiam conlaudantes. Synodum namque congregavit rex ad eandem civitatem ...« Is it stretching a point to suggest that the favouring of Worms as the »Lieblingsresidenz«[46] (I will not say capital) during these years resulted from Fastrada's influence? One further sign of that influence may be the raising to the archbishopric of Mainz of the former royal chaplain Riculf whose appointment

---

41 *Ibid.*, 66. The revised version adds the fact that Fastrada was the daughter of Count Radolf, but omits the location of the wedding, and also the word »queen«. This latter detail is present in *Annales Mosellani* (LAPPENBERG 497).

42 *Annales regni Francorum* s.a. (KURZE 68). (The English translations, here and elsewhere, owe much to those of P.D. KING, *Charlemagne*. Translated Sources, Lancaster 1987).

43 *Annales regni Francorum* s.a. (KURZE, 76). Cf. revised version, 77: »At Worms he joined his wife Fastrada ... and decided to hold his assembly there.« Pippin of Italy was apparently also present at this assembly.

44 *Ibid.*, 77: »... et omnem comitatum.« I owe to the kindness of Donald Bullough the interesting observation that this seems to be the earliest usage of the term *comitatus* in any annals of the Carolingian period.

45 *Ibid.*, 91, 94-95. The Moselle Annals and the Lorsch Annals too record her death.

46 BRÜHL (cf. n. 6) 22.

possibly, and consecration certainly, took place while Charlemagne was away in Italy[47]. If he had functioned as chief of the court chaplains from about the time Fastrada became queen[48], Riculf may have been among her *comitatus* of 786–787.

The second kind of evidence is represented by a single item: the one and only personal letter of Charlemagne's to survive (not counting the letters written in his name by Alcuin). It was written on or very shortly after 8 September 791 at Charlemagne's camp on the River Enns, and it is addressed to Fastrada »our beloved and most loving wife«[49]. First Charlemagne greets his wife, »our darling daughters and our other *fideles* who are with you.« The substance of the letter is the transmission of two reports: one from Pippin of Italy, Charlemagne's third son, of a great victory against the Avars and the plundering of an Avar fortress; and the other from Charlemagne himself detailing the just-completed three days of litanies, prayer and fasting performed by himself, his army and the clergy accompanying them[50]. Charlemagne then requests Fastrada to make arrangements for the performance of similar litanies and fasts at Regensburg, though Fastrada herself is to do no more than she can manage given her *infirmitas* (which I take to refer not to her gender but to an illness)[51]. He ends with a request for more news about his wife's health »and other matters you may think necessary.« It sounds as if Fastrada was acting at Regensburg effectively as a regent during her husband's absence: in September 791 there could be nothing more important to be entrusted with than the saying of the litanies which Charlemagne believed might ensure »a happy and successful outcome to the war.«

The third item in the dossier comes in c. 6 of the Astronomer's *Life* of Louis the Pious, and it relates to the same period as the texts just considered, that is, winter 791–792. Louis had joined his father on campaign against the Avars, and gone as far as the Wienerwald

---

47 I am much indebted to Donald Bullough for drawing to my attention the date of Riculf's consecration, 4 March 787 (Marianus Scotus, *Chronicon*, MGH *SS* V, 548, using an earlier source) and its possible implications.

48 That is, after the death of Fulrad in 784.

49 *Epistolae variorum Karolo regnante scriptae*, ed. E. Dümmler, MGH *Epp.* IV, no. 20, 528–529. This letter survives uniquely in MS. BN lat. 2777, from St-Denis during the abbacy of Fardulf (c.793–806). According to the revised *Annales regni Francorum* s.a. 792 (Kurze 91–93): »after the conspiracy had been exposed by the Lombard Fardulf he was presented with the monastery of St-Denis as a reward for keeping faith.«

50 *Annales regni Francorum* s.a., both versions (Kurze 88-89); *Annales Mettenses Priores* s.a. (Simson 78-79). See M. McCormick, *The liturgy of war in the early Middle Ages: crisis, litanies and the Carolingian monarchy*, in: *Viator* 15 (1984) 1-23.

51 Cf. the use of *infirmitas* in the sense of illness a few lines above in the same letter.

»before being ordered to go back and stay with Queen Fastrada until his father's return. So he spent that winter with her while his father continued campaigning. But after Charles returned he ordered Louis to return to Aquitaine and then to proceed to Italy to help his brother ... invade Benevento ...«[52].

The next piece of information to be given by the Astronomer is the news of the Hunchback's revolt. Fastrada had perhaps intervened crucially in the tangled politics around Charlemagne's sons: promoting Pippin of Italy's career (remember he had been with Fastrada and Charlemagne at Worms in 787); keeping Louis under careful surveillance but offering him a combination of stick and carrot; and, by implication (this, admittedly, is an argument from silence) encouraging a highly discriminatory family policy which denied Pippin the Hunchback any share in the spoils on either the Avar or the Beneventan front, and by further implication, denying him any sub-kingdom either. This, I suggest, was the »cruelty« against which Charlemagne's eldest son rebelled, his aim »to kill not only his father but also his half-brothers and to reign in (his father's) place«[53]. This cruelty was laid at Fastrada's door. I return to Pippin's motives in a moment.

Meanwhile, the fourth and last item of the dossier on Fastrada brings us back by a roundabout route to Frankfort. Here, some months before the famous council, we find, again, Fastrada. The evidence comes, rather unexpectedly, in one of the *Formulae Imperiales* of Louis the Pious which documents Louis's return of lands to a man named Richard *vassallus noster*[54]. According to Richard's testimony, the lands in question had belonged to his grandfather Hortlaicus.

»When Fastrada, the queen of our lord Charles had come from Bavaria to winter at Frankfort, Hortlaicus was slain in her presence by mischance (»casu accidente«), because before this he had himself slain a man called Ruotmund. And for this reason (»hac occasione«) all his property (which he had at ...) had been resumed into the public fisc.«

This wording seems to suggest that it was Fastrada herself who had ordered the confiscation of Hortlaicus's property, because a dispute had turned to violence in her presence, and led to two killings[55]. However we read *hac occasione*, it's surely reasonable to infer that Fastrada had a major hand in this decision.

This evidence is significant for two reasons: first because it shows Fastrada holding court on her own, in the judicial as well as the social sense, thus bearing

---

52 ASTRONOMER, *Vita Hludowici* (PERTZ 610).

53 *Annales Laureshamenses* s.a. 792, ed. G.H. PERTZ, MGH *SS* I, 33.

54 *Formulae Imperiales*, ed. K. ZEUMER, MGH *Formulae*, Hannover 1882, no. 49, 323.

55 It seems likely that had Charlemagne been the confiscator, the text would have said so. Perhaps too, a queen's confiscating was easier to challenge and reverse.

out what's implied by the rest of the dossier: namely, that she was politically an important figure, and arguably becoming increasingly so. I underline this, not to claim that she was the only significant person in Charlemagne's life, but to register surprise that so many studies of Charlemagne's reign simply leave her out, as they do other women at Charlemagne's court, when the evidence is plain for Fastrada's political importance. If she appears in the textbooks at all, she does so on the margin, as part of Charlemagne's private life, as one on the list of his sexual partners, quite separate from the political world inhabited exclusively it seems by men. To give just one example: in Ganshof's *Carolingians and the Frankish Monarchy*, Fastrada is not mentioned once. In other and otherwise excellent overviews of Charlemagne's reign, women and their political roles are as good as ignored. Silvia Konecny had much useful information on Carolingian queens including Fastrada; but because she l i m i t e d herself to them Konecny did not fully bring out their involvement in politics generally. Charlemagne's court was — surely? — a »höfische Gesellschaft«[56]. Women belonged.

Secondly, then, the evidence for Fastrada's political activity has some implications for this conference. For the episode of Hortlaicus's death and dispossession is most plausibly dated to the winter of 793-4. Fastrada, the Formulae-text says, had »come f r o m Bavaria to winter ....« She had evidently come alone. Yet she and Charlemagne had apparently spent the Christmases of 791–792, and 792–793, together in Bavaria at Regensburg[57]. Fastrada came to Frankfort before Charlemagne, who spent Christmas 793 at Würzburg. She was already there when he arrived sometime between Christmas and 22 February[58]. Why did she make for Frankfort, a place wholly unrecorded in the written sources before this date? Non-written evidence may come to the rescue. In 1991 archaeologists excavating beneath Frankfort's splendid cathedral found a late-seventh-century girl's grave. The grave-goods and particularly the girl's necklace indicated her aristocratic, perhaps even princely, status[59]. A noble Frankish family had evidently been settled near this site for a century or so before 793/94. Could Fastrada have

---

56 I borrow Norbert Elias's evocative phrase.

57 For 791-792, this is an inference from (i) Charlemagne's letter addressed to Fastrada in September when she seems to have remained behind at Regensburg, and (ii) the revised *Annales regni Francorum* for 792, which show Charlemagne returning from campaign to winter at Regensburg. Charlemagne stayed in Bavaria, mostly at Regensburg, throughout 792 and nearly the whole of 793.

58 See above, 150.

59 A. HAMPEL, *Der Kaiserdom zu Frankfurt am Main. Ausgrabungen 1991–1993* (*Beiträge zum Denkmalschutz* 8), Nußloch 1994.

been a scion of this family? At all events, there was somewhere for her to stay, some appropriate residence for her and her *comitatus*, her »court«, when she came from Bavaria to Frankfort to winter. Two further points about Fastrada are relevant. One we have already noted: that she had a recent history of ill-health. The other is that she died, at Frankfort, on 10 August 794. Among the reasons why the great council of 794 was summoned to Frankfort – and I am not claiming it as the only reason though I think that it's both significant and hitherto neglected – was Fastrada's presence here. Given her central role, and perhaps her central importance for him, Charlemagne preferred to summon all those *proceres* and prelates and papal legates here, to Frankfort, rather than either make Fastrada move (I am tempted to say, the dying Fastrada) or hold his assembly without her. Did the great council represent a great act of propitiation, which Charlemagne intended, or hoped, might call down a divine reprieve?

Thus, for the question, why did Charlemagne choose Frankfort? we must substitute a prior question: why did Fastrada choose Frankfort? She could after all have gone to Aachen, where she and Charlemagne had wintered in 788–789, and where Charlemagne would winter in 794–795[60]. Why not Worms, where despite the burning-down of the palace before Christmas, the court had nevertheless remained all winter in 790–791, spending Easter 791 there too? Charlemagne and his *fideles* were used to camping out. In 798, the Annals enthusiastically record the gift from the king of the Asturias of an extraordinarily beautiful tent. Frankfort in 793–794 can hardly have been a very well-equipped residence as yet. Thirty years later when Louis the Pious had it refitted for his pregnant wife Judith (she gave birth to her son Charles there in June 823), there was evidently much work to do[61]. So, it was not that Frankfort was so much more comfortable than Worms in 793. It is hard to see that it was more accessible: yes, the famine of that year no doubt made it necessary to bring in food from further afield, but Worms as well as Frankfort could be supplied by boat. Fastrada's choice was perhaps determined by something more basic. Her father Radulf came from this area; she herself was »of the *gens* of the Eastern Franks, that is, Germans.« She came from east of the Rhine: she was *facta in Germania*. Frankfort lay in her *Heimat*[62].

In the last part of this paper I want to suggest what implications the choice of Frankfort had for Charlemagne's growing sense of imperial status. For such a

---

60 But now with a new wife, the Alaman Liutgard.

61 See J.L NELSON, *Charles the Bald*, London 1992, 76.

62 Her body was taken for burial to St-Alban Mainz, however. Perhaps Riculf's position there had something to do with this decision; cf. above, 158-159.

sense surely was developing, and the Council of Frankfort did indeed signal it, as has often enough been claimed, by Ganshof for one, and recently by Judith Herrin[63]. The aim of Pippin the Hunchback's revolt in 792 had been the retention of the unity of the Reich by the elimination of all contenders, that is, of Pippin's own close kin. What was the alternative? A Merovingian-style division of the *regnum Francorum*, a traditional parcelling-out of the patrimony? In 806 Charlemagne took a middle way: the peripheral *regna* were to remain distinct, and yes, they were parcelled out; but Francia, eastern as well as western, including the Rhine-Main region therefore, was to remain intact. The beneficiary was to be Charles the Younger, not Pippin the Hunchback. If Pippin's revolt had been the result of Fastrada's cruelty, that means that her cruelty could be construed as determination to exclude him from the succession, to maintain the existing four-way division of the empire, with Charlemagne ruling the heartlands while his three sons by Hildegard ruled the *regna* of Italy, Aquitaine, Neustria. The three-way division once Charlemagne had passed on would simply reunite Neustria with the heartlands. Fastrada probably had other hopes in the 780s; but her own lack of sons, and her ill-health, could have meant that, from 792 at any rate, she was committed to the sort of plan just described. The encouragement of Pippin of Italy to engage his forces against the Avars was tantamount to the promise of Bavaria. That was to be exactly the scheme of 806. Pippin the Hunchback rebelled because he was left out of a family-arrangement which his step-mother Fastrada had personally fostered and finessed. The failure of his revolt, the ruthless crushing of his adherents, surely owed much to Fastrada's determination too. The consequences were far-reaching. It was precisely in the period between c. 787 and 794 that the future of Charlemagne's empire in the next generation began to be addressed, and a pattern began to emerge. At its heart was a non-Roman imperial idea.

Where would be the seat (»sedes«) of this new empire? In 794 Frankfort had, perhaps, its first great moment of opportunity. At that council, a whole agenda of imperial action was sketched, and an imperial power-base was foreshadowed. It had nothing to do with geographic Rome. It reflected the power-politics of Charlemagne's realm, and his determination to retain the heartlands undivided, with the *Schwerpunkt* of his realm in the Rhine-Main area. Fastrada, it can now be seen, played a part in that. Had she lived, perhaps Frankfort would have become the imperial *sedes*, as it was to become a royal one in the ninth-century kingdom of Louis the German. Fastrada's life was thus important in shaping a realm, but

63 J. HERRIN, *The Formation of Christendom*, Princeton 1988, 434-444.

not an empire. For Fastrada's death meant that Charlemagne reverted to an alternative possibility: Aachen. It was more squarely within the Carolingian heartlands; and it had Roman resonance. Nevertheless, a degree of eastwards shift proved permanent for the *regnum Francorum*. The centre of balance of the expanded realm had shifted. And the Rhine-Main area would remain close to its heart. In that sense the empire too was indeed *facta in Germania*. Fastrada had something (I claim no more) to do with that[64].

THE ITINERARY OF CHARLEMAGNE, 768–801

	Easter	Summer assembly	Christmas
768			Aachen
769	Rouen	Angoulême	Düren
770	Liège	Worms	Mainz
771	Herstal	Valenciennes	Attigny
772	Herstal	Worms	Herstal
773	Herstal		Rome
774	Rome	? Ingelheim	Quierzy
775	Quierzy	Düren	Sélestat
776	Treviso	Worms	Herstal
777	Nijmegen	Paderborn	Douzy
778	Chasseneuil		Herstal
779	Herstal	Düren	Worms
780	Worms	(near Paderborn)	Pavia
781	Rome		Quierzy
782	Quierzy	(near Paderborn)	Thionville
783	Thionville		Herstal

64 My warm thanks go to Rainer Berndt for his help in the preparation of this paper for publication, and to Donald Bullough for his advice and encouragement.

	Easter	Summer assembly	Christmas
784	Herstal		Lügde
785	Eresburg	Paderborn	Attigny
786	Attigny	Worms	Florence
787	Rome	Worms	Ingelheim
788	Ingelheim	Ingelheim	Aachen
789	Aachen		Worms
790	Worms	(no campaign)	Worms
791	Worms	Regensburg	Regensburg
792	Regensburg	(no campaign)	Regensburg
793	Regensburg		Würzburg
794	Frankfort	Frankfort	Aachen
795	Aachen	Kostheim (Mainz)	Aachen
796	Aachen	? Aachen	
797	Aachen		(Saxony)
798	(Saxony)		Aachen
799	Aachen	? Paderborn	Aachen
800	St-Riquier	Mainz	Rome
801	Rome		Aachen

XIV

LA COUR IMPÉRIALE DE CHARLEMAGNE

Je commence par décrire une grande maison. Charlemagne, revenu de Rome au mois de juillet 801, s'installa à Aix-la-Chapelle, plus ou moins en permanence. Les années suivantes, il passa tous les hivers à Aix, sauf un. L'auteur des *Annales Regni Francorum* signale à l'année 811 que les grands conciles d'été se réunissent à Aix par *consuetudo* [1]. À Aix, l'empereur reçut plus fréquemment des ambassades, venues de pays plus divers qu'auparavant — de Constantinople, de Venise et de Dalmatie, de Bagdad et Jérusalem, de la Northumbrie, de Scandinavie, de Saragosse et de Cordoue, du pays des Slaves et des Avars, et bien sûr de Rome : le pape lui-même se trouvait à Aix pour fêter Noël, en 804 [2]. Charlemagne rassembla à Aix les trésors du *regnum*, y compris la statue de Théodoric, statue qu'on fit apporter de Ravenne, puis réinstaller tout près du palais [3]. Dans les espaces publiques fourmillaient des foules de mendiants, des clients des grands, des plaideurs, des gens en quête de justice [4]. À Aix il y avait un marché, un hôtel de la monnaie, les *mansiones* des ministres et des officiers royaux, les *domus* de leurs serviteurs, une cour. Au centre, le palais, et le *cubiculum regium* [5], quartier de logement personnel de Char-

---

1. *Annales Regni Francorum*, éd. F. KURZE, *MGH SSRG*, Hannover, 1895, s.a. 811, p. 134. Je voudrais remercier de tout cœur les organisateurs, et l'assistance du colloque de Lille de mars 1997, pour leurs critiques sagaces, et surtout Régine Le Jan pour m'avoir donné l'aide indispensable à l'établissement de mon texte français et, une fois encore, beaucoup de conseils avisés et son appui moral.

2. Les *Annales Regni Francorum* donnent tous ces détails ; voir surtout s.a. 802, 807, p. 117, 123-4, les ambassades et les dons exotiques de Bagdad, y compris l'éléphant Abboul Abas.

3. *Chron. Moissiacense*, s.a. 796, éd. G.H. PERTZ, *MGH SS* I, Hannover, 1826, p. 302 ; Agnellus, *Liber pontificalis ecclesiae Ravennatis*, c. 94, éd. O. HOLDER-EGGER, *MGH SSRL*, Hannover, 1878, p. 338 ; voir l'étude fondamentale de L. FALKENSTEIN, « Charlemagne et Aix-la-Chapelle », dans *Byzantion* 61, 1991, p. 231-289 à 247-248, 250-251.

4. Éd. A. BORETIUS et V. KRAUSE, *MGH Capit.* I, Hannover, 1883, n°.146, p. 297-298.

5. ÉGINHARD, *Translatio SS Marcellinus et Petrus*, II, 1, éd. G. WAITZ, *MGH SS* XV, I, Hannover, 1888, p. 245.

lemagne et de ses proches. À l'origine théoriquement un *vicus*, Aix devint, grâce au palais, une ville, un emplacement urbain, voire impérial, un centre de pouvoir. Lieu de fidélité ? Eh bien, pour la fidélité c'est autre chose... Dans les années 880, Notker fit l'éloge des très grands bâtiments que Charlemagne, à l'exemple de Salomon, avait fait construire à Aix : si les *mansiones* des grands étaient assez vastes et d'une grande hauteur, elles étaient construites autour du palais de telle façon que Charlemagne, homme astucieux, pouvait surveiller des fenêtres de son appartement tout ce que les grands faisaient, tous leurs va-et-vient, sans que personne ne l'aperçût. Personne ne pouvait échapper aux yeux d'un Charlemagne, tellement perspicace *(peritissimus)* [6]. Donc la fidélité ne naissait pas naturellement, il fallait la cultiver.

La chose est donc entendue : Charlemagne devint le centre de l'empire. Voilà ce dont il s'était agi en créant une *sedes*, et avec elle un régime sédentarisé. À la différence du regretté Ganshof (je suis, non sans hésitation, en désaccord avec lui), je ne considère pas que les années impériales ont été des années d'affaiblissement, de désordres grandissants. Certes, le palais était comble — Ganshof imaginait une masse de documents, sans ordre, donc sans objet réel. Moi, j'ai l'impression qu'il y avait là une certaine organisation, une forme de système, une main d'œuvre spécialisée [7]. Éginhard, qui fréquenta la cour pendant ces mêmes années, se réfère aux *amici*, aux *ministri festinantes*. Les gens du palais, les *comites*, les *actores*, les *mansionarii*, les *camerarii*, les sous-officiers du comte de palais, durent faire preuve de nouveaux talents administratifs [8]. Un jugement royal de 806 montre un *camera-*

---

6. NOTKER, *Gesta Karoli* I, 30, éd. H.F. HAEFELE, *MGH SSRG*, Berlin, 1962, p. 41.

7. F.L. GANSHOF, « The use of the written word in Charlemagne's administration », traduction anglaise par J. SONDHEIMER, dans F.L. GANSHOF, *The Carolingians and the Frankish Monarchy*, London, 1971, p. 125-142, surtout 134-135 ; cf. J.-L. NELSON, « Literacy in Carolingian Government », dans R. MCKITTERICK éd., *The Uses of Literacy in Early Medieval Europe*, Cambridge, 1990, p. 258-296 (réimpr dans J.-L. NELSON, *The Frankish World*, London, 1996, p. 1-36).

8. K.-F. WERNER, « *Missus — marchio — comes* », dans W. PARAVICINI et K.F. WERNER éd., *Histoire comparée de l'administration,* Beiheft der *Francia,* 9, 1980, p. 191-239. J. FLECKENSTEIN, « Die Struktur des Hofes Karls des Grossen im Spiegel von Hinkmars "De ordine palatii" », dans *Zeitschrift des Aachener Geschichtsvereins,* 83, 1976, p. 5-22. B. KASTEN, *Adalhard von Corbie*, Düsseldorf, 1986, p. 72-79, qui donne d'autres bonnes raisons pour placer le *de Ordine Palatii* « vor 814 » (p. 76). De plus, on doit remarquer que « die organisatorische Seite der wirtschaftlichen Versorgung eines reisenden Königshofes » (B. KASTEN, p. 78) se référerait moins bien à la cour de Charlemagne des années postérieures à 801 qu'avant ; et en tout cas, quelques détails terminologiques se réfèrent clairement au royaume lombard. B. KASTEN, p. 79, en suivant C.-R. BRÜHL, « Hinkmariana 1 », dans *Deutsches Archiv,* 29, 1964, p. 48-77, à 54, a justement émis l'hypothèse qu'Adalard écrivit pour Bernard d'Italie. Reste à expliquer l'esquisse du rôle important de la reine dans c. 22, éd. T. GROSS et R. SCHIEFFER, *MGH Fontes Iuris Germanici Antiquae*, Hannover, 1980, p. 74 : est-ce qu'on doit le rapprocher du mariage de Bernard avec Cunigonde, mariage d'ailleurs

rius, Évrard ; un jugement de 812 nous fait connaître trois officiers inconnus par ailleurs, tous trois délégués du comte du palais [9]. Ces deux affaires font intervenir quatorze comtes régionaux : ils avaient pris la peine de venir à Aix, lieu d'accord, de règlement, de résolution des conflits.

Lieu de travail, lieu des affaires, avec des hommes très occupés. Ensuite et en même temps, lieu de détente, de sociabilité. De la natation (pour les hommes), de la chasse dans le breuil, parc royal (peut-être pour les femmes aussi) [10]. Parfois des fêtes, des banquets — des banquets modérés, selon Eginhard, plutôt que les soûleries gargantuesques qu'imagine un archéologue de la fin du vingtième siècle [11]. Dans une grande maison comme celle-là (je cite Dhuoda, qui connaissait bien la vie à la cour sous le règne de Louis le Pieux), beaucoup de conversations (*collationes multae*) [12]. Donc de ce fait, processus d'apprentissage. Le jeune *comilito* qui se trouvait à la cour devait apprendre son métier auprès des *maiores*, se perfectionner, jusqu'à ce qu'il mérite d'être appelé au conseil des fidèles — même les jeunes pouvaient donner - s'ils étaient prudents, à l'exemple de Samuel et Daniel - des conseils fidèles au milieu des grands. À ce moment, le *comilito* connaîtrait déjà les grands : il aurait

---

voulu par Adalard lui-même, selon la *Translatio sancti Viti* (voir P. Depreux, « Das Königtum Berhards von Italien », dans *Quellen und Forschungen aus Italienischen Archiven und Bibliotheken,* 72, 1992, p. 1-25, p. 5) ? Ou est-ce qu'Adalard l'a lui-même ajoutée en revoyant son ouvrage dans les années c. 821-5, dans le contexte d'un rapprochement avec Louis et Judith (on rappelle l'intérêt de celle-là pour la nouvelle fondation de Corvey, en 823) ? Autre hypothèse : le c. 22 a été, soit écrit soit augmenté par Hincmar.

9. *MGH DD Karol.* I, éd. E. Mühlbacher, Hannover, 1906, n°s. 204, 216, p. 273-274, 288-289.

10. Natation : Éginhard, *Vita Karoli*, éd. O. Holder-Egger, *MGH SSRG*, Hannover, 1911, c. 22, p. 27 : « ob hoc etiam Aquisgrani regiam exstruxit ibique extremis vitae annis usque ad obitum perpetim habitavit » ; breuil (*brogilus*) : *Cap. de villis, MGH Capit.* I, n° 32, c. 46, p. 87, parle en général des breuils des *villae regales*. À Aix, où, se demande L. Falkenstein, p. 252, sinon dans le breuil, était logé Abboul Abas ? Voir aussi K. Hauck, « Tiergärten im Pfalzbereich », dans *Deutsche Königspfalzen* I, Göttingen, 1963, p. 39-42, 45-47.

11. R. Samson, « Carolingian palaces and the poverty of ideology », dans M. Lowcock éd., *Meaningful Architecture*, Woodbridge, 1995, p. 99-131. Cf. le commentaire plus subtile de S. Airlie, « The view from Maastricht », dans B.E. Crawford éd., *Scotland in Dark Age Europe*, St Andrews, 1994, p. 33-46.

12. Dhuoda, *Liber Manualis*, éd. avec trad. française par P. Riché, Paris, 1975, III, 9, p. 170. Elle s'était mariée, dit-elle, *in Aquisgrani palatio* le 29 juin 824, *praefatio*, p. 84, avec commentaire de Riché, p. 85, n. 2. *Pace* P. Riché, Introd., p. 16, Dhuoda ne fait pas mention explicite de la chapelle. Selon les *Annales Regni Francorum*, s.a. 824, Louis le Pieux avait annoncé son *conventum* pour Compiègne *circiter* le 24 juin, et partit tout de suite pour la Bretagne. Est-ce que l'empereur n'assista pas au mariage de Bernard et Dhuoda ? Ou faut-il penser que l'annaliste s'est trompé ? La distance d'Aix à Compiègne est d'environ 300 km.

accepté leurs invitations à dîner, il aurait déjà beaucoup appris de leurs conversations [13].

Parmi les *fulgentes in aula,* Dhuoda distingue un groupe particulier celui des parents royaux — les *parentes et proximi.* Ils possédaient ensemble, semble-t-il, le *regni imperium* : « Deus enim eos... elegit et praelegit in regno... Que le Père tout-puissant... leur inspire même conduite et mêmes sentiments ! Qu'il leur fasse... chercher la paix, brillamment réussir... » [14]. Rappelons que Dhuoda connaissait bien la cour des années huit cent vingt. Est-ce que ses remarques s'appliquent aussi aux années impériales de Charlemagne ? Donald Bullough a bien noté le rôle des *parentes* dans l'entourage de Charlemagne, son *aula renovata,* pendant les premières années du règne, en particulier le rôle de son *propinquus* Thierry, et son oncle Bernard, fils de Charles Martel [15]. Les proches de Charlemagne avaient toujours eu une certaine influence, et parmi eux, les enfants. Eginhard avait de quoi se féliciter en reconnaissant le *nutrimentum* de Charlemagne et la *perpetua amicitia postquam in aula eius conversari coepi, cum ipso ac liberis eius* — entre lui et ses enfants.[16] *Conversari* signifiait plus que vivre, établir sa demeure. Le mot impliquait toute une manière de vivre : des conversations, bien sûr, mais des conversations sérieuses, y compris politiques [17]. Si on cherche à saisir de l'intérieur la vie de la cour comme centre de pouvoir, il faut donc voir la place et le rôle qu'y tenaient les enfants et les parents royaux.

Durant les années impériales, une affaire agita ces personnes plus que toute autre : une question qui impliquait et le pouvoir et la fidélité, la question de la succession au *regnum.* Parce que, même s'il est anachronique de traiter ces années comme les dernières années du règne [18], il faut quand même reconnaître que Char-

---

13. DHUODA, *Liber,* III, 5, p. 156 (conseils) ; III, 9, p. 170 (les grands) ; III, 11, p. 194 (repas avec *honesti sacerdotes*). Voir le *de Ordine Palatii,* c. 27, p. 00 : les *capitanei ministeriales* invitaient à dîner les jeunes *milites* dans leurs *mansiones* du palais.

14. DHUODA, *Liber,* III, 8, p. 168.

15. D. BULLOUGH, « *Albuinus deliciosus Karoli regis* : Alcuin of York and the shaping of the early Carolingian court », dans L. FENSKE, W. RÖSENER et T. ZOTZ éd., *Institutionen, Kultur und Gesellschaft im Mittelalter. Festschrift für J. Fleckenstein,* Sigmaringen, 1984, p. 73-92, en particulier p. 87-88. Sur Bernard, voir aussi J.-L. NELSON, « La famille de Charlemagne », dans *Byzantion,* 61, 1991, p. 194-212, à 198 ; et pour le fils de Bernard, Adalhard, *ibid.,* p. 205.

16. ÉGINHARD, *Vita Karoli,* préface, p. 2.

17. Sur le sens du mot *conversatio* comme manière de vivre en train de se perfectionner, voir H. HOPPENBROUWERS, « *Conversatio* », dans *Graecitas et latinitatis christianorum primaeva,* supplem. 1, Nimègue, 1964, p. 47-95.

18. J'ai fait quelques remarques comparables à propos de Louis le Pieux, « The last years of Louis the Pious », dans P. GODMAN et R. COLLINS éd., *Charlemagne's Heir. New Perspectives on the Reign of Louis the Pious (814-840),* Oxford, 1990, p. 147-160 (repr. dans

lemagne était déjà, en 801, un homme d'un certain âge : il avait en effet 53 ans [19] et il ne rajeunissait pas. Les gens de la cour le savaient bien : on peut donc supposer que la santé de l'empereur était le sujet de beaucoup de conversations.

À la fin de l'année 805, Charlemagne accueillit ses trois fils, Charles, Pépin et Louis, non à Aix mais à Thionville — endroit moins chargé. C'était la première fois depuis de longues années que la famille se trouvait réunie, au moins physiquement. Les textes du début de l'année suivante, la *Divisio regnorum,* le capitulaire de Nimègue, comme les *Annales Regni Francorum* elles-mêmes, indiquent tous des circonstances très tendues qui risquaient de mettre en cause la stabilité de l'empire. Si on insiste sur l'établissement de la paix, c'est, n'est-ce-pas, que la paix a été perturbée [20]. Selon les *Annales,* il avait fallu convoquer ce *conventum cum primoribus et optimatibus Francorum.* Le capitulaire de Nimègue ajoute : *propter pacis concordiam* ; et il fallut le poursuivre par une expédition des *missi* afin de recueillir en plus les serments de « tous » pour démontrer leur « accord » au projet [21]. De la célèbre *Divisio,* voici le dix-huitième chapitre : « qu'aucun de nos fils, sous aucun prétexte, ne fasse tuer... aucun de nos petits-fils (c'est à dire, le fils ou le neveu d'un tel fils), ni le mutiler, ni l'aveugler, ni le fasse tonsurer contre son gré, sans procès judiciaire... » (Ainsi, tout était en règle...) Le professeur Mohr, grand savant allemand, pensait qu'une telle stipulation était anachroniquement barbare pour le règne de Charlemagne, donc que ce chapitre devait être un faux datant du règne suivant [22]. Le professeur Schlesinger émit d'autres soupçons : Charlemagne aurait été pris de remords (un peu tardifs, doit-on dire) pour le sort de ses propres neveux... [23]

J.-L. NELSON, *Frankish World,* p. 37-50), et d'Alfred de Wessex, « Reconstructing a royal family : reflections on Alfred from Asser, chapter 2 », dans I. WOOD et N. LUND éds., *People and Places in Northern Europe, 500-1600. Studies presented to Peter H. Sawyer,* Woodbridge, 1991, p. 47-66. Il semble donc qu'un roi ayant des fils déjà adultes doive toujours trouver de nouvelles stratégies pour les contenir.

19. Pour la date de naissance de Charlemagne, le 2 avril 748, j'ai bien envie d'accepter les précisions de M. BECHER, « Neue Überlegungen zum Geburtsdatum Karls des Großen », dans *Francia,* 19, 1992, p. 37-60. L'étude de K.-F. WERNER, « Das Geburtsdatum Karls des Großen », dans *Francia,* 1, 1973, p. 115-137 (réimp. avec quelques développements, « La date de naissance de Charlemagne », dans *Bulletin de la Société nationale des Antiquaires de France,* année 1972, Paris 1975, réimp. dans K.-F. WERNER, *Structures politiques du monde franc (VIe-XIIe siècles),* Londres, 1979), était le travail pionnier à cet égard.

20. *Annales Regni Francorum,* s.a. 806, p. 121 : «... de pace constituenda et conservanda inter filios... » ; *MGH Capit.* I, n° 45, pref., p. 127 ; n. 46, c. 2, p. 131.

21. *MGH Capit.* I, n° 46, c. 2, p. 131 : « pleniter omnes consentire debeant ».

22. W. MOHR, « Bemerkungen zur *Divisio regnorum* von 806 », dans *Archivum latinitatis medii aevi,* 24, 1954, p. 121-157.

23. W. SCHLESINGER, « Kaisertum und Reichsteilung. Zur *Divisio regnorum* von 806 », dans W. SCHLESINGER éd., *Beiträge zur deutschen Verfassungsgeschichte des Mittelalter,* 2 vol., Göttingen 1963, I, p. 196. Cf. aussi K. SPRIGADE, « Zur Frage der Verfälschung von

Mais le bénéficiaire principal de la *Divisio*, Charles le Jeune, le *primogenitus*, celui qui devait acquérir, après la mort de son père, la Francie entière, n'avait pas de fils, autant qu'on sache [24]. On se demande si, durant les semaines d'hiver, entre la Noël 805 et la fête de la purification de la Vierge 806, les membres de la famille carolingienne firent un pacte entre eux à l'instar, peut-être, des princes anglo-saxons du siècle suivant, ou même des princes royaux asturiens contemporains de Charlemagne [25]. S'il est vrai que Charles le Jeune était célibataire, est-ce que ce mode de vie avait été, au moins jusque-là, le prix de son avancement ? Traits civilisés chez les Barbares ? Ou s'agit-il de quelques dispositions provisoires ? Charles le Jeune espérait-il que son père mourrait bientôt ? Pour l'instant, du moins, les fils cadets, Pépin et Louis, étaient calmés. Ils quittèrent Thionville. La paix familiale carolingienne était rétablie. C'était la dernière fois que cette famille se trouvait ainsi rassemblée.

Le 6 juin 810, la fille de Charlemagne, Rotrude, *qui natu maior erat*, mourut ; puis le 8 juillet, ce fut le tour du fils de Charlemagne, Pépin, qui mourut dans l'Italie lointaine. Les dates exactes ont été soigneusement enregistrées dans les *Annales* [26]. La même année, le 7 juin, puis le 30 novembre, survinrent deux éclipses solaires, également précisées dans les *Annales*. Chez l'empereur, comment interpréter ces événements ? Et comment réagir ? On saisit un peu l'atmosphère de la cour en lisant la lettre écrite par l'irlandais Dungal en 811 pour expliquer ces phénomènes astronomiques [27]. Dungal s'adressait à Charlemagne, c'est vrai, mais je

---

Karls des Großens *Divisio regnorum* », dans *Zeitschrift der Savigny-Stiftung für Rechtsgeschichte*, 81, 1964, *Germ. Abt.*, p. 305-317.

24. L'étude de P. CLASSEN, « Karl der Große und der Thronfolge im Frankenreich », dans *Festschrift für H. Heimpel*, Göttingen, 1972, vol. III, p. 109-134, reste tout à fait indispensable. C'est vrai que ce qu'on sait des femmes de Pépin d'Italie ou de Bernard d'Italie ne tient qu'à un fil. Mais quand même, le manque total de renseignement sur le lieu de sépulture de Charles le Jeune soulève quelques soupçons. A-t-il été soumis à une espèce de *damnatio memoriae* sous le règne de Louis ?

25. Pour la possibilité d'un accord parmi les fils d'Edouard de Wessex, voir P. STAFFORD, *Unification and Conquest. A Political and Social History of England in the Tenth and Eleventh Centuries*, London, 1989, p. 42. On remarque que, selon la chronologie de M. BECHER (*supra*, n. 19), on aurait à faire à une entente assez semblable entre Pépin et Carloman pendant l'automne 747 — mais (et c'est ma seule réserve quant à la reconstitution de M. BECHER) avec Bertrade enceinte ?

26. *Annales Regni Francorum*, p. 131, 132. Je veux ici corriger une erreur de ma part que j'ai répétée plusieurs fois en diverses livres et articles en réutilisant mon tableau généalogique (en « Macdraw ») de la famille de Charlemagne où j'ai fait, à tort, mourir Rotrude « après 839 ». Une fois pour toutes, je m'excuse ; et je rétablis la date correcte : 810.

27. Voir B.S. EASTWOOD, « The astronomy of Macrobius in Carolingian Europe : Dungal's letter of 811 to Charles the Great », dans *Early Medieval Europe* 3, 1994, p. 117-134 ; voir déjà la belle discussion (non citée par B.S. EASTWOOD) de WERNER, « *Hludovicus Augustus* », dans P. GODMAN et R. COLLINS éd., *Charlemagne's Heir*, p. 28.

crois que lorsque Charlemagne lut cette lettre, son entourage impérial était présent. À voir la lettre que Fridugise, ancien élève d'Alcuin, envoya aux *fideles in sacro palatio* à une date indéterminée de la dernière décennie du règne de Charlemagne, les fidèles, qui souffraient, paraît-il, d'une peur existentielle, avaient « très longtemps discuté », pour savoir si le néant était ou n'était pas un être, avant d'abandonner la question comme intranchable [28]. La lettre de Dungal, qui expose très clairement la science astronomique de Macrobe, la *scientia* pour se munir de la *praescientia*, avait été évoquée par l'empereur lui-même mais, j'ose le dire, pas *que* pour lui-même. Il ne fallait pas voir les éclipses comme des présages de malheur : en flattant la science, la formation des fidèles, des *palatini*, on les soulageait. La cour, la même cour qui admettait les débats religieux et qui, en cette même année 811, bouillonnait sous les impulsions réformatrices de Charlemagne, lui qui, cette même année, envisageait la possibilité de se retirer du monde [29], cette cour était à la fois le foyer du rationalisme carolingien permettant de diriger le personnel, et le foyer de la prévention de la crise.

En 811, Charles le Jeune mourut à son tour. L'Astronome, le biographe le plus révélateur, décrit la réponse de Louis le Pieux, toujours installé en Aquitaine : « il éprouva un vif espoir de tout maîtriser » — *spes universitatis potiundae*. Il envoya un officier, Gerric le fauconnier, à Aix : alors que Gerric attendait au palais (*cum in palatio moraretur* — on sait bien que les gens de cour doivent apprendre l'art d'attendre) il rencontra des *Franci* et des *Germani*, gens qui parlaient le français et le germanique, qui lui donnèrent leur avis : Louis devait venir tout de suite au palais. Mais Louis fut plus sage : il attendit jusqu'à ce que son père le fasse venir [30]. Les biographes de Louis racontent tous, et avec enthousiasme, le grand concile de 813, le *festiva dies* où Charlemagne, en présence de tous ses *proceres, nostro nutri-*

---

28. *De substantia nihili*, MGH Epp IV, p. 552-555. Pour la datation de ce petit ouvrage, j'accepte 804-814, en suivant DÜMMLER, *ibid.* Voir J. MARENBON, *From the Circle of Alcuin to the School of Auxerre*, Cambridge, 1981, p. 62 (« 800 at the earliest »), avec references à n. 90. M. COLISH, « Carolingian debates over *Nihil* and *Tenebrae* », dans *Speculum*, 59, 1984, p. 757-795, à 759, prend un *terminus ante quem* en avril 800. C'est vrai que Fridugise dans le *De substantia* se qualifie de « diacré », alors qu'il a été promu archidiacre, paraît-il, en 800 (Alcuin, *Ep.* 210, p. 351) ; mais il qualifie ici Charlemagne de *serenissimus princeps*, ce qui, à mon avis, plaide pour les années impériales. Alcuin, *Ep.* 251, p. 406, datée « 801-802 » par DÜMMLER, qualifie également Fridugise de « diacre ».

29. ÉGINHARD, *Vita Karoli*, c. 33, p. 39 : dans son testament, l'empereur s'est rendu compte d'une possible *voluntaria saecularium rerum carentia*.

30. ASTRONOME, *Vita Hludovici Pii*, c. 20, éd. E. TREMP, *MGH SSRG*, Hannover, 1995, p. 342-343. J'ai beaucoup appris des aperçus de S. AIRLIE, « Bonds of Power and Bonds of Association », dans P. GODMAN et R. COLLINS éd., *Charlemagne's Heir*, p. 191-204.

mine freti, fit de Louis son héritier [31]. Mais ensuite, une fois de plus, Louis quitta aussitôt la cour.

Durant les années impériales, qui étaient ceux qui se trouvaient plus ou moins en permanence au palais pour offrir leur *amicitia* à Eginhard et aux autres ? Qui entourait l'empereur ? Qui étaient les parents royaux parmi les *palatini* ? Jusqu'en 804, il y eut Guillaume, cousin et *familiaris* de Charlemagne [32]. D'autres cousins y restèrent jusque dans les dernières années. Les trois fils de Bernard, l'oncle de Charlemagne, Adalard, Wala, et pour quelque temps Bernhar, étaient tous *palatini*. Adalard, selon son biographe Paschase Radbert, donnait à Charlemagne son *familiare consilium* [33]. Le fait qu'Adalard et Bernhar étaient moines n'empêchait pas qu'ils accomplissent des services politiques. Wala, en particulier, atteignit un *locus summus apud imperatorem* [34]. Il possédait, dit encore Paschase, *eloquentia utrarumque linguarum* — la langue romaine (proto-français ?) et le germanique [35]. Il en avait besoin à la cour. On le voit en tête des témoins du testament de l'empereur en 811 [36]. Le groupe de *parentes* devait être plus large qu'on ne le voit à travers nos maigres sources. C'est par pur hasard, par exemple, qu'on entrevoit deux Carolingiens, par ailleurs tout à fait inconnus, dans deux sources du début des années 840 [37]. Surtout, après la mort d'Alcuin en 804, on manque, sauf quelques très rares exceptions, des lettres et des poésies palatines qui mirent en lumière la vie de la cour pendant les décennies précédentes [38].

Mais grâce à Eginhard, et à quelques sources plus tardives, nous savons qu'il y avait aussi des petits *parentes* et *aulici*, enfants et petits enfants illégitimes de Charlemagne : pendant les années impériales, une partie de la *domus regalis* devint une sorte de crèche. Il y avait les enfants des concubines : Drogon, Hugues, Richbodon, et Ruothild et Adaltrude ; il y avait aussi les petits-fils illégitimes : Nithard, Hartnid, et Louis ; il y eut après 810 une bande de petites-filles italiennes ; en

31. ERMOLD, *In honorem Hludovici Pii*, éd. E. FARAL, *Ermold le Noir, Poème sur Louis le Pieux*, Paris 1964, vers 652-735, p. 52-59 ; cf. THEGAN, *Gesta Hludowici imperatoris*, c. 6, éd. E. TREMP, *MGH SSRG*, Hannover, 1995, p. 180-185.

32. *Vita Benedicti Abbatis Anianensis*, c. 30, éd. G. WAITZ, *MGH SS* XV (i), Hannover, 1887, p. 211.

33. PASCHASE RADBERT, *Vita Adalhardi*, c. 32, *PL* 120, col. 1526.

34. ASTRONOME, *Vita Hludovici*, c. 21, p. 346-347.

35. PASCHASE, *Epitaphium Arsenii*, I, 1, éd. E. DÜMMLER, *Abhandlungen d. königl. preuß. Akademie zu Berlin*, 1900, p. 22. L. WEINRICH, *Wala. Graf, Mönch und Rebell*, Hamburg, 1963, p. 25, pense plutôt à « lateinischen Amtssparche ».

36. ÉGINHARD, *Vita Karoli*, c. 33, p. 41.

37. Bernon : LOUP DE FERRIÈRES, *Epistolae*, éd. P. MARSHALL, Leipzig, 1984, *Ep.* 81, p. 80 ; Lothaire : éd. T. SCHIEFFER, *MGH DD Lotharii* I, Berlin, 1966, n.°86, p. 210 (ici la parenté n'est pas explicite, mais je la déduis du nom lui-même).

38. Voir P. GODMAN, *Poetry of the Carolingian Renaissance*, London, 1985, p. 8.

somme une douzaine d'enfants au moins se trouvaient à la maternelle palatine [39]. Voilà quelque chose d'inattendu chez un souverain quinquagénaire ou sexagénaire. Qui cherche les enfants cherche les femmes... Il y en avait pas mal à Aix. Dans les premières années du règne de Louis le Pieux, on essaya de nettoyer l'intérieur des *mansiones* en chassant les *meretrices* qui s'y cachaient [40]. *Meretrices* peut-être... Mais dans ces *mansiones*, qui étaient les maisons familiales aristocratiques, devaient aussi habiter les femmes et les filles des grands. De cette présence de jeunes filles nobles pendant les années impériales, on trouve trace dans une des dernières lettres d'Alcuin : il s'adresse à Gondrade, sœur de Wala, donc cousine de Charlemagne. Elle était moniale, mais elle se trouvait évidemment au palais, puisque Alcuin lui demande de faire ses excuses à Charlemagne, de détourner sa colère. Elle aussi était une personne d'une grande influence *apud imperatorem*. Et ailleurs : « *Esto ceteris in palatio virginibus exemplar* », demande Alcuin, « qu'elles soient aussi nobles dans leur conduite que dans leur naissance » [41]. Alcuin s'adressa aussi à une autre moniale d'un certain âge qui se trouvait évidemment au palais, à Gisèle, la sœur de Charlemagne lui-même. Abbesse de Chelles, Gisèle ne restait pas toujours dans son monastère [42], pas plus que sa nièce qui était elle aussi moniale à Chelles. Selon les lettres d'Alcuin et selon les poésies palatines des années 790, Rotrude, fille aînée (née vers 775) de Charlemagne, se trouvait souvent à la cour [43]. Elle prit un amant, et mit au monde un fils. On lui donna le nom de Louis : fait intéressant, parce que c'était le nom du frère de la mère, nom qui impliquait un droit d'hériter [44]. La paternité du petit Louis n'est attestée, comme dit justement Georges Tessier, par aucun témoignage direct [45]. Toute une historiographie fait de Louis le fils de Rorgon, noble de souche neustrienne dont on ne sait absolument rien jusqu'en 819 [46]. À

---

39. Voir généalogie dans J.-L. NELSON, « La famille... », *op. cit.*
40. *Capit. de disciplina palatii Aquisgranensis*, MGH *Capit.* I, n°. 146, p. 298.
41. MGH *Epp.* IV, n°. 241, p. 387. Cf. aussi *Ep.* 204, p. 337-339, et 309, p. 473-475. (P. GODMAN, *Poetry*, p. 121, n. 41, fait une petite erreur en décrivant Gondrade comme « Charlemagne's daughter »).
42. Pour la relation entre Alcuin et Gisèle, voir J.-L. NELSON, « Perceptions du pouvoir chez les historiennes du haut moyen âge », dans M. ROUCHE et J. HEUCLIN éd., *La Femme au Moyen Âge*, Maubeuge, 1990, p. 75-87.
43. Alcuin s'adresse à Rotrude (ou avec Berthe, ou avec sa tante) dans *Ep.* 72, 195, 213, 214, 216, 228, p. 114-5, 322-323, 354-360, 371-372, et peut-être dans *Ep.* 32 et 279, p. 73-74, 435-436 ; Rotrude, avec sa tante, s'adresse à Alcuin dans *Ep.* 196, pp. 323-5 ; Alcuin fait mention de Rotrude dans *Ep.* 262, p. 420, et peut-être dans *Ep.* 244, p. 392. Pour le témoignage des poètes, voir P. GODMAN, *Poetry*, p. 114-5, 154-5 ; et *supra*, p. 184.
44. Je suis particulièrement reconnaissante à Stuart Airlie qui a bien voulu souligner la signification particulièrement « royale » d'un tel nom.
45. Éd. G. TESSIER, *Recueil des chartes de Charles II*, 3 vol., Paris, 1945-55, III, p. 39.
46. K.-F. WERNER, « Bedeutende Adelsfamilien im Reich Karls des Großen », dans W. BRAUNFELS éd., *Karl der Große. Lebenswerk und Nachleben*, 5 vol., Düsseldorf, 1965-67, vol. I, p. 138 avec n. 8, se réfère au Cartulaire de Redon pour cette première parution de Ror-

XIV

partir de 839, Rorgon est bien attesté comme père de Gauzlin qui deviendra longtemps après le chancelier de Charles le Chauve à la place de Louis, abbé de St-Denis
depuis 840/1, décédé en 867. La base unique de l'hypothèse d'une demi-fraternité
entre Louis et Gauzlin est une notice des *Annales Bertiniani* de 858 où Gauzlin,
moine de St-Denis, est dit « frater ipsius [Louis] » [47]. Je me demande s'il faut prendre le mot « frère » dans son acception biologique. Admettons plutôt, peut-être, que
le nom de l'amant de Rotrude est inconnu. Mais je crois que l'homme était loin
d'être un inconnu. La fille aînée de Charlemagne ne pouvait s'offrir — même si on
croit que son père n'était pour rien dans l'affaire — à n'importe quel jeune Lothario.
Non ! L'amant de Rotrude devait être un homme d'une certaine influence. Mêmes
incertitudes autour de la date de naissance du petit Louis. Aux alentours de 800 ? Ou
(et je le suggère comme hypothèse, sans plus) quelques années plus tard, peut-être
même aussi tard que 810 ? Est-ce que Rotrude, âgée de 35 ans, mourut en couches ?
Qui, en tout cas, choisit le nom du bébé ? À coup sûr, n'est-ce pas Charlemagne lui-
même ? Ou pour être clair, si ce n'est pas Charlemagne qui a choisi, avouons que
tout un peloton d'historiens (dont je fais partie) s'est complètement égaré, au sujet
des années impériales...

Le professeur Tessier a écrit une belle épitaphe pour Rotrude, qui « devait
mourir... laissant une réputation de lettrée, voire de théologienne » [48]. Un poète
contemporain laissa un portrait non moins enthousiaste de Rotrude comme *mentis
clarissima virgo/virgo decora satis, et moribus inclita virgo* [49]. Le poète était Angilbert, du sobriquet Homère — qui témoigne ainsi de sa participation au *inner circle*
de la cour. Jeune palatin, élève d'Alcuin, Angilbert devint *manualis nostrae familia-
ritatis auricolarius* de Charlemagne [50]. Il devint abbé de St-Riquier : le fils est devenu père, plaisante Alcuin [51]. Le père-abbé devint également père de fils charnels,
étant devenu l'amant de Berthe, la deuxième des filles les plus célèbres de Charlemagne [52]. Les historiens (et les historiennes) modernes ont trouvé ici une situation
un peu problématique. Angilbert était abbé laïque, selon Beumann ; selon Lauer,

gon en 819. Cf. pour la carrière postérieure de Rorgon, R. LE JAN, « *Prosopographica
Neustrica* : les agents du roi en Neustrie de 639 à 840 », dans H. ATSMA éd., *La Neustrie*,
2 vols., Beihefte der *Francia*, 16/1 et 16/2, Sigmaringen, 1989, vol. I, p. 231-269, à n.°253,
p. 263.

47. *Annales Bertiniani*, éd. F. GRAT *et al.*, *Les Annales de Saint-Bertin*, Paris, 1964,
p. 77.

48. Éd. G. TESSIER, *Recueil*, vol. III, p. 40.

49. P. GODMAN, *Poetry*, p. 114-115.

50. ALCUIN, *Ep.* 93, p. 137 (lettre de Charlemagne au pape, 796).

51. ALCUIN, *Ep.* 9, p. 35 (lettre d'Alcuin à Adalhard de Corbie) : ici, parmi d'autres références aux *patres*, pas le moindre soupçon d'un statut irrégulier pour Angilbert, ni dans les
autres lettres d'Alcuin.

52. NITHARD, *Histoire des fils de Louis le Pieux*, IV, 5, éd. et trad. P. LAUER, Paris, 1926,
p. 138-139.

Angilbert et Berthe s'étaient mariés [53]. Selon Susan Rabe, ce fut un mariage d'amour : elle nous rappelle que « conditions at court were quite fluid » [54]. En effet ! Et sérieusement. Chez Rotrude et Berthe, les affaires de cœur (si c'est le mot juste) étaient aussi les affaires de la cour, donc des affaires politiques. Si les sources strictement contemporaines, et, plus tard Éginhard également, traitent ces liaisons d'une façon si peu explicite, c'est à cause de leur extrême sensibilité : en d'autres termes, on ne passait pas sous silence les affaires sans importance, c'est l'inverse.

Écoutons encore une fois la voix d'un poète, l'auteur de la célèbre *Épopée de Paderborn*, connue sous le titre *Karolus Magnus et Leo Papa* [55]. On trouve ici quelques vers mal connus par les anglophones, parce que n'étant traduits ni par M. Godman [56] ni par M. Dutton : c'est une description, pour l'essentiel assez stéréotypée (beaucoup de Virgile, beaucoup de Venance), d'un grand cortège de la cour royale qui part à la chasse. La scène se passe en 799 — mais la datation du poème, selon les avis savants récents, est des alentours de l'an 806. Voilà qu'apparaît dans ces vers un deuxième niveau contextuel et chronologique de la fa-

---

53. H. BEUMANN, art. « Angilbert », dans *Lexikon des Mittelalters*, Munich-Zürich, 1980, I, col. 635 (à comparer, col. 534 : « nicht-sanktionierte Ehe ») ; P. LAUER, voir n. 52, *supra*, traduit « [Angilbertus] ex ejusdem magni regis filia nomine Berta Hartnidum fratrem meum et me Nithardum genuit » : « de la fille de ce grand roi, appelée Berte, qu'il épousa [!], il eut Hartnid, mon frère, et moi Nithard » (voir n. 52, dessus). M. GARRISON, « The emergence of Carolingian Latin literature at the court of Charlemagne », dans R. MCKITTERICK éd., *Carolingian Culture. Emulation and Innovation*, Cambridge 1994, p. 119, désigne aussi Angilbert comme « lay-abbot ». Cf. D. BULLOUGH, « *Aula renovata*. The Carolingian Court before the Aachen Palace », dans D. BULLOUGH, *Carolingian Renewal*, Manchester, 1991, p. 158, n. 62 : « his appointment to St-Riquier (conventionally, as « lay abbot »)... », où l'adverbe suppose quelque réserve.

54. S.A. RABE, *Faith, Art and Politics at Saint-Riquier. The Symbolic Vision of Angilbert*, Philadelphia, PA, 1995, p. 74. Cf. p. 73, où l'auteur suppose « a marital relationship... [which] was most likely *Friedelehe*, an ancient Germanic custom ». Je n'ai jamais pu trouver aucun témoignage de l'existence d'une telle « coutume ». Si elle a bien existé, je ne vois pas son rapport avec le cas de Berthe et Angilbert. S.A. RABE, p. 175, n. 5, 180, n. 48, nomme d'une façon utile des historiens français et cléricaux du XIXᵉ siècle qui ont démontré que « amishness with Angilbert's marriage (sic) and children ». Des vers :

carta [c'est à dire, le poème] cito hortos percurris amoenos
cum pueris quos iam habitare solebat Homerus,

S.A. RABE entend, p. 73, 74, Angilbert « describing his boys, i.e. his sons, playing in the garden of their home » : image délicieuse qui évoque peut-être plus la vie de banlieue américaine du XXᵉ siècle tardif que l'Aix des années 790. Voir P. GODMAN, *Poetry*, p. 118, et son Introduction p. 10 : les « jardins » sont une métaphore pour l'école palatine, les *pueri* sont les élèves. (Mais qui sait ? Les maisons des grands avaient peut-être aussi leurs jardins)

55. Éd. E. DÜMMLER, *MGH Poetae* I, p. 366-79, où le poème est attribué à Angilbert.

56. Qui en traduit, néanmoins, une bonne partie, *Poetry*, p. 196-207, avec un commentaire utile : p. 22-4. Voir aussi D. SCHALLER, « Das Aachener Epos für Karl den Kaiser », dans *Frühmittelalterliche Studien*, 10, 1976, p. 136-68.

mille de Charlemagne [57]. D'abord viennent les garçons, Charles et Pépin (Louis est absent, comme d'habitude). Ils sont décrits d'un façon stylisée : Charles s'illustre par le nom de son père, Pépin par celui de son grand-père. Puis « suit la bande éclatante des jeunes filles ». Rotrude passe rapidement devant, « à la tête de la troupe... à cheval, elle s'avance calmement, elle prend la première place... » Puis vient Berthe, qui rayonne brillamment, en compagnie de maintes jeunes filles. Virile dans sa voix, mais aussi dans son esprit, avec un aspect et un visage resplendissants, elle a une bouche, un maintien, des yeux, un cœur qui reproduisent les attraits de son père » [58].

Le poème continue avec les autres filles de Charlemagne, trois filles adultes légitimes, une illégitime. Mais c'est évidemment Rotrude et Berthe qui apparaissent comme les chefs féminins. Surtout, il n'y a rien de stéréotypé dans le portrait de Berthe, femme virile, véritable enfant de son père. C'est elle, non ses frères, qui, selon le poète, ressemble à Charlemagne, et physiquement et par caractère [59].

Je crois qu'on peut trouver d'autres allusions à l'influence de ces femmes pendant les années impériales. Par exemple, un capitulaire raconte que les *missi* trouvent aussi difficile de *distringere* les *homines* des filles de l'empereur que les *homines* des fils [60]. Ou dans la *Divisio regnorum*, Charlemagne insiste pour que ses filles aient le droit de choisir (*licentia eligendi*) dans quel royaume elles s'installeront après la mort de leur père ; elles devront y vivre dans l'honneur (*honorifice*) ; si elles veulent alors se marier et qu'elles donnent leurs *consensus*, il sera interdit à leurs frères de s'y opposer [61]. Enfin, selon Éginhard, Charlemagne ne pouvait se passer du *contubernium* de ses filles : c'est pour cela qu'il ne les laissa pas se marier de son vivant[62]. Éginhard ajoute des détails intéressants au sujet du testament

---

57. Ici on trouve Liutgarde, femme de Charlemagne : le poète reconstruit d'une façon vraisemblable l'année 799.

58. *MGH Poetae* I, éd. E. DÜMMLER, p. 371, vers 220-223 : «... Berta nitet, multis sociata puellis./ Voce, virili animo, habitu vultuque corusco/Os, mores, oculos imitantia pectora patris/Fert... »

59. Je me permets de vous rappeler la jolie histoire folklorique de Berthe, qui, une nuit d'hiver, après une soudaine tombée de neige, s'inquiétait à cause de son amant qui lui rendait visite dans sa chambre au palais d'Aix. Comment éviter la découverte ? Elle sut porter Angilbert sur son dos à travers la cour du palais, afin qu'une seule paire d'empreintes de pas puisse tromper les yeux paternels. (Vain espoir ! Mais Charlemagne était indulgent.) Voir R. FOLZ, *Le souvenir et la légende de Charlemagne dans l'empire germanique médiéval*, Paris, 1950, p. 342-343. P.E. DUTTON, *The Politics of Dreaming in the Carolingian Empire*, Lincoln NE et London, 1995, p. 13-14, suppose une toilette à l'extérieur des appartements royaux, à l'extrémité de la cour en face de la chambre de Berthe. Dans la mémoire sociale du moyen âge tardif donc, Berthe était vraiment une fille assez bien bâtie, à l'instar de son père.

60. *MGH Capit.* I, n°. 51, c. 13, p. 139.

61. *MGH Capit.* I, n°. 45, c. 17, p. 129.

62. ÉGINHARD, *Vita Karoli*, c. 19, p. 25. Voir J.-L. NELSON, « Women at the court of Charlemagne : a case of monstrous regiment ? », dans J.-C. PARSONS éd., *Medieval*

que Charlemagne avait l'intention de faire mais qu'il ne fit jamais : il voulait *heredes facere* ses filles légitimes [63].

Durant ces années, Charlemagne se montra un vieil opiniâtre. Il est possible qu'il n'ait pas beaucoup aimé Louis ; mais il est certain qu'il n'entendait pas perdre sa liberté de père en matière de politique familiale. La promotion de son petit-fils Bernard en 812 dut être ressentie par Louis le Pieux comme une gifle vraiment injurieuse [64]. Pas moins peut-être que la décision du vieil empereur de faire de son petit-fils l'homonyme de Louis. Étant données ces « fluid conditions », le patriarche devait surtout user de mystification, afin de laisser tout le monde, et surtout le fils aquitain qu'il ne connaissait guère, dans un état d'incertitude. Charlemagne réussit ainsi à se maintenir au centre du pouvoir. Mais il n'était pas seul, il ne pouvait se maintenir dans toute son autorité qu'avec des collaborateurs. Il les trouva chez lui, à la cour, dans sa *domus*, sa maison. Je crois que la fluidité, voire la volatilité qui existait à la cour offrait un espace permettant les interventions des femmes influentes et d'un certain âge, de l'une en particulier, je veux parler de Berthe, celle qui ressemblait tellement à son père.

Le 28 janvier 814, Charlemagne lui-même mourut. Louis se trouvait toujours en Aquitaine. Donc, selon l'Astronome, ce furent les enfants et les grands du palais (*liberi et proceres palatini* — je me demande si l'adjectif s'attache aussi bien aux *liberi* qu'aux *proceres*) qui s'occupèrent des funérailles du vieil empereur le jour même de sa mort. Parmi les enfants, il n'y avait que des filles adultes, et parmi elles, la principale, Berthe ; parmi les *proceres*, le principal : Wala. C'est l'Astronome qui s'exprime explicitement : Louis le Pieux, le nouvel empereur, avait très peur de Wala, qui avait eu une considérable influence *apud Carolum imperatorem* ; Louis soupçonnait Wala de préparer contre lui une sinistre tentative[65]. Je pense qu'il s'agissait d'une prise de pouvoir. Infidélité contre Louis, bien sûr — de la lointaine Aquitaine, Louis le Pieux avait dû longtemps regarder avec méfiance les habitants d'Aix — mais vu de la cour, aux yeux des *palatini* contemporains d'après 811, une telle tentative ne se présentait pas nécessairement comme une infidélité à Charlemagne.

Je n'entre pas dans les détails (vous connaissez tous le récit de l'Astronome) : je souligne seulement que Louis le Pieux ne prit pas le contrôle du palais sans violence. Il fallut presque un coup d'État, une marche sur Aix. Wala avait déjà cédé le terrain, et Louis, avec une astuce malveillante, se servit de lui pour se venger de ses propres compagnons d'hier. Parmi les hommes tués, il y eut un certain Hodoinus. Ni E. Tremp ni d'autres n'ont pu l'identifier. On l'écarte en le présentant comme

---

Queenship, New York, 1993, p. 43-61 (réimp. dans J.-L. NELSON, *Frankish World*, p. 223-242).

63. ÉGINHARD, *Vita Karoli*, c. 33, p. 37.
64. Commentaire très judicieux de P. DEPREUX, « Das Königtum Bernhards », p. 6-10.
65. L'ASTRONOME, c. 21, p. 346-347.

« amant d'une des filles de Charlemagne »,[66] une espèce de gigolo. Mais il y avait probablement un autre cousin de Charlemagne qui s'appelait Oduin, lui aussi petit-fils de Charles Martel [67]. Je propose de voir en Hoduinus un des parents — *encore un des parents* — qui entouraient le vieux Charlemagne, et dont la fidélité (avec d'autres motivations moins désintéressées, sans doute) le poussa, finalement, à essayer de garder dans ses mains les leviers du pouvoir.

Et, enfin, les femmes. Selon l'Astronome, ce qui inquiétait vraiment Louis le Pieux (*moverat animum*), c'était *illud quod a sororibus illius in contubernio exercebatur paterno* : de cette large tache qui souillait la *domus paterna* [68], Louis craignait un *scandalum :* non pas un quelconque scandale, mais précisément la répétition du *scandalum* qui s'était passé 70 ans auparavant mais qu'on se rappelait toujours bien, celui de la sœur de Pépin, Hiltrude, modèle de *licentia eligendi,* qui s'était mariée avec Odilon de Bavière sans le consentement de son frère [69]. Histoire qui risquait de se reproduire. Personne n'avait su mieux que Charlemagne que le mariage d'une fille royale était un acte politique par excellence et personne n'avait compris aussi bien que lui la politique de la crèche. Cette réserve d'enfants au palais offrait l'embarras du choix et pouvait susciter des conflits. Les femmes du palais pouvaient facilement paraître monstrueuses parce qu'elle étaient affranchies de tout ordre.

Pour les abattre, pour nettoyer le palais, il fallait chasser ce *coetus femineus qui permaximus erat* [70]. Il fallait souiller toutes les femmes - *virgines, filiae, ancillae* - de la même tache, en les désignant comme *meretrices.* En se présentant comme un purificateur Louis s'offrait aussi comme rénovateur de tout un système de représentation fondé sur l'autorité masculine. C'était rassurant. Parce que les femmes de la cour inquiétaient les hommes. Alcuin était un peu dubitatif lorsqu'il saluait Gisèle comme *verbipotens* [71]. Quand il écrivit à un jeune homme à la cour au sujet des problèmes moraux qu'il y trouverait, des obstacles à une *conversatio honesta,* il lui conseilla : *non veniant coronatae columbae ad fenestras tuas quae volant per cameras palatii...* [72] Calembour, peut-être, sur le sobriquet de Rotrude, Columba ? En tout cas, avertissement : « Women at work ! » Quelque chose d'équivoque, de dan-

---

66. K.-F. WERNER, « *Hludowicus Augustus* », p. 30, n. 100.

67. Fils de Jérôme, demi-frère de Pépin. Les sources sont tardives : les *Gesta abbatum sancti Bertini* ; la *Vita Folquini,* mais je crois que Régine LE JAN, *Famille et pouvoir dans le monde franc (VIIe-Xe siècle)*, Paris, 1995, p. 454, avec les références en n. 1, a raison en les croyant valables.

68. L'ASTRONOME, c. 21, p. 348-349. À remarquer, la réutilisation du mot *contubernium.* L'Astronome connaissait certainement et utilisait le texte d'Éginhard.

69. *Continuateur de Frédégaire* c. 25, éd. J.-M. WALLACE-HADRILL, *The Fourth Book of the Chronicle of Fredegar with its Continuations*, London, 1960, p. 98.

70. L'ASTRONOME, c. 23, p. 350-351. Bien sûr, il fallait aussi envoyer aux monastères les concurrents possibles : d'abord Wala et peut-être Louis, puis (en 817) Drogon, Hugues et Thierry, petits bâtards de Charlemagne (NITHARD, *Histoire*, I, 2, p. 6-9).

71. ALCUIN, Poème XII, vers 6, *MGH Poetae* I, p. 237.

72. ALCUIN, *Ep.* 244, p. 392 (avec allusion à Isaïe 60 : 8).

gereux, s'attachait aux colombes qui volaient à basse altitude. L'image de Berthe dans l'*Épopée de Paderborn* résonne, je crois, des inquiétudes comparables d'un *palatinus* (non sans raison voit-on comme auteur Éginhard) face à une femme qui exerçait un véritable pouvoir à la cour de son père, père auquel la fille rassemblait si visiblement *voce vultuque*. Le pouvoir de cette femme empiétait sur les structures d'autorité. Le fils du père devait incarner la stabilité, la continuité. Mais la fille du père ? Les valeurs dynastiques, centrées sur la succession de père en fils, s'accommodaient mal de règles patriarcales accordant au père le droit de s'appuyer sur ses filles autant que sur ses fils. Histoire de tous les jours, peut-être, dans la vie de la cour, et d'une société de cour. Histoire d'un pouvoir mal relié à l'autorité, histoire d'une fidélité fondée non sur les serments et les rituels publiques, mais sur les mystères des *cubicula*, des chambres intérieures. Éginhard, je crois, l'avait clairement perçu. Afin de détruire ce pouvoir féminin, il fut au moins le complice de ceux qui murmuraient contre Charlemagne l'accusation d'inceste : accusation à peine voilée dans la *Vita Karoli* avec l'idée d'un *contubernium filiarum in domo*, mais devenue tout à fait explicite dans la *Visio Wettini* des années 820 [73]. Je ne veux pas dire que Charlemagne a été incestueux [74], mais qu'une telle accusation avait quelque chose de vraisemblable, que de tels ragots, au fond très misogynes, avaient une portée réelle dans la bouche et sous la plume des propagandistes du nouveau régime. Donc, rien de fortuit dans les prodiges qui, selon Éginhard, annoncèrent la mort de l'empereur, et parmi ces *signa* (et le moins souvent cité) le plus sinistre pour les oreilles de celles qui écoutaient au palais : *Accessit creber Aquensis palatii tremor et in domibus ubi conversabatur assiduus laqueariorum crepitus* [75]. Les grincements des poutres des plafonds devaient annoncer une fois pour toutes le dérèglement des colombes de Charlemagne.

---

73. K.-F. WERNER, « *Hludovicus Augustus* », p. 30-31 ; voir maintenant le commentaire très suggestif de DUTTON, *The Politics of dreaming*, p. 63-67.

74. À la différence de M. ROUCHE, « Charlemagne, polygame et incestueux », dans *L'Histoire, 4*, 1984, p. 18-24. À noter la riposte impérative de K.-F. WERNER, « *Hludovicus Augustus* », p. 31, n. 101, pour lequel ces témoignages « nous permettent de reconstituer, au moins partiellement, l'attitude mentale... de Louis et ses amis avant 814 ». En reconnaissant la perspicacité de K.-F. WERNER, j'ajouterais : en et après 814. Je voudrais insister, en revanche, sur l'efficacité de la propagande quant aux accusations de mauvaise conduite sexuelle. Les filles de l'empereur et leurs amis étaient la vraie cible ; et selon le dicton anglais : mud sticks.

75. ÉGINHARD, *Vita Karoli*, c. 32, p. 37.

Early Medieval Rites of Queen-Making and the Shaping of Medieval Queenship

'We wish you to know, brethren, that our *dominus et senior* the glorious king Charles besought the devotion of our humility, that, through the authority of the ministry conferred on us by God, just as he has been anointed and consecrated king by episcopal authority with sacred unction and blessing, just as we read that the Lord commanded in the Scriptures that kings be anointed and consecrated to royal power, in the same way we should bless (*benedicamus*) his wife our lady in the title of queen (*in nomine reginae*), as we have learned has previously been done by the apostolic see and by our predecessors for other [queens] (*de aliis*).'[1]

Thus Hincmar and colleague[2] in August 866, presenting, a shade self-

---

1 I translate from the edition of R. A. Jackson, *Ordines Coronationis Franciae: Texts and Ordines for the Coronation of Frankish and French Kings and Queens in the Middle Ages*, i (Philadelphia, 1995), Ordo VI, pp. 80–6, at pp. 82–3. Among recent historiography on Carolingian coronations, I would signal in particular G. Lanoë, 'L'*ordo* de couronnement de Charles le Chauve', in *Kings and Kingship in Medieval Europe*, ed. A. J. Duggan, King's College London Medieval Studies, x (London, 1993), pp. 41–68 (noting, p. 52 n. 40, that 'le couronnement des reines pose dès l'origine bien des problèmes', and promising to return to this subject). See also R.-H. Bautier, 'Sacres et couronnements sous les Carolingiens et les premiers Capetiens', *Annuaire-Bulletin de la Société d'Histoire de la France* (1987), pp. 7–56 (repr. in Bautier's collected papers, *Recherches sur l'histoire de la France médiévale* [London, 1991], ch. 2), an important study which does not deal very fully with queens' consecrations, and regrettably cites no recent anglophone historiography. Neither do many contributors to *Le Sacre des rois: Actes du Colloque international d'histoire sur les sacres . . . Reims 1975* (Paris, 1985), nor R. Folz, 'Les Trois couronnements de Charles le Chauve', *Byzantion*, lxi (1991), 93–111.

2 Archbishop Herard of Tours was the colleague. Two different manuscripts were apparently available to J. Sirmond in the seventeenth century: in one, containing a dossier of material on the Council of Soissons, printed in Sirmond's edition of *Concilia antiqua Galliae* (Paris, 1629), and reprinted by Mansi, xv (Venice, 1770), cols 703–60, the *adlocutio*, preceding Ermentrude's consecration, at 725–8, was attributed to Herard and tacked onto a longer speech on another topic; the other, a now-lost Liège manuscript, edited by Sirmond in *Capitula Caroli Calvi* (Paris, 1623), and repr. by A. Boretius, *MGH, Capitularia regum Francorum*, edd. A. Boretius and V. Krause, 2 vols (Hanover, 1883–97; repr. 1957), ii, 453–5 no. 301, attributed the *adlocutio* to 'duo episcopi', evidently Hincmar and Herard; cf. Jackson, p. 82 n. 5. Ermentrude's *ordo* was preserved in the Liège manuscript alongside Hincmar's *ordines* for Judith, see below, pp. 306–8, for Charles the Bald (869) and for Louis the Stammerer (877), the four treated here as a set: see J. L. Nelson, *Politics and Ritual in*

consciously, the justification for what was clearly a rather unexpected performance – the consecration of Ermentrude, who had been Charles the Bald's wife for nearly twenty-four years and borne him eleven children. The particular circumstances of her consecration are not my prime concern here.[3] Instead I would stress the intimate linkage of king and queen in Charles's and Hincmar's wider and longer-term concerns with monarchic representation. The anointing of kings could be, and had been, justified by appeal to Scripture; but, as Hincmar acknowledged, there were no queenly equivalents to David and Solomon and Josiah. Hincmar had to invent a tradition, claiming precedents for the making of Carolingian queens and empresses by popes and bishops. Real enough though these precedents were, and important sources of inspiration, they had left little trace in the written record; they lacked continuity and hence formal stability; and their dependence on modern history rather than Scripture left some ideological spadework to be done. These drawbacks were mitigated, if not overcome, when queenly consecration found an anchorage in liturgy between the mid-ninth century and the early tenth. The aim of the present paper is to assess the significance of these developments in reflecting, and perhaps engendering, a firmer delineation, or institutionalisation, of the queen's function.

Queenly consecration in context

Queens had indeed been blessed before the mid-ninth century. Yet the evidence goes back no further than the advent of the Carolingian dynasty in 751. According to what is probably the most nearly-contemporary source, 'Pippin . . . by the consecration of bishops and by the subjection of lay magnates, together with the queen Bertrada as the rules of ancient tradition require was elevated into the kingdom.'[4] Three years later, Bertrada was consecrated at St-Denis along with her husband and two sons, by Pope Stephen II.[5] Consecration or coronation is possible,

Early Medieval Europe (London, 1986), pp. 138, 343. I think that the Liège manuscript's version should be preferred to that of the Soissons dossier, and that the 866 *adlocutio*, with the *ordo* itself, bears the stamp of Hincmar's authorship. I hope to return in a future paper to Sirmond and his work.

3 See now the wide-ranging study of F.-R. Erkens, ' "Sicut Esther regina": Die westfränk-ische Königin als *consors regni'*, *Francia*, xx/1 (1993), 15–38, plausibly suggesting, pp. 33–7, Charles's intent to contrast his own marital rectitude with the scandal of Lothar II's 'two wives'. Ermentrude's anointing represented a strengthening of marriage as well as 'a sacral elevation of the queen' (p. 35). Lotharingia was certainly in Charles's sights in 866.

4 Continuator of Fredegar, c. 33: *The Fourth Book of the Chronicle of Fredegar and its Continuators* , ed. J. M. Wallace-Hadrill (London, 1960), p. 102. See now R. Collins, 'Deception and Misrepresentation in Early Eighth-Century Frankish Historiography: Two Case Studies', in *Karl Martell in seiner Zeit*, edd. J. Jarnut, U. Nonn and M. Richter (Sigmaringen, 1992), pp. 227–47, at 243–6, arguing convincingly that Count Hildebrand's section of the Continuation was presented to Pippin at his accession, and is a highly tendentious work.

5 Codex Carolinus, no. 11, ed. W. Gundlach, *MGH Epp.*, iii (Berlin, 1892), 505. The arguments of A. Stoclet, 'La "Clausula de unctione Pippini regis": mises au point et nouvelles hypothèses', *Francia*, viii (1980), 1–42, stressing the tenth-century date of the manuscript,

if perhaps improbable, for Charlemagne's wife Fastrada in 783.[6] Louis the Pious's first wife Irmengard was crowned with a golden crown at Reims by Pope Stephen III in 816,[7] and Louis' second wife Judith was probably crowned by Louis himself and 'acclaimed by all as empress (*augusta*)' in 819.[8] In place of all these possibilities, we reach certainty, at last, when we come to the mid-ninth century. It is no coincidence that the history of queenly *ordines* begins and flourishes at this point. The Carolingian family, even before 751, had been keen patrons of church reform. They encouraged clergy and monks to perform their sacramental and intercessory functions correctly, and be seen to do so.[9] Key agents were bishops, and a key instrument was liturgy. Thanks to regular and relatively frequent synodal meetings, and the multiplication of the means to produce and distribute liturgical books,[10] the bishops became increasingly active, collectively self-conscious and self-propelled. Hincmar, archbishop of Reims from 845 to 882, was perhaps their most articulate and loquacious spokesman, an exemplary if not quite representative figure.[11] Few traditional forms of liturgy escaped his attention, and he pioneered several new ones.[12] He was not alone, however. Many other bishops took an active interest in reform, liturgy, and the written word. The archbishops of Sens, in particular, rivalled their confrères for the leadership of the church in the West Frankish realm; and the role of Archbishop Walter (887–923), almost as long in post as Hincmar, merits special attention.[13] Furthermore, the Carolingian rulers themselves were increasingly interested in the ideology of rulership, as articulated in texts but also as represented in symbolism and public ritual. Here a

have persuaded me that the *Clausula* cannot be accepted as unproblematic evidence for what happened in 754. Stoclet's work is not cited by G. Wolf, 'Königinnen-Krönungen des frühen Mittelalters bis zum Beginn des Investiturstreits', *Zeitschrift für Rechtsgeschichte, Kan. Abt.*, lxxvi (1990), 62–88, at p. 63.

6 *Annales regni Francorum*, ed. F. Kurze, *MGH SRG*, vi (Hanover, 1895), 66.

7 Thegan, *Gesta Hludowici imperatoris*, c. 17, ed. G. Pertz, *MGH SS*, ii (Hanover, 1829), 594; cf. Ermold, *In Honorem Hludowici Pii*, ed. and trans. E. Faral, *Ermold le Noir: Poème sur Louis le Pieux* (Paris, 1964), lines 1101–5. Ermold's evidence seems to me to be accepted too enthusiastically by Wolf, 'Königinnen-Krönungen', pp. 81–2.

8 *Annales Mettenses Priores*, ed. B. Simson, *MGH SRG*, x (Hanover, 1905), 95–6.

9 As explicitly stated in Charlemagne's capitulary *de litteris colendis*, ed. A. Boretius, *MGH, Capitularia*, i, 79 no. 29: '. . . ut quicumque vos propter nomen Domini et sanctae conversationis nobilitatem ad videndum expetierit, sicut de aspectu vestro aedificetur visus, ita quoque de sapientia vestra, quam in legendo seu cantando perceperit, instructus . . . redeat'. For the wider context, see W. Ullmann, *The Carolingian Renaissance and the Idea of Reform* (Cambridge, 1969), R. McKitterick, *The Frankish Church and the Carolingian Reforms* (London, 1977), and G. Brown, 'Introduction: The Carolingian Renaissance', in *Carolingian Culture*, ed. R. McKitterick (Cambridge, 1994), pp. 1–51.

10 R. McKitterick, *The Carolingians and the Written Word* (Cambridge, 1989), pp. 135–64, discusses book-production in general.

11 J. M. Wallace-Hadrill, *The Frankish Church* (Oxford, 1984), pp. 292–303, is the classic account. See now also the fine monograph of M. Stratmann, *Hinkmar von Reims als Verwalter von Bistum und Kirchenprovinz* (Sigmaringen, 1991). Cf. Bautier, 'Sacres', pp. 42–3.

12 Nelson, *Politics and Ritual*, esp. chs 7 and 15.

13 Below, p. 310.

crucial figure was Charles the Bald (840–77).[14] During his reign, there was increasing stress, in a battery of media, on the active functions of the king, as provider of justice and equity as well as war-leader, and as protector and regulator of the church in his realm. At the same time, the dynastic element of kingship came to be amplified. It was hardly surprising that alongside this enhanced concern with the king's function went an increased interest in the queen's.

Already in the 820s, the *de Ordine Palatii* described the queen's centrally important roles.[15] She was responsible for the 'good order of the palace' (*honestas palatii*), and in particular for the *ornamentum regale*, that is, the *regalia*, the royal insignia and cemeronial equipment, also the annual gifts for the *milites*, the king's military household. It was also the queen's job, with the help of the chamberlain, to supervise the provisioning of the court, so that all would be made ready for a royal visit in good time (*tempore congruo, opportuno tempore*). Finally, while the chamberlain normally arranged the giving of gifts to foreign envoys, sometimes the queen might involve herself there too, should the king command it. Here then, in the palace, the queen operated as the materfamilias, 'the lady with a mead-cup', perhaps with a certain ritualised role to play at royal feasts.[16]

The West Franks by the mid-ninth century were certainly very familiar with the position and status of queen. The ruler's wife was routinely called queen in letters and in charters.[17] Sedulius Scottus ('the Irishman'), in his *Liber de rectoribus*

---

[14] See the fundamental study of the late and much lamented R. Deshman, 'The Exalted Servant: The Ruler Theology of the Prayer-Book of Charles the Bald', *Viator*, xi (1980), 385–417; also L. Nees, *A Tainted Mantle: Hercules and the Classical Tradition at the Carolingian Court* (Philadelphia, 1991); N. Staubach, *Rex christianus: Hofkultur und Herrschaftspropaganda im Reich Karls des Kahlen, Teil II: Die Grundlegen der 'religion royale'* (Cologne/Weimar/Vienna, 1993); J. L. Nelson, *Charles the Bald* (London, 1992), and *eadem*, *The Frankish World* (London, 1996), especially chs 5–7, and 9.

[15] Edd. T. Gross and R. Schieffer, *MGH Fontes*, NS (Hanover, 1980), pp. 72–3, c. 22. A form of this work was written in the 820s by Adalard of Corbie, but the extant version is as revised by Hincmar of Reims in 881. See B. Kasten, *Adalard von Corbie: Die Biographie eines karolingischen Politikers und Klostervorstehers* (Düsseldorf, 1986), pp. 72–84, arguing that Adalard's Italian experience influenced his writing. The section on the queen could, it seems to me, refer equally to the 820s and the 870s.

[16] Cf. M. J. Enright, 'Lady with a Mead-Cup: Ritual, Group Cohesion and Hierarchy in the Germanic Warband', *Frühmittelalterliche Studien*, xxii (1988), 170–203.

[17] E.g. Lupus of Ferrières, *epp.* 6 (referring to Judith), 89 and 95 (written for Ermentrude), ed. P. Marshall (Leipzig, 1984), pp. 16, 88, and 93; Nithard, *Historiarum Libri IV*, i.3, 3rd edn, ed. E. Müller, *MGH SRG*, xliv (Hanover, 1907), 4; *Annales de Saint Bertin*, edd. F. Grat, J. Vielliard and S. Clémencet (Paris, 1964), *s.a.* 840, p. 36: *augusta* (Judith); *s.a.* 857, p. 74: *regina* (Theutberga); Hincmar, letters to queens and empresses, summarised in Flodoard, *Historia Remensis Ecclesiae*, iii.27, edd. I. Heller and G. Waitz, *MGH SS*, xiii (Hanover, 1881), 547–50. For the charter evidence, see the convenient summary in Erkens, ' "Sicut Esther regina" ', pp. 18, 24–5. Worth noting, therefore, are cases where a queenly title is not accorded. That Nithard calls Judith queen only once, for instance, and elsewhere refers to her simply as Louis' wife or Charles the Bald's mother, could suggest personal hostility to her. That in a series of letters, *epp.* 50, 90, 96, 102, 149 (?), 150, 190, 197, ed. E. Dümmler, *MGH Epp.*, iv (Berlin, 1895), 94, 134, 140, 149, 244, 246, 317, 326, Alcuin never calls Liutgard queen or refers to her as such could suggest some doubt about her status; cf. *ep.* 62

christianis, written in 869 for Charles the Bald, devoted practically a whole chapter (c. 5) to the queen.[18] First in relation to her husband: he performs his royal office (*regendi ministerium gerit*) in ruling himself, then his wife, his children and the *domestici* of his household. But it was not enough for the king alone to be virtuous, his wife too had to be so: indeed she had to be 'adorned with purity'. 'And as the moon shines with the splendour of the stars around it, so the king adorns himself with his entourage, and, above all, with the queen. 'It is for her to concern herself *disciplinariter* with whatever is necessary, it is for her to regulate *pacifice* the children and the household, with modest face and cheerful words (*humili facie hilarique sermone*). She must be the beauty of the *familia*; at the same time she must have the prudence of the good counsellor. If the bad wife was characterised by *persuasio,* the good one had *consilium.* Notwithstanding feminine frailty, the husband of a prudent queen should be grateful for her advice. St Paul had said, 'the pagan husband (*infidelis*) will be sanctified (*sanctificatus erit*) by his believing wife'.[19] Sedulius's version has: 'the husband will be saved (*salvabitur*) by his wife'. Beside her husband, the wife should flourish in her prudence, like Queen Esther of old:

> Princeps et rectrix, populum si rite gubernant, suam regant prosapiam.
>
> (If king and queen govern the people justly, they will rule their own off-spring.)[20]

Note here that the queen has the title of *rectrix.* Even in a poetic text, this counts for something: alongside the prince, the queen 'governs' and 'rules'. Furthermore, ruling the people, and ruling the children, were indeed two intimately linked spheres of queenly activity. The troubles of Louis the Pious's reign had shown some possible drawbacks in this area.[21] Charles the Bald's wife Ermentrude, on the other hand, performed her queenly roles, apparently with discretion and success.[22]

---

where he does call Cynethryth of Mercia *regina* (though in *epp.* 101, referring to Cynethryth, and 122, he seems to avoid using the term queen for an Anglo-Saxon king's wife too).

[18] Ed. S. Hellmann, *Sedulius Scottus,* Quellen und Untersuchungen zur lateinischen Philologie des Mittelalters, i/1 (Munich, 1906), 35–7. I am very grateful to my colleague Evelyn Cornell for tracking down King's College Library's long-lost copy of this book. On the significance of Sedulius's work, Staubach, *Rex christianus,* supersedes earlier studies, and argues cogently that Charles was Sedulius's addressee, the Lotharingian succession the context.

[19] I Cor. 7:14.

[20] Ed. Hellmann, pp. 35–7.

[21] E. Ward, 'Caesar's Wife: The Career of the Empress Judith 819–29', in *Charlemagne's Heir: New Perspectives on the Reign of Louis the Pious,* edd. P. Godman and R. Collins (Oxford, 1990), pp. 205–27; cf. *eadem,* 'Agobard of Lyons and Paschasius Radbertus as Critics of the Empress Judith', *SCH,* xxvii (1990), 15–25.

[22] J. Hyam, 'Ermentrude and Richildis', in *Charles the Bald: Court and Kingdom,* edd. M. T. Gibson and J. L. Nelson, 2nd rev. edn (London, 1990), pp. 154–68. For the telling argument that ninth-century accusations of queenly adultery were symptomatic of queens' increased

The *ordines*

The case of Judith, daughter of Charles the Bald, in 856 is the first queenly consecration for which there is not only relatively full contemporary documentation but a surviving *ordo*.[23] This was not, strictly speaking, a West Frankish queen-making, for the occasion was Judith's marriage to King Æthelwulf of the West Saxons and hence Judith's becoming a West Saxon queen. Nevertheless, the setting was a West Frankish royal palace, Verberie on the Oise, and one officiant a West Frankish prelate. According to the *Annals of St-Bertin*:

> Æthelwulf . . . received Judith in marriage, and after Bishop Hincmar of Reims had consecrated her and placed a diadem on her head, he [Æthelwulf] formally conferred on her the title of queen, which was something not customary before then to him or to his people.[24]

Four points can be noted here. First, the conferring of the queenly title is done by the king, not the bishop. Second, however, the bishop's acts precede the king's conferring of the title, thus strongly suggesting that Judith's becoming queen depended on her consecration and coronation: these made the queen, and the king set the seal on what has been done; in other words, Æthelwulf did not simply declare his wife queen without a prior change in her status. Third, although the Latin *benedicere* need not mean consecration, it clearly does so here, for the central *benedictio* was accompanied by a prayer, 'Deus electorum', derived from the blessing of holy oils and borrowed directly – as a glance at the parallel texts will show – from an equivalent prayer for the anointing of a king.[25] Hence Judith's consecration was clearly envisaged by those who designed and witnessed it as a status-changing rite. Fourth, the *nomen* of 'queen' was something already familiar to the West Franks and borrowed from them in 856 by Æthelwulf. Judith thus had to be made queen before leaving her father's kingdom.[26] A king's wife could of course bear the title 'queen' without having been consecrated. The fact that Hincmar had to adapt a king's *ordo* for Judith suggests that no queen's *ordo* was available to him.

political significance, see G. Bührer-Thierry, 'Les reines adultères', *Cahiers de civilisation médiévale*, xxxv (1992), 299–312.

[23] See Appendix, Text A. Earlier editions are now largely superseded by that of Jackson, *Ordines*, pp. 73–9 no. V. Unfortunately Wolf, 'Königinnen-Krönungen', pp. 66–7, discusses Judith's consecration without citing any historiography in English.

[24] *The Annals of St-Bertin, s.a.* 856, trans. J. L. Nelson (Manchester, 1991), p. 83. The Latin reads: 'Ediluulf . . . Iudith . . . in matrimonium accipit, et eam, Ingmaro Durocortori Remorum episcopo benedicente, inposito capiti eius diademate, reginae nomine insignit, quod sibi suaeque genti eatenus fuerat insuetum', ed. Grat, p. 73.

[25] See below, p. 313. I think I established this derivation and this borrowing in 'The Earliest Royal *ordo*', in *Authority and Power: Studies in Medieval Law and Government presented to Walter Ullmann*, edd. P. Linehan and B. Tierney (Cambridge, 1980), pp. 29–48, reprinted in my *Politics and Ritual*, pp. 341–60.

[26] Pointed out already by W. Stevenson in his editorial notes to Asser, *De Rebus Gestis Ælfredi* (Oxford, 1904; repr. 1959), p. 201.

This contrast between Frankish and West Saxon treatment of the king's wife deserves to be explored a little further. It is attested not only by the *Annals of St-Bertin* but by the *Life of Alfred*, whose author, Asser, claimed to be writing in 893, and, as regards this very issue, on evidence supplied by Alfred himself. The coincidence of these two sources here seems to me to support the argument for the *Life*'s authenticity as a ninth-century work.[27] It may be that the West Saxons' 'custom' was not of very long standing. The one-year reign, in 672, of King Cenwalh's widowed *cuen*, Seaxburh, was retained in the social memory of some late-ninth-century West Saxons.[28] Further, the West Saxons' neighbours and rivals, the Mercians, certainly had queens in the later eighth and ninth centuries; and while it is not certain that Eadburh, daughter of the Mercian king Offa was also daughter of Offa's wife Queen Cynethryth,[29] it seems quite likely that when Eadburh married the West Saxon king Beohrtric in 789, she too received the title of queen. Yet the new dynasty established by Egbert, Beohrtric's successor, in 802, seems from the outset to have downplayed the status of the king's wife.[30] Hence the need for a special enhancement of Judith's position, a declaration of her *nomen*, at Verberie in 856, and her further honouring in Wessex by being publicly accorded a seat 'beside her husband on a royal throne'.[31]

What light does the 856 *Ordo* throw on the nature of Judith's honourable *nomen*? She was anointed with chrism, like the king. Borrowing and modifying the king's anointing-prayer 'Deus electorum', Hincmar omitted references to 'the people subjected to [him]', to 'attaining the height of the kingdom in the counsels of knowledge and the equity of judgement', and to 'presenting a face of joy to the whole people'. In place of these phrases, Hincmar inserted two biblical allusions to explain the meaning of the anointing:

> [God] who by this unction made joyful the face of your maidservant Judith for the liberating of your servants and the confounding of their enemies, and who so made radiant the face of your handmaiden Esther by this spiritual anointing of your mercy that by her prayers you inclined the fierce heart of

---

[27] A. P. Smyth, *Alfred the Great* (Oxford, 1995), pp. 149–367, takes the contrary view.

[28] *Anglo-Saxon Chronicle 'A'*, ed. J. Bately (Cambridge, 1985), p. 31: 'Seaxburg an gear ricsode his cuen æfter him'. See further the comments of Nelson, 'Reconstructing a Royal Family: Reflections on Alfred from Asser, ch. 2', in *People and Places in Northern Europe, 500–1600: Essays in Honour of P. H. Sawyer*, edd. I. Wood and N. Lund (Woodbridge, 1991), pp. 47–66, at 55–6, 65.

[29] For Cynethryth as *regina* on coins issued in her name, see M. Archibald, 'The Mercian Supremacy: Coins', in *The Making of England: Anglo-Saxon Art and Culture, AD 600–900*, edd. J. Backhouse and L. Webster (London, 1991), pp. 245–6, and for Alcuin addressing Cynethryth as *regina*, see n. 17, above.

[30] P. Stafford, 'The King's Wife in Wessex, 800–1066', *Past and Present*, xci (1981), 3–27.

[31] Asser, *De Rebus Gestis Ælfredi*, c. 13, p. 11. For differing interpretations of the political context of this episode, see Stafford, 'Charles the Bald, Judith and England', in *Charles the Bald*, edd. Gibson and Nelson, pp. 139–53; M. J. Enright, 'Charles the Bald and Æthelwulf of Wessex: The Alliance of 856 and Strategies of Royal Succession', *Journal of Medieval History*, v (1979), 291–302; Nelson, *Charles the Bald*, p. 182. For Judith's 'liberating' role, see the Vulgate book of Judith, 13:20.

the king to mercy and to the salvation of those who believed in you, we ask you, omnipotent God, . . . to make her fittingly lovely[32] with chastity.

Through these changes, Hincmar gendered the function and qualities of the queen. The reference to the 'face' of both the Old Testament women, and the final reference to the 'beauty of chastity', suggest the importance of the queen's physical appearance and demeanour in the representation of monarchy. Where the king was to show 'equity of judgement', the queen was characterised by 'mercy': two distinct if complementary aspects of justice.[33] While mentions of the *populus* and the *plebs* were dropped, Esther's role as intercessor with her husband was spelled out, and the concluding phrase highlighted chastity as the queenly virtue *par excellence*. Gender played a key part in the stories of both Judith and Esther: each traded on her feminity to defeat or sway a powerful man.[34] There is nothing about fertility in this prayer, however. Neither Judith nor Esther would have been an apt model of maternity. The choice of these two biblical women was of course determined on the one hand by the name Charles's daughter bore (she had been named for her grandmother),[35] on the other by the fittingness of a queenly exemplar. Yet both Judith and Esther were women imbued with power, and Hincmar's prayer is explicit on the significance of their divinely-inspired interventions: the *liberatio* and *salvatio* of the chosen people. Their individual 'private' actions had the most public of consequences.

In 866, before a great assembly in a major Carolingian cult-site, Hincmar's claims about the historicity of queen-making rites had implications also for the role and functions of the queen. He stated explicitly that there was a queenly *nomen*.[36] In the coronation-prayer itself, that idea was amplified: the queen was to remain stalwart *in hoc seculo* 'in merits, in *nomen* and in *virtus*', that is, in official title and in necessary attributes. The queen was 'crowned with a crown of justice, crowned with glory'. Like Charles the Bald himself, his wife surely wore a crown, now a prime symbol of royalty, and among the insignia handed on by Charles on his deathbed to his son and heir. In Charles's own inauguration-rite as king of the (Lotharingian) Franks in 869, the coronation-prayer drew on that composed for Ermentrude three years before. The inspiration, to be sure, was biblical: Pss. 8:7; 20:4; 44:8, and Heb. 1:9. But it is surely significant that the

---

[32] The adjective *decora* combines the senses of appropriateness and beauty. See Appendix, Text A.

[33] See for illuminating comment on the implications of this for later ritual practice, J. C. Parsons, 'Ritual and Symbol in the English Queenship to 1500', in *Women and Sovereignty*, ed. L. O. Fradenburg (Edinburgh, 1992), pp. 60–77.

[34] The Vulgate sources are Judith, chs 10–13, and Esther, 2:15–18; 5:1–8.

[35] For this widespread naming-practice, see C. Bouchard, 'Patterns of Women's Names in Royal Lineages: Ninth–Eleventh Centuries', *Medieval Prosopography*, ix/1 (1988), 1–32.

[36] Appendix, Text B; Jackson, *Ordines*, p. 83. For the same expression already applied to Judith in 856 by the author of the *Annals of St-Bertin*, *s.a.* 856, see above, p. 306. Whether the author of this passage was Prudentius, responsible for the annals between 835 and 861, or Hincmar, who continued the annals down to 882, and may have made interpolations in the earlier annals, must remain for now an open question, on which more work needs to be done.

formula 'Coronet te Dominus' was first used for a queen (and last used for a queen too, since the amplified 869 version of the prayer, translated into English, was used in 1953 for Elizabeth II)[37] – significant because the virtues here specified are not *gender*-specific.[38] Queen and king alike need faith manifested in good works. For queen and king alike, virtues that accompany an earthly crown prefigure the wearing of a heavenly crown (*in futuro*; in the *regnum perpetuum*). The notion of co-rulership in heaven[39] is equally applied to the queen and king, only the queen will sit at the right hand of another, heavenly, king. Important though the theme of fertility was in the 866 *ordo*, Ermentrude's consecration was, after all, more than a piece of fertility-magic.[40] One important difference between the officiants in the act of coronation nevertheless signalled the queen's ancillary position as consort: whereas Charles was consecrated by clergy, he himself joined the clergy in crowning the queen. Did he have a Byzantine model in mind?[41]

In Hincmar's *ordines* queenly status was high, but imprecise. Another queen's *ordo*, produced apparently at Sens, intimated the conferment of a more clearly functional authority. This *ordo*, the so-called Erdmann *Ordo*, is the first queen's *ordo* to be presented in a liturgical book alongside that of the king.[42] There is no continuity with Hincmar's *ordines*: instead the composer[43] had turned to another source. The prayer to be said over the newly-anointed queen is clearly taken almost word-for-word from the prayer over the newly-ordained abbess. Here, although the phrase *regimen animarum* from the abbess's rite is not used, a queenly office

---

37 E. C. Ratcliffe, *The Coronation Service of Queen Elizabeth II* (Cambridge, 1953), p. 49.

38 Cf. also the *ordo*, dating from the third quarter of the ninth century, recently published by R. Elze, 'Ein karolingischer Ordo für die Krönung eines Herrscherpaares', *Bullettino dell'Istituto Storico Italiano per il Medio Evo e Archivio Muratorio*, lxxxviii (1992), 417–23.

39 P. E. Schramm, 'Mittherrschaft im Himmel: ein Topos der Herrscherkults in christlicher Einkleidung', in Schramm, *Kaiser, Könige und Päpste, Gesammelte Aufsätze*, i (Stuttgart, 1968), 79–85.

40 The interpretation of Ermentrude's consecration as a *Fruchtbarkeitszauber* was first offered by E. H. Kantorowicz, 'The Carolingian King in the Bible of San Paolo Fuori le Mura', in *Late Classical and Medieval Studies in Honour of A. M. Friend* (Princeton, 1955), pp. 287–300, at 290 (cf. also A. Wintersig, 'Zur Königinnenweihe', *Jahrbuch für Liturgiewissenschaft*, v [1925], 150–3 at p. 152: 'eine Weihe der Thronfolgermutter'), and has recently been taken up again by Erkens, ' "Sicut Esther regina" ', p. 28.

41 Cf. Wolf, 'Königinnen-Krönungen', pp. 81–2, with reference to 816.

42 Appendix, Text C. Cf. Jackson, *Ordines*, no. XIII, pp. 151–2. Schramm named the *ordo* after Carl Erdmann (d. 1944), and although Erdmann himself objected, the name has stuck: Jackson, p. 143. The older of the two manuscripts, a pontifical from Sens, has generally been dated to *c.* 900, but for the still unpublished arguments of P. Konakov and G. Lobrichon for a date 'about 875 or even from the middle of the century', see Jackson, p. 26, with some further general remarks ('that there was no generally accepted coronation rite in ninth-century Francia, that each coronation ceremony was an *ad hoc* ceremony, that a rite was devised for each coronation and used on that occasion alone . . . [and that] Louis the Stammerer's *Ordo* [of 877] would play a crucial role in standardizing the ceremony'). The mid-ninth century should, however, be highlighted as the period during which a continuous tradition took shape, and the importance of Hincmar's *ordines* as a group deserves emphasis too: see above, p. 301, n. 2.

43 See below, p. 310.

is evoked in the idea of the queen's being 'instituted' and remaining 'worthy' (*digna*). The position of abbess was the most authoritative one available to women, not least in the Carolingian period when abbesses, like abbots, were subject to the institutionalised demands of the realm, owing military service, for instance, holding military strongpoints, and sometimes being summoned to assemblies.[44] Abbesses were also *magistrae*, female-teachers.[45] This combination of functions likewise characterised the later Carolingian queen.

The prayer for the conferring of the ring in this same queen's *ordo* has struck some modern commentators as anomalous (Appendix, Text D). Walter Ullmann argued that the ring here 'has the function of a knuckle-duster'.[46] It has been claimed, too, that this prayer must have been borrowed from a rite for a king, or even for a bishop.[47] This ring is not a wedding-ring, but an amulet, a charm, not necessarily conceived as gender-specific, that is, for men only. Avoiding heresy and summoning barbarous *gentes* to acknowledgement of the truth of the faith could be queenly functions. Patronage of missionaries, support for the church, care for the spiritual wellbeing of the household, were characteristic responsibilities of powerful women, and of queens par excellance.[48] Thus by the tenth century, here again a queenly office is being outlined.

If the 'Erdmann' composer should be located at Sens, as the earliest manuscript might suggest, there is a problem in supplying a plausible occasion for the first use of the king's and queen's *ordines* as a pair. The contemporary evidence for the consecration of Odo (Eudes) by Archbishop Walter of Sens on 29 February 888 makes no mention of Odo's queen Theodrada. Further, an *ordo* for Odo's consecration is extant, and it is not 'Erdmann'.[49] Similar problems surround a second possibility: King Ralph was consecrated at St-Médard, Soissons, by Archbishop Walter on 13 July 923, but Ralph's wife Emma was consecrated later in the year by Archbishop Seulf at Reims. My tentative solution is that since the extant *ordo* for Odo clearly represents only a part of what took place, 'Erdmann' too might have been used for the royal couple in February 888.[50] I would stress the likelihood

---

[44] Nelson, *Politics and Ritual*, pp. 122–4, and cf. *eadem, The Frankish World*, pp. 19–29, 209.

[45] Nelson, 'Les Femmes et l'évangelisation', *Revue du Nord*, lxviii (1986), 471–85.

[46] *Principles of Government and Politics in the Middle Ages* (London, 1961), pp. 181–2.

[47] C. A. Bouman, *Sacring and Crowning* (Groningen, 1957), p. 131, and cf. pp. 129–30.

[48] See Nelson, 'Les reines carolingiennes au XIe siècle', in *Femmes et pouvoirs des femmes à Byzance et en Occident*, edd. A. Dierkens, J. M. Sansterre, S. Lebecq and R. Le Jan (forthcoming).

[49] Jackson, *Ordines*, Ordo XI, pp. 133–8. Cf. also Schramm, *Könige*, ii, 211–14.

[50] Cf. the fundamental study by O. Guillot, 'Les Etapes de l'accession d'Eudes au pouvoir royal', in *'Media in Francia . . .': Recueil de mélanges offert à Karl Ferdinand Werner* (Maulévrier, 1989), pp. 199–223. Cf. also Bautier, 'Sacres', pp. 47–8. I cannot wholly share the view of Jackson, p. 142, that 'the king's and queen's *ordines* have nothing to do with each other either in the Erdmann *Ordo* or in other early *ordines*, and their juxtaposition in no way reflects a joint coronation or implies that the two were to be used for a joint coronation'. These propositions may be true at some times and places, but do not hold universally. They reflect the situation once pontificals had assumed more generalised, standardised form and function. In the ninth and tenth centuries, when royal *ordines* were

of Theodrada's consecration alongside her husband: a clear statement of dynastic intent.[51] The twin 'Erdmann' *ordines* might then have been reused for Ralph and Emma, even though they were consecrated separately, Ralph at Soissons in July 923, and Emma at Reims later that year.[52] Again I think Emma's consecration was very significant: Ralph's acceptability to the *primates* of West Francia had much to do with the fact that his wife was 'the daughter of King Robert', his immediate predecessor.[53]

A fourth and final queen's *ordo* to consider briefly here is that associated with the 'Seven Forms' king's *ordo*.[54] It may have been used for Gerberga, wife of Louis IV 'd'Outremer'. Gerberga, sister of Otto I, and widow of the recently-dead Duke Giselbert of Lotharingia, married Louis in 939, and was consecrated by Archbishop Artold of Reims.[55] The hypothesis of use for Gerberga, given the

---

still at an early stage of formation and diffusion, the presence of a queen's *ordo* does seem to me a potentially important indication of historical context.

51 A hagiographer writing before 894 called Theodrada *regina*: *Vita Rignoberti*, ed. W. Levison, *MGH, Scriptores rerum Merovingicarum*, vii (Hanover/Leipzig, 1920), 55.

52 The suggestion of Bautier, 'Sacres', p. 50 n. 152, that a set of blessings for a king's investiture with ring, sword, crown, sceptre and staff, which follows the queen's *ordo* in the Sens Pontifical, Jackson, Ordo XIIIB, was used for Ralph's *Festkrönung* on the occasion of Emma's consecration, deserves further consideration, if the date of the manuscript does not preclude it (see above, n. 42). It does not seem to me implausible that Seulf of Reims would have used a queen's *ordo* emanating from Sens: Robert was consecrated by Walter of Sens (Bautier, 'Sacres', p. 49 n. 50) as Seulf's predecessor Harvey of Reims lay dying (Flodoard says 'he died three days after Robert was made king', *Historia Remensis Ecclesiae*, iv.17, p. 577), and as Seulf was a firm adherent of Robert and Ralph, he might well have been willing to signal this, and the continuity of the two regimes, by re-using for Ralph the *ordo* used for Robert. Reims-Sens rivalry was not a constant, and other factors affected particular situations, as in this case. The prayer-texts of Ordo XIIIB are brief, but I do not see any evidence to support Jackson's idea, p. 144, that their content represents 'a primitive . . . survival . . . from the early ninth or even the late eighth century'. *Pace* Jackson, p. 143 n. 2, Bautier, 'Sacres', pp. 49–50, did *not* suggest that 'Erdmann' was composed for a 'double coronation' of Robert and Ralph in 923.

53 Flodoard, *Annales*, ann. 923, ed. P. Lauer (Paris, 1906), p. 17, notes the relationship. For the importance of the consecration of the Anglo-Saxon King Edgar's wife Ælfthryth in 973, see Nelson, *Politics and Ritual*, pp. 296–303, 370–4.

54 Jackson, Ordo XIV, pp. 159–67, suggesting, p. 154, renaming as 'the Ordo of Eleven Forms', in order to signal the presence of the queen's *ordo*, of four formulae, following the king's. Yet it is clear that the queen's *ordo* sometimes travelled independently of the king's, and *vice versa*. Moreover, Carl Erdmann's original name of 'Seven Forms *Ordo*' is now well established: I therefore retain it here while using Jackson's edition. This is the place to observe that while I much admire the ingenuity of Lanoë, 'L'ordo de couronnement' (cf. above n. 1), arguing that an abbreviated, five-form, version of the king's *ordo* preserved in a Leyden manuscript of *c*. 1000 represents the *ordo* used for Charles the Bald in 848, I am not convinced, chiefly because (a) the 877 form of the consecration prayer, 'Omnipotens sempiterne deus creator' seems to me older than that of the Leyden manuscript, and (b) the original form of the 'two peoples' mentioned in the Leyden consecration prayer were, in my view, the Angles and Saxons (rather than the Franks and Aquitanians), and so derive from an Anglo-Saxon model which travelled to the Continent in the tenth century (see my *Politics and Ritual*, pp. 361–6, a discussion not cited by Lanoë in this context).

55 Flodoard, *Annales*, ann. 939, p. 74 (suggesting that the location was in Lotharingia);

importance of the Ottonian connection, would help explain why the 'Seven Forms' queen's *ordo* was incorporated into the Romano-Germanic Pontifical and other Ottonian pontificals in Italy as well as in Germany.[56] Artold had also consecrated Louis himself,[57] and may have composed new *ordines* for both king and queen, or used *ordines* which he found already at Reims, rather than continue following the Sens tradition embodied in 'Erdmann'. The queen's *ordo* (like the king's) clearly picks up on a Reims tradition. References to both Judith and Esther models are recapitulated, and amplified. God 'once willed to entrust the triumph of [his] glory and strength into the hands of a woman, Judith, for the sake of the Jewish people';[58] and brought about Esther's marriage 'for the sake of Israel's salvation from its captivity'.[59] The queen's crown is said to be 'of royal excellence', its outward glitter the sign of wisdom as well as virtues within. More important still, blessing is sought for 'your servant whom we have elected to be queen'; and God is requested 'for the sake of the salvation of your Christian people, to make [the queen] enter into worthy and sublime union with our king'. There are, moreover, several strong parallels in wording between this *ordo* and the king's.[60] All this adds up to a representation of the queen as involved in 'a partnership of [the king's] realm (*regni sui participium*)', even if, at the same time, the prayers differentiated clearly between the king's office of ruling and the queen's supporting role.

In the tenth-century narrative and charter evidence, queens and empresses are conspicuous for their political activities in all the kingdoms of Latin Christendom for which adequate documentation survives. Theophano, coming from Byzantium as Otto II's bride, and later seizing the opportunies of a regency, found a position and a status ready-made.[61] If her high profile was exceptional, her impact as a consort was typical.[62] The composers and performers of queenly *ordines* were

Flodoard, *Historia Remensis Ecclesiae*, iv.35, p. 585, quotes the letter of Artold to the Council of Ingelheim in 948: 'Postquam Ludovicum regem, favente Hugone cunctisque regni principibus, Gerbergam quoque reginam benedixeram et sacro perfuderam chrismate'; cf. also Richer, *Historiarum Libri IV*, 2nd edn, ed. G. Waitz, *MGH SRG*, li (Hanover, 1877), ii.19, p. 49: 'Ludowicus rex Gislebertum extinctum comperiens . . . in Belgicam profectus, eius uxorem Gerbergam, Ottonis sororem, coniugio duxit eamque secum reginam in regnum coronavit.'

56 *Ordines coronationis imperialis: Die Ordines für die Weihe und Krönung des Kaisers und der Kaiserin*, ed. R. Elze, *MGH Fontes*, ix (Hanover, 1960), *Ordo III*, pp. 6–9; *Le Pontifical romano-germanique du dixième siècle*, edd. C. Vogel and R. Elze, 3 vols, Studi e Testi, 226–7, 269 (Vatican City, 1963–72), i, 246–63.

57 Flodoard, *Annales*, pp. 63–4; Richer, *Historiarum Libri IV*, ii.4, p. 42.

58 Appendix, Text E. The prayer continues with allusions to the fertility of Sarah, Rebecca, Leah and Rachel. The examples of Sarah, Rebecca and Rachel were also invoked in the *Ordo* of Ermentrude (866).

59 Cf. above, n. 34.

60 Note the notion of 'election into being queen/king' in prayer 1; and repeated references to the mediation of the officiating bishops in prayers 3 and 4.

61 See *Kaiserin Theophanu: Begegnung des Ostens und Westens um die Wende des ersten Jahrtausends*, edd. A. von Euw and P. Schreiner (Cologne, 1991), and *The Empress Theophano*, ed. A. Davids (Cambridge, 1995).

62 The literature on tenth-century queens and empresses is now extensive: see *Frauen im*

responding to the real world about them: queens were not only mothers of future kings, but acted in partnership with their husbands, and perhaps did so because they knew themselves to have been consecrated to that end. In incorporating allusions to such roles and functions into the most solemn formulae of the queen's inauguration, formulae used from the tenth-century onwards in much of Latin Christendom, the queen-makers were also giving shape – and permanent shape – to medieval queenship.

Appendix

EARLY *ORDINES* FOR KINGS AND QUEENS

A. The earliest king's *ordo*

Deus electorum fortitudo et humilium celsitudo, qui in primordio per effusionem diluvii crimina mundi castigare voluisti et per columbam, ramum olivae portantem, pacem terris redditam demonstrasti, iterumque Aaron famulum tuum per unctionem olei sacerdotem sanxisti, et postea per huius unguenti infusionem ad regendum populum Israeliticum sacerdotes, reges et prophetas perfecisti, vultumque ecclesiae in oleo exhilarandum per propheticam famuli tui voce David esse praedixisti: ita, quaesumus, omnipotens pater, ut per huius creaturae pinguedinem hunc servum tuum sanctificare tua benedictione digneris, eumque in similitudinem *columbae pacem simplicitatis* populo sibi subdito praestare, et exempla Aaron in Dei servitio diligenter imitari, regnique fastigia in consiliis scientiae et aequitate iudicii semper assequi,*

The Judith *Ordo* (856)

Deus electorum fortitudo et humilium celsitudo, qui in primordio per effusionem diluvii crimina mundi purgari voluisti et per columbam, ramum olivae portantem, pacem terris redditam demonstrasti, iterum Aaron famulum tuum per unctionem olei sacerdotem unxisti et postea per huius unguenti infusionem ad regendum populum Israeliticum sacerdotes, reges et prophetas perfecisti, vultumque ecclesiae in oleo exhilarandum prophetica famuli tui voce David esse praedixisti: qui hoc etiam unguento famulae tuae Iudith ad liberationem servorum tuorum et confusionem inimicorum vultum exhilarasti et ancillae tuae Hester faciem hac spiritali misericordiae tuae unctione adeo lucifluam reddidisti, ut efferatum cor regis ad misericordiam et salvationem in te credentium ipsius precibus inclinares: te *quaesumus, omnipotens Deus, ut per huius*

Frühmittelalter: Eine ausgewählte, kommentierte Bibliographie, edd. W. Affeldt, C. Nolte, S. Reiter and U. Vorwerk (Frankfurt, 1990), Section 9, pp. 225–66. T. Vogelsang, *Die Frau als Herrscherin im hohen Mittelalter* (Frankfurt, 1954), still provides a valuable starting-point; and P. Stafford, *Queens, Concubines and Dowagers* (Athens, Ga/London, 1983) is indispensable. See further J. Verdon, 'Les Femmes et la politique en France au Xe siècle', in *Economies et sociétés au moyen âge: Mélanges offerts à E. Perroy* (Paris, 1973), pp. 108–19. See now also R. Collins, 'Queens-Dowager and Queens-Regent in Tenth-Century León and Navarre', in *Medieval Queenship*, ed. Parsons, pp. 79–92; Stafford, 'The Portrayal of Royal Women in England, Mid-Tenth to Mid-Twelfth Centuries', *ibid.*, pp. 143–68; and *eadem*, in the present volume, with further references. For tenth-century Italian queens, see the perceptive analysis of P. Buc, 'Italian Hussies and German Matrons: Liutprand of Cremona on Dynastic Legitimacy', *Frühmittelalterliche Studien*, xxix (1995), 207–25; and for the most recent comment on Ottonian queenly consecration and its implications, H. Keller, 'Widukind's Bericht über die Aachener Wahl und Krönung Ottos I', *Frühmittelalterliche Studien*, xxix (1995), 390–453, at 418–19.

vultumque hilaritatis per hanc olei unctionem tuamque benedictionem, te adiuvante, toti plebi paratum habere facias.

B. *Ordo* of Queen Ermentrude (866)

. . . *Corona* eam, *Domine, corona iustitiae,* corona eam *fructibus* sanctis et operibus benedictis. Sit meritis et nomine atque virtute regina adsistens in hoc seculo *fide recta* et operibus *bonis,* et in futuro honore et *gloria coronata* a dextris regis, in vestitu bonorum operum, circumdata virtutum varietate. . . . *Coronet te Dominus gloria* et honore et sempiterna protectione. Qui vivit et regnat.

C. Eighth-Century Gelasian Sacramentary of Gellone

Oratio quando abbas vel abbatissa ordinatur . . .

O.s.d. divinum *tuae benedictionis spiritum famulæ tuae* N. nobis *propitiatus infunde, ut quae per manus nostrae impositionem hodie* abbatissa constituitur *sanctificatione tua digna* a te *electa permaneat . . .*

D. 'Erdmann' *Ordo* (*c.* 875/*c.* 900)

Ordo ad ordinandam reginam . . .

Tunc summus episcoporum accipiens anulum et digito illius imponens dicat.
Accipe anulum fidei, signaculum sanctae Trinitatis, quo possis omnes hereticas pravitates devitare, barbaras quoque gentes virtute tibi praestita ad agnitionem veritatis advocare.

E. Ordo of Seven Forms (early tenth century)

Queen's *Ordo*

Incipit benedictio regine in ingressu ecclesie

Omnipotens eterne Deus, fons et origo totius bonitatis, qui feminei sexus fragilitatem nequaquam reprobando aversaris, sed dignanter comprobando potius eligis, et qui infirma mundi eligendo fortia queque confundere decrevisti, quique etiam glorie virtutisque tue triumphum in manu Iudith femine olim Iudaice plebi de hoste sevissimo resignare voluisti, *respice, quesumus, ad preces humilitatis nostre, et super hanc famulam tuam N. quam supplici devotione in reginam eligimus,*

creatura pinguedinem, columbae pace, simplicitate, ac pudicitia decoram efficias.

Ordo of Charles the Bald (869)

Coronet te Dominus corona gloriae atque *iustitiae,* ut cum *fide recta* et multiplici bonorum operum fructu, ad coronam pervenias regni perpetui.

'Erdmann' *Ordo* (*c.* 875/*c.* 900)

Ordo ad ordinandam reginam

O.s.d. affluentem *spiritum tuae benedictionis* super *hanc famulam tuam* nostra oratione *propitiatus infunde, ut quae per manus nostrae impositionem hodie* regina instituitur *sanctificatione tua digna* et *electa permaneat . . .*

King's *Ordo*

Ordo qualiter rex ordinari debet

O.e.D. creator omnium, imperator angelorum, rex regnantium dominusque dominantium, qui Habraham fidelem famulum tuum de hostibus triumphare fecisti, Moysi et Iosue populo prelatis multiplicem victoriam tribuisti, humilemque David puerum tuum regni fastigio sublimasti,

respice, quesumus, ad preces humilitatis nostre, et super hunc famulum tuum N. quem suplici devotione in regem eligimus, be+nedictionum tuarum dona multiplica, eamque dextera tua potentie semper et ubique circumda, ut umbone muniminis tui undique secus firmiter protecta, *visibilis seu invisibilis hostis* nequitias triumphaliter expugnare valeat, et una cum Sara atque Rebecca, Lia et Rachel, beatis reverendisque feminis, fructu uteri sui fecundari seu gratulari mereatur ad decorem totius regni statumque sancte Dei ecclesie regendum necnon protegendum. Per Christum . . .

Item alia oratio eiusdem ante altare

Deus qui solus habes immortalitatem lucemque inhabitas inaccessibilem . . . qui superbos equo moderamine de principatu deicis atque humiles dignanter in sublime provehis, ineffabilem misericordiam tuam supplices exoramus, ut sicut Hester reginam Israhelis causa salutis de captivitatis sue compede solutam ad regis Assueri talamum regnique sui consortium transire fecisti, ita hanc famulam tuam N. humilitatis nostre be+nedictione christiane plebis gratia salutis ad dignam sublimemque regis nostri copulam regnique sui *participium* misercorditer transire concedas, et ut in regalis federe coniugii semper manens pudica proximam virginitati palmam continere queat, tibique Deo vivo et vero in omnibus et super omnia iugiter placere desideret, et te inspirante que tibi placita sunt toto corde perficiat. . . .

Corone inpositio

Officio indignitatis nostre seu congregationis in reginam bene+dicta, *accipe coronam regalis excellentie, que licet ab indignis episcoporum tamen manibus capiti tuo imponitur* . . .

benedicti+onum tuarum dona in eo multiplica eumque dextera tue potentie semper et ubique circumda, quatinus predicti Habrae fidelitate firmatus, Moysi mansuetudine fretus, Salomonis sapientia decoratus, tibi in omnibus placeat et per tramitem iustitie inoffenso gressu semper incedat, ecclesiamque tuam deinceps cum plebibus sibi annexis ita enutriat ac doceat, muniat et instruat, contraque omnes *visibiles et invisibiles hostes* eidem potenter regaliterque tue virtutis regimen administret et ad vere fidei pacisque concordiam eorum animos te opitulante reformet, ut horum populorum debita subiectione fultus, cum digno amore glorificetur, et ad paternum decenter solium tua miseratione conscendere mereatur, tue quoque protectionis galea munitus et scuto insuperabili iugiter protectus armisque celestibus circumdatus, optabilis victorie triumphum fideliter vel feliciter capiat terroremque sue potentie infidelibus inferat et pacem tibi militantibus letanter reportet, per dominum nostrum . . .

Corone regalis impositio

Accipe coronam regni, que licet ab indignis episcoporum tamen manibus capiti tuo imponitur. . . . *et per hanc te participem ministerii nostri non ignores* . . .

XVI

A TALE OF TWO PRINCES: POLITICS, TEXT AND IDEOLOGY IN A CAROLINGIAN ANNAL[1]

In chapters 24 through 26 of Book V of the *City of God,* Augustine sketched a picture of the happy Christian emperors who ruled justly. These chapters have been condemned as shoddy, but reprieved as unrepresentative.[2] Elsewhere in the same work, Augustine's mature reflection on the *saeculum* seemed to convince him that justice could be attained in no kingdom save God's. In 873, in a *Mirror of Princes* written for the Carolingian king Charles the Bald, Archbishop Hincmar of Rheims wrote: "Nothing is happier for human affairs than when those men rule who have the science of ruling . . ."; and he then quoted from chapter 24 of Book V of the *City of God:* "We call Christian kings happy if they rule justly".[3] Hincmar did not go on to spurn such ideas: he and other Carolingian churchmen encouraged their kings to provide peace and justice for the Christian people in the Frankish realm.

Modern scholars have tended to conclude that the sheer difficulty of Augustine's political thought defeated his early medieval *epigoni.* It is often implied that from the sixth century, after Gelasius' advocacy of an unworkable dualism between priestly authority and royal power, until the eleventh century, when, one day in March 1081, Gregory VII rediscovered a genuinely Augustinian objectivity, churchmen evaded the problem of secular power in a Christian world. They deluded themselves that the City of God could be built on earth. Either they cultivated an enthusiastic collaboration with divinely-appointed rulers, who could seem latter-day incarnations of Augustine's happy Christian emperors; or, in a travesty of Augustine that has been labelled *l'Augustinisme politique,* they proposed the absorption of the state by the church.[4] Carolingian writers are portrayed as veering between these positions, or confusing them: either way, fundamentally misunderstanding Augustine's conception of the two cities. The genre to have received most attention from modern commentators is that of the *Mirrors of Princes*, works by their very nature one-sided, even sycophantic. Carolingian political thought, where it has been written of at all, has thus tended to be written off. Inconsistency, muddle, and naivety are damning traits.

But a reprieve can be sought, for not all the relevant evidence has yet been taken into account. The so-called *Annals of St. Bertin*, in fact a continuation of the *Royal Frankish Annals* and the major Carolingian annalistic text of the ninth century, have been almost completely ignored in standard works on medieval political ideas. From 861 to 882, the author of these annals was Hincmar of Rheims.[5] Though he has been accused of the intellectual vices listed above, little appreciation has been shown for the subtlety of his thought, least of all as displayed in his historical writing. In what follows, a truer assessment will be sought through an examination of just one of Hincmar's annals, that for 873. First of all, its opening two sections will be quoted in full. They concern two princes, both rebels against their respective fathers: Carloman against the West Frankish king Charles the Bald, Charles the Fat against the East Frankish king Louis the German.

*   *   *   *   *

"There were many in Charles's realm who expected that Carloman would wreak still further evils in the Holy Church of God and in the other realms in which Charles discharged the office of a king. Therefore, with the advice of his faithful men and according to the custom of his predecessors and of his ancestors, Charles promulgated laws relevant to the peace of the Church and the internal strengthening of the realm, and he decreed that everyone was to obey them. He also gave orders that the bishops of his realm were to assemble at Senlis where Carloman still was, so that they might carry out their episcopal responsibility concerning him, in accordance with the sacred canons from which, as Pope Leo says, they are not permitted to depart through any negligence or presumption. The bishops did what had to be done: they deposed Carloman from all ecclesiastical rank, according to the sacred rules, and left him only the communion of a layman. When this had been done, the ancient cunning Enemy incited Carloman and his accomplices to exploit another argument, namely, that because he no longer held any ecclesiastical orders, he could be all the more free to assume the title and power of a king, and that because, by the bishops' judgement, he had lost his clerical rank, he could all the more readily abandon his clerical tonsure. So it came about that, following his deposition, his former accomplices began to rally to him again, more enthusiastically than ever, and to seduce as many others as they could into joining him: their plan was that, as soon as they got the chance, they would snatch him out of the prison where he was being held, and set him up as their king. It was therefore necessary to bring out again into the open all those charges on which he had not been judged by the bishops, and according to what was laid down in the sacred laws, he was condemned to death for his crimes. But so that he might have time and opportunity for doing penance, yet not have the power to commit the still worse offences he was planning, the death sentence was commuted, by the public assent of all present, to a sentence of blinding, in order that the pernicious hope in him on the part of those men who hated peace, might be deceived, and the Church of God and the Christian religion in Charles's realm might not be thrown into disorder by deadly sedition in addition to the attacks of the pagans.

Louis, king of Germany, came before Christmas to the palace of Frankfurt, where he celebrated Christmas and gave notice that his assembly would be held there at the beginning of February. He gave orders that his sons Louis and Charles [the Fat], with his other faithful men, were to attend this meeting, and also the men of the late Lothar's kingdom who had commended themselves to him. While Louis waited there, the Devil in the guise of an Angel of Light came to his son Charles and told him that his father, who was trying to ruin him for the sake of his brother Karlmann, had offended God and would soon lose his kingdom, and that God had arranged that that kingdom was to be held by none other than Charles and that he would have it very soon. Charles was terror-stricken as the apparition clung to the house in which he was staying. He went into a church, but the Devil followed him in, and said: 'Why are you so frightened? And why do you run away? If I who foretell to you what is soon to happen had not come from God, I would not be able to follow you into this house of the Lord ' By these and other smooth arguments, the Devil persuaded him to receive from his hand the communion which [he said] God had sent him. Charles did so; and passing inside his mouth, Satan entered into him. Charles then came to his father, and was sitting in the council-hall with his brothers and the other faithful men, both bishops and laymen, when he leapt up, suddenly possessed, and said that he wanted to abandon the world and would not touch his wife in carnal intercourse. Taking his sword from his belt, he let it fall to the ground. As he tried to undo his sword-belt and take off his cloak, he began to shake violently. He was firmly held by the bishops and other men and, with his father much distressed and all present thunderstruck, he was led into a church. Archbishop Liutbert put on his priestly vestments and began to chant the Mass: when he got as far as the Gospel, Charles began to shout out with loud cries in his native language: 'Woe! Woe!'—like that, over and over again, until the whole of Mass was finished. His father handed him over to the bishops and other faithful men, and gave orders that he was to be led about from one sacred place of holy martyrs to another, so that their merits and prayers might free him from the demon and he might be able, by God's mercy, to recover his sanity. Then he planned to send Charles to Rome, but various other affairs intervened, and the idea of this journey was given up."

This opening section of the 873 entry in the *AB* will now be examined under three heads:

1. as a pair of historical narratives
2. as a literary text—a single tale—within the context of the 873 annal as a whole
3. as an ideological statement.

Historians have generally used only the first of these readings: I hope to show that the second and third can complement and inform the first.

I. Two histories.

The information on Carloman here is virtually the end of a story: the rest can be reconstructed from scraps of evidence, including some earlier entries in the *AB*.[6] Carloman was the third son of the West Frankish king Charles the Bald (840–877) and his queen, Ermentrude. He was born in 848 or 849, and given a name that marked him a full, throne-worthy member of the Carolingian family: hence a prince in the modern sense.[7] In 854 he was offered to the Church and tonsured as a cleric—a new destiny for the legitimate son of a Carolingian king. Every dynasty sooner or later faces the choice of either dividing the realm or shedding some of those eligible for the succession, or both.[8] The Carolingian Empire was divided in 843 among three brothers. In the next generation—Carloman's generation—options became more limited in the West Frankish kingdom: it had two historic components, Neustria and Aquitaine. Charles the Bald envisaged these as inheritances for his first and second sons: the Church, previously the destination of illegitimate Carolingians, was now to house the legitimate who were surplus to the supply of kingdoms. Carloman's three younger brothers all seem to have been tonsured in their turn.[9]

Carloman was given the best-available education.[10] In 860, he was consecrated to minor orders, as a deacon: half a century later, with the benefit of hindsight, a chronicler claimed that Carloman had been ordained "unwillingly and under compulsion"[11], but perhaps his father's intention had been to open up prospects of a career for him in the secular church. A precedent might have been seen in the case of Carloman's cousin, Charles of Aquitaine, who after being tonsured as a cleric in 850, was ordained a deacon in 854 and became archbishop of Mainz in 856.[12] Carloman, aged perhaps fifteen, was given the rich abbacy of St. Médard Soissons in 863, in 866 he succeeded his younger brother as abbot of St Germain Auxerre, and, about the same time, he acquired the abbacy of St Amand. Significantly, in none of these cases was Carloman the regular abbot: though technically a cleric not a layman, and hence not strictly (like Charles the Bald himself, and like a growing number of magnates) a lay-abbot, Carloman operated just like one, administering, or exploiting, the monasteries' economic resources, and leaving religious matters to a regular abbot who held office in tandem with him.[13]

The death of Carloman's elder brother, the sub-king of Aquitaine, in September of 866 caused his father Charles the Bald to rethink the family's arrangements. There may briefly have been a plan to deploy Carloman in Aquitaine; but in 867 Charles the Bald's eldest son Louis was sent there as sub-king. [14] Perhaps Charles was reconsidering the future of Neustria. In 868

his son Carloman, deacon and abbot, was sent with a crack force of household troops, as [the Breton leader] Salomon had requested. . . across the Seine . . . to attack the Northmen based on the Loire.[15]

Carloman had a military following, like many other Carolingian prelates—and like any king's son with aspirations to secular power. Some of the lands of his monasteries were probably used to provide warriors with benefices. It is possible that Charles the Bald at this point envisaged the return of Carloman to lay status. Again, there was a recent precedent: Charles' nephew Pippin II of Aquitaine, forcibly tonsured in 852 (like his younger brother in 850) to remove him from the ranks of those eligible for kingship, had briefly been accepted publicly in 858 as "a layman now" and given "some counties and monasteries in Aquitaine."[16] But Pippin II had not been granted a kingdom, or the title of king. Perhaps some similar deal was planned for Carloman, who, moreover, unlike Pippin, had never taken monastic vows.[17]

In 869, however, two things dramatically altered Charles the Bald's, and hence Carloman's, situation. First, Charles's nephew Lothar II of the Middle Kingdom, died without a legitimate heir, and Charles made a strong bid for the succession: at Metz on 9 September, he had himself consecrated king of Lothar's kingdom.[18] On the same day, he gave Carloman the abbacy (effectively the lay-abbacy) of St Arnulf, Metz.[19] This was a significant grant, for Arnulf was an ancestor and patron of the royal family, his church the chosen burial-place of Carloman's grandfather Louis the Pious, and Metz a center of the Carolingian cult.[20] Now or soon after, Carloman was given another major abbacy in the western part of the Middle Kingdom, the rich royal monastery of Lobbes. He also received the abbacy of St. Riquier in West Francia.[21] A second change in Carloman's situation swiftly followed: his mother Queen Ermentrude died on 6 October. Within days her place in the royal bed of Charles the Bald was taken by Richildis, a young woman whose family had lands in the region of Metz and powerful connexions elsewhere in the Middle Kingdom too.[22] For Carloman, the first of these developments yielded welcome new resources. The second threatened to foreclose the possibility of Carloman's inheriting a kingdom: any son of Richildis would be eligible for royal succession alongside Carloman's surviving elder brother Louis.

In the course of the winter that followed, Charles the Bald took steps to secure Lotharingia. After spending Christmas at Aachen, he went to Nijmegen to meet the Viking lord of Frisia, Roric, formerly the faithful man of Lothar II and hoped-for protector of the northern frontier of what had been Lothar's kingdom.[23]

But Charles's prospects of acquiring the whole of that kingdom were blighted. Many nobles in the area between the rivers Meuse and Rhine proved unwilling to accept Charles, while Louis the German, gravely ill the previous September and hence unable to forestall Charles's move into the Middle Kingdom, recovered and pressed his claims. In the early summer of 870, Charles held an assembly at the palace of Attigny, where negotiations began for a partition of the Middle Kingdom between himself and Louis the German. Carloman was there. [24] Perhaps he tried lobbying on his own account, having spent the previous months using the lands of Lobbes to win himself supporters in the region. His father reacted with characteristic decisiveness:

> Carloman . . . was alleged to have been stirring up plots against his father, in a faithless way. He was deprived of his abbacies and imprisoned at Senlis. [25]

The partition of Lotharingia proceeded. At Meersen in July, Charles's acquisitions north of the Rhone valley were limited to the lands west of the rivers Meuse and Ourthe: he lost Metz, but kept Toul, Verdun and Mouzon.[26]

Carloman won sympathy in high places. His imprisonment was brief: at St Denis on 9 October (St Denis' day), at the request of "the pope's envoys and some of Charles' faithful men," Charles decided to release Carloman on condition that he "stayed at his father's side."[27] But when Charles moved south to Lyons, against opponents in the Rhone valley,

> Carloman one night ran away from his father, and reached the Belgic province. Gathering around him many accomplices and sons of Belial, he wrought such cruelty and devastation at Satan's prompting that it could only be believed by those who actually saw and suffered that destruction.[28]

Carloman's base for these activities may well have been Lobbes, for the abbey's Annals imply that he retained control of it in 871.[29] Lobbes lay in the diocese of Cambrai in the ecclesiastical province of Rheims: hence close enough to Hincmar's heart to elicit the pained tone of the *AB* passage just quoted.

XVI

After a successful campaign in Burgundy, Charles moved north again to St Denis early in 871. Carloman went with his "accomplices" southwards to Mouzon and "laid waste that stronghold and the surrounding estates." He then sent envoys to his father, while he himself went to the Toul area. Charles, unimpressed by his son's tactics, ordered harsh reprisals against Carloman's supporters. Carloman fled across the Jura Mountains. In late summer 871, Charles "through the good offices of Louis the German" received more envoys from his son. In November, Carloman came to his father at Besançon

> with a show of humility. [Charles] received him, and ordered him to stay with him; and said that, when he had a chance to go to the Belgic province to speak with his faithful men there, he would decide with their counsel what honors he had best grant to Carloman.[30]

The reference to the "Belgic province" echoes the 870 annal, and gives a clue to what had been Carloman's intentions perhaps as early as 869, probably in early summer 870 (assuming the allegations had some basis), and surely by the end of that year. He had responded to the enlargement of his father's realm by staking a claim for a kingdom of his own in Lotharingia. In this context, the "Belgic province" should be understood to mean not only the area of modern Belgium[31], where Lobbes lay, but also the places where the *AB* locates Carloman's activities and supporters, namely, the regions of Toul and Mouzon. It may have been to forestall such a bid that Charles had, from the outset, made Carloman a sharer of the spoils—to the extent of giving him yet more abbacies in the newly-acquired lands. It was not enough; and Carloman seems to have been supported by some powerful men in the western part of the *regnum Hlotharii*—men who may have viewed with distaste the rise of Richildis' and her brother Boso's influence. Carloman may have hoped to work out from this base to attract more backers in the heartlands of the Middle Kingdom. There is evidence from the 860s that the "men of Lothar" were beginning to think of themselves as a group and sought to preserve "their" kingdom as a discrete bloc, against the ambitions of both East and West Frankish kings.[32] Carloman had a ready-made constituency. He failed because his father was determined to salvage as much of his Lotharingian acquisition as possible: for himself, in the short run, but in the long run for the new son he hoped Richildis would bear him.

Charles too could practise deceit: having promised Carloman some kind of deal involving "honors", perhaps including Lobbes, Charles:

> travelled to Servais. There he held an assembly with his counsellors, and on their advice he again consigned Carloman to prison at Senlis, while his accomplices he ordered to be bound by a solemn oath of fidelity, each in his own county; and on condition that each received a lord, whomever he wished, from among the king's faithful men, and that each expressed his willingness to live in peace, Charles allowed them to live in his kingdom.[33]

This passage again implies that Carloman's supporters were in Lotharingia: hence they had not yet got lords among the magnates in Charles's kingdom. Hincmar's first entry for 872 points in the same direction: in January, Charles went to Moustier near Namur "to speak with the Northmen Roric and Rodulf," presumably to secure their continued support for himself rather than his son. In October a further meeting ended in an open breach between Charles and Rodulf who, Hincmar says,

> had been plotting acts of unfaithfulness and making excessive demands.

From such strong language, it is tempting to infer that Rodulf had been intriguing with Carloman, or on his behalf. Eight years before, that same Rodulf had received a large payment, in cash and kind, from Lothar II for services rendered; and other Carolingian princes, including Charles the Bald, had found Viking allies and collaborators.[34] Charles, having sent Rodulf away empty-handed, knew that retaliation could be expected. But he may well have hoped that one particularly dangerous spin-off from Carloman's defection had been checked.

We hear no more of Carloman himself until the 873 annal (there is no mention of him under 872), which reveals that "evils were reviving." The same note is sounded in the capitulary that survives from the January assembly at Quierzy, reported in the annal: "evils still remained to be cut down."[35] The theme of this capitulary, not new, of course, but notably insistent here, is the combatting of lawlessness: "the greatest effort" was called for. "Malefactors" who refused to be brought to justice were to be outlawed. With c.4, giving point to all this, came an explicit reference to "those who were with Carloman." Those of them who had not yet chosen a lord, "as ordered," were to have their allodial lands confiscated, i.e., taken into the royal fisc. This was the most serious penalty, short of a death sentence, that an early medieval ruler could impose. It was rarely threatened, still more rarely demonstrably carried out.[36] In this case we do not even know the names of the condemned, let alone how or if they were punished. But the threat was symptomatic of the acute perception of danger: Charles and his "counsellors" were very seriously worried. All the gains of 870 may have seemed at risk. It can be no coincidence that the capitulary went on to record that "male witches and female witches are rising up in many places in our realm" and to recall, and expand, Moses' injunction (*Exodus* xxii.18): "it is the king's office not to permit witches and poisoners to live"; and finally to decree that, should no firm evidence, or witnesses, be forthcoming in cases of alleged witchcraft, then the accused should be put to the ordeal—the "judgement of God."[37] This is the work of a jittery regime; and the 873 annal links the capitulary of Quierzy very firmly with the problem of Carloman.

The first solution was for the king to perform his royal office (again the annal echoes the capitulary); the second was for the bishops to perform theirs, by publicly trying and condemning Carloman. The danger of Carloman's escaping was evidently so great that Charles did not dare locate the synod anywhere else than his most secure stronghold: Senlis. Carloman, demoted from his grade of deacon, was left merely with his clerial tonsure. Did Charles, and the bishops who collaborated with him, intend Carloman to live out his days in prison at Senlis, in an exact repeat of Pippin II's fate in 864? If that was their plan, they would indeed have been shocked when Carloman and his supporters, far from admitting defeat, were given new heart, arguing now that Carloman as a layman was "freer" to "ascend to the title and power of a king." The supporters, more enthusiastic than ever, attracted recruits and planned to spring Carloman from jail. Their aim, explicit and immediate now as apparently it had not been before, was to "make Carloman their king" (*illum . . . sibi regem constituere*).

The 873 annal presents this outcome as unforeseen by Charles and his counsellors: a mess-up requiring hurried recourse to a new tactic. Now a new secular assembly had to be convened to deal with "the matters on which the bishopos had not judged" and Carloman, "according to the decrees of the sacred laws," i.e, the legislation of Roman emperors, was condemned to death.

Mess-up—or conspiracy? Could an experienced Frankish king like Charles the Bald, who had bound his son in clerical status precisely to render him unkingworthy, or experienced Frankish bishops, who had used precisely the same bonds for both Pippin II of Aquitaine and his brother, and for Carloman's brother too[38], really have failed to foresee the consequences of undoing the knot? Such carelessness is, frankly, incredible. What we should see here is a series of legal procedures adopted, quite deliberately, to result in the death sentence, which only a secular court, not an ecclesiastical one, could pass: this could then be commuted to the "gentler" one of blinding, though such commutations often brought death in any case[39].

The rest of Carloman's story is predictably brief.[40] Once blind, he could be transferred to a more open monastic prison at Corbie. From there he was rescued a few months later by "former supporters," and taken to Louis the German "in order to harm Charles' interests." Charles was "not greatly upset" by the news of his escape: he may have presumed a blind man to be disqualified for kingship, or may simply have known the extent of Carloman's injuries.[41] Louis the German consigned Carloman to monastic care, but, according to the *AB*, did not disguise his disapproval of Carloman's misdeeds. Louis accepted the *fait accompli*. Carloman's career was finished, its poignant epilogue the provision made by his lone surviving brother, Louis the Stammerer, for his posthumous liturgical commemoration at St Medard, Soissons.[42]

*   *   *   *   *   *

If Carloman was a king's son whose father may never have intended him to become a king, and whom the sources accord no titles other than "deacon and abbot," Charles the Fat was a real prince.[43] Born in 839, the third and youngest son of Louis the German, king of the East Frankish realm, Charles was marked out for a royal future, along with his brothers, almost as soon as he came of age. For Louis the German, unlike his West Frankish brother Charles the Bald, seems consistently to have planned to partition his lands into three, so that each son could succeed to a kingdom. Perhaps Louis was lucky, in having as many *regna*—Bavaria, Alamannia and Franconia—as he had legitimate sons. But the signs are that all his sons would have been considered kingworthy, and hence shared the succession, however many there had been of them: not until the tenth century would an East Frankish king put his son into the church. In 859, Charles the Fat was assigned the county of Breisgau in Alamannia; but he appears in documents with the title of, not "count," but *princeps:* "prince." (The existing count seems to have stayed on as his subordinate.)[44] The implications for his royal future became clear in 865 when his father formally announced a prospective division of his kingdom among his sons, assigning Alamannia and Rhaetia to Charles. The eldest, Karlmann, was to get Bavaria, and Louis, the second son, Franconia. The plan was to come fully into effect after the father's death: meanwhile each son was to hold certain royal lands in his future kingdom, and judge minor cases, with major cases, control of the fisc, and appointments to bishoprics, abbeys and countships, being retained by Louis the German.[45]

The East Frankish king has been much praised by modern historians for this sensible arrangement. But it did not prevent filial resentment and rebellion. Adult sons, with their own followings generating demand for loot and lands, inevitably had priorities of their own. Karlmann had rebelled already in 861–2, seeking allies on the eastern frontiers of Bavaria. Lothar II's continuing lack of a legitimate heir, making the future of the Middle Kingdom uncertain, tempted the East Frankish king's sons to look westwards. When Karlmann rebelled again in 863–4, he seems to have prodded an archenemy of Lothar II, his erstwhile brother-in-law Hubert, into seizing the abbey of Lobbes in the west of Lothar's kingdom.[46] In 865, soon after the succession-plan was announced, Louis the Younger got betrothed without his father's consent to the daughter of a magnate with important holdings in Lotharingia and connexions also in West Francia. Only under the combined pressure of his father and Charles the Bald was Louis made to give up the match.[47] By comparison with these unruly brothers, Charles the Fat has been seen as the "good boy" of the 860s. Yet his marriage in 860 or 861 to Richgard, daughter of an influential count in Alsace, could suggest his own initiative, hence his own perception of prospects in the Middle Kingdom, rather than, as generally asumed, his father's.[48] If Louis the German was interested in Alsace (he had, after all, extracted a grant, or promise, of some kind of authority there in 860 from Lothar II), so too was his son Charles, whose position in Alamannia would be strengthened by contacts west of the Rhine. True, Louis stumped up the lavish morning-gift for Charles's bride; but he did so at Charles's request.[49] Perhaps this signified the father coming to terms with the son's bid.

Lacking an eastern frontier against the Slavs, Charles had less opportunity than his brothers to exploit the frontier's potential as a source of plunder and warlike renown, or of political allies. But in 869, when Louis the German himself was too ill to campaign, "compelled by necessity" he put Charles in charge of the army of Franks and (significantly) of Alamans which had already been collected. "The youngest son," as the Annals of Fulda call him—though he was now thirty—won a great victory over the Moravians, and carried off a good deal of loot.[50]

Charles certainly did rebel against his father in 871, when, in alliance with his brother Louis, he reacted fiercely to a rumor that their father was planning to give to Karlmann "parts of the kingdoms he had agreed they should have on his death."[51] The rebellion was serious, not least because it was encouraged by Charles's and Louis's uncle, Charles the Bald, and perhaps, too, by their mother.[52] According to the *AB*, they embarked on a "devastation of the realm."[53] But their father Louis the German was old—nearly 60—and for most of 870–1, seriously ill. His sons could hope soon to come into their inheritance. When the father made them an immediate grant of "benefices," they agreed to a reconciliation.[54]

There was another factor: Louis the German's nephew, the Emperor Louis II of Italy, was sonless and nearing fifty. In late summer 871 a rumor of his death spread north of the Alps. According to the East Frankish *AF*, Louis the German was "sad": the West Frankish *AB* report a different reaction:

he despatched his son Charles [the Fat] to the territory [which Louis II] used to hold beyond the Jura Mountains, to bind as many men as he could to his allegiance with solemn oaths: and this young Charles duly did.[55]

The move fitted into Charles's planned future as king of Alamannia and Rhaetia: the "territory beyond the Jura" had been transferred by Lothar II to the emperor Louis back in 859, but real control of the region had been disputed between rival magnates.[56] Charles the Fat was to try to make a reality of royal power in this region contiguous to his own prospective realm, perhaps by allying with his mother's relatives, the grandsons of Count Welf. But the resentments of Louis the German's younger sons had only been soothed, not healed. At Forchheim in March 872, the reaffirmation of the 865 division-plan produced only sham submissions from Charles and his brother. [57] Plots were rife: if the succession to Lothar II had been the great open question of the 860s, in the early 870s Carolingian rivalries focused on the future of Louis II's Italian realm. And here, it was Charles the Fat rather than his brother Louis the Younger who had real prospects: he also had most cause for jealousy of his eldest brother Karlmann, whom he rightly suspected of aspiring to the imperial inheritance for himself.

In this atmosphere of tension and intrigue, Louis the German summoned the assembly at Frankfurt where took place the events recorded in the *AB* as a second item for 873. The *AF* give a rather different account of what happened when Charles the Fat came into the royal council-meeting on 26 January:

> a wicked spirit entered into him and tortured him severely, so that he could scarcely be held down by six of the strongest men . . .And justly so: for he who had wished to deceive the king chosen and ordained by God was himself deceived: he who had treacherously set traps for his father fell himself into the snares of the Devil. . . . When he was led into a church . . . he screamed, sometimes weakly, sometimes at the top of his voice, and threatened with open mouth to bite those who were holding him. The king [Louis the German] then turned to the young Louis and said: 'Don't you see, my son, whose lordship you accepted, you and your brother [Charles], when you thought to carry out wickedness against me? Now you may understand . . . that, as the saying of Truth has it [Matt.10.26]: "Nothing is hidden that is not laid bare". Confess your sins, therefore, and do penance and pray humbly to God that they may be forgiven you. I also, as far as lies in me, grant you forgiveness.' After the attack of the Devil was over, Charles said aloud in the hearing of many, that as many times as he had plotted against his father, just so many times had he been delivered into the power of the Enemy.[58]

The *AF*'s account is paralleled in another contemporary report: according to the *Annals of Xanten,* Charles's aim was "to deprive his father of the realm and to imprison him"; Charles's possession by the malign spirit was 'a great miracle' which moved young Louis to fall at his father's feet and confess all.[59] The contrast between the *AB* version, and that of the other two annalists, will repay further attention.

Charles did "recover his sanity": the role of the clergy's exorcisms and ministrations in his recovery can only be surmised. Three months after his attack, he was judging disputes, under his father's eye; in 874 he was acting as his father's envoy to the West Franks; in 875, when the emperor Louis II died, he was sent on campaign to Italy to oppose Charles the Bald—unsuccessfully, as it proved; and in 876, when Louis the German died, the 865 plan finally came into effect, and Charles received his kingdom.[60] A reputation for incompetence has been cast over Charles's whole career by hindsight focussed on his last years from 885 onwards; but it is worth noting that contemporary writers of the early 880s record an able and assertive ruler.[61] There is no justification for regarding Charles as psychologically unstable then or in the 870s. His experiences in 873 ought not to be dismissed as symptoms of permanent mental disorder. More light is thrown on them by two further pieces of information about Charles's private life. The first is that, in 887, according to Regino, Charles summoned his wife Richgard before an assembly to answer charges of adultery with the arch-chancellor Bishop Liutward: Charles publicly alleged, *mirabile dictu*, that "in more than ten years' legitimate marriage," he had not had intercourse with his wife. Richgard's response was that she had not had intercourse with anyone, and was indeed still a virgin. She offered to prove this by ordeal of hot ploughshares, and, apparently having done so successfully, was permitted to retire to a convent.[62] The second significant fact is that in 880 or 881, Charles became the father of an illegitimate son, Bernard, and in 885 tried unsuccessfully to enlist papal help in having the boy recognised as *haeres regni*.[63]

* * * * *

The histories of Carloman and Charles the Fat that culminated in the episodes of 873, have been told separately; in fact they are connected in several ways. First, both princes were affected by the configuration of the Carolingian family at a particular point in time: for both, crises resulted from the conjunction of long reigns in two of the Carolingian kingdoms with problematic successions in the other two. The sons of Charles the Bald in West Francia and of Louis the German in East Francia were both frustrated by their fathers' longevity, and both sons responded with a new assertiveness to new dynastic openings in Lotharingia and Italy. The two-way division of Lotharingia in 870 reaffirmed the older generation's control and blasted the hopes of both younger men. Both princes sought new fields "across the Jura Mountains," but with limited success. The coincidence of princely rebellion in East and West Frankish kingdoms was therefore not fortuitous.

The second connection between the princes' stories lay in the encouragement given to their rebellious nephews by both the East and West Frankish kings. Charles the Bald went eastwards to meet his namesake in 871, and helped arrange a reconciliation between Charles the Fat and Louis the German later in the same year. At the same time, Louis the German appeared as a "go-between" for his brother's rebellious son Carloman, and had evidently responded to Carloman's request for moral support. After Carloman's blinding, his supporters still looked to Louis the German for help. Axes of solidarity between uncles and nephews crosscut the tense relationships between royal fathers and sons.

The stories of the rebel princes are linked in a third way, revealing the tensions in Carolingian family politics from another angle. Each story is documented largely by a single annalist writing in the kingdom affected by the rebellion and clearly hostile to the rebel. Thus the *AB* writer condemns Carloman and affirms Charles the Bald's authority, while the *AF* writer affirms Louis the German's authority and condemns Charles the Fat. But each writer, while within his own kingdom firmly siding with father against son, shows a sympathy for the rebel prince in the other kingdom. Both writers, in other words, when not constrained by their own personal allegiances, recognise the inevitability of conflict within the royal family; both writers, while identifying their own interests with those of their respective kings, can share a prince's point of view. This dual perspective is at least hinted at in the *AF*'s brief reference to Carloman's fate: "Charles, the tyrant of Gaul, put aside his paternal feelings and had his son Carloman, who had been ordained deacon, blinded."[64]

But the development of a true counterpoint between paternal and filial themes is to be found in the *AB*, in the 873 annal, to which we must now return.

II The 873 annal as a literary text.

It is already clear from the accounts of Charles the Fat's experience that even in what is often considered the dry–as–dust genre of annalistic writing, presentations of the same event can differ significantly. In this section I want to explore the *AB* passage I began with, as a text within a literary context. I shall argue that the two stories, of Carloman and Charles the Fat, can be construed as a single tale, and that the tale must be read in the setting of the 873 annal as a whole.

The question of authorial intention is fundamental. Archbishop Hincmar of Rheims took over the writing of the *AB* in 861, and continued it till his death in 882.[65] He had known of the existence of a continuation of the *Royal Frankish Annals*, kept up from 835 to 861 by Bishop Prudentius of Troyes. Hincmar borrowed the manuscript from King Charles the Bald, into whose hands it had come when Prudentius died. Hincmar made his own copy and kept it at Rheims where he added to it year by year. Modern historians (insofar as they have shown any interest at all in Hincmar as a historian) have commented on the wealth of historical material in Hincmar's annals.[66] They have also lamented his bias and selectivity: it has been noted, for instance, that in 873 his relations with Charles the Bald were very close—an entente born of a common interest in preserving for the West Frankish kingdom the territorial gains of 870 and hence in blocking Carloman's ambitions—and that his eventual role in Carloman's condemnation may explain why he made no mention in the *AB* of his involvement in attempts to reconcile Carloman with his father in 872.[67] But Hincmar's literary method in the *AB* has scarcely been studied. The following examination of the structure of a single annal will, I hope, help in evaluating its historical data, and also, perhaps, open up the rest of the *AB* to similar analysis.

The 873 annal, like most of the annals after 870, is relatively short: roughly half the length, on average, of the annals in the 860s. Though some topics are still dealt with quite lengthily, there are relatively fewer items of information per year. The 873 annal illustrates this. It consists of four quite long episodes, plus four smaller items inserted at intervals into the last and longest of the episodes:

1. Carloman
2. Charles the Fat
3. the political difficulties of the emperor Louis in southern Italy

4. the political and military success of Charles the Bald against the Northmen in the Loire valley, plus
   (a) the blinded Carloman's escape from Corbie to Louis the German
   (b) the death of the Northman Rodulf in East Francia
   (c) a plague of locusts (or grasshoppers)[68]
   (d) Louis the German's activities including his treatment of Carloman.

Items 4. (a) and 4. (b) are presented as news that reached Charles in the course of his campaign.[69]

   All these items are also documented independently of the *AB*; and the examples of items (1) and (2) have already suggested comparisons between the treatments of material in the *AB* and in other sources. In the Carloman case the close similarities of wording, and of stance, between the *AB* and the Quierzy capitulary strongly support the hypothesis that Hincmar wrote at least parts of the capitulary.[70] Other contemporary annalists record Carloman's sentence laconically, but with evident disapproval of Charles the Bald's action.[71] Hincmar's presentation in the *AB* is designed wholly to condemn Carloman and in various ways to justify Charles the Bald's response. Again, other evidence on item (4) shows that the successes against the Northmen on the Loire owed a good deal more to Charles the Bald's Breton allies than the *AB* account implies. The taking of Angers may indeed have been a Breton rather than a Frankish victory.[72] Item 4b identifies Rodulf in terms of the "many evils he had inflicted on Charles' realm," and notes his death "in the realm of Louis [the German] along with 500 of his accomplices"; the *AF* (dating the appearance of Rodulf's fleet to June) tells a much fuller story, in which 800 Northmen are slain, and the rest are said (twice) to have departed from Louis's realm swearing never to return.[73] As for the locusts (or grasshoppers), the *AB*'s reference is brief and unemotional: for Hincmar, it is only the *scale* of the attack that invites comparison with the plague of Egypt (Exodus x.12–15.), whereas the *AF* give a long and lurid account (". . . they had a wide mouth and a long stomach and two teeth harder than stone . . ."etc.) and like the Annals of Xanten, interpret this plague as a divine punishment for "our sins."[74] Further, where the other contemporary witnesses say that Gaul, or "the Franks," bore the brunt of the attack, Hincmar, uniquely, claims not only that the insects went on to Spain, but that

Spain was the place worst-affected. If the plague was a sign of God's anger against sinners, Hincmar implied that those sinners were not the Franks of Charles's kingdom.

One phrase in the *AB* for 873 strikes the reader forcibly: Charles the Bald besieged the Northmen in Angers *viriliter ac strenue* ("manfully and energetically"). Such language applied to this king is unprecedented in Hincmar's section of the *AB*. It is a clue to the theme of the whole 873 annal—in what we call the *AB* but Hincmar called *The Deeds of Kings*.[75] The annal begins with "the king's office" embodied in legislation: the long description of the Angers campaign shows the king actually doing the job. The Northmen have been "ravaging towns, razing fortresses to the ground, burning churches and monasteries and turning cultivated land into a desert."[76]

Charles besieges them. The Bretons collaborate—on Charles's terms: Duke Salomon's own son swears an oath of fidelity. Charles "thoroughly tames" the Northmen: their leading men come over to him, swear "exactly the solemn oaths he ordered" and hand over "as many, and as important, hostages as he demanded"; finally, they agree either to leave Charles's realm forever, or to become Christians.[77]

> After all this, Charles, together with the bishops and people, with the greatest demonstration of religious fervour restored to their rightful places, with rich offerings, the bodies of SS Albinus and Licinius, which had been disinterred from their graves through fear fear of the Northmen.

Angers, its saints returned to it, could be left in safe hands. The annal ends with a description of Charles's route northwards to Francia: "via the city of Le Mans, and the town of Evreux, and passing close to the new fortress at Pîtres," and after hunting on the royal estate of Orville, "he reached St. Vaast where he celebrated Christmas."[78] The listing, with its careful gradation of settlements, is far from haphazard: Charles's royal journey signifies a direct inversion of the Northmen's activities—evoking patronage of urban life, responsibility for fortress-construction, devotion to the church, and (where the summertime cultivation of crops would be inappropriate) the hunting economy of winter.

The fourth episode, devoted to Charles's actions against the

Northmen, is neatly offset by the third, devoted to Louis II's difficulties in dealing with the Beneventans. Those old enemies of the Franks posed a new threat when sent help by "the emperor of the Greeks": against them, the "emperor of Italy" (Hincmar's use of this imperial title is tinged with irony) now had to mobilise the pope as a conciliator, cloaking his dependence by a show of deference to the vicar of St. Peter. [79] Louis, according to Hincmar, had sworn to capture the Beneventan duke Adalgis, "but in reality he was incapable of achieving this by his own strength."[80] Louis's lack of *virtus* contrasts with the very qualities Hincmar· goes on to attribute to Charles the Bald: "manliness and energy."

The smaller sections of (4) are woven into its main story. In (4a) Charles is *en route* for Angers when he hears of Carloman's escape, "with the connivance of two false monks," allegedly "as a result of the scheming of . . . Louis king of Germany," and "with the object of harming Charles's interests."[81] There can be no doubt of where the reader's sympathies are being led. In (4b) Charles has begun the siege of the Northmen in Angers when he hears of the death of his old enemy, the Northman Rodulf. But this item resonates with the preceding one: Rodolf had very probably been suspected of colluding with Carloman.[82] In (4c) while the fact of the plague of locusts is not suppressed, it is implicitly attributed to the sins of others, and especially of pagans. This points forward to Charles's ensuing success. In (4d) Louis the German's activities in fact mirror those of Charles—naturally, on a lesser scale. Louis's pagan enemies are the Wends. He heads for the frontier and, through envoys, wins over some of them; then he receives envoys of the Bohemians who plan to deceive him, and flings them into prison. As for Louis's reception of Carloman, it turns out that, though showing pity, Louis totally condemns "the evil deeds committed by Carloman against the holy church of God, against the Christian people, and against his own father."[83]

This brings us back to the episodes we began with. The stories of Carloman and Charles the Fat belong together. Both deal with the fraught relationship between a royal father and his son. Both show how the breakdown of the relationship endangers the right order of things. Carloman's rebellion and the acts of violence that accompany it threaten "the church of God and the Christian religion in Charles's realm": sacred laws (that is, the laws of Christian emperors) and sacred canons alike condemn Carloman. Despite being degraded from clerical rank, he remains bound by the canonical rules: the "ecclesiastical tonsure" has irreversible consequences. But Carloman is a criminal who persistently refuses to accept the restraints of law. Set apart from the world, he wilfully attempts to reenter it, fleeing from the church. Having been forbidden kingship, he seeks royal title and power. Where tonsure failed, blindness must ensure his ineligibility.

Charles the Fat, in Hincmar's presentation here, makes a comparable, yet contrasting case. As a king's son he is wide open to the temptation to rebel: so far the sources agree. But where the other sources go on to tell the story of a rebel unmasked, getting his just deserts, Hincmar in the *AB* depicts Charles the Fat as hardly responsible for his own actions. Tempted, the king's son is "terror-stricken" and flees to a church. When, possessed by the devil, he confronts his father, has action is the opposite of Carloman's: he seeks to abandon the world, renouncing the two kinds of activity, sex and war, that differentiate the worldly from the spiritual order.[84] This is madness. The royal father is acutely distressed; the attendant faithful men are "thunderstruck."

I shall return in section IV to the implications of these contrasting modes of filial defiance. For the present, I want to establish the link between the two within the structure of the 873 annal. They are parts of a single story: a tale of two princes. Each is an implicit comment on the other, just as the impotent Louis II is a foil to the manful Charles the Bald. Thus the whole annal forms a coherent whole. It opens with Charles the Bald, "in the manner of his ancestors," discharging the office of king, ensuring through law the peace of the church and the internal strengthening of the realm. Two princes are shown subverting this right order. Both fail, and two king-fathers reaffirm both that order and their own authority. Far away to the South, in Italy two emperors squabble over the Beneventans' allegiance, owed in the past to the emperors of Francia. Even the Carolingian Louis II lacks the strength to punish the faithless duke of a people once subject to the Franks. We return to Francia and the kings with strength. One asserts his authority over peoples on the eastern frontier. The other, with yet more conspicuous success, extracts due fidelity from the Bretons in the West and tames the men from the North. He restores the saints to "their rightful places." Amid images of re-established order, the annal ends with the calm resumption of royal routine.

III Ideology

Historians who have tried to extract from Hincmar's works a consistent political theory, whether of royalism or hierocracy, have been consistently unsuccessful. [85] The annals that Hincmar wrote from 861 to 882 have scarcely been considered at all in the context of political ideas. Yet they represent more clearly and consistently than do any of his other works, a set of ideological statements: responses to observed uses (and abuses) of power that attempt to accommodate these within the framework of heterogeneous beliefs and values which made up Carolingian culture.

Power is the central theme of the 873 annal; but Hincmar's concern here is not simply with the triumphant affirmation of patrimonial regalian authority. Power, for Hincmar, is complex and problematic. It has multiple sources, hence can be legitimized in more than one way. Kingship, its dominant secular form, may be "a scarce resource" but given partible royal succession, not as scarce as all that.[86] The transmission of royal power between generations is as negotiable as its distribution within each generation. The interests of individual royals crosscut those of the royal family; and are crosscut, in turn, by the interests of individual nobles and groups (often family-groups) of nobles. Already there exists a courtly society; but by no means all transactions of power are conducted at court. Hincmar would have agreed with his contemporary Notker (and both learned it from Augustine) that amidst all such uncertainties, only one thing was certain: "Nowhere and never is anything safe in this world of space and time (*in saeculo*), but always and everywhere is security an illusion."[87]

The tale of two princes highlights, first, the problem of power's recreation in space: how and when could a new king be validly made, to rule alongside his father? Within an existing kingdom could lie a potential one: what modern historians term the "sub-kingdoms" of this period were, for contemporaries, kingdoms whose noble families only awaited suitable princes for their distinctive political identity to be resumed. [88] The map could be redrawn with each generation. No Carolingian division, certainly not Verdun, had foreclosed subsequent rearrangements. Even if, as in Charles the Bald's case, the number of king's sons exceeded available kingdoms, (hence Carloman's tonsuring), kings had nephews as well as sons; and if a nephew himself died sonless, his uncle could validly claim a residual right to the orphaned kingdom. Hincmar presents the intended setting-up of Carloman by a group of Lotharingian nobles as invalid, not because of the incapacity of the would-be kingmakers but because of their candidate's personal ineligibility. In the *De Divortio* Hincmar considered the three ways that a man could "be set up in rulership" (*principatus* covers holy men as well as kings[89]): through the intervention of God, through God via men, or through men acting of their own choice (though always, Hincmar believed, with God's permission and foreknowledge). In the third and last category, a further distinction could be made. Men might collaborate with "angels," that is, with divine ministers—as when David ordered Solomon to be consecrated by Zadoch the priest and Nathan the prophet; or the king might be set up directly by men—and Hincmar was clearly thinking of the contemporary category of laymen: "by the support of citizens and soldiers," "by the succession of son to father," or through an individual's "tyrannical usurpation."[90] Solomon's inauguration was the prototype of the kind of procedure that Hincmar himself pioneered in Francia: where consecration by God's ministers operated in conjunction with the decision of a royal father (or in Queen Ermentrude's case, a royal husband) and the consent of the king's faithful men, the "people."[91] With the remaining man-made settings-up of kings, Hincmar evidently had in mind both Frankish (as well as Roman and Biblical) history and contemporary experience. For all his disctinction between angels and men, reflecting that between priesthood and laity in the Frankish world, and for all his preference for angelic participation, Frankish kingmakings, as Hincmar well knew, had been, and in the main still were, the work of laymen. And as such, he acknowledged, they were perfectly legitimate. Carloman was debarred from accepting "the support of citizens and soldiers" because of his clerical status: his crime turned potential kingmakers into "accomplices."

The story of Charles the Fat explores the problem of the timing of royal succession. Charles, validly designated to succeed his father, was tempted to jump the gun. Where other sources make it clear that there was a plot to remove Louis the German from his kingship, and present Charles's horrific experience as God's means of at once exposing and punishing him, Hincmar neither accuses the prince of actual rebellion, nor does he mention the unveiling of the plot as the sequel to Charles's fit. Instead, Hincmar repeats the claim, mentioned in the 870 annal, that Charles's eldest brother was being

given unfair preference, threatening Charles's own promised in-
heritance.No doubt Hincmar's presentation reflects his bias in Charles's favor: Hincmar's closeness to Charles the Bald in 873 prejudiced
him against Louis the German, who had so recently thwarted the
West Frankish king's hopes of acquiring the whole Middle Kingdom.
Hincmar hints, without perceptible disapproval, at Charles the Bald's
encouragement of Louis's sons in their rebellion against their father.
It is even possible that Hincmar retouched the 873 annal years later,
when he had come to view Charles the Fat as a potential ally against
his own rivals for influence in the West Frankish kingdom.[92] But as
the foregoing discussion of the annals' form has suggested, Hincmar
here intended more than a display of personal feeling. In juxtaposing
the very different outcomes of the two princes' filial misbehavior,
Hincmar contrasts the incorrigible with the contrite. At the same
time, he seems to invite sympathy for the temptation that inevitably
beset an adult king-to-be. Recent Frankish history could offer parallels: Hincmar had the evidence under his nose in the shape of the
Royal Frankish Annals and the earlier sections of the *AB*.

The tale of two princes has another theme: the bringing out
into the open of dangerous secrets. To make such things public was to
allow them to be defused, bad power to be replaced by good. In
Carloman's case, all the criminal charges against him had to be rehearsed, by implication, before a court of Charles the Bald's faithful
men. This is reminiscent of the legislation of 873, requiring the
prosecution of witches before Frankish courts. In the case of Charles
the Fat, the means of exposure was an agonising seizure which happened "in the council-hall, before the king, Charles's brothers and
all their faithful men." The rebellion of Carloman, and the seizure of
Charles both constituted intrusions of wild power into the ordered
structures of a kingdom. Both had to be tamed and held within those
structures: hence the king used assemblies, and the counsel of faithful
men, to reassert control. Hincmar emphasises here the efficacy of
kingship working through consensus politics.[93]

But all this would not be enough: "man-made" remedies
could not cope with threats that were in fact diabolical. Twice, and in
phrases that are not mere formal expressions of disapproval, Hincmar attributes Carloman's actions to the devil's instigation. Indeed
Carloman and his supporters, "sons of Belial," replicated the action of
that archetypal son of pride, Satan himself: in a capitulary only ten
years before, Hincmar had castigated contemporary Frankish mag-

nates for being the Devil's imitators in refusing to subject themselves to the power constituted by God or to acknowledge others as their "fellows and equals in the kingdom."[94] The annal's reference to Belial is as precisely apt: Deuteronomy xiii linked sedition with sin against God:

> If thou shalt hear say in one of thy cities, which the Lord thy God hath given thee to dwell there, saying,
> Certain men, the children of Belial, are gone out from among you, and have withdrawn the inhabitants of their city, saying, Let us go and serve other gods which ye have not known;
> Then shalt thou inquire, and make search, and ask diligently; and behold, if it be truth, and the thing certain, that such abomination is wrought among you;
> Thou shalt surely smite the inhabitants of that city with the edge of the sword, destroying it utterly, and all that is therein . . .
> And thou shalt gather all the spoil of it into the midst of the street thereof, and shalt burn with fire the city, and all the spoil thereof every whit, for the Lord thy God . . .
> And there shall cleave nought of the cursed thing to thine hand: that the Lord may turn from thee the fierceness of his anger, and shew thee mercy, and have compassion upon thee, and multiply thee, as he hath sworn unto thy fathers.[95]

Carloman too had attempted to withdraw the inhabitants of cities from their allegiance; the people had suffered divine wrath; so had the king, who now urgently sought the multiplication of his seed. For men who knew their Old Testament, and believed themselves part of the new Israel, such parallels did not need laying on with a trowel. The Lord would be appeased only by the exposure and total extinction of "the cursed thing."

Satan reappears in the story of Charles the Fat. What makes this story so terrifying is the way in which evil is disguised as good. The prince's supplanting of his father is presented to him by the "angelic" apparition as reasonable and morally justified, his self-interest coinciding with God's decision: since Louis the German favors his firstborn unfairly, denying Charles what has been promised him, God, offended, will remove power from Louis and transfer it to Charles. Indeed the decision has already been made: the transfer is imminent, and inevitable. This is the most insidious form of temptation: Satan looks like an Angel of Light. Charles's response does him some credit. He mistrusts what he sees. The projection of his own ambition produces not assent but terror—presumably the terror of guilt. He links danger with his secular environment, his house; he seeks safety in a church. But a second time, appearances deceive: the "Angel" pursues him in, confronting Charles with an argument that seems irrefutable in terms of the prince's own faith: "If I hadn't come from God, would I have been able to enter?" This time the prince is persuaded: understandably so, for the church is a consecrated place, fortified against the Devil's attacks. Where if not in a church can asylum be found? But the third and worst deception is to come: the "Angel" now offers Charles the Host from his own hand. With the prince's acceptance of that mouthful, the Devil is in him. It is impossible to imagine a more complete inversion of right order, a more cruel denial of devout expectations: what looked like the sacrament, the means of God's salvation, turns out to purvey the Devil instead. "Nowhere and never is anything safe. . . ."

Here too Hincmar had a Biblical model: the terrible story of Judas in John xiii.27, where after the very mouthful of bread that Christ gave him, Satan entered into the false disciple. [96] Hincmar more than once used this text to convey a warning: to the *simplices* to alert them to the dangers of predestination to damnation; to the evil-living palace clergy to warn that the very act of taking the sacrament "into a stomach full of sin" could rebound against the recipient.[97] The apparent contradiction, the fatal consequence of taking what gave life, could in fact be resolved: the wicked already belonged to Satan, so for them, as for Judas, taking the sacrament only confirmed his grip. Bede in his *Commentary on John* had wrestled with the problem, and offered such an explanation.[98] Hincmar's return to the text on several occasions suggests its significance for him, and helps to explain why he evoked it in trying to make sense of Charles the Fat's experience.

But, in the tale of two princes, Hincmar assaulted false confidence, in order to restore true faith. God had appointed mediators of the means of salvation, genuinely "angelic" ministers. They were the ordained priests of the Church's hierarchy, and specifically the bishops. The efficacy of their services could be relied on; the laws they observed were fixed beyond dispute. In the thirty-six lines of Latin text covering the Carloman story, Hincmar mentioned the bishops and their functions four times, the Church three times, the canons and holy orders twice each. This insistence has a crucial function in the text, and in the elaboration of an ideology. Hincmar wanted to show that the denial of Carloman's kingship was righteous. In practice, Hincmar knew, a secular penalty—blinding—ensured that no one would ever again support Carloman for king. That penalty followed Carloman's condemnation for his crimes by a secular court. But Hincmar sought to establish a prior ineligibility, and this could be done by invoking the immutable rules of canon law. At one level, this was a test case, which proved the effectiveness of Charles the Bald's putting his son into the Church as a means of extinguishing the young man's king-worthiness. At another level, the strategy worked by removing Carloman from a secular area of confliction and uncertain claims to an ecclesiastical area where clear-cut rules applied. The strategy could only work because laymen were willing to collude with it, recognising these rules, and their purview, absorbing the message of men like Hincmar that there were two orders, priestly and lay, mutually dependent, mutually supportive, each with its own rules, both within one Christian people: it was the old teaching of Gelasius, and it had a long run ahead of it.[99] But the scene was not just one of active clerics and passive laity. If churchmen knew that in the *saeculum* there was no doing without secular power, laymen— beset by uncertain and conflicting secular loyalties, by guilt, by fears of enemies within—sought from the Church a power without ambiguity. In the fraught divisions of the Carolingian Empire, they looked to the advice of bishops and priests "as if to a divine presence" to supply "a solution and an authoritive judgment." This is not Hincmar speaking, but the layman, Nithard.[100] And it was laymen who wanted, and accepted, the Church's lead in judging Carloman.

The denouement of Charles the Fat's story makes sense as part of the same bipartite ideology. Hincmar noted the involvement of the two orders, that is, of bishops and laymen together, in all three stages: they witnessed the prince's fit in the council hall; they held him firm and got him into a church; they took charge of him on the road to recovery. Charles's behavior during his fit was a kind of confounding of the orders: he tried to renounce his functions as husband and as warrior, and to take off his cloak *(vestimentum)*, the clothing that marked his status. The sequel reversed this violation of categories: the archbishop put on his priestly vestments *(vestes sacerdotales)* and began to perform Mass, the defining function of the priesthood. While he "chanted," that is, intoned in Latin, Charles "shouted out in the language of his ancestors." The ritual performance presented and reestablished the duality of orders and, implicitly, of functions. Charles would recover by following a sacred itinerary, defined by local cult-centers. The story, like the annal as a whole, after its dramatic climax ended on a quiet note. The restoration of right order had been possible, thanks to the Church's mediation of sacred power.

Hincmar and his contemporaries have been accused of blurring and softening Augustine's sharp vision of a violent and confused world in which no regime could be called just.[101] Of course, texts can be cited that seem to support this judgement. But it is both one-sided—for no Carolingian thinker consistently advocated mere facile conformism (though many had occasion to flatter royal patrons); and unhistorical—for it ignores the changes of the ninth century, and hence the variability of responses to them. Among those changes was the internalisation by at least some members of the literate lay elite of the essentialy monastic spirituality preached by the leaders of the Carolingian Reform. I do not think Charles the Fat's dilemma was Hincmar's invention.[102] It was not Charles's alone: from within a few years of 873 comes evidence of two other young men who shared it. Gerald of Aurillac and Alfred of Wessex, though born to secular power, and perhaps ambitious for it, rejected the carnality it required.[103] Hincmar took the dilemma seriously. He unmasked "angelic" temptation: lay power required and hence legitimised marriage and weapons.

The tale of two cities affirmed royal and paternal authority: the kings' triumph over filial rebellion was the triumph of God over the Devil, and the Church with law and ritual served the kings' interests. But in the annals that were perhaps not quite such a private work as has recently been claimed, Hincmar was no mere apologist for kings.[104] To "the historian's instinctive control of material"[105], Hincmar added the writer's conscious control and the statesman's recognition of the gulf between writing and reality. Hincmar the annalist, like Hincmar the draftsman of capitularies, recognised the ambivalence of human power. Alongside law and ritual, as forms of power, was coercion. When consensus failed, force was necessary: it was the king's job to wield it and so thwart the Devil and give "peace to the Church and Christendom in the realm." The order of the pure, the priesthood, required the exercise of impure power as a condition of its existence in the *saeculum*. The dilemma could not be evaded, as Charles the Fat had sought to evade it. Marriage and weapons had their uses—and kings had to use them. Worldly power would always be flawed, uncertain; but it acquired a conditional value. This had been Augustine's view: the judge conscious of his fallibility, of the necessary evil inherent in judging, had to get on with the job: "he must serve."[106] Hincmar's tale of two princes was also a tale of two cities. As such, it was realistic about power, but it was uncompromising about duty—and not without hope.

NOTES

[1] My thanks are due to Stuart Airlie, John Gillingham, Timothy Reuter, Richard Unger, and Patrick Wormald for help and criticism, and to Janos Bak for his patience and encouragement.

[2] Accusation and defence of Augustine are to be found in P. Brown, 'Saint Augustine', in B. Smalley, ed., *Trends in Medieval Political Thought* (Oxford, 1965), pp. 1–21, at p. 8 (reprinted in Brown, *Religion and Politics in the Age of St. Augustine* (London, 1972), pp. 25–45). v R. Markus, *Saeculum. History and Society in the Theology of St Augustine* (Cambridge, 1970).

[3] Hincmar of Rheims, *De Persona Regis et Regio Ministerio*, c. 5, ed. J. -P. Migne, *Patrologia Latina* (hereafter PL) 125, cols. 839–40.

[4] Critical, on the whole, of Carolingian political thought are R. W. and A. J. Carlyle, *A History of Medieval Political Theory*, 4th. ed. (Edinburgh, London, 1950) I; H. X. Arquilliere, *L'Augustinisme politique* (Paris, 1934). More sympathetic, yet also critical, are J. M. Wallace-Hadrill, "The *Via Regia* of the Carolingian Age," in Smalley, ed., *Trends*, pp. 22–41 (reprinted in Wallace-Hadrill, *Early Medieval History* (Oxford, 1975), pp. 181–200), and H. H. Anton, *Fürstenspiegel und Herrscherethos in der Karolingerzeit* (Bonn, 1968).

[5] *Annales Bertiniani*, ed. (F. Grat as *Annales de Saint Bertin*), J. Vielliard and S. Clemencet (Paris, 1965), hereafter referred to as *AB*. I use my own translation, to be published along with Timothy Reuter's translation of the *Annales Fuldenses* (hereafter *AF*), ed. F. Kurze, *Monumenta Germaniae Historica* (hereafter *MGH*), *Scriptores rerum Germanicarum in usum scholarum* (hereafter *SS rer. Germ. i.u.s.*) 7 (Hannover, 1891). v H. Lowe, "Geschichtschreibung der ausgehenden Karolingerzeit," in *Deutsches Archiv* 23 (1967), 1–30, at p. 3, 7–11; M. McCormick, *Les Annales du Haut Moyen Age* (Turnhout, 1975), pp. 18, 41, 46; J. L. Nelson, "The Annals of St. Bertin," in M. Gibson and J. Nelson, eds., *Charles the Bald: Court and Kingdom*, B.A.R. International Series 101 (Oxford, 1981), pp. 15–36 (reprinted in Nelson, *Politics and Ritual in Early Medieval Europe* (London, 1986), pp. 173–94). Hincmar's life and works are sensitively discussed by Wallace-Hadrill, "History in the mind of Archbishop Hincmar," in R.H.C. Davis and J. M. Wallace-Hadrill, eds., *The Writing of History in the Middle Ages* (Oxford, 1981), pp. 43–70; idem, *The Frankish Church* (Oxford, 1983), pp. 292–303. Interesting new perspectives on Hincmar's thought are opened up by K. F. Morrison, *Unum ex multis:* Hincmar of Rheims' medical and aesthetic rationales for unification," in *Nascita dell'Europa ed Europa Carolingia: un'equazione da verificare*. Settimane di Studio del Centro Italiano di Studi sull'Alto Medioevo 27 (Spoleto, 1981), pp. 583–712, esp. pp. 674ff. (reprinted in Morrison,

Holiness and Politics in Early Medieval Thought [London, 1985], no. II). For a first-rate critical survey of recent literature on Hincmar, *v* N. Staubach, *Das Herrscherbild Karls des Kahlen. Formen und Fulktionen monarchischer Reprasentation im fruheren Mittelalter*, diss. Munster, (1981), pt. II, with notes at pp. 366ff. The *AB* are scarcely mentioned in the otherwise exhaustive account of J. Devisse, *Hincmar, Archeveque de Reims (845–882)*, 3 vols. (Geneva, 1975–76); nor by Nelson, "Kingship, law and liturgy in the political thought of Hincmar," *EHR* 363 (1977), pp. 241–79 (reprinted in Nelson, *Politics and Ritual*, pp. 133–71). For an excellent survey of Hincmar's life and works, with an up-to-date bibliography, *v* "Hinkmar von Reims," by R. Schieffer, *Theologische Realenzyklopadie*, 15, pp. 355–60.

[6] *AB*, s.a. 873, pp. 189–92.

[7] Since E. Dummler, *Geschichte des ostfrankischen Reiches*, 3 vols. (Leipzig, 1887–88, repr. Darmstadt, 1960), II, pp. 320–23, 337–38, 356–59, there has been no adequate treatment of Carloman's revolt. But *v* P. McKeon, *Hincmar of Laon and Carolingian Politics* (Urbana-Chicago-London, 1978), ch. 7; and, for brief accounts, K. Brunner, *Oppositionelle Gruppen im Karolingerreich* (Wien-Köln-Graz, 1979), pp. 134–35; and K. Bund, *Thronsturz und Herrscherabsetzung im Fruhmittelalter* (Bonn, 1979), pp. 466–67. In the title of this paper, I use the term "prince" in the modern sense of king's son, though I am aware of the variety of meanings of *princeps* in the Carolingian period: *v* K. F. Werner, "Les principautes peripheriques," in Werner, *Structures politiques du monde franc (VIe–XIIe siecles)* (London, 1979), ch. 2; H. Wolfram, "The shaping of the early medieval principality," *Viator* 2 (1971), pp. 33–51; *idem, Intitulatio I: Lateinische Konigs- und Furstentitel bis zum Ende des 8. Jhdt.* (Wien, 1967), pp. 148–51; K. Brunner, "Der frankische Furstentitel im neunten und zehnten Jhdt.," in Wolfram, ed., *Intitulatio II* (Wien, 1973), pp. 183–85. Special "family-names" were used to indicate the status and throneworthiness of kings' sons: Carloman was such a name for the Carolingians. Stuart Airlie will discuss the evidence in a forthcoming paper.

[8] Cf. J. Goody, *Succession to High Office* (Cambridge, 1966), pp. 29–39.

[9] For details, *v* Nelson, *Politics and Ritual*, pp. 81–82.

[10] On Carloman's tutor, Wulfad, *v* J. Marenbon, "Wulfad, Charles the Bald and John Scottus Eriugena," in Gibson and Nelson, ed., *Charles the Bald*, pp. 375–83, at 375.

[11] Regino of Prum, *Chronicon*, ed. F. Kurze, *MGH SS rer. Germ. i.u.s.* 50 (Hannover, 1890), s.a. 870, p. 101.

[12] *v* T. Schieffer, 'Karl von Aquitanien. Der Weg eines karolingischen Prinzen auf den Stuhl des heiligen Bonifatius', in L. Lenhart, ed., *Universitas. Festschrift fur A. Stohr*, 2 vols. (Mainz, 1960), II, pp. 42–54.

[13] For Carloman's lay abbacies in the 860s, *v* G. Tessier, ed., *Receuil des Actes de Charles II le Chauve*, 3 vols. (Paris, 1943–55), II, nos. 303, 338; J. Wollasch, "Das Patrimonium Beati Germani in Auxerre," in G. Tellenbach, ed., *Studien und Vorarbeiten zur Geschichte des grossfrankischen und fruhdeutschen Adels* (Freiburg, 1957), pp. 185–224, at pp. 215–7. W. Wattenbach and W. Levison, *Deutschlands Geschichtsquellen im Mittelalter*, 5, rev. ed., H. Lowe (Weimar, 1973), pp. 548, n. 224, 552, 563. The monks of St. Medard complained to Charles the Bald about the violence done to the monastery's resourced by their lord (*senior*) Carloman and his following (*sequaces*): *MGH Epp.* 6, pp. 179–80.

[14] *AB*, s.a. 866, p. 130; 867, p. 135.

[15] *AB*, s.a. 868, p. 151. F. Prinz, *Klerus und Krieg* (Stuttgart, 1971), p. 124, treats Carloman as a typical example of the military service of the higher clergy of this period.

[16] *AB*, s.a. 852, pp. 64–65; 858, p. 78.

[17] *AB*, s.a. 853, pp. 66–67; "*Pippinus . . . habitum monachi suscipit requlaeque observationem more monachis solito promittit*"; cf. 854, p. 69. Later Pippin was accused of being an "apostate," i.e., runaway monk: *AB*, s.a. 864, p. 105; Hincmar, Ep. 170, *MGH Epp.* VIII, p. 163. This charge was never levelled against Carloman. The difference between his status and Pippin's is ignored by Devisse, *Hincmar*, vol. 2, p. 752 ("*moine gyrovaque*").

[18] *AB*, s.a. 869, pp. 157–64. *v* W. Schlesinger, "Zur Erhebung Karls des Kahlen zum Konig von Lothringen, 869" in Metz', in *Festschrift fur F. Petri* (Bonn, 1970), pp. 454–75; Staubach, *Herrscherbild*, pp. 239–71; Tessier, *Actes de Charles le Chauve*, II, no. 328, pp. 224–6.

[19] Tessier, *Actes de Charles le Chauve*, II, no. 333, pp. 236–38; Folcuin, *Gesta Abbatum Lobbiensium*, ed. G. H. Pertz, *MGH Scriptores* IV (Hannover, 1841), p. 61.

[20] O. G. Oexle, "Die Karolinger und die Stadt des heiligen Arnulf," *Frühmittelalterliche Studien* 1 (1967), pp. 250–64.

[21] A. Dierkens, *Abbayes et Chapitres entre Sambre et Meuse (VIIe–XIe siècles)* (Sigmaringen, 1985), pp. 110, 130; *Carmina Centulensia*, no. 105, ed. L. Traube, *MGH Poetae Latinae* (Berlin, 1896), III, pp. 336–37.

[22] *AB*, s.a. 869, p. 167; 870, p. 169. On Richildis and her family, see Brunner, *Oppositionelle Gruppen*, pp. 134, 137–40; J. Hyam, "Ermentrude and Richildis," in Gibson and Nelson, ed., *Charles the Bald*, pp. 153–68; S. Airlie, *The Political Behaviour of Secular Magnates in Francia*, unpub. D. Phil. (Oxford), 1985, ch. 5.

[23] *AB*, s.a. 870, p. 168. *v* W. Vogel, *Die Normannen und das frankische Reich* (Heidelberg, 1906), p. 235.

[24] J. -D. Mansi, ed., *Sacrorum Conciliorum Nova et Amplissima Collectio*, 31 vols. (Florence, Venice, 1758–98), XVI, col. 860. The implication that Carloman was taken by surprise is noted by McKeon, *Hincmar of Laon*, p. 121 and n. 15.

[25] *AB*, s.a. 870, p. 171.

[26] *AB*, s.a. 870, pp. 172–74. *v* Map. Cf. H. Henze, "Zur kartographischen Darstellung der Westgrenze des deutschen Reiches in karolingischer Zeit," *Rheinische Vierteljahrsblattёr* 9 (1939), pp. 207–54, at 219–21, 236–43.

[27] *AB*, s.a. 870, p. 177; cp. ibid. p. 179: Pope Hadrian II's envoys came with envoys from Emperor Louis II of Italy. Hadrian had written to Charles the Bald and Louis the German taking the emperor's part in protesting against the two kings' appropriation of the Middle Kingdom: *MGH Epp.* VI, no. 21, 25, pp. 724, 730. Hadrian protested to Charles about his treatment of Carloman: ibid., no. 31, pp. 735–36; perhaps again the emperor was involved in an attempt to embarrass Charles. I am not sure who else McKeon, *Hincmar of Laon*, p. 157, had in mind in referring to "influential parties in Italy" as among Carloman's sympathisers.

[28] *AB*, s.a. 870, p. 178: '*Karlomannus . . . in Belgicam provinciam venit, et congregatis secum plurimis satellitibus ac filiis Belial, tantam crudelitatem et devastationem secundum operationem Satanae exercuit ut non possit credi. . . .* '

[29] *Annales Laubienses*, s.a. 870, 873, ed. Pertz, *MGH Scriptores* IV, p. 15.

[30] *AB*, s.a. 871, p. 179.

[31] So, Devisse, *Hincmar*, vol. 2,, p. 787, n. 497; McKeon, *Hincmar of Laon*, p. 123; R. McKitterick, *The Frankish Kingdoms under the Carolingians* (London, 1983), p. 186; and by implication Brunner, *Oppositionelle Gruppen*, pp. 134–35. Both McKeon and Brunner assume that the men on whom Charles the Bald and Hincmar of Rheims relied to deal with Carloman were in fact Carloman's supporters: assumptions that seem to depend, respectively, on a mistranslation of *AB*, s.a. 871, p. 179 (McKeon, pp. 121, 124, has Baldwin of Flanders as an envoy of Carloman's, where the *AB* clearly name him as an envoy of Charles the Bald to Carloman), and on the unsupported assertion (Brunner, p. 135, n. 85) that Charles's chamberlain Engilramn was Baldwin's brother. Carloman's supporters seem to have been active in the ecclesiastical province of Sens as well as those of Rheims and Trier: *v* Tessier, *Actes de Charles le Chauve*, II, no. 368, pp. 320–21, where the king complains about attacks on the see of Meaux.

[32] E. Hlawitschka, *Lotharingien und das Reich* (Stuttgart, 1968), pp. 15–19; Airlie, *Political Behaviour*, ch. 4.

[33] *AB*, s.a. 871, p. 184.

[34] *AB*, s.a. 872, pp. 184–85 (January), 188 (October); cf. the payment of Lothar II to Rodolf, s.a. 864, p. 105. For the alliances of Lothar II with Roric, see *AF*, s.a. 857, p. 47; of Lothar I with Harald, *AB*, s.a. 841, p. 39; and of Pippin II of Aquitaine with unnamed Northmen, *AB* s.a. 857, 864, pp. 74, 105. For the probable alliance of Charles the Bald with Ragnar, perhaps in 840, *v Vita Anskarii*, ed. G. Waitz, *MGH SS rer. Germ. i.u.s.* (Hannover, 1884) c. 21, p. 46; and for Charles's alliance with Weland, *v AB* s.a. 862, p. 89. *AF* s.a. 883, p. 100 and Regino, *Chronicon*, s.a. 885, p. 123 show Hugh, son of Lothar II, allied with the Viking Godfrid. A shrewd appraisal of the context of such relations is provided by Ian Wood, "Christians and Pagans in Ninth-century Scandinavia," in B. Sawyer, P. Sawyer and I. Wood, eds., *The Christianization of Scandinavia* (Alingsås, 1987), pp. 36–67. I am very grateful to Ian Wood and Simon Coupland for helpful discussion of the *AB* evidence.

[35] *MGH Capitularia Regum Francorum*, eds. A. Boretius and V. Krause (Hannover, 1897), II, no. 278 (Quierzy, 4 Jan., 873), c. 1, p. 343.

[36] Ibid., c. 4, pp. 344–5. For confiscation as a penalty, *v* Nelson, " 'A King across the Sea': Alfred in Continental Perspective," *Transactions of the Royal Historical Society* 5th. ser., 36 (1986), pp. 45–68, at 53–4.

[37] *MGH Capit.* II, no. 278, c. 7, p. 345:"Et quia audivimus quod malefici homines et sortiariae per plura loca in nostro regno insurgunt, quorum maleficiis iam multi homines infirmati et plures mortui sunt, quoniam, sicut sancti Dei homines scripserunt, regis ministerium est impios de terra perdere, maleficos et veneficos non sinere vivere, expresse praecipimus, ut unusquisque comes in suo comitatu magnum studium adhibeat, ut tales perquirantur et comprehendantur. Et si iam inde comprobati masculi vel comprobatae feminae sunt, sicut lex et iustitia docet, disperdantur. Si vero nominati vel suspecti et necdum inde comprobati sunt vel per testes veraces comprobari non possunt, Dei iudicio examinentur; et sic per illud Dei iudicium aut liberentur aut condemnentur. Et non solum tales istius mali auctores, sed et conscii ac complices eorum, sive masculorum sive feminarum, disperdantur, ut una cum eis scientia tanti mali de terra nostra pereat." On the significance of this as the first Carolingian legislation specifying the death-penalty for witchcraft, *v* J. B. Russell, *Witchcraft in the Middle Ages* (Ithaca, 1972), pp. 72–73, noting the influence of late Roman models.

[38] Above, nn. 9, 12, 16.

[39] Examples include Bernard of Italy, *Annales regni Francorum*, ed. F. Kurze, *MGH SS rer. germ. i.u.s.* (Hanover, 1895), s.a. 818, p. 148; the Breton *dux* Salomon, *AB*, s.a. 874, p. 196; and Lothar II's son Hugh, *AF*, s.a. 885, p. 103. H. Schaab's dissertation on blinding as a penalty in the early Middle Ages has unfortunately been inaccessible.

[40] *AB*, s.a. 873, pp. 192–3. Cf. *Annals of Xanten*, ed. B. v. Simson, *MGH SS rer. Germ. i.u.s.* 12 (Hanover, 1909), p. 32. (On these annals, see below, n. 59.) Regino, s.a. 870, p. 102, adds that Carloman died not long after. McKeon, *Hincmar of Laon*, p. 158 and n. 17, cited evidence for 887.

[41] McKeon, *Hincmar of Laon*, p. 158, mistranslates in suggesting that Charles the Bald "learned with alarm" of Carloman's rescue. But Brunner, *Oppositionelle Gruppen*, p. 135, notes that Charles could have been worried by Adalard's role here. Serious physical handicap seems to have been considered a bar to kingship: hence the noting of the lameness of Charles the Bald's son Lothar, tonsured in 861, in *AB*, s.a., p. 84. Cf. Charlemagne's eldest son Pippin, a hunchback, according to Einhard, *Vita Karoli*, ed. G. Waitz, *MGH SS rer. Germ. i.u.s.* (Hanover, 1911), c. 20, p. 25, and also a dwarf, according to Notker, *Gesta Karoli*, ed. H. F. Haefele, *MGH SS rer. Germ. i.u.s.*, n.s. 13 (Berlin, 1959), II, c. 12, p. 72. The Franks may have found this a useful criterion for dynastic shedding. Cf. P. Wormald, "Celtic and Anglo-Saxon Kingship: Some Further Thoughts," in P. E. Szarmach, ed., *Sources of Anglo-Saxon Culture*, Studies in Medieval Culture 20 (Kalamazoo, 1986), pp. 151–83, at 160, 162.

[42] R. H. Bautier, ed., *Receuil des Actes de Louis II le Begue* (Paris, 1978), no. 30 (8 February, 879), p. 91.

[43] For Charles the Fat's early career, *v* Dummler, *Geschichte*, vol. 2, pp. 36, 352–55; G. Eiten, *Das Unterkonigtum im Reiche der Merowinger und Karolinger* (Heidelberg, 1907), pp. 158–65.

[44] M. Borgolte, *Die Grafen Alemanniens in merowingischer und karolingischer Zeit* (Sigmaringen, 1986), p. 162.

[45] Dummler, *Geschichte*, II, p. 119. The *AF*, s.a. 865, do not mention this division, but the 866 entry, p. 64, assumes it.

[46] This is implied in a charter of Arnulf, ed. P. Kehr, *MGH Diplomata regum Germaniae ex stirpe Karolinorum*, III (Berlin, 1955), no. 64 (15 November, 889). *v* Dierkens, *Abbayes et Chapitres*, pp. 109, 112–13.

[47] Karlmann: *AF*, s.a. 861, p. 55; 863, pp. 56–57; Louis the Younger: *AB*, s.a. 865, pp. 123–24; *AF*, s.a. 866, pp. 64–65. *v* J. Fried, *Konig Ludwig der Jungere in seiner Zeit* (Lorsch, 1984), pp. 8–11.

[48] Brunner, *Oppositionelle Gruppen*, p. 145; Borgolte, *Grafen*, p. 106.

[49] *MGH Diplomata Regum Germaniae*, I, ed. P. Kehr (Berlin, 1937), no. 108 (1 August 861 or 862), pp. 155–56.

[50] *AF*, s.a. 869, pp. 68–69.

[51] *AF*, s.a. 871, pp. 72–73.

[52] *AB*, s.a. 870, p. 176: "[Louis the German] suosque filios Hludouuicum et Karolum ad se venire praecepit. Qui sentientes. satagente matre, inclinatiorem esse voluntatem patris erga Karlomannum quam erga se, ad illum venire detrectaverunt". I take this to mean that the princes' mother sided with her two younger sons; Fried, *Konig Ludwig*, p. 8, that she encouraged her husband to favor their first-born.

[53] *AB*, s.a. 870, p. 176.

[54] *AF*, s.a. 871, p. 74.

[55] *AB*, s.a. 871, p. 183. Cp. *AF*, 871, p. 74.

[56] *AB*, s.a. 859, p. 82. *v* Brunner, *Oppositionelle Gruppen*, p. 140, though he admits that the conflicts in this area cannot be reduced to a struggle between "Bosonids" and "Welfs."

[57] *AB*, s.a. 872, p. 186 seems more plausible than the bland statement of *AF*, s.a. 872, p. 75. The *AF* at this point are virtually an "official" source, consistently favouring Louis the German.

[58] *AF*, s.a. 873, pp. 77–78.

[59] *Annals of Xanten*, s.a. 873, pp. 31–32. Written at this time in Cologne, these originally Lotharingian annals show a bias in the late 860s and early 870s towards Louis the German. *v* H. Lowe, "Studien zu den *Annales Xantenses*," *Deutsches Archiv* 5 (1950), pp. 59–99.

[60] *AF*, s.a. 873, p. 78; *AB*, s.a. 874, p. 196; *AB*, s.a. 875, p. 198; *AF*, s.a. 876, p. 89.

[61] Dummler, *Geschichte*, vol. 3, p. 291, n.2, points out that there is no evidence for the nickname "the Fat" before the twelfth century. I have followed Dummler in using it for convenience to distinguish this Charles from his uncle, the West Frankish king. For confusion in early medieval sources between the two Charleses, *v* K. U. Jaschke, "Die Karolingergenealogien aus Metz," *Rheinische Vierteljahrsblatter* 34 (1970), pp. 190–218, at 198, 214–27. For positive views of Charles the Fat's career down to 886, *v AF*, first continuator, pp. 107–14, and *Annales Vedastini* (Ann. St. Vaast), ed. B. v. Simson, *MGH SS rer. Germ. i.u.s.* 12 (Hanover, 1909), pp. 51–60. The main *AF* author is more critical, but does not disguise Charles's success in some traditional royal roles: s.a. 882, p. 98; 883, p. 100; 885, p. 103. It seems unreasonable to link the fact that Charles was trepanned in 887 after suffering headaches (*AF*, first continuator, s.a., p. 115), with his fit in 873, and conclude that he had suffered from a nervous disorder throughout the intervening period.

[62] Regino, s.a. 887, p. 127, where, at n.5, the editor (Kurze) says that the imputation of "ten years" to Charles's and Richgard's marriage is an error for twenty-five years. But Regino (and Charles) may have been calculating from 873. The broader significance of Richgard's case is nicely brought out by P. Stafford, *Queens, Concubines, and Dowagers: The King's Wife in the Early Middle Ages* (Athens, Georgia, 1983), pp. 94–96.

[63] *AF*, s.a. 885, p. 103; Notker, *Gesta Karoli*, II, c. 12, p. 74, c. 14, p. 78.

[64] *AF*, s.a. 873, p. 78.

[65] *v* Nelson, "Annals of St. Bertin," pp. 22–29.

[66] Lowe, '*Geschichtschreibung der ausgehenden Karolingerzeit*', pp. 3, 7–10; Wallace-Hadrill, "History in the Mind of Archbishop Hincmar," pp. 52–54. By contrast, the *AB* are virtually neglected by Anton, *Furstenspiegel und Herrscherethos* (a fleeting mention, p. 285), and, more curiously, by Devisse, *Hincmar*, where the remarks at vol. 2, pp. 974, n. 34 ("*document officiel*"), and 1054 ("l'oeuvre la plus anonyme du prelat") betray a failure to give this text the same careful attention accorded Hincmar's other works.

[67] Nelson, "Annals of St. Bertin," p. 27; Devisse, *Hincmar*, vol. 2, p. 787, n. 497.

[68] *AB*, s.a. 873, p. 193, n. 2. the word *locusta*, with its obvious Biblical connotations, was also used for this pest in the 873 annals of *AF*, p. 79, *Annals of Xanten*, p. 83, and Regino, p. 105.

[69] It is tempting to infer that Hincmar was with Charles the Bald on this campaign. Cf.

his insistence in 867 on the regularity with which he performed his due military service: *v* Nelson, "The Church's Military Service in the Ninth Century," *Studies in Church History* 20 (1983), pp. 15–30, at 29 (reprinted in Nelson, *Politics and Ritual*, pp. 117–32).

[70] For the manuscript evidence of Hincmar's involvement, see Nelson, "Legislation and Consensus in the Reign of Charles the Bald," in P. Wormald, ed., *Ideal and Reality. Studies in Frankish and Anglo-Saxon Society presented to J. M. Wallace-Hadrill* (Oxford, 1983), pp. 202–27, at 205–8, 225 (reprinted in Nelson, *Politics and Ritual*, pp. 94–97, 114).

[71] *AF*, s.a. 873, p. 78; *Annals of Xanten*, p. 32. Regino, s.a. 870, p. 102, is evenhanded.

[72] Compare the well-informed account of the siege by Regino, s.a. 873, pp. 105–7. *v* Werner, "Zur Arbeitsweise des Regino von Prum," *Die Welt als Geschichte* 19 (1959), pp. 96–116.

[73] *AF*, s.a. 873, p. 80. (The *Annals of Xanten*, s.a. 873, p. 32, like the *AB*, give the figure of 500 slain.)

[74] Cf. n. 68 above.

[75] *MGH Epp* VIII, i, ed. E. Perels (Berlin, 1939), no. 187, p. 194.

[76] *AB*, s.a. 873, p. 193.

[77] Ibid., pp. 194–95.

[78] Ibid., p. 195.

[79] Ibid., p. 192. Cf. *AB*, s.a. 864, p. 105, where Louis II is "so-called emperor of Italy" (*imperator Italiae nominatus*).

[80] Ibid., s.a. 873, p. 192: " . . . *rem re vera virtute sua obtinere non posset.*"

[81] Ibid., pp. 192–93.

[82] *v* above, p. 113, and n. 34.

[83] *AB*, s.a. 873, p. 194.

[84] Cf. Notker, *Gesta Karoli* II, c. 10, p. 66: "[res et negotia] sine quibus res publica terrena non subsistit, coniugio videlicet usuque armorum."

[85] For some valiant attempts, *v* Anton, *Furstenspiegel*, pp. 281–355; Devisse, *Hincmar*, vol. 2, pp. 671–723; W. Ullmann, *The Carolingian Renaissance and the Idea of Kingship* (London, 1971), pp. 83–101; Nelson, "Kingship, Law and Liturgy in the Political Thought of Hincmar of Rheims," *EHR*, 92 (1977), pp. 241–79 (reprinted in Nelson, *Politics and Ritual*, pp. 133–71). All of these effectively ignore the *AB*.

[86] Cf. Goody, *Succession*, pp. 170–72.

[87] Notker, *Gesta Karoli* I, 22, p. 31: "[in cautelam] nusquam et numquam in hoc saeculo tutae sed semper et ubique vanae securitatis." For the central Augustinian concept here, *v* R. A. Markus, *Saeculum*, esp. pp. 101–2, 133–34, 150–53.

[88] Werner, *"Principautés peripheriques,"* pp. 490ff; idem, "La génese des duchés en France et en Allemagne," in *Nascita dell' Europa ed Europa Carolingia: un'equazione da verificare, Settimane di studio del Centro Italiano di Studi sull'alto medioevo*, 27 (1981), pp. 175–207, at pp. 176–80.

[89] For non-royal *principatus* in the Frankish world, *v* the works cited above, n. 7.,

[90] Hincmar, *De Divortio Lotharii regis et Tetbergae reginae*, PL 125, col. 758. Anton, *Furstenspiegel*, pp. 295–96 (followed by Wallace-Hadrill, "History in the mind of Hincmar", p. 57), misleadingly says that Hincmar "lists six types of ruler." The sixfold classification is Anton's inference only: Hincmar seems (though without enumerating) to start with three types, and the third, when he reaches it, prompts

further sub-division. The whole passsage is a riposte to those who argue that Lothar "could be constituted king . . . by God alone." After considering the various ways in which men have in fact become kings, Hincmar concludes with filial succession, and comments: "The king ought rather to fear divine judgements and show respect for human judgements, than take vast pride in acquiring the kingdom, if he does not imitate his father's good behaviour . . . ." Note that human as well as divine judgment is here threatened as a sanction.

91 *v* Nelson, "Inauguration Rituals," in P. Sawyer and I. N. Wood, eds., *Early Medieval Kingship* (Leeds, 1977), pp. 50–71, at 61–63 (reprinted in Nelson, *Politics and Ritual*, pp. 283–307, at 294–96); idem, "Carolingian Royal Ritual," in D. Cannadine and S. Price, eds., *Rituals of Royalty* (Cambridge, 1987), pp. 137–80.

92 Devisse, *Hincmar*, II, pp. 982–83.

93 Cf. Hincmar's views in the *AB* and in the *de Ordine Palatii*: Nelson, "Legislation and Consensus," pp. 214–22 (reprinted *Politics and Ritual*, pp. 103–11).

94 *MGH Capit.* II, no. 272, pp. 305–6 (and, for Hincmar's authorship, the editor's note, ibid., p. 303).

95 Deuteronomy xiii, 12–17.

96 *John* xiii, 26–27: "Respondit Jesus: ille est [qui me tradet] cui ego intinctum panem porrexero. Et cum intinxisset panem, dedit Judae Simonis Iscariotae. Et post buccellam, introivit in eum Satanas."

97 *MGH Epp.* VIII, i, no. 37, p. 22; no. 127, p. 66. Cf. *de Cavendis Vitiis* (addressed to Charles the Bald probably in 869), PL 125, col. 925. Further references (though without details) ar indicated in Devisse, *Hincmar*, III, p. 1267.

98 Bede, *In S. Ioannis Evangelium Expositio*, PL 92, cols. 810–12. Cf. Walafrid Strabo, *de Exordiis et Incrementis* c. 18, ed. Krause, *MGH Capit.* II, p. 491, where the fate of Judas is cited to justify withholding the sacrament from those in a state of mortal sin.

99 Cf. Wallace-Hadrill, "History in the Mind of Hincmar," p. 56: "Hincmar remained a Gelasian"; also Anton, *Furstenspiegel*, pp. 319–55.

100 Nithard, *Historiarum Libri* IV, ed. E. Muller, *MGH SS rer. Germ. i.u.s.* (Hannover, 1907), IV, 1, p. 40: " . . . ut illorum [i.e., bishops and priests] consultu veluti numine divino harum rerum exordium atque auctoritas proderetur'. On Nithard's ideas, see Nelson, "Public *Histories* and Private History in the Work of Nithard," *Speculum* 60 (1985), pp. 273, 284–85 (reprinted Nelson, *Politics and Ritual*, pp. 217, 228–29); and idem, "Carolingian Royal Ritual" pp. 160–61.

101 *v* above, p. 105. Markus, *Saeculum*, p. 153, rightly notes that later developments were "scarcely in line with the grain of Augustine's own thought."

102 Hincmar's account of Charles's aspiration to celibacy in 873 is unique. But cf. Regino, s.a. 887, p. 127, cited above, p. 119 with n. 62. An important aspect of the context of Charles's behavior is explored by K. Leyser, "Early Medieval Canon Law and the Beginnings of Knighthood," in L. Fenske, ed., *Festschrift für J. Fleckenstein* (Sigmaringen, 1984), pp. 549–66 (with a reference to Charles's case at p. 563).

103 A comparison between Gerald and Alfred was suggested by Patrick Wormald in a lecture to the Anglo-American Conference of Historians, London, 1985. I hope in a future paper to consider Charles's case along with these.

104 He often criticises individual kings in the *AB* but never hints here at any hierocratic idea of episcopal jurisdiction over kings.

105 Wallace-Hadrill, "History in the Mind of Hincmar," p. 54.

106 Augustine, *De Civitate Dei* XIX, 6.

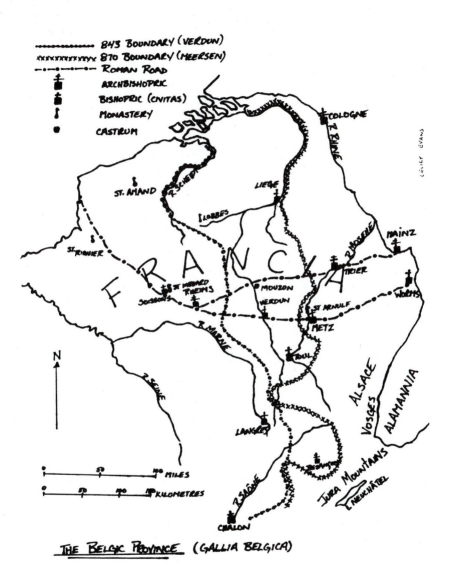

━━━━━━━━━ 843 BOUNDARY (VERDUN)
xxxxxxxxxxx 870 BOUNDARY (MEERSEN)
━·━·━·━·━·━ ROMAN ROAD
♦ ARCHBISHOPRIC
♦ BISHOPRIC (CIVITAS)
♦ MONASTERY
● CASTRUM

CECILY EVANS

COLOGNE
R. RHINE
ST. AMAND
R. SCHELDT
LIEGE
LOBBES
MAINZ
R. MOSELLE
ST RIQUIER
F R A N C I A
TRIER
ST MEDARD
RHEIMS
MOUZON
WORMS
SOISSONS
VERDUN
ST ARNULF
R. MARNE
METZ
N
TOUL
R. SEINE
ALSACE
VOSGES
ALAMANNIA
LANGRES
JURA MOUNTAINS
L. NEUCHÂTEL
0   50   100 MILES
0   50   100 150 KILOMETRES
R. SAÔNE
CHALON

THE BELGIC PROVINCE (GALLIA BELGICA)

Hincmar of Reims on King-making: The Evidence of the *Annals of St. Bertin*, 861–882

Hincmar of Reims wrote voluminously—on theology, on canon law, and on the conduct of the powerful. Modern historians of medieval political thought have ransacked these works with an energy worthy of the Vikings and have amassed a disparate hoard of fragmentary discussions of how kings ought to act.[1] Among this hacksilver can be found a rare gem of Hincmarian political analysis: a typology of king-making.[2] Its original location was in a series of ripostes to a list of objectionable propositions, which Hincmar appended to his bulky treatise on the divorce of Lothar II and Theutberga. As so often, controversy sharpened Hincmar's cutting edge. "Some wise ones," he noted sardonically, had alleged that Lothar II was "a king, and subject to no human laws or judgements but only those of God, who constituted him king in the realm which his father had left him."[3] Hincmar first tackled the issue of the king's subjection to law: "The law is not laid down for the just man, but for the unjust." Hence a just king would be judged, and rewarded, by Christ alone, but a bad king would be judged by bishops "either secretly or in public."[4] The related, but distinct, proposition that the king was "set up" by God through the workings of filial inheritance then received separate discussion. There were three ways, said Hincmar, that a man could be "set up in rulership": by God, like Moses, Samuel, and Josias; by God through men, like Joshua and David; and by man "but not without the divine nod [of permission]," like Solomon "on the orders of his father David, and by means of Zadoch the prophet and Nathan the priest." Hincmar went on to elaborate further subtypes of the third category: kings constituted "by the support of citizens and soldiers," and kings who succeeded to their fathers, as can be found, said Hincmar, "in the case of all those in the *Histories* and *Chronicles*, and even in the *Lives of the Caesars*."[5] The *Histories* and

Chronicles Hincmar had in mind were presumably Frankish ones; and Lothar II, succeeding his father, thus clearly came into this section of Hincmar's third category. But of the timing or form of Lothar's becoming king, Hincmar said not a word, preferring, instead, to spell out the Biblical lesson that a bad king (and he hastily disclaimed any allegation that Lothar's father had been a bad king) would see the succession depart from his line.[6] In other words, characteristically, Hincmar slid away from analyzing into moralizing.

This passage has been discussed by several modern commentators. It has been excerpted, taken from its immediate context, sometimes misconstrued.[7] Above all, it has not been set against the broader context of Hincmar's own political experience. Yet, as a man who for a generation and more was at the heart of events in the oft-divided Frankish realm, Hincmar observed many settings-up of rulers. His personal interest in the practicalities of royal inauguration is documented in the consecration *ordines* he himself produced for Carolingian rulers.[8] But most ninth-century Frankish kings received no ecclesiastical consecration. How important was such a ritual in Hincmar's view? How otherwise did a man become a king? Who, other than bishops, could participate? Did Hincmar have consistent criteria for gauging the legitimacy of a king's accession? Given that he regarded "tyrannical usurpers" as divinely ordained ("whether to fill up the number of their own sins, or to allow vengeance on the people's sins"), yet clearly identified the tyrant as one who acquired kingship in a wrongful manner, how did Hincmar distinguish in practice between the usurper and the rightful king? In canonical treatises, and in Mirrors of Princes, such questions could be sidestepped. What forced Hincmar to address them, however briefly and often obliquely, was the writing of contemporary history. His sustained essay in the genre, virtually disregarded by historians who have dealt at length with his political ideas, and even dismissed as "the prelate's most anonymous work," was the last section of the so-called *Annals of St. Bertin*, covering the years 861–882; it was a work that Hincmar himself designated "the Deeds of Our Kings."[9]

In the *AB*, Hincmar mentions some twenty-six acquisitions of regnal power, some abortive, mere attempted coups, some confirming previously established tenure, some inaugurating effective reigns.[10] The twenty years of his authorship of the *AB* were years of unprecedented disruption in the transmission of Carolingian power. A generation of long-lived kings gave way to a series of reigns cut short by illness or accident. Filial succession, whether to a subkingdom during a royal father's lifetime, or to the father's whole kingdom after his death, was no statistical norm, even if contemporaries considered it normal. As frequent as cases of sons succeeding fathers were those where another close kinsman made a bid for the succession.[11] Even where a son was available, the timing of his succession could be problematic: more than one prince was tempted to jump the gun and "usurped part of the realm" as a rebel against his father.[12] The fact that conflict was, with a single exception, contained within the dynastic circle of those descended from Charlemagne in the male line did not remove its intensity. A brother might pit his "hereditary right" against an uncle's claim: the rules of family inheritance in any case allowed room for maneuver.[13]

In the *AB*, Hincmar recorded nearly all of the settings up (successful or otherwise) of rulers known to have occurred during the decades 861–882.[14] Though his accounts were mostly terse, he indicated for some cases distinct elements or stages in the ruler's inauguration. Hereditary right clearly underlay nearly every case, for all save one of the claimants were Carolingians born; yet Hincmar scarcely even mentions it. It was commonplace, uncontroversial: only a Carolingian, and a king's son, was eligible for kingship. By contrast, in nearly all the cases of filial succession not said to involve usurpation of power, Hincmar expressly mentions paternal designation.[15] Still more striking is the stress on the participation of the aristocracy in every type of dynastic succession. The quest of a would-be king for aristocratic support, or aristocratic initiative in inviting a hoped-for king, is mentioned explicitly in well over half the cases Hincmar covered.[16] His silence in certain cases may thus be significant. An elective element could occur, of course, alongside others, such as paternal designation or fraternal division. But rarely was it wholly absent. In fact, Hincmar presents nearly every king-to-be, or would-be king, whatever his position in the dynasty, as dependent on the support of aristocrats for the timing, course, and outcome of his bid for rulership.[17] The emphasis is worth noting, since it has been argued on the basis of Hincmar's ordines that his basic view was hierocratic—that he was trying to establish the authority of bishops, and especially the archbishop of Reims, as king-makers. The performance of royal consecration rites, on this argument, gave Hincmar the means to control the king. But Hincmar the recorder of royal *Gesta* expresses no such view and is, as we shall see, capable of realism about the political forces that could underlie, and belie, episcopal role-playing.[18]

The status of the *AB* as evidence of Hincmar's opinions is also worth noting. This was an "unofficial," private work in which Hincmar gave vent to some very personal views on, for example, the interventions of Pope Nicholas I in the affairs of the Frankish Church, or the promotion of the archbishop of Sens to the primacy of Gaul.[19] For Hincmar, perhaps even more than for any of his contemporaries, the writing of royal *Gesta* was a self-conscious and subjective business: it involved selectivity and (in both senses of the word) discrimination.[20] In the *AB*, Hincmar did not seek anonymity: his own preferences, and prejudices, shine through almost every page. Hence, if we want to know what Hincmar "really" thought about king-making, his section of the *AB* seems a good place to look. A brief examination of four cases follows.

THE ATTEMPTED SETTING UP OF CARLOMAN AS KING IN 873

This is Hincmar's account of the final phase in the rebellion of Charles the Bald's son Carloman. Three years before Carloman was first alleged to have been "plotting against his father, thereby breaching his fidelity."[21] He had been put into the Church as a child of five or six and tonsured as a cleric, subsequently receiving minor orders as a deacon. He had then been given several abbacies, which he held in the manner of a lay abbot, having a regular abbot in office alongside to supervise the monasteries' religious life. In 868, Hincmar records Charles the Bald's sending of Carloman "with a crack force of household troops" to Neustria to fight the Vikings on the Loire.[22] In 869, when Charles made a strong bid for the succession to his nephew Lothar II, he endowed Carloman with further abbacies in the newly acquired western part of Lothar's kingdom. But the new situation had evoked a new ambition in Carloman: his rebellion was surely a response to the potential availability of a Lotharingian kingdom for himself. Though Hincmar does not say that Carloman aspired to kingship in 870 or 871, his record of Carloman's activities in these years strongly suggests such an ambition. The annal for 873 makes this explicit. Life imprisonment was the punishment intended by Charles for his faithless son. But when the bishop had

> deposed Carloman from all ecclesiastical rank, and left him only the communion of a layman, . . . the ancient cunning Enemy incited Carloman and his accomplices to exploit another argument, namely, that because he no longer held any ecclesiastical orders, he could be all the more free to assume the title and power of a king. . . So it came about that, following his deposition, his former accomplices began to rally to him again, more enthusiastically than ever. . . : their plan was that, as soon as they got the chance, they would snatch him out of the prison where he was being held, and set him up as their king.[23]

Charles the Bald then had Carloman hailed before a secular court and condemned to death for his crimes—a sentence commuted to blinding "in order to deceive the pernicious hope in him on the part of those men who hated peace."[24]

There are two implications here for Hincmar's view of ninth-century Frankish king-making. First, however much Hincmar disapproved of Carloman's supporters, he did not challenge their capacity to "set up a king."[25] It was Carloman's personal ineligibility that made his elevation to kingship impossible: the would-be king-makers' qualifications for their role were implicitly accepted. Significantly, there is no hint here or in Hincmar's letters that Carloman's supporters included any bishop. Second, in affirming here Charles's right to override filial claims in making his arrangements for the future, Hincmar was asserting (and perhaps wished to assure Charles the Bald) that the Church could offer a workable method for excluding a legitimate son from a share in the royal succession. Consecration to holy orders, was indelible: hence Carloman, by receiving tonsure as a cleric, had been removed permanently from the ranks of those eligible for kingship.[26] Carloman's supporters sinned in ignoring this. In the end, the Church's rule was vindicated, even if secular power and a secular judgment were needed to enforce it.[27] Thus the Church, which increasingly stressed the obligations of Christian marriage, and hence, by implication, the claims of all legitimate sons, was offering at the same time an escape route from the ensuing intensification of problems arising from partible inheritance. In practice, previous kings too had recognized that partibility had limits: the kingdom of the Franks had never been treated just like a family holding. But the Carolingian dynasty in the middle decades of the ninth century seemed to risk a crisis of overproduction. Hincmar was clearsighted about the threat further partition might pose to royal power in a kingdom reduced to a mere "fragment."[28] Carloman could, perhaps should, receive *honores* that would enable him to maintain high social status. But the "title and power of a king" would be denied him. Hincmar was no less clearsighted about Charles's need to buttress the new method of exclusion by a traditional one. Only by blinding was Carloman's fate sealed, and his supporters' hopes thereby finally dashed. Hincmar recorded the sentence without comment. In his view, it was justified by Carloman's faithlessness towards his father and by the overriding need to forestall any further partition of the Frankish heartlands.[29]

The rest of the 873 annal sets Carloman's story in a context that also suggests its meaning for Hincmar. Alongside it is placed the story of the East Frankish prince Charles the Fat, tempted doubly by the devil, on the one hand, to rebellion against his father, and on the other, to renounce the world. Both temptations had to be spurned, in Hincmar's view: royal power must be transmitted legitimately, from father to son, and, thus acquired, must be used.[30] The annal goes on to highlight Charles the Bald's success in defeating the Vikings at Angers. Here was a king acting "manfully and strenuously," and carrying out his royal function to the full. His judgment on his faithless son was amply vindicated in a triumphant affirmation at once of his paternal and regal authority, and of the integrity of his realm.

THE ROYAL CONSECRATIONS OF LOUIS III AND CARLOMAN

Another view of Hincmar on king-making can be noted in the consecration of Louis III and Carloman, sons of Louis the Stammerer at Ferrières in 879. The context of this event was the complex situation that arose in the West Frankish kingdom after the death of Louis the Stammerer at Compiègne on 10 April. Hincmar began the 879 annal with an account of the arrangements made by Louis during his final illness for the sole succession of his elder son, the future Louis III. Though the boy was already of age, a sort of regency council was set up for him. Then the dying father sent his son "crown and sword and the rest of the royal gear, and ordered those who were with his son to have him consecrated and crowned king."[31] According to Hincmar, these paternal plans were blocked by the interests of two powerful factions, the one inviting the intervention of the East Frankish king Louis the Younger to take over the West Frankish realm, the other wishing to see the realm divided between the Stammerer's two sons.[32] To avert the former's success, "Abbot Hugh and the other magnates who were with the sons of their late lord Louis (the Stammerer) . . . , namely, Louis and Carloman, sent certain bishops, Ansegis and others, to the monastery of Ferrières, and there had Louis and Carloman consecrated and crowned kings."[33]

The tone of this account is markedly reserved, as if Hincmar were detaching himself from proceedings that constituted a plain violation of Louis the Stammerer's plans for the single succession of his eldest son; the consequence would be a new division of the realm, as described in the next annal.[34] Note the pointed reminder that the magnates who acted were with "the sons of their late lord," whose last wishes they were disregarding. No doubt Hincmar was motivated by personal rancor: his deepest hostility was to Louis the Younger's main partisan, Abbot Gauzlin, whose motives and support he blatantly misrepresents; but Abbot Hugh and Archbishop Ansegis of Sens were also his rivals and supplanters in influence at court.[35] Hincmar may well have thought that he, if anyone, ought to have performed the consecrations of the Stammerer's sons, as he had their father's.[36] Nevertheless, the *AB*'s account stresses the need for haste. For Hincmar (unlike the other main source for these events) records the impending invasion of Louis the Younger, which justified the action of Abbot Hugh and the other magnates. Further, Hincmar, though absent from the consecrations, sent envoys to convey his consent to what was done.[37] In the *AB* thereafter, the Stammerer's sons are referred to as kings. The king-makings at Ferrières were valid, then, in Hincmar's eyes; and his account indicates that their validity derived from the magnates' initiative and role therein. They are the subjects of the two main verbs of Hincmar's key sentence: they "sent" the bishops, and they "caused" the late king's sons to be consecrated and crowned. Hincmar seems to be suggesting that when paternal designation and aristocratic choice did not coincide, in the last resort the latter sufficed to authorize the setting up of king's sons as kings. Again, his prime concern was to preserve the separate existence of a West Frankish realm.

BOSO'S CONSECRATION, 879

Hincmar sets the scene for his account of Boso's king-making by another explicit attribution of initiative: Boso was "persuaded by his wife, who kept on saying that she no longer wanted to live if, daughter as she was of the emperor of Italy, and former betrothed of the emperor of Greece, she did not make her husband a king."[38] The statement gains its point from the account that immediately precedes it in Hincmar's annal (and the word "meanwhile" signals the synchronicity of the two events) of the king-making of the Stammerer's sons. There the subject of the verb (regem) *facere* was the *primores*; here the subject is Boso's wife! After this travesty of correct proceedings, we are not surprised to read that Boso "persuaded the bishops of those regions, who had in part been constrained by threats, in part drawn in by greed for the abbacies and estates promised them and later given them, to anoint and crown him king."[39] Hincmar's single long sentence is carefully constructed: the final verbs "anoint and crown" are drained of their usual meaning, and rendered positively ironic, by what precedes them.

Further, as in the case of Carloman's fate in 873, the Boso episode needs to be read in the context of a whole annal. In fact it is framed by accounts of two other king-makings. Not only is it immediately preceded by the description of the consecrations at Ferrières, as we have seen, but it is immediately followed by this statement: "And also Hugh, son of Lothar II by Waldrada, collected a great gang of brigands and tried to seize the realm of his father."[40] The use of the words "meanwhile" and "also" to introduce the successive sentences dealing with Boso and Hugh suggests that Hincmar means us to link these episodes. Boso's attempted coup "in those parts" has as complement the bastard Hugh's abortive "invasion" of Lotharingia. Only in the next sentence, with its neutral statement that Charles the Fat "obtained the kingdom" of Lombardy, does Hincmar recover his composure; he can go on to conclude this annal with an upbeat account of the young West Frankish kings' encounter with the Vikings, "and the army of the Franks, by God's will, returned home safe with victory."[41]

Both in his record of Boso's consecration, and in his setting of it, Hincmar has packed a judgment. The omission of reference to primores (though other sources imply just such backing for Boso) is surely deliberate. For a man who lacked any hereditary right, only aristocratic invitation could have supplied legitimacy. A consecration performed by bishops under such circumstances was inoperative as far as Hincmar was concerned: in his remaining annals, he pointedly denies Boso the title of king. Far from elevating episcopal consecration to the cardinal constitutive act of king-making, Hincmar shows here his contempt for what the relationship of king to bishops could all too easily become: a mere matter of bribes and threats. By juxtaposing this to the very different case of the Stammerer's sons, Hincmar highlights the absence of the primores from Boso's inauguration and hence implies that no true king-making was effected.

THE KING-MAKING OF CHARLES THE BALD IN LOTHARINGIA, 869

Hincmar's account of Charles the Bald's assumption of power in the Middle Kingdom is the great set-piece of the *AB*. It occupies more space than almost any other single episode. This is not only because Hincmar here quotes more texts in full than elsewhere; nor does Hincmar give this event such prominence simply because he himself had "stage-managed" it. In fact, the theatrical metaphor diverts us from Hincmar's purpose in writing up these events as he does: precisely what he seeks to emphasize are the spontaneous actions of many powerful men, clerical and lay.[42]

Hincmar acknowledges that the news of Lothar II's death in Italy without a legitimate heir produced divergent responses among the Lotharingian aristocracy. Two sets of envoys, he says, came to Charles at Attigny: a minority of the bishops and magnates (primores) of the late Lothar's kingdom sent word that Charles should await his brother Louis the German's agreement to a partition of Lotharingia before himself advancing into that kingdom; but a majority invitied Charles to move into Lotharingia as swiftly as possible, promising to meet him either en route to Metz or on his arrival at that city. Hincmar reveals his own preference: the latter counsel was "sounder" (sanior), and Charles thought it "more acceptable and healthier [salubrius] for him."[43] These adjectives are redolent of the language of church councils, and evoke the role of consensus therein.[44] Sounder, healthier proposals naturally prevail: a vote carried by the part that is greater both in quantity and quality entails unanimous compliance.

Charler's calculation, so Hincmar wishes to imply, proved correct: at Verdun, Charles was met by "many men" from Lotharingia, and at Metz received "many others" into his lordship. All these persons participated in the ensuing rituals (cohibentibus omnibus) in the church of St. Stephen at Metz. Hincmar gives the full texts of two speeches. The first was by Bishop Adventius of Metz. His theme was the divinely inspired unanimity that activated all present. He quoted St. Paul: "[God] hath made us to live of one mind in one house, and broken down the middle wall of partition between us."[45] Adventius also stressed the hereditary right by which Charles succeeded as "legitimate heir" to his nephew's kingdom. Now therefore, he said, it was "worthy for Charles and necessary for us" that the "faithful people" should hear what was fitting from "the most Christian king." Charles responded with the desired assurances: "You know that I will keep for each his due law and justice, as long as each of you offers the royal honour due obedience and subjection.[46]

Hincmar now addressed the Lotharingian bishops present, to justify his officiating at Metz, which was outside his province. He could advance good canonical reasons for an archbishop of Reims to act during a vacancy in the neighboring province "in his Belgic region." On receiving the bishops' collective assent, Hincmar proceeded to a second, general speech. Charles, he said, who had "usefully been in charge of and benefited" his people in the West Frankish kingdom, has come to Metz "led by God" (deo ducente). Like Adventius, Hincmar stressed unanimity. But his accent was not just on the support of the Lotharingians, but on its voluntary, spontaneous character:

"Just as all the animals came together into Noah's ark, with no one compelling them," so "you have flowed together here by divine inspiration." What men could perceive as an unforced, collective assembling ("you have come together on your own volition") signified the action of God through them.[47]

Hincmar invoked two earlier occasions. One was in the remote past, when Clovis, "famous king of the Franks," converted by St. Remigius, "apostle of the Franks," with "his whole people," was baptized "with 3000 Franks (not counting their women and children)," and was anointed king with oil brought from heaven. The other occasion was within living memory, when Clovis's "descendant" and namesake, Louis the Pious, Charles's own father, was "restored to rulership and crowned with the crown of the realm by the priests of the Lord with the acclamation of the faithful people in this very church, as we saw who were present there!"[48] Hincmar could telescope the whole of Frankish history: the same heavenly oil "of which we still have some" was to be used for Charles as had been divinely supplied for Clovis, while Charles's coronation recalled that of his father in the same place a generation before. Both models, of oiling and of crowning, were to be taken up and fused in the ritual that followed.[49] The common factor linking the three occasions was the manifestation of God's will through the participation of the Franks, "the faithful people," as well of Frankish bishops, in the elevation of their rulers.

Hincmar ended by letting the "people" speak for themselves:

"If this pleases you, make a noise together with your own voices." And at this all shouted out together. The bishop [i.e. Hincmar] then said: "Let us give thanks with one mind to the Lord, singing 'Te deum laudamus.'" And after this [Charles] was crowned king by the bishops.[50]

In thus allowing us to "hear" the aristocracy's consent to Charles's king-making, Hincmar conveys the indispensability of their collaboration with the bishops. Louis the Pious's restoration, still vivid in Hincmar's memory, Clovis's anointing, no less vivid in Hincmar's historical imagination, both seemed to him to show God working through the Franks to give them the rulers that were good for them. The king-making of 869 too represented, for Hincmar, a Judgment of God.

In his section of the *AB*, Hincmar supplied his contemporary audience with something other than objective reporting. What they could perceive as apologia or propaganda or self-conscious myth-making, we modern historians tend to read as a genre familiar to us: history as fact. This short paper's sampling of just one theme has suggested that each annal may be a more skillful literary construct than hitherto suspected and would thus repay careful textual analysis.[51] But the historian's further aim must be to get behind the text to ninth-century political realities. The more closely we scrutinize

XVII

the *AB* in the light of other literary sources of the period, the stronger our impression that its "facts" are refracted—that inconvenient realities have been distorted, even obscured altogether. This is clear, for instance, in the case of the *AB*'s presentation of Charles's inauguration at Metz: where the *AB* shows unanimity, divisions remained; where spontaneity is depicted, political pressures were rife; where the historic unity of the Frankish *gens* is evoked, only a localized fraction of that people were involved; where Charles's success is implied, in fact only months later, Metz, and much of Lotharingia, were in the hands of his rival Louis the German.[52]

But we need not give up the quest for truth of a kind in the *AB*. Hincmar's original audience, a coterie of sympathizers sharing his local concerns, would have expected bias, but not cynicism. For them, the writing of *Gesta*, based, so to speak, on "real life" details, was an opportunity to express, and evoke, more general assumptions and values. Hincmar's accounts of king-makings are evidence of consistent views as to how power might legitimately be acquired in the Frankish realm. The *AB* is a work of ideology. The power to shape the past is itself an historical fact. In the case of the *AB*, the early medieval historian can know more than usual of the wielder of this power, his methods and his purposes.

The political ideas of the mature Hincmar touched his theological views at a crucial point. He had fought hard, and successfully, against the predestinarian teachings of Gottschalk: "How could it be that each will receive according to his works on the day of Judgement, if there were no Free Will?"[53] Hincmar wanted to affirm the responsibility of individuals for their own actions, hence for their own salvation. The alternative, as Hincmar saw it, was social disintegration. Hincmar was "above all a pastor."[54] Like Gottschalk, he was acutely aware of the ubiquity of coercion in the temporal world: unlike Gottschalk, he could conceive of truly voluntary human actions and understood divine grace as enabling rather than constraining. Hence Hincmar could set a high value on decision-making that was unforced. Of course, he was no egalitarian democrat: those directly involved in the choosing of Frankish kings were the leaders of the Franks, the aristocracy, to which Hincmar himself belonged. Nevertheless the assumption was that they spoke for the rest.[55] Hincmar has been regarded as a less true Augustinian than Gottschalk; but his appreciation of the role of consensus as the expression of the community of faithful men accords with Augustine's definition of the commonwealth as an association of wills.[56] For Hincmar, God worked through the church and its sacraments, but he could also work "through soldiers and citizens." In old age, responding to what he perceived as new threats both to the kingdom that he had struggled so long to defend, and to his personal influence in its government, Hincmar laid new stress on the politics of consensus. His annals (and he was nearly sixty when he took up the job of writing them) convey, intermittently, the same message as his revision of the *de Ordine Palatii*, or the letter written in 879 to a great lay magnate reminding him that "the general disposition of the realm" must depend, not on any one man, but on "the judgement and consent of many."[57] Such ideas had long underlain the political practice of the Franks. Hincmar gave them clearer expression and a new coherence and social force: "The Deeds of Our Kings" were the pastor's teaching aid. Whether addressing his intimates at Reims, in the *AB*, or reaching out in capitularies and manifestos to a wider audience, Hincmar had a very clear perception of "the useful past."[58]

Hincmar saw in the Carolingian dynasty a divinely placed bulwark of social order for the Franks. Boso, the non-Carolingian, was to be rejected. The dynasty's discarded members deserved some sympathy and some share in its *honores*. But discarded they must be. The overriding problem of past and present was to transmit the dynasty's power safely over time. In a letter to Charles the Bald, Hincmar pointed anxiously to "the loss of many capital places as a result of the multiple divisions of the Frankish realm. For the sake of the royal *honor*, there must be no diminution of the resources your predecessors used to be able to have from those places." The king and the faithful men in his household needed those *portiuncula* for their upkeep.[59] The solution was to avoid further division of the Frankish heartlands (the tripartite arrangement agreed at Verdun by the leading men of the Franks along with their kings became for Hincmar both model and limiting case), and if possible to reintegrate what had previously been divided.[60] Hincmar supported Charles the Bald's efforts in this direction, opposing distractions in far-off Italy; he supported Louis the Stammerer's plan for an undivided succession in 879. But another equally urgent requirement had to be set alongside this one: namely, to maintain the aristocratic support on which the dynasty's power depended. Hincmar sought to square these imperatives, presenting Charles in 869 as having such support, Boso in 879 as lacking it. But in the last resort, as in the case of the Stammerer's sons, or as in 876 when Charles sought to acquire his nephew's inherited kingdom, it was the expressed will of the local *primores* that must prevail. Without their consent, Hincmar implied, no realm could be acquired, in fact or in right. Contemporary history taught prudence, recognition of the fundamental reality of aristocratic power. But for Hincmar, it also showed the role of the faithful men in king-making, not opposed to, but the vehicle of, God's intervention in the world.

NOTES

1. See H. H. Anton, *Fürstenspiegel und Herrscherethos in der Karolingerzeit* (Bonn, 1968), 281–356; U. Penndorf, *Das Problem des "Reichseinheitsidee" nach der Teilung von Verdun (843)* (Munich, 1974), 77–88; J. Devisse, *Hincmar archevêque de Reims, 845–882*, 3 vols. (Geneva, 1975–1976) 2: 671–723; J. L. Nelson, "Kingship, Law and Liturgy in

the Political Thought of Hincmar of Rheims," *English Historical Review* 92 (1977): 241–279 (reprinted in Nelson, *Politics and Ritual in Early Medieval Europe* (London, 1986), chap. 7); J. M. Wallace-Hadrill, "History in the Mind of Archbishop Hincmar," in *The Writing of History in the Middle Ages. Essays Presented to R. W. Southern*, ed. R. H. C. Davis and J. M. Wallace-Hadrill (Oxford, 1981), 43–70.

2. Cf. Anton, *Fürstenspiegel*, 295–296, with references at n. 756 to earlier literature; Wallace-Hadrill, "History in the Mind of Hincmar," 57.

3. *De Divortio Lotharii regis et Tetbergae reginae*, quaestio vi, PL 125, col. 756.

4. The reference here is clearly to the imposition of penance on the king as an individual, rather than to deposition from office: see Nelson, "Kingship, Law and Liturgy," 243–245.

5. PL 125, col. 758 ". . . sicut de his omnibus in historiis et chronicis et etiam in libro qui inscribitur Vita Caesarum invenitur." Tyrannical usurpers constituted a third subgroup.

6. Ibid.: "Non sufficit ad suffragium liberis paterna nobilitas. Vitia siquidem vicerunt naturae privilegia." To the Biblical exempla mentioned by Hincmar here may be added the influence of Pseudo-Cyprian, *De XII abusivis saeculi*, chap. 9, ed. S. Hellmann, *Texte und Untersuchungen* 34 (Leipzig, 1910), 52: ". . . regis iniustitia non solum praesentis imperii faciem fuscat, sed etiam filios suos et nepotes ne post se regni hereditatem teneant obscurat." (The text goes on to cite the case of Solomon.) Lothar II's inauguration occurred, curiously, under his uncle's auspices, outside his own kingdom, but with the support of its *principes* and *optimates*; see *Annales Fuldenses*, ed. F. Kurze, MGH Scriptores rerum Germanicarum in usum scholarum 7 (Hanover, 1891), s.a. 855, 46.

7. Cf. above, n. 2 (followed by Wallace-Hadrill) claims that Hincmar distinguished "six types of ruler," when in fact the distinction is between three types of ruler-making.

8. Anton and Devisse say very little about these. But see. C. A. Bouman, *Sacring and Crowning* (Groningen, 1957), 103, 112–114; see also Nelson, "Kingship, Law and Liturgy," 246 and nn. 1 and 4.

9. Ep. 187, MGH Epp. KA VI, i, p. 196. The *Annals of St. Bertin* are referred to below as the *AB* and cited in the edition of F. Grat, J. Vieilliard and S. Clemencet (Paris, 1964). The comment quoted is that of Devisse, vol. 2: 1054.

10. See Appendix. Cf. the list of "coronations" in C. R. Bruhl, "Fränkischer Krönungsbrauch," *Historische Zeitschrift* 194 (1962): 265–326, at 321–326.

11. Filial succession: see Appendix, items 1, 4, 5, 6, 13, 14, 16, 18, 19, 21; succession to brother, uncle, nephew, or cousin: see items 2, 3, 7, 8, 9, 10, 12, 17, 22, 25, 26.

12. See Appendix, items 1, 10. Cf. the case of Louis the Stammerer in 862, *AB*, s.a., p. 88, where Hincmar hints at, but does not specify, the aim of usurping royal power; and the sons of Louis the German, *Annales Fuldenses*, s.a. 861, 863, 866, 871, 873, pp. 55, 56, 64, 72–73, 77–78. See K. Bund, *Thronsturz und Herrscherabsetzung im Frühmittelalter* (Bonn, 1979), 469–470, 528–529.

13. See Appendix, item 8. On family inheritance, see J. L. Nelson, "Public Histories and Private History in the Work of Nithard," *Speculum* 60 (1985): 251–293, at 264, 272–273 (reprinted in *Politics and Ritual*, chap. 9).

14. Among the few not mentioned by Hincmar are some of the East Frankish cases listed above, n. 11. Hincmar may not have taken the unrest of Louis the Ger-

man's sons as seriously as the authors of the East Frankish *Annals of Fulda*. It is of course not always easy to distinguish usurpation from a ritual of rebellion, in the case of kings' sons, nor from a probing-exercise, such as Louis the German's attack on West Francia in 875; see Bund, *Thronsturz*, 467–468. My list in the Appendix follow Hincmar's interpretation, with all the possibilities of arbitrariness that implies.

15. See Appendix, items 4, 5, 6, 13, 14, 16.

16. See Appendix, items 2, 3, 4, 7, 9, 12, 13, 14, 16, 17, 19, 23, 25, 26. Excluding the three papally performed coronations (two of them involving emperors), the figures are thus 14/23. Note that Hincmar does not mention aristocratic support for filial usurpations: See Appendix items 1, 10, 18, 21, though he does talk of "accomplices" (item 10) and "brigands" (item 21).

17. A helpful survey of such situations in the ninth century can be found in W. Schlesinger, "Karlingische Königswahlen," in his *Beiträge zur deutschen Verfassungsgeschichte des Mittelalters*, 2 vols. (Göttingen, 1963), 1: 88–138. But whereas Schlesinger, pp. 97, 132, sees a "winning-back" of aristocratic influence after 814, I would see expectations as constant throughout the period. Cf. K. Brunner, *Oppositionelle Gruppen im Karolingerreich* (Vienna-Cologne-Graz, 1979). G. Tellenbach, "Die geistigen und politischen Grundlagen der karolingischen Thronfolge," *Frühmittelalterliche Studien* 13 (1979): 184–302, offers penetrating observations on the creation of consensus between king and aristocracy, esp. at pp. 253–257, despite the unpleasant ring of some of his terminology. (The first part of this study was written in 1944/1945.)

18. For the view that Hincmar expounded hierocracy or episcopalism, see W. Ullmann, *The Carolingian Renaissance and the Idea of Kingship* (London, 1979), 82–124.

19. *AB*, s.a. 865, p. 118–119, 121; 866, pp. 128–129; 876, pp. 201–202. Cf. J. L. Nelson, "The Annals of St. Bertin," in M. Gibson and J. L. Nelson, *Charles the Bald: Court and Kingdom* (B.A.R., International Series 101, Oxford, 1981), 15–36 (reprinted in *Politics and Ritual*, chap. 8, pp. 24–29).

20. Cf. Wallace-Hadrill, "History in the Mind of Hincmar," [54: ". . . the entire account of public life as he sees it over more than twenty years betrays the historian's instinctive control of material"]. For some reservations about Hincmar the historian, see below.

21. *AB*, s.a. 870, p. 171: ". . . reputatus quoniam insidias erga patrem suum infideliter moliebatur . . ." On the revolt of Carloman, E. Dümmler, *Geschichte des ostfränkischen Reiches*, 2d ed., 3 vols. (Leipzig, 1888) 2: 320–323, 337–338, 356–359 remains fundamental. See also P. McKeon, *Hincmar of Laon and Carolingian Politics* (Urbana, 1978), chap. 7, and J. L. Nelson, "A Tale of Two Princes: Politics, Text and Ideology in a Carolingian Annal," *Studies in Medieval and Renaissance History* 10(1988): 105–141. Hincmar left three different types of information on Carloman's revolt: the *AB*; references in letters, excerpted by Flodoard; and the Capitulary of Quierzy (January, 873). A hint in a letter, Flodoard, *Historia Ecclesiae Remensis* iii, chap. 18, MGH Scriptores XIII, p. 508, indicates that Hincmar attempted to negotiate with Carloman on Charles's behalf in 871.

22. *AB*, s.a. 868, p. 151: "Karlomannum filium suum, diaconum et abbatem, cum scara e vestigio . . . [Karolus] misit . . ." Carloman's abbacies included St. Médard, Soissons, St. Germain, Auxerre, and St. Amand: lucrative *honores*.

23. *AB*, s.a. 873, pp. 189–190: ". . . antiquus et callidus Adversarius [Karloman-

num] et suos complices ad argumentum aliud excitavit, videlicet quia liberius ad
nomen et potentiam regiam conscendere posset quia ordinem ecclesiasticam non
haberet. . . . Unde post depositionem eius complices illius ardentius coeperunt se ei
iterum reconiugere et alios quos valebant in societatem suam abducere, quatenus,
mox ut locum invenire possent, illum a custodia in qua servabatur educerent et sibi
regem constituerent. . ."

 24. *AB*, s.a. 873, p. 180: "quatenus pernitiosa spes pacem odientium de illo frus-
traretur."

 25. The location of Carloman's supporters is indicated by his itinerary: *AB*, s.a.
870, p. 178; 871, pp. 179, 182–183; and by several of Hincmar's letters: Flodoard, iii,
chap. 21, p. 515; chap. 26, p. 543. On the difficulty of identifying these supporters, see
Nelson, "Tale of Two Princes," p. 112 Pope Hadrian II's interventions (probably at
the instance of the Emperor Louis) are in MGH Epp. VI, nos. 32, 33, pp. 736, 737.

 26. For earlier use of similar strategies in 849 and 852 for Charles's nephews, see
AB, s.a., pp. 58, 65. See. T. Schieffer, "Karl von Aquitanien. Der Weg eines karoling-
ischen Prinzen auf den Stuhl des heiligen Bonifatius," in *Universitas. Festschrift für A.
Stohr*, ed. L. Lenhart, 2 vols. (Mainz, 1960) 2: 42–54, at 47–48. Before the ninth
century, of course, as during it, kings' illegitimate sons were often put into the
Church.

 27. As Hincmar recognized in Flodoard, iii, chap. 26, MGH SS XIII, p. 543:
ecclesiastical sanctions would need backing by *alia* (i.e., royal) *potestas*.

 28. Letter to King Carloman (881), PL 125, col. 1045: "particula regni." Cf.
below, n. 58. On earlier attempts to limit partibility, see J. L. Nelson, "Queens as
Jezebels" in *Medieval Women*, ed. D. Baker (Oxford: Blackwell, 1977), 45, 48 (reprinted in Nelson, *Politics and Ritual*, chap. 1). Cf. Schlesinger, "Karlingische Königswahlen," 95, 101.

 29. Blinding, widely used as a punishment for political crimes in the early Middle
Ages, had special consequences in the case of royals: generally it removed them definitively from the circle of eligibles. (The dissertation of M. Schaab has unfortunately
been inaccessible.)

 30. For the structure of the rest of the 873 annal, and the story of Charles the Fat,
see Nelson, "Tale of Two Princes."

 31. *AB*, s.a. 879, pp. 234–235: ". . . coronam et spatam ac reliquum regium
apparatum filio suo Hludouuico misit, mandans illis qui cum eo erant ut eum in
regem sacrari ac coronari facerent." The political conflicts following Louis the Stammerer's death are lucidly examined by K. F. Werner, "Gauzlin von Saint-Denis und
die westfränkische Reichsteilung von Amiens (880)," *Deutsches Archiv* 35 (1979): 395–
462. Hincmar's stance is discussed by Penndorf, *Das Problem des "Reichseinheitsidee,"*
pp. 77–88.

 32. *AB*, s.a. 879, pp. 236, 239. See J. Fried, "König Ludwig der Jüngere in seiner
Zeit," *Geschichtsblätter für den Kreis Bergstrasse* 16 (1983): 5–32, at 15–17.

 33. *AB*, s.a. 879, pp. 238–239: ". . . Hugo abbas et ceteri primores, qui cum filiis
quondam senioris sui Hludouuici . . . agebant, . . . quosdam episcopos, Ansegisum et
alios, miserunt ad Ferrarias monasterium, et ibi eos consecrari ac coronari in reges
fecerunt."

 34. *AB*, s.a. 880, pp. 241–242. Hincmar had also recorded the agreement made

with Louis the Younger at Fouron in November 878, when Louis the Stammerer had apparently envisaged a divided succession between his sons: *AB*, s.a. 878, pp. 230–234, esp. chap. 3, p. 232. But it is not clear that Hincmar himself approved this plan.

35. See Werner, "Gauzlin," pp. 426, 449–450; also G. Schmitz, "Hinkmar von Reims, die Synode von Fismes (881) und der Streit um das Bistum Beauvais," *Deutsches Archiv* 35 (1979): 463–486, at 471, n. 31, 478, n. 51. It may have been Hincmar's resentment of Abbots Hugh and (especially) Gauzlin which occasioned his new emphasis on episcopal authority in writings of these last years, e.g., the decrees of the Synod of Fismes, PL 125, cols. 1071, 1087–1088; and letter to Louis III, PL 126, col. 119. Bishops (and not abbots) could consecrate kings.

36. Hincmar's ordo for Louis the Stammerer: MGH Capitularia II, no. 304, pp. 461–462.

37. Flodoard, iii, chap. 23. MGH SS XIII, p. 532: Hincmar to the bishop of Soissons. Evidently the initiative had come from the magnates with the young kings, however. Hincmar later had to protest his support for the "election" of Louis III and Carloman: ibid., chap. 19, p. 510. The differing accounts of the *AB* and the *Annals of St. Vaast* are discussed by Werner, "Gauzlin," pp. 428–431. The problem of dating and placing the "electoral assembly" implied by Hincmar disappears if his reference is seen as ideological rather than literal.

38. *AB*, s.a. 879, p. 239: "Interea Boso, persuadente uxore sua, quae nolle vivere se dicebat, si filia imperatoris Italiae et desponsata imperatori Greciae, maritum suum regem non faceret . . ." This is often taken as a statement of fact: cf. W. Mohr, "Boso von Vienne und die Nachfolgerfrage," *Archivum Latinitatis Medii Aevi* 26 (1956): 141–165, at 158–160; but for an alternative view, see P. Stafford, *Queens, Concubines and Dowagers* (Athens, 1983), p. 24.

39. *AB*, s.a. 879, p. 239: ". . . partim comminatione constrictis, partim cupiditate illectis pro abbatiis et villis eis promissis et postea datis, episcopis illarum partium persuasit ut eum in regem ungerent et coronarent." On Boso's installation, see R. H. Bautier, "Aux origines du royaume de Provence. De la sédition avortée de Boso à la royauté légitime de Louis," *Provence Historique* 23 (1973): 41–68; See also Bund, *Thronsturz*, 499–503.

40. *AB*, s.a. 879, p. 239: "Hugo etiam, filius iunioris Hlotharii ex Vualdrada, collecta praedonum multitudine, regnum patris sui est molitus invadere." For other sources, see Bund, *Thronsturz*, 447–478. Hincmar's attitude is further revealed in Flodoard, iii chap. 26, pp. 545–546, where he warns Hugh against "any flatterer who urges him to attempt the usurpation of a realm" (*pervasio regni*), but also recalls his friendship with Hugh's father and grandfather, and urges Hugh to accept the honores promised him by Charles the Fat.

41. *AB*, s.a. 879, p. 240. The structure of this annal shows some parallels to that of 873; see n. 23 above.

42. *AB*, s.a. 869, pp. 157–164. See W. Schlesinger, "Zur Erhebung Karls des Kahlen zum König von Lothringen," in *Festschrift für F. Petri* (Bonn, 1970), 454–475; and N. Staubach, "Das Herrscherbild Karls des Kahlen. Formen und Funktionen monarchischer Repräsentation im früheren Mittelalter" (diss. Münster, 1982), 239–271. Staubach, p. 555, n. 672, stresses that the rituals of 869 should also be looked at from Charles's standpoint as having "die Funktion herrscherlicher Selbstdarstellung." Thus the *AB* account can be seen as the representation of a representation, in

another medium. (L. Riefenstahl's film of the 1936 Olympics comes to mind as a modern parallel.)

43. *AB*, s.a. 869, p. 157: "...plures autem saniore consilio illi mandaverunt ut quantotius commode posset usque Mettis properare satageret.... Quorum consilium Karolus acceptabilius et sibi salubrius esse intellegens...festinavit." Cf. the prologue to the *Ordinatio imperii* of 817, MGH Capitularia I, no. 136, p. 270: "hi qui sanum sapiunt."

44. J. Hannig, *Consensus Fidelium* (Stuttgart, 1982).

45. *AB*, s.a. 869, pp. 158–159, quoting Eph. 2: 14.

46. Ibid., p. 160: "...sciatis me...unicuique in suo ordine secundum sibi competentem leges...legem et iustitiam conservare." This echoes the promise of Coulaine (843): see Nelson, "Kingship, Law and Liturgy," 255–256.

47. *AB*, s.a. 869, pp. 162–164: "...quo etiam vos eius inspiratione confluxistis et ipsi vos sponte commendastis, cuius instinctu animata omnia in arcam Noe...nullo cogente convenerunt." (The allusion is to Gen. 7: 8–9, but the idea of the animals moving without human compulsion is Hincmar's own.) "...non incongruum videtur...ut in obtentu regni, unde vos ad illum sponte convenistis...coronetur."

48. *AB*, s.a. 869, pp. 162–163. The two precedents are described in a single lengthy clause, beginning with "because" (quia) and covering nineteen lines of the printed text! The second "cause" adduced is the Biblical precedent of I Macc. 2: 13, for a repeated coronation when a king acquires a second kingdom. P. E. Schramm, "Die Krönung bei den Westfranken und den Franzosen," *Archiv für Urkundenforschung* 15 (1938): 3–55, at 13, n. 6, noted that seven bishops officiated both in 835 and in 869. On the myth of Carolingian descent from Clovis, see O. G. Oexle, "Die Karolinger und die Stadt des heiligen Arnulf," *Frühmittelalterliche Studien* 1 (1967): 250–364; on the holy oil, see Ullmann, *Carolingian Renaissance*, p. 92; and on the meaning of all this for Hincmar, see Wallace-Hadrill, "History in the Mind of Hincmar," 54–55.

49. The prayers for the anointing and the crowning both begin with same phrase, "Coronet te dominus corona gloriae": MGH Capitularia II, no. 302, p. 457. Hincmar's personal involvement in the two rituals, of 835 and 869, partly explains this association. For some further considerations, see J. L. Nelson, "The Lord's Anointed and the People's Choice: Carolingian Royal Ritual," in *Rituals of Royalty*, ed. D. Cannadine and S. Price (Cambridge, 1987), 137–180.

50. *AB*, s.a. 869, p. 164.

51. I have attempted this for the 873 annals in "Tale of Two Princes." For some suggestions about the original audience of Hincmar's *AB*, see Nelson, "Annals of St. Bertin," pp. 24, 28.

52. The evidence is sensitively discussed by Schlesinger, "Zur Erhebung," 460–464, and Staubach, *Herrscherbild*, 252–253. In this case, other contemporary annals have little to say. For 873, the *Annuals of Fulda* and other evidence can be set against the *AB*: see Nelson, "Tale of Two Princes." For 879, the Annals of St. Vaast give a very different picture from the *AB*'s, while papal letters offer a corrective to the *AB* on both Carloman and Boso: see references above, notes 24, 36, 37.

53. Hincmar, *Third Treatise on Predestination*, PL 125, col. 191, quoting the *Hypomnesticon* which he believed to be by Augustine (iii, chap. 10, PL 45, col. 1631): "...quomodo autem unicuique secundum opera sua redderetur in die iudicii nisi liberum esset arbitrium?" For Hincmar's use of this probably fifth-century work, see

Devisse, *Hincmar* 1: 234–236.

54. Devisse, *Hincmar* 1: 256; and see also the thought-provoking comparison between the psychologies of Gottschalk and Hincmar, pp. 265–268.

55. *De Ordine Palatii*, ed. T. Gross and R. Schieffer, MGH Fontes Iuris Germanici Antiqui (Hanover, 1980), chap. 29, pp. 84–85. See J. L. Nelson, "Legislation and Consensus in the Reign of Charles the Bald," in *Ideals and Reality. Studies in Frankish and Anglo-Saxon Society presented to J. M. Wallace-Hadrill*, ed. P. Wormald (Oxford, 1983), 202–227 (reprinted in *Politics and Ritual*, chap. 5).

56. See P. Brown, "St. Augustine," in *Trends in Medieval Political Thought*, ed. B. Smalley (Oxford, 1965), 1–21, at 12–16; R. Markus, *Saeculum* (Cambridge, 1970), 59–71.

57. Flodoard, iii, chap. 26, MGH SS XIII, p. 545 (to Count Theuderic): ". . . ne moleste acciperet si eum commoneret . . . quia non solum grandis presumptio, sed etiam magnum periculum est, uni soli generalem regni dispositionem tractare sine consultu et consensu plurimorum . . ." Cf. *De Ordine Palatii*, chaps. 29–34, pp. 82–93; *Instruction to Louis the Stammerer*, chap. 8, PL 125, col. 987–988; *Acta* of Synod of Fismes, PL 125, cols. 1085–1086. Note that the letter of warning to Theuderic ends by harking back to the three-fold division of 843. On Theuderic's role in the late 870s, see Werner, "Gauzlin," 416, n. 74. The *primores*' "utilitarian" values are given particularly clear expression in Hincmar's very first annal: *AB* 861, p. 87.

58. Wallace-Hadrill, "History in the Mind of Hincmar," 58–59, also noting the appeal to dynastic history, and to Verdun as a model settlement, in the *Instruction to Louis the Stammerer*, PL 125, chap. 4, col. 986.

59. MGH Epp. KA VI, no. 126, p. 65.

60. Cf. Hincmar's letters cited above, notes 56, 57; and note the regretful tone of *AB*, s.a. 880, p. 241: in the division of Amiens, Louis III received "quod de Francia residuum erat ex paterno regno . . ."

Appendix

The following is a list of acquisitions of rulership (claimed or achieved) mentioned in Hincmar's section of the *Annals of St. Bertin*. (Page references are to the edition of F. Grat, J. Vielliard, and S. Clemencet, Paris, 1964.) Note: Consecrations of consorts are not included in this list.

1. 861, p. 85: Karlmann, son of Louis the German "magnam sibi partem . . . paterni regni praesumit."

2. 861, p. 87: Charles the Bald "a quibusdam invitatus quasi regnum Provintiae adepturus."

3. 863, p. 96: Louis II "Provintiam venit et quos potuit ipsius regni primores sibi conciliavit."

4. 865, pp. 117–118: Charles the Bald "Aquitaniae primores suscepit. Ad quorum multam petitionem filium suum Karolum . . . in Aquitaniam cum regio nomine ac potestate redire permittit."

5. 865, p. 123: Charles the Bald "Hludouuicum filium suum in Neustraim dirigit, nec reddito nec interdicto sibi nomine regio."

6. 867, p. 135: Charles the Bald "primores Aquitaniorum sibi obviam accersivit et filium suum Hludouuicum . . . eisdem Aquitanis regem praefecit."

7. 869, pp. 106–111: Charles the Bald in Lotharingia.

8. 869, pp. 167–168: Louis II "regnum quondam regis Hlotharii . . . Hludouuico imperatori . . . hereditario iure debetur."

9. 870, pp. 169, 172: Louis the German/Charles the Bald "talem portionem de regno Hlotharii regis consensit habere, qualem aut ipsi iustiorem et aequiorem aut communes fideles eorum inter se invenerint . . . Reges . . . convenerunt, et . . . regnum Hlotharii inter se diviserunt."

10. 873, p. 190: Carloman's bid for a kingdom.

11. 875–876, pp. 199–200: Charles the Bald "quibusdam de primoribus ex Italia ad se non venientibus, pluribus autem receptis, Roman invitante papa Iohanne perrexit et . . . in imperatorem unctus et coronatus atque imperator Romanorum est appellatus."

12. 876, pp. 206–207: Charles the Bald "dispositum habens . . . episcopos et primores regni quondam fratris sui ad se venientes recipere."

13. 876, p. 207: Louis the Younger uses Judgment of God to assert "plus per rectum ille habere deberet portionem de regno [Hlotharii] quam pater suus dimisit."

14. 877, pp. 218–221: Louis the Stammerer's accession to West Frankish kingdom, receiving "praeceptum per quod pater suus illi regnum ante mortem suum tradiderat," and *regalia*; "coronatus est"; *promissio* to bishops; *professio* to clergy and people.

15. 878, p. 227: Louis the Stammerer "coronatus Hluduuicus a papa Iohanne" at Troyes.

16. 879, pp. 234–235: Louis the Stammerer designates Louis III.

17. 879, p. 236: Gauzlin and others persuade "potentes homines . . . ut Hludouuicum Germaniae rege, in hoc regno convocarent."

18. 879, p. 238: Louis the Younger hears that his late brother's illegitimate son Arnulf "partem regni illius occupasse."

19. 879, p. 239: The consecrations of Louis III and Carloman.

20. 879, p. 239: Boso's consecration.

21. 879, p. 239: Hugh's bid for Lotharingia.

22. 879, p. 240: Charles the Fat "in Longobardiam perrexit et ipsum regnum obtinuit."

23. 880, p. 241: Louis III and Carloman "sicut fideles illorum invenerunt regnum paternum inter se diviserunt."

24. 880, p. 243: Charles the Fat "a Iohanne papa se . . . in imperatorem consecrari obtinuit."

25. 882, p. 245: "Venientes autem primores partis illius regni [Lotharingia] voluerunt se [to Louis III] commendare. Sed . . . non eos in commendatione suscepit."

26. 882, pp. 246–247: "Primores autem regni [of Louis III] nuntium miserunt ad Karlomannum, mandantes ut . . . ipse quantotius ad eos venire festinaret. . . . Ipsi autem parati erant illum recipere et se illi commendare, sicut et fecerunt."

INDEX